THE MIDDLE AGES
David / Donaldson

THE SIXTEENTH CENTURY
Logan / Greenblatt

THE EARLY SEVENTEENTH CENTURY
Lewalski / Adams

THE RESTORATION AND THE EIGHTEENTH CENTURY
Lipking / Monk

THE ROMANTIC PERIOD
Abrams / Stillinger

THE VICTORIAN AGE
Christ / Ford

THE TWENTIETH CENTURY
Stallworthy / Daiches

The Norton Anthology of English Literature

SEVENTH EDITION

VOLUME 1A

THE MIDDLE AGES

The Norton Anthology
of English Literature

SEVENTH EDITION
VOLUME 1A
THE MIDDLE AGES

Alfred David

PROFESSOR OF ENGLISH EMERITUS,
INDIANA UNIVERSITY

M. H. Abrams, *General Editor*

CLASS OF 1916 PROFESSOR OF ENGLISH EMERITUS,
CORNELL UNIVERSITY

Stephen Greenblatt, *Associate General Editor*

COGAN UNIVERSITY PROFESSOR OF THE HUMANITIES,
HARVARD UNIVERSITY

W • W • NORTON & COMPANY • *New York* • *London*

Copyright © 2000, 1993, 1990, 1986, 1979, 1974, 1968, 1962
by W. W. Norton & Company, Inc.

The text of this book is composed in Fairfield Medium
with the display set in Bernhard Modern.
Composition by Binghamton Valley Composition.
Manufacturing by R. R. Donnelley & Sons, Inc.
Cover illustration: Luttrell Psalter (14th century). The British Library, London.
Photo: The Bridgeman Art Library International Ltd.

Editor: Julia Reidhead
Developmental Editor/Associate Managing Editor: Marian Johnson
Production Manager: Diane O'Connor
Manuscript and Project Editors: Candace Levy, Barry Katzen, David Hawkins,
Ann Tappert, Will Rigby
Editorial Assistant: Christa Grenawalt
Permissions Manager: Kristin Sheerin
Cover and Text Design: Antonina Krass
Art Research: Neil Ryder Hoos

Library of Congress Cataloging-in-Publication Data

The Norton anthology of English literature / M. H. Abrams, general
editor : Stephen Greenblatt, associate general editor. — 7th ed.
p.   cm.
Includes bibliographical references and index.

ISBN 0-393-97486-3 (v. 1). — ISBN 0-393-97487-1 (pbk.: v. 1).
ISBN 0-393-97490-1 (v. 2). — ISBN 0-393-97491-X (pbk.: v. 2).

1. English literature.   2. Great Britain—Literary collections.
I. Abrams, M. H. (Meyer Howard), 1912– .   II. Greenblatt, Stephen, 1943– .
III.   Title: Anthology of English literature.
PR1109.A2   1999
820.8—dc21   99-43298
CIP

Volume 1A, The Middle Ages:
ISBN 0-393-97565-7 (pbk.)

W. W. Norton & Company, Inc., 500 Fifth Avenue, New York, N.Y. 10110
www.wwnorton.com

W. W. Norton & Company Ltd., 10 Coptic Street, London WC1A 1PU

3 4 5 6 7 8 9 0

PERMISSIONS ACKNOWLEDGMENTS

Ancrene Riwle: Excerpt (ca. 1200 words) from MEDIEVAL ENGLISH PROSE FOR WOMEN, edited by Bella Millett and Jocelyn Wogan-Browne (1990). Reprinted by permission of Oxford University Press.

Beowulf: A new translation by Seamus Heaney. Copyright © 2000 by Seamus Heaney. Reprinted with permission of W. W. Norton & Company, Inc.

Geoffrey Chaucer: All excerpts are from CHAUCER'S POETRY: AN ANTHOLOGY FOR THE MODERN READER, 2nd ed. by E. T. Donaldson. Copyright © 1958, 1975 by John Wiley & Sons, Inc. Reprinted by permission of Addison Wesley Longman Educational Publishers, Inc.

Sir Gawain: Complete text of SIR GAWAIN AND THE GREEN KNIGHT: A New Verse Translation by Marie Boroff, translator. Copyright © 1967 by W. W. Norton & Company, Inc. Reprinted by permission of W. W. Norton & Company, Inc.

Thomas Gray: From the manuscript of *Elegy Written in a Country Churchyard*. Transcribed by kind permission of the Provost and Fellows of Eton College.

Robert Henryson: *The Cock and the Fox* from ROBERT HENRYSON: THE POEMS, edited by Denton Fox (1987). Reprinted by permission of Oxford University Press.

Samuel Johnson: Excerpt from the manuscript of *The Vanity of Human Wishes*. Reprinted with permission.

Julian of Norwich: Excerpts reprinted from Julian of Norwich, A BOOK OF SHOWINGS, edited by Edmund Colledge and James Walsh, by permission of the publisher. Copyright © 1978 by the Pontifical Institute of Mediaeval Studies, Toronto.

Margery Kempe: Excerpts from THE BOOK OF MARGERY KEMPE, edited by Meech and Allen. Reprinted by permission of The Council of the Early English Text Society.

William Langland: Excerpts from PIERS PLOWMAN: An Alliterative Verse Translation, translated by E. Talbot Donaldson. Translation copyright © 1990 by W. W. Norton & Company, Inc. Reprinted by permission of W. W. Norton & Company, Inc.

Layamon: Excerpts from Layamon's BRUT translated by Rosamund Allen. Reprinted by permission of The Orion Publishing Group Ltd. on behalf of the publisher, Everyman.

The Mabinogi: From THE MABINOGI AND OTHER WELSH TALES by Patrick Ford. Copyright © 1977 by the Regents of the University of California. Reprinted by permission of the University of California Press.

Marie de France: Translation of LANVAL by Alfred David. Copyright © 2000 by Alfred David. Reprinted with the permission of the translator. *The Wolf and the Lamb* and *The Wolf and the Sow* from FABLES, translated by Harriet Spiegel. Copyright © 1987. Reprinted by permission of the University of Toronto Press.

John Milton: Lines from the manuscript of Milton's LYCIDAS. Reprinted with the permission of the Masters and Fellows of Trinity College, Cambridge.

Mystery Plays: *The Chester Play of Noah's Flood* from THE CHESTER MYSTERY CYCLE, edited by R. M. Lumiansky and David Mills. Copyright © 1974. *The Wakefield Second Shepherd's Play* based on the edition by A. C. Cawley and Martin Stevens. Reprinted by permission of The Council of the Early English Text Society.

Alexander Pope: From the manuscript of AN ESSAY ON MAN, MS Eng 233.21 transcribed by permission of the Houghton Library, Harvard University, and The Pierpont Morgan Library/Art Resource, NY.

Tain Epic: *Exile of the Sons of Uisliu* from THE TAIN. Translated from the Irish Epic *Tain Bo Cuailinge*, translated by T. Kinsella. Reprinted by permission of the translator.

Every effort has been made to contact the copyright holders of each of the selections. Rights holders of any selections not credited should contact W. W. Norton & Company, Inc., 500 Fifth Avenue, New York, NY 10110, in order for a correction to be made in the next reprinting of our work.

Contents

PERMISSIONS ACKNOWLEDGMENTS   ix
PREFACE TO THE SEVENTH EDITION   xvii
ACKNOWLEDGMENTS   xxvii

The Middle Ages (to ca. 1485)   1

Introduction   1
    Anglo-Saxon England   3
    Anglo-Norman England   7
    Middle English Literature in the Fourteenth and Fifteenth
        Centuries   9
    Medieval English   14
    Old and Middle English Prosody   19
Timeline   21

ANGLO-SAXON ENGLAND   23

BEDE (ca. 673–735) and CÆDMON'S HYMN   23
    An Ecclesiastical History of the English People   24
        [The Story of Cædmon]   24

THE DREAM OF THE ROOD   26

BEOWULF   translated by Seamus Heaney   29

THE WANDERER   99

THE WIFE'S LAMENT   102

THE BATTLE OF MALDON   103

ANGLO-NORMAN ENGLAND   110

THE ANGLO-SAXON CHRONICLE   110
    [Obituary for William the Conqueror]   110
    [Henry of Poitou Becomes Abbot of Peterborough]   113
    [The reign of King Stephen]   114

LEGENDARY HISTORIES OF BRITAIN   115

GEOFFREY OF MONMOUTH   115
    The History of the Kings of Britain   116
      [The Story of Brutus and Diana's Prophecy]   116

WACE   118
    Le Roman de Brut   118
      [The Roman Challenge]   118

LAYAMON   122
    Brut   122
      [Arthur's Dream]   122

THE MYTH OF ARTHUR'S RETURN   124
    Geoffrey of Monmouth: From History of the Kings of Britain   125
    Wace's: From Roman de Brut   125
    Layamon: From Brut   125

MARIE DE FRANCE   126
    Lanval   127
    FABLES   140
    The Wolf and the Lamb   140
    The Wolf and the Sow   141

CELTIC CONTEXTS   142

EXILE OF THE SONS OF UISLIU   142

LLUDD AND LLEUELYS   150

ANCRENE RIWLE (Rule for Anchoresses)   153
    [The Parable of the Christ-Knight]   154

MIDDLE ENGLISH LITERATURE IN THE FOURTEENTH
AND FIFTEENTH CENTURIES   156

SIR GAWAIN AND THE GREEN KNIGHT (ca. 1375–1400)   156

GEOFFREY CHAUCER (ca. 1343–1400)   210
    THE CANTERBURY TALES   213
    The General Prologue   215
    The Miller's Prologue and Tale   235
      The Prologue   236
      The Tale   237
    The Man of Law's Epilogue   252

The Wife of Bath's Prologue and Tale   253
   The Prologue   253
   The Tale   272
The Pardoner's Prologue and Tale   281
   The Introduction   281
   The Prologue   282
   The Tale   285
   The Epilogue   295
The Nun's Priest's Tale   296
[Close of Canterbury Tales]   310
The Parson's Tale   311
   The Introduction   311
Chaucer's Retraction   313

LYRICS AND OCCASIONAL VERSE   313
Troilus's Song   314
Truth   315
To His Scribe Adam   315
Complaint to His Purse   316

WILLIAM LANGLAND (ca. 1330–1387)   317
The Vision of Piers Plowman   319
   The Prologue   319
      [The Field of Folk]   319
   Passus 5   322
      [The Confession of Envy]   322
      [The Confession of Gluttony]   323
      [Piers Plowman Shows the Way to Saint Truth]   325
   Passus 6   328
      [The Plowing of Piers's Half-Acre]   328
   Passus 18   336
      [The Harrowing of Hell]   336
   The C-Text   346
      [The Dreamer Meets Conscience and Reason]   346

MIDDLE ENGLISH LYRICS   349
The Cuckoo Song   350
Alison   351
My Lief Is Faren in Londe   352
Western Wind   352
I Am of Ireland   352
What is he, this lordling, that cometh from the fight   352
Ye That Pasen by the Weye   353
Sunset on Calvary   353
I Sing of a Maiden   353
Adam Lay Bound   354
The Corpus Christi Carol   354

JULIAN OF NORWICH (1342–ca. 1416)   355
A Book of Showings to the Anchoress Julian of Norwich   356
   [The First Revelation]   356
      Chapter 3   356

Chapter 4   357
Chapter 5   358
From Chapter 7   359
Chapter 27   360
[Jesus as Mother]   361
From Chapter 58   361
From Chapter 59   362
Chapter 60   363
Chapter 61   364
[Conclusion]   366
Chapter 86   366

MARGERY KEMPE (ca. 1373–1438)   366
    The Book of Margery Kempe   367
        [The Birth of Her First Child and Her First Vision]   367
        [Her Pride and Attempts to Start a Business]   369
        [Margery and Her Husband Reach a Settlement]   370
        [A Visit with Julian of Norwich]   371
        [Pilgrimage to Jerusalem]   372
        [Examination before the Archbishop]   374
        [Margery Nurses Her Husband in His Old Age]   377

MYSTERY PLAYS   379
    The Chester Play of Noah's Flood   380
    The Wakefield Second Shepherds' Play   391

SIR THOMAS MALORY (ca. 1405–1471)   419
    Morte Darthur   421
        [The Conspiracy against Lancelot and Guinevere]   421
        [War Breaks Out between Arthur and Lancelot]   426
        [The Death of Arthur]   430
        [The Deaths of Lancelot and Guinevere]   435

ROBERT HENRYSON (ca. 1425–ca. 1500)   439
    The Cock and the Fox   439

EVERYMAN (after 1485)   445

POEMS IN PROCESS   A-1
    John Milton   A-2
        Lycidas   A-2
    Alexander Pope   A-4
        The Rape of the Lock   A-4
        An Essay on Man   A-5
    Samuel Johnson   A-6
        The Vanity of Human Wishes   A-7
    Thomas Gray   A-8
        Elegy Written in a Country Churchyard   A-8

SELECTED BIBLIOGRAPHIES   A-11
    Suggested General Readings   A-11
    The Middle Ages   A-13

"The Persistence of English" by Geoffrey Nunberg   A-19

GEOGRAPHIC NOMENCLATURE   A-35

BRITISH MONEY   A-36

THE BRITISH BARONAGE   A-39
   The Royal Lines of England and Great Britain   A-41

RELIGIONS IN ENGLAND   A-44

POETIC FORMS AND LITERARY TERMINOLOGY   A-46

ILLUSTRATION
   The Universe According to Ptolemy   A-62

INDEX   A-65

Preface to the Seventh Edition

The outpouring of English literature overflows all boundaries, including the capacious boundaries of *The Norton Anthology of English Literature*. But these pages manage to contain many of the most remarkable works written in English during centuries of restless creative effort. We have included epic poems and short lyrics; love songs and satires; tragedies and comedies written for performance on the commercial stage and private meditations meant to be perused in silence; prayers, popular ballads, prophecies, ecstatic visions, erotic fantasies, sermons, short stories, letters in verse and prose, critical essays, polemical tracts, several entire novels, and a great deal more. Such works generally form the core of courses that are designed to introduce students to the history of English literature, a history not only of gradual development, continuity, and dense internal echoes, but also of radical contingency, sudden change, and startling innovation.

One of the joys of literature in English is its spectacular abundance. Even from within the geographical confines of Great Britain and Ireland, where the majority of texts brought together in this collection originated, there are more than enough distinguished and exciting works to fill the pages of this anthology many times over. The abundance is all the greater if one takes, as the editors of these volumes do, a broad understanding of the term *literature*. The meaning of the term has in the course of several centuries shifted from the whole body of writing produced in a particular language to a subset of that writing consisting of works that claim special attention because of their formal beauty or expressive power. But any individual text's claim to attention is subject to constant debate and revision; established texts are jostled both by new arrivals and by previously neglected claimants; and the boundaries between the literary and whatever is thought to be "non-literary" are constantly challenged and redrawn. The heart of this collection consists of poems, plays, and prose fiction, but these categories are themselves products of ongoing historical transformations, and we have included many texts that call into question any conception of literature as denoting only a limited set of particular kinds of writing.

The designation "English" provides some obvious limits to the unwieldy, unstable, constantly shifting field of literature, but these limits are themselves in constant flux, due in part to the complexity of the territory evoked by the term (as explained in our appendix on "Geographical Nomenclature") and in part to the multinational, multicultural, and hugely expansive character of the language. As Geoffrey Nunberg's informative essay "The Persistence of English" (p. A-19), commissioned for this Seventh Edition, makes clear, the variations in the forms of the spoken language that all go by the name of English are so great as to call into question the very notion of a single tongue, and the complex history and diffusion of the language have helped ensure that its literature is enormous. In the momentous process that transformed England into Great Britain and eventually into the center of a huge empire, more and more writers from outside England, beginning with the strong Irish and Scottish presence in the eighteenth century and gradually fanning out into the colonies, were absorbed into "English literature." Moreover, English has constantly interacted with other languages and has been transformed by this interaction. The scope of the cross-currents may be gauged by our medieval section, which includes selections in Old Irish and Middle Welsh, along with works by Bede, Geoffrey of Monmouth, Wace, and Marie de France—all of them authors living in the British Isles writing in languages other than English. Their works are important in themselves and also provide cultural contexts for understanding aspects of what we have come to think of as "English literature." Certain literary texts—many of them included in these volumes—have achieved sufficient prominence to serve as widespread models for other writers and as objects of enduring admiration, and thus to constitute a loose-boundaried canon. But just as there have never been academies in English-speaking countries established to regulate the use of language, so too there have never been firm and settled guidelines for canonizing particular texts. English literature as a field arouses not a sense of order but what the poet Yeats calls "the emotion of multitude."

The term "English Literature" in our title designates two different things. First, it refers to all the literary productions of a particular part of the world: the great preponderance of the works we include were written by authors living in England, Scotland, Wales, and Ireland. Second, it refers to literary works in the English language, a language that has extended far beyond the boundaries of its point of origin. Following the lead of most college courses, we have separated off, for purposes of this anthology, English literature from American literature, but in the selections for the latter half of the twentieth century we have incorporated a substantial number of texts by authors from other countries.

The linguistic mobility and cultural intertwining reflected in these twentieth-century texts are not new. It is fitting that among the first works in this anthology is *Beowulf,* a powerful epic written in the Germanic language known as Old English about a singularly restless Scandinavian hero, an epic newly translated for this edition by the Irish poet Seamus Heaney. Heaney, who was awarded the Nobel Prize for Literature in 1995, is one of the contemporary masters of English literature, but it would be potentially misleading to call him an "English poet," for he was born in Northern Ireland and is not in fact English. It would be still more misleading to call him a "British poet," as if his having been born in a country that was part of the British Empire were the most salient fact about the language he speaks and writes or the culture by which he was shaped. What does matter is that the language in which Heaney writes is English, and this fact links him powerfully with the authors assembled in these volumes, a linguistic community that stubbornly refuses to fit comfortably within any firm geographical or ethnic or national boundaries. So too, to glance at authors and writings included in the anthology, in the sixteenth century William Tyndale, in exile in the Low Countries and inspired by German religious reformers, translated the New

Testament from Greek and thereby changed the course of the English language; in the seventeenth century Aphra Behn touched her readers with a story that moves from Africa, where its hero is born, to South America, where she may have witnessed some of the tragic events she describes; and early in the twentieth century Joseph Conrad, born in Ukraine of Polish parents, wrote in eloquent English a celebrated novella whose vision of European empire was trenchantly challenged at the century's end by the Nigerian-born writer in English, Chinua Achebe.

A vital literary culture is always on the move. The Seventh Edition of *The Norton Anthology of English Literature* has retained the body of works that have traditionally been taught as the principal glories of English literature, but many of our new selections reflect the fact that the *national* conception of literary history, the conception by which English Literature meant the literature of England or at most of Great Britain, has begun to give way to something else. Writers like William Butler Yeats (born in Dublin), Hugh MacDiarmid (born in Dumfriesshire, Scotland), Virginia Woolf (born in London), and Dylan Thomas (born in Swansea, Wales) are now being taught, and are here anthologized, alongside such writers as Nadine Gordimer (born in the Transvaal, South Africa), Alice Munro (born in Wingham, Ontario), Derek Walcott (born on Saint Lucia in the West Indies), Chinua Achebe (born in Ogidi, Nigeria), and Salman Rushdie (born in Bombay, India). English literature, like so many other collective enterprises in our century, has ceased to be principally the product of the identity of a single nation; it is a global phenomenon.

A central feature of *The Norton Anthology of English Literature*, established by its original editors, was a commitment to provide periodic revisions in order to take advantage of newly recovered or better-edited texts, reflect scholarly discoveries and the shifting interests of readers, and keep the anthology in touch with contemporary critical and intellectual concerns. To help us honor this commitment we have, as in past years, profited from a remarkable flow of voluntary corrections and suggestions proposed by students, as well as teachers, who view the anthology with a loyal but critical eye. Moreover, we have again solicited and received detailed information on the works actually assigned, proposals for deletions and additions, and suggestions for improving the editorial matter, from over two hundred reviewers from around the world, almost all of them teachers who use the books in a course. In its evolution, then, this anthology has been the product of an ongoing collaboration among its editors, teachers, and students.

The active participation of an engaged community of readers has been crucial as the editors grapple with the challenging task of retaining (and indeed strengthening) the selection of more traditional texts even while adding many texts that reflect the transformation and expansion of the field of English studies. The challenge is heightened by the wish to keep each volume manageable, in size and weight, so that students will actually carry the book to class. The final decisions on what to include were made by the editors, but we were immeasurably assisted, especially in borderline cases, by the practical experience and the detailed opinions of teachers and scholars.

In addition to the new translation of *Beowulf* and to the greatly augmented global approach to twentieth-century literature in English, several other features of this Seventh Edition merit special mention. We have greatly expanded the selection of writing by women in all of the historical periods. The extraordinary work of scholars in recent years has recovered dozens of significant authors who had been marginalized or neglected by a male-dominated literary tradition and has deepened our understanding of those women writers who had managed, against considerable odds, to claim a place in that tradition. The First Edition of the *Norton Anthology* was ahead of its time in including six women writers; this Seventh Edition includes sixty, of whom twenty-one are newly added and twenty are reselected or expanded. Poets and prose writers whose names were scarcely mentioned even in the specialized literary histories of earlier generations—Isabella Whitney, Aemilia Lanyer, Lady Mary Wroth, Elizabeth Cary, Margaret Cavendish, Mary Leapor, Anna Letitia Barbauld, Charlotte Smith, Letitia Elizabeth Landon, and many others—now appear in the company of their male contemporaries. There are in addition three complete long prose works by women: Aphra Behn's *Oroonoko*, Mary Shelley's *Frankenstein*, and Virginia Woolf's *A Room of One's Own*.

The novel is, of course, a stumbling block for an anthology. The length of many great novels defies their incorporation in any volume that hopes to include a broad spectrum of literature. At the same time it is difficult to excerpt representative passages from narratives whose power often depends upon amplitude or upon the slow development of character or upon the on-rushing urgency of the story. Therefore, better to represent the remarkable achievements of novelists, the publisher is making available, in inexpensive and well-edited Norton Anthology Editions, a range of novels, including Jane Austen's *Pride and Prejudice*, Charles Dickens's *Hard Times*, Charlotte Brontë's *Jane Eyre*, and Emily Brontë's *Wuthering Heights*.

A further innovation in the Seventh Edition is our inclusion of new and expanded clusters of texts that resonate with one another culturally and thematically. Using the "Victorian Issues" section long featured in *The Norton Anthology of English Literature* as our model, we devised for each period groupings that serve to suggest some ways in which the pervasive concepts, images, and key terms that haunt major literary works can often be found in other written traces of a culture. Hence, for example, the adventures of Edmund Spenser's wandering knights resonate with the excerpts from Elizabethan travel accounts brought together in "The Wider World": Frobisher's violent encounters with the Eskimos of Baffin Island, Drake's attempt to lay claim to California, Amadas and Barlowe's idealizing vision of the Indians as the inhabitants of the Golden Age, and Hariot's subtle attempt to analyze and manipulate native beliefs. Similarly, the millenarian expectations voiced in the texts grouped in "The French Revolution and the 'Spirit of the Age' " helped shape the major writings of poets from William Blake to Percy Bysshe Shelley, while the historical struggles reflected in texts by Jawaharlal Nehru and others in "The Rise and Fall of Empire" echo in the fiction of Chinua Achebe, V. S. Naipaul, and J. M. Coetzee. We supplement the clusters for each period with several more topical groupings of texts and copious illustrations on the *Norton Anthology* Web site.

Period-by-Period Revisions

The scope of the revisions we have undertaken, the most extensive in the long publishing history of *The Norton Anthology of English Literature,* can be conveyed more fully by a list of some of the principal additions.

The Middle Ages. Better to represent the complex multilingual situation of the period, the section has been reorganized and divided into three parts: Anglo-Saxon England, Anglo-Norman England, and Middle English Literature of the Fourteenth and Fifteenth Centuries. Nearly fifteen years in the making, Seamus Heaney's translation of *Beowulf* comes closer to conveying the full power of the Anglo-Saxon epic than any existing rendering and will be of major interest as well to students of modern poetry. The selection of Anglo-Saxon poems has also been augmented by *The Wife's Lament.* We have added a new section, Anglo-Norman England, which provides a key bridge between the Anglo-Saxon period and the time of Chaucer, highlighting a cluster of texts that trace the origins of Arthurian romance. This section includes selections from the chronicle account of the Norman conquest; legendary histories by Geoffrey of Monmouth, Wace, and Layamon; Marie de France's *Lanval* (a Breton lay about King Arthur's court, here in a new verse translation by Alfred David), along with two of her fables; a selection from the *Ancrene Riwle* (Rule for Anchoresses); and two Celtic narratives: the Irish *Exile of the Sons of Uisliu* and the Welsh *Lludd and Lleuelys.* To Chaucer's works we have added *The Man of Law's Epilogue* and *Troilus's Song*; we have added to the grouping of Late Middle English lyrics and strengthened the already considerable selection from the revelations of the visionary anchoress Julian of Norwich; and we have included for the first time a work by Robert Henryson, *The Cock and the Fox.*

The Sixteenth Century. Shakespeare's magnificent comedy of cross-dressing and cross-purposes, *Twelfth Night,* is for the first time included in the *Norton Anthology,* providing a powerful contrast with his bleakest tragedy, *King Lear.* The raucous *Tunning of Elinour Rumming* has been added to Skelton's poems and the somber *Stand whoso list* to Wyatt's, while Gascoigne is now represented by his poem *Woodmanship.* Additions in poetry and prose works have similarly been made to Roger Ascham, Henry Howard, Earl of Surrey, Sir Walter Ralegh, Fulke Greville, Samuel Daniel, Thomas Campion, and Thomas Nashe. Along with the grouping of travel texts described above, another new cluster, "Literature of the Sacred," brings together contrasting Bible translations; writings by William Tyndale and Richard Hooker; Anne Askew's account, smuggled from the Tower, of her interrogation and torture, along with the martyrologist John Foxe's account of her execution; selections from the Book of Common Prayer and the Book of Homilies; and an Elizabethan translation of John Calvin's influential account of predestination. In addition to Anne Askew, another Elizabethan woman writer, Isabella Whitney, makes her appearance in the *Norton Anthology,* along with a new selection of texts by Mary Herbert and a newly added speech and letters by Queen Elizabeth.

The Early Seventeenth Century. In response to widespread demand and to our own sense of the work's commanding importance, both in its own time and in the history of English literature, we have for the first time included the whole of Milton's *Paradise Lost.* Other substantial works that newly appear in this section include Ben Jonson's *Masque of Blackness* and Andrew Marvell's *Upon Appleton House,* extensive selections from Elizabeth Cary's *Tragedy of Mariam,* and poetry and prose by Aemilia Lanyer and Margaret Cavendish. Additions have been made to the works of John Donne, Jonson, Lady Mary Wroth, George Herbert, Henry Vaughan, Richard Crashaw, Robert Herrick, and John Suckling. The "Voices of the War" cluster, introduced in the last edition, now includes Anna Trapnel's narrative of her eventful voyage from London to Cornwall; and a new cluster, "The Science of Self and World," brings together meditative texts, poems, and essays by Francis Bacon, Martha Moulsworth, Robert Burton, Rachel Speght, Sir Thomas Browne, Izaak Walton, and Thomas Hobbes.

The Restoration and the Eighteenth Century. John Gay's *The Beggar's Opera*—familiar to modern audiences as the source of Bertolt Brecht's *Threepenny Opera*—makes its appearance in the *Norton Anthology,* along with William Hogarth's illustration of a scene from the play. Hogarth's "literary" graphic art is represented by his satiric *Marriage A-la-Mode.* Two new clusters of texts enable readers to engage more fully with key controversies in the period. "Debating Women: Arguments in Verse" presents the war between the sexes in spirited poems by Jonathan Swift, Lady Mary Wortley Montagu, Alexander Pope, Anne Finch, Anne Ingram, and Mary Leapor. The period's sexual politics is illuminated as well in added texts by Samuel Pepys, John Wilmot, Second Earl of Rochester, and Aphra Behn. "Slavery and Freedom" brings together the disquieting exchange on the enslavement of African peoples between Ignatius Sancho and Laurence Sterne, along with Olaudah Equiano's ground-breaking history of his own enslavement. The narrative gifts of Frances Burney, whose long career spans this period and the next, are newly presented by six texts, including her famous, harrowing account of her mastectomy.

The Romantic Period. The principal changes here center on the greatly increased representation of women writers in the period: Mary Robinson and Letitia Elizabeth Landon are included for the first time, and there are substantially increased selections by Anna Letitia Barbauld, Charlotte Smith, Joanna Baillie, Dorothy Wordsworth, and Felicia Hemans; to Mary Wollstonecraft's epochal *Vindication of the Rights of Women,* we have now added a selection from her *Letters Written in Sweden.* Conjoined with Mary Shelley's *Frankenstein,* presented here in its entirety, these texts restore women writers, once marginalized in literary histories of the period, to the significant place they in fact occupied. A new thematic cluster focusing on the period's cataclysmic event, the French Revolution, brings together texts in prose and verse by Richard Price, Edmund Burke, Mary Wollstonecraft, Thomas Paine, Elhanan Winchester, Joseph Priestley, William Black, Robert Southey, William Wordsworth, Samuel Taylor Coleridge, and Percy Bysshe Shelley. The selection of poems by the peasant poet John Clare has been expanded and is printed in a new text prepared for this edition. We have also added to Sir Walter Scott the introductory chapter of his *Heart of Midlothian,* and to William Wordsworth his long and moving lyrical ballad *The Thorn.*

The Victorian Age. The important novelist, short story writer, and biographer Elizabeth Gaskell makes her appearance in the *Norton Anthology,* along with two late-nineteenth-century poets, Michael Field and Mary Elizabeth Coleridge. Rudyard Kipling's powerful story *The Man Who Would Be King* is a significant new addition, as is the selection from Oscar Wilde's prison writings, *De Profundis*. Dickens's somber reflection *A Visit to Newgate* has been added. There are new texts in the selections of many authors as well, including John Henry Cardinal Newman, Elizabeth Barrett Browning, Alfred, Lord Tennyson, Elizabeth Gaskell, George Eliot, Dante Gabriel Rossetti, William Morris, and Gerard Manley Hopkins. Bernard Shaw's play *Mrs. Warren's Profession* has been moved to its chronological place in this section. New texts have also been added to the "Victorian Issues" clusters on evolution, industrialism, and the debate about gender.

The Twentieth Century. The principal addition here, in length and in symbolic significance, is Chinua Achebe's celebrated novel *Things Fall Apart*, presented in its entirety, and, with Joseph Conrad's *Heart of Darkness* and Virginia Woolf's *A Room of One's Own*, the third complete prose work in this section. But there are many other changes as well, in keeping with a thoroughgoing rethinking of this century's literary history. We begin with Thomas Hardy (now shown as fiction writer as well as poet) and Joseph Conrad, both liminal figures poised between two distinct cultural worlds. These are followed by groupings of texts that articulate some of the forces that helped pull these worlds asunder. A cluster on "The Rise and Fall of Empire" brings together John Ruskin, John Hobson, the Easter Proclamation of the Irish Republic, Richard Mulcahy, James Morris, Jawaharlal Nehru, and Chinua Achebe, and these texts of geo-political crisis in turn resonate with "Voices from World War I" and "Voices from World War II," both sections newly strengthened by prose texts. We have added selections to E. M. Forster, James Joyce, and T. S. Eliot, among others, and for the first time present the work of the West Indian writer Jean Rhys and the Irish poet Paul Muldoon. Samuel Beckett is now represented by the complete text of his masterful tragicomedy, *Endgame*. Above all, the explosion of writing in English in "postcolonial" countries around the world shapes our revision of this section, not only in our inclusion of Achebe but also in new texts by Derek Walcott, V. S. Naipaul, Anita Desai, Les Murray, J. M. Coetzee, Eavan Boland, Alice Munro, and Salman Rushdie. Seamus Heaney's works, to which another poem has been added, provide the occasion to look back again to the beginning of these volumes with Heaney's new translation of *Beowulf*. This translation is a reminder that the history of literature is not a straightforward sequence, that the most recent works can double back upon the distant past, and that the words set down by men and women who have crumbled into dust can speak to us with astonishing directness.

Editorial Procedures

The scope of revisions to the editorial apparatus in the Seventh Edition is the most extensive ever undertaken in *The Norton Anthology of English Literature*. As in past editions, period introductions, headnotes, and annotation are designed to give students the information needed, without imposing an interpretation. The aim of these editorial materials is to make the anthology self-sufficient, so that it can be read anywhere—in a coffeehouse, on a bus, or under a tree. In this edition, this apparatus has been thoroughly revised in response to new scholarship. The period introductions and many headnotes have been either entirely or substantially rewritten to be more helpful to students, and all the Selected Bibliographies have been thoroughly updated.

Several new features reflect the broadened scope of the selections in the anthology. The new essay, "The Persistence of English" by Geoffrey Nunberg, Stanford University and Xerox Palo Alto Research Center, explores the emergence and spread of English and its apparent present-day "triumph" as a world language. It provides a lively point of departure for the study of literature in English. The endpaper maps have been reconceived and redrawn. New timelines following each period introduction help students place their reading in historical and cultural context. So that students can explore literature as a visual medium, the anthology introduces visual materials from several periods—Hogarth's *Marriage A-la-Mode*, engravings by Blake, and Dante Gabriel Rossetti's illustrations for poems by Tennyson, Christina Rossetti, and Rossetti himself. These illustrations can be supplemented by the hundreds of images available on Norton Topics Online, the Web companion to the *Norton Anthology*.

Each volume of the anthology includes an appendix, "Poems in Process," which reproduces from manuscripts and printed texts the genesis and evolution of a number of poems whose final form is printed in that volume. Each volume contains a useful section on "Poetic Forms and Literary Terminology," much revised in the Seventh Edition, as well as brief appendices on the intricacies of English money, the baronage, and religions. A new appendix, "Geographic Nomenclature," has been added to clarify the shifting place-names applied to regions of the British Isles.

Students, no less than scholars, deserve the most accurate texts available; in keeping with this policy, we continue to introduce improved versions of the selections where available. In this edition, for example, in addition to Seamus Heaney's new verse translation of *Beowulf*, we introduce Alfred David's new verse translation of Marie de France's *Lanval*, the Norton/Oxford text of *Twelfth Night*; and Jack Stillinger's newly edited texts of the poems of John Clare. To ease a student's access, we have normalized spelling and capitalization in texts up to and including the Victorian period to follow the conventions of modern English; we leave unaltered, however, texts in which modernizing would change semantic or metrical qualities and those texts for which we use specially edited versions (identified in a headnote or footnote); these include Wollstonecraft's *Vindication*, William Wordsworth's *Ruined Cottage* and *Prelude*, Dorothy Wordsworth's *Journals*, the verse and prose of P. B. Shelley and Keats, and Mary Shelley's *Frankenstein*. In The Twentieth Century, we have restored original spelling and punctuation to selections retained from the previous edition in the belief that the authors' choices, when they pose no difficulties for student readers, should be respected.

We continue other editorial procedures that have proved useful in the past. After each work, we cite (when known) the date of composition on the left and the date of first publication on the right; in some instances, the latter is followed by the date of a revised edition for which the author was responsible. We have used square brackets to indicate titles supplied by the editors for the convenience of readers. Whenever a portion of a text has been omitted, we have indicated that omission with three asterisks. If the omitted portion is important for following the plot or argument, we have provided a brief summary within the text or in a footnote. We have extended our longstanding practice of providing marginal glossing of single words and short phrases from medieval and dialect poets (such as Robert Burns) to all the poets in the anthology. Finally, we have adopted a bolder typeface and redesigned the page, so as to make the text more readable.

The Course Guide to Accompany "The Norton Anthology of English Literature," by Katherine Eggert and Kelly Hurley, University of Colorado at Boulder, based on an earlier version by Alfred David, Indiana University, has been thoroughly revised and expanded; it contains detailed syllabi for a variety of approaches to the course, teaching notes on individual authors, periods, and works, study and essay questions, and suggested ways to integrate the printed texts with material on the Norton Web site. A copy of the *Guide* may be obtained on request from the publisher.

Two cardinal innovations, one print and one electronic, greatly increase the anthology's flexibility: The book is now available both in the traditional two-volume format, in clothbound and paperback versions, and in a new six-volume paperback version comprised of volume 1A, *The Middle Ages,* volume 1B, *The Sixteenth Century/The Early Seventeenth Century,* volume 1C, *The Restoration and the Eighteenth Century,* volume 2A, *The Romantic Period,* volume 2B, *The Victorian Age,* and volume 2C, *The Twentieth Century.* By maintaining the same pagination as in the original two volumes, the six-volume format offers a more portable option for students in survey courses and allows the individual volumes to be used in period courses.

Extending beyond the printed page, the Norton Topics Online Web site (*www.wwnorton.com/nael*) augments the anthology's already broad representation of the sweep of English literature and greatly enlarges the representation of graphic materials that are relevant to literary studies. For students who wish to deepen their exploration of literary and cultural contexts, the Web site offers a huge range of related texts, prepared by the anthology editors, and by Myron Tuman, University of Alabama, and Philip Schwyzer, University of California, Berkeley. An ongoing venture, the Web site currently offers twenty-one thematic clusters—three per period—of texts and visual images, cross-referenced to the anthology, together with overviews, study explorations, and annotated links to related sites. The site also includes an electronic archive of over 185 texts to supplement the anthology. In addition, the Audio Companion to *The Norton Anthology of English Literature* is available without charge upon request by teachers who adopt the anthology. It consists of two compact discs of readings by the authors of the works represented in the anthology, readings of poems in Old and Middle English and in English dialects, and performances of poems that were written to be set to music.

The editors are deeply grateful to the hundreds of teachers worldwide who have helped us to improve *The Norton Anthology of English Literature.* A list of the advisors who prepared in-depth reviews and of the instructors who replied to a detailed questionnaire follows on a separate page, under Acknowledgments. The editors would like to express appreciation for their assistance to Tiffany Beechy (Harvard University), Mitch Cohen (Wissenschaftskolleg zu Berlin), Sandie Byrne (Oxford University), Sarah Cole (Columbia University), Dianne Ferriss (Cornell University), Robert Folkenflik (University of California, Irvine), Robert D. Fulk (Indiana University), Andrew Gurr (The University of Reading), Wendy Hyman (Harvard University), Elissa Linke (Wissenschaftskolleg zu Berlin), Joanna Lipking (Northwestern University), Linda O'Riordan (Wissenschaftskolleg zu Berlin), Ruth Perry (M.I.T.), Leah Price (Harvard University), Ramie Targoff (Yale University), and Douglas Trevor (Harvard University). The editors give special thanks to Paul Leopold, who drafted the appendix on Geographic Nomenclature and revised the appendix on Religions in England, and to Philip Schwyzer (University of California, Berkeley), whose wide-ranging contributions include preparing texts and study materials for the Web site, assisting with the revision of numerous headnotes, and updating appendices on the British baronage and British money. We also thank the many people at Norton who contributed to the Seventh Edition: Julia Reidhead, who served not only as the inhouse supervisor but also as an unfailingly wise and effective collaborator in every aspect of planning and accomplishing this Seventh Edition; Marian Johnson, developmental editor, who kept the project moving forward with a remarkable blend of focused energy, intelligence, and common sense; Candace Levy, Ann Tappert, Barry Katzen, David Hawkins, and Will Rigby, project and manuscript editors; Anna Karvellas and Kirsten Miller, Web site editors; Diane O'Connor, production manager; Kristin Sheerin, permissions manager; Toni Krass, designer; Neil Ryder Hoos, art researcher; and Christa Grenawalt, editorial assistant and map coordinator. All these friends provided the editors with indispensable help in meeting the challenge of representing the unparalleled range and variety of English literature.

M. H. ABRAMS
STEPHEN GREENBLATT

Acknowledgments

Among our many critics, advisors, and friends, the following were of especial help toward the preparation of the Seventh Edition, either with advice or by providing critiques of particular periods of the anthology: Judith H. Anderson (Indiana University), Paula Backsheider (Auburn University), Elleke Boehmer (Leeds University), Rebecca Brackmann (University of Illinois), James Chandler (University of Chicago), Valentine Cunningham (Oxford University), Lennard Davis (SUNY Binghamton), Katherine Eggert (University of Colorado), P. J. C. Field (University of Wales), Vincent Gillespie (Oxford University), Roland Greene (University of Oregon), A. C. Hamilton (Queen's University), Emrys Jones (Oxford University), Laura King (Yale University), Noel Kinnamon (Mars Hill College), John Leonard (University of Western Ontario), William T. Liston (Ball State University), F. P. Lock (Queen's University), Lee Patterson (Yale University), Jahan Ramazani (University of Virginia), John Regan (Oxford University), John Rogers (Yale University), Herbert Tucker (University of Virginia), Mel Wiebe (Queen's University).

The editors would like to express appreciation and thanks to the hundreds of teachers who provided reviews: Porter Abbott (University of California, Santa Barbara), Robert Aguirre (University of California, Los Angeles), Alan Ainsworth (Houston Community College Central), Jesse T. Airaudi (Baylor University), Edward Alexander (University of Washington), Michael Alexander (University of St. Andrews), Gilbert Allen (Furman University), Jill Angelino (George Washington University), Linda M. Austin (Oklahoma State University), Sonja S. Baghy (State University of West Georgia), Vern D. Bailey (Carleton College), William Barker (Fitchburg State University), Carol Barret (Northridge Campus, Austin Community College), Mary Barron (University of North Florida), Jackson Barry (University of Maryland), Dean Bevan (Baker University), Carol Beran (St. Mary's College), James Biester (Loyola University, Chicago), Nancy B. Black (Brooklyn College), Alan Blackstock (Wharton Community Junior College), Alfred F. Boe (San Diego State University), Cheryl D. Bohde (McLennan Community College), Karin Boklund-Lagopouloou (Aristotle University of Thessaloniki), Scott Boltwood (Emory and Henry College), Troy Boone (University of California, Santa Cruz), James L. Boren (University of Oregon), Ellen Brinks (Princeton University), Douglas Bruster (University of Texas, San Antonio), John Bugge (Emory University), Maria Bullon-Fernandez (Seattle University), John J. Burke (University of Alabama), Deborah G. Burks (Ohio State University), James Byer (Western Carlonia University), Gregory Castle (Arizona State University), Paul William Child (Sam Houston State University), Joe R. Christopher (Tarleton State University), A. E. B. Coldiron (Towson State University), John Constable (University of Leeds), C. Abbott Conway (McGill University), Patrick Creevy (Mississippi State University), Thomas M. Curley (Bridgewater State College), Clifford Davidson (Western Michigan University), Craig R. Davis (Smith College), Frank Day (Clemson University), Marliss Desens (Texas Tech University), Jerome Donnelly (University of Central Florida), Terrance Doody (Rice University), Max Dorsinville (McGill University), David Duff (University of Aberdeen), Alexander Dunlop (Auburn University), Richard J. DuRocher (St. Olaf College), Dwight Eddins (University of Alabama), Caroline L. Eisner (George Washington University), Andrew Elfenbein (University of Minnesota), Doris Williams Elliott (University of Kansas), Nancy S. Ellis (Mississippi State University), Kevin Eubanks (University of Tennessee), Gareth Euridge (Denison University), Deanna Evans (Bemidji State University), Julia A. Fesmire (Middle Tennessee State University), Michael Field (Bemidji State University), Judith L. Fisher (Trinity University), Graham Forst (Capilano College), Marilyn Francus (West Virginia University), Susan S. Frisbie (Santa Clara University), Shearle Furnish (West Texas A&M University), Arthur Ganz (City College of CUNY; The New School), Stephanie Gauper (Western Michigan University), Donna A. Gessell (North Georgia College and State University), Reid Gilbert (Capilano College), Jonathan C. Glance (Mercer University), I. Gopnik (McGill University), William Gorski (Northwestern State University of Louisiana), Roy Gottfried (Vanderbilt University), Timothy Gray (University of California, Santa Barbara), Patsy Griffin (Georgia Southern University), M. J. Gross (Southwest Texas State University), Gillian Hanson (University of Houston), Linda Hatchel (McLennan Community College), James Heldman (Western Kentucky University), Stephen Hemenway (Hope College), Michael Hennessy (Southwest Texas State University), Peter C. Herman (San Diego State University), James Hirsh (Georgia State University), Diane Long Hoeveler (Marquette University), Jerrold E. Hogle (University of Arizona), Brian Holloway (College of West Virginia), David Honick (Bentley College), Catherine E. Howard (University of Houston), David Hudson (Augsburg College), Steve Hudson (Portland Community College), Clark Hulse (University of Illinois, Chicago), Jefferson Hunter (Smith College), Vernon Ingraham (University of Massachusetts, Dartmouth), Thomas Jemielity (University of Notre Dame), R. Jothiprakash (Wiley College), John M. Kandl (Walsh University), David Kay (University of Illinois, Urbana-Champaign), Richard Kelly (University of Tennessee), Elizabeth Keyser (Hollins College), Gail Kienitz (Wheaton College), Richard Knowles (University of Wisconsin, Madison), Deborah Knuth (Colgate University), Albert Koinm (Sam Houston State University), Jack Kolb (University of California, Los Angeles), Valerie Krishna (City College, CUNY), Richard Kroll (University of California, Irvine), Jameela Lares (University of Southern Mississippi), Beth Lau (California State University, Long Beach), James Livingston (Northern Michigan University), Christine Loflin (Grinnell College), W. J. Lohman Jr. (University of Tampa), Suzanne H. MacRae (University of Arkansas, Fayettesville), Julia Maia (West Valley College), Sarah R. Marino (Ohio Northern University), Louis Martin (Elizabethtown College), Irene Martyniuk (Fitchburg State College), Frank T. Mason (University of South Florida), Mary Massirer (Baylor University), J. C. C. Mays (University College, Dublin), James McCord (Union College), Brian McCrea (University of Florida), Claie McEachern (University of California, Los Angeles), Joseph McGowan (University of San Diego), Alexander Menocal (University of North Florida), John Mercer (Northeastern State University),

Teresa Michals (George Mason University), Michael Allen Mikolajezak (University of St. Thomas), Jonathan Middlebrook (San Francisco State University), Sal Miroglotta (John Carroll University), James H. Morey (Emory University), Maryclaire Moroney (John Carroll University), William E. Morris (University of South Florida), Charlotte C. Morse (Virginia Commonwealth University), Alan H. Nelson (University of California, Berkeley), Jeff Nelson (University of Alabama, Huntsville), Richard Newhauser (Trinity University), Ashton Nichols (Dickinson College), Noreen O'Connor (George Washington University), Peter Okun (Davis and Elkins College), Nora M. Olivares (San Antonio College), Harold Orel (University of Kansas), Sue Owen (University of Sheffield), Diane Parkin-Speer (Southwest Texas State University), C. Patton (Texas Tech University), Paulus Pimoma (Central Washington University), John F. Plummer (Vanderbilt University), Alan Powers (Bristol Community College), William Powers (Michigan Technological University), Nicholas Radel (Furman University), Martha Rainbolt (DePauw University), Robert L. Reid (Emory and Henry College), Luke Reinsina (Seattle Pacific University), Cedric D. Reverand II (University of Wyoming), Mary E. Robbins (Georgia State University), Mark Rollins (Ohio University, Athens), Charles Ross (Purdue University), Donelle R. Ruwe (Fitchburg State College), John Schell (University of Central Florida), Walter Scheps (SUNY Stony Brook), Michael Schoenfeldt (University of Michigan), Robert Scotto (Baruch College), Asha Sen (University of Wisconsin, Eau Claire), Lavina Shankar (Bates College), Michael Shea (Southern Connecticut State University), R. Allen Shoaf (University of Florida), Michael N. Stanton (University of Vermont), Massie C. Stinson Jr. (Longwood College), Andrea St. John (University of Miami), Donald R. Stoddard (Anne Arundel Community College), Joyce Ann Sutphen (Gustavas Adolphus College), Max K. Sutton (University of Kansas), Margaret Thomas (Wilberforce University), John M. Thompson (U.S. Naval Academy), Dinny Thorold (University of Westminster), James B. Twitchell (University of Florida), J. K. Van Dover (Lincoln University), Karen Van Eman (Wayne State University), Paul V. Voss (Georgia State University), Leon Waldoff (University of Illinois, Urbana-Champaign), Donald J. Weinstock (California State University, Long Beach), Susan Wells (Temple University), Winthrop Wetherbee (Cornell University), Thomas Willard (University of Arizona), J. D. Williams (Hunter College), Charles Workman (Stanford University), Margaret Enright Wye (Rockhurst College), R. O. Wyly (University of Southern Florida), James J. Yoch (University of Oklahoma), Marvin R. Zirker (Indiana University, Bloomington).

The Norton Anthology of English Literature

SEVENTH EDITION

VOLUME 1A

THE MIDDLE AGES

The Middle Ages
to ca. 1485

43–ca. 420:	Roman invasion and occupation of Britain
ca. 450:	Anglo-Saxon Conquest
597:	St. Augustine arrives in Kent; beginning of Anglo-Saxon conversion to Christianity
871–899:	Reign of King Alfred
1066:	Norman Conquest
1154–1189:	Reign of Henry II
ca. 1200:	Beginnings of Middle English literature
1360–1400:	Geoffrey Chaucer; *Piers Plowman; Sir Gawain and the Green Knight*
1485:	William Caxton's printing of Sir Thomas Malory's *Morte Darthur*, one of the first books printed in England

The Middle Ages designates the time span roughly from the collapse of the Roman Empire to the Renaissance. The adjective "medieval," coined from Latin *medium* (middle) and *aevum* (age), refers to whatever was made, written, or thought during the Middle Ages. The Renaissance was so named by nineteenth-century historians and critics because they associated it with an outburst of creativity attributed to a "rebirth" or revival of Latin and, especially, of Greek learning and literature. The Renaissance was seen as spreading from Italy in the fourteenth and fifteenth centuries to the rest of Europe. The very idea of a "rebirth," however, implies something dormant or lacking in the preceding era. More recently, there has been a tendency to emphasize the continuities between the Middle Ages and the later time now often called the Early Modern period. Medieval authors, of course, did not think of themselves as living in the "middle"; they sometimes expressed the idea that the world was growing old and that theirs was a declining age, close to the end of time. Yet art, literature, and science flourished during the Middle Ages, rooted in the Christian culture that preserved, transmitted, and transformed classical tradition.

The works covered in this section of the anthology encompass a period of more than eight hundred years, from Cædmon's *Hymn* at the end of the seventh century to *Everyman* at the beginning of the sixteenth. The date 1485, the year of the accession of Henry VII and the beginning of the Tudor dynasty, is an arbitrary but convenient one to mark the "end" of the Middle Ages.

Although the Roman Catholic Church provided continuity, the period was one of enormous historical, social, and linguistic change. To emphasize these changes and the events underlying them, we have divided the period into three primary sections: Anglo-Saxon England, Anglo-Norman England, and

1

Middle English Literature in the Fourteenth and Fifteenth Centuries. The Anglo-Saxon invaders, who began their conquest of the southeastern part of Britain around 450, spoke an early form of the language we now call Old English. Old English displays its kinship with other Germanic languages (German or Dutch, for example) much more clearly than does contemporary British and American English, of which Old English is the remote ancestor. As late as the tenth century, part of an Old Saxon poem written on the Continent was transcribed and transliterated into the West Saxon dialect of Old English without presenting problems to its English readers. In form and content Old English literature also has much in common with other Germanic literatures with which it shared a body of heroic as well as Christian stories. The major characters in *Beowulf* are pagan Danes and Geats, and the only connection to England is an obscure allusion to the ancestor of one of the kings of the Angles.

The changes already in progress in the language and culture of Anglo-Saxon England were greatly accelerated by the Norman Conquest of 1066. The ascendancy of a French-speaking ruling class had the effect of adding a vast number of French loan words to the English vocabulary. The conquest resulted in new forms of political organization and administration, architecture, and literary expression. In the twelfth century, through the interest of the Anglo-Normans in British history before the Anglo-Saxon Conquest, not only England but all of Western Europe became fascinated with a legendary hero named Arthur who makes his earliest appearances in Celtic literature. King Arthur and his knights became a staple subject of medieval French, English, and German literature. Selections from French, Old Irish, and Middle Welsh as well as from Early Middle English have been included here to give a sense of the cross-currents of languages and literatures in Anglo-Norman England and to provide background for later English literature in all periods.

Literature in English was performed orally and written throughout the Middle Ages, but the awareness of and pride in a uniquely *English* literature does not actually exist before the late fourteenth century. In 1336 Edward III began a war to enforce his claims to the throne of France; the war continued intermittently for one hundred years until finally the English were driven from all their French territories except for the port of Calais. One result of the war and these losses was a keener sense on the part of England's nobility of their English heritage and identity. Toward the close of the fourteenth century English finally began to displace French as the language for conducting business in Parliament and in the courts of law. Although the high nobility continued to speak French by preference, they were certainly bilingual, whereas some of the earlier Norman kings had known no English at all. It was becoming possible to obtain patronage for literary achievement in English. Chaucer's decision to emulate French and Italian poetry in his own vernacular is an indication of the change taking place in the status of English, and Chaucer's works were greatly to enhance the prestige of English as a vehicle for important literature. He was acclaimed by fifteenth-century poets as the embellisher of the English tongue; later writers called him the English Homer and the father of English poetry. His friend John Gower (1325?–1408) wrote long poems in French and Latin before producing his last major work, the *Confessio Amantis* (The Lover's Confession), which in spite of its Latin title is composed in English. The third and longest of the three primary sections, Middle English Literature in the Fourteenth and Fifteenth Centuries, is thus not only a chronological and linguistic division but implies a new sense of English as a literary medium that could compete with French and Latin in elegance and seriousness.

Texts in Old English, Early Middle English, and the more difficult texts in later Middle English (*Sir Gawain and the Green Knight, Piers Plowman*) and other languages are given in translation. Chaucer and other Middle English works may be read in the original, even by the beginner, with the help of marginal glosses and notes. These texts have been spelled in a way that is intended to aid the reader. Analyses of the sounds and grammar of Middle English and of Old and Middle English prosody are discussed on pages 15–20.

ANGLO-SAXON ENGLAND

From the first to the fifth century, England was a province of the Roman Empire and was named Britannia after its Celtic-speaking inhabitants, the Britons. The Britons adapted themselves to Roman civilization, of which the ruins survived to impress the poet of *The Wanderer*, who refers to them as "the old works of giants." The withdrawal of the Roman legions during the fifth century, in a vain attempt to protect Rome itself from the threat of Germanic conquest, left the island vulnerable to seafaring Germanic invaders. These belonged primarily to three related tribes, the Angles, the Saxons, and the Jutes. The name *English* derives from the Angles, and the names of the counties Essex, Sussex, and Wessex refer to the territories occupied by the East, South, and West Saxons.

The Anglo-Saxon occupation was no sudden conquest but extended over decades of fighting against the native Britons. The latter were finally confined to the mountainous region of Wales, where the modern form of their language is spoken alongside English to this day. The Britons had become Christians in the fourth century after the conversion of Emperor Constantine along with most of the rest of the Roman Empire, but for about 150 years after the beginning of the invasion, Christianity was maintained only in the remoter regions where the as yet pagan Anglo-Saxons failed to penetrate. In the year 597, however, a Benedictine monk (afterward St. Augustine of Canterbury) was sent by Pope Gregory as a missionary to King Ethelbert of Kent, the most southerly of the kingdoms into which England was then divided, and about the same time missionaries from Ireland began to preach Christianity in the north. Within 75 years the island was once more predominantly Christian. Before Christianity there had been no books. The impact of Christianity on literacy is evident from the fact that the first extended written specimen of the Old English (Anglo-Saxon) language is a code of laws promulgated by Ethelbert, the first English Christian king.

In the centuries that followed the conversion, England produced many distinguished churchmen. One of the earliest of these was Bede, whose Latin *Ecclesiastical History of the English People*, which tells the story of the conversion and of the English church, was completed in 731; this remains one of our most important sources of knowledge about the period. In the next generation Alcuin (735–804), a man of wide culture, became the friend and adviser of the Frankish emperor Charlemagne, whom he assisted in making the Frankish court a great center of learning; thus by the year 800 English culture had developed so richly that it overflowed its insular boundaries.

In the ninth century the Christian Anglo-Saxons were themselves sub-jected to new Germanic invasions by the Danes who in their longboats repeatedly ravaged the coast, sacking Bede's monastery among others. Such a raid in the tenth century inspired *The Battle of Maldon*, the last of the Old English heroic poems. The Danes also occupied the northern part of the island, threatening to overrun the rest. They were stopped by Alfred, king of the West Saxons from 871 to 899, who for a time united all the kingdoms of southern England. This most active king was also an enthusiastic patron of literature. He himself translated various works from Latin, the most important of which was Boethius's *Consolation of Philosophy*, a sixth-century Roman work also translated in the fourteenth century by Chaucer. Alfred probably also instigated a translation of Bede's *History* and the beginning of the *Anglo-Saxon Chronicle*: this year-by-year record in Old English of impor-tant events in England was maintained at one monastery until the middle of the twelfth century. Practically all of Old English poetry is preserved in cop-ies made in the West Saxon dialect after the reign of Alfred.

Old English Poetry

The Anglo-Saxon invaders brought with them a tradition of oral poetry (see "Bede and Cædmon's *Hymn*," p. 23). Because nothing was written down before the conversion to Christianity, we have only circumstantial evidence of what that poetry must have been like. Aside from a few short inscriptions on small artifacts, the earliest records in the English language are in man-uscripts produced at monasteries and other religious establishments, begin-ning in the seventh century. Literacy was mainly restricted to servants of the church, and so it is natural that the bulk of Old English literature deals with religious subjects and is mostly drawn from Latin sources. Manuscripts were costly and time-consuming to produce, because they required the copying of texts word by word onto parchment, a durable material made from the prepared skins of domestic animals (paper would not be used in Europe before the twelfth century). Under these difficult circumstances, few texts were written down that did not pertain directly to the work of the church. Most of Old English poetry is contained in just four manuscripts.

Germanic heroic poetry continued to be performed orally in alliterative verse and was at times used to describe current events. *The Battle of Brun-aburh*, which celebrates an English victory over the Danes in traditional alliterative verse, is preserved in the *Anglo-Saxon Chronicle*. *The Battle of Maldon* commemorates a Viking victory in which the Christian English invoke the ancient code of honor that obliges a warrior to avenge his slain lord or to die beside him.

These poems show that the aristocratic heroic and kinship values of Ger-manic society continued to inspire both clergy and laity in the Christian era. As represented in the relatively small body of Anglo-Saxon heroic poetry that survives, this world shares many characteristics with the heroic world described by Homer. Nations are reckoned as groups of people related by kinship rather than by geographical areas, and kinship is the basis of the heroic code. The tribe is ruled by a chieftain who is called *king*, a word that has "kin" for its root. The *lord* (a word derived from Old English *hlaf*, "loaf," plus *weard*, "protector") surrounds himself with a band of retainers (many of them his blood kindred) who are members of his household. He leads his men in battle and rewards them with the spoils; royal generosity was one of the most important aspects of heroic behavior. In return, the retainers are obligated to fight for their lord to the death, and if he is slain, to avenge him or die in the attempt. Blood vengeance is regarded as a sacred duty, and in poetry, everlasting shame awaits those who fail to observe it.

Even though the heroic world of poetry could be invoked to rally resistance to the Viking invasions, it was already remote from the Christian world of Anglo-Saxon England. Nevertheless, Christian writers like the *Beowulf* poet were fascinated by the distant culture of their pagan ancestors and by the inherent conflict between the heroic code and a religion that teaches that we should "forgive those who trespass against us" and that "all they that take the sword shall perish with the sword." The *Beowulf* poet looks back on that ancient world with admiration for the courage of which it was capable and at the same time with elegiac sympathy for its inevitable doom.

For Anglo-Saxon poetry, it is difficult and probably futile to draw a line between "heroic" and "Christian," for the best poetry crosses that boundary. Much of the Christian poetry is also cast in the heroic mode: although the Anglo-Saxons adapted themselves readily to the ideals of Christianity, they did not do so without adapting Christianity to their own heroic ideal. Thus Moses and St. Andrew, Christ and God the Father are represented in the style of heroic verse. In the *Dream of the Rood*, the Cross speaks of Christ as "the young hero, . . . strong and stouthearted." In Cædmon's *Hymn* the creation of heaven and earth is seen as a mighty deed, an "establishment of wonders." Anglo-Saxon heroines, too, are portrayed in the heroic manner. St. Helena, who leads an expedition to the Holy Land to discover the true Cross, is described as a "battle-queen." Christian and heroic ideals are poignantly blended in *The Wanderer*, which laments the separation from one's lord and kinsmen and the transience of all earthly treasures. Love between man and woman, as described by the female speaker of *The Wife's Lament*, is disrupted by separation, exile, and the malice of kinfolk.

The world of Old English poetry is predominantly harsh. Men are said to be cheerful in the mead hall, but even there they think of struggle in war, of possible triumph but more possible failure. Romantic love—one of the principal topics of later literature—appears hardly at all. Even so, at some of the bleakest moments, the poets powerfully recall the return of spring. The blade of the magic sword with which Beowulf has killed Grendel's mother in her sinister underwater lair begins to melt, "as ice melts / when the Father eases the fetters off the frost / and unravels the water ropes, He who wields power."

The poetic diction, formulaic phrases, and repetitions of parallel syntactic structures, which are determined by the versification, are difficult to reproduce in modern translation. A few features may be anticipated here and studied in the text of Cædmon's *Hymn*, printed below (pp. 24–25) with interlinear translation.

Poetic language is created out of a special vocabulary that contains a multiplicity of terms for *lord, warrior, spear, shield*, and so on. Synecdoche and metonymy are common figures of speech as when *keel* is used for "ship" or *iron*, for "sword." A particularly striking effect is achieved by the kenning, a compound of two words in place of another as when *sea* becomes "whale-road" or *body* is called "life-house." The figurative use of language finds playful expression in poetic riddles, of which about one hundred survive. Common (and sometimes uncommon) creatures, objects, or phenomena are described in an enigmatic passage of alliterative verse, and the reader must guess their identity. Sometimes they are personified and ask, "What is my name?"

Because special vocabulary and compounds are among the chief poetic effects, the verse is constructed in such a way as to show off such terms by creating a series of them in apposition. In the second sentence of Cædmon's *Hymn*, for example, God is referred to five times appositively as "he," "holy Creator," "mankind's Guardian," "eternal Lord," and "Master Almighty." This use of parallel and appositive expressions, known as *variation*, gives the verse a highly structured and musical quality.

The overall effect of the language is to formalize and elevate speech. Instead of being straightforward, it moves at a slow and stately pace with steady indirection. A favorite mode of this indirection is irony. A grim irony pervades heroic poetry even at the level of diction where *fighting* is called "battle-play." A favorite device, known by the rhetorical term *litotes*, is ironic understatement. After the monster Grendel has slaughtered the Danes in the great hall Heorot, it stands deserted. The poet observes, "It was easy then to meet with a man / shifting himself to a safer distance."

More than a figure of speech, irony is also a mode of perception in Old English poetry. In a famous passage, the Wanderer articulates the theme of *Ubi sunt* (where are they now): "Where has the horse gone? Where the young warrior? Where the giver of treasure? . . ." *Beowulf* is full of ironic balances and contrasts—between the aged Danish king and the youthful Beowulf, and between Beowulf, the high-spirited young warrior at the beginning, and Beowulf, the gray-haired king at the end, facing the dragon and death.

The formal and dignified speech of Old English poetry was always distant from the everyday language of the Anglo-Saxons, and this poetic idiom remained remarkably uniform throughout the roughly three hundred years that separate Cædmon's *Hymn* from *The Battle of Maldon*. This clinging to old forms—grammatical and orthographic as well as literary—by the Anglo-Saxon church and aristocracy conceals from us the enormous changes that were taking place in the English language and the diversity of its dialects. The dramatic changes between Old and Middle English did not happen overnight or over the course of a single century. The Normans displaced the English ruling class with their own barons and clerics, whose native language was a dialect of Old French that we call Anglo-Norman. Without a ruling literate class to preserve English traditions, the custom of transcribing vernacular texts in an earlier form of the West-Saxon dialect was abandoned, and both language and literature were allowed to develop unchecked in new directions.

ANGLO-NORMAN ENGLAND

The Normans, who took possession of England after the decisive Battle of Hastings (1066), were, like the Anglo-Saxons, descendants of Germanic adventurers who at the beginning of the tenth century had seized a wide part of northern France. Their name is actually a contraction of "Norsemen." A highly adaptable people, they had adopted the French language of the land they had settled in and its Christian religion. Both in Normandy and in Britain they were great builders of castles, with which they enforced their political dominance, and magnificent churches. Norman bishops, who held land and castles like the barons, wielded both political and spiritual authority. The earlier Norman kings of England, however, were often absentee rulers, as much concerned with defending their Continental possessions as with ruling over their English holdings. The English Crown's French territories were enormously increased in 1154 when Henry II, the first of England's Plantagenet kings, ascended the throne. Through his marriage with Eleanor of Aquitaine, the divorced wife of Louis VII of France, Henry had acquired vast provinces in the south of France.

The presence of a French-speaking ruling class in England created exceptional opportunities for linguistic and cultural exchange. Four languages coexisted in the realm of Anglo-Norman England: Latin, as it had been for Bede, remained the international language of learning, used for theology, science, and history. It was not by any means a written language only but a lingua franca by which different nationalities communicated in the church and the newly founded universities. The Norman aristocracy for the most part spoke French, but intermarriage with the native English nobility and the business of daily life between masters and servants encouraged bilingualism. Different branches of the Celtic language group were spoken in Scotland, Ireland, Wales, Cornwall, and Brittany.

Inevitably there was also literary intercourse among the different languages. The Latin Bible and Latin saints' lives provided subjects for a great deal of Old English as well as Old French poetry and prose. The first medieval drama in the vernacular, *The Play of Adam*, with elaborate stage directions in Latin and realistic dialogue in the Anglo-Norman dialect of French, was probably produced in England during the twelfth century.

The Anglo-Norman aristocracy was especially attracted to Celtic legends and tales that had been circulating orally for centuries. The twelfth-century poets Marie de France and Chrétien de Troyes both claim to have obtained their narratives from Breton storytellers, who were probably bilingual performers of native tales for French audiences. "Breton" may indicate that they came from Brittany, or it may have been a generic term for a Celtic bard. Marie speaks respectfully of the storytellers; Chrétien accuses them of marring their material, which, he boasts, he has retold with an elegant fusion of form and meaning. Marie wrote a series of short romances, which she refers to as "lays" originally told by Bretons. Her versions are the most original and sophisticated examples of the genre that came to be known as the Breton lay, represented here by Marie's *Lanval*. It is very likely that Henry II is the "noble king" to whom she dedicated her lays and that they were written for his court. Chrétien is the principal creator of the romance of chivalry in which knightly adventures are a means of exploring psychological and ethical dilemmas that the knights must solve, in addition to displaying martial prowess in saving ladies from monsters, giants, and wicked knights. Chrétien, like Marie, is thought to have spent time in England at the court of Henry II. Both Marie de France and Chrétien de Troyes were innovators of the genre that has become known as "romance." The word *roman* was initially applied in French to a work written in the French vernacular. Thus the thirteenth-century *Roman de Troie* is a long poem about the Trojan War in French. While this work deals mainly with the siege of Troy, it also includes stories about the love of Troilus for Cressida and of Achilles for the Trojan princess Polyxena. Eventually "romance" acquired the generic associations it has for us as a story about love and adventure. In the late twelfth century, Andreas Capellanus (Andrew the Chaplain) wrote a Latin treatise, the title of which may be translated *The Art of Loving Correctly* [*honeste*]. In one part, Eleanor of Aquitaine, her daughter, the countess Marie de Champagne, and other noble women are cited as a supreme court rendering decisions on difficult questions of love—for example, whether there is greater passion between lovers or between married couples. Whether such "courts of love" were purely imaginary or whether they represent some actual court entertainment, they imply that the literary taste and judgment of women had a significant role in determining the rise of romance in France and Anglo-Norman England.

In Marie's *Lanval* and in Chrétien's romances, the court of King Arthur had already acquired for French audiences a reputation as the most famous center of chivalry. That eminence is owing in large measure to a remarkable book in Latin, *The History of the Kings of Britain*, completed by Geoffrey of Monmouth, ca. 1136–38. Geoffrey claimed to have based his "history" on a book in the British tongue (i.e., Welsh), but no one has ever found such a book. He drew on a few earlier Latin chronicles, but the bulk of his history was probably fabricated from Celtic oral tradition, his familiarity with Roman history and literature, and his own fertile imagination. The climax of the book is the reign of King Arthur, who defeats the Roman armies but is forced to turn back to Britain to counter the treachery of his nephew Mordred. Geoffrey's Latin was rendered into French rhyme by an Anglo-Norman poet called Wace, and Wace's poem was turned by Layamon, an English priest, into a much longer poem that combines English alliterative verse with sporadic rhyme.

Layamon's work is one of many instances where English receives new material directly through French sources, which may be drawn from Celtic or Latin sources. There are two Middle English versions of Marie's *Lanval*, and the English romance called *Yvain and Gawain* is a cruder version of Chrétien's *Le Chevalier au Lion* (The Knight of the Lion). There is a marvelous English lay, *Sir Orfeo*, a version of the Orpheus story in which Orpheus succeeds in rescuing his wife from the other world, for which a French original, if there was one, has never been found. Romance, stripped of its courtly, psychological, and ethical subtleties, had an immense popular appeal for English readers and listeners. Many of these romances are simplified adaptations of more aristocratic French poems and recount in a rollicking and rambling style the adventures of heroes like Guy of Warwick, a poor steward who must prove his knightly worth to win the love of Fair

Phyllis. The ethos of many romances, aristocratic and popular alike, involves a knight proving his worthiness through nobility of character and brave deeds rather than through high birth. In this respect romances reflect the aspirations of a lower order of the nobility to rise in the world, as historically some of these nobles did. William the Marshall, for example, the fourth son of a baron of middle rank, used his talents in war and in tournaments to become tutor to the oldest son of Henry II and Eleanor of Aquitaine. He married a great heiress and became one of the most powerful nobles in England and the subject of a verse biography in French, which often reads like a romance.

Of course not all writing in Early Middle English depends on French sources or intermediaries. The *Anglo-Saxon Chronicle* continued to be written at the monastery of Peterborough. It is an invaluable witness for the changes taking place in the English language and allows us to see Norman rule from an English point of view. *The Owl and the Nightingale* is a witty and entertaining poem in which these two birds engage in a fierce debate about the benefits their singing brings to humankind. The owl grimly reminds his rival of the sinfulness of the human condition, which his mournful song is intended to amend; the nightingale sings about the pleasures of life and love when lord and lady are in bed together. The poet, who was certainly a cleric, is well aware of the fashionable new romance literature; he specifically has the nightingale allude to Marie de France's lay *Laüstic*, the Breton word, she says, for "rossignol" in French and "nightingale" in English. The poet does not side with either bird; rather he has amusingly created a dialectic between the discourses of religion and romance that is carried on throughout medieval literature.

There is also a body of Early Middle English religious prose aimed at women. Three saints' lives celebrate the heroic combats of virgin martyrs who suffer dismemberment and death; a tract entitled "Holy Maidenhead" paints the woes of marriage not from the point of view of the husband, as in standard medieval antifeminist writings, but from that of the wife. Related to these texts, named the Katherine Group after one of the virgin martyrs, is a religious work also written for women but in a very different spirit. The *Ancrene Riwle* (Anchoresses' Rule), or *Ancrene Wisse* (Anchoresses' Guide) as it is called in another manuscript, is one of the finest works of English religious prose in any period. It is a manual of instruction written at the request of three sisters who have chosen to live as religious recluses. The author, who may have been their personal confessor, addresses them with affection, with kindness, and, at times, with humor. He is also profoundly serious in his analyses of sin, penance, and love. In the selection included here from his chapter on love, he, too, tells a tale of romance in a strikingly different way.

MIDDLE ENGLISH LITERATURE IN THE FOURTEENTH AND FIFTEENTH CENTURIES

The styles of *The Owl and the Nightingale* and *Ancrene Riwle* show that around the year 1200 both poetry and prose were being written for sophisticated and well-educated readers whose primary language was English. Throughout the thirteenth and early fourteenth centuries, there are many kinds of evidence that, although French continued to be the principal language of Parliament, law, business, and high culture, English was gaining ground. Several authors of religious and didactic works in English state that they are writing for the benefit of those who do not understand Latin or French. Anthologies are made of miscellaneous works adapted from French for English readers and original pieces in English. Most of the nobility are by now bilingual, and the author of an English romance written early in the fourteenth century declares that he has seen many nobles who cannot speak French. Children of the nobility and the merchant class are now learning French as a second language. By the 1360s the linguistic, political, and cultural climate had been prepared for the flowering of Middle English literature in the writings of Chaucer, Langland, and the *Gawain* poet.

The Fourteenth Century

War and disease were prevalent throughout the Middle Ages but never more devastatingly than during the fourteenth century. In the wars against France, the gains of two spectacular English victories, at Crécy in 1346 and Poitiers in 1356, were gradually frittered away in futile campaigns that ravaged the French countryside without obtaining any clear advantage for the English. In 1348 the first and most virulent epidemic of the bubonic plague—the Black Death—swept Europe, wiping out a quarter to a third of the population. The toll was higher in crowded urban centers. Giovanni Boccaccio's description of the plague in Florence, with which he introduces the *Decameron*, vividly portrays its ravages: "So many corpses would arrive in front of a church every day and at every hour that the amount of holy ground for burials was certainly insufficient for the ancient custom of giving each body its individual place; when all the graves were full, huge trenches were dug in all of the cemeteries of the churches and into them the new arrivals were dumped by the hundreds; and they were packed in there with dirt, one on top of another, like a ship's cargo, until the trench was filled." The resulting scarcity of labor and a sudden expansion of the possibilities for social mobility fostered popular discontent. In 1381 attempts to enforce wage controls and to collect oppressive new taxes provoked a rural uprising in Essex and Kent that dealt a profound shock to the English ruling class. The participants were for the most part tenant farmers, day laborers, apprentices, and rural workers not attached to the big manors. A few of the lower clergy sided with the rebels against their wealthy church superiors; the priest John Ball was among the leaders. The movement was quickly suppressed, but not before sympathizers in London had admitted the rebels through two city gates, which had been barred against them. The insurgents burned down the palace of the hated duke of Lancaster, and they summarily beheaded the archbishop of Canterbury and the treasurer of England, who had taken refuge in the Tower of London. The church had become the target of popular resentment because it was among the greatest of the oppressive landowners and because of the wealth, worldliness, and venality of many of the higher clergy.

These calamities and upheavals nevertheless did not stem the growth of international trade and the influence of the merchant class. In the portrait of Geoffrey Chaucer's merchant, we see the budding of capitalism based on credit and interest. Cities like London ran their own affairs under politically powerful mayors and aldermen. Edward III, chronically in need of money to finance his wars, was obliged to negotiate for revenues with the Commons in the English Parliament, an institution that became a major political force during this period. A large part of the king's revenues depended on taxing the profitable export of English wool to the Continent. The Crown thus became involved in the country's economic affairs, and this involvement led to a need for capable administrators. These were no longer drawn mainly from the church, as in the past, but from a newly educated laity that occupied a rank somewhere between that of the lesser nobility and the upper bourgeoisie. The career of Chaucer, who served Edward III and his successor Richard II in a number of civil posts, is typical of this class—with the exception that Chaucer was also a great poet.

In the fourteenth century, a few poets and intellectuals achieved the status and respect formerly accorded only to the ancients. Marie de France and Chrétien de Troyes had dedicated their works to noble patrons and, in their role as narrators, address themselves as entertainers and sometimes as instructors to court audiences. Dante (1265–1321) made himself the protagonist of *The Divine Comedy*, the sacred poem, as he called it, in which he revealed the secrets of the afterlife. After his death, manuscripts of the work were provided with lengthy commentaries as though it were Scripture, and public readings and lectures were devoted to it. Francesco Petrarch (1304–1374) won an international reputation as a man of letters. He wrote primarily in Latin and contrived to have himself crowned "poet laureate" in emulation of the Roman poets whose works he imitated, but his most famous work is the sonnet sequence he wrote in Italian. Giovanni Boccaccio (1313–1375) was among Petrarch's most ardent admirers and carried on a literary correspondence with him.

Chaucer read these authors along with the ancient Roman poets and drew on them in his own works. Chaucer's *Clerk's Tale* is based on a Latin version Petrarch made from the last tale in Boccaccio's *Decameron*; in his prologue, the Clerk refers to Petrarch as "lauriat poete" whose sweet rhetoric illuminated all Italy with his poetry. Yet in his own time, the English poet Chaucer never attained the kind of laurels that he and others accorded to Petrarch. In his earlier works, Chaucer portrayed himself comically as a diligent reader of old books, as an aspiring apprentice writer, and as an eager spectator on the fringe of a fashionable world of courtiers and poets. In *The House of Fame*, he relates a dream of being snatched up by a huge golden eagle (the eagle and many other things in this work were inspired by Dante), who transports him to the palace of the goddess of Fame. There he gets to see phantoms, like the shades in Dante's poem, of all the famous authors of antiquity. At the end of his romance *Troilus and Criseyde*, Chaucer asks his "litel book" to kiss the footsteps where the great ancient poets had passed before. Like Dante and Petrarch, Chaucer had an ideal of great poetry and, in his *Troilus* at least, strove to emulate it. But in *The House of Fame* and in his final work, *The Canterbury Tales*, he also views that ideal ironically and distances himself from it. The many surviving documents that record Geoffrey Chaucer's career as a civil servant do not contain a single word to show that he was also a poet. Only in the following centuries would he be canonized as the father of English poetry.

Chaucer is unlikely to have known his contemporary William Langland, who says in an autobiographical passage (see p. 346), added to the third and last version of his great poem *Piers Plowman*, that he lived in London on Cornhill (a poor area of the city) among "lollers." "Loller" was a slang term for the unemployed and transients; it was later applied to followers of the religious and social reformer John Wycliffe (see p. 252), some of whom were burned at the stake for heresy in the next century. Langland assailed corruption in church and state, but he was certainly no radical. It is thought that he may have written the third version of *Piers Plowman*, which tones down his attacks on the church, after the rebels of 1381 invoked Piers as one of their own. Although Langland does not condone rebellion and his religion is quite orthodox, he nevertheless presents the most clear-sighted vision of social and religious issues in the England of his day. *Piers Plowman* is also a painfully honest search for the right way that leads to salvation. Though learned himself, Langland and the dreamer who represents him in the poem arrive at the insight that learning can be one of the chief obstacles on that way.

Langland came from the west of England, and his poem belongs to the "Alliterative Revival," a final flowering in the late fourteenth century of the verse form that goes all the way back to Anglo-Saxon England. Native traditions held out longest in the west and north, away from London, where Chaucer and his audience were more open to literary fashions from the Continent. Admiration for Chaucer's poetry and the controversial nature of Langland's writing assured the survival of their work in many manuscripts. The work of a third major fourteenth-century English poet, who remains anonymous, is known only through a single manuscript, which contains four poems all thought to be by a single author: *Cleanness* and *Patience*, two biblical narratives in alliterative verse; *Pearl*, a moving dream vision in which a grief-stricken father is visited and consoled by his dead child, who has been transformed into a queen in the kingdom of heaven; and *Sir Gawain and the Green Knight*, the finest of all English romances. The plot of *Gawain* involves a folklore motif of a challenge by a supernatural visitor, first found in an Old Irish tale. The poet has made this motif a challenge to King Arthur's court and has framed the tale with allusions at the beginning and end to the legends that link Arthur's reign with the Trojan War and the founding of Rome and of Britain. The poet has a sophisticated awareness of romance as a literary genre and plays a game with both the hero's and the readers' expectations of what is supposed to happen in a romance. One could say that the broader subject of *Sir Gawain and the Green Knight* is "romance" itself, and in this respect the poem resembles Chaucer's *Canterbury Tales* in its author's interest in literary form.

The Fifteenth Century

In 1399 Henry Bolingbroke, the duke of Lancaster, deposed his cousin Richard II, who was murdered in prison. As Henry IV, he successfully defended his crown against several insurrections and passed it on to Henry V, who briefly united the country once more and achieved one last apparently decisive victory over the French at the Battle of Agincourt (1415). The premature death of Henry V, however, left England exposed to the civil wars known as the Wars of the Roses, the red rose being the emblem of the house of Lancaster; the white, of York. These wars did not end until 1485, when Henry Tudor defeated Richard III at Bosworth Field and acceded to the throne as Henry VII.

Social, economic, and literary life continued as they had throughout all of the previous wars. The prosperity of the towns was shown by performances of the mystery plays—a sequence or "cycle" of plays based on the Bible and produced by the city guilds, the organizations representing the various trades and crafts. The cycles of several towns are lost, but those of York, Wakefield, and Chester have been preserved. Under the guise of dramatizing biblical history, playwrights such as the Wakefield Master manage to comment satirically on the social ills of the times. The century also saw the development of the morality play, in which personified vices and virtues struggle for the soul of "Mankind" or "Everyman." Performed by strolling players, the morality plays were precursors of the professional theater in the reign of Elizabeth I.

While religious works of all kinds continued to be produced, the fourteenth and fifteenth centuries are notable (both in England and on the Continent) for mystical writings in which the authors, many of whom were women, tell of their direct personal experience of God. The anchoress Julian of Norwich spent her life meditating and writing about a series of visions, which she called "showings," that she had received in 1373, when she was thirty years old. Early in the fifteenth century she was still in her cell, attached to a church in Norwich, when she was consulted by Margery Kempe, whom a series of visions had directed to lead a spiritual life. Kempe, a controversial figure, made a pilgrimage to the Holy Land and during the 1430s dictated the first autobiography in English. Both Julian of Norwich and Margery Kempe, in highly individual ways, allow us to see the medieval church and its doctrines from female points of view.

The most prolific poet of the fifteenth century was the monk John Lydgate (1370?–1451?), who produced dream visions; a life of the Virgin; translations of French religious allegories; a *Troy Book*; *The Siege of Thebes*, which he framed as a "new" Canterbury tale; and a thirty-six-thousand-line poem called *The Fall of Princes*, a free translation of a French work, itself based on a Latin work by Boccaccio. The last illustrates the late medieval idea of tragedy, namely that emperors, kings, and other famous men enjoy power and fortune only to be cast down in misery. Lydgate shapes these tales as a "mirror" for princes, i.e., as object lessons to the powerful men of his own day, several of whom were his patrons. A self-styled imitator of Chaucer, Lydgate had a reputation almost equal to Chaucer's in the fifteenth century. The best of Chaucer's imitators was the "Scottish Chaucerian," Robert Henryson (1425?–1508?), who wrote *The Testament of Cresseid*, a continuation of Chaucer's great poem *Troilus and Criseyde*. He also wrote the *Moral Fabilis of Esope*, among which *The Cock and the Fox*, included here, is a remake of Chaucer's *Nun's Priest's Tale*. The works of Sir Thomas Malory gave the definitive form in English to the saga of King Arthur and his knights. Malory spent years in prison Englishing a series of Arthurian romances that he translated and abridged chiefly from several enormously long thirteenth-century French prose romances. Malory was a passionate devotee of chivalry, which he personified in his hero Sir Lancelot. In the jealousies and rivalries that finally break up the round table and destroy Arthur's kingdom, Malory saw a distant image of the civil wars of his own time. A manuscript of Malory's works fell into the hands of William Caxton (1422?–1491), who had introduced the new art of printing by movable type to England in 1476. Caxton divided Malory's tales into the chapters and books of a single long work, as though it were a chronicle history, and gave it the title *Morte Darthur*, which has stuck to it ever since. Caxton also printed *The Canterbury Tales*, some of Chaucer's earlier works, and Gower's *Confessio Amantis*. Caxton himself translated many of the works he printed for English readers: a history of Troy, a book on chivalry, Aesop's fables, and *The Game and Playe of Chesse*. The new technology extended literacy and made books more easily accessible to new classes of readers. Printing made the production of literature a business and made possible the bitter political and doctrinal disputes that, in the sixteenth century, were waged in print as well as on the field of battle.

MEDIEVAL ENGLISH

The medieval works in this book were composed in different states of our language. Old English, the language that took shape among the Germanic settlers of England, preserved its integrity until the Norman Conquest radically altered English civilization. Middle English, the earliest records of which date from the early twelfth century, was continually changing. Shortly after the introduction of printing at the end of the fifteenth century, it attained the form designated as Early Modern English. Old English is a very heavily inflected language. (That is, the words change form to indicate changes in usage, such as person, number, tense, case, mood, and so on. Most languages have some inflection—for example, the personal pronouns in Modern English have different forms when used as objects—but a "heavily inflected" language is one in which almost all classes of words undergo elaborate patterns of change.) The vocabulary of Old English is almost entirely Germanic. In Middle English, the inflectional system was weakened, and a large number of words were introduced into it from French, so that many of the older native words disappeared. Because of the difficulty of Old English, all selections from it in this book have been given in translation. So that the reader may see an example of the language, Cædmon's *Hymn* and a passage from *The Battle of Maldon* have been printed in the original, together with interlinear translations. The present discussion, then, is concerned primarily with the relatively late form of Middle English used by Chaucer and the East Midland dialect in which he wrote.

The chief difficulty with Middle English for the modern reader is caused not by its inflections so much as by its spelling, which may be described as a rough-and-ready phonetic system, and by the fact that it is not a single standardized language, but consists of a number of regional dialects, each with its own peculiarities of sound and its own systems for representing sounds in writing. The Midland dialect—the dialect of London and of Chaucer, which is the ancestor of our own standard speech—differs greatly from the dialect spoken in the west of England (the original dialect of *Piers Plowman*), from that of the northwest (*Sir Gawain* and *the Green Knight*), and from that of the north (*The Second Shepherds' Play*). In this book, the long texts composed in the more difficult dialects have been translated or modernized, and those that—like Chaucer, *Everyman*, the lyrics, and the ballads—appear in the original, have been re-spelled in a way that is designed to aid the reader. The remarks that follow apply chiefly to Chaucer's Midland English, although certain non-Midland dialectal variations are noted if they occur in some of the other selections.

I. The Sounds of Middle English: General Rules

The following general analysis of the sounds of Middle English will enable the reader who has not time for detailed study to read Middle English aloud so as to preserve some of its most essential characteristics, without, however, giving heed to many important details. The next section, "Detailed Analysis," is designed for the reader who wishes to go more deeply into the pronunciation of Middle English.

Middle English differs from Modern English in three principal respects: (1) the pronunciation of the long vowels *a*, *e*, *i* (or *y*), *o*, and *u* (spelled *ou*, *ow*); (2) the fact that Middle English final *e* is often sounded; and (3) the fact that all Middle English consonants are sounded.

1. LONG VOWELS

Middle English vowels are long when they are doubled (*aa*, *ee*, *oo*) or when they are terminal (*he*, *to*, *holy*); *a*, *e*, and *o* are long when followed by a single consonant plus a vowel (*name*, *mete*, *note*). Middle English vowels are short when they are followed by two consonants.

Long *a* is sounded like the *a* in Modern English "father": *maken*, *madd*.

Long *e* may be sounded like the *a* in Modern English "name" (ignoring the distinction between the close and open vowel): *be*, *sweete*.

Long *i* (or *y*) is sounded like the *i* in Modern English "machine": *lif*, *whit*; *myn*, *holy*.

Long *o* may be sounded like the *o* in Modern English "note" (again ignoring the distinction between the close and open vowel): *do*, *soone*.

Long *u* (spelled *ou*, *ow*) is sounded like the *oo* in Modern English "goose": *hous*, *flowr*.

Note that in general Middle English long vowels are pronounced like long vowels in modern European languages other than English. Short vowels and diphthongs, however, may be pronounced as in Modern English.

2. FINAL E

In Middle English syllabic verse, final *e* is sounded like the *a* in "sofa" to provide a needed unstressed syllable: *Another Nonnë with hire haddë she*. But (cf. *hire* in the example) final *e* is suppressed when not needed for the meter. It is commonly silent before words beginning with a vowel or *h*.

3. CONSONANTS

Middle English consonants are pronounced separately in all combinations—*gnat*: *g-nat*; *knave*: *k-nave*; *write*: *w-rite*; *folk*: *fol-k*. In a simplified system of pronunciation the combination *gh* as in *night* or *thought* may be treated as if it were silent.

II. The Sounds of Middle English: Detailed Analysis

1. SIMPLE VOWELS

Sound	Pronunciation	Example
long *a* (spelled *a*, *aa*)	*a* in "father"	*maken*, *maad*
short *a*	*o* in "hot"	*cappe*
long *e* close (spelled *e*, *ee*)	*a* in "name"	*be*, *sweete*

long *e* open (spelled *e, ee*)	*e* in "there"	*mete, heeth*
short *e*	*e* in "set"	*setten*
final *e*	*a* in "sofa"	*large*
long *i* (spelled *i, y*)	*i* in "machine"	*lif, mym*
short *i*	*i* in "wit"	*wit*
long *o* close (spelled *o, oo*)	*o* in "note"	*do, soone*
long *o* open (spelled *o, oo*)	*oa* in "broad"	*go, goon*
short *o*	*o* in "oft"	*pot*
long *u* when spelled *ou, ow*	*oo* in "goose"	*hous, flowr*
long *u* when spelled *u*	*u* in "pure"	*vertu*
short *u* (spelled *u, o*)	*u* in "full"	*ful, love*

Doubled vowels and terminal vowels are always long, whereas single vowels before two consonants other than *th, ch* are always short. The vowels *a*, *e*, and *o* are long before a single consonant followed by a vowel: *nāmë, sēkë* (sick), *hōly*. In general, words that have descended into Modern English reflect their original Middle English quantity: *liven* (to live), but *līf* (life).

The close and open sounds of long *e* and long *o* may often be identified by the Modern English spellings of the words in which they appear. Original long close *e* is generally represented in Modern English by *ee*: "sweet," "knee," "teeth," "see" have close *e* in Middle English, but so does "be"; original long open *e* is generally represented in Modern English by *ea*: "meat," "heath," "sea," "great," "breath" have open *e* in Middle English. Similarly, original long close *o* is now generally represented by *oo*: "soon," "food," "good," but also "do," "to"; original long open *o* is represented either by *oa* or by *o*: "coat," "boat," "moan," but also "go," "bone," "foe," "home." Notice that original close *o* is now almost always pronounced like the *oo* in "goose," but that original open *o* is almost never so pronounced; thus it is often possible to identify the Middle English vowels through Modern English sounds.

The nonphonetic Middle English spelling of *o* for short *u* has been preserved in a number of Modern English words ("love," "son," "come"), but in others *u* has been restored: "sun" (*sonne*), "run" (*ronne*).

For the treatment of final *e*, see "General Rules," "Final *e*."

2. DIPHTHONGS

Sound	Pronunciation	Example
ai, ay, ei, ay	between *ai* in "aisle" and *ay* in "day"	*saide, day, veine, preye*
au, aw	*ou* in "out"	*chaunge, bawdy*
eu, ew	*ew* in "few"	*newe*
oi, oy	*oy* in "joy"	*joye, point*
ou, ow	*ou* in "thought"	*thought, lowe*

Note that in words with *ou, ow* that in Modern English are sounded with the *ou* of "about," the combination indicates not the diphthong but the simple vowel long *u* (see "Simple Vowels").

3. CONSONANTS

In general, all consonants except *h* were always sounded in Middle English, including consonants that have become silent in Modern English, such as the *g* in *gnaw*, the *k* in *knight*, the *l* in *folk*, and the *w* in *write*. In noninitial *gn*, however, the *g* was silent as in Modern English "sign." Initial *h* was silent in short common English words and in words borrowed from French and may have been almost silent in all words. The combination *gh* as in *night* or *thought* was sounded like the *ch* of German *ich* or *nach*. Note that Middle English *gg* represents both the hard sound of "dagger" and the soft sound of "bridge."

III. Parts of Speech and Grammar

1. NOUNS

The plural and possessive of nouns end in *es*, formed by adding *s* or *es* to the singular: *knight, knightes; roote, rootes*; a final consonant is frequently doubled before *es: bed, beddes*. A common irregular plural is *yën*, from *yë, eye*.

2. PRONOUNS

The chief differences from Modern English are as follows:

Modern English	Middle English
I	*I, ich* (*ik* is a northern form)
you (singular)	*thou* (subjective); *thee* (objective)
her	*hir(e), her(e)*
its	*his*
you (plural)	*ye* (subjective); *you* (objective)
their	*hir*
them	*hem*

In formal speech, the second person plural is often used for the singular. The possessive adjectives *my, thy* take *n* before a word beginning with a vowel or *h: thyn yë, myn host*.

3. ADJECTIVES

Adjectives ending in a consonant add final *e* when they stand before the noun they modify and after another modifying word such as *the, this, that*, or nouns or pronouns in the possessive: *a good hors*, but *the* (*this, my, the kinges*) *goode hors*. They also generally add *e* when standing before and modifying a plural noun, a noun in the vocative, or any proper noun: *goode men, oh goode man, faire Venus*.

Adjectives are compared by adding *er(e)* for the comparative, *est(e)* for the superlative. Sometimes the stem vowel is shortened or altered in the process: *sweete, swettere, swettest; long, lenger, lengest*.

4. ADVERBS

Adverbs are formed from adjectives by adding *e, ly*, or *liche*; the adjective *fair* thus yields *faire, fairly, fairliche*.

5. VERBS

Middle English verbs, like Modern English verbs, are either "weak" or "strong." Weak verbs form their preterites and past participles with a *t* or *d* suffix and preserve the same stem vowel throughout their systems, although it is sometimes shortened in the preterite and past participle: *love, loved; bend, bent; hear, heard; meet, met*. Strong verbs do not use the *t* or *d* suffix, but vary their stem vowel in the preterite and past participle: *take, took, taken; begin, began, begun; find, found, found*.

The inflectional endings are the same for Middle English strong verbs and weak verbs except in the preterite singular and the imperative singular. In the following paradigms, the weak verbs *loven* (to love) and *heeren* (to hear), and the strong verbs *taken* (to take) and *ginnen* (to begin) serve as models.

	Present Indicative	Preterite Indicative
I	*love, heere*	*loved(e), herde*
	take, ginne	*took, gan*
thou	*lovest, heerest*	*lovedest, herdest*
	takest, ginnest	*tooke, gonne*
he, she, it	*loveth, heereth*	*loved(e), herde*
	taketh, ginneth	*took, gan*
we, ye, they	*love(n) (th), heere(n) (th)*	*loved(e) (en), herde(n)*
	take(n) (th), ginne(n) (th)	*tooke(n), gonne(n)*

The present plural ending *eth* is southern, whereas the *e(n)* ending is Midland and characteristic of Chaucer. In the north, *s* may appear as the ending of all persons of the present. In the weak preterite, when the ending *e* gave a verb three or more syllables, it was frequently dropped. Note that in certain strong verbs like *ginnen* there are two distinct stem vowels in the preterite; even in Chaucer's time, however, one of these had begun to replace the other, and Chaucer occasionally writes *gan* for all persons of the preterite.

	Present Subjunctive	Preterite Subjunctive
Singular	*love, heere*	*lovede, herde*
	take, ginne	*tooke, gonne*
Plural	*love(n), heere(n)*	*lovede(n), herde(n)*
	take(n), ginne(n)	*tooke(n), gonne(n)*

In verbs like *ginnen*, which have two stem vowels in the indicative preterite, it is the vowel of the plural and of the second person singular that is used for the preterite subjunctive.

The imperative singular of most weak verbs is *e: (thou) love*, but of some weak verbs and all strong verbs, the imperative singular is without termination: *(thou) heer, taak, gin*. The imperative plural of all verbs is either *e* or *eth: (ye) love(th), heere(th), take(th), ginne(th)*.

The infinitive of verbs is *e* or *en: love(n), heere(n), take(n), ginne(n)*.

The past participle of weak verbs is the same as the preterite without inflectional ending: *loved, herd*. In strong verbs the ending is either *e* or *en: take(n), gonne(n)*. The prefix *y* often appears on past participles: *yloved, yherd, ytake(n)*.

OLD AND MIDDLE ENGLISH PROSODY

All the poetry of Old English is in the same verse form. The verse unit is the single line, because rhyme was not used to link one line to another, except very occasionally in late Old English. The organizing device of the line is alliteration, the beginning of several words with the same sound ("Foemen fled"). The Old English alliterative line contains, on the average, four principal stresses and is divided into two half-lines of two stresses each by a strong medial caesura, or pause. These two half-lines are linked to each other by the alliteration; at least one of the two stressed words in the first half-line, and often both of them, begin with the same sound as the first stressed word of the second half-line (the second stressed word is generally nonalliterative). The fourth line of *Beowulf* is an example (*sc* has the value of modern *sh*; þ is a runic symbol with the value of modern *th*):

Oft Scyld Scefing   sceaþena þreatum.

For further examples, see Cædmon's *Hymn* and the passage from *The Battle of Maldon*. It will be noticed that any vowel alliterates with any other vowel. In addition to the alliteration, the length of the unstressed syllables and their number and pattern is governed by a highly complex set of rules. When sung or intoned—as it was—to the rhythmic strumming of a harp, Old English poetry must have been wonderfully impressive in the dignified, highly formalized way that aptly fits both its subject matter and tone.

The majority of Middle English verse is either in alternately stressed rhyming verse, adapted from French after the conquest, or in alliterative verse that is descended from Old English. The latter preserves the caesura of Old English and in its purest form the same alliterative system, the two stressed words of the first half-line (or at least one of them) alliterating with the first stressed word in the second half-line. But most of the alliterative poets allowed themselves a number of deviations from the norm. All four stressed words may alliterate, as in the first line of *Piers Plowman*:

In a summer season   when soft was the sun.

Or the line may contain five, six, or even more stressed words, of which all or only the basic minimum may alliterate:

A *fair field full* of   *folk found* I there between.

There is no rule determining the number of unstressed syllables, and at times some poets seem to ignore alliteration entirely. As in Old English, any vowel may alliterate with any other vowel; furthermore, since initial *h* was silent or lightly pronounced in Middle English, words beginning with *h* are treated as though they began with the following vowel.

There are two general types of stressed verse with rhyme. In the more common, stressed and unstressed syllables alternate regularly as x X x X x X or, with two unstressed syllables intervening as x x X x x X x x X or a combination of the two as x x X x X x x X (of the reverse patterns, only X x X x X x is common in English). There is also a line that can only be defined as containing a predetermined number of stressed syllables but an irregular number and pattern of unstressed syllables. Much Middle English verse has to be read without expectation of regularity; some of this was evidently composed in the irregular meter, but some was probably originally composed according to a strict metrical system that has been obliterated by scribes careless of fine points. One receives the impression that many of the lyrics— as well as the *Second Shepherds' Play*—were at least composed with regular syllabic alternation. In the play *Everyman*, only the number of stresses is generally predetermined but not the number or placement of unstressed syllables.

In pre-Chaucerian verse the number of stresses, whether regularly or irregularly alternated, was most often four, although sometimes the number was three and rose in some poems to seven. Rhyme in Middle English (as in Modern English) may be either between adjacent or alternate lines, or may occur in more complex patterns. Most of the *Canterbury Tales* are in rhymed couplets, the line containing five stresses with regular alternation—technically known as iambic pentameter, the standard English poetic line, perhaps introduced into English by Chaucer. In reading Chaucer and much pre-Chaucerian verse one must remember that the final *e*, which is silent in Modern English, could be pronounced at any time to provide a needed unstressed syllable. Evidence seems to indicate that it was also pronounced at the end of the line, even though it thus produced a line with eleven syllables. Although he was a very regular metricist, Chaucer used various conventional devices that are apt to make the reader stumble until he or she understands them. Final *e* is often not pronounced before a word beginning with a vowel or *h*, and may be suppressed whenever metrically convenient. The same medial and terminal syllables that are slurred in Modern English are apt to be suppressed in Chaucer's English: *Canterb'ry* for *Canterbury*; *ev'r* (perhaps *e'er*) for *evere*. The plural in *es* may either be syllabic or reduced to *s* as in Modern English. Despite these seeming irregularities, Chaucer's verse is not difficult to read if one constantly bears in mind the basic pattern of the iambic pentameter line.

THE MIDDLE AGES

TEXTS	CONTEXTS
	43–ca. 420 Romans conquer Britons; Brittania a province of the Roman Empire
	307–37 Reign of Constantine the Great leads to adoption of Christianity as official religion of the Roman Empire
ca. 405 St. Jerome completes *Vulgate,* Latin translation of the Bible that becomes standard for the Roman Catholic Church	
	432 St. Patrick begins mission to convert Ireland
	ca. 450 Anglo-Saxon conquest of Britons begins
523 Boethius, *Consolation of Philosophy* (Latin)	
	597 St. Augustine of Canterbury's mission to Kent begins conversion of Anglo-Saxons to Christianity
ca. 658–80 *Cædmon's Hymn,* earliest poem recorded in English	
731 Bede completes *Ecclesiastical History of the English People*	
? ca. 750 *Beowulf* composed	
	ca. 787 First Viking raids on England
	871–99 Reign of King Alfred
ca. 1000 Unique *Beowulf* manuscript written	
	1066 Norman Conquest by William I establishes French-speaking ruling class in England
	1095–1221 Crusades
ca. 1135–38 Geoffrey of Monmouth's Latin *History of the Kings of Britain* gives pseudohistorical status to Arthurian and other legends	
	1152 Future Henry II marries Eleanor of Aquitaine, bringing vast French territories to the English crown
1154 End of *Peterborough Chronicle,* last branch of the *Anglo-Saxon Chronicle*	
? ca. 1165–80 Marie de France, *Lais* in Anglo-Norman French from Breton sources	
ca. 1170–91 Chrétien de Troyes, chivalric romances about knights of the Round Table	**1170** Archbishop Thomas Becket murdered in Canterbury Cathedral
	1182 Birth of St. Francis of Assisi
? ca. 1200 Layamon's *Brut*	
? ca. 1215–25 *Ancrene Riwle*	**1215** Fourth Lateran Council requires annual confession. English barons force King John to seal Magna Carta (the Great Charter) guaranteeing baronial rights

TEXTS	CONTEXTS
ca. 1304–21 Dante Alighieri writing *Divine Comedy*	
	ca. 1337–1453 Hundred Years' War
	1348 Black Death ravages Europe
	1362 English first used in law courts and Parliament
1368 Chaucer, *Book of the Duchess*	
	1372 Chaucer's first journey to Italy
ca. 1375–1400 *Sir Gawain and the Green Knight*	
	1376 Earliest record of performance of drama at York
1377–79 William Langland, *Piers Plowman* (B-Text)	
ca. 1380 John Wycliffe and his followers begin first complete translation of the Bible into English	
	1381 People's uprising briefly takes control of London before being suppressed
ca. 1385–87 Chaucer, *Troilus and Criseyde*	
ca. 1387–89 Chaucer working on *The Canterbury Tales*	
ca. 1390–92 John Gower, *Confessio Amantis*	
	1399 Richard II deposed by his cousin, who succeeds him as Henry IV
	1400 Richard II murdered
	1401 Execution of William Sawtre, first Lollard burned at the stake under new law against heresy
	1415 Henry V defeats French at Agincourt
	1431 English burn Joan of Arc at Rouen
ca. 1432–38 Margery Kempe, *The Book of Margery Kempe*	
ca. 1450–75 Wakefield mystery cycle, *Second Shepherds' Play*	
	1455–85 Wars of the Roses
ca. 1470 Sir Thomas Malory in prison working on *Morte Darthur*	
	1476 William Caxton sets up first printing press in England
1485 Caxton publishes *Morte Darthur*, one of the first books in English to be printed	1485 The earl of Richmond defeats the Yorkist king, Richard III, at Bosworth Field and succeeds him as Henry VII, founder of the Tudor dynasty
ca. 1510 *Everyman*	
	1575 Last performance of mystery plays at Chester

Anglo-Saxon England

BEDE (ca. 673–735) and CÆDMON'S HYMN

The Venerable Bede (the title by which he is known to posterity) became a novice at the age of seven and spent the rest of his life at the neighboring monasteries of Wearmouth and Jarrow. Although he may never have traveled beyond the boundaries of his native district of Northumbria, he achieved an international reputation as one of the greatest scholars of his age. Writing in Latin, the learned language of the era, Bede produced many theological works as well as books on science and rhetoric, but his most popular and enduring work is the *Ecclesiastical History of the English People* (completed 731). The *History* tells about the Anglo-Saxon conquest and the vicissitudes of the petty kingdoms that comprised Anglo-Saxon England; Bede's main theme, however, is the spread of Christianity and the growth of the English church. The latter were the great events leading up to Bede's own time, and he regarded them as the unfolding of God's providence. The *History* is, therefore, also a moral work and a hagiography—that is, it contains many stories of saints and miracles meant to testify to the grace and glory of God.

The story we reprint preserves what is probably the earliest extant Old English poem (composed sometime between 658 and 680) and the only biographical information, outside of what is said in the poems themselves, about any Old English poet. Bede tells how Cædmon, an illiterate cowherd employed by the monastery of Whitby, miraculously received the gift of song, entered the monastery, and became the founder of a school of Christian poetry. Cædmon was clearly an oral-formulaic poet, one who created his work by combining and varying formulas—units of verse developed in a tradition transmitted by one generation of singers to another. In this respect he resembles the singers of the Homeric poems and oral-formulaic poets recorded in the twentieth century, especially in the Balkan countries. Although Bede tells us that Cædmon had never learned the art of song, we may suspect that he concealed his skill from his fellow workmen and from the monks because he was ashamed of knowing "vain and idle" songs, the kind Bede says Cædmon never composed. Cædmon's inspiration and the true miracle, then, was to apply the meter and language of such songs, presumably including pagan heroic verse, to Christian themes.

Although most Old English poetry was written by lettered poets, they continued to use the oral-formulaic style. The *Hymn* is, therefore, a good short example of the way Old English verse, with its traditional poetic diction and interwoven formulaic expressions, is constructed. Eight of the poem's eighteen half-lines contain epithets describing various aspects of God: He is *Weard* (Guardian), *Meotod* (Measurer), *Wuldor-Fæder* (Glory-Father), *Drihten* (Lord), *Scyppend* (Creator), and *Frea* (Master). God is *heofonrices Weard* or *mancynnes Weard* (heaven's or mankind's Guardian), depending on the alliteration required. This formulaic style provides a richness of texture and meaning difficult to convey in translation. As Bede said about his own Latin paraphrase of the *Hymn*, no literal translation of poetry from one language to another is possible without sacrifice of some poetic quality.

Several manuscripts of Bede's *History* contain the Old English text in addition to Bede's Latin version. The poem is given here in a West Saxon form with a literal

23

interlinear translation. In Old English spelling, æ (as in Cædmon's name and line 3) is a vowel symbol that represents the vowel of Modern English *cat*; þ (line 2) and ð (line 7) both represented the sound *th*. The spelling *sc* (line 1) = *sh*; ġ (line 1) = *y* in *yard*; ċ (line 1) = *ch* in *chin*; c (line 2) = *k*. The large space in the middle of the line indicates the caesura. The alliterating sounds that connect the half-lines have been italicized.

From An Ecclesiastical History of the English People

[THE STORY OF CÆDMON]

Heavenly grace had especially singled out a certain one of the brothers in the monastery ruled by this abbess,[1] for he used to compose devout and religious songs. Whatever he learned of holy Scripture with the aid of inter-preters, he quickly turned into the sweetest and most moving poetry in his own language, that is to say English. It often happened that his songs kindled a contempt for this world and a longing for the life of Heaven in the hearts of many men. Indeed, after him others among the English people tried to compose religious poetry, but no one could equal him because he was not taught the art of song by men or by human agency but received this gift through heavenly grace. Therefore, he was never able to compose any vain and idle songs but only such as dealt with religion and were proper for his religious tongue to utter. As a matter of fact, he had lived in the secular estate until he was well advanced in age without learning any songs. Therefore, at feasts, when it was decided to have a good time by taking turns singing, whenever he would see the harp getting close to his place,[2] he got up in the middle of the meal and went home.

Once when he left the feast like this, he went to the cattle shed, which he had been assigned the duty of guarding that night. And after he had stretched himself out and gone to sleep, he dreamed that someone was standing at his side and greeted him, calling out his name. "Cædmon," he said, "sing me something."

And he replied, "I don't know how to sing; that is why I left the feast to come here—because I cannot sing."

"All the same," said the one who was speaking to him, "you have to sing for me."

"What must I sing?" he said.

And he said, "Sing about the Creation."

At this, Cædmon immediately began to sing verses in praise of God the Creator, which he had never heard before and of which the sense is this:

Nu sculon *heri*ġean	*heo*fonriċes Weard
Now we must praise	heaven-kingdom's Guardian,
*Meo*todes *mea*hte	and his *mod*ġeþanc
the Measurer's might	and his mind-plans,

1. Abbess Hilda (614–680), a grandniece of the first Christian king of Northumbria, founded Whitby, a double house for monks and nuns, in 657 and ruled over it for twenty-two years.

2. Oral poetry was performed to the accompani-ment of a harp; here the harp is being passed from one participant of the feast to another, each being expected to perform in turn.

weorc Wuldor-Fæder	swa he wundra ġehwæs
the work of the Glory-Father,	when he of wonders of every one,
eċe Drihten	or onstealde
eternal Lord,	the beginning established.[3]

5

He ærest sceop	ielda[4] bearnum
He first created	for men's sons
heofon to hrofe	haliġ Scyppend
heaven as a roof,	holy Creator;
ða middanġeard	moncynnes Weard
then middle-earth	mankind's Guardian,
eċe Drihten	æfter teode
eternal Lord,	afterwards made—
firum foldan	Frea ælmihtiġ
for men earth,	Master almighty.

This is the general sense but not the exact order of the words that he sang in his sleep;[5] for it is impossible to make a literal translation, no matter how well-written, of poetry into another language without losing some of the beauty and dignity. When he woke up, he remembered everything that he had sung in his sleep, and to this he soon added, in the same poetic measure, more verses praising God.

The next morning he went to the reeve,[6] who was his foreman, and told him about the gift he had received. He was taken to the abbess and ordered to tell his dream and to recite his song to an audience of the most learned men so that they might judge what the nature of that vision was and where it came from. It was evident to all of them that he had been granted the heavenly grace of God. Then they expounded some bit of sacred story or teaching to him, and instructed him to turn it into poetry if he could. He agreed and went away. And when he came back the next morning, he gave back what had been commissioned to him in the finest verse.

Therefore, the abbess, who cherished the grace of God in this man, instructed him to give up secular life and to take monastic vows. And when she and all those subject to her had received him into the community of brothers, she gave orders that he be taught the whole sequence of sacred history. He remembered everything that he was able to learn by listening, and turning it over in his mind like a clean beast that chews the cud,[7] he converted it into sweetest song, which sounded so delightful that he made his teachers, in their turn, his listeners. He sang about the creation of the

3. I.e., established the beginning of every one of wonders.
4. The later manuscript copies read eorþan, "earth," for ælda (West Saxon ielda), "men's."
5. Bede is referring to his Latin translation for which we have substituted the Old English text with interlinear translation.
6. Superintendent of the farms belonging to the monastery.
7. In Mosaic law "clean" animals, those that may be eaten, are those that both chew the cud and have a cloven hoof (cf. Leviticus 11.3 and Deuteronomy 14.6).

world and the origin of the human race and all the history of Genesis; about the exodus of Israel out of Egypt and entrance into the promised land; and about many other stories of sacred Scripture, about the Lord's incarnation, and his passion,[8] resurrection, and ascension into Heaven; about the advent of the Holy Spirit and the teachings of the apostles. He also made many songs about the terror of the coming judgment and the horror of the punishments of hell and the sweetness of the heavenly kingdom; and a great many others besides about divine grace and justice in all of which he sought to draw men away from the love of sin and to inspire them with delight in the practice of good works.[9] * * *

8. The suffering of Christ on the Cross and during his trial leading up to the Crucifixion.
9. The great majority of extant Old English poems are on religious subjects like those listed here, but most are thought to be later than Cædmon.

THE DREAM OF THE ROOD

The *Dream of the Rood* (i.e., of the Cross) is the finest of a rather large number of religious poems in Old English. Neither its author nor its date of composition is known. It appears in a late tenth-century manuscript located in Vercelli in northern Italy, a manuscript made up of Old English religious poems and sermons. The poem may antedate its manuscript, because some passages from the Rood's speech were carved, with some variations, in runes on a stone cross at some time after its construction early in the eighth century; this is the famous Ruthwell Cross, which is preserved near Dumfries in southern Scotland. The precise relation of the poem to this cross is, however, uncertain.

The experience of the Rood—its humiliation at the hands of those who changed it from tree to instrument of punishment for criminals, its humility when the young hero Christ mounts it, and its pride as the restored "tree of glory"—has a suggestive relevance to the condition of the sad, lonely, sin-stained Dreamer. His isolation and melancholy is typical of exile figures in Old English poetry. For the Rood, however, glory has replaced torment, and at the end, the Dreamer's description of Christ's triumphant entry into heaven with the souls He has liberated from hell reflects the Dreamer's response to the hope that has been brought to him.

The Dream of the Rood[1]

Listen, I will speak of the best of dreams, of what I dreamed at midnight when men and their voices were at rest. It seemed to me that I saw a most rare tree reach high aloft, wound in light, brightest of beams. All that beacon[2] was covered with gold; gems stood fair where it met the ground, five were above about the crosspiece. Many hosts of angels gazed on it, fair in the form created for them. This was surely no felon's gallows, but holy spirits beheld it there, men upon earth, and all this glorious creation. Wonderful was the triumph-tree, and I stained with sins, wounded with wrongdoings. I saw the

1. This prose translation, by E. T. Donaldson, has been based in general on the edition of the poem by John C. Pope, *Seven Old English Poems* (1966).
2. The Old English word *beacen* also means token or sign and battle standard.

tree of glory shine splendidly, adorned with garments, decked with gold: jewels had worthily covered the Lord's tree. Yet through that gold I might perceive ancient agony of wretches, for now it began to bleed on the right side.[3] I was all afflicted with sorrows, I was afraid for that fair sight. I saw that bright beacon change in clothing and color: now it was wet with moisture, drenched with flowing of blood, now adorned with treasure. Yet I, lying there a long while troubled, beheld the Saviour's tree until I heard it give voice: the best of trees began to speak words.

"It was long ago—I remember it still—that I was hewn down at the wood's edge, taken from my stump. Strong foes seized me there, hewed me to the shape they wished to see, commanded me to lift their criminals. Men carried me on their shoulders, then set me on a hill; foes enough fastened me there. Then I saw the Lord of mankind hasten with stout heart, for he would climb upon me. I dared not bow or break against God's word when I saw earth's surface tremble. I might have felled all foes, but I stood fast. Then the young Hero stripped himself—that was God Almighty—strong and stouthearted. He climbed on the high gallows, bold in the sight of many, when he would free mankind. I trembled when the Warrior embraced me, yet I dared not bow to earth, fall to the ground's surface; but I must stand fast. I was raised up, a cross; I lifted up the Mighty King, Lord of the Heavens: I dared not bend. They pierced me with dark nails: the wounds are seen on me, open gashes of hatred. Nor did I dare harm any of them. They mocked us both together. I was all wet with blood, drenched from the side of that Man after he had sent forth his spirit. I had endured many bitter happenings on that hill. I saw the God of Hosts cruelly racked. The shades of night had covered the Ruler's body with their mists, the bright splendor. Shadow came forth, dark beneath the clouds. All creation wept, bewailed the King's fall; Christ was on Cross.

"Yet from afar some came hastening to the Lord.[4] All that I beheld. I was sore afflicted with griefs, yet I bowed to the men's hands, meekly, eagerly. Then they took Almighty God, lifted him up from his heavy torment. The warriors left me standing, covered with blood. I was all wounded with arrows. They laid him down weary of limb, stood at the body's head, looked there upon Heaven's Lord; and he rested there a while, tired after the great struggle. Then warriors began to build him an earth-house in the sight of his slayer,[5] carved it out of bright stone; they set there the Wielder of Triumphs. Then they began to sing him a song of sorrow, desolate in the evening. Then they wished to turn back, weary, from the great Prince; he remained with small company.[6] Yet we[7] stood in our places a good while, weeping. The voice of the warriors departed. The body grew cold, fair house of the spirit. Then some began to fell us to earth—that was a fearful fate! Some buried us in a deep pit. Yet thanes[8] of the Lord, friends, learned of me there. . . . decked me in gold and silver.[9]

3. The wound Christ received on the Cross was supposed to have been on the right side.
4. According to John 19.38–39, it was Joseph of Arimathea and Nicodemus who received Christ's body from the Cross.
5. I.e., the Cross.
6. I.e., alone (an understatement).
7. I.e., Christ's Cross and those on which the two thieves were crucified.
8. Members of the king's body of warriors.
9. A number of lines describing the finding of the Cross have apparently been lost here. According to the legend, St. Helen, the mother of Constantine the Great, the first Christian emperor, led a Roman expedition that discovered the true Cross in the 4th century.

"Now you might understand, my beloved man, that I had endured the work of evildoers, grievous sorrows. Now the time has come that men far and wide upon earth honor me—and all this glorious creation—and pray to this beacon. On me God's Son suffered awhile; therefore I tower now glorious under the heavens, and I may heal every one of those who hold me in awe. Of old I became the hardest of torments, most loathed by men, before I opened the right road of life to those who have voices. Behold, the Lord of Glory honored me over all the trees of the wood, the Ruler of Heaven, just as also he honored his mother Mary, Almighty God for all men's sake, over all woman's kind.

"Now I command you, my beloved man, that you tell men of this vision. Disclose with your words that it is of the tree of glory on which Almighty God suffered for mankind's many sins and the deeds Adam did of old. He tasted death there; yet the Lord arose again to help mankind in his great might. Then he climbed to the heavens. He will come again hither on this earth to seek mankind on Doomsday, the Lord himself, Almighty God, and his angels with him, for then he will judge, he who has power to judge, each one just as in this brief life he has deserved. Nor may any one be unafraid of the word the Ruler will speak. Before his host he will ask where the man is who in the name of the Lord would taste bitter death as he did on the Cross. But then they will be afraid, and will think of little to begin to say to Christ. There need none be afraid who bears on his breast the best of tokens, but through the Cross shall the kingdom be sought by each soul on this earthly journey that thinks to dwell with the Lord."

Then I prayed to the tree, blithe-hearted, confident, there where I was alone with small company. My heart's thoughts were urged on the way hence. I endured many times of longing. Now is there hope of life for me, that I am permitted to seek the tree of triumph, more often than other men honor it well, alone. For it my heart's desire is great, and my hope of protection is directed to the Cross. I do not possess many powerful friends on earth, but they have gone hence from the delights of the world, sought for themselves the King of Glory. They live now in the heavens with the High Father, dwell in glory. And every day I look forward to when the Lord's Cross that I beheld here on earth will fetch me from this short life and bring me then where joy is great, delight in the heavens, where the Lord's folk are seated at the feast, where bliss is eternal. And then may it place me where thenceforth I may dwell in glory, fully enjoy bliss with the saints. May the Lord be my friend, who once here on earth suffered on the gallows-tree for man's sins: he freed us and granted us life, a heavenly home. Hope was renewed, with joys and with bliss, to those who endured fire.[1] The Son was victorious in that foray, mighty and successful. Then he came with his multitude, a host of spirits, into God's kingdom, the Almighty Ruler; and the angels and all the saints who dwelt then in glory rejoiced when their Ruler, Almighty God, came where his home was.

---

1. This and the following sentences refer to the Harrowing (i.e., pillaging) of Hell; after His death on the Cross, Christ descended into Hell, from which He released the souls of certain of the patriarchs and prophets, conducting them triumphantly to Heaven.

BEOWULF

Beowulf, the oldest of the great long poems written in English, may have been composed more than twelve hundred years ago, in the first half of the eighth century, although some scholars would place it as late as the tenth century. As is the case with most Old English poems, the title has been assigned by modern editors, for the manuscripts do not normally give any indication of title or authorship. Linguistic evidence shows that the poem was originally composed in the dialect of what was then Mercia, the Midlands of England today. But in the unique late-tenth-century manuscript preserving the poem, it has been converted into the West-Saxon dialect of the southwest in which most of Old English literature survives. In 1731, before any modern transcript of the text had been made, the manuscript was seriously damaged in a fire that destroyed the building in London that housed the extraordinary collection of medieval English manuscripts made by Sir Robert Bruce Cotton (1571–1631). As a result of the fire and subsequent deterioration, a number of lines and words have been lost from the poem.

It is possible that *Beowulf* may be the lone survivor of a genre of Old English long epics, but it must have been a remarkable and difficult work even in its own day. The poet was reviving the heroic language, style, and pagan world of ancient Germanic oral poetry, a world that was already remote for his contemporaries and that is stranger to the modern reader, in many respects, than the epic world of Homer and Virgil. With the help of *Beowulf* itself, a few shorter heroic poems in Old English, and later poetry and prose in Old Saxon, Old Icelandic, and Middle High German, we can only conjecture what Germanic oral epic must have been like when performed by the Germanic *scop*, or bard. The *Beowulf* poet himself imagines such oral performances by having King Hrothgar's court poet recite a heroic lay at a feast celebrating Beowulf's defeat of Grendel. Many of the words and formulaic expressions in *Beowulf* can be found in other Old English poems, but there are also an extraordinary number of what linguists call *hapax legomena*—that is, words recorded only once in a language. The poet may have found them elsewhere, but the high incidence of such words suggests that he was an original wordsmith in his own right.

Although the poem itself is English in language and origin, it deals not with native Englishmen but with their Germanic forebears, especially with two south Scandinavian tribes, the Danes and the Geats, who lived on the Danish island of Zealand and in southern Sweden. Thus the historical period the poem concerns—insofar as it may be said to refer to history at all—is some centuries before it was written—that is, a time after the initial invasion of England by Germanic tribes in the middle of the fifth century but before the Anglo-Saxon migration was completed. The one datable fact of history mentioned in the poem is a raid on the Franks in which Hygelac, the king of the Geats and Beowulf's lord, was killed, and this raid occurred in the year 520. Yet the poet's elliptical references to quasihistorical and legendary material show that his audience was still familiar with many old stories, the outlines of which we can only infer, sometimes with the help of later analogous tales in other Germanic languages. This knowledge was probably kept alive by other heroic poetry, of which little has been preserved in English, although much may once have existed.

It is now widely believed that *Beowulf* is the work of a single poet who was a Christian and that his poem reflects well-established Christian tradition. The conversion of the Germanic settlers in England had been largely completed during the seventh century. The Danish king Hrothgar's poet sings a song about the Creation (lines 87–98) reminiscent of Cædmon's *Hymn*. The monster Grendel is said to be a descendant of Cain. There are allusions to God's judgment and to fate (*wyrd*) but none to pagan deities. References to the New Testament are notably absent, but Hrothgar and Beowulf often speak of God as though their religion is monotheistic. With sadness the poet relates that, made desperate by Grendel's attacks, the Danes pray for help at heathen shrines—apparently backsliding as the children of Israel had sometimes lapsed into idolatry.

Although Hrothgar and Beowulf are portrayed as morally upright and enlightened pagans, they fully espouse and frequently affirm the values of Germanic heroic poetry. In the poetry depicting this warrior society, the most important of human relationships was that which existed between the warrior—the thane—and his lord, a relationship based less on subordination of one man's will to another's than on mutual trust and respect. When a warrior vowed loyalty to his lord, he became not so much his servant as his voluntary companion, one who would take pride in defending him and fighting in his wars. In return, the lord was expected to take care of his thanes and to reward them richly for their valor; a good king, one like Hrothgar or Beowulf, is referred to by such poetic epithets as "ring-giver" and as the "helmet" and "shield" of his people.

The relationship between kinsmen was also of deep significance to this society. If one of his kinsmen had been slain, a man had a moral obligation either to kill the slayer or to exact the payment of *wergild* (man-price) in compensation. Each rank of society was evaluated at a definite price, which had to be paid to the dead man's kin by the killer if he wished to avoid their vengeance—even if the killing had been an accident. In the absence of any legal code other than custom or any body of law enforcement, it was the duty of the family (often with the lord's support) to execute justice. The payment itself had less significance as wealth than as proof that the kinsmen had done what was right. The failure to take revenge or to exact compensation was considered shameful. Hrothgar's anguish over the murders committed by Grendel is not only for the loss of his men but also for the shame of his inability either to kill Grendel or to exact a "death-price" from the killer. "It is always better / to avenge dear ones than to indulge in mourning" (lines 1384–85), Beowulf says to Hrothgar, who has been thrown back into despair by the revenge-slaying of his old friend Aeschere by Grendel's mother.

Yet the young Beowulf's attempt to comfort the bereaved old king by invoking the code of vengeance may be one of several instances of the poet's ironic treatment of the tragic futility of the never-ending blood feuds. The most graphic example in the poem of that irony is the Finnsburg episode, the lay sung by Hrothgar's hall-poet. The Danish princess Hildeburh, married to the Frisian king Finn—probably to put an end to a feud between those peoples—loses both her brother and her son when a bloody fight breaks out in the hall between a visiting party of Danes and her husband's men. The bodies are cremated together on a huge funeral pyre: "The glutton element flamed and consumed / the dead of both sides. Their great days were gone" (lines 1124–25).

Such feuds, the staple subject of Germanic epic and saga, have only a peripheral place in the poem. Instead, the poem turns on Beowulf's three great fights against preternatural evil, which inhabits the dangerous and demonic space surrounding human society. He undertakes the fight against Grendel to save the Danes from the monster and to exact vengeance for the men Grendel has slain. Another motive is to demonstrate his strength and courage and thereby to enhance his personal glory. Hrothgar's magnificent gifts become the material emblems of that glory. Revenge and glory also motivate Beowulf's slaying of Grendel's mother. He undertakes his last battle against the dragon, however, only because there is no other way to save his own people.

A somber and dignified elegiac mood pervades *Beowulf*. The poem opens and closes with the description of a funeral and is filled with laments for the dead. Our first view of Beowulf is of an ambitious young hero. At the end, he has become an old king, facing the dragon and death. His people mourn him and praise him, as does the poet, for his nobility, generosity, courage, and, what is less common in Germanic heroes, kindness to his people. The poet's elegiac tone may be informed by something more than the duty to "praise a prince whom he holds dear / and cherish his memory when that moment comes / when he has to be convoyed from his bodily home" (lines 3175–

77). The entire poem could be viewed as the poet's lament for heroes like Beowulf who went into the darkness without the light of his own Christian faith.

The present verse translation is by the Irish poet Seamus Heaney, who received the Nobel Prize for literature in 1995. Selections from Heaney's own poems appear in Volume 2 of the anthology. His *Beowulf* is both a translation of one of the oldest English poems and a personal response to a work that speaks to a modern poet about the violence of our own century and the courage with which some men and women have faced up to it.

TRIBES AND GENEALOGIES

1. The Danes (Bright-, Half-, Ring-, Spear-, North-, East-, South-, West-Danes; Shield-ings, Honor-, Victor-, War-Shieldings; Ing's friends)

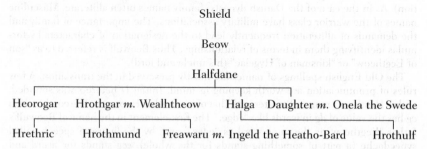

Shield

Beow

Halfdane

Heorogar   Hrothgar *m.* Wealhtheow   Halga   Daughter *m.* Onela the Swede

Hrethric   Hrothmund   Freawaru *m.* Ingeld the Heatho-Bard   Hrothulf

2. The Geats (Sea-, War-, Weather-Geats)

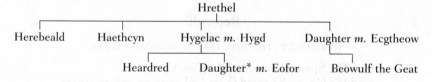

Hrethel

Herebeald   Haethcyn   Hygelac *m.* Hygd   Daughter *m.* Ecgtheow

Heardred   Daughter* *m.* Eofor   Beowulf the Geat

3. The Swedes

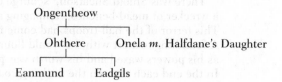

Ongentheow

Ohthere   Onela *m.* Halfdane's Daughter

Eanmund   Eadgils

4. Miscellaneous

A. The Half-Danes (also called Shieldings) involved in the fight at Finnsburg may represent a different tribe from the Danes described above. Their king Hoc had a son, Hnaef, who succeeded him, and a daughter Hildeburh, who married Finn, king of the Jutes.

B. The Jutes or Frisians are represented as enemies of the Danes in the fight at Finnsburg and as allies of the Franks or Hugas at the time Hygelac the Geat made the attack in which he lost his life and from which Beowulf swam home. Also allied with the Franks at this time were the Hetware.

* The daughter of Hygelac who was given to Eofor may have been born to him by a former wife, older than Hygd.

C. The Heatho-Bards (i.e., "Battle-Bards") are represented as inveterate enemies of the Danes. Their king Froda had been killed in an attack on the Danes, and Hrothgar's attempt to make peace with them by marrying his daughter Freawaru to Froda's son Ingeld failed when the latter attacked Heorot. The attack was repulsed, although Heorot was burned.

A NOTE ON NAMES

Old English, like Modern German, contained many compound words, most of which have been lost in Modern English. Most of the names in *Beowulf* are compounds. Hrothgar is a combination of words meaning "glory" and "spear"; the name of his older brother, Heorogar, comes from "army" and "spear"; Hrothgar's sons Hrethric and Hrothmund contain the first elements of their father's name combined, respectively, with *ric* (kingdom, empire; Modern German *Reich*) and *mund* (hand, protection). As in the case of the Danish dynasty, family names often alliterate. Masculine names of the warrior class have military associations. The importance of family and the demands of alliteration frequently lead to the designation of characters by formulas identifying them in terms of relationships. Thus Beowulf is referred to as "son of Ecgtheow" or "kinsman of Hygelac" (his uncle and lord).

The Old English spellings of names are mostly preserved in the translation. A few rules of pronunciation are worth keeping in mind. Initial *H* before *r* was sounded, and so Hrothgar's name alliterates with that of his brother Heorogar. The combination *cg* has the value of *dg* in words like "edge." The first element in the name of Beowulf's father "Ecgtheow" is the same word as "edge," and, by the figure of speech called synecdoche (a part of something stands for the whole), *ecg* stands for *sword* and Ecgtheow means "sword-servant."

Beowulf

[PROLOGUE: THE RISE OF THE DANISH NATION]

So. The Spear-Danes[1] in days gone by
and the kings who ruled them had courage and greatness.
We have heard of those princes' heroic campaigns.
    There was Shield Sheafson,[2] scourge of many tribes,
5   a wrecker of mead-benches, rampaging among foes.
This terror of the hall-troops had come far.
A foundling to start with, he would flourish later on
as his powers waxed and his worth was proved.
In the end each clan on the outlying coasts
10 beyond the whale-road had to yield to him
and begin to pay tribute. That was one good king.
    Afterward a boy-child was born to Shield,
a cub in the yard, a comfort sent
by God to that nation. He knew what they had tholed,[3]

---

1. There are different compound names for tribes, often determined by alliteration in Old English poetry. Line 1 reads, "*Hwæt, we Gar-dena in geardagum,*" where alliteration falls on *Gar* (spear) and *gear* (year). Old English hard and soft g (spelled y in Modern English) alliterate. The compound *geardagum* derives from "year," used in the special sense of "long ago," and "days" and survives in the archaic expression "days of yore."

2. Shield is the name of the founder of the Danish royal line. Sheafson translates *Scefing*, i.e., *sheaf* + the patronymic suffix *-ing*. Because Sheaf was a "foundling" (line 7: *feasceaft funden*, i.e., found destitute) who arrived by sea (lines 45–46), it is likely that as a child Shield brought with him only a sheaf, a symbol of fruitfulness.

3. Suffered, endured.

15   the long times and troubles they'd come through
      without a leader; so the Lord of Life,
      the glorious Almighty, made this man renowned.
      Shield had fathered a famous son:
      Beow's name was known through the north.
20   And a young prince must be prudent like that,
      giving freely while his father lives
      so that afterward in age when fighting starts
      steadfast companions will stand by him
      and hold the line. Behavior that's admired
25   is the path to power among people everywhere.
          Shield was still thriving when his time came
      and he crossed over into the Lord's keeping.
      His warrior band did what he bade them
      when he laid down the law among the Danes:
30   they shouldered him out to the sea's flood,
      the chief they revered who had long ruled them.
      A ring-whorled prow rode in the harbor,
      ice-clad, outbound, a craft for a prince.
      They stretched their beloved lord in his boat,
35   laid out by the mast, amidships,
      the great ring-giver. Far-fetched treasures
      were piled upon him, and precious gear.
      I never heard before of a ship so well furbished
      with battle-tackle, bladed weapons
40   and coats of mail. The massed treasure
      was loaded on top of him: it would travel far
      on out into the ocean's sway.
      They decked his body no less bountifully
      with offerings than those first ones did
45   who cast him away when he was a child
      and launched him alone out over the waves.[4]
      And they set a gold standard up
      high above his head and let him drift
      to wind and tide, bewailing him
50   and mourning their loss. No man can tell,
      no wise man in hall or weathered veteran
      knows for certain who salvaged that load.
          Then it fell to Beow to keep the forts.
      He was well regarded and ruled the Danes
55   for a long time after his father took leave
      of his life on earth. And then his heir,
      the great Halfdane,[5] held sway
      for as long as he lived, their elder and warlord.
      He was four times a father, this fighter prince:
60   one by one they entered the world,
          Heorogar, Hrothgar, the good Halga,
          and a daughter, I have heard, who was Onela's queen,

4. See n. 2, above. Since Shield was found destitute, "no less bountifully" is litotes or understatement; the ironic reminder that he came with
nothing (line 43) emphasizes the reversal of his
fortunes.
5. Probably named so because, according to one
source, his mother was a Swedish princess.

a balm in bed to the battle-scarred Swede.
The fortunes of war favored Hrothgar.
65 Friends and kinsmen flocked to his ranks,
young followers, a force that grew
to be a mighty army. So his mind turned
to hall-building: he handed down orders
for men to work on a great mead-hall
70 meant to be a wonder of the world forever;
it would be his throne-room and there he would dispense
his God-given goods to young and old—
but not the common land or people's lives.[6]
Far and wide through the world, I have heard,
75 orders for work to adorn that wallstead
were sent to many peoples. And soon it stood there
finished and ready, in full view,
the hall of halls. Heorot was the name[7]
he had settled on it, whose utterance was law.
80 Nor did he renege, but doled out rings
and torques at the table. The hall towered,
its gables wide and high and awaiting
a barbarous burning.[8] That doom abided,
but in time it would come: the killer instinct
85 unleashed among in-laws, the blood-lust rampant.[9]

[HEOROT IS ATTACKED]

Then a powerful demon,[1] a prowler through the dark,
nursed a hard grievance. It harrowed him
to hear the din of the loud banquet
every day in the hall, the harp being struck
90 and the clear song of a skilled poet
telling with mastery of man's beginnings,
how the Almighty had made the earth
a gleaming plain girdled with waters;
in His splendor He set the sun and the moon
95 to be earth's lamplight, lanterns for men,
and filled the broad lap of the world
with branches and leaves; and quickened life
in every other thing that moved.
So times were pleasant for the people there
100 until finally one, a fiend out of hell,
began to work his evil in the world.
Grendel was the name of this grim demon
haunting the marches, marauding round the heath
and the desolate fens; he had dwelt for a time
105 in misery among the banished monsters,

---

6. The king could not dispose of land used by all, such as a common pasture, or of slaves.
7. I.e., "Hart," from antlers fastened to the gables or because the crossed gable-ends resembled a stag's antlers; the hart was also an icon of royalty.
8. An allusion to the future destruction of Heorot by fire, probably in a raid by the Heatho-Bards.

9. As told later (lines 2020–69), Hrothgar plans to marry a daughter to Ingeld, chief of the Heatho-Bards, in hopes of resolving a long-standing feud. See previous note.
1. The poet withholds the name for several lines. He does the same with the name of the hero as well as others.

Cain's clan, whom the Creator had outlawed
and condemned as outcasts.[2] For the killing of Abel
the Eternal Lord had exacted a price:
Cain got no good from committing that murder
110 because the Almighty made him anathema
and out of the curse of his exile there sprang
ogres and elves and evil phantoms
and the giants too who strove with God
time and again until He gave them their reward.
115 So, after nightfall, Grendel set out
for the lofty house, to see how the Ring-Danes
were settling into it after their drink,
and there he came upon them, a company of the best
asleep from their feasting, insensible to pain
120 and human sorrow. Suddenly then
the God-cursed brute was creating havoc:
greedy and grim, he grabbed thirty men
from their resting places and rushed to his lair,
flushed up and inflamed from the raid,
125 blundering back with the butchered corpses.
　　　Then as dawn brightened and the day broke,
Grendel's powers of destruction were plain:
their wassail was over, they wept to heaven
and mourned under morning. Their mighty prince,
130 the storied leader, sat stricken and helpless,
humiliated by the loss of his guard,
bewildered and stunned, staring aghast
at the demon's trail, in deep distress.
He was numb with grief, but got no respite
135 for one night later merciless Grendel
struck again with more gruesome murders.
Malignant by nature, he never showed remorse.
It was easy then to meet with a man
shifting himself to a safer distance
140 to bed in the bothies,[3] for who could be blind
to the evidence of his eyes, the obviousness
of the hall-watcher's hate? Whoever escaped
kept a weather-eye open and moved away.
　　　So Grendel ruled in defiance of right,
145 one against all, until the greatest house
in the world stood empty, a deserted wallstead.
For twelve winters, seasons of woe,
the lord of the Shieldings[4] suffered under
his load of sorrow; and so, before long,
150 the news was known over the whole world.
Sad lays were sung about the beset king,
the vicious raids and ravages of Grendel,
his long and unrelenting feud,
nothing but war; how he would never

---

2. See Genesis 4.9–12.
3. Huts, outlying buildings. Evidently Grendel
wants only to dominate the hall.

4. The descendants of Shield, another name for
the Danes.

155   parley or make peace with any Dane
     nor stop his death-dealing nor pay the death-price.[5]
     No counselor could ever expect
     fair reparation from those rabid hands.
     All were endangered; young and old
160   were hunted down by that dark death-shadow
     who lurked and swooped in the long nights
     on the misty moors; nobody knows
     where these reavers from hell roam on their errands.
       So Grendel waged his lonely war,
165   inflicting constant cruelties on the people,
     atrocious hurt. He took over Heorot,
     haunted the glittering hall after dark,
     but the throne itself, the treasure-seat,
     he was kept from approaching; he was the Lord's outcast.
170   These were hard times, heartbreaking
     for the prince of the Shieldings; powerful counselors,
     the highest in the land, would lend advice,
     plotting how best the bold defenders
     might resist and beat off sudden attacks.
175   Sometimes at pagan shrines they vowed
     offerings to idols, swore oaths
     that the killer of souls[6] might come to their aid
     and save the people. That was their way,
     their heathenish hope; deep in their hearts
180   they remembered hell. The Almighty Judge
     of good deeds and bad, the Lord God,
     Head of the Heavens and High King of the World,
     was unknown to them. Oh, cursed is he
     who in time of trouble has to thrust his soul
185   in the fire's embrace, forfeiting help;
     he has nowhere to turn. But blessed is he
     who after death can approach the Lord
     and find friendship in the Father's embrace.

[THE HERO COMES TO HEOROT]

     So that troubled time continued, woe
190   that never stopped, steady affliction
     for Halfdane's son, too hard an ordeal.
     There was panic after dark, people endured
     raids in the night, riven by the terror.
       When he heard about Grendel, Hygelac's thane
195   was on home ground, over in Geatland.
     There was no one else like him alive.
     In his day, he was the mightiest man on earth,
     highborn and powerful. He ordered a boat
     that would ply the waves. He announced his plan:
200   to sail the swan's road and seek out that king,

---

5. I.e., *wergild* (man-price); monetary compensation for the life of the slain man is the only way, according to Germanic law, to settle a feud peacefully.

6. I.e., the devil. Heathen gods were thought to be devils.

the famous prince who needed defenders.
Nobody tried to keep him from going,
no elder denied him, dear as he was to them.
Instead, they inspected omens and spurred
205   his ambition to go, whilst he moved about
like the leader he was, enlisting men,
the best he could find; with fourteen others
the warrior boarded the boat as captain,
a canny pilot along coast and currents.
210   Time went by, the boat was on water,
in close under the cliffs.
Men climbed eagerly up the gangplank,
sand churned in surf, warriors loaded
a cargo of weapons, shining war-gear
215   in the vessel's hold, then heaved out,
away with a will in their wood-wreathed ship.
Over the waves, with the wind behind her
and foam at her neck, she flew like a bird
until her curved prow had covered the distance,
220   and on the following day, at the due hour,
those seafarers sighted land,
sunlit cliffs, sheer crags
and looming headlands, the landfall they sought.
It was the end of their voyage and the Geats vaulted
225   over the side, out on to the sand,
and moored their ship. There was a clash of mail
and a thresh of gear. They thanked God
for that easy crossing on a calm sea.
    When the watchman on the wall, the Shieldings' lookout
230   whose job it was to guard the sea-cliffs,
saw shields glittering on the gangplank
and battle-equipment being unloaded
he had to find out who and what
the arrivals were. So he rode to the shore,
235   this horseman of Hrothgar's, and challenged them
in formal terms, flourishing his spear:
"What kind of men are you who arrive
rigged out for combat in your coats of mail,
sailing here over the sea-lanes
240   in your steep-hulled boat? I have been stationed
as lookout on this coast for a long time.
My job is to watch the waves for raiders,
any danger to the Danish shore.
Never before has a force under arms
245   disembarked so openly—not bothering to ask
if the sentries allowed them safe passage
or the clan had consented. Nor have I seen
a mightier man-at-arms on this earth
than the one standing here: unless I am mistaken,
250   he is truly noble. This is no mere
hanger-on in a hero's armor.
So now, before you fare inland

as interlopers, I have to be informed
about who you are and where you hail from.
255   Outsiders from across the water,
I say it again: the sooner you tell
where you come from and why, the better."
    The leader of the troop unlocked his word-hoard;
the distinguished one delivered this answer:
260   "We belong by birth to the Geat people
and owe allegiance to Lord Hygelac.
In his day, my father was a famous man,
a noble warrior-lord named Ecgtheow.
He outlasted many a long winter
265   and went on his way. All over the world
men wise in counsel continue to remember him.
We come in good faith to find your lord
and nation's shield, the son of Halfdane.
Give us the right advice and direction.
270   We have arrived here on a great errand
to the lord of the Danes, and I believe therefore
there should be nothing hidden or withheld between us.
So tell us if what we have heard is true
about this threat, whatever it is,
275   this danger abroad in the dark nights,
this corpse-maker mongering death
in the Shieldings' country. I come to proffer
my wholehearted help and counsel.
I can show the wise Hrothgar a way
280   to defeat his enemy and find respite—
if any respite is to reach him, ever.
I can calm the turmoil and terror in his mind.
Otherwise, he must endure woes
and live with grief for as long as his hall
285   stands at the horizon on its high ground."
    Undaunted, sitting astride his horse,
the coast-guard answered: "Anyone with gumption
and a sharp mind will take the measure
of two things: what's said and what's done.
290   I believe what you have told me, that you are a troop
loyal to our king. So come ahead
with your arms and your gear, and I will guide you.
What's more, I'll order my own comrades
on their word of honor to watch your boat
295   down there on the strand—keep her safe
in her fresh tar, until the time comes
for her curved prow to preen on the waves
and bear this hero back to Geatland.
May one so valiant and venturesome
300   come unharmed through the clash of battle."
    So they went on their way. The ship rode the water,
broad-beamed, bound by its hawser
and anchored fast. Boar-shapes[7] flashed

---

7. Carved images of boars were placed on helmets, probably as good luck charms to protect the warriors.

above their cheek-guards, the brightly forged
305 work of goldsmiths, watching over
those stern-faced men. They marched in step,
hurrying on till the timbered hall
rose before them, radiant with gold.
Nobody on earth knew of another
310 building like it. Majesty lodged there,
its light shone over many lands.
So their gallant escort guided them
to that dazzling stronghold and indicated
the shortest way to it; then the noble warrior
315 wheeled on his horse and spoke these words:
"It is time for me to go. May the Almighty
Father keep you and in His kindness
watch over your exploits. I'm away to the sea,
back on alert against enemy raiders."
320   It was a paved track, a path that kept them
in marching order. Their mail-shirts glinted,
hard and hand-linked; the high-gloss iron
of their armor rang. So they duly arrived
in their grim war-graith[8] and gear at the hall,
325 and, weary from the sea, stacked wide shields
of the toughest hardwood against the wall,
then collapsed on the benches; battle-dress
and weapons clashed. They collected their spears
in a seafarers' stook, a stand of grayish
330 tapering ash. And the troops themselves
were as good as their weapons.
                              Then a proud warrior
questioned the men concerning their origins:
"Where do you come from, carrying these
decorated shields and shirts of mail,
335 these cheek-hinged helmets and javelins?
I am Hrothgar's herald and officer.
I have never seen so impressive or large
an assembly of strangers. Stoutness of heart,
bravery not banishment, must have brought you to Hrothgar."
340   The man whose name was known for courage,
the Geat leader, resolute in his helmet,
answered in return: "We are retainers
from Hygelac's band. Beowulf is my name.
If your lord and master, the most renowned
345 son of Halfdane, will hear me out
and graciously allow me to greet him in person,
I am ready and willing to report my errand."
      Wulfgar replied, a Wendel chief
renowned as a warrior, well known for his wisdom
350 and the temper of his mind: "I will take this message,
in accordance with your wish, to our noble king,
our dear lord, friend of the Danes,
the giver of rings. I will go and ask him

8. "Graith": archaic for apparel.

about your coming here, then hurry back
355 with whatever reply it pleases him to give."
  With that he turned to where Hrothgar sat,
an old man among retainers;
the valiant follower stood foursquare
in front of his king: he knew the courtesies.
360 Wulfgar addressed his dear lord:
"People from Geatland have put ashore.
They have sailed far over the wide sea.
They call the chief in charge of their band
by the name of Beowulf. They beg, my lord,
365 an audience with you, exchange of words
and formal greeting. Most gracious Hrothgar,
do not refuse them, but grant them a reply.
From their arms and appointment, they appear well born
and worthy of respect, especially the one
370 who has led them this far: he is formidable indeed."
  Hrothgar, protector of Shieldings, replied:
"I used to know him when he was a young boy.
His father before him was called Ecgtheow.
Hrethel the Geat⁹ gave Ecgtheow
375 his daughter in marriage. This man is their son,
here to follow up an old friendship.
A crew of seamen who sailed for me once
with a gift-cargo across to Geatland
returned with marvelous tales about him:
380 a thane, they declared, with the strength of thirty
in the grip of each hand. Now Holy God
has, in His goodness, guided him here
to the West-Danes, to defend us from Grendel.
This is my hope; and for his heroism
385 I will recompense him with a rich treasure.
Go immediately, bid him and the Geats
he has in attendance to assemble and enter.
Say, moreover, when you speak to them,
they are welcome to Denmark."
                                    At the door of the hall,
390 Wulfgar duly delivered the message:
"My lord, the conquering king of the Danes,
bids me announce that he knows your ancestry;
also that he welcomes you here to Heorot
and salutes your arrival from across the sea.
395 You are free now to move forward
to meet Hrothgar in helmets and armor,
but shields must stay here and spears be stacked
until the outcome of the audience is clear."
  The hero arose, surrounded closely
400 by his powerful thanes. A party remained
under orders to keep watch on the arms;
the rest proceeded, led by their prince
under Heorot's roof. And standing on the hearth

9. Hygelac's father and Beowulf's grandfather.

in webbed links that the smith had woven,
405 the fine-forged mesh of his gleaming mail-shirt,
resolute in his helmet, Beowulf spoke:
"Greetings to Hrothgar. I am Hygelac's kinsman,
one of his hall-troop. When I was younger,
I had great triumphs. Then news of Grendel,
410 hard to ignore, reached me at home:
sailors brought stories of the plight you suffer
in this legendary hall, how it lies deserted,
empty and useless once the evening light
hides itself under heaven's dome.
415 So every elder and experienced councilman
among my people supported my resolve
to come here to you, King Hrothgar,
because all knew of my awesome strength.
They had seen me boltered[1] in the blood of enemies
420 when I battled and bound five beasts,
raided a troll-nest and in the night-sea
slaughtered sea-brutes. I have suffered extremes
and avenged the Geats (their enemies brought it
upon themselves; I devastated them).
425 Now I mean to be a match for Grendel,
settle the outcome in single combat.
And so, my request, O king of Bright-Danes,
dear prince of the Shieldings, friend of the people
and their ring of defense, my one request
430 is that you won't refuse me, who have come this far,
the privilege of purifying Heorot,
with my own men to help me, and nobody else.
I have heard moreover that the monster scorns
in his reckless way to use weapons;
435 therefore, to heighten Hygelac's fame
and gladden his heart, I hereby renounce
sword and the shelter of the broad shield,
the heavy war-board: hand-to-hand
is how it will be, a life-and-death
440 fight with the fiend. Whichever one death fells
must deem it a just judgment by God.
If Grendel wins, it will be a gruesome day;
he will glut himself on the Geats in the war-hall,
swoop without fear on that flower of manhood
445 as on others before. Then my face won't be there
to be covered in death: he will carry me away
as he goes to ground, gorged and bloodied;
he will run gloating with my raw corpse
and feed on it alone, in a cruel frenzy
450 fouling his moor-nest. No need then
to lament for long or lay out my body:[2]
if the battle takes me, send back
this breast-webbing that Weland[3] fashioned

1. Clotted, sticky.
2. I.e., for burial. Hrothgar will not need to give
Beowulf an expensive funeral.
3. Famed blacksmith in Germanic legend.

and Hrethel gave me, to Lord Hygelac.
455 Fate goes ever as fate must."
    Hrothgar, the helmet of Shieldings, spoke:
"Beowulf, my friend, you have traveled here
to favor us with help and to fight for us.
There was a feud one time, begun by your father.
460 With his own hands he had killed Heatholaf
who was a Wulfing; so war was looming
and his people, in fear of it, forced him to leave.
He came away then over rolling waves
to the South-Danes here, the sons of honor.
465 I was then in the first flush of kingship,
establishing my sway over the rich strongholds
of this heroic land. Heorogar,
my older brother and the better man,
also a son of Halfdane's, had died.
470 Finally I healed the feud by paying:
I shipped a treasure-trove to the Wulfings,
and Ecgtheow acknowledged me with oaths of allegiance.
    "It bothers me to have to burden anyone
with all the grief that Grendel has caused
475 and the havoc he has wreaked upon us in Heorot,
our humiliations. My household-guard
are on the wane, fate sweeps them away
into Grendel's clutches—but God can easily
halt these raids and harrowing attacks!
480 "Time and again, when the goblets passed
and seasoned fighters got flushed with beer
they would pledge themselves to protect Heorot
and wait for Grendel with their whetted swords.
But when dawn broke and day crept in
485 over each empty, blood-spattered bench,
the floor of the mead-hall where they had feasted
would be slick with slaughter. And so they died,
faithful retainers, and my following dwindled.
Now take your place at the table, relish
490 the triumph of heroes to your heart's content."

[FEAST AT HEOROT]

    Then a bench was cleared in that banquet hall
so the Geats could have room to be together
and the party sat, proud in their bearing,
strong and stalwart. An attendant stood by
495 with a decorated pitcher, pouring bright
helpings of mead. And the minstrel sang,
filling Heorot with his head-clearing voice,
gladdening that great rally of Geats and Danes.
    From where he crouched at the king's feet,
500 Unferth, a son of Ecglaf's, spoke
contrary words. Beowulf's coming,
his sea-braving, made him sick with envy:

　　　　he could not brook or abide the fact
　　　　that anyone else alive under heaven
505　　might enjoy greater regard than he did:
　　　　"Are you the Beowulf who took on Breca
　　　　in a swimming match on the open sea,
　　　　risking the water just to prove that you could win?
　　　　It was sheer vanity made you venture out
510　　on the main deep. And no matter who tried,
　　　　friend or foe, to deflect the pair of you,
　　　　neither would back down: the sea-test obsessed you.
　　　　You waded in, embracing water,
　　　　taking its measure, mastering currents,
515　　riding on the swell. The ocean swayed,
　　　　winter went wild in the waves, but you vied
　　　　for seven nights; and then he outswam you,
　　　　came ashore the stronger contender.
　　　　He was cast up safe and sound one morning
520　　among the Heatho-Reams, then made his way
　　　　to where he belonged in Bronding country,
　　　　home again, sure of his ground
　　　　in strongroom and bawn.[4] So Breca made good
　　　　his boast upon you and was proved right.
525　　No matter, therefore, how you may have fared
　　　　in every bout and battle until now,
　　　　this time you'll be worsted; no one has ever
　　　　outlasted an entire night against Grendel."
　　　　　　Beowulf, Ecgtheow's son, replied:
530　　"Well, friend Unferth, you have had your say
　　　　about Breca and me. But it was mostly beer
　　　　that was doing the talking. The truth is this:
　　　　when the going was heavy in those high waves,
　　　　I was the strongest swimmer of all.
535　　We'd been children together and we grew up
　　　　daring ourselves to outdo each other,
　　　　boasting and urging each other to risk
　　　　our lives on the sea. And so it turned out.
　　　　Each of us swam holding a sword,
540　　a naked, hard-proofed blade for protection
　　　　against the whale-beasts. But Breca could never
　　　　move out farther or faster from me
　　　　than I could manage to move from him.
　　　　Shoulder to shoulder, we struggled on
545　　for five nights, until the long flow
　　　　and pitch of the waves, the perishing cold,
　　　　night falling and winds from the north
　　　　drove us apart. The deep boiled up
　　　　and its wallowing sent the sea-brutes wild.
550　　My armor helped me to hold out;
　　　　my hard-ringed chain-mail, hand-forged and linked,

4. Fortified outwork of a court or castle. The word was used by English planters in Ulster to describe fortified dwellings they erected on lands confiscated from the Irish [Translator's note].

a fine, close-fitting filigree of gold,
kept me safe when some ocean creature
pulled me to the bottom. Pinioned fast
555 and swathed in its grip, I was granted one
final chance: my sword plunged
and the ordeal was over. Through my own hands,
the fury of battle had finished off the sea-beast.
    "Time and again, foul things attacked me,
560 lurking and stalking, but I lashed out,
gave as good as I got with my sword.
My flesh was not for feasting on,
there would be no monsters gnawing and gloating
over their banquet at the bottom of the sea.
565 Instead, in the morning, mangled and sleeping
the sleep of the sword, they slopped and floated
like the ocean's leavings. From now on
sailors would be safe, the deep-sea raids
were over for good. Light came from the east,
570 bright guarantee of God, and the waves
went quiet; I could see headlands
and buffeted cliffs. Often, for undaunted courage,
fate spares the man it has not already marked.
However it occurred, my sword had killed
575 nine sea-monsters. Such night dangers
and hard ordeals I have never heard of
nor of a man more desolate in surging waves.
But worn out as I was, I survived,
came through with my life. The ocean lifted
580 and laid me ashore, I landed safe
on the coast of Finland.

                      Now I cannot recall
any fight you entered, Unferth,
that bears comparison. I don't boast when I say
that neither you nor Breca were ever much
585 celebrated for swordsmanship
or for facing danger on the field of battle.
You killed your own kith and kin,
so for all your cleverness and quick tongue,
you will suffer damnation in the depths of hell.
590 The fact is, Unferth, if you were truly
as keen or courageous as you claim to be
Grendel would never have got away with
such unchecked atrocity, attacks on your king,
havoc in Heorot and horrors everywhere.
595 But he knows he need never be in dread
of your blade making a mizzle of his blood
or of vengeance arriving ever from this quarter—
from the Victory-Shieldings, the shoulderers of the spear.
He knows he can trample down you Danes
600 to his heart's content, humiliate and murder
without fear of reprisal. But he will find me different.
I will show him how Geats shape to kill

in the heat of battle. Then whoever wants to
may go bravely to mead, when the morning light,
605   scarfed in sun-dazzle, shines forth from the south
and brings another daybreak to the world."
     Then the gray-haired treasure-giver was glad;
far-famed in battle, the prince of Bright-Danes
and keeper of his people counted on Beowulf,
610   on the warrior's steadfastness and his word.
So the laughter started, the din got louder
and the crowd was happy. Wealhtheow came in,
Hrothgar's queen, observing the courtesies.
Adorned in her gold, she graciously saluted
615   the men in the hall, then handed the cup
first to Hrothgar, their homeland's guardian,
urging him to drink deep and enjoy it
because he was dear to them. And he drank it down
like the warlord he was, with festive cheer.
620   So the Helming woman went on her rounds,
queenly and dignified, decked out in rings,
offering the goblet to all ranks,
treating the household and the assembled troop,
until it was Beowulf's turn to take it from her hand.
625   With measured words she welcomed the Geat
and thanked God for granting her wish
that a deliverer she could believe in would arrive
to ease their afflictions. He accepted the cup,
a daunting man, dangerous in action
630   and eager for it always. He addressed Wealhtheow;
Beowulf, son of Ecgtheow, said:
"I had a fixed purpose when I put to sea.
As I sat in the boat with my band of men,
I meant to perform to the uttermost
635   what your people wanted or perish in the attempt,
in the fiend's clutches. And I shall fulfill that purpose,
prove myself with a proud deed
or meet my death here in the mead-hall."
This formal boast by Beowulf the Geat
640   pleased the lady well and she went to sit
by Hrothgar, regal and arrayed with gold.
     Then it was like old times in the echoing hall,
proud talk and the people happy,
loud and excited; until soon enough
645   Halfdane's heir had to be away
to his night's rest. He realized
that the demon was going to descend on the hall,
that he had plotted all day, from dawn-light
until darkness gathered again over the world
650   and stealthy night-shapes came stealing forth
under the cloud-murk. The company stood
as the two leaders took leave of each other:
Hrothgar wished Beowulf health and good luck,
named him hall-warden and announced as follows:

655   "Never, since my hand could hold a shield
     have I entrusted or given control
     of the Danes' hall to anyone but you.
     Ward and guard it, for it is the greatest of houses.
     Be on your mettle now, keep in mind your fame,
660   beware of the enemy. There's nothing you wish for
     that won't be yours if you win through alive."

[THE FIGHT WITH GRENDEL]

    Hrothgar departed then with his house-guard.
     The lord of the Shieldings, their shelter in war,
     left the mead-hall to lie with Wealhtheow,
665   his queen and bedmate. The King of Glory
     (as people learned) had posted a lookout
     who was a match for Grendel, a guard against monsters,
     special protection to the Danish prince.
     And the Geat placed complete trust
670   in his strength of limb and the Lord's favor.
     He began to remove his iron breast-mail,
     took off the helmet and handed his attendant
     the patterned sword, a smith's masterpiece,
     ordering him to keep the equipment guarded.
675   And before he bedded down, Beowulf,
     that prince of goodness, proudly asserted:
     "When it comes to fighting, I count myself
     as dangerous any day as Grendel.
     So it won't be a cutting edge I'll wield
680   to mow him down, easily as I might.
     He has no idea of the arts of war,
     of shield or sword-play, although he does possess
     a wild strength. No weapons, therefore,
     for either this night: unarmed he shall face me
685   if face me he dares. And may the Divine Lord
     in His wisdom grant the glory of victory
     to whichever side He sees fit."
    Then down the brave man lay with his bolster
     under his head and his whole company
690   of sea-rovers at rest beside him.
     None of them expected he would ever see
     his homeland again or get back
     to his native place and the people who reared him.
     They knew too well the way it was before,
695   how often the Danes had fallen prey
     to death in the mead-hall. But the Lord was weaving
     a victory on His war-loom for the Weather-Geats.
     Through the strength of one they all prevailed;
     they would crush their enemy and come through
700   in triumph and gladness. The truth is clear:
     Almighty God rules over mankind
     and always has.
                 Then out of the night

came the shadow-stalker, stealthy and swift.
The hall-guards were slack, asleep at their posts,
705   all except one; it was widely understood
that as long as God disallowed it,
the fiend could not bear them to his shadow-bourne.
One man, however, was in fighting mood,
awake and on edge, spoiling for action.
710   In off the moors, down through the mist-bands
God-cursed Grendel came greedily loping.
The bane of the race of men roamed forth,
hunting for a prey in the high hall.
Under the cloud-murk he moved toward it
715   until it shone above him, a sheer keep
of fortified gold. Nor was that the first time
he had scouted the grounds of Hrothgar's dwelling—
although never in his life, before or since,
did he find harder fortune or hall-defenders.
720   Spurned and joyless, he journeyed on ahead
and arrived at the bawn.[5] The iron-braced door
turned on its hinge when his hands touched it.
Then his rage boiled over, he ripped open
the mouth of the building, maddening for blood,
725   pacing the length of the patterned floor
with his loathsome tread, while a baleful light,
flame more than light, flared from his eyes.
He saw many men in the mansion, sleeping,
a ranked company of kinsmen and warriors
730   quartered together. And his glee was demonic,
picturing the mayhem: before morning
he would rip life from limb and devour them,
feed on their flesh; but his fate that night
was due to change, his days of ravening
had come to an end.
735   Mighty and canny,
Hygelac's kinsman was keenly watching
for the first move the monster would make.
Nor did the creature keep him waiting
but struck suddenly and started in;
740   he grabbed and mauled a man on his bench,
bit into his bone-lappings, bolted down his blood
and gorged on him in lumps, leaving the body
utterly lifeless, eaten up
hand and foot. Venturing closer,
745   his talon was raised to attack Beowulf
where he lay on the bed, he was bearing in
with open claw when the alert hero's
comeback and armlock forestalled him utterly.
The captain of evil discovered himself
750   in a handgrip harder than anything
he had ever encountered in any man

5. See p. 43, n. 4.

on the face of the earth. Every bone in his body
quailed and recoiled, but he could not escape.
He was desperate to flee to his den and hide
755 with the devil's litter, for in all his days
he had never been clamped or cornered like this.
Then Hygelac's trusty retainer recalled
his bedtime speech, sprang to his feet
and got a firm hold. Fingers were bursting,
760 the monster back-tracking, the man overpowering.
The dread of the land was desperate to escape,
to take a roundabout road and flee
to his lair in the fens. The latching power
in his fingers weakened; it was the worst trip
765 the terror-monger had taken to Heorot.
And now the timbers trembled and sang,
a hall-session[6] that harrowed every Dane
inside the stockade: stumbling in fury,
the two contenders crashed through the building.
770 The hall clattered and hammered, but somehow
survived the onslaught and kept standing:
it was handsomely structured, a sturdy frame
braced with the best of blacksmith's work
inside and out. The story goes
775 that as the pair struggled, mead-benches were smashed
and sprung off the floor, gold fittings and all.
Before then, no Shielding elder would believe
there was any power or person upon earth
capable of wrecking their horn-rigged hall
780 unless the burning embrace of a fire
engulf it in flame. Then an extraordinary
wail arose, and bewildering fear
came over the Danes. Everyone felt it
who heard that cry as it echoed off the wall,
785 a God-cursed scream and strain of catastrophe,
the howl of the loser, the lament of the hell-serf
keening his wound. He was overwhelmed,
manacled tight by the man who of all men
was foremost and strongest in the days of this life.
790   But the earl-troop's leader was not inclined
to allow his caller to depart alive:
he did not consider that life of much account
to anyone anywhere. Time and again,
Beowulf's warriors worked to defend
795 their lord's life, laying about them
as best they could, with their ancestral blades.
Stalwart in action, they kept striking out
on every side, seeking to cut
straight to the soul. When they joined the struggle
800 there was something they could not have known at the time,

6. In Hiberno-English the word "session" (*seissiún* in Irish) can mean a gathering where musicians and
singers perform for their own enjoyment [Translator's note].

that no blade on earth, no blacksmith's art
could ever damage their demon opponent.
He had conjured the harm from the cutting edge
of every weapon.[7] But his going away
805   out of this world and the days of his life
would be agony to him, and his alien spirit
would travel far into fiends' keeping.
    Then he who had harrowed the hearts of men
with pain and affliction in former times
810   and had given offense also to God
found that his bodily powers failed him.
Hygelac's kinsman kept him helplessly
locked in a handgrip. As long as either lived,
he was hateful to the other. The monster's whole
815   body was in pain; a tremendous wound
appeared on his shoulder. Sinews split
and the bone-lappings burst. Beowulf was granted
the glory of winning; Grendel was driven
under the fen-banks, fatally hurt,
820   to his desolate lair. His days were numbered,
the end of his life was coming over him,
he knew it for certain; and one bloody clash
had fulfilled the dearest wishes of the Danes.
The man who had lately landed among them,
825   proud and sure, had purged the hall,
kept it from harm; he was happy with his nightwork
and the courage he had shown. The Geat captain
had boldly fulfilled his boast to the Danes:
he had healed and relieved a huge distress,
830   unremitting humiliations,
the hard fate they'd been forced to undergo,
no small affliction. Clear proof of this
could be seen in the hand the hero displayed
high up near the roof: the whole of Grendel's
835   shoulder and arm, his awesome grasp.

[CELEBRATION AT HEOROT]

    Then morning came and many a warrior
gathered, as I've heard, around the gift-hall,
clan-chiefs flocking from far and near
down wide-ranging roads, wondering greatly
840   at the monster's footprints. His fatal departure
was regretted by no one who witnessed his trail,
the ignominious marks of his flight
where he'd skulked away, exhausted in spirit
and beaten in battle, bloodying the path,
845   hauling his doom to the demons' mere.[8]
The bloodshot water wallowed and surged,

---

7. Grendel is protected by a charm against metals.
8. A lake or pool, although we learn later that it has an outlet to the sea. Grendel's habitat.

there were loathsome upthrows and overturnings
of waves and gore and wound-slurry.
With his death upon him, he had dived deep
850 into his marsh-den, drowned out his life
and his heathen soul: hell claimed him there.
  Then away they rode, the old retainers
with many a young man following after,
a troop on horseback, in high spirits
855 on their bay steeds. Beowulf's doings
were praised over and over again.
Nowhere, they said, north or south
between the two seas or under the tall sky
on the broad earth was there anyone better
860 to raise a shield or to rule a kingdom.
Yet there was no laying of blame on their lord,
the noble Hrothgar; he was a good king.
  At times the war-band broke into a gallop,
letting their chestnut horses race
865 wherever they found the going good
on those well-known tracks. Meanwhile, a thane
of the king's household, a carrier of tales,
a traditional singer deeply schooled
in the lore of the past, linked a new theme
870 to a strict meter.[9] The man started
to recite with skill, rehearsing Beowulf's
triumphs and feats in well-fashioned lines,
entwining his words.
      He told what he'd heard
repeated in songs about Sigemund's exploits,[1]
875 all of those many feats and marvels,
the struggles and wanderings of Waels's son,[2]
things unknown to anyone
except to Fitela, feuds and foul doings
confided by uncle to nephew when he felt
880 the urge to speak of them: always they had been
partners in the fight, friends in need.
They killed giants, their conquering swords
had brought them down.
      After his death
Sigemund's glory grew and grew
885 *because of his courage when he killed the dragon,*
the guardian of the hoard. Under gray stone
he had dared to enter all by himself
to face the worst without Fitela.
But it came to pass that his sword plunged
890 *right through those radiant scales*
and drove into the wall. The dragon died of it.

---

9. I.e., an extemporaneous heroic poem in alliterative verse about Beowulf's deeds.
1. Tales about Sigemund, his nephew Sinfjotli
(Fitela), and his son Sigurth are found in a 13th-
century Old Icelandic collection of legends known
as the *Volsung Saga*. Analogous stories must have
been known to the poet and his audience, though
details differ.
2. Waels is the father of Sigemund.

His daring had given him   total possession
of the treasure-hoard,   his to dispose of
however he liked.   He loaded a boat:
895   Waels's son   weighted her hold
with dazzling spoils.   The hot dragon melted.
     Sigemund's name   was known everywhere.
He was utterly valiant   and venturesome,
a fence round his fighters   and flourished therefore
900   after King Heremod's[3]   prowess declined
and his campaigns slowed down.   The king was betrayed,
ambushed in Jutland,   overpowered
and done away with.   The waves of his grief
had beaten him down,   made him a burden,
905   a source of anxiety   to his own nobles:
that expedition   was often condemned
in those earlier times   by experienced men,
men who relied   on his lordship for redress,
who presumed that the part   of a prince was to thrive
910   on his father's throne   and defend the nation,
the Shielding land   where they lived and belonged,
its holdings and strongholds.   Such was Beowulf
in the affection of his friends   and of everyone alive.
But evil entered   into Heremod.
915   Meanwhile, the Danes kept racing their mounts
down sandy lanes. The light of day
broke and kept brightening. Bands of retainers
galloped in excitement to the gabled hall
to see the marvel; and the king himself,
920   guardian of the ring-hoard, goodness in person,
walked in majesty from the women's quarters
with a numerous train, attended by his queen
and her crowd of maidens, across to the mead-hall.
     When Hrothgar arrived at the hall, he spoke,
925   standing on the steps, under the steep eaves,
gazing toward the roofwork and Grendel's talon:
"First and foremost, let the Almighty Father
be thanked for this sight. I suffered a long
harrowing by Grendel. But the Heavenly Shepherd
930   can work His wonders always and everywhere.
Not long since, it seemed I would never
be granted the slightest solace or relief
from any of my burdens: the best of houses
glittered and reeked and ran with blood.
935   This one worry outweighed all others—
a constant distress to counselors entrusted
with defending the people's forts from assault
by monsters and demons. But now a man,
with the Lord's assistance, has accomplished something
940   none of us could manage before now

---

3. Heremod was a bad king, held up by the bard as the opposite of Beowulf, as Sigemund is held up as a
heroic prototype of Beowulf.

for all our efforts. Whoever she was
who brought forth this flower of manhood,
if she is still alive, that woman can say
that in her labor the Lord of Ages
945 bestowed a grace on her. So now, Beowulf,
I adopt you in my heart as a dear son.
Nourish and maintain this new connection,
you noblest of men; there'll be nothing you'll want for,
no worldly goods that won't be yours.
950 I have often honored smaller achievements,
recognized warriors not nearly as worthy,
lavished rewards on the less deserving.
But you have made yourself immortal
by your glorious action. May the God of Ages
955 continue to keep and requite you well."
    Beowulf, son of Ecgtheow, spoke:
"We have gone through with a glorious endeavor
and been much favored in this fight we dared
against the unknown. Nevertheless,
960 if you could have seen the monster himself
where he lay beaten, I would have been better pleased.
My plan was to pounce, pin him down
in a tight grip and grapple him to death—
have him panting for life, powerless and clasped
965 in my bare hands, his body in thrall.
But I couldn't stop him from slipping my hold.
The Lord allowed it, my lock on him
wasn't strong enough; he struggled fiercely
and broke and ran. Yet he bought his freedom
970 at a high price, for he left his hand
and arm and shoulder to show he had been here,
a cold comfort for having come among us.
And now he won't be long for this world.
He has done his worst but the wound will end him.
975 He is hasped and hooped and hirpling with pain,
limping and looped in it. Like a man outlawed
for wickedness, he must await
the mighty judgment of God in majesty."
    There was less tampering and big talk then
980 from Unferth the boaster, less of his blather
as the hall-thanes eyed the awful proof
of the hero's prowess, the splayed hand
up under the eaves. Every nail,
claw-scale and spur, every spike
985 and welt on the hand of that heathen brute
was like barbed steel. Everybody said
there was no honed iron hard enough
to pierce him through, no time-proofed blade
that could cut his brutal, blood-caked claw.
990   Then the order was given for all hands
to help to refurbish Heorot immediately:
men and women thronging the wine-hall,

getting it ready. Gold thread shone
in the wall-hangings, woven scenes
995 that attracted and held the eye's attention.
But iron-braced as the inside of it had been,
that bright room lay in ruins now.
The very doors had been dragged from their hinges.
Only the roof remained unscathed
1000 by the time the guilt-fouled fiend turned tail
in despair of his life. But death is not easily
escaped from by anyone:
all of us with souls, earth-dwellers
and children of men, must make our way
1005 to a destination already ordained
where the body, after the banqueting,
sleeps on its deathbed.
               Then the due time arrived
for Halfdane's son to proceed to the hall.
The king himself would sit down to feast.
1010 No group ever gathered in greater numbers
or better order around their ring-giver.
The benches filled with famous men
who fell to with relish; round upon round
of mead was passed; those powerful kinsmen,
1015 Hrothgar and Hrothulf, were in high spirits
in the raftered hall. Inside Heorot
there was nothing but friendship. The Shielding nation
was not yet familiar with feud and betrayal.[4]
    Then Halfdane's son presented Beowulf
1020 with a gold standard as a victory gift,
an embroidered banner; also breast-mail
and a helmet; and a sword carried high,
that was both precious object and token of honor.
So Beowulf drank his drink, at ease;
1025 it was hardly a shame to be showered with such gifts
in front of the hall-troops. There haven't been many
moments, I am sure, when men exchanged
four such treasures at so friendly a sitting.
An embossed ridge, a band lapped with wire
1030 arched over the helmet: head-protection
to keep the keen-ground cutting edge
from damaging it when danger threatened
and the man was battling behind his shield.
Next the king ordered eight horses
1035 with gold bridles to be brought through the yard
into the hall. The harness of one
included a saddle of sumptuous design,
the battle-seat where the son of Halfdane
rode when he wished to join the sword-play:
1040 wherever the killing and carnage were the worst,

4. Probably an ironic allusion to the future usur-
pation of the throne from Hrothgar's sons by Hrothulf, although no such treachery is recorded of
Hrothulf, who is the hero of other Germanic stories.

he would be to the fore, fighting hard.
Then the Danish prince, descendant of Ing,
handed over both the arms and the horses,
urging Beowulf to use them well.
1045 And so their leader, the lord and guard
of coffer and strongroom, with customary grace
bestowed upon Beowulf both sets of gifts.
A fair witness can see how well each one behaved.
The chieftain went on to reward the others:
1050 each man on the bench who had sailed with Beowulf
and risked the voyage received a bounty,
some treasured possession. And compensation,
a price in gold, was settled for the Geat
Grendel had cruelly killed earlier—
1055 as he would have killed more, had not mindful God
and one man's daring prevented that doom.
Past and present, God's will prevails.
Hence, understanding is always best
and a prudent mind. Whoever remains
1060 for long here in this earthly life
will enjoy and endure more than enough.

They sang then and played to please the hero,
words and music for their warrior prince,
harp tunes and tales of adventure:
1065 there were high times on the hall benches,
and the king's poet performed his part
with the saga of Finn and his sons, unfolding
the tale of the fierce attack in Friesland
where Hnaef, king of the Danes, met death.[5]

Hildeburh
1070   had little cause
to credit the Jutes:
                           son and brother,
she lost them both
                           on the battlefield.
She, bereft
                           and blameless, they
foredoomed, cut down
                           and spear-gored. She,
the woman in shock,
1075   waylaid by grief,
Hoc's daughter—
                           how could she not

---

5. The bard's lay is known as the Finnsburg Episode. Its allusive style makes the tale obscure in
many details, although some can be filled in from
a fragmentary Old English lay, which modern editors have entitled *The Fight at Finnsburg*. Hildeburh, the daughter of the former Danish king Hoc,
was married to Finn, king of Friesland, presumably
to help end a feud between their peoples. As the
episode opens, the feud has already broken out
again when a visiting party of Danes, led by Hildeburh's brother Hnaef, who has succeeded their
father, is attacked by a tribe called the Jutes. The
Jutes are subject to Finn but may be a clan distinct
from the Frisians, and Finn does not seem to have
instigated the attack. In the ensuing battle, both
Hnaef and the son of Hildeburh and Finn are
killed, and both sides suffer heavy losses.

lament her fate
                    when morning came
and the light broke
                    on her murdered dears?
And so farewell
                    delight on earth,
war carried away
                    Finn's troop of thanes
all but a few.
                    How then could Finn
hold the line
                    or fight on
to the end with Hengest,
                    how save
the rump of his force
                    from that enemy chief?
So a truce was offered
                    as follows:[6] first
separate quarters
                    to be cleared for the Danes,
hall and throne
                    to be shared with the Frisians.
Then, second:
                    every day
at the dole-out of gifts
                    Finn, son of Focwald,
should honor the Danes,
                    bestow with an even
hand to Hengest
                    and Hengest's men
the wrought-gold rings,
                    bounty to match
the measure he gave
                    his own Frisians—
to keep morale
                    in the beer-hall high.
Both sides then
                    sealed their agreement.
With oaths to Hengest
                    Finn swore
openly, solemnly,
                    that the battle survivors
would be guaranteed
                    honor and status.
No infringement
                    by word or deed,
no provocation
                    would be permitted.
Their own ring-giver
                    after all

6. The truce was offered by Finn to Hengest, who succeeded Hnaef as leader of the Danes.

was dead and gone,
>they were leaderless,
in forced allegiance
>to his murderer.
So if any Frisian
>stirred up bad blood
1105 with insinuations
>or taunts about this,
the blade of the sword
>would arbitrate it.
A funeral pyre
>was then prepared,
effulgent gold
>brought out from the hoard.
The pride and prince
>of the Shieldings lay
1110 awaiting the flame.
>Everywhere
there were blood-plastered
>coats of mail.
The pyre was heaped
>with boar-shaped helmets
forged in gold,
>with the gashed corpses
of wellborn Danes—
>many had fallen.
1115 Then Hildeburh
>ordered her own
son's body
>be burnt with Hnaef's,
the flesh on his bones
>to sputter and blaze
beside his uncle's.
>The woman wailed
and sang keens,
>the warrior went up.[7]
1120 Carcass flame
>swirled and fumed,
they stood round the burial
>mound and howled
as heads melted,
>crusted gashes
spattered and ran
>bloody matter.
The glutton element
>flamed and consumed
1125 the dead of both sides.
>Their great days were gone.
Warriors scattered

---

7. The meaning may be, the warrior was placed up on the pyre, or went up in smoke. "Keens": lamentations or dirges for the dead.

to homes and forts
all over Friesland,
                    fewer now, feeling
loss of friends.
                    Hengest stayed,
lived out that whole
                    resentful, blood-sullen
winter with Finn,
1130   homesick and helpless.
No ring-whorled prow
                    could up then
and away on the sea.
                    Wind and water
raged with storms,
                    wave and shingle
were shackled in ice
                    until another year
appeared in the yard
1135   as it does to this day,
the seasons constant,
                    the wonder of light
coming over us.
                    Then winter was gone,
earth's lap grew lovely,
                    longing woke
in the cooped-up exile
                    for a voyage home—
but more for vengeance,
1140   some way of bringing
things to a head:
                    his sword arm hankered
to greet the Jutes.
                    So he did not balk
once Hunlafing
                    placed on his lap
Dazzle-the-Duel,
                    the best sword of all,[8]
whose edges Jutes
1145   knew only too well.
Thus blood was spilled,
                    the gallant Finn
slain in his home
                    after Guthlaf and Oslaf[9]
back from their voyage
                    made old accusation:
the brutal ambush,
                    the fate they had suffered,
all blamed on Finn.

8. Hunlafing may be the son of a Danish warrior called Hunlaf. The placing of the sword in Hengest's lap is a symbolic call for revenge.
9. It is not clear whether the Danes have traveled home and then returned to Friesland with reinforcements, or whether the Danish survivors attack once the weather allows them to take ship.

1150
                    The wildness in them
had to brim over.
                    The hall ran red
with blood of enemies.
                              Finn was cut down,
the queen brought away
                         and everything
the Shieldings could find
                         inside Finn's walls—
1155 *the Frisian king's*
                    gold collars and gemstones—
swept off to the ship.
                         Over sea-lanes then
back to Daneland
                    the warrior troop
bore that lady home.

                    The poem was over,
the poet had performed, a pleasant murmur
1160 started on the benches, stewards did the rounds
with wine in splendid jugs, and Wealhtheow came to sit
in her gold crown between two good men,
uncle and nephew, each one of whom
still trusted the other;[1] and the forthright Unferth,
1165 admired by all for his mind and courage
although under a cloud for killing his brothers,
reclined near the king.
                    The queen spoke:
"Enjoy this drink, my most generous lord;
raise up your goblet, entertain the Geats
1170 duly and gently, discourse with them,
be open-handed, happy and fond.
Relish their company, but recollect as well
all of the boons that have been bestowed on you.
The bright court of Heorot has been cleansed
1175 and now the word is that you want to adopt
this warrior as a son. So, while you may,
bask in your fortune, and then bequeath
kingdom and nation to your kith and kin,
before your decease. I am certain of Hrothulf.
1180 He is noble and will use the young ones well.
He will not let you down. Should you die before him,
he will treat our children truly and fairly.
He will honor, I am sure, our two sons,
repay them in kind, when he recollects
1185 all the good things we gave him once,
the favor and respect he found in his childhood."
She turned then to the bench where her boys sat,
Hrethric and Hrothmund, with other nobles' sons,

1. See n. 4, p. 53.

all the youth together; and that good man,
1190 Beowulf the Geat, sat between the brothers.
The cup was carried to him, kind words
spoken in welcome and a wealth of wrought gold
graciously bestowed: two arm bangles,
a mail-shirt and rings, and the most resplendent
1195 torque of gold I ever heard tell of
anywhere on earth or under heaven.
There was no hoard like it since Hama snatched
the Brosings' neck-chain and bore it away
with its gems and settings to his shining fort,
1200 away from Eormenric's wiles and hatred,[2]
and thereby ensured his eternal reward.
Hygelac the Geat, grandson of Swerting,
wore this neck-ring on his last raid;[3]
at bay under his banner, he defended the booty,
1205 treasure he had won. Fate swept him away
because of his proud need to provoke
a feud with the Frisians. He fell beneath his shield,
in the same gem-crusted, kingly gear
he had worn when he crossed the frothing wave-vat.
1210 So the dead king fell into Frankish hands.
They took his breast-mail, also his neck-torque,
and punier warriors plundered the slain
when the carnage ended; Geat corpses
covered the field.
                    Applause filled the hall.
1215 Then Wealhtheow pronounced in the presence of the company:
"Take delight in this torque, dear Beowulf,
wear it for luck and wear also this mail
from our people's armory: may you prosper in them!
Be acclaimed for strength, for kindly guidance
1220 to these two boys, and your bounty will be sure.
You have won renown: you are known to all men
far and near, now and forever.
Your sway is wide as the wind's home,
as the sea around cliffs. And so, my prince,
1225 I wish you a lifetime's luck and blessings
to enjoy this treasure. Treat my sons
with tender care, be strong and kind.
Here each comrade is true to the other,
loyal to lord, loving in spirit.
1230 The thanes have one purpose, the people are ready:
having drunk and pledged, the ranks do as I bid."
She moved then to her place. Men were drinking wine

2. The necklace presented to Beowulf is compared to one worn by the goddess Freya in Germanic mythology. In another story it was stolen by Hama from the Gothic king Eormenric, who is treated as a tyrant in Germanic legend, but how Eormenric came to possess it is not known.
3. Later we learn that Beowulf gave the necklace to Hygd, the queen of his lord Hygelac. Hygelac is here said to have been wearing it on his last expedition. This is the first of several allusions to Hygelac's death on a raid up the Rhine, the one incident in the poem that can be connected to a historical event documented elsewhere.

at that rare feast; how could they know fate,
the grim shape of things to come,
1235 the threat looming over many thanes
as night approached and King Hrothgar prepared
to retire to his quarters? Retainers in great numbers
were posted on guard as so often in the past.
Benches were pushed back, bedding gear and bolsters
1240 spread across the floor, and one man
lay down to his rest, already marked for death.
At their heads they placed their polished timber
battle-shields; and on the bench above them,
each man's kit was kept to hand:
1245 a towering war-helmet, webbed mail-shirt
and great-shafted spear. It was their habit
always and everywhere to be ready for action,
at home or in the camp, in whatever case
and at whatever time the need arose
1250 to rally round their lord. They were a right people.

[ANOTHER ATTACK]

They went to sleep. And one paid dearly
for his night's ease, as had happened to them often,
ever since Grendel occupied the gold-hall,
committing evil until the end came,
1255 death after his crimes. Then it became clear,
obvious to everyone once the fight was over,
that an avenger lurked and was still alive,
grimly biding time. Grendel's mother,
monstrous hell-bride, brooded on her wrongs.
1260 She had been forced down into fearful waters,
the cold depths, after Cain had killed
his father's son, felled his own
brother with a sword. Branded an outlaw,
marked by having murdered, he moved into the wilds,
1265 shunned company and joy. And from Cain there sprang
misbegotten spirits, among them Grendel,
the banished and accursed, due to come to grips
with that watcher in Heorot waiting to do battle.
The monster wrenched and wrestled with him,
1270 but Beowulf was mindful of his mighty strength,
the wondrous gifts God had showered on him:
he relied for help on the Lord of All,
on His care and favor. So he overcame the foe,
brought down the hell-brute. Broken and bowed,
1275 outcast from all sweetness, the enemy of mankind
made for his death-den. But now his mother
had sallied forth on a savage journey,
grief-racked and ravenous, desperate for revenge.
She came to Heorot. There, inside the hall,
1280 Danes lay asleep, earls who would soon endure
a great reversal, once Grendel's mother

attacked and entered. Her onslaught was less
only by as much as an amazon warrior's
strength is less than an armed man's
1285 when the hefted sword, its hammered edge
and gleaming blade slathered in blood,
razes the sturdy boar-ridge off a helmet.
Then in the hall, hard-honed swords
were grabbed from the bench, many a broad shield
1290 lifted and braced; there was little thought of helmets
or woven mail when they woke in terror.
    The hell-dam was in panic, desperate to get out,
in mortal terror the moment she was found.
She had pounced and taken one of the retainers
1295 in a tight hold, then headed for the fen.
To Hrothgar, this man was the most beloved
of the friends he trusted between the two seas.
She had done away with a great warrior,
ambushed him at rest.
                Beowulf was elsewhere.
1300 Earlier, after the award of the treasure,
the Geat had been given another lodging.
    There was uproar in Heorot. She had snatched their trophy,
Grendel's bloodied hand. It was a fresh blow
to the afflicted bawn. The bargain was hard,
1305 both parties having to pay
with the lives of friends. And the old lord,
the gray-haired warrior, was heartsore and weary
when he heard the news: his highest-placed adviser,
his dearest companion, was dead and gone.
1310   Beowulf was quickly brought to the chamber:
the winner of fights, the arch-warrior,
came first-footing in with his fellow troops
to where the king in his wisdom waited,
still wondering whether Almighty God
1315 would ever turn the tide of his misfortunes.
So Beowulf entered with his band in attendance
and the wooden floorboards banged and rang
as he advanced, hurrying to address
the prince of the Ingwins, asking if he'd rested
1320 since the urgent summons had come as a surprise.
    Then Hrothgar, the Shieldings' helmet, spoke:
"Rest? What is rest? Sorrow has returned.
Alas for the Danes! Aeschere is dead.
He was Yrmenlaf's elder brother
1325 and a soul-mate to me, a true mentor,
my right-hand man when the ranks clashed
and our boar-crests had to take a battering
in the line of action. Aeschere was everything
the world admires in a wise man and a friend.
1330 Then this roaming killer came in a fury
and slaughtered him in Heorot. Where she is hiding,
glutting on the corpse and glorying in her escape,

I cannot tell; she has taken up the feud
because of last night, when you killed Grendel,
1335 wrestled and racked him in ruinous combat
since for too long he had terrorized us
with his depredations. He died in battle,
paid with his life; and now this powerful
other one arrives, this force for evil
1340 driven to avenge her kinsman's death.
Or so it seems to thanes in their grief,
in the anguish every thane endures
at the loss of a ring-giver, now that the hand
that bestowed so richly has been stilled in death.
1345   "I have heard it said by my people in hall,
counselors who live in the upland country,
that they have seen two such creatures
prowling the moors, huge marauders
from some other world. One of these things,
1350 as far as anyone ever can discern,
looks like a woman; the other, warped
in the shape of a man, moves beyond the pale
bigger than any man, an unnatural birth
called Grendel by the country people
1355 in former days. They are fatherless creatures,
and their whole ancestry is hidden in a past
of demons and ghosts. They dwell apart
among wolves on the hills, on windswept crags
and treacherous keshes, where cold streams
1360 pour down the mountain and disappear
under mist and moorland.
                              A few miles from here
a frost-stiffened wood waits and keeps watch
above a mere; the overhanging bank
is a maze of tree-roots mirrored in its surface.
1365 At night there, something uncanny happens:
the water burns. And the mere bottom
has never been sounded by the sons of men.
On its bank, the heather-stepper halts:
the hart in flight from pursuing hounds
1370 will turn to face them with firm-set horns
and die in the wood rather than dive
beneath its surface. That is no good place.
When wind blows up and stormy weather
makes clouds scud and the skies weep,
1375 out of its depths a dirty surge
is pitched toward the heavens. Now help depends
again on you and on you alone.
The gap of danger where the demon waits
is still unknown to you. Seek it if you dare.
1380 I will compensate you for settling the feud
as I did the last time with lavish wealth,
coffers of coiled gold, if you come back."

[BEOWULF FIGHTS GRENDEL'S MOTHER]

Beowulf, son of Ecgtheow, spoke:
"Wise sir, do not grieve. It is always better
1385 to avenge dear ones than to indulge in mourning.
For every one of us, living in this world
means waiting for our end. Let whoever can
win glory before death. When a warrior is gone,
that will be his best and only bulwark.
1390 So arise, my lord, and let us immediately
set forth on the trail of this troll-dam.
I guarantee you: she will not get away,
not to dens under ground nor upland groves
nor the ocean floor. She'll have nowhere to flee to.
1395 Endure your troubles today. Bear up
and be the man I expect you to be."
    With that the old lord sprang to his feet
and praised God for Beowulf's pledge.
Then a bit and halter were brought for his horse
1400 with the plaited mane. The wise king mounted
the royal saddle and rode out in style
with a force of shield-bearers. The forest paths
were marked all over with the monster's tracks,
her trail on the ground wherever she had gone
1405 across the dark moors, dragging away
the body of that thane, Hrothgar's best
counselor and overseer of the country.
So the noble prince proceeded undismayed
up fells and screes, along narrow footpaths
1410 and ways where they were forced into single file,
ledges on cliffs above lairs of water-monsters.
He went in front with a few men,
good judges of the lie of the land,
and suddenly discovered the dismal wood,
1415 mountain trees growing out at an angle
above gray stones: the bloodshot water
surged underneath. It was a sore blow
to all of the Danes, friends of the Shieldings,
a hurt to each and every one
1420 of that noble company when they came upon
Aeschere's head at the foot of the cliff.
    Everybody gazed as the hot gore
kept wallowing up and an urgent war-horn
repeated its notes: the whole party
1425 sat down to watch. The water was infested
with all kinds of reptiles. There were writhing sea-dragons
and monsters slouching on slopes by the cliff,
serpents and wild things such as those that often
surface at dawn to roam the sail-road
1430 and doom the voyage. Down they plunged,
lashing in anger at the loud call
of the battle-bugle. An arrow from the bow
of the Geat chief got one of them

as he surged to the surface: the seasoned shaft
1435 stuck deep in his flank and his freedom in the water
got less and less. It was his last swim.
He was swiftly overwhelmed in the shallows,
prodded by barbed boar-spears,
cornered, beaten, pulled up on the bank,
1440 a strange lake-birth, a loathsome catch
men gazed at in awe.
                              Beowulf got ready,
donned his war-gear, indifferent to death;
his mighty, hand-forged, fine-webbed mail
would soon meet with the menace underwater.
1445 It would keep the bone-cage of his body safe:
no enemy's clasp could crush him in it,
no vicious armlock choke his life out.
To guard his head he had a glittering helmet
that was due to be muddied on the mere bottom
1450 and blurred in the upswirl. It was of beaten gold,
princely headgear hooped and hasped
by a weapon-smith who had worked wonders
in days gone by and adorned it with boar-shapes;
since then it had resisted every sword.
1455 And another item lent by Unferth
at that moment of need was of no small importance:
the brehon[4] handed him a hilted weapon,
a rare and ancient sword named Hrunting.
The iron blade with its ill-boding patterns
1460 had been tempered in blood. It had never failed
the hand of anyone who hefted it in battle,
anyone who had fought and faced the worst
in the gap of danger. This was not the first time
it had been called to perform heroic feats.
1465   When he lent that blade to the better swordsman,
Unferth, the strong-built son of Ecglaf,
could hardly have remembered the ranting speech
he had made in his cups. He was not man enough
to face the turmoil of a fight under water
1470 and the risk to his life. So there he lost
fame and repute. It was different for the other
rigged out in his gear, ready to do battle.
     Beowulf, son of Ecgtheow, spoke:
"Wisest of kings, now that I have come
1475 to the point of action, I ask you to recall
what we said earlier: that you, son of Halfdane
and gold-friend to retainers, that you, if I should fall
and suffer death while serving your cause,
would act like a father to me afterward.
1480 If this combat kills me, take care
of my young company, my comrades in arms.

---

4. One of an ancient class of lawyers in Ireland [Translator's note]. The Old English word for Unferth's office, *thyle*, has been interpreted as "orator" and "spokesman."

And be sure also, my beloved Hrothgar,
to send Hygelac the treasures I received.
Let the lord of the Geats gaze on that gold,
1485 let Hrethel's son take note of it and see
that I found a ring-giver of rare magnificence
and enjoyed the good of his generosity.
And Unferth is to have what I inherited:
to that far-famed man I bequeath my own
1490 sharp-honed, wave-sheened wonder-blade.
With Hrunting I shall gain glory or die."
    After these words, the prince of the Weather-Geats
was impatient to be away and plunged suddenly:
without more ado, he dived into the heaving
1495 depths of the lake. It was the best part of a day
before he could see the solid bottom.
    Quickly the one who haunted those waters,
who had scavenged and gone her gluttonous rounds
for a hundred seasons, sensed a human
1500 observing her outlandish lair from above.
So she lunged and clutched and managed to catch him
in her brutal grip; but his body, for all that,
remained unscathed: the mesh of the chain-mail
saved him on the outside. Her savage talons
1505 failed to rip the web of his war-shirt.
Then once she touched bottom, that wolfish swimmer
carried the ring-mailed prince to her court
so that for all his courage he could never use
the weapons he carried; and a bewildering horde
1510 came at him from the depths, droves of sea-beasts
who attacked with tusks and tore at his chain-mail
in a ghastly onslaught. The gallant man
could see he had entered some hellish turn-hole
and yet the water there did not work against him
1515 because the hall-roofing held off
the force of the current; then he saw firelight,
a gleam and flare-up, a glimmer of brightness.
    The hero observed that swamp-thing from hell,
the tarn-hag in all her terrible strength,
1520 then heaved his war-sword and swung his arm:
the decorated blade came down ringing
and singing on her head. But he soon found
his battle-torch extinguished; the shining blade
refused to bite. It spared her and failed
1525 the man in his need. It had gone through many
hand-to-hand fight, had hewed the armor
and helmets of the doomed, but here at last
the fabulous powers of that heirloom failed.
    Hygelac's kinsman kept thinking about
1530 his name and fame: he never lost heart.
Then, in a fury, he flung his sword away.
The keen, inlaid, worm-loop-patterned steel
was hurled to the ground: he would have to rely

on the might of his arm. So must a man do
1535 who intends to gain enduring glory
in a combat. Life doesn't cost him a thought.
Then the prince of War-Geats, warming to this fight
with Grendel's mother, gripped her shoulder
and laid about him in a battle frenzy:
1540 he pitched his killer opponent to the floor
but she rose quickly and retaliated,
grappled him tightly in her grim embrace.
The sure-footed fighter felt daunted,
the strongest of warriors stumbled and fell.
1545 So she pounced upon him and pulled out
a broad, whetted knife: now she would avenge
her only child. But the mesh of chain-mail
on Beowulf's shoulder shielded his life,
turned the edge and tip of the blade.
1550 The son of Ecgtheow would have surely perished
and the Geats lost their warrior under the wide earth
had the strong links and locks of his war-gear
not helped to save him: holy God
decided the victory. It was easy for the Lord,
1555 the Ruler of Heaven, to redress the balance
once Beowulf got back up on his feet.
    Then he saw a blade that boded well,
a sword in her armory, an ancient heirloom
from the days of the giants, an ideal weapon,
1560 one that any warrior would envy,
but so huge and heavy of itself
only Beowulf could wield it in a battle.
So the Shieldings' hero hard-pressed and enraged,
took a firm hold of the hilt and swung
1565 the blade in an arc, a resolute blow
that bit deep into her neck-bone
and severed it entirely, toppling the doomed
house of her flesh; she fell to the floor.
The sword dripped blood, the swordsman was elated.
1570   A light appeared and the place brightened
the way the sky does when heaven's candle
is shining clearly. He inspected the vault:
with sword held high, its hilt raised
to guard and threaten, Hygelac's thane
1575 scouted by the wall in Grendel's wake.
Now the weapon was to prove its worth.
The warrior determined to take revenge
for every gross act Grendel had committed—
and not only for that one occasion
1580 when he'd come to slaughter the sleeping troops,
fifteen of Hrothgar's house-guards
surprised on their benches and ruthlessly devoured,
and as many again carried away,
a brutal plunder. Beowulf in his fury
1585 now settled that score: he saw the monster

in his resting place, war-weary and wrecked,
a lifeless corpse, a casualty
of the battle in Heorot. The body gaped
at the stroke dealt to it after death:
1590   Beowulf cut the corpse's head off.
        Immediately the counselors keeping a lookout
with Hrothgar, watching the lake water,
saw a heave-up and surge of waves
and blood in the backwash. They bowed gray heads,
1595   spoke in their sage, experienced way
about the good warrior, how they never again
expected to see that prince returning
in triumph to their king. It was clear to many
that the wolf of the deep had destroyed him forever.
1600   The ninth hour of the day arrived.
The brave Shieldings abandoned the cliff-top
and the king went home; but sick at heart,
staring at the mere, the strangers held on.
They wished, without hope, to behold their lord,
Beowulf himself.
1605   Meanwhile, the sword
began to wilt into gory icicles
to slather and thaw. It was a wonderful thing,
the way it all melted as ice melts
when the Father eases the fetters off the frost
1610   and unravels the water-ropes, He who wields power
over time and tide: He is the true Lord.
        The Geat captain saw treasure in abundance
but carried no spoils from those quarters
except for the head and the inlaid hilt
1615   embossed with jewels; its blade had melted
and the scrollwork on it burned, so scalding was the blood
of the poisonous fiend who had perished there.
Then away he swam, the one who had survived
the fall of his enemies, flailing to the surface.
1620   The wide water, the waves and pools,
were no longer infested once the wandering fiend
let go of her life and this unreliable world.
        The seafarers' leader made for land,
resolutely swimming, delighted with his prize,
1625   the mighty load he was lugging to the surface.
His thanes advanced in a troop to meet him,
thanking God and taking great delight
in seeing their prince back safe and sound.
Quickly the hero's helmet and mail-shirt
1630   were loosed and unlaced. The lake settled,
clouds darkened above the bloodshot depths.
        With high hearts they headed away
along footpaths and trails through the fields,
roads that they knew, each of them wrestling
1635   with the head they were carrying from the lakeside cliff,
men kingly in their courage and capable

of difficult work. It was a task for four
to hoist Grendel's head on a spear
and bear it under strain to the bright hall.
1640   But soon enough they neared the place,
fourteen Geats in fine fettle,
striding across the outlying ground
in a delighted throng around their leader.
       In he came then, the thanes' commander,
1645   the arch-warrior, to address Hrothgar:
his courage was proven, his glory was secure.
Grendel's head was hauled by the hair,
dragged across the floor where the people were drinking,
a horror for both queen and company to behold.
1650   They stared in awe. It was an astonishing sight.

[ANOTHER CELEBRATION AT HEOROT]

       Beowulf, son of Ecgtheow, spoke:
"So, son of Halfdane, prince of the Shieldings,
we are glad to bring this booty from the lake.
It is a token of triumph and we tender it to you.
1655   I barely survived the battle under water.
It was hard-fought, a desperate affair
that could have gone badly; if God had not helped me,
the outcome would have been quick and fatal.
Although Hrunting is hard-edged,
1660   I could never bring it to bear in battle.
But the Lord of Men allowed me to behold—
for He often helps the unbefriended—
an ancient sword shining on the wall,
a weapon made for giants, there for the wielding.
1665   Then my moment came in the combat and I struck
the dwellers in that den. Next thing the damascened
sword blade melted; it bloated and it burned
in their rushing blood. I have wrested the hilt
from the enemies' hand, avenged the evil
1670   done to the Danes; it is what was due.
And this I pledge, O prince of the Shieldings:
you can sleep secure with your company of troops
in Heorot Hall. Never need you fear
for a single thane of your sept or nation,
1675   young warriors or old, that laying waste of life
that you and your people endured of yore."
       Then the gold hilt was handed over
to the old lord, a relic from long ago
for the venerable ruler. That rare smithwork
1680   was passed on to the prince of the Danes
when those devils perished; once death removed
that murdering, guilt-steeped, God-cursed fiend,
eliminating his unholy life
and his mother's as well, it was willed to that king
1685   who of all the lavish gift-lords of the north

was the best regarded between the two seas.
   Hrothgar spoke; he examined the hilt,
that relic of old times. It was engraved all over
and showed how war first came into the world
1690 and the flood destroyed the tribe of giants.
They suffered a terrible severance from the Lord;
the Almighty made the waters rise,
drowned them in the deluge for retribution.
In pure gold inlay on the sword-guards
1695 there were rune-markings correctly incised,
stating and recording for whom the sword
had been first made and ornamented
with its scrollworked hilt. Then everyone hushed
as the son of Halfdane spoke this wisdom:
1700 "A protector of his people, pledged to uphold
truth and justice and to respect tradition,
is entitled to affirm that this man
was born to distinction. Beowulf, my friend,
your fame has gone far and wide,
1705 you are known everywhere. In all things you are even-tempered,
prudent and resolute. So I stand firm by the promise of friendship
we exchanged before. Forever you will be
your people's mainstay and your own warriors'
helping hand.
             Heremod was different,
1710 the way he behaved to Ecgwela's sons.
His rise in the world brought little joy
to the Danish people, only death and destruction.
He vented his rage on men he caroused with,
killed his own comrades, a pariah king
1715 who cut himself off from his own kind,
even though Almighty God had made him
eminent and powerful and marked him from the start
for a happy life. But a change happened,
he grew bloodthirsty, gave no more rings
1720 to honor the Danes. He suffered in the end
for having plagued his people for so long:
his life lost happiness.
             So learn from this
and understand true values. I who tell you
have wintered into wisdom.
             It is a great wonder
1725 how Almighty God in His magnificence
favors our race with rank and scope
and the gift of wisdom; His sway is wide.
Sometimes He allows the mind of a man
of distinguished birth to follow its bent,
1730 grants him fulfillment and felicity on earth
and forts to command in his own country.
He permits him to lord it in many lands
until the man in his unthinkingness
forgets that it will ever end for him.

1735 He indulges his desires; illness and old age
mean nothing to him; his mind is untroubled
by envy or malice or the thought of enemies
with their hate-honed swords. The whole world
conforms to his will, he is kept from the worst
1740 until an element of overweening
enters him and takes hold
while the soul's guard, its sentry, drowses,
grown too distracted. A killer stalks him,
an archer who draws a deadly bow.
1745 And then the man is hit in the heart,
the arrow flies beneath his defenses,
the devious promptings of the demon start.
His old possessions seem paltry to him now.
He covets and resents; dishonors custom
1750 and bestows no gold; and because of good things
that the Heavenly Powers gave him in the past
he ignores the shape of things to come.
Then finally the end arrives
when the body he was lent collapses and falls
1755 prey to its death; ancestral possessions
and the goods he hoarded are inherited by another
who lets them go with a liberal hand.
        "O flower of warriors, beware of that trap.
Choose, dear Beowulf, the better part,
1760 eternal rewards. Do not give way to pride.
For a brief while your strength is in bloom
but it fades quickly; and soon there will follow
illness or the sword to lay you low,
or a sudden fire or surge of water
1765 or jabbing blade or javelin from the air
or repellent age. Your piercing eye
will dim and darken; and death will arrive,
dear warrior, to sweep you away.
        "Just so I ruled the Ring-Danes' country
1770 for fifty years, defended them in wartime
with spear and sword against constant assaults
by many tribes: I came to believe
my enemies had faded from the face of the earth.
Still, what happened was a hard reversal
1775 from bliss to grief. Grendel struck
after lying in wait. He laid waste to the land
and from that moment my mind was in dread
of his depredations. So I praise God
in His heavenly glory that I lived to behold
1780 this head dripping blood and that after such harrowing
I can look upon it in triumph at last.
Take your place, then, with pride and pleasure,
and move to the feast. Tomorrow morning
our treasure will be shared and showered upon you."
1785   The Geat was elated and gladly obeyed
the old man's bidding; he sat on the bench.

And soon all was restored, the same as before.
Happiness came back, the hall was thronged,
and a banquet set forth; black night fell
and covered them in darkness.
1790   Then the company rose
for the old campaigner: the gray-haired prince
was ready for bed. And a need for rest
came over the brave shield-bearing Geat.
He was a weary seafarer, far from home,
1795 so immediately a house-guard guided him out,
one whose office entailed looking after
whatever a thane on the road in those days
might need or require. It was noble courtesy.

[BEOWULF RETURNS HOME]

    That great heart rested. The hall towered,
1800 gold-shingled and gabled, and the guest slept in it
until the black raven with raucous glee
announced heaven's joy, and a hurry of brightness
overran the shadows. Warriors rose quickly,
impatient to be off: their own country
1805 was beckoning the nobles; and the bold voyager
longed to be aboard his distant boat.
Then that stalwart fighter ordered Hrunting
to be brought to Unferth, and bade Unferth
take the sword and thanked him for lending it.
1810 He said he had found it a friend in battle
and a powerful help; he put no blame
on the blade's cutting edge. He was a considerate man.
    And there the warriors stood in their war-gear,
eager to go, while their honored lord
1815 approached the platform where the other sat.
The undaunted hero addressed Hrothgar.
Beowulf, son of Ecgtheow, spoke:
"Now we who crossed the wide sea
have to inform you that we feel a desire
1820 to return to Hygelac. Here we have been welcomed
and thoroughly entertained. You have treated us well.
If there is any favor on earth I can perform
beyond deeds of arms I have done already,
anything that would merit your affections more,
1825 I shall act, my lord, with alacrity.
If ever I hear from across the ocean
that people on your borders are threatening battle
as attackers have done from time to time,
I shall land with a thousand thanes at my back
1830 to help your cause. Hygelac may be young
to rule a nation, but this much I know
about the king of the Geats: he will come to my aid
and want to support me by word and action
in your hour of need, when honor dictates

1835　　that I raise a hedge of spears around you.
　　　　Then if Hrethric should think about traveling
　　　　as a king's son to the court of the Geats,
　　　　he will find many friends. Foreign places
　　　　yield more to one who is himself worth meeting."
1840　　　　Hrothgar spoke and answered him:
　　　　"The Lord in his wisdom sent you those words
　　　　and they came from the heart. I have never heard
　　　　so young a man make truer observations.
　　　　You are strong in body and mature in mind,
1845　　impressive in speech. If it should come to pass
　　　　that Hrethel's descendant dies beneath a spear,
　　　　if deadly battle or the sword blade or disease
　　　　fells the prince who guards your people
　　　　and you are still alive, then I firmly believe
1850　　the seafaring Geats won't find a man
　　　　worthier of acclaim as their king and defender
　　　　than you, if only you would undertake
　　　　the lordship of your homeland. My liking for you
　　　　deepens with time, dear Beowulf.
1855　　What you have done is to draw two peoples,
　　　　the Geat nation and us neighboring Danes,
　　　　into shared peace and a pact of friendship
　　　　in spite of hatreds we have harbored in the past.
　　　　For as long as I rule this far-flung land
1860　　treasures will change hands and each side will treat
　　　　the other with gifts; across the gannet's bath,
　　　　over the broad sea, whorled prows will bring
　　　　presents and tokens. I know your people
　　　　are beyond reproach in every respect,
1865　　steadfast in the old way with friend or foe."
　　　　　　Then the earls' defender furnished the hero
　　　　with twelve treasures and told him to set out,
　　　　sail with those gifts safely home
　　　　to the people he loved, but to return promptly.
1870　　And so the good and gray-haired Dane,
　　　　that highborn king, kissed Beowulf
　　　　and embraced his neck, then broke down
　　　　in sudden tears. Two forebodings
　　　　disturbed him in his wisdom, but one was stronger:
1875　　nevermore would they meet each other
　　　　face to face. And such was his affection
　　　　that he could not help being overcome:
　　　　his fondness for the man was so deep-founded,
　　　　it warmed his heart and wound the heartstrings
　　　　tight in his breast.
1880　　　　　　　　　　The embrace ended
　　　　and Beowulf, glorious in his gold regalia,
　　　　stepped the green earth. Straining at anchor
　　　　and ready for boarding, his boat awaited him.
　　　　So they went on their journey, and Hrothgar's generosity
1885　　was praised repeatedly. He was a peerless king
　　　　until old age sapped his strength and did him

mortal harm, as it has done so many.
Down to the waves then, dressed in the web
of their chain-mail and war-shirts the young men marched
1890 in high spirits. The coast-guard spied them,
thanes setting forth, the same as before.
His salute this time from the top of the cliff
was far from unmannerly; he galloped to meet them
and as they took ship in their shining gear,
1895 he said how welcome they would be in Geatland.
Then the broad hull was beached on the sand
to be cargoed with treasure, horses and war-gear.
The curved prow motioned; the mast stood high
above Hrothgar's riches in the loaded hold.
1900 The guard who had watched the boat was given
a sword with gold fittings, and in future days
that present would make him a respected man
at his place on the mead-bench.
                                        Then the keel plunged
and shook in the sea; and they sailed from Denmark.
1905 Right away the mast was rigged with its sea-shawl;
sail-ropes were tightened, timbers drummed
and stiff winds kept the wave-crosser
skimming ahead; as she heaved forward,
her foamy neck was fleet and buoyant,
1910 a lapped prow loping over currents,
until finally the Geats caught sight of coastline
and familiar cliffs. The keel reared up,
wind lifted it home, it hit on the land.
The harbor guard came hurrying out
1915 to the rolling water: he had watched the offing
long and hard, on the lookout for those friends.
With the anchor cables, he moored their craft
right where it had beached, in case a backwash
might catch the hull and carry it away.
1920 Then he ordered the prince's treasure-trove
to be carried ashore. It was a short step
from there to where Hrethel's son and heir,
Hygelac the gold-giver, makes his home
on a secure cliff, in the company of retainers.
1925 The building was magnificent, the king majestic,
ensconced in his hall; and although Hygd, his queen,
was young, a few short years at court,
her mind was thoughtful and her manners sure.
Haereth's daughter behaved generously
1930 and stinted nothing when she distributed
bounty to the Geats.
                         Great Queen Modthryth
perpetrated terrible wrongs.[5]

---

5. The story of Queen Modthryth's vices is abruptly introduced as a foil to Queen Hygd's virtues. A transitional passage may have been lost, but the poet's device is similar to that of using the earlier reference to the wickedness of King Heremod to contrast with the good qualities of Sigemund and Beowulf.

If any retainer ever made bold
to look her in the face, if an eye not her lord's[6]
1935   stared at her directly during daylight,
the outcome was sealed: he was kept bound,
in hand-tightened shackles, racked, tortured
until doom was pronounced—death by the sword,
slash of blade, blood-gush, and death-qualms
1940   in an evil display. Even a queen
outstanding in beauty must not overstep like that.
A queen should weave peace, not punish the innocent
with loss of life for imagined insults.
But Hemming's kinsman[7] put a halt to her ways
1945   and drinkers round the table had another tale:
she was less of a bane to people's lives,
less cruel-minded, after she was married
to the brave Offa, a bride arrayed
in her gold finery, given away
1950   by a caring father, ferried to her young prince
over dim seas. In days to come
she would grace the throne and grow famous
for her good deeds and conduct of life,
her high devotion to the hero king
1955   who was the best king, it has been said,
between the two seas or anywhere else
on the face of the earth. Offa was honored
far and wide for his generous ways,
his fighting spirit and his farseeing
1960   defense of his homeland; from him there sprang Eomer,
Garmund's grandson, kinsman of Hemming,[8]
his warriors' mainstay and master of the field.

    Heroic Beowulf and his band of men
crossed the wide strand, striding along
1965   the sandy foreshore; the sun shone,
the world's candle warmed them from the south
as they hastened to where, as they had heard,
the young king, Ongentheow's killer
and his people's protector,[9] was dispensing rings
1970   inside his bawn. Beowulf's return
was reported to Hygelac as soon as possible,
news that the captain was now in the enclosure,
his battle-brother back from the fray
alive and well, walking to the hall.
1975   Room was quickly made, on the king's orders,
and the troops filed across the cleared floor.

6. This could refer to her husband or her father before her marriage. The story resembles folktales about a proud princess whose unsuccessful suitors are all put to death, although the unfortunate victims in this case seem to be guilty only of looking at her.
7. I.e., Offa I, a legendary king of the Angles. We know nothing about Hemming other than that Offa was related to him. Offa II (757–96) was king of Mercia, and although the story is about the second Offa's ancestor on the Continent, this is the only English connection in the poem and has been taken as evidence to date its origins to 8th-century Mercia.
8. I.e., Eomer, Offa's son. See previous note. Garmund was presumably the name of Offa's father.
9. I.e., Hygelac. Ongentheow was king of the Swedish people called the Shylfings. This is the first of the references to wars between the Geats and the Swedes. One of Hygelac's war party named Eofer was the actual slayer of Ongentheow.

After Hygelac had offered greetings
to his loyal thane in a lofty speech,
he and his kinsman, that hale survivor,
1980   sat face to face. Haereth's daughter
moved about with the mead-jug in her hand,
taking care of the company, filling the cups
that warriors held out. Then Hygelac began
to put courteous questions to his old comrade
1985   in the high hall. He hankered to know
every tale the Sea-Geats had to tell:
"How did you fare on your foreign voyage,
dear Beowulf, when you abruptly decided
to sail away across the salt water
1990   and fight at Heorot? Did you help Hrothgar
much in the end? Could you ease the prince
of his well-known troubles? Your undertaking
cast my spirits down, I dreaded the outcome
of your expedition and pleaded with you
1995   long and hard to leave the killer be,
let the South-Danes settle their own
blood-feud with Grendel. So God be thanked
I am granted this sight of you, safe and sound."
      Beowulf, son of Ecgtheow, spoke:
2000   "What happened, Lord Hygelac, is hardly a secret
any more among men in this world—
myself and Grendel coming to grips
on the very spot where he visited destruction
on the Victory-Shieldings and violated
2005   life and limb, losses I avenged
so no earthly offspring of Grendel's
need ever boast of that bout before dawn,
no matter how long the last of his evil
family survives.
                          When I first landed
2010   I hastened to the ring-hall and saluted Hrothgar.
Once he discovered why I had come,
the son of Halfdane sent me immediately
to sit with his own sons on the bench.
It was a happy gathering. In my whole life
2015   I have never seen mead enjoyed more
in any hall on earth. Sometimes the queen
herself appeared, peace-pledge between nations,
to hearten the young ones and hand out
a torque to a warrior, then take her place.
2020   Sometimes Hrothgar's daughter distributed
ale to older ranks, in order on the benches:
I heard the company call her Freawaru
as she made her rounds, presenting men
with the gem-studded bowl, young bride-to-be
2025   to the gracious Ingeld,[1] in her gold-trimmed attire.
The friend of the Shieldings favors her betrothal:

1. King of the Heatho-Bards; his father, Froda, was killed by the Danes.

the guardian of the kingdom sees good in it
and hopes this woman will heal old wounds
and grievous feuds.
              But generally the spear
2030 is prompt to retaliate when a prince is killed,
no matter how admirable the bride may be.
    "Think how the Heatho-Bards are bound to feel,
their lord, Ingeld, and his loyal thanes,
when he walks in with that woman to the feast:
2035 Danes are at the table, being entertained,
honored guests in glittering regalia,
burnished ring-mail that was their hosts' birthright,
looted when the Heatho-Bards could no longer wield
their weapons in the shield-clash, when they went down
2040 with their beloved comrades and forfeited their lives.
Then an old spearman will speak while they are drinking,
having glimpsed some heirloom that brings alive
memories of the massacre; his mood will darken
and heart-stricken, in the stress of his emotion,
2045 he will begin to test a young man's temper
and stir up trouble, starting like this:
'Now, my friend, don't you recognize
your father's sword, his favorite weapon,
the one he wore when he went out in his war-mask
2050 to face the Danes on that final day?
After Withergeld[2] died and his men were doomed,
the Shieldings quickly claimed the field;
and now here's a son of one or other
of those same killers coming through our hall
2055 overbearing us, mouthing boasts,
and rigged in armor that by right is yours.'
And so he keeps on, recalling and accusing,
working things up with bitter words
until one of the lady's retainers lies
2060 spattered in blood, split open
on his father's account.[3] The killer knows
the lie of the land and escapes with his life.
Then on both sides the oath-bound lords
will break the peace, a passionate hate
2065 will build up in Ingeld, and love for his bride
will falter in him as the feud rankles.
I therefore suspect the good faith of the Heatho-Bards,
the truth of their friendship and the trustworthiness
of their alliance with the Danes.
              But now, my lord,
2070 I shall carry on with my account of Grendel,
the whole story of everything that happened
in the hand-to-hand fight.
              After heaven's gem

---

2. One of the Heatho-Bard leaders.
3. I.e., the young Danish attendant is killed
because his father killed the father of the young

Heatho-Bard who has been egged on by the old
veteran of that campaign.

had gone mildly to earth, that maddened spirit,
the terror of those twilights, came to attack us
2075   where we stood guard, still safe inside the hall.
There deadly violence came down on Hondscio
and he fell as fate ordained, the first to perish,
rigged out for the combat. A comrade from our ranks
had come to grief in Grendel's maw:
2080   he ate up the entire body.
There was blood on his teeth, he was bloated and dangerous,
all roused up, yet still unready
to leave the hall empty-handed;
renowned for his might, he matched himself against me,
2085   wildly reaching. He had this roomy pouch,
a strange accoutrement, intricately strung
and hung at the ready, a rare patchwork
of devilishly fitted dragon-skins.
I had done him no wrong, yet the raging demon
2090   wanted to cram me and many another
into this bag—but it was not to be
once I got to my feet in a blind fury.
It would take too long to tell how I repaid
the terror of the land for every life he took
2095   and so won credit for you, my king,
and for all your people. And although he got away
to enjoy life's sweetness for a while longer,
his right hand stayed behind him in Heorot,
evidence of his miserable overthrow
2100   as he dived into murk on the mere bottom.
   "I got lavish rewards from the lord of the Danes
for my part in the battle, beaten gold
and much else, once morning came
and we took our places at the banquet table.
2105   There was singing and excitement: an old reciter,
a carrier of stories, recalled the early days.
At times some hero made the timbered harp
tremble with sweetness, or related true
and tragic happenings; at times the king
2110   gave the proper turn to some fantastic tale,
or a battle-scarred veteran, bowed with age,
would begin to remember the martial deeds
of his youth and prime and be overcome
as the past welled up in his wintry heart.
2115   "We were happy there the whole day long
and enjoyed our time until another night
descended upon us. Then suddenly
the vehement mother avenged her son
and wreaked destruction. Death had robbed her,
2120   Geats had slain Grendel, so his ghastly dam
struck back and with bare-faced defiance
laid a man low. Thus life departed
from the sage Aeschere, an elder wise in counsel.
But afterward, on the morning following,

2125　the Danes could not burn the dead body
　　　　nor lay the remains of the man they loved
　　　　on his funeral pyre. She had fled with the corpse
　　　　and taken refuge beneath torrents on the mountain.
　　　　It was a hard blow for Hrothgar to bear,
2130　harder than any he had undergone before.
　　　　And so the heartsore king beseeched me
　　　　in your royal name to take my chances
　　　　underwater, to win glory
　　　　and prove my worth. He promised me rewards.
2135　Hence, as is well known, I went to my encounter
　　　　with the terror-monger at the bottom of the tarn.
　　　　For a while it was hand-to-hand between us,
　　　　then blood went curling along the currents
　　　　and I beheaded Grendel's mother in the hall
2140　with a mighty sword. I barely managed
　　　　to escape with my life; my time had not yet come.
　　　　But Halfdane's heir, the shelter of those earls,
　　　　again endowed me with gifts in abundance.
　　　　　"Thus the king acted with due custom.
2145　I was paid and recompensed completely,
　　　　given full measure and the freedom to choose
　　　　from Hothgar's treasures by Hrothgar himself.
　　　　These, King Hygelac, I am happy to present
　　　　to you as gifts. It is still upon your grace
2150　that all favor depends. I have few kinsmen
　　　　who are close, my king, except for your kind self."
　　　　Then he ordered the boar-framed standard to be brought,
　　　　the battle-topping helmet, the mail-shirt gray as hoar-frost,
　　　　and the precious war-sword; and proceeded with his speech:
2155　"When Hrothgar presented this war-gear to me
　　　　he instructed me, my lord, to give you some account
　　　　of why it signifies his special favor.
　　　　He said it had belonged to his older brother,
　　　　King Heorogar, who had long kept it,
2160　but that Heorogar had never bequeathed it
　　　　to his son Heoroward, that worthy scion,
　　　　loyal as he was. Enjoy it well."
　　　　　I heard four horses were handed over next.
　　　　Beowulf bestowed four bay steeds
2165　to go with the armor, swift gallopers,
　　　　all alike. So ought a kinsman act,
　　　　instead of plotting and planning in secret
　　　　to bring people to grief, or conspiring to arrange
　　　　the death of comrades. The warrior king
2170　was uncle to Beowulf and honored by his nephew:
　　　　each was concerned for the other's good.
　　　　　I heard he presented Hygd with a gorget,
　　　　the priceless torque that the prince's daughter,
　　　　Wealhtheow, had given him; and three horses,
2175　supple creatures brilliantly saddled.
　　　　The bright necklace would be luminous on Hygd's breast.

Thus Beowulf bore himself with valor;
he was formidable in battle yet behaved with honor
and took no advantage; never cut down
2180 a comrade who was drunk, kept his temper
and, warrior that he was, watched and controlled
his God-sent strength and his outstanding
natural powers. He had been poorly regarded
for a long time, was taken by the Geats
2185 for less than he was worth:[4] and their lord too
had never much esteemed him in the mead-hall.
They firmly believed that he lacked force,
that the prince was a weakling; but presently
every affront to his deserving was reversed.
2190 The battle-famed king, bulwark of his earls,
ordered a gold-chased heirloom of Hrethel's[5]
to be brought in; it was the best example
of a gem-studded sword in the Geat treasury.
This he laid on Beowulf's lap
2195 and then rewarded him with land as well,
seven thousand hides; and a hall and a throne.
Both owned land by birth in that country,
ancestral grounds; but the greater right
and sway were inherited by the higher born.

[THE DRAGON WAKES]

2200 A lot was to happen in later days
in the fury of battle. Hygelac fell
and the shelter of Heardred's shield proved useless
against the fierce aggression of the Shylfings:[6]
ruthless swordsmen, seasoned campaigners,
2205 they came against him and his conquering nation,
and with cruel force cut him down
so that afterwards
                           the wide kingdom
reverted to Beowulf. He ruled it well
for fifty winters, grew old and wise

---

4. There is no other mention of Beowulf's
unpromising youth. This motif of the "Cinderella
hero" and others, such as Grendel's magic pouch,
are examples of folklore material, probably circulating orally, that made its way into the poem.
5. Hygelac's father and Beowulf's grandfather.
6. There are several references, some of them
lengthy, to the wars between the Geats and the
Swedes. Because these are highly allusive and not
in chronological order, they are difficult to follow
and keep straight. This outline, along with the
Genealogies (p. 31), may serve as a guide. *Phase 1*:
After the death of the Geat patriarch, King Hrethel
(lines 2462–70), Ohthere and Onela, the sons of
the Swedish king Ongentheow, invade Geat territory and inflict heavy casualties in a battle at
Hreosnahill (lines 2472–78). *Phase 2*: The Geats
invade Sweden under Haethcyn, King

Hrethel's son who has succeeded him. At the battle
of Ravenswood, the Geats capture Ongentheow's
queen, but Ongentheow counterattacks, rescues
the queen, and kills Haethcyn. Hygelac, Haethcyn's younger brother, arrives with reinforcements;
Ongentheow is killed in savage combat with two of
Hygelac's men; and the Swedes are routed (lines
2479–89 and 2922–90). *Phase 3*: Eanmund and
Eadgils, the sons of Ohthere (presumably dead),
are driven into exile by their uncle Onela, who is
now king of the Swedes. They are given refuge by
Hygelac's son Heardred, who has succeeded his
father. Onela invades Geatland and kills Heardred;
his retainer Weohstan kills Eanmund; and after
the Swedes withdraw, Beowulf becomes king (lines
2204–8, which follow, and 2379–90). *Phase 4*:
Eadgils, supported by Beowulf, invades Sweden
and kills Onela (lines 2391–96).

2210   as warden of the land
                     until one began
    to dominate the dark, a dragon on the prowl
    from the steep vaults of a stone-roofed barrow
    where he guarded a hoard; there was a hidden passage,
    unknown to men, but someone[7] managed
2215   to enter by it and interfere
    with the heathen trove. He had handled and removed
    a gem-studded goblet; it gained him nothing,
    though with a thief's wiles he had outwitted
    the sleeping dragon. That drove him into rage,
2220   as the people of that country would soon discover.
        The intruder who broached the dragon's treasure
    and moved him to wrath had never meant to.
    It was desperation on the part of a slave
    fleeing the heavy hand of some master,
2225   guilt-ridden and on the run,
    going to ground. But he soon began
    to shake with terror;[8] . . . . . . in shock
    the wretch . . . .
    . . . . panicked and ran
2230   away with the precious . . . . . .
    metalwork. There were many other
    heirlooms heaped inside the earth-house,
    because long ago, with deliberate care,
    somebody now forgotten
2235   had buried the riches of a highborn race
    in this ancient cache. Death had come
    and taken them all in times gone by
    and the only one left to tell their tale,
    the last of their line, could look forward to nothing
2240   but the same fate for himself: he foresaw that his joy
    in the treasure would be brief.
                       A newly constructed
    barrow stood waiting, on a wide headland
    close to the waves, its entryway secured.
    Into it the keeper of the hoard had carried
2245   all the goods and golden ware
    worth preserving. His words were few:
    "Now, earth, hold what earls once held
    and heroes can no more; it was mined from you first
    by honorable men. My own people
2250   have been ruined in war; one by one
    they went down to death, looked their last
    on sweet life in the hall. I am left with nobody
    to bear a sword or to burnish plated goblets,
    put a sheen on the cup. The companies have departed.
2255   The hard helmet, hasped with gold,

---

7. The following section was damaged by fire. In lines 2215–31 entire words and phrases are missing or indicated by only a few letters. Editorial attempts to reconstruct the text are conjectural and often disagree.

8. Lines 2227–30 are so damaged that they defy guesswork to reconstruct them.

will be stripped of its hoops; and the helmet-shiner
who should polish the metal of the war-mask sleeps;
the coat of mail that came through all fights,
through shield-collapse and cut of sword,
2260　decays with the warrior. Nor may webbed mail
range far and wide on the warlord's back
beside his mustered troops. No trembling harp,
no tuned timber, no tumbling hawk
swerving through the hall, no swift horse
2265　pawing the courtyard. Pillage and slaughter
have emptied the earth of entire peoples."
And so he mourned as he moved about the world,
deserted and alone, lamenting his unhappiness
day and night, until death's flood
2270　brimmed up in his heart.
　　　　　　　　　　　　Then an old harrower of the dark
happened to find the hoard open,
the burning one who hunts out barrows,
the slick-skinned dragon, threatening the night sky
with streamers of fire. People on the farms
2275　are in dread of him. He is driven to hunt out
hoards under ground, to guard heathen gold
through age-long vigils, though to little avail.
For three centuries, this scourge of the people
had stood guard on that stoutly protected
2280　underground treasury, until the intruder
unleashed its fury; he hurried to his lord
with the gold-plated cup and made his plea
to be reinstated. Then the vault was rifled,
the ring-hoard robbed, and the wretched man
2285　had his request granted. His master gazed
on that find from the past for the first time.
　　　When the dragon awoke, trouble flared again.
He rippled down the rock, writhing with anger
when he saw the footprints of the prowler who had stolen
2290　too close to his dreaming head.
So may a man not marked by fate
easily escape exile and woe
by the grace of God.
　　　　　　　　　　The hoard-guardian
scorched the ground as he scoured and hunted
2295　for the trespasser who had troubled his sleep.
Hot and savage, he kept circling and circling
the outside of the mound. No man appeared
in that desert waste, but he worked himself up
by imagining battle; then back in he'd go
2300　in search of the cup, only to discover
signs that someone had stumbled upon
the golden treasures. So the guardian of the mound,
the hoard-watcher, waited for the gloaming
with fierce impatience; his pent-up fury
2305　at the loss of the vessel made him long to hit back

and lash out in flames. Then, to his delight,
the day waned and he could wait no longer
behind the wall, but hurtled forth
in a fiery blaze. The first to suffer
2310   were the people on the land, but before long
it was their treasure-giver who would come to grief.
   The dragon began to belch out flames
and burn bright homesteads; there was a hot glow
that scared everyone, for the vile sky-winger
2315   would leave nothing alive in his wake.
Everywhere the havoc he wrought was in evidence.
Far and near, the Geat nation
bore the brunt of his brutal assaults
and virulent hate. Then back to the hoard
2320   he would dart before daybreak, to hide in his den.
He had swinged the land, swathed it in flame,
in fire and burning, and now he felt secure
in the vaults of his barrow; but his trust was unavailing.
   Then Beowulf was given bad news,
2325   the hard truth: his own home,
the best of buildings, had been burned to a cinder,
the throne-room of the Geats. It threw the hero
into deep anguish and darkened his mood:
the wise man thought he must have thwarted
2330   ancient ordinance of the eternal Lord,
broken His commandment. His mind was in turmoil,
unaccustomed anxiety and gloom
confused his brain; the fire-dragon
had razed the coastal region and reduced
2335   forts and earthworks to dust and ashes,
so the war-king planned and plotted his revenge.
The warriors' protector, prince of the hall-troop,
ordered a marvelous all-iron shield
from his smithy works. He well knew
2340   that linden boards would let him down
and timber burn. After many trials,
he was destined to face the end of his days,
in this mortal world, as was the dragon,
for all his long leasehold on the treasure.
2345   Yet the prince of the rings was too proud
to line up with a large army
against the sky-plague. He had scant regard
for the dragon as a threat, no dread at all
of its courage or strength, for he had kept going
2350   often in the past, through perils and ordeals
of every sort, after he had purged
Hrothgar's hall, triumphed in Heorot
and beaten Grendel. He outgrappled the monster
and his evil kin.
               One of his cruelest
2355   hand-to-hand encounters had happened
when Hygelac, king of the Geats, was killed

in Friesland: the people's friend and lord,
Hrethel's son, slaked a sword blade's
thirst for blood. But Beowulf's prodigious
2360   gifts as a swimmer guaranteed his safety:
he arrived at the shore, shouldering thirty
battle-dresses, the booty he had won.
There was little for the Hetware[9] to be happy about
as they shielded their faces and fighting on the ground
2365   began in earnest. With Beowulf against them,
few could hope to return home.
        Across the wide sea, desolate and alone,
the son of Ecgtheow swam back to his people.
There Hygd offered him throne and authority
2370   as lord of the ring-hoard: with Hygelac dead,
she had no belief in her son's ability
to defend their homeland against foreign invaders.
Yet there was no way the weakened nation
could get Beowulf to give in and agree
2375   to be elevated over Heardred as his lord
or to undertake the office of kingship.
But he did provide support for the prince,
honored and minded him until he matured
as the ruler of Geatland.
                                Then over sea-roads
2380   exiles arrived, sons of Ohthere.[1]
They had rebelled against the best of all
the sea-kings in Sweden, the one who held sway
in the Shylfing nation, their renowned prince,
lord of the mead-hall. That marked the end
2385   for Hygelac's son: his hospitality
was mortally rewarded with wounds from a sword.
Heardred lay slaughtered and Onela returned
to the land of Sweden, leaving Beowulf
to ascend the throne, to sit in majesty
2390   and rule over the Geats. He was a good king.
        In days to come, he contrived to avenge
the fall of his prince; he befriended Eadgils
when Eadgils was friendless, aiding his cause
with weapons and warriors over the wide sea,
2395   sending him men. The feud was settled
on a comfortless campaign when he killed Onela.
        And so the son of Ecgtheow had survived
every extreme, excelling himself
in daring and in danger, until the day arrived
2400   when he had to come face to face with the dragon.
The lord of the Geats took eleven comrades
and went in a rage to reconnoiter.
By then he had discovered the cause of the affliction
being visited on the people. The precious cup
2405   had come to him from the hand of the finder,

---

9. A tribe of the Franks allied with the Frisians.   1. See p. 79, n. 6, Phases 3 and 4.

the one who had started all this strife
and was now added as a thirteenth to their number.
They press-ganged and compelled this poor creature
to be their guide. Against his will
2410   he led them to the earth-vault he alone knew,
an underground barrow near the sea-billows
and heaving waves, heaped inside
with exquisite metalwork. The one who stood guard
was dangerous and watchful, warden of the trove
2415   buried under earth: no easy bargain
would be made in that place by any man.
      The veteran king sat down on the cliff-top.
He wished good luck to the Geats who had shared
his hearth and his gold. He was sad at heart,
2420   unsettled yet ready, sensing his death.
His fate hovered near, unknowable but certain:
it would soon claim his coffered soul,
part life from limb. Before long
the prince's spirit would spin free from his body.
2425   Beowulf, son of Ecgtheow, spoke:
"Many a skirmish I survived when I was young
and many times of war: I remember them well.
At seven, I was fostered out by my father,
left in the charge of my people's lord.
2430   King Hrethel kept me and took care of me,
was openhanded, behaved like a kinsman.
While I was his ward, he treated me no worse
as a wean[2] about the place than one of his own boys,
Herebeald and Haethcyn, or my own Hygelac.
2435   For the eldest, Herebeald, an unexpected
deathbed was laid out, through a brother's doing,
when Haethcyn bent his horn-tipped bow
and loosed the arrow that destroyed his life.
He shot wide and buried a shaft
2440   in the flesh and blood of his own brother.
That offense was beyond redress, a wrongfooting
of the heart's affections; for who could avenge
the prince's life or pay his death-price?
It was like the misery felt by an old man
2445   who has lived to see his son's body
swing on the gallows. He begins to keen
and weep for his boy, watching the raven
gloat where he hangs: he can be of no help.
The wisdom of age is worthless to him.
2450   Morning after morning, he wakes to remember
that his child is gone; he has no interest
in living on until another heir
is born in the hall, now that his first-born
has entered death's dominion forever.
2455   He gazes sorrowfully at his son's dwelling,

2. A young child [Northern Ireland; Translator's note].

the banquet hall bereft of all delight,
the windswept hearthstone; the horsemen are sleeping,
the warriors under ground; what was is no more.
No tunes from the harp, no cheer raised in the yard.
2460 Alone with his longing, he lies down on his bed
and sings a lament; everything seems too large,
the steadings and the fields.
                                        Such was the feeling
of loss endured by the lord of the Geats
after Herebeald's death. He was helplessly placed
2465 to set to rights the wrong committed,
could not punish the killer in accordance with the law
of the blood-feud, although he felt no love for him.
Heartsore, wearied, he turned away
from life's joys, chose God's light
2470 and departed, leaving buildings and lands
to his sons, as a man of substance will.
      "Then over the wide sea Swedes and Geats
battled and feuded and fought without quarter.
Hostilities broke out when Hrethel died.[3]
2475 Ongentheow's sons were unrelenting,
refusing to make peace, campaigning violently
from coast to coast, constantly setting up
terrible ambushes around Hreosnahill.
My own kith and kin avenged
2480 these evil events, as everybody knows,
but the price was high: one of them paid
with his life. Haethcyn, lord of the Geats,
met his fate there and fell in the battle.
Then, as I have heard, Hygelac's sword
2485 was raised in the morning against Ongentheow,
his brother's killer. When Eofor cleft
the old Swede's helmet, halved it open,
he fell, death-pale: his feud-calloused hand
could not stave off the fatal stroke.
2490   "The treasures that Hygelac lavished on me
I paid for when I fought, as fortune allowed me,
with my glittering sword. He gave me land
and the security land brings, so he had no call
to go looking for some lesser champion,
2495 some mercenary from among the Gifthas
or the Spear-Danes or the men of Sweden.
I marched ahead of him, always there
at the front of the line; and I shall fight like that
for as long as I live, as long as this sword
2500 shall last, which has stood me in good stead
late and soon, ever since I killed
Dayraven the Frank in front of the two armies.
He brought back no looted breastplate
to the Frisian king but fell in battle,

3. See p. 79, n. 6, Phases 1 and 2.

2505 their standard-bearer, highborn and brave.
No sword blade sent him to his death:
my bare hands stilled his heartbeats
and wrecked the bone-house. Now blade and hand,
sword and sword-stroke, will assay the hoard."

[BEOWULF ATTACKS THE DRAGON]

2510   Beowulf spoke, made a formal boast
for the last time: "I risked my life
often when I was young. Now I am old,
but as king of the people I shall pursue this fight
for the glory of winning, if the evil one will only
2515 abandon his earth-fort and face me in the open."
    Then he addressed each dear companion
one final time, those fighters in their helmets,
resolute and highborn: "I would rather not
use a weapon if I knew another way
2520 to grapple with the dragon and make good my boast
as I did against Grendel in days gone by.
But I shall be meeting molten venom
in the fire he breathes, so I go forth
in mail-shirt and shield. I won't shift a foot
2525 when I meet the cave-guard: what occurs on the wall
between the two of us will turn out as fate,
overseer of men, decides. I am resolved.
I scorn further words against this sky-borne foe.
    "Men-at-arms, remain here on the barrow,
2530 safe in your armor, to see which one of us
is better in the end at bearing wounds
in a deadly fray. This fight is not yours,
nor is it up to any man except me
to measure his strength against the monster
2535 or to prove his worth. I shall win the gold
by my courage, or else mortal combat,
doom of battle, will bear your lord away."
    Then he drew himself up beside his shield.
The fabled warrior in his war-shirt and helmet
2540 trusted in his own strength entirely
and went under the crag. No coward path.
    Hard by the rock-face that hale veteran,
a good man who had gone repeatedly
into combat and danger and come through,
2545 saw a stone arch and a gushing stream
that burst from the barrow, blazing and wafting
a deadly heat. It would be hard to survive
unscathed near the hoard, to hold firm
against the dragon in those flaming depths.
2550 Then he gave a shout. The lord of the Geats
unburdened his breast and broke out
in a storm of anger. Under gray stone

his voice challenged and resounded clearly.
Hate was ignited. The hoard-guard recognized
2555 a human voice, the time was over
for peace and parleying. Pouring forth
in a hot battle-fume, the breath of the monster
burst from the rock. There was a rumble under ground.
Down there in the barrow, Beowulf the warrior
2560 lifted his shield: the outlandish thing
writhed and convulsed and viciously
turned on the king, whose keen-edged sword,
an heirloom inherited by ancient right,
was already in his hand. Roused to a fury,
2565 each antagonist struck terror in the other.
Unyielding, the lord of his people loomed
by his tall shield, sure of his ground,
while the serpent looped and unleashed itself.
Swaddled in flames, it came gliding and flexing
2570 and racing toward its fate. Yet his shield defended
the renowned leader's life and limb
for a shorter time than he meant it to:
that final day was the first time
when Beowulf fought and fate denied him
2575 glory in battle. So the king of the Geats
raised his hand and struck hard
at the enameled scales, but scarcely cut through:
the blade flashed and slashed yet the blow
was far less powerful than the hard-pressed king
2580 had need of at that moment. The mound-keeper
went into a spasm and spouted deadly flames:
when he felt the stroke, battle-fire
billowed and spewed. Beowulf was foiled
of a glorious victory. The glittering sword,
2585 infallible before that day,
failed when he unsheathed it, as it never should have.
For the son of Ecgtheow, it was no easy thing
to have to give ground like that and go
unwillingly to inhabit another home
2590 in a place beyond; so every man must yield
the leasehold of his days.
                                        Before long
the fierce contenders clashed again.
The hoard-guard took heart, inhaled and swelled up
and got a new wind; he who had once ruled
2595 was furled in fire and had to face the worst.
No help or backing was to be had then
from his highborn comrades; that hand-picked troop
broke ranks and ran for their lives
to the safety of the wood. But within one heart
2600 sorrow welled up: in a man of worth
the claims of kinship cannot be denied.
     His name was Wiglaf, a son of Weohstan's,
a well-regarded Shylfing warrior

related to Aelfhere.[4] When he saw his lord
2605   tormented by the heat of his scalding helmet,
he remembered the bountiful gifts bestowed on him,
how well he lived among the Waegmundings,
the freehold he inherited from his father[5] before him.
He could not hold back: one hand brandished
2610   the yellow-timbered shield, the other drew his sword—
an ancient blade that was said to have belonged
to Eanmund, the son of Ohthere, the one
Weohstan had slain when he was an exile without friends.
He carried the arms to the victim's kinfolk,
2615   the burnished helmet, the webbed chain-mail
and that relic of the giants. But Onela returned
the weapons to him, rewarded Weohstan
with Eanmund's war-gear. He ignored the blood-feud,
the fact that Eanmund was his brother's son.[6]
2620   Weohstan kept that war-gear for a lifetime,
the sword and the mail-shirt, until it was the son's turn
to follow his father and perform his part.
Then, in old age, at the end of his days
among the Weather-Geats, he bequeathed to Wiglaf
innumerable weapons.
2625   And now the youth
was to enter the line of battle with his lord,
his first time to be tested as a fighter.
His spirit did not break and the ancestral blade
would keep its edge, as the dragon discovered
2630   as soon as they came together in the combat.
     Sad at heart, addressing his companions,
Wiglaf spoke wise and fluent words:
"I remember that time when mead was flowing,
how we pledged loyalty to our lord in the hall,
2635   promised our ring-giver we would be worth our price,
make good the gift of the war-gear,
those swords and helmets, as and when
his need required it. He picked us out
from the army deliberately, honored us and judged us
2640   fit for this action, made me these lavish gifts—
and all because he considered us the best
of his arms-bearing thanes. And now, although
he wanted this challenge to be one he'd face
by himself alone—the shepherd of our land,
2645   a man unequaled in the quest for glory
and a name for daring—now the day has come
when this lord we serve needs sound men
to give him their support. Let us go to him,

---

4. Although Wiglaf is here said to be a Shylfing
(i.e., a Swede), in line 2607 we are told his family
are Waegmundings, a clan of the Geats, which is
also Beowulf's family. It was possible for a family
to owe allegiance to more than one nation and to
shift sides as a result of feuds. Nothing is known
of Aelfhere.
5. I.e., Weohstan, who, as explained below, was
the slayer of Onela's nephew Eanmund. Possibly,

Weohstan joined the Geats under Beowulf after
Eanmund's brother, with Beowulf's help, avenged
Eanmund's death on Onela and became king of the
Shylfings. See p. 79, n. 6, Phase 2.
6. An ironic comment: since Onela wanted to kill
Eanmund, he rewarded Weohstan for killing his
nephew instead of exacting compensation or
revenge.

help our leader through the hot flame
2650 and dread of the fire. As God is my witness,
I would rather my body were robed in the same
burning blaze as my gold-giver's body
than go back home bearing arms.
That is unthinkable, unless we have first
2655 slain the foe and defended the life
of the prince of the Weather-Geats. I well know
the things he has done for us deserve better.
Should he alone be left exposed
to fall in battle? We must bond together,
2660 shield and helmet, mail-shirt and sword."
Then he waded the dangerous reek and went
under arms to his lord, saying only:
"Go on, dear Beowulf, do everything
you said you would when you were still young
2665 and vowed you would never let your name and fame
be dimmed while you lived. Your deeds are famous,
so stay resolute, my lord, defend your life now
with the whole of your strength. I shall stand by you."
After those words, a wildness rose
2670 in the dragon again and drove it to attack,
heaving up fire, hunting for enemies,
the humans it loathed. Flames lapped the shield,
charred it to the boss, and the body armor
on the young warrior was useless to him.
2675 But Wiglaf did well under the wide rim
Beowulf shared with him once his own had shattered
in sparks and ashes.
Inspired again
by the thought of glory, the war-king threw
his whole strength behind a sword stroke
2680 and connected with the skull. And Naegling snapped.
Beowulf's ancient iron-gray sword
let him down in the fight. It was never his fortune
to be helped in combat by the cutting edge
of weapons made of iron. When he wielded a sword,
2685 no matter how blooded and hard-edged the blade,
his hand was too strong, the stroke he dealt
(I have heard) would ruin it. He could reap no advantage.
Then the bane of that people, the fire-breathing dragon,
was mad to attack for a third time.
2690 When a chance came, he caught the hero
in a rush of flame and clamped sharp fangs
into his neck. Beowulf's body
ran wet with his life-blood: it came welling out.
Next thing, they say, the noble son of Weohstan
2695 saw the king in danger at his side
and displayed his inborn bravery and strength.
He left the head alone,[7] but his fighting hand
was burned when he came to his kinsman's aid.

7. I.e., he avoided the dragon's flame-breathing head.

He lunged at the enemy lower down
2700   so that his decorated sword sank into its belly
and the flames grew weaker.
                    Once again the king
gathered his strength and drew a stabbing knife
he carried on his belt, sharpened for battle.
He stuck it deep in the dragon's flank.
2705   Beowulf dealt it a deadly wound.
They had killed the enemy, courage quelled his life;
that pair of kinsmen, partners in nobility,
had destroyed the foe. So every man should act,
be at hand when needed; but now, for the king,
2710   this would be the last of his many labors
and triumphs in the world.
                    Then the wound
dealt by the ground-burner earlier began
to scald and swell; Beowulf discovered
deadly poison suppurating inside him,
2715   surges of nausea, and so, in his wisdom,
the prince realized his state and struggled
toward a seat on the rampart. He steadied his gaze
on those gigantic stones, saw how the earthwork
was braced with arches built over columns.
2720   And now that thane unequaled for goodness
with his own hands washed his lord's wounds,
swabbed the weary prince with water,
bathed him clean, unbuckled his helmet.
    Beowulf spoke: in spite of his wounds,
2725   mortal wounds, he still spoke
for he well knew his days in the world
had been lived out to the end—his allotted time
was drawing to a close, death was very near.
    "Now is the time when I would have wanted
2730   to bestow this armor on my own son,
had it been my fortune to have fathered an heir
and live on in his flesh. For fifty years
I ruled this nation. No king
of any neighboring clan would dare
2735   face me with troops, none had the power
to intimidate me. I took what came,
cared for and stood by things in my keeping,
never fomented quarrels, never
swore to a lie. All this consoles me,
2740   doomed as I am and sickening for death;
because of my right ways, the Ruler of mankind
need never blame me when the breath leaves my body
for murder of kinsmen. Go now quickly,
dearest Wiglaf, under the gray stone
2745   where the dragon is laid out, lost to his treasure;
hurry to feast your eyes on the hoard.
Away you go: I want to examine
that ancient gold, gaze my fill

on those garnered jewels; my going will be easier
2750 for having seen the treasure, a less troubled letting-go
of the life and lordship I have long maintained."
And so, I have heard, the son of Weohstan
quickly obeyed the command of his languishing
war-weary lord; he went in his chain-mail
2755 under the rock-piled roof of the barrow,
exulting in his triumph, and saw beyond the seat
a treasure-trove of astonishing richness,
wall-hangings that were a wonder to behold,
glittering gold spread across the ground,
2760 the old dawn-scorching serpent's den
packed with goblets and vessels from the past,
tarnished and corroding. Rusty helmets
all eaten away. Armbands everywhere,
artfully wrought. How easily treasure
2765 buried in the ground, gold hidden
however skillfully, can escape from any man!
And he saw too a standard, entirely of gold,
hanging high over the hoard,
a masterpiece of filigree; it glowed with light
2770 so he could make out the ground at his feet
and inspect the valuables. Of the dragon there was no
remaining sign: the sword had dispatched him.
Then, the story goes, a certain man
plundered the hoard in that immemorial howe,
2775 filled his arms with flagons and plates,
anything he wanted; and took the standard also,
most brilliant of banners.
                    Already the blade
of the old king's sharp killing-sword
had done its worst: the one who had for long
2780 minded the hoard, hovering over gold,
unleashing fire, surging forth
midnight after midnight, had been mown down.
Wiglaf went quickly, keen to get back,
excited by the treasure. Anxiety weighed
2785 on his brave heart—he was hoping he would find
the leader of the Geats alive where he had left him
helpless, earlier, on the open ground.
So he came to the place, carrying the treasure
and found his lord bleeding profusely,
2790 his life at an end; again he began
to swab his body. The beginnings of an utterance
broke out from the king's breast-cage.
The old lord gazed sadly at the gold.
"To the everlasting Lord of all,
2795 to the King of Glory, I give thanks
that I behold this treasure here in front of me,
that I have been allowed to leave my people
so well endowed on the day I die.
Now that I have bartered my last breath

2800 to own this fortune, it is up to you
to look after their needs. I can hold out no longer.
Order my troop to construct a barrow
on a headland on the coast, after my pyre has cooled.
It will loom on the horizon at Hronesness[8]
2805 and be a reminder among my people—
so that in coming times crews under sail
will call it Beowulf's Barrow, as they steer
ships across the wide and shrouded waters."
Then the king in his great-heartedness unclasped
2810 the collar of gold from his neck and gave it
to the young thane, telling him to use
it and the war-shirt and gilded helmet well.
"You are the last of us, the only one left
of the Waegmundings. Fate swept us away,
2815 sent my whole brave highborn clan
to their final doom. Now I must follow them."
That was the warrior's last word.
He had no more to confide. The furious heat
of the pyre would assail him. His soul fled from his breast
2820 to its destined place among the steadfast ones.

[BEOWULF'S FUNERAL]

It was hard then on the young hero,
having to watch the one he held so dear
there on the ground, going through
his death agony. The dragon from underearth,
2825 his nightmarish destroyer, lay destroyed as well,
utterly without life. No longer would his snakefolds
ply themselves to safeguard hidden gold.
Hard-edged blades, hammered out
and keenly filed, had finished him
2830 so that the sky-roamer lay there rigid,
brought low beside the treasure-lodge.
Never again would he glitter and glide
and show himself off in midnight air,
exulting in his riches: he fell to earth
2835 through the battle-strength in Beowulf's arm.
There were few, indeed, as far as I have heard,
big and brave as they may have been,
few who would have held out if they had had to face
the outpourings of that poison-breather
2840 or gone foraging on the ring-hall floor
and found the deep barrow-dweller
on guard and awake.
The treasure had been won,
bought and paid for by Beowulf's death.
Both had reached the end of the road
through the life they had been lent.
2845   Before long

---

8. A headland by the sea. The name means "Whalesness."

the battle-dodgers abandoned the wood,
the ones who had let down their lord earlier,
the tail-turners, ten of them together.
When he needed them most, they had made off.
2850 Now they were ashamed and came behind shields,
in their battle-outfits, to where the old man lay.
They watched Wiglaf, sitting worn out,
a comrade shoulder to shoulder with his lord,
trying in vain to bring him round with water.
2855 Much as he wanted to, there was no way
he could preserve his lord's life on earth
or alter in the least the Almighty's will.
What God judged right would rule what happened
to every man, as it does to this day.
2860   Then a stern rebuke was bound to come
from the young warrior to the ones who had been cowards.
Wiglaf, son of Weohstan, spoke
disdainfully and in disappointment:
"Anyone ready to admit the truth
2865 will surely realize that the lord of men
who showered you with gifts and gave you the armor
you are standing in—when he would distribute
helmets and mail-shirts to men on the mead-benches,
a prince treating his thanes in hall
2870 to the best he could find, far or near—
was throwing weapons uselessly away.
It would be a sad waste when the war broke out.
Beowulf had little cause to brag
about his armed guard; yet God who ordains
2875 who wins or loses allowed him to strike
with his own blade when bravery was needed.
There was little I could do to protect his life
in the heat of the fray, but I found new strength
welling up when I went to help him.
2880 Then my sword connected and the deadly assaults
of our foe grew weaker, the fire coursed
less strongly from his head. But when the worst happened
too few rallied around the prince.
    "So it is good-bye now to all you know and love
2885 on your home ground, the open-handedness,
the giving of war-swords. Every one of you
with freeholds of land, our whole nation,
will be dispossessed, once princes from beyond
get tidings of how you turned and fled
2890 and disgraced yourselves. A warrior will sooner
die than live a life of shame."
    Then he ordered the outcome of the fight to be reported
to those camped on the ridge, that crowd of retainers
who had sat all morning, sad at heart,
2895 shield-bearers wondering about
the man they loved: would this day be his last
or would he return? He told the truth

and did not balk, the rider who bore
news to the cliff-top. He addressed them all:

2900 "Now the people's pride and love,
the lord of the Geats, is laid on his deathbed,
brought down by the dragon's attack.
Beside him lies the bane of his life,
dead from knife-wounds. There was no way

2905 Beowulf could manage to get the better
of the monster with his sword. Wiglaf sits
at Beowulf's side, the son of Weohstan,
the living warrior watching by the dead,
keeping weary vigil, holding a wake
for the loved and the loathed.

2910   Now war is looming
over our nation, soon it will be known
to Franks and Frisians, far and wide,
that the king is gone. Hostility has been great
among the Franks since Hygelac sailed forth

2915 at the head of a war-fleet into Friesland:
there the Hetware harried and attacked
and overwhelmed him with great odds.
The leader in his war-gear was laid low,
fell among followers: that lord did not favor

2920 his company with spoils. The Merovingian king
has been an enemy to us ever since.
    "Nor do I expect peace or pact-keeping
of any sort from the Swedes. Remember:
at Ravenswood,[9] Ongentheow

2925 slaughtered Haethcyn, Hrethel's son,
when the Geat people in their arrogance
first attacked the fierce Shylfings.
The return blow was quickly struck
by Ohthere's father.[1] Old and terrible,

2930 he felled the sea-king and saved his own
aged wife, the mother of Onela
and of Ohthere, bereft of her gold rings.
Then he kept hard on the heels of the foe
and drove them, leaderless, lucky to get away

2935 in a desperate rout into Ravenswood.
His army surrounded the weary remnant
where they nursed their wounds; all through the night
he howled threats at those huddled survivors,
promised to axe their bodies open

2940 when dawn broke, dangle them from gallows
to feed the birds. But at first light
when their spirits were lowest, relief arrived.
They heard the sound of Hygelac's horn,
his trumpet calling as he came to find them,

2945 the hero in pursuit, at hand with troops.

9. The messenger describes in greater detail the
Battle of Ravenswood. See the outline of the Swedish wars on p. 79, n. 6.
1. I.e., Ongentheow.

"The bloody swathe that Swedes and Geats
cut through each other was everywhere.
No one could miss their murderous feuding.
Then the old man made his move,
2950 pulled back, barred his people in:
Ongentheow withdrew to higher ground.
Hygelac's pride and prowess as a fighter
were known to the earl; he had no confidence
that he could hold out against that horde of seamen,
2955 defend his wife and the ones he loved
from the shock of the attack. He retreated for shelter
behind the earthwall. Then Hygelac swooped
on the Swedes at bay, his banners swarmed
into their refuge, his Geat forces
2960 drove forward to destroy the camp.
There in his gray hairs, Ongentheow
was cornered, ringed around with swords.
And it came to pass that the king's fate
was in Eofor's hands,[2] and in his alone.
2965 Wulf, son of Wonred, went for him in anger,
split him open so that blood came spurting
from under his hair. The old hero
still did not flinch, but parried fast,
hit back with a harder stroke:
2970 the king turned and took him on.
Then Wonred's son, the brave Wulf,
could land no blow against the aged lord.
Ongentheow divided his helmet
so that he buckled and bowed his bloodied head
2975 and dropped to the ground. But his doom held off.
Though he was cut deep, he recovered again.
"With his brother down, the undaunted Eofor,
Hygelac's thane, hefted his sword
and smashed murderously at the massive helmet
2980 past the lifted shield. And the king collapsed,
the shepherd of people was sheared of life.
Many then hurried to help Wulf,
bandaged and lifted him, now that they were left
masters of the blood-soaked battle-ground.
2985 One warrior stripped the other,
looted Ongenteow's iron mail-coat,
his hard sword-hilt, his helmet too,
and carried the graith[3] to King Hygelac,
he accepted the prize, promised fairly
2990 that reward would come, and kept his word.
For their bravery in action, when they arrived home,
Eofor and Wulf were overloaded
by Hrethel's son, Hygelac the Geat,

2. I.e., he was at Eofor's mercy. Eofor's slaying of Ongetheow was described in lines 2486–89, where no mention is made of his brother Wulf's part in the battle. They are the sons of Wonred. *Eofor* means boar, and *Wulf* is the Old English spelling of wolf.
3. Possessions, apparel.

with gifts of land and linked rings
2995   that were worth a fortune. They had won glory,
so there was no gainsaying his generosity.
And he gave Eofor his only daughter
to bide at home with him, an honor and a bond.
    "So this bad blood between us and the Swedes,
3000   this vicious feud, I am convinced,
is bound to revive; they will cross our borders
and attack in force when they find out
that Beowulf is dead. In days gone by
when our warriors fell and we were undefended,
3005   he kept our coffers and our kingdom safe.
He worked for the people, but as well as that
he behaved like a hero.
                We must hurry now
to take a last look at the king
and launch him, lord and lavisher of rings,
3010   on the funeral road. His royal pyre
will melt no small amount of gold:
heaped there in a hoard, it was bought at heavy cost,
and that pile of rings he paid for at the end
with his own life will go up with the flame,
3015   be furled in fire: treasure no follower
will wear in his memory, nor lovely woman
link and attach as a torque around her neck—
but often, repeatedly, in the path of exile
they shall walk bereft, bowed under woe,
3020   now that their leader's laugh is silenced,
high spirits quenched. Many a spear
dawn-cold to the touch will be taken down
and waved on high; the swept harp
won't waken warriors, but the raven winging
3025   darkly over the doomed will have news,
tidings for the eagle of how he hoked and ate,
how the wolf and he made short work of the dead."[4]
    Such was the drift of the dire report
that gallant man delivered. He got little wrong
in what he told and predicted.
3030   The whole troop
rose in tears, then took their way
to the uncanny scene under Earnaness.[5]
There, on the sand, where his soul had left him,
they found him at rest, their ring-giver
3035   from days gone by. The great man
had breathed his last. Beowulf the king
had indeed met with a marvelous death.
    But what they saw first was far stranger:
the serpent on the ground, gruesome and vile,

---

4. The raven, eagle, and wolf—the scavengers who will feed on the slain—are "the beasts of battle," a common motif in Germanic war poetry. "Hoked": rooted about [Northern Ireland, Translator's note].

5. The site of Beowulf's fight with the dragon. The name means "Eaglesness."

3040 lying facing him. The fire-dragon
was scaresomely burned, scorched all colors.
From head to tail, his entire length
was fifty feet. He had shimmered forth
on the night air once, then winged back
3045 down to his den; but death owned him now,
he would never enter his earth-gallery again.
Beside him stood pitchers and piled-up dishes,
silent flagons, precious swords
eaten through with rust, ranged as they had been
3050 while they waited their thousand winters under ground.
That huge cache, gold inherited
from an ancient race, was under a spell—
which meant no one was ever permitted
to enter the ring-hall unless God Himself,
3055 mankind's Keeper, True King of Triumphs,
allowed some person pleasing to Him—
and in His eyes worthy—to open the hoard.
    What came about brought to nothing
the hopes of the one who had wrongly hidden
3060 riches under the rock-face. First the dragon slew
that man among men, who in turn made fierce amends
and settled the feud. Famous for his deeds
a warrior may be, but it remains a mystery
where his life will end, when he may no longer
3065 dwell in the mead-hall among his own.
So it was with Beowulf, when he faced the cruelty
and cunning of the mound-guard. He himself was ignorant
of how his departure from the world would happen.
The highborn chiefs who had buried the treasure
3070 declared it until doomsday so accursed
that whoever robbed it would be guilty of wrong
and grimly punished for their transgression,
hasped in hell-bonds in heathen shrines.
Yet Beowulf's gaze at the gold treasure
3075 when he first saw it had not been selfish.
    Wiglaf, son of Weohstan, spoke:
"Often when one man follows his own will
many are hurt. This happened to us.
Nothing we advised could ever convince
3080 the prince we loved, our land's guardian,
not to vex the custodian of the gold,
let him lie where he was long accustomed,
lurk there under earth until the end of the world.
He held to his high destiny. The hoard is laid bare,
3085 but at a grave cost; it was too cruel a fate
that forced the king to that encounter.
I have been inside and seen everything
amassed in the vault. I managed to enter
although no great welcome awaited me
3090 under the earthwall. I quickly gathered up
a huge pile of the priceless treasures

handpicked from the hoard and carried them here
where the king could see them. He was still himself,
alive, aware, and in spite of his weakness
3095   he had many requests. He wanted me to greet you
and order the building of a barrow that would crown
the site of his pyre, serve as his memorial,
in a commanding position, since of all men
to have lived and thrived and lorded it on earth
3100   his worth and due as a warrior were the greatest.
Now let us again go quickly
and feast our eyes on that amazing fortune
heaped under the wall. I will show the way
and take you close to those coffers packed with rings
3105   and bars of gold. Let a bier be made
and got ready quickly when we come out
and then let us bring the body of our lord,
the man we loved, to where he will lodge
for a long time in the care of the Almighty."
3110   Then Weohstan's son, stalwart to the end,
had orders given to owners of dwellings,
many people of importance in the land,
to fetch wood from far and wide
for the good man's pyre:
                                        "Now shall flame consume
3115   our leader in battle, the blaze darken
round him who stood his ground in the steel-hail,
when the arrow-storm shot from bowstrings
pelted the shield-wall. The shaft hit home.
Feather-fledged, it finned the barb in flight."
3120   Next the wise son of Weohstan
called from among the king's thanes
a group of seven: he selected the best
and entered with them, the eighth of their number,
under the God-cursed roof; one raised
3125   a lighted torch and led the way.
No lots were cast for who should loot the hoard
for it was obvious to them that every bit of it
lay unprotected within the vault,
there for the taking. It was no trouble
3130   to hurry to work and haul out
the priceless store. They pitched the dragon
over the cliff-top, let tide's flow
and backwash take the treasure-minder.
Then coiled gold was loaded on a cart
3135   in great abundance, and the gray-haired leader,
the prince on his bier, borne to Hronesness.
      The Geat people built a pyre for Beowulf,
stacked and decked it until it stood foursquare,
hung with helmets, heavy war-shields
3140   and shining armor, just as he had ordered.
Then his warriors laid him in the middle of it,
mourning a lord far-famed and beloved.

On a height they kindled the hugest of all
funeral fires; fumes of woodsmoke
3145 billowed darkly up, the blaze roared
and drowned out their weeping, wind died down
and flames wrought havoc in the hot bone-house,
burning it to the core. They were disconsolate
and wailed aloud for their lord's decease.
3150 A Geat woman too sang out in grief;
with hair bound up, she unburdened herself
of her worst fears, a wild litany
of nightmare and lament: her nation invaded,
enemies on the rampage, bodies in piles,
3155 slavery and abasement. Heaven swallowed the smoke.
      Then the Geat people began to construct
a mound on a headland, high and imposing,
a marker that sailors could see from far away,
and in ten days they had done the work.
3160 It was their hero's memorial; what remained from the fire
they housed inside it, behind a wall
as worthy of him as their workmanship could make it.
And they buried torques in the barrow, and jewels
and a trove of such things as trespassing men
3165 had once dared to drag from the hoard.
They let the ground keep that ancestral treasure,
gold under gravel, gone to earth,
as useless to men now as it ever was.
Then twelve warriors rode around the tomb,
3170 chieftains' sons, champions in battle,
all of them distraught, chanting in dirges,
mourning his loss as a man and a king.
They extolled his heroic nature and exploits
and gave thanks for his greatness; which was the proper thing,
3175 for a man should praise a prince whom he holds dear
and cherish his memory when that moment comes
when he has to be convoyed from his bodily home.
So the Geat people, his hearth-companions,
sorrowed for the lord who had been laid low.
3180 They said that of all the kings upon earth
he was the man most gracious and fair-minded,
kindest to his people and keenest to win fame.

THE WANDERER

The lament of *The Wanderer* is an excellent example of the elegiac mood so common
in Old English poetry. The loss of a lord, of companions in arms, of a mead hall (in
which Anglo-Saxon life realized itself to the full) are themes that enhance the melancholy tone of *Beowulf* as they are the emotional basis for such a poem as the present
one. But nowhere more poignantly expressed than in *The Wanderer* is the loneliness
of the exile in search of a new lord and hall; this is what Beowulf's father, Ecgtheow,

would have suffered, had it not been for Hrothgar's hospitality. To the wretched seeker all weather is wintry, for nature seems to conspire to match a man's mood as he moves over the water from one land to another, yearning for a home and kin to replace those vanished ones that still fill his thoughts.

As is true of most Old English elegiac laments, both the language and the structure of *The Wanderer* are difficult. At the beginning the speaker (whom the poet identifies as an "earth-walker") voices hope of finding comfort after his many tribulations. After the poet's interruption, the wanderer continues to speak—to himself—of his long search for a new home, describing how he must keep his thoughts locked within him while he makes his search. But these thoughts form the most vivid and moving part of his soliloquy—how, floating on the sea, dazed with sorrow and fatigue, he imagines that he sees his old companions, and how, as he wakens to reality, they vanish over the water like seabirds. The second part of the poem, beginning with the seventh paragraph ("Therefore I cannot think why . . ."), expands the theme from one man to all human beings in a world wasted by war and time, and the speaker draws philosophical implications from his harsh experiences (presumably now in the past). He derives such cold comfort as he can from asking the old question *Ubi sunt?*—where are they who were once so glad to be alive? And he concludes with the thought that "all this earthly habitation shall be emptied" of humankind. The narrator communes with himself in private, apparently as an indication of his detachment from life. The poem concludes with a characteristic Old English injunction to practice restraint on earth, place hope only in heaven.

The Wanderer is preserved only in the Exeter Book, a manuscript copied about 975, which contains the largest surviving collection of Old English poetry.

The Wanderer[1]

"He who is alone often lives to find favor, mildness of the Lord, even though he has long had to stir with his arms the frost-cold sea, troubled in heart over the water-way had to tread the tracks of exile. Fully-fixed is his fate."

So spoke the earth-walker, remembering hardships, fierce war-slaughters—the fall of dear kinsmen.

"Often before the day dawned I have had to speak of my cares, alone: there is now none among the living to whom I dare clearly express the thought of my heart. I know indeed that it is a fine custom for a man to lock tight his heart's coffer, keep closed the hoard-case of his mind, whatever his thoughts may be. Words of a weary heart may not withstand fate, nor those of an angry spirit bring help. Therefore men eager for fame shut sorrowful thought up fast in their breast's coffer.

"Thus I, wretched with care, removed from my homeland, far from dear kinsmen, have had to fasten with fetters the thoughts of my heart—ever since the time, many years ago, that I covered my gold-friend in the darkness of the earth; and from there I crossed the woven waves, winter-sad, downcast for want of a hall, sought a giver of treasure—a place, far or near, where I might find one in a mead-hall who should know of my people, or would comfort me friendless, receive me with gladness. He who has experienced it

---

1. This translation by E. T. Donaldson is based on the text as edited by John C. Pope in *Seven Old English Poems* (1966).

knows how cruel a companion sorrow is to the man who has no beloved protectors. Exile's path awaits him, not twisted gold—frozen thoughts in his heart-case, no joy of earth. He recalls the hall-warriors and the taking of treasure, how in youth his gold-friend made him accustomed to feasting. All delight has gone.

"He who has had long to forgo the counsel of a beloved lord knows indeed how, when sorrow and sleep together bind the poor dweller-alone, it will seem to him in his mind that he is embracing and kissing his liege lord and laying his hands and his head on his knee, as it some times was in the old days when he took part in the gift-giving. Then he wakens again, the man with no lord, sees the yellow waves before him, the sea-birds bathe, spread their feathers, frost and snow fall, mingled with hail.

"Then the wounds are deeper in his heart, sore for want of his dear one. His sorrow renews as the memory of his kinsmen moves through his mind: he greets them with glad words, eagerly looks at them, a company of warriors. Again they fade, moving off over the water; the spirit of these fleeting ones brings to him no familiar voices. Care renews in him who must again and again send his weary heart out over the woven waves.

"Therefore I cannot think why the thoughts of my heart should not grow dark when I consider all the life of men through this world—with what terrible swiftness they forgo the hall-floor, bold young retainers. So this middle-earth each day fails and falls. No man may indeed become wise before he has had his share of winters in this world's kingdom. The wise man must be patient, must never be too hot-hearted, nor too hasty of speech, nor too fearful, nor too glad, nor too greedy for wealth, nor ever too eager to boast before he has thought clearly. A man must wait, when he speaks in boast, until he knows clearly, sure-minded, where the thoughts of his heart may turn.

"The wise warrior must consider how ghostly it will be when all the wealth of this world stands waste, just as now here and there through this middle-earth wind-blown walls stand covered with frost-fall, storm-beaten dwellings. Wine-halls totter, the lord lies bereft of joy, all the company has fallen, bold men beside the wall. War took away some, bore them forth on their way; a bird carried one away over the deep sea; a wolf shared one with Death; another a man sad of face hid in an earth-pit.

"So the Maker of mankind laid waste this dwelling-place until the old works of giants[2] stood idle, devoid of the noise of the stronghold's keepers. Therefore the man wise in his heart considers carefully this wall-place and this dark life, remembers the multitude of deadly combats long ago, and speaks these words: 'Where has the horse gone? Where the young warrior? Where is the giver of treasure? What has become of the feasting seats? Where are the joys of the hall? Alas, the bright cup! Alas, the mailed warrior! Alas, the prince's glory! How that time has gone, vanished beneath night's cover, just as if it never had been! The wall, wondrous high, decorated with snake-likenesses, stands now over traces of the beloved company. The ash-spears' might has borne the earls away—weapons greedy for slaughter, Fate the mighty; and storms beat on the stone walls, snow, the herald of winter, falling thick binds the earth when darkness comes and the night-shadow falls, sends

2. Probably a reference to Roman ruins.

harsh hailstones from the north in hatred of men. All earth's kingdom is wretched, the world beneath the skies is changed by the work of the fates. Here wealth is fleeting, here friend is fleeting, here man is fleeting, here woman is fleeting—all this earthly habitation shall be emptied.' "

So the wise man spoke in his heart, sat apart in private meditation. He is good who keeps his word; a man must never utter too quickly his breast's passion, unless he knows first how to achieve remedy, as a leader with his courage. It will be well with him who seeks favor, comfort from the Father in heaven, where for us all stability resides.

THE WIFE'S LAMENT

In modern English translation, the speaker of this poem sounds much like the speaker in *The Wanderer*, lamenting his exile, isolation, and the loss of his lord. But in Old English the grammatical gender of the pronouns reveals that this speaker is a woman; the man she refers to as "my lord" must, therefore, be her husband. The story behind the lament remains obscure. All that can be made out for certain is that the speaker was married to a nobleman of another country; that her husband has left her (possibly forced into exile as a result of a feud); that his kinsmen are hostile to her; and that she is now living alone in a wilderness. Although the circumstances are shadowy, it is reasonable to conjecture that the wife may have been a "peace-weaver" (a woman married off to make peace between warring tribes), like Hildeburh and Freawaru, whose politically inspired marriages only result in further bloodshed (see *Beowulf*, pp. 54 and 75). The obscurity of the Old English text has led to diametrically opposed interpretations of the husband's feeling toward his wife. One interpretation holds that, for unexplained reasons, possibly because of his kinsmen's hostility to her, he has turned against her. The other, which is adopted in this translation, is that, in her mind at least, they share the suffering of his exile and their separation. Thus in the line here rendered "I must suffer the feud of my much-beloved," *fœhðu* (feud) is read by some as the technical term for a blood feud—the way it is used in *Beowulf* when Hrothgar says he settled a great feud started by Beowulf's father with *feo* (fee), i.e., monetary compensation (p. 40). Others take the word in a more general sense as referring to the man's enmity toward his wife. In either case, the woman's themes and language resemble those of male "wræccas" (outcasts or exiles; the Old English root survives in modern *wretch* and *wretched*) in the Old English poems called "elegies" because of their elegiac content and mood.

The Wife's Lament[1]

Full of grief, I make this poem about myself, my own fate. I have the right to say what miseries I have endured since I grew up, new or old—never greater than now. Endlessly I have suffered the wretchedness of exile.

First my lord went away from his people here across the storm-tossed sea. At daybreak I worried in what land my lord might be. Then I set out—a

1. Translated by Alfred David.

friendless exile—to seek a household to shelter me against wretched need. Hiding their thoughts, the man's kinfolk hatched a plot to separate us so that we two should live most unhappy and farthest from one another in this wide world. And I felt longing.

My lord commanded me to stay in this place. I had few dear ones, faithful friends, in this country; that is why I am sad. Then I found my husband like-minded—luckless, gloomy, hiding murderous thoughts in his heart. With glad countenance, how often we vowed that death alone—nothing else—would drive us apart. That vow has been overthrown. Our friendship is as if it had never been. Far and near, I must suffer the feud of my much-beloved.

I was told to live in an earth-cave beneath an oak tree amid the forest. This earthen hall is old. I am overcome with longing. These dales are dark, and hills high, bitter bulwarks overgrown with briers, a joyless dwelling. Here very often my lord's going away has wrenched me. There are couples on earth, lovers lying together in bed, while at dawn I come out of this cave to sit under the oak tree the summerlong day alone. There I weep my exile, the many burdens. Therefore I can never set my cares at rest, nor still all this life's longing, which is my lot.

Should a young person ever be sad, harsh care at heart, he must then at one and the same time have heartache and a glad countenance, although he suffers endless surging sorrows. Whether my friend has all the world's joy at his bidding or whether, outlawed from his homeland, he sits covered with storm-frost beneath a rocky cliff—my weary-minded friend, drenched in some dreary hall—he suffers great anguish. Too often he remembers a happier place. Woe is the one who, languishing, waits for a lover.

THE BATTLE OF MALDON

The *Battle of Maldon* celebrates an event of the year 991, when a large party of Scandinavian raiders met the English defense forces on the estuary of the Blackwater River (the Pant of the poem), near Maldon in Essex. The Vikings had made a number of successful raids on seaports in the vicinity, after which they had encamped on an island near the mouth of the river. The island, because it was accessible from the mainland by a causeway that might be used only at low tide, provided a natural base from which the Vikings could continue their hit-and-run depredations on the countryside. Birhtnoth, the earl of Essex, who was leader of the English militia, took up his position at the end of the causeway and from there was able to prevent the enemy from crossing to the mainland. As the poem relates, however, in his "overconfidence" he allowed them free passage so that a battle might take place. As a result, he was himself killed, and many of the defenders took to their heels, but the members of the earl's retinue—his close associates and retainers—continued to fight bravely until they were overwhelmed. In the incomplete form in which the poem has come down to us, we do not hear of the ultimate defeat of the English, although the grim tone and in particular the famous speech of Birhtwold prepare us for the disaster.

The unknown poet of late Anglo-Saxon times was apparently well versed in heroic English poetry of the type of *Beowulf*, and he does a brilliant job of adapting traditional epic mannerisms to his description of a local battle of no particular historical importance, which involved people with whom he was acquainted. The defense forces were actually no more than a home guard: inexperienced farmers and laborers conscripted for the local defense, together with a small group of aristocrats who were acquainted with heroic martial tradition. Godric and his brothers, who, according to the poem, fled from the battle, are representative of those Englishmen who preferred to pay tribute rather than to fight. But Birhtnoth and his retinue are of the traditional tough fiber, and it is especially in their speeches and single combats that the poet uses the epic style. After Birhtnoth is killed, his loyal companions make speeches that express the heroic ethic, each in his own way. Last and most eloquent, Birhtwold, an old retainer, speaks these memorable lines, set down here, as Cædmon's *Hymn* was, in the original with interlinear translation that, where possible, provides the modern form of the Old English word. For the pronunciation of the consonants as marked, see page 24.

> "Hyġe sceal þy heardra,   heorte þy cenre,
> Spirit must be by as much the harder,   heart by as much the keener,

> Mod sceal þy mare   þy ure mæġen lytlaþ.
> Mood must be by as much the more,   by as much as our strength lessens.

> Her liġeþ ure ealdor   eall forheawen,
> Here lieth our elder   all hewn to pieces,

> god on greote.   A mæġ gnornian
> good (man) on (the) sand.   Ever may he be sorry

> se-þe nu fram þys wiġ-plegan   wendan þenċeþ
> who now from this battle-play   thinks to turn.

> Iċ eom frod feores;   fram iċ ne wille
> I am old of life;   I do not want (to go away) from (here),

> Ac iċ me be healfe   minum hlaforde,
> But I myself beside   my lord,

> be swa leofum menn,   licgan þenċe.
> By so beloved (a) man,   think to lie (dead)."

Birhtnoth's decision to let the Vikings cross the river is treated in the epic manner as an instance of heroic overconfidence, like Beowulf's refusal to use his sword against the unarmed Grendel—but in this case it is a gesture that leads to tragic doom. Probably Birhtnoth had a practical motive for his rashness: if the Vikings were prevented from raiding here, they would simply sail along the coast to a less well-defended spot to continue their depredations. Only their destruction would ensure general peace, but from the local point of view, Birhtnoth's permitting the enemy to come where he could fight with them might well appear as the rashly noble act of a traditional hero.

The poem was written down in a manuscript that was reduced to charred fragments in the same fire that damaged the *Beowulf* manuscript. Fortunately, a transcript had been made of it before the fire, and on this modern editions depend. Even before the manuscript was burned, the poem must have lacked a number of lines at its beginning and end, although most scholars believe that nothing very substantial has been lost.

The Battle of Maldon[1]

Then he[2] commanded each of his warriors to leave his horse, drive it far away, and walk forward, trusting in his hands and in his good courage. When Offa's kinsman[3] understood that the earl would not put up with cowardice, he let his beloved hawk fly from his hand toward the woods and advanced to the battle: by this men might know that the youth would not weaken in the fight once he had taken up his weapons. Eadric wished also to serve his lord the earl in the battle; he carried his spear forward to the conflict. He was of good heart as long as he might hold shield and broadsword in his hands; he carried out the vow that he had made, now that he was to fight before his lord.

Then Birhtnoth began to place his men at their stations; he rode about and advised them, taught the troops how they should stand and hold the place and bade them grasp their shields aright, firm in their hands, and have no fear. When he had arranged his folk properly, he alighted among them where it seemed best to him, where he knew his retainers to be most loyal.

Then the Vikings' herald stood on the river bank, cried out loudly, spoke words, boastfully proclaimed the seafarers' message to the earl where he stood on the shore: "Bold seamen have sent me to you, have commanded me to say to you that you must quickly send treasure in order to protect yourself; and it is better for you to buy off this spear-assault with tribute than to have us give you harsh war. There is no need for us to destroy one another, if you are rich enough to pay. With the gold we will confirm truce. If you that are highest here decide upon this, that you will ransom your people, and in return for peace give the seamen money in the amount they request, and receive peace from us, we will go to ship with the tribute, set sail on the sea, and keep peace with you."

Birhtnoth spoke, raised his shield, his slender ash-spear, uttered words, angry and resolute gave him answer: "Do you hear, seafarer, what this folk says? They will give you spears for tribute, poisoned point and old sword, heriot[4] that avails you not in battle. Sea-wanderers' herald, take back our answer, speak to your people a message far more hateful, that here stands with his host an undisgraced earl who will defend this country, my lord Æthelred's[5] homeland, folk and land. Heathen shall fall in the battle. It seems to me too shameful that you should go unfought to ship with our tribute, now that you have come thus far into our land. Not so easily shall you get treasure: point and edge shall first reconcile us, grim battle-play, before we give tribute."

Then he ordered the men to bear their shields, go forward so that they all stood on the river bank. Because of the water neither band could come to the other: after the ebb, the floodtide came flowing in; currents met and

1. In this prose translation by E. T. Donaldson, a few liberties have been taken with the text to make clear the references of some of the loosely used Old English terms for *warrior*. The translation is in general based on the text in John C. Pope's *Seven Old English Poems* (1966).
2. Earl Birhtnoth, commander of the English defense forces.

3. Offa is mentioned later in the poem as one of Birhtnoth's principal retainers; his young kinsman is not otherwise identified.
4. The weapons a tenant received from his lord; they were returned to the lord upon the tenant's death.
5. King Ethelred reigned from 978 to 1016.

crossed. It seemed to them too long a time before they might bear their spears together. On the river Pant they stood in proud array, the battle-line of the East Saxons and the men from the ash-ships. Nor might any of them injure another, unless one should receive death from the flight of an arrow.

The tide went out. The seamen stood ready, many Vikings eager for war. The earl, protector of men, bade a war-hard warrior—he was named Wulfstan, of bold lineage—to hold the bridge:[6] he was Ceola's son, who with his spear pierced the first man bold enough to step upon the bridge. There stood with Wulfstan fearless fighters, Ælfhere and Maccus, bold men both who would not take flight from the ford, but defended themselves stoutly against the enemy as long as they might wield weapons.

When the loathed strangers saw that, and understood clearly that they would face bitter bridge-defenders there, they began to prefer words to deeds,[7] prayed that they might have access to the bank, pass over the ford and lead their forces across. Then in his overconfidence the earl began to yield ground—too much ground—to the hateful people: Birhthelm's son began to call over the cold water while warriors listened: "Now the way is laid open for you. Come straightway to us, as men to battle. God alone knows which of us may be master of the field."

The slaughter-wolves advanced, minded not the water, a host of Vikings westward over the Pant, over the bright water bore their shields: sailors to land brought shields of linden. Opposite stood Birhtnoth with his warriors, ready for the fierce invaders. He ordered his men to form a war-hedge[8] with their shields and to hold the formation fast against the enemy. Now was combat near, glory in battle. The time had come when doomed men should fall. Shouts were raised; ravens circled, the eagle eager for food. On earth there was uproar.

They let the file-hard spears fly from their hands, grim-ground javelins. Bows were busy, shield felt point. Bitter was the battle-rush. On either side warriors fell, young men lay dead. Wulfmær was wounded, chose the slaughter-bed: kinsman of Birhtnoth—his sister's son—he was cruelly hewn down with swords. Then requital was made to the Vikings: I have heard that Eadweard struck one fiercely with his sword, withheld not the stroke, so that the warrior fell doomed at his feet; for this his lord gave the chamberlain[9] thanks when he had opportunity. Thus men stood firm in the battle, stern of purpose. Eagerly all these armed fighters contended with one another to see who could be the first with his weapon's point to take life from doomed man. The slain fell, carrion, to the earth. The defenders stood fast; Birhtnoth urged them on, bade each man who would win glory from the Danes to give his whole heart to the battle.

A war-hard Viking advanced, raised up his weapon, his shield to defend himself, moved against Birhtnoth. As resolute as the churl,[1] the earl advanced toward him. Each of them meant harm to the other. Then the seaman threw his southern-made[2] spear so that the fighters' chief was

---

6. Not a bridge in the modern sense, but probably a stone causeway, underwater even at low tide; immediately below, it is called a ford.
7. Literally, "to practice deception"—an overstatement due to the poet's scorn for fighters who refused to do things the hard heroic way.
8. A wall of shields (a common defensive formation).
9. I.e., Eadweard.
1. A common soldier, in contrast to "earl" Birhtnoth.
2. Apparently the Vikings preferred weapons made in England or France—the "south."

wounded. But he thrust the spear with his shield so that the shaft split and the spearhead broke off and sprang away.[3] The war-chief was maddened; with his spear he stabbed the proud Viking that had given him the wound. Wise in war was the host's leader: he let his spear go through the man's neck, guided his hand so that he mortally wounded the raider. Then he quickly stabbed another, breaking through the mail-shirt: in the breast, quite through the corselet, was this one wounded; at his heart stood the deadly point. The earl was the blither; the bold man laughed, gave thanks to God that the Lord had given him this day's work.

One of the Vikings loosed a javelin from his hand, let it fly from his fist, and it sped its way through Æthelred's noble thane. By the earl's side stood a lad not yet grown, a boy in the battle, son of Wulfstan, Wulfmær the young, who plucked full boldly the bloody spear from the warrior. He sent the hard spear flying back again: its point went in, and on the earth lay the man who had sorely wounded his lord. Then an armed Viking stepped toward the earl. He wished to seize the earl's war-gear, make booty of rings and ornamented sword. Then Birhtnoth took his sword from its sheath, broad and bright-edged, and struck at his assailant's coat of mail. Too soon one of the seafarers hindered him, wounded the earl in his arm. Then the gold-hilted sword fell to the earth: he might not hold the hard blade, wield his weapon. Yet he spoke words, the hoar battle-leader, encouraged his men, bade them go forward stoutly together. He might no longer stand firm on his feet. He looked toward Heaven and spoke: "I thank thee, Ruler of Nations, for all the joys that I have had in the world. Now, gentle Lord, I have most need that thou grant my spirit grace, that my soul may travel to thee—under thy protection, Prince of Angels, depart in peace. I beseech thee that fiends of hell harm it not." Then the heathen warriors slew him and both the men who stood by him; Ælfnoth and Wulfmær both were laid low; close by their lord they gave up their lives.

Then there retired from the battle those who did not wish to be there. The son of Odda was the first to flee: Godric went from the fight and left the good man that had given him many a steed. He leaped upon the horse that his lord had owned, upon trappings that he had no right to, and both his brothers galloped with him, Godwine and Godwig cared not for battle, but went from the war and sought the wood, fled to its fastness and saved their lives—and more men than was in any way right, if they remembered all the favors he had done for their benefit. So Offa had said to him that day at the meeting he had held in the place, that many there spoke boldly who would not remain firm at need.

The folk's leader had fallen, Æthelred's earl: all his hearth-companions saw that their lord lay dead. Then the proud thanes advanced; men without fear pressed eagerly on. They all desired either of two things, to leave life or avenge the man they loved. Thus Ælfric's son urged them on; the warrior young of winters spoke words; Ælfwine it was who spoke, and spoke boldly: "Remember the speeches we have spoken so often over our mead,[4] when we raised boast on the bench, heroes in the hall, about hard fighting. Now may the man who is bold prove that he is. I will make my noble birth known to

---

3. The maneuver described frees the spear from the wounded man's body and enables him to take retaliatory action.

4. Boasting of prowess while drinking is a common element in Old English poetry.

all, that I was of great kin in Mercia. My grandfather was named Ealhelm, a wise earl, worldly-prosperous. Thanes among that people shall not have reason to reproach me that I would go from this band of defenders, seek my home, now that my lord lies hewn down in battle. To me that is greatest of griefs: he was both my kinsman and my lord." Then he went forward, bent on revenge, and with the point of his spear pierced one of the pirate band, so that he lay on the earth, destroyed by the weapon. Then Ælfwine began to encourage his comrades, friends and companions, to go forward.

Offa spoke, shook his ash-spear: "Lo, you, Ælfwine, have encouraged us all, thanes in need. Now that our lord the earl lies on the earth, there is need for us all that each one of us encourage the other, warriors to battle, as long as he may have and hold weapon, hard sword, spear and good blade. The coward son of Odda, Godric, has betrayed us all; when he rode off on that horse, on that proud steed, many a man thought that he was our lord. Therefore here on the field folk were dispersed, the shield-wall broken. Curses on his action, by which he caused so many men here to flee."

Leofsunu spoke, raised the linden buckler, his shield to defend himself; he answered the warrior: "I promise that I will not flee a footstep hence, but I will go forward, avenge my dear lord in the fight. Steadfast warriors about Sturmer[5] need not reproach me with their words that now that my patron is dead I would go lordless home, abandon the battle. But weapon, point and iron, shall take me." Full wrathful he went forward, fought fiercely; flight he despised.

Then Dunnere spoke, shook his spear; humble churl,[6] he cried over all, bade each warrior avenge Birhtnoth: "He who intends to avenge his lord on the folk may not hesitate nor care for life." Then they advanced: they cared not for life. The retainers began to fight hardily, fierce spear-bearers, and prayed God that they might avenge their patron and bring destruction to their enemies.

The hostage[7] began to help them eagerly. He was of bold kin among the Northumbrians, the son of Ecglaf: his name was Æscferth. He did not flinch at the war-play, but threw spears without pause. Now he hit shield, now he pierced man: each moment he caused some wound, as long as he might wield weapons.

Eadweard the Long still stood in the line, ready and eager, spoke boasting words, how he would not flee a footstep nor turn back, now that his chief lay dead. He broke the shield-wall and fought against the foe until he had worthily avenged his treasure-giver on the seamen—before he himself lay on the slaughter-bed.

So also did Æthelric, noble companion, eager and impetuous; he fought most resolutely, this brother of Sibirht, as did many another: they split the hollow shield and defended themselves boldly,[8] . . . The shield's rim broke and the mail-shirt sang one of horror's songs. Then in the battle Offa struck the seafarer so that he fell on the earth, and there Gadd's kinsman himself sought the ground: Offa was quickly hewn down in the fight. He had, however, performed what he had promised his lord, what he had vowed before

5. The Essex village where the speaker lived.
6. I.e., freeman of the lowest rank.
7. Among Germanic peoples, hostages of high rank generally fought on the side of the warriors

who held them in hostage.
8. Apparently a description of a Viking's attack on Offa has been lost.

to his ring-giver, that they should either both ride to the town, hale to their home, or fall among the host, die of wounds in the slaughter-place. He lay as a thane should, near his lord.

Then there was a crash of shields. The seamen advanced, enraged by the fight. Spear oft pierced life-house of doomed man. Then Wistan advanced: Thurstan's son fought against the men. He was the slayer of three of them in the throng before the son of Wighelm[9] lay dead in the carnage. There was stubborn conflict. Warriors stood fast in the fight. Fighting men fell, worn out with wounds: slain fell among slain.

All the while Oswold and Eadwold, brothers both, encouraged the men, with their words bade their dear kinsmen that they should stand firm at need, wield their weapons without weakness.

Birhtwold spoke, raised his shield—he was an old retainer—shook his ash spear; full boldly he exhorted the men: "Purpose shall be the firmer, heart the keener, courage shall be the more, as our might lessens. Here lies our lord all hewn down, good man on ground. Ever may he lament who now thinks to turn from war-play. I am old of life; from here I will not turn, but by my lord's side, by the man I loved, I intend to lie."

So also the son of Æthelgar encouraged them all to the battle: this Godric oft let spear go, slaughter-shaft fly on the Vikings; thus he advanced foremost among the folk, hewed and laid low until he died in the fighting: he was not that Godric who fled the battle.

9. Identification uncertain.

Anglo-Norman England

THE ANGLO-SAXON CHRONICLE

The Anglo-Saxon Chronicle is a historical record in English, which takes the form of annals—that is, an annual summary of important events. Entries begin with variations of the formula "Ðis gear" (This year) and may be brief or, occasionally, extended narratives. Copies of the original *Chronicle*, which was started in 891, were distributed to centers of learning where they were carried on independently. Seven manuscripts survive. The following selections are from the *Peterborough Chronicle* (named for the monastery where it was kept), which was continued until 1154.

The *Peterborough Chronicle* provides an English perspective on the rule of the Normans after the conquest. In recording the death of William the Conqueror, the chronicler begins with conventional pious observations about the transitory nature of fortune in this world and the expected eulogy of the late king. But the rhetorical praise of the great man shifts into criticism and finally into doggerel rhyme satirizing William's greed and arbitrary exercise of power—especially his cruel game laws.

Since the *Chronicle* was written by monks, much space is devoted to church politics. The resentment of English monks at French exploitation clearly shows in the chronicler's barbed account of Henry of Poitou, an enterprising French churchman who pulled strings to get himself appointed abbot of Peterborough even though he was already abbot of a monastery in Normandy.

The Conqueror's iron rule, which, according to the *Chronicle*, provided a measure of peace and security, did not last. After the death of Henry I in 1135, Henry's nephew, Stephen of Blois, crossed the English Channel and succeeded in having himself crowned. He thus displaced his cousin Matilda, Henry's daughter, who had been the designated heir. Matilda had been married at the age of twelve to the emperor Henry V and, upon the latter's death, was remarried to Geoffrey Plantagenet, count of Anjou, whose raids in Normandy made him extremely unpopular with the Anglo-Norman barons who owned lands in that province. Stephen, however, soon managed to alienate his supporters, and a bitter civil war ensued. The chronicler gives an apocalyptic account of King Stephen's reign. Although people unquestionably suffered greatly during this period, the chronicler's descriptions of torture, famine, and robbery perhaps reflect a rhetorical excess considered appropriate to descriptions of evil times, the other side of which may be seen in the idealization of a legendary past in the twelfth-century Arthurian chronicles of Geoffrey of Monmouth, Robert Wace, and Layamon (see pp. 115–26).

The Anglo-Saxon Chronicle[1]

[OBITUARY FOR WILLIAM THE CONQUEROR]

[1087] In the same year, before the feast of the Assumption of Saint Mary,[2] King William went from Normandy into France with an army and made war

---

1. Translated by Alfred David.   2. August 15.

on his own lord King Philip,[3] and killed a great number of his men, and burned down the city of Mantes and all the holy churches that were in the city; and two holy men, who served God, living there in an anchorite's cell, were burned to death. When he had done this, King William returned to Normandy. He did a wretched thing, and one more wretched happened to him. In what way more wretched? He got sick and suffered severely. Bitter death, which spares neither the powerful nor the lowly, seized him. He died in Normandy the day after the feast of the birth of Saint Mary,[4] and they buried him in Caen at the abbey of St. Stephen. He had had it built and then endowed it richly. Oh, how false and how fickle is the wealth of this world! He who had been a powerful king and lord of many lands, of all the land then held no more than seven feet. He who was once clothed in gold and gems, now lay covered with earth. He left three sons: the oldest was called Robert, who succeeded him as duke of Normandy; the second was called William who bore the crown of England after him; the third was called Henry to whom the father bequeathed countless treasures.

If anyone wishes to know what kind of man he was, or what honor he possessed, or how many lands he was lord of, we will write about him just as he appeared to us, who beheld him and formerly lived in his court. This King William we are speaking about was a very wise man, and very powerful, and worthier and stronger than any of his predecessors. He was mild to good men who loved God and extremely harsh to men who crossed his will. On that site where God had granted him to gain possession of England, he established a famous monastery[5] and set up monks in it and endowed it well. In his days the famous church of Canterbury was built and also many others throughout England. Moreover, this land was filled with a great many monks, and they led their life according to the rule of St. Benedict. And Christianity was such in his day that every man who wished was able to perform the duties that pertained to his religious order. Also he attached great importance to ceremony: he wore his crown three times a year as often as he was in England—at Easter he wore it at Winchester, at Pentecost at Westminster, and at Christmas at Gloucester. And at those times all the powerful men in England attended him—archbishops and bishops, abbots and earls, thanes and knights. He was also a very harsh and violent man so that no one dared do anything against his will. He put earls who acted against his will in fetters; he removed bishops from their bishoprics and abbots from their abbacies; and he threw thanes into prison. And he did not spare even his own brother, who was called Odo. The latter was a very powerful bishop in Normandy— his see was at Bayeux—and he was the foremost man next to the king. He had an earldom in England, and when the king was in Normandy, then he was master in this land. The king threw him in prison. Among other things, one must not forget the good peace that he made in this land so that any man of property might travel safely throughout the kingdom with his purse full of gold. No man dared to kill another, no matter how much harm that one had done to him. And if a man raped a woman, he immediately lost those parts with which he took pleasure.

He ruled over England and because of his management contrived that

---

3. The king of France was lord of the dukes of Normandy.
4. September 9.

5. Battle Abbey where the Battle of Hastings took place.

there was not a hide of land in England that he did not know who owned it and what it was worth; and he set it down in his record.[6] The land of the Britons[7] was in his power, and he built castles in it and completely dominated that people. Likewise he subjected Scotland because of his great strength. Normandy was his by inheritance, and he ruled over the county called Maine.[8] And if he had lived another two years, he would have conquered Ireland with no weapon other than astute diplomacy. Truly in his time men suffered much hardship and very many injuries.

> He built fortresses
> And caused poor men great distress.
> This king was very hard.
> He took many a gold mark
> From his subjects and did purloin
> Hundreds more of silver coin.
> He extorted it by pounds
> On most illegal grounds.
> His people he would bleed,
> Not from any need.
> Into avarice he fell
> And loved greed above all.
> He laid laws severe
> To protect the deer.
> Whoever killed a hart or hind
> Was to be made blind.
> The harts were forbidden, and
> The wild boars were also banned.
> He loved the tall deer
> As if he were their father.
> And the hares, he made a decree,
> That they should go free.
> His rich men lamented it,
> And his poor men resented it,
> But so stern a man was he
> He cared not for all their enmity.
> But they must in everything
> Follow the will of the king
> If they wished to live or planned
> To own any land—
> Estates or goods to embrace
> And to remain in his good grace.
> Alas, that any man should be
> So filled with arrogance that he
> Exalts himself above all the rest
> And holds himself to be the highest.
> May almighty God be merciful
> And grant forgiveness to his soul.

We have written these things about him, both the good and the bad, so that good men may take after the good and shun the bad in every respect and follow the path that leads us to the kingdom of heaven.

---

6. Reference to the Domesday Book, a census and survey of land ordered by William. A hide of land is roughly equivalent to 120 acres.

7. Wales.
8. Province in France adjoining Normandy.

[HENRY OF POITOU BECOMES ABBOT OF PETERBOROUGH]

[1127] This same year [King Henry I] gave the abbacy of Peterborough to an abbot called Henry of Poitou, who held the abbey of St. Jean d'Angely[9] in his possession. And all the archbishops and bishops said that it was illegal and that he might not hold two abbacies. But this same Henry gave the king to understand that he had given up his abbey because of the great unrest that was in that country, and that he did this on the advice and with the consent of the pope of Rome and the abbot of Cluny, and because he was the papal tax collector.[1] But it was no more true for all he said, but he wanted to have both monasteries in his possession, and so he had it as long as it was God's will. As a priest, he had been bishop of Soissons; then he became a monk at Cluny and afterwards prior of that same monastery; and then he became prior at Savigny. Thereupon, because he was related to the king of England and to the count of Poitou, the count made him abbot of St. Jean d'Angely. Then, as a result of his elaborate stratagems, he got the archbishopric of Besançon and held it for three days; then he justly lost it because he had obtained it unjustly. Then he got the bishopric of Saintes, which is five miles from the monastery of which he was abbot. He had that for almost a week. The abbot of Cluny got him out of there, as he had previously out of Besançon. Then he considered that if he could put down roots in England, he could have all his will. He sought out the king and told him that he was a broken-down old man, and that he could not put up with great injustices and strife in their land. Then he asked specifically for the abbey of Peterborough on his own behalf and that of all his friends. And the king granted it to him because he was his kinsman and had been the chief cleric to swear an oath and bear witness when the son of the count of Normandy and daughter of the count of Anjou were divorced because of consanguinity.[2]

Thus miserably was the abbacy given away between Christmas and Candlemas at London. And so he traveled with the king to Winchester and then he came to Peterborough. And there he lived like the drones in the hive. All that the bees drag in the drones devour and drag out—so did he. All that he might take, inside and outside, from churchmen or laymen, he sent across the sea. He did no good there and left nothing good there.

Let no one think strange the truth that we declare, for it was well-known throughout the entire country that as soon as he arrived there—that is, on the Sunday on which one sings, "Exurge, quare obdormis, Domine?"[3] immediately thereafter many men saw and heard many huntsmen hunting. These hunters were black and big and ugly, and all their dogs were black and ugly with wide eyes, and they rode on black horses and black goats.[4] This was seen in the deer park itself in the town of Peterborough and in all the woods between Peterborough and Stamford. And the monks heard the horns blowing, which they blew at night. Reliable witnesses observed them at night. They said it seemed to them there might well have been twenty to thirty

---

9. Monastery in Normandy.
1. For the tax popularly known in England as "Peter's Pence."
2. The divorce was promoted by Henry I to allow the count's son (Henry's nephew) to marry the sister of the king of France, who, in return, made him count of Flanders. Such a divorce or annulment required the endorsement of the church, usually on grounds that the marriage had violated the permissible degree of kinship between the partners.
3. Awake, why sleepest thou, Oh Lord? (Latin); Psalm 43 [44].23, sung at the beginning of the mass on the second Sunday before Lent, February 6 in 1127.
4. The Wild Hunt, a motif in Germanic mythology, is here given a diabolical twist.

blowing horns. This was seen and heard from the time he came here all that Lent up to Easter. This was his arrival. Of his departure we cannot yet speak. May God provide!

[THE REIGN OF KING STEPHEN]

[1135] In [King Stephen's] time all was warfare, wickedness, and robbery, for right away all the powerful men who were traitors rose up against him[5] * * * [1137] When the traitors discovered that he was a mild man, and gentle and good, and did not enforce justice they committed every sort of atrocity. They had done homage to him and sworn oaths, but they kept no faith. They were all forsworn and broke their oaths, for every powerful man built castles and held them against him. And they filled the land full of castles.

They oppressed the wretched people greatly with forced labor on castle works. When the castles were built, they filled them with devils and evil men. Night and day they seized anyone who they thought possessed any wealth (both men and women), and put them in prison, and tortured them with unspeakable tortures to get their gold and silver. For never were any martyrs so tortured as these were. They were hung up by the feet and smoked with foul smoke. They were hung up by the thumbs or by the head with armor attached to the feet. Knotted cords were tied around their heads and twisted till they cut into the brain. They were incarcerated with adders, snakes, and toads and killed in that way. Some were put into a torture box—that is, in a chest that was short, narrow, and shallow—into which they put sharp stones, and pressed the man in it so that all his limbs were broken. Many of the castles had a "strangle-trap": that was a device made up of chains so heavy that it was all two or three men could do to carry one of them. It worked like this—they fitted a sharp iron, which was fastened to a beam, around a man's throat and neck so that he could not move in any direction, nor sit, nor lie down, nor sleep but had to bear up all that iron. Many thousands they starved to death.

I do not know how nor would it be possible to tell all the atrocities and tortures they inflicted upon the wretched people of this land. And that lasted nineteen winters for as long as Stephen was king. And the whole time it went from bad to worse. They were constantly making the villages pay taxes, which they called "protection money." When the wretched people had nothing more to give, they pillaged and burned all the villages so that you could easily do a day's journey without ever seeing an inhabitant in a village or land under cultivation. Then grain was expensive, and meat and cheese and butter, for there was none in the land. Wretched people starved to death. Some, who had once been wealthy, went begging. Some fled the country. Never before in the land had there been more misery, nor did ever heathens do worse things than they did.

Contrary to civilized behavior, they spared neither church nor churchyard but took all the valuables therein and then burned church and all together. They did not spare bishop's land, nor abbot's nor priest's, but robbed monks and clerics, and every man robbed the other if he was the stronger. If two or

5. Though dated the year of Stephen's accession, these entries, which later refer to the entire reign of nineteen years, were written after 1154. In fact, Stephen at first had considerable support from the city of London and among the baronage. Many of the barons—traitors according to this chronicler, who regards Stephen as an ineffectual but legitimate monarch—soon switched to Matilda's cause.

three men rode into a village, the entire village would flee them because they thought they were robbers. The bishops and clergy kept excommunicating them, but they did not care about that since they were all totally accursed, perjured, and abandoned.

Wherever the ground was tilled, the earth bore no grain, for the land was ruined by such acts. It was openly said that Christ and his saints were asleep. Such things—and more than we can tell—we suffered nineteen winters for our sins.

LEGENDARY HISTORIES OF BRITAIN

During the twelfth century, three authors, who wrote in Latin, Anglo-Norman French, and Middle English, respectively, created a mostly legendary history of Britain for their Norman overlords (see pp. 7–8). This "history" was set in the remote past, beginning with a foundation myth—a heroic account of national origins—modeled on Virgil's *Aeneid* and ending with the Anglo-Saxon conquest of the native islanders, the Britons, in the fifth and sixth centuries. The chief architect of the history is Geoffrey of Monmouth, who was writing his *History of the Kings of Britain* in Latin prose ca. 1136–38. His work was freely translated into French verse by Wace in 1155, and Wace in turn was translated into English alliterative poetry by Layamon.

Geoffrey of Monmouth and Wace wrote their histories of Britain primarily for an audience of noblemen and prelates who were descendants of the Norman conquerors of the Anglo-Saxons. Geoffrey wrote several dedications of his *History*, first to supporters of Matilda, the heiress presumptive of Henry I, and, when the Crown went instead to Stephen of Blois, to the new king's allies and to Stephen himself. Layamon tells us that Wace wrote his French version for Eleanor of Aquitaine, queen of Stephen's successor, Henry II. The prestige and power of ancient Rome still dominated the historical and political imagination of the feudal aristocracy, and the legendary history of the ancient kings of the Britons, especially of King Arthur, who had defeated Rome itself, served to flatter the self-image and ambitions of the Anglo-Norman barons. Perhaps the destruction of Arthur's kingdom also provided a timely object lesson of the disastrous consequences of civil wars such as those over the English succession in which these lords were engaged.

The selections from Geoffrey of Monmouth and Wace are translated by Alfred David. The Layamon selections are translated by Rosamund Allen.

GEOFFREY OF MONMOUTH

The author of the *History of the Kings of Britain* was a churchman, probably of Welsh or Breton ancestry, who spent much of his life at Oxford. One of his motives in writing the work was undoubtedly to obtain advancement in the church. In the dedications of the *History*, Geoffrey claims that it is merely a translation into Latin of "a very old book in the British language [i.e., Welsh]," which had been loaned to him by his friend Walter, archdeacon of Oxford, but scholars have discounted this story as another one of Geoffrey's many fictions.

Geoffrey began his history with a British foundation myth modeled upon Virgil's

Aeneid. Out of legends that Rome had been founded by refugees from the fall of Troy, the poet Virgil had created his epic poem the *Aeneid* for Augustus Caesar. Aeneas, carrying his father upon his back, had escaped from the ruins of Troy and, fulfilling prophecies, became the founding father of a new Troy in Italy. The Britons had developed an analogous foundation myth in which a great-grandson of Aeneas called Brutus had led another band of Trojan exiles to establish another Troy, which was named Britain after him. Geoffrey drew upon earlier Latin chronicles and Welsh oral tradition, but he himself provided his history with a chronology, a genealogy, a large cast of both historical and legendary characters (among many other stories, he is the first to tell of King Lear and his daughters), and a cyclical sense of the rise and fall of empires. The longest and most original part of the work (over one-fifth of the *History*) is devoted to the birth and reign of King Arthur. In the first part of Arthur's reign, he defeats and drives out the pagan Anglo-Saxon invaders. At the end of his reign the Saxons return at the invitation of the traitor Mordred and, though defeated again by Arthur in his last battle, they ultimately triumph over his successors.

The historicity of Geoffrey's book, although questioned by some of Geoffrey's contemporary historians, was widely accepted and not fully discredited until the seventeenth century. In the course of time Arthur was adopted as a national and cultural hero by the English against whose ancestors he had fought, and his court became the international ideal of a splendid chivalric order in the past of which contemporary knighthood was only a faint imitation. Geoffrey of Monmouth himself already declares that in Arthur's time, "Womenfolk became chaste and more virtuous and for their love the knights were ever more daring."

In the following selections, Geoffrey relates the British foundation myth, which he historicizes, amplifies, and fleshes out with details that he regards as classical.

From The History of the Kings of Britain

[THE STORY OF BRUTUS AND DIANA'S PROPHECY]

After the Trojan War, Aeneas with his son Ascanius fled from the destruction of the city and sailed to Italy. Although King Latinus would have received him there with honor, Turnus, the king of the Rutuli, was envious and made war on him. In their rivalry Aeneas prevailed and, having slain Turnus, obtained the kingdom of Italy and Latinus's daughter, Lavinia.

At the end of Aeneas's days, Ascanius was elevated to royal power and founded the city of Alba on the banks of the Tiber. He fathered a son whose name was Silvius. The latter had a secret love affair with a niece of Lavinia's whom he married and got with child. When his father Ascanius learned about this he ordered his wise men to find out the sex of the child that the girl had conceived. When the wise men had made sure of the truth, they said that she would bear a son who would be the death of his father and mother. After travelling through many lands as an exile, he would nevertheless attain to the highest honor. Their prophecies did not turn out to be mistaken. For when her time had come, the woman bore a boy and died in childbirth. The boy was handed over to the midwife and named Brutus. At last, after fifteen years had gone by, the boy went hunting with his father and killed him with a misdirected bowshot. For as the servants were driving some stags into their path, Brutus, believing that he was aiming at them, hit his father below the breast. On account of this death, his relatives, outraged that he should have done such a deed, drove him from Italy.* * *

[The exiled Brutus travels to Greece, where he discovers descendants of Trojan prisoners of war living in slavery. He organizes a successful rebellion against their Greek masters and, like Aeneas before him, leads them on a quest for a new homeland.]

Driven by favorable winds, the Trojans sailed for two days and one night until they made land on an island called Leogetia, which was uninhabited because long ago it had been devastated by pirate raids. So Brutus sent three hundred armed men to explore the island and see whether anything was living on it. They found no one but they killed several kinds of wild animals that they came across in the woods and thickets.

They came to a deserted city where they found a temple of Diana in which a statue of the goddess rendered oracles if someone should consult it. At last they returned to their ships, loaded down with game, and told their comrades about the land and the city. They suggested to their chief that he go to the temple and, after making propitiatory sacrifices, inquire of the goddess what land might afford them a permanent home. When everyone agreed, Brutus with the soothsayer Gero and twelve elders set out for the temple, taking along everything necessary for the sacrifice. When they got there, they bound their brows with headbands and, in preparation of the most ancient rite, they erected three hearths to three gods, namely to Jupiter, Mercury, and Diana. They poured out libations to each one in turn. Before the altar of the goddess, Brutus himself, holding a sacrificial vessel filled with wine and the blood of a white doe in his right hand, raised his face to her statue and broke the silence with these words:[1]

> Mighty goddess of woodlands, terror of the wild boar,
> Thou who art free to traverse the ethereal heavens
> And the mansions of hell, disclose my rights on this earth
> And say what lands it is your wish for us to inhabit,
> What dwelling-place where I shall worship you all my life,
> Where I shall dedicate temples to you with virgin choirs.

After he had spoken this prayer nine times, he walked four times around the altar and poured out the wine he was holding upon the hearth. Then he spread out the hide of the doe before the altar and lay down on it. He tried to doze off and finally fell asleep. It was now the third hour of the night when sweetest slumber overcomes mortals. Then it seemed to him that the goddess was standing before him and speaking to him like this:

> Brutus, where the sun sets beyond the kingdoms of Gaul
> Is an isle in the ocean, closed all around by the sea.
> Once on a time giants lived on that isle in the ocean,
> But now it stands empty and fit to receive your people.
> Seek it out, for it shall be your homeland forever;
> It shall be a second Troy for your descendants.
> There kings shall be born of your seed and to them
> All nations of the round earth shall be subject.

When the vision vanished, Brutus remained in doubt whether what he had seen was only a phantom or whether the actual voice of the goddess had

1. Brutus's prayer and Diana's prophecy are written as Latin poetry and employ a more formal diction than the prose narrative. The entire episode is meant to show off Geoffrey's classical learning and familiarity with pagan ritual.

foretold the homeland to which he was to travel. Finally he called his comrades and told them point by point what had happened to him while he slept. Waves of great joy swept over them, and they urged that they return to the ships and, while the wind blew behind them, head with swiftest sail toward the ocean to seek out what the goddess had promised. Without delay they rejoined their comrades and set out on the high seas.

WACE

Wace (ca. 1110–ca. 1180) was a Norman cleric, born on the island of Jersey in the English Channel, which was then part of the dukedom of Normandy. Although educated for the church, he seems to have served the laity, perhaps in a secretarial function. All of his extant works, which include saints' lives, Le Roman de Brut, and Le Roman de Rou, were written in French verse for a lay audience that would have included women like Eleanor of Aquitaine, to whom he dedicated the Brut, and Marie de France, who drew on that work in her lays. Roman in these titles refers to the fact that they are, respectively, chronicles in French verse about the dynasties of Brutus (first of the kings of Britain) and Rollo (first of the dukes of Normandy).

The Roman de Brut is a very free translation in eight-syllable couplets of Geoffrey of Monmouth's Latin prose History of the Kings of Britain. Wace has cut some details and added a good deal, including the first mention of the Round Table. He is far more interested than Geoffrey in creating an atmosphere of courtliness—in the way his characters dress, think, speak, and behave. The following selection covers a challenge delivered to Arthur by the Roman emperor Lucius and Arthur's response. This climactic sequence follows an elaborate coronation scene attended by a large gathering of kings and dukes from Britain and overseas who owe allegiance to Arthur and whose lands comprise what might be called the Arthurian Empire. At the feast following his coronation, Arthur's authority is challenged by ambassadors who present an insulting letter from Lucius. Arthur's reply is a masterpiece of feudal rhetoric that would have been admired by Wace's audience.

From Le Roman de Brut

[THE ROMAN CHALLENGE]

Arthur was seated on a dais surrounded by counts and kings when a dozen white-haired, very well-dressed men came into the hall in pairs, one holding the other's hand. Each held an olive branch. They crossed the hall very slowly in an orderly and solemn procession, approached the king and hailed him. They said they had come from Rome as messengers. They unfolded a letter, which one of them gave to Arthur on behalf of the Roman emperor. Listen to what it said:

"Lucius who holds Rome in his domain and is sovereign lord of the Romans, proclaims to King Arthur, his enemy, what he has deserved. I am disdainful in amazement and am amazed with disdain at the inordinate and insane pride with which you have set your sights on Rome. With disdain and amazement I ask myself at whose prompting and from what quarters you have undertaken to pick a quarrel with Rome as long as a single Roman remains alive. You have acted with great recklessness in attacking us who have the right to rule the world and hold supremacy over it. You still don't know, but we shall teach you; you are blind, but we shall make you see what a great thing it is to anger Rome, which has the power to rule over everything. You have presumed beyond your place and crossed the bounds of your authority! Have you any idea who you are and where you come from—you who are taking and holding back the tribute that belongs to us? You are taking our tribute and our lands: why do you hold them, why don't you turn them over, why do you keep them, what right do you have to them? If you keep them any longer, you will be acting most recklessly. And if you are capable of holding them without our forcing you to give them up, you might as well say—an unprecedented miracle!—that the lion flees from the lamb, the wolf from the goat, the greyhound from the hare. But that could never happen, for Nature would not suffer it. Julius Caesar, our ancestor—but maybe you have little respect for him—conquered Britain and imposed a tribute that our people have collected since that time. And we have also been receiving tribute for a long time from the other islands surrounding you. And you have foolishly presumed to take tribute from both of them. Already you were guilty of senseless behavior, but you have committed an even greater insult that touches us still more closely than the losses we have sustained: you killed our vassal Frollo[1] and illegally occupied France. Therefore, since you are not afraid of Rome nor its great power, the Senate summons and orders you—for the summons is an order—to come before it in mid-August, ready, at whatever cost, to make full restitution of what you have taken from them. And thus you will give satisfaction for the wrongs of which we accuse you. But if you delay in any fashion to do what I command you, I will cross the Alps with an army and will deprive you of Britain and France. But I can't imagine that you will await my coming or will defend France against me. I don't think you will dare to face me on this side of the Channel. And even if you stay over there, you will never await my coming. You won't know a place to hide where I won't flush you out. I'll lead you to Rome in chains and hand you over to the Senate."

At these words there was a great uproar, and all were greatly enraged. You could have heard the Britons shouting loudly, calling God as witness and swearing by his name that they were going to punish the messengers. They would have showered them with abuse and insults, but the king rose to his feet and called out to them, "Silence! Silence! Don't lay a hand on these men. They are messengers; they have a master, they are bringing his message; they can say whatever they like. No one shall do them the slightest harm."

When the noise quieted down and the retainers recovered their composure, the king ordered his dukes and counts and his personal advisers to accompany him to a stone tower called the Giant Tower. There he wanted to seek advice on what to reply to the messengers. Side by side the barons and counts were already mounting the stairs, when Cador, the duke of Cornwall, with a smile spoke to the king, who was in front of him, as follows: "I've been afraid," he said, "and have often thought that leisure and peace might spoil the Britons, for leisure is conducive to bad habits and causes many a man to become lazy. Leisure diminishes prowess, leisure promotes lechery, leisure kindles clandestine love affairs. Through prolonged repose and leisure

---

1. Roman governor of France.

youth gets preoccupied with entertainment and pleasure and backgammon and other games of diversion. By staying put and resting for a long time, we could lose our reputation. Well, we've been asleep, but God has given us a little wake-up call—let us thank him for encouraging the Romans to challenge our country and the others we have conquered. Should the Romans find it in themselves to carry out what they say in that letter, the Britons will still retain their reputation for valor and strength. I never like peace for long, nor shall I love a peace that lasts a long time."

"My lord," said Gawain, "in faith, you're getting upset over nothing. Peace after war is a good thing. The land is better and more beautiful on account of it. It's very good to amuse oneself and to make love. It's for love and for their ladies that knights perform chivalrous deeds."

While bantering in this way, they entered the tower and took their seats. When Arthur saw them sitting down and waiting in silence with full attention, he paused for a moment in thought, then raised his head and spoke:

"Barons," he said, "you who are here, my companions and friends, you have stood by me in good times and bad; you have supported me when I had to go to war; you have taken my part whether I won or lost; you have been partners in my loss, and in my gain when I conquered. Thanks to you and your help, I have won many a victory. I have led you through many dangers by land and by sea, in places near and far. I have found you loyal in action and in counsel. I have tested your mettle many times and always found it good. Thanks to you the neighboring countries are subject to me. You have heard the Romans' order, the tenor of the letter, and the overbearingness and arrogance of their demands. They have provoked and threatened us enough, but if God protects us, we shall do away with the Romans. They are rich and have great power, and now we must carefully consider what we can properly and reasonably say and do. Trouble is dealt with better when a strategy has been worked out in advance. If someone sees the arrow in flight, he must get out of the way or shield himself. That is how we must proceed. The Romans want to shoot at us, and we must get ready so that they cannot wound us. They demand tribute from Britain and must have it, so they tell us; they demand the same from the other islands and from France.

"But first I shall reply how matters stand with regard to Britain. They claim that Caesar conquered it; Caesar was a powerful man and carried out his will by force. The Britons could not defend themselves against him, and he exacted tribute from them by force. But might is not right; it is force and superior power. A man does not possess by right what he has taken by force. Therefore, we are allowed to keep by right what they formerly took by force. They have held up to us the damages, losses, humiliations, the sufferings and fears that they inflicted on our ancestors. They boasted that they conquered them and extorted tribute and rents from them. We have all the more right to make them suffer; they have all the more restitution to make to us. We ought to hate those who hated our ancestors and to injure those who injured them. They remind us that they made them suffer, got tribute from them, and demand tribute from us. They want us to suffer the same shame and extortion as our ancestors. They once got tribute from Britain, and so they want to get it from us. By the same reason and with equal cause we can challenge the Romans and dispute our rights. Belinus, who was king of the

Britons, and Brennus,[2] duke of the Burgundians, two brothers born in Britain, valiant and wise knights, marched on Rome, laid siege to the city, and took it by assault. They hanged twenty-four hostages in plain sight of their families. When Belinus returned from Rome, he entrusted the city to his brother.

"I won't dwell on Belinus and Brennus but will speak of Constantine. He was British by birth, the son of Helen; he held Rome in his own right. Maximian, king of Britain, conquered France and Germany, crossed the Alps and Lombardy and reigned over Rome. These were my ancestors by direct descent, and each one held Rome in his possession. Now you may hear and understand that we have just as much right to possess Rome as they do to possess Britain. The Romans had our tribute, and my ancestors had theirs. They claim Britain, and I claim Rome. This is the gist of my counsel: that they may have the land and tribute who can take it away from another. As for France and the other lands we have taken from them, they have no right to dispute them since they would not or could not defend them, or perhaps had no right to them because they held them in bondage through force and greed. So let he who can hold all. There is no need to look for any other kind of right. The emperor threatens us. God forbid that he should do us any harm. He says that he will take away our lands and lead me to Rome as a prisoner. He has small regard or fear of me. But, God willing, if he comes to this land, before he leaves again he'll have no stomach to make threats. He defies me, and I defy him: may he possess the lands who is able to take them!"

When King Arthur had spoken what he wanted to his barons, the others spoke in turn while the rest listened. Hoël, king of Brittany, spoke next: "Sire," he said, "in faith, you have spoken many just words; none could have said it better. Send after and mobilize your forces along with us who are here at court. Without delay pass over the sea, pass through Burgundy and France, pass the Alps, conquer Lombardy! Throw the emperor who is defying you into confusion and panic so that he will not have the chance to cause you harm. The Romans have begun a suit that will ruin them. God wants to exalt you: don't hold back and lose any time! Make yourself master of the empire, which is ready to surrender to you of its own will. Remember what is written in the Sibyl's prophecies.[3] Three Britons will be born in Britain who shall conquer Rome by might. Two have already lived and been sovereigns over Rome. The first was Belinus and the second, Constantine. You shall be the third to possess Rome and conquer it by force; in you the Sibyl's prophecy will be fulfilled. Why delay to seize that which God wants to bestow on you? Increase your glory and ours to which we aspire. We may say truly that we are not afraid of blows or wounds or death or hardship or prison so

2. Brennus was not a Briton but a Gaulish chieftain who sacked Rome in the 4th century. Belinus is fictional. Constantine I, who adopted Christianity as the official religion of the Roman Empire, was believed to be British. Maximian (Maximus) was a 5th-century Roman general serving in Britain who abandoned the island when his army proclaimed him emperor and usurped the imperium in civil wars that weakened Rome and left Britain at the mercy of attacks by the Picts, Scots, and Germanic tribes. Geoffrey of Monmouth's earlier accounts of these personages had conflated a tiny amount of fact with a great deal of fiction.

3. Reference to the Sibylline books containing prophecies of the Roman Sibyl of Cumae, but these no longer existed and could have been known only by reputation. This prophecy was probably invented by Geoffrey of Monmouth.

long as we strive for honor. As long as you are in danger, I will lead ten
thousand armed knights in your host, and if that should not be enough, I
shall mortgage all my lands and give you the gold and silver. I won't keep
back a farthing so long as you have need of it!"

LAYAMON

Layamon, an English priest, adapted Wace's *Roman de Brut* into Middle English
alliterative verse. His *Brut* (ca. 1190) runs to 16,095 lines, expanding on Wace and
adding much new material.

After winning the continental campaign against Lucius, Arthur is forced to return
to Britain upon learning that his nephew, Mordred, whom he had left behind as
regent, has usurped Arthur's throne and queen. The following selection, a passage
added by Layamon, presents Arthur's dream of Mordred's treachery.

Layamon employs a long alliterative line that harks back to Old English poetry, but
the two halves of his line are often linked by rhyme as well as by alliteration. Layamon
reveals his ties with Germanic literary tradition in other ways. In Arthur's nightmare,
the king and Gawain are sitting astride the roof beam of a building like the mead hall
Heorot in *Beowulf*—a symbol of the control a king wields over his house and kingdom.
On the ground below, Mordred is chopping away at the foundations like the gigantic
rodent in Norse mythology that is gnawing away at the roots of Yggdrasil, the great
tree, which holds together earth, heaven, and hell.

From Brut

[ARTHUR'S DREAM]

Then came to pass what Merlin spoke of long before,
13965   That the walls of Rome would fall down before Arthur;
This had already happened there in relation to the emperor
Who had fallen in the fighting with fifty thousand men:
That's when Rome with her power was pushed to the ground.
    And so Arthur really expected to possess all of Rome,
13970   And the most mighty of kings remained there in Burgundy.
    Now there arrived at this time a bold man on horseback;
News he was bringing for Arthur the king
From Modred, his sister's son: to Arthur he was welcome,
For he thought that he was bringing very pleasant tidings.
13975   Arthur lay there all that long night, talking with the young knight,
Who simply did not like to tell him the truth of what had happened.
The next day, as dawn broke, the household started moving,
And then Arthur got up, and, stretching his arms,
He stood up, and sat down again, as if he felt very sick.
    Then a good knight questioned him: "My Lord, how did you get on
13980   last night?"
Arthur responded (his heart was very heavy):
"Tonight as I was sleeping, where I was lying in my chamber,

There came to me a dream which has made me most depressed:
I dreamed someone had lifted me right on top of some hall
13985 And I was sitting on the hall, astride, as if I was going riding;
All the lands which I possess, all of them I was surveying,
And Gawain sat in front of me, holding in his hands my sword.
Then Modred came marching there with a countless host of men,
Carrying in his hand a massive battle-axe.
13990 He started to hew, with horrible force,
And hacked down all the posts which were holding up the hall.
I saw Guinevere there as well, the woman I love best of all:
The whole roof of that enormous hall with her hands she was
        pulling down;
The hall started tottering, and I tumbled to the ground,
13995 And broke my right arm, at which Modred said 'Take that!'
Down then fell the hall and Gawain fell as well,
Falling on the ground where both his arms were broken,
So with my left hand I clutched my beloved sword
And struck off Modred's head and it went rolling over the ground,
14000 And I sliced the queen in pieces with my beloved sword,
And after that I dropped her into a dingy pit.
And all my fine subjects set off in flight,
And what in Christendom became of them I had no idea,
Except that I was standing by myself in a vast plain,
14005 And then I started roaming all around across the moors;
There I could see griffins and really gruesome birds.
    "Then a golden lioness came gliding over the downs,
As really lovely a beast as any Our Lord has made.
The lioness ran up to me and put her jaws around my waist,
14010 And off she set, moving away towards the sea,
And I could see the waves, tossing in the sea,
And taking me with her, the lioness plunged into the water.
When we two were in the sea, the waves swept her away from me;
Then a fish came swimming by and ferried me ashore.
14015 Then I was all wet and weary, and I was sick with sorrow.
And upon waking, I started quaking,
And then I started to shudder as if burning up with fire,
And so all night I've been preoccupied with my disturbing dream,
For I know of a certainty this is the end of my felicity,
14020 And all the rest of my life I must suffer grief.
O alas that I do not have here my queen with me, my Guinevere!"
    Then the knight responded: "My Lord, you are mistaken;
Dreams should never be interpreted as harbingers of sorrow!
You are the most mighty prince who has rule in any land,
14025 And the most intelligent of all inhabitants on the earth.
If it should have happened—as may Our Lord not allow it—
That your sister's son, Lord Modred, your own queen might have
        wedded,
And all your royal domains might have annexed in his own name,
Those which you entrusted to him when you intended going to
        Rome,
14030 And if he should have done all this by his treacherous deeds,
Even then you might avenge yourself honorably with arms,

And once again possess your lands and rule over your people,
And destroy your enemies who wish you so much evil,
And slay them, every one alive, so that there is none who survives!"

14035   Then Arthur answered him, most excellent of all kings:
"For as long as is for ever, I have no fear whatever,
That Modred who is my relative, the man I love best,
Would betray all my trust, not for all of my realm,
Nor would Guinevere, my queen, weaken in her allegiance,
14040 She will not begin to, for any man in the world!"
Immediately after these words, the knight gave his answer:
"I am telling you the truth, dear king, for I am merely your
    underling:
Modred has done these things: he has adopted your queen,
And has placed in his own hands your lovely land;
14045 He is king and she is queen; they don't expect your return,
For they don't believe it will be the case that you'll ever come back
    from Rome.
I am your loyal liegeman, and I did see this treason,
And so I have come to you in person to tell you the truth.
Let my head be as pledge of what I have told you,
14050 The truth and no lie, about your beloved queen,
And about Modred, your sister's son, and how he has snatched
    Britain from you."
    Then everything went still in King Arthur's hall;
There was great unhappiness for the excellent king,
And because of it the British men were utterly depressed;
14055 Then after a while came the sound of a voice;
All over could be heard the reactions of the British
As they started to discuss in many kinds of expression
How they wished to condemn Modred and the queen
And destroy all the population who had supported Modred.
14060 Most courteous of all Britons, Arthur then called out aloud,
"Sit down quietly, my knights in this assembly,
And then I shall tell you some very strange tales.
Now tomorrow when daylight is sent by our Lord to us,
I wish to be on my way toward entering Britain,
14065 And there I shall kill Modred and burn the queen to death,
And I shall destroy all of them who gave assent to the treason."

THE MYTH OF ARTHUR'S RETURN

Folklore and literature provide examples of a recurrent myth about a leader or hero
who has not really died but is asleep somewhere or in some state of suspended life
and will return to save his people. Evidently, the Bretons and Welsh developed this
myth about Arthur in oral tradition long before it turns up in medieval chronicles.
Geoffrey of Monmouth, Wace, and Layamon, and subsequent writers about Arthur,
including Malory (see p. 434), allude to it with varying degrees of skepticism.

GEOFFREY OF MONMOUTH: *From* History of the Kings of Britain

But also the famous King Arthur himself was mortally wounded. When he was carried off to the island of Avalon to have his wounds treated, he bestowed the crown on his cousin Constantine, the son of Duke Cador in the year 542 after the Incarnation of our lord. May his soul rest in peace.

WACE: *From* Roman de Brut

Arthur, if the story is not false, was mortally wounded; he had himself carried to Avalon to be healed of his wounds. He is still there and the Britons expect him as they say and hope. He'll come from there if he is still alive. Master Wace, who made this book, won't say more about Arthur's end than the prophet Merlin rightly said once upon a time that one would not know whether or not he were dead. The prophet spoke truly: ever since men have asked and shall always ask, I believe, whether he is dead or alive. Truly he had himself taken to Avalon 542 years after the Incarnation. It was a pity that he had no offspring. He left his realm to Constantine, the son of Cador of Cornwall, and asked him to reign until his return.

LAYAMON: *From* Brut

Arthur was mortally wounded, grievously badly;
To him there came a young lad who was from his clan,
He was Cador the Earl of Cornwall's son;
The boy was called Constantine; the king loved him very much.
14270 Arthur gazed up at him, as he lay there on the ground,
And uttered these words with a sorrowing heart:
"Welcome, Constantine; you were Cador's son;
Here I bequeath to you all of my kingdom,
And guard well my Britons all the days of your life
14275 And retain for them all the laws which have been extant in my days
And all the good laws which there were in Uther's days.
And I shall voyage to Avalon, to the fairest of all maidens,
To the Queen Argante, a very radiant elf,
And she will make quite sound every one of my wounds,
14280 Will make me completely whole with her health-giving potions.
And then I shall come back to my own kingdom
And dwell among the Britons with surpassing delight."
After these words there came gliding from the sea
What seemed a short boat, moving, propelled along by the tide
14285 And in it were two women in remarkable attire,
Who took Arthur up at once and immediately carried him
And gently laid him down and began to move off.
And so it had happened, as Merlin said before:

That the grief would be incalculable at the passing of Arthur.
14290 The Britons even now believe that he is alive
And living in Avalon with the fairest of the elf-folk,
And the Britons are still always looking for when Arthur comes
          returning.
Yet once there was a prophet and his name was Merlin:
He spoke his predictions, and his sayings were the truth,
14295 Of how an Arthur once again would come to aid the English.

MARIE DE FRANCE

Much of twelfth-century French literature was composed in England in the Anglo-Norman dialect (see pp. 7–8). Prominent among the earliest poets writing in the French vernacular, who shaped the genres, themes, and styles of later medieval European poetry, is the author who, in an epilogue to her *Fables*, calls herself Marie de France. That signature tells us only that her given name was Marie and that she was born in France, but circumstantial evidence from her writings shows that she spent much of her life in England. A reference to her in a French poem written in England around 1180 speaks of "dame Marie" who wrote "lais" much loved and praised, read, and heard by counts, barons, and knights and indicates that her poems also appealed to ladies who listened to them gladly and joyfully.

Three works can be safely attributed to Marie, probably written in the following order: the *Lais* [English "lay" refers to a short narrative poem in verse], the *Fables*, and *St. Patrick's Purgatory*. Marie's twelve lays are short romances (they range from 118 to 1,184 lines), each of which deals with a single event or crisis in the affairs of noble lovers. In her prologue, Marie tells us that she had heard these *performed*, and in several of the lays she refers to the Breton language and Breton storytellers—that is, professional minstrels from the French province of Brittany or the Celtic parts of Great Britain. Because no sources of Marie's stories have survived, it is not possible to determine the exact nature of the materials she worked from, but they were probably oral and were presented with the accompaniment of a stringed instrument. Marie's lays provide the basis of the genre that came to be known as the "Breton lay." In the prologue Marie dedicates the work to a "noble king," who is most likely to have been Henry II of England, who reigned from 1154 to 1189.

In an epilogue to her *Fables*, Marie claims to have translated the stories into "romance" (i.e., French) from an English version by King Alfred, who translated them from a Latin translation that was translated from the Greek by Aesop, for whom the book is named. No such collection in English or any other vernacular prior to Marie's time is known, but of course fables have been transmitted from time immemorial in oral tradition as well as in translations. In the Middle Ages the classical fables, ascribed to the legendary Aesop, were used for teaching elementary Latin. *St. Patrick's Purgatory* is a verse translation for the laity of a moralistic twelfth-century monastic poem in Latin about a knight's descent to the underworld through an entryway first found by St. Patrick.

The portrait of the author that emerges from the combination of these works is of a highly educated noblewoman, proficient in Latin and English as well as her native French, with ideas of her own and a strong commitment to writing. Scholars have proposed several Maries of the period who fit this description to identify the author. A likely candidate is Marie, abbess of Shaftesbury, an illegitimate daughter of Geoffrey of Anjou and thus half-sister of Henry II. Correct or not, such an identification points to the milieu in which Marie moved and to the kind of audience she was addressing.

Many of Marie's lays contain elements of magic and mystery. Medieval readers would recognize that *Lanval* is about a mortal lover and a fairy bride, although the word "fairy" is not used in the tale. In the Middle Ages fairies were not thought of as the small creatures they became in Elizabethan and later literature. Fairies are supernatural, sometimes dangerous, beings who possess magical powers and inhabit another world. Their realm in some respects resembles the human (fairies have kings and queens), and fairies generally keep to themselves and disappear when humans notice them. But the tales are often about crossovers between the human and fairy worlds. Chaucer's *Wife of Bath's Tale* is such a story. In *Lanval* the female fairy world eclipses King Arthur's chivalric court (which Marie had read about in Wace's *Roman de Brut*) in splendor, riches, and generosity.

With Chrétien de Troyes, Marie is among the twelfth-century writers who made love the means of analyzing the individual's relation to his or her society. The only woman writer known to be among the creators of this literature, Marie explores both female and male desire. Her lays portray different kinds of love relationships, both favorably and unfavorably, with both happy and tragic resolutions. They resist reduction to a pattern.

In fables, animals stand for types of human characters, and a succinct moral is spelled out at the end. Some of Marie's fables, like the two printed here, are exceptional in the way they criticize feudal society and sympathize with the female against the male animals.

Two Middle English versions of Marie's *Lanval* exist, but we prefer to offer a modern verse translation of the original. Marie wrote in eight-syllable couplets, which was the standard form of French narrative verse, employed also by Wace and Chrétien de Troyes. Here is what the beginning of Marie's prologue to the *Lais* says about her view of a writer's duty and, implicitly, of her own talent:

Ki Deu ad duné escïence	He to whom God has given knowledge
E de parler bon' eloquence	And the gift of speaking eloquently,
Ne s'en deit taisir ne celer,	Must not keep silent nor conceal the gift,
Ainz se deit volunters mustrer.	But he must willingly display it.

Lanval[1]

Another lay to you I'll tell,
Of the adventure that befell
A noble vassal whom they call
In the Breton tongue Lanval.
5   Arthur, the brave and courtly king,
At Carlisle was sojourning
Because the Scots and Picts allied
Were ravaging the countryside;
Of Logres° they had crossed the border   *Arthur's kingdom*
10 Where often they caused great disorder.
He had come there with his host
That spring to hold the Pentecost.
He lavished ample patronage
On all his noble baronage—

---

1. The translation is by Alfred David and is based on *Marie de France: Lais*, edited by Alfred Ewert (1947).

15 That is the knights of the Round Table
(In all the world none are so able).
Lands and wives he gave outright
To all his servants save one knight:
That was Lanval; him he forgot.
20 His men disliked him, too; the lot
Were envious of his handsomeness,
His strength, his courage, his largesse.
There were a few who friendship feigned,
But would by no means have complained
25 Had Lanval met some evil fate.
He was a prince of great estate,
But all his personal property
He gave away for amity,
And he got nothing from the king,
30 Nor would he ask for anything.
Now Lanval is much preoccupied,
Gloomy, seeing the darker side.
My lords, please do not think it rare:
A foreigner is filled with care
35 And sadness in a distant land,
Finding no help at any hand.
    The knight of whom I'm telling you,
In the king's service tried and true,
Mounting upon his steed one day,
40 For pleasure's sake set on his way.
Outside the town he went to ride
Alone into the countryside.
He got off by a running brook,
But there his horse trembled and shook.
45 He unlaced the saddle, set it free,
And let it ramble on the lee.
He folded up his riding gown
To make a pillow and lay down.
Much troubled by his luck's declining,
50 He can't see any silver lining.
There as he lay without a clue,
Two damoiselles hove into view,
The fairest he had ever eyed,
Riding along the riverside.
55 Their clothes were in expensive taste,
Close-fitting tunics, tightly laced,
Made of deep-dyed purple wool.
Their faces were most beautiful.
The elder bore a well-made pair
60 Of basins; of purest gold they were.
My lords, I swear that I'm not lying!
The other held a towel for drying.
The two of them went straightaway
Right to the spot where the knight lay.
65 Lanval, the soul of courtesy,
Rose to his feet immediately.

They greeted him first by his name
And told the reason why they came.
"Sir Lanval, our damoiselle,
70 Who is so worthy, wise, and *belle*,[2]
Dispatched us to come after you,
For she has come here with us, too.
We shall bring you safely to her:
See, her pavillion's over there."
75 The knight followed without regard
For the horse left grazing on the sward.
The tent to which they bring the knight
Was fairly pitched, a beauteous sight.
Not Queen Semiramis of yore,
80 Had she been owner of even more
Wealth, power, and *savoir*,°   *wisdom, know-how*
Nor Octavian, the emperor,
Could have afforded to pay for
The right-hand flap of the front door.
85 On top was set an eagle of gold,
The cost of which cannot be told,
Nor of the cords and poles which brace
That structure and hold it in place.
No earthly king could own this tent
90 For any treasure that he spent.
Inside the tent the maiden was:
Not rose nor lily could surpass
Her beauty when they bloom in May.
The sumptuous bed on which she lay
95 Was beautiful. The drapes and tassel,
Sheets and pillows were worth a castle.
The single gown she wore was sheer
And made her shapely form appear.
She'd thrown, in order to keep warm,
100 An ermine stole over her arm,
White fur with the lining dyed
Alexandrian purple. But her side,
Her face, her neck, her bosom
Showed whiter than the hawthorn blossom.
105 The knight moved toward the bed's head.
She asked him to sit down and said,
"Lanval, fair friend, for you I've come,
For you I've traveled far from home.
If you are brave and courteous,
110 You'll be more glad and prosperous
Than ever was emperor or king,
For I love you over everything."
Her loveliness transfixed his gaze.
Love pierced his eyes with its bright rays,
115 Set fire to and scorched his heart.

2. Beautiful. Several words and phrases are in French, partly for the sake of rhyme but also as an indication of the great influence that the French language exercised on English. Most of these words can be found in a modern English dictionary.

He gave fair answer on his part.
"Lady," he said, "if this should be
Your wish (and such joy meant for me),
To have me for your paramour,
120 There's no command, you may be sure,
Wise or foolish, what you will,
Which I don't promise to fulfill.
I'll follow only your behest.
For you I'll give up all the rest."
125 When the lady heard him say
That he would love her in this way,
She bestowed on him her heart
And her body, every part.
Now Lanval is on easy street!
130 Whatever his needs are she will meet:
As a gift to him she granted
He should get whatever he wanted—
Money, as fast as he can spend it,
No matter how much, she will send it.
135 The more largesse he gives, the more
Gold and silver in his store.
Now Sir Lanval is harbored well.
To him then spoke the damoiselle:
"*Ami*,"[3] she said, "please understand,
140 I warn and pray you and command:
You must never tell anyone
About the love that you have won.
The consequence I shall declare:
Should people learn of this affair,
145 You shall never again see me,
Nor have my body in your fee."
He promised her that he would do
Whatever thing she told him to.
He lay beside her on the bed:
150 Now is Lanval well bestead.
He stayed with her all afternoon
Until it would be evening soon
And gladly would have stayed all night
Had she consented that he might.
155 But she told him, "Rise up, *Ami*.
You may no longer stay with me.
Get on your way; I shall remain.
But one thing I will tell you plain:
When you would like to talk to me
160 At any rendezvous that's free
Of blame or of unseemliness,
Where one his true love may possess,
I shall attend you at your will
All your wishes to fulfill."
165 These words gave him great happiness.

---

3. Literally "friend," but used as a term of endearment for a lover. The feminine form is *amie*.

He kissed her, then got up to dress.
The damsels who had brought him there
Gave him expensive clothes to wear.
This world has no such comely squire
170 As Lanval in his new attire.
He was no simpleton or knave.
Water to wash his hands they gave,
Also the towel with which he dried,
And next he was with food supplied.
175 His love ate supper with Lanval,
A thing he did not mind at all.
They served him with great courtesy,
Which he accepted with much glee.
There were many special dishes
180 That the knight found most delicious.
And many times the gallant knight
Kissed his love and held her tight.
After they had cleared the table,
They fetched his horse out of the stable,
185 Harnessed just as it should be.
He had been served luxuriously.
He took his leave, mounted the horse,
And toward town he held his course,
Oftentimes looking to his rear.
190 Lanval was very much in fear
As he went thinking about the maiden,
And his heart with doubts was laden.
What to believe he's all astir;
He thinks he's seen the last of her.
195 Arrived back home, Sir Lanval sees
His men dressed in new liveries.
That night the lavish host he plays,
But no one knows from whence he pays.
In town there is no _chevalier_[4]
200 Who badly needs a place to stay
Whom Lanval doesn't make his guest
And serves him richly of the best.
Lanval gives expensive presents;
Lanval remits the captive's sentence;
205 Lanval puts minstrels in new dress;
Lanval does honors in excess.
There's no stranger nor private friend
On whom Lanval does not spend.
He lives in joy and in delight,
210 Whether it be by day or night.
He sees his lady often, and
Has all the world at his command.
     That same summer, I would say,
After the feast of St. John's Day,
215 Thirty knights made an excursion,

4. Knight. Rhymes with -_ay_ in French pronunciation.

For the sake of their diversion,
To a garden beneath the tower
In which the queen had her bower.
Among that party was Gawain
220 And his cousin, the good Yvain.
Sir Gawain spoke, brave and sincere,
Whom everybody held so dear,
"By God, my lords, we've not done right
By our companion, that good knight—
225 Lanval, so free, courtly, and loyal,
Son of a king who's rich and royal—
To leave that nobleman behind."
And straightway they turn back and find
Sir Lanval at his residence
230 And beg that they might take him thence.
    From a window with fine molding
The queen herself leaned out beholding
(Waited on by damsels three)
King Arthur's festive company.
235 She gazed at Lanval and knew him well.
She called out to one damoiselle
And sent her for her maids-in-waiting,
The fairest and most captivating.
With her into the garden then
240 They went to relax with the men.
Thirty she took along and more,
Down the stairs and out the door.
Rejoiced to have the ladies meet them,
The *chevaliers* advance to greet them.
245 Each girl by a knight's hand is led:
Such pleasant talk is not ill-bred.
Lanval goes off alone and turns
Aside from all the rest. He yearns
To hold his love within his arms,
250 To kiss, embrace, and feel her charms.
The joy of others is less pleasant
To him, his own not being present.
When she perceives him stand alone,
The queen straightway to him has gone
255 To sit beside him and reveals
All the passion that she feels:
"Lanval, I've honored you sincerely,
Have cherished you and loved you dearly.
All my love is at your disposal.
260 What do you say to my proposal?
Your mistress I consent to be;
You should receive much joy from me."
"Lady," he said, "hold me excused
Because your love must be refused.
265 I've served the king for many a day;
My faith to him I won't betray.
Never for love, and not for you,

Would I be to my lord untrue."
Made angry by these words, the queen
270 Insultingly expressed her spleen.
"Lanval," she said, "It's evident
That to such pleasures you have no bent.
Often I have heard men aver
That women are not what you prefer.
275 But you have many pretty boys
With whom you like to take your joys.
Faithless coward of low degree,
My lord was badly served when he
Suffered your person to come near.
280 For that he could lose God, I fear."
      Hearing this, Lanval was dismayed;
His answer was not long delayed.
With spite, as he was much upset,
He spoke what soon he would regret.
285 "My lady queen," was his retort,
"I know nothing about that sport.
But I love one, and she loves me;
From every woman I know of, she
Deserves to bear the prize away.
290 And one more thing I wish to say,
So that you may know it plain:
Each serving-maid in her domain,
The poorest girl of the whole crew,
My lady, is worth more than you
295 In beauty of both figure and face,
In good breeding and bounteous grace."
In tears the queen at once repairs
Back to her chamber up the stairs.
Dolorous she is and mortified
300 To be by him thus villified.
She goes to bed where sick she lies,
Vowing never again to rise,
Unless the king grants her redress
For that which caused her such distress.
305   The king had come back from the wood
Cheerful because the day was good.
To the queen's bedroom he attained;
As soon as she saw him, she complained.
Fallen at his feet, she cried, "Merci![5]
310 Lanval has done me infamy."
To be her lover he had affected.
When his advances were rejected,
He had reviled her shamefully
And boasted he had an *amie*
315 So chic, noble, and proud, he said,
That even her lowliest chambermaid,
The poorest one that might be seen,

---

5. Exclamation appealing for compassion and favor.

Was worthier than she—the queen.
The king grew marvelously wroth,
320 And solemnly he swore an oath:
Unless the knight proved what he'd boasted,
The king would have him hanged or roasted.
Leaving the chamber, the king then
Summoned three of his noblemen.
325 After Lanval they were to go,
Who, feeling enough of grief and woe,
Had returned to his habitation,
Well aware of his situation.
Since he had told of their *amour,*
330 He had lost his love for sure.
In his room alone he languished,
Melancholy and sorely anguished.
He calls his love time and again,
But all his pleadings are in vain.
335 Sighs he utters and complaints,
And from time to time he faints.
A hundred times he cries *merci*
And begs her speak to her *ami.*
He curses both his heart and tongue;
340 A wonder 'tis he lives so long
Without committing suicide.
However much he roared and cried,
Fought with himself and scratched his face,
She would not show him any grace—
345 Even to see her once again.
Alas, how can he bear the pain?
  The king's men have arrived to say
He must to court without delay.
The king had summoned him for this reason:
350 The queen had charged the knight with treason.
Lanval went with them very sadly.
Should he be killed, he'd bear it gladly.
The knight was brought before the king,
Grief-stricken, not saying anything,
355 Like someone in great misery.
The king spoke out indignantly:
"Vassal, you've done lèse-majesté.[6]
You have begun a churlish play,
Me to dishonor and demean
360 And to speak slander of the queen.
It was a foolish boast to call
Your love the noblest one of all,
And her servant—to declare her
Worthier than the queen and fairer.
365   Lanval protested, word for word,
Any dishonor done to his lord
Respecting the queen's accusation

6. Treason against the highest authority.

Of a guilty solicitation.
But of his speech—to give her due—
370 He confessed that it was true.
The mistress he had boasted of
He mourned, for he had lost her love.
Regarding that, he said he'd do
Whatever the court told him to.
375 This put the king in a great fury.
He summoned his knights to act as jury
To tell how to proceed by law
So none might catch him in a flaw.[7]
They obeyed him—the entire lot,
380 Whether they wanted to or not.
They met together to consult
And deemed and judged with this result:
A court day set, Lanval goes free
But must find pledges to guarantee
385 His lord that judgment he'll abide,
Return to court and there be tried
By Arthur's entire baronage,
Not just the palace entourage.[8]
Back to the king the barons bring
390 The judgment of their parleying.
The king demands his sureties,
Thus putting Lanval ill at ease.
A foreigner, he felt chagrin
Since he had neither friend nor kin.
395 Gawain stepped forth and pledged that he
Would stand as Lanval's surety.
And his companions in succession
Each one made the same profession.
The king replied, "He's in your hands
400 At risk to forfeit all your lands
And fiefs, whatever they may be,
Which each of you obtained from me."
The pledges made, the court adjourned,
And Lanval to his place returned.
405 The knights escort him on his way.
They blame and warn him, and they say
To shun excessive melancholy;
And they lay curses on love's folly.
Worried about his mental state,
410 Each day they go investigate
Whether he's taking nourishment
Or to himself is violent.
    On the day that had been set,
All King Arthur's barons met.

415   Attending were the king and queen;
      Pledges brought Lanval on the scene.
      They were all sad on his account—
      A hundred of them I could count
      Who would have done their best to see
420   Him without trial go scot-free,
      For he'd been wrongfully arraigned.
      On the charge, the king maintained,
      And his response, he must be tried:
      And now the barons must decide.
425   To the judgment they go next
      Greatly worried and perplexed,
      Since the noble foreign guest
      In their midst is so hard-pressed.
      Some were willing to condemn
430   To oblige their sovereign.
      The Duke of Cornwall counselled thus:
      "No fault shall be ascribed to us:
      Though some may weep and some may play,
      Justice must take its lawful way.
435   A vassal by the king denounced,
      Whose name—'Lanval'—I heard pronounced,
      Has been accused of felony
      And charged that mischievously he
      To a mistress had pretended
440   And Madame the Queen offended.
      By the faith I owe you duly,
      In this case, should one speak truly,
      The king being the sole adversary,
      No defense were necessary,
445   Save for the sake of his lord's name
      A man must never speak him shame.
      Sir Lanval by his oath must stand,
      And the king quitclaim our land,
      If the knight can guarantee
450   The coming here of his *amie*.
      Should it prove true what he has claimed,
      By which the queen felt so defamed,
      Of that he'll be judged innocent,
      Since he spoke without base intent.
455   But if he cannot prove it so,
      In that case we must let him know,
      All the king's service he must lose
      And banished say his last adieus."
      The knight was sent the court's decree
460   And informed by them that he
      Must summon his *amie* and send her
      To be his witness and defender.
      The knight responded that he could not:
      To his rescue come she would not.
465   To the judges they made report
      That he looked for no support.

The king pressed them to make an ending
And not to keep the queen attending.
   When they came to lay down the law,
470 Two maidens from afar they saw
On two fine steeds, riding apace,
Who were extremely fair of face.
Of purple taffeta a sheath
They wore with nothing underneath.
475 The men took pleasure in the view.
Sir Gawain and three of his crew
Went to Sir Lanval to report
And show the girls coming to court.
Happy, he asked him earnestly
480 If one of them were his *amie*.
He told them that he knew not who
They were, where from, or going to.
The damoiselles rode on withal
Upon their mounts into the hall,
485 And they got off before the dais
There where the king sat at his place.
Their features were of beauty rare;
Their form of speech was debonair:
"King, clear your chambers, if you please,
490 And hang them with silk draperies,
Where my lady may make arrest,
For she wishes to be your guest."
The king gladly gave his consent.
Two of his courtiers he sent
495 To show them to their rooms upstairs.
No more was said of these affairs.
   The king ordered his retinue
To render up their judgment due.
The long procrastination had,
500 He said, made him extremely mad.
"My lord," they answered, "we have acted.
But our attention was distracted
By those ladies we have seen.
But now the court shall reconvene."
505 They reassembled much perturbed,
By too much noise and strife disturbed.
   While they engaged in this debate,
Two damoiselles of high estate—
In silks produced in Phrygia,
510 On mules from Andalusia—
Came riding up the street just then.
This gave great joy to Arthur's men,
Who told each other this must be
The worthy Lanval's remedy.
515 To him there hastened Sir Gawain
With his companions in his train.
"Sir knight," he said, "be of good cheer.
For God's sake speak to us! See here,

Two maidens are approaching us,
520 Most beautiful and decorous;
Surely one must be your *amie*."
Lanval made answer hastily.
He said that he recognized neither.
He didn't know or love them either.
525 Meanwhile the damaiselles had gone
And dismounted before the throne
Where the king was sitting on the dais.
From many there they won great praise
For figure, visage, and complexion.
530 They came much nearer to perfection
Than did the queen, so people said.
The elder was courteous and well-bred.
She spoke her message with much flair:
"King, tell your household to prepare
535 A suite to lodge my lady, who
Is coming here to speak with you."
The king had them conducted where
His men had lodged the previous pair.
As soon as they were from him gone,
540 He told his barons to have done
And give their verdict right away.
There had been far too much delay;
The queen had found it most frustrating
That they so long had kept her waiting.
545   When they were just about to bring
Judgment, a girl was entering
The town, whose beauty, it was clear,
In all the world could have no peer.
She rode upon a milkwhite horse,
550 Which bore her gently down the course.
Its neck and head were shapeliest;
Of all creatures, it was the best.
Splendidly furnished was this mount:
Beneath the heavens, no king or count
555 Could have afforded gear so grand
Unless he sold or pawned his land.
And this is how she was arrayed:
A white linen shift displayed—
There where it was with laces tied—
560 Her slender flanks on either side.
Slim-hipped, her form was *comme il faut*;[9]
Her neck, whiter than branch in snow;
Her eyes were gray; her face was bright;
Her mouth, lovely; nose, set just right;
565 Eyebrows black, forehead fair;
Blonde and curly was her hair.
Golden wire sheds no such ray
As did her locks against the day.

---

9. As required, perfectly correct.

A mantle was around her drawn,
570 A cloak of deep-dyed purple lawn.
A falcon on her wrist sat still;
A greyhound followed her at will.
In town was neither high nor low,
Old man or child, who did not go
575 And line the streets along the way
To watch as she made her entrée.
And as they stood gazing at her,
Her beauty was no laughing matter.
She rode up to the castle slowly.
580 The judges, seeing her, were wholly
Astonished at that spectacle
And held it for a miracle.
The heart of every single knight
Among them warmed with sheer delight.
585 Those who loved Sir Lanval well
Quickly went to him to tell
About the maiden who perchance,
Please God, brought him deliverance.
"Comrade," they said, "here comes one,
590 Who is neither swart nor dun.
Of all women by land and sea,
She is the fairest that may be."
Lanval heard and raised his eye;
He knew her well and gave a sigh.
595 The blood shot up into his cheeks,
And somewhat hastily he speaks:
"In faith," he said, "that's my *amie*!
Now I don't care if they kill me
If but her mercy is assured,
600 For when I see her, I am cured."
The maid rode through the palace door,
So fair came never there before.
In front of Arthur she got down
With the whole company looking on.
605 Softly she let her mantle fall,
The better to be seen by all.
King Arthur, who was most discreet,
To greet her got up on his feet.
In turn, to honor her the rest
610 Offered their service to the guest.
When they had satisfied their gaze
And greatly sung her beauty's praise,
She made her speech in such a way
As she did not intend to stay:
615 "King, I have loved one of your band—
It's Lanval, there you see him stand.
I would not have the man ill-used—
In your court he has been accused
Of lies he spoke. Take it from me,
620 The queen committed perjury;

He never asked her for her love.
As for the things he boasted of,
If I may be his warranty,
Your barons ought to speak him free."
625 The king agreed he would abide
By what they lawfully decide.
Among them there was no dissent;
Lanval was pronounced innocent.
The damoiselle set off again,
630 Though the king asked her to remain.
Outside there stood a marble rock
With steps to make a mounting block,
From which armed men would get astride
When they from court set out to ride.
635 Lanval climbed up on it before
The damoiselle rode out the door.
Swiftly he sprang the horse to straddle
And sat behind her on the saddle.
To Avalon they came away,
640 Which Breton storytellers say
An island is, most ravishing,
There Lanval has gone, vanishing.
No man has heard more of his fate;
I've nothing further to relate.

FINIS

FABLES[1]

The Wolf and the Lamb

This tells of wolf and lamb who drank
Together once along a bank.
The wolf right at the spring was staying
While lambkin down the stream was straying.
5 The wolf then spoke up nastily,
For argumentative was he,
Saying to lamb, with great disdain,
"You give me such a royal pain!"
The lamb made this reply to him,
10 "Pray sir, what's wrong?"—"Are your eyes dim!
You've so stirred up the water here,
I cannot drink my fill, I fear.
I do believe I should be first,
Because I've come here dying of thirst."
15 The little lamb then said to him,
"But sir, 'twas you who drank upstream.
My water comes from you, you see."
"What!" snapped the wolf. "You dare curse me?"
"Sir, I had no intention to!"

1. The translation is by Harriet Spiegel, *Fables* (1987).

20 The wolf replied, "I know what's true.
Your father treated me just so
Here at this spring some time ago—
It's now six months since we were here."
"So why blame me for that affair?
25 I wasn't even born, I guess."
"So what?" the wolf responded next;
"You really are perverse today—
You're not supposed to act this way."
The wolf then grabbed the lamb so small,
30 Chomped through his neck, extinguished all.
    And this is what our great lords do,
The viscounts and the judges too,
With all the people whom they rule:
False charge they make from greed so cruel.
35 To cause confusion they consort
And often summon folk to court.
They strip them clean of flesh and skin,
As the wolf did to the lambkin.

The Wolf and the Sow

Once long ago a wolf strolled down
A path and chanced to come upon
A sow who was with piglets big.
He hastily approached the pig.
5 He'd give her peace, he told the sow,
If quickly she'd bear piglets now—
Her piglet babes he wished to have.
With wisdom, this response she gave:
"My lord, how can you hurry me?'
10 When you, so close to me I see,
I cannot bear my young outright;
I'm so ashamed when in your sight.
Do you not sense the implication?
All women suffer degradation
15 If male hands should dare to touch
At such a time, or even approach!"
With this the wolf hid in retreat
Who'd sought the baby pigs to eat.
The mother pig could now proceed
20 Who through her cleverness was freed.
    All women ought to hear this tale
And should remember it as well:
Merely to avoid a lie,
They should not let their children die!

CELTIC CONTEXTS

The changes European literature underwent during the twelfth and thirteenth centuries are greatly indebted to Celtic influences. The legends about King Arthur and his knights, although they were assimilated to the feudal culture of the Anglo-Normans and transmitted by texts written in Latin, French, and English (see pp. 7–8), were originally products of Celtic myth and legend. The folkloric otherworld elements and the major role played by women in those stories profoundly shaped and colored the literature we now think of as "romance." The French Tristan romances, the romances of Marie de France and Chrétien de Troyes, and even the legends of the Holy Grail could not have been imagined without their Celtic components.

The Celts overran central Europe, Spain, and the British Isles during the first millennium B.C.E. On the Continent and in Great Britain, south of the wall built by the emperor Hadrian (see the map inside the front cover), they were absorbed into the Roman Empire. However, the Celtic vernacular continued to be spoken as the native language, and Ireland never became a Roman province. The Anglo-Saxon invasions in the fifth and early sixth centuries, and the Danish invasions after the eighth, displaced Celtic in England, but Celtic language and culture continued to flourish in Wales (Welsh), in Cornwall (Cornish), across the English Channel in Brittany (Breton), and, of course, in Ireland (Gaelic). While still part of the Roman Empire, Britain and, in consequence, Ireland had been converted to Christianity. As portrayed in the Arthurian legend, the Christian Britons fought against barbaric Germanic invaders. Irish and Welsh missionaries, along with Roman ones, brought about the conversion of the Anglo-Saxons.

The earliest Celtic literature, like that of the Anglo-Saxons, was transmitted orally and little was copied down before the twelfth century. Nevertheless, the surviving monuments indicate its richness and its significance for the development of French and English medieval literature.

EXILE OF THE SONS OF UISLIU

The Old Irish tale of the *Exile of the Sons of Uisliu* [ísh-lu] is believed on linguistic grounds to date back to at least the eighth century, although the earliest text is found in a mid-twelfth-century manuscript known as the Book of the Dun Cow. As is typical in Old Irish narrative, many of the characters' speeches are in verse that is probably even older. The *Exile* is one of several tales leading up to the epic *Táin Bó Cuailnge* (The Cattle Raid of Cooley), which tells of the war between the kingdoms of Connacht and Ulster. Its heroine Derdriu [dér-dru] is one of the passionate and strong-willed women, whose prototypes may have been ancient divinities, for which Old Irish literature is noted. In some respects the triangle of Derdriu, Conchobor [kón-chor: *ch* is guttural as in Scots *loch*], and Noisiu [nói-shu] resembles that of Isolt, King Mark, and Tristan, told in twelfth-century poetic versions by Thomas, who probably wrote for the court of Henry II, and by the Norman Béroul. The Tristan story has antecedents in Irish, Welsh, and Breton. The story of Derdriu is the source of modern plays by William Butler Yeats and John Millington Synge and a novel by James Stephens.[1]

---

1. The translation and notes 2, 4, 6–8 are by Thomas Kinsella, *The Táin* (1969).

Exile of the Sons of Uisliu

What caused the exile of the sons of Uisliu? It is soon told.
The men of Ulster were drinking in the house of Conchobor's storyteller,
Fedlimid mac Daill. Fedlimid's wife was overseeing everything and looking
after them all. She was full with child. Meat and drink were passed round,
and a drunken uproar shook the place. When they were ready to sleep the
woman went to her bed. As she crossed the floor of the house the child
screamed in her womb and was heard all over the enclosure. At that scream
everyone in the house started up, staring at each other. Sencha mac Ailella
said:

"No one move! Bring the woman here. We'll see what caused this noise."
So the woman was brought before them. Her husband Fedlimid said:

> Woman,
> what was that fierce shuddering sound
> furious in your troubled womb?
> The weird uproar at your waist
> hurts the ears of all who hear it.
> My heart trembles at some great terror
> or some cruel injury.

She turned distracted to the seer Cathbad:

> Fair-faced Cathbad, hear me
> —prince, pure, precious crown,
> grown huge in druid spells.
> I can't find the fair words
> that would shed the light of knowledge
> for my husband Fedlimid,
> even though it was the hollow
> of my own womb that howled.
> No woman knows what her womb bears.

Then Cathbad said:

> A woman with twisted yellow tresses,
> green-irised eyes of great beauty
> and cheeks flushed like the foxglove
> howled in the hollow of your womb.
> I say that whiter than the snow
> is the white treasure of her teeth;
> Parthian-red,[2] her lip's luster.
> Ulster's chariot-warriors
> will deal many a blow for her.
> There howled in your troubled womb
> a tall, lovely, long-haired woman.
> Heroes will contend for her,
> high kings beseech on her account;

---

2. A word of doubtful meaning. It has been suggested that it derives from "Parthica"—Parthian leather
dyed scarlet.

then, west of Conchobor's kingdom
a heavy harvest of fighting men.
High queens will ache with envy
to see those lips of Parthian-red
opening on her pearly teeth,
and see her pure perfect body.

Cathbad placed his hand on the woman's belly and the baby wriggled under it.

"Yes," he said, "there is a girl there. Derdriu shall be her name. She will bring evil."

Then the daughter was born and Cathbad said:

Much damage, Derdriu, will follow
your high fame and fair visage:
Ulster in your time tormented,
demure daughter of Fedlimid.

And later, too, jealousy
will dog you, woman like a flame,
and later still—listen well—
the three sons of Uisliu exiled.

Then again, in your lifetime,
a bitter blow struck in Emain.
Remorse later for that ruin
wrought by the great son of Roech;[3]

Fergus exiled out of Ulster
through your fault, fatal woman,
and the much-wept deadly wound
of Fiachna, Conchobor's son.

Your fault also, fatal woman,
Gerrce felled, Illadan's son,
and a crime that no less cries out,
the son of Durthacht, Eogan, struck.

Harsh, hideous deeds done
in anger at Ulster's high king,
and little graves everywhere
—a famous tale, Derdriu.

"Kill the child!" the warriors said.

"No," Conchobor said. "The girl will be taken away tomorrow. I'll have her reared for me. This woman I'll keep to myself."

The men of Ulster didn't dare speak against him.

And so it was done. She was reared by Conchobor and grew into the loveliest woman in all Ireland. She was kept in a place set apart, so that no

---

3. Fergus, a great hero of Ulster. One consequence of this episode is that he will side with Connacht in the war against Ulster.

Ulsterman might see her until she was ready for Conchobor's bed. No one was allowed in the enclosure but her foster-father and her foster-mother, and Leborcham, tall and crooked, a satirist, who couldn't be kept out.[4]

One day in winter, the girl's foster-father was skinning a milk-fed calf on the snow outside, to cook it for her. She saw a raven drinking the blood on the snow. She said to Leborcham:

"I could desire a man who had those three colors there: hair like the raven, cheeks like blood and his body like snow."

"Good luck and success to you!" Leborcham said. "He isn't too far away, but close at hand—Noisiu, Uisliu's son."

"I'll be ill in that case," she said, "until I see him." This man Noisiu was chanting by himself one time near Emain,[5] on the rampart of the stronghold. The chanting of the sons of Uisliu was very sweet. Every cow or beast that heard it gave two-thirds more milk. Any person hearing it was filled with peace and music. Their deeds in war were great also: if the whole province of Ulster came at them at once, they could put their three backs together and not be beaten, their parrying and defense were so fine. Besides this they were swift as hounds in the chase, killing the wild beasts in flight.

While Noisiu was out there alone, therefore, she slipped out quickly to him and made as though to pass him and not recognize him.

"That is a fine heifer going by," he said.

"As well it might," she said. "The heifers grow big where there are no bulls."

"You have the bull of this province all to yourself," he said, "the king of Ulster."

"Of the two," she said, "I'd pick a game young bull like you."

"You couldn't," he said. "There is Cathbad's prophecy."

"Are you rejecting me?"

"I am," he said.

Then she rushed at him and caught the two ears of his head.

"Two ears of shame and mockery," she said, "if you don't take me with you."

"Woman, leave me alone!" he said.

"You will do it," she said, binding him.[6]

A shrill cry escaped him at that. The men of Ulster nearby, when they heard it, started up staring at each other. Uisliu's other sons went out to quieten their brother.

"What is wrong?" they said. "Whatever it is, Ulstermen shouldn't kill each other for it."

He told them what had happened.

"Evil will come of this," the warriors said. "But even so, you won't be shamed as long as we live. We can bring her with us to some other place. There's no king in Ireland who would deny us a welcome."

They decided on that. They left that night, with three times fifty warriors and three times fifty women and the same of hounds and menials. Derdriu was among them, mingling with the rest.

---

4. Through fear that her verses might bring harm. Leborcham, as a satirist, would have more than usual freedom.

5. Emain Macha [év-in-má-cha], Conchobor's royal stronghold.

6. The words "binding him" are not in the text. Her words put Noisiu under bond, or *geasa*, to do what she asked.

They traveled about Ireland for a long time, under protection. Conchobor tried to destroy them often with ambushes and treachery. They went round southwestward from the red cataract at Es Ruaid, and to the promontory at Benn Etair, northeastward. But still the men of Ulster pursued them until they crossed the sea to the land of Alba.[7]

They settled there in the waste places. When the mountain game failed them they turned to take the people's cattle. A day came when the people of Alba went out to destroy them. Then they offered themselves to the king of Alba, who accepted them among his people as hired soldiers. They set their houses on the green. They built their houses so that no one could see in at the girl in case there might be killing on her account.

It happened that a steward came looking around their house early one morning. He saw the couple sleeping. Then he went and woke the king:

"I never found a woman fit for you until today," he said. "There is a woman with Noisiu mac Uislenn who is fit for a king over the Western World. If you have Noisiu killed, you can have the woman to sleep with," the steward said.

"No," the king said, "but go and ask her every day in secret."

He did this, but every day he came she told Noisiu about it that night. Since nothing could be done with her, the sons of Uisliu were ordered into all kinds of traps and dangerous battles to have them killed. But they were so hard in the carnage that nothing came of it.

They tried her one last time. Then the men of Alba were called together to kill them. She told Noisiu this.

"Go away from here," she said. "If you don't leave here this night, you will be dead tomorrow."

So they left that night and reached an island in the sea.

This news reached Ulster.

"Conchobor," everyone said, "it would be shameful if the sons of Uisliu fell in enemy lands by the fault of a bad woman. Better to forgive and protect them—to save their lives and let them come home—than for enemies to lay them low."

"Let them come," Conchobor said. "Send for them, with guarantees of safety."

This news was brought to them.

"It is welcome," they said. "We'll go if Fergus comes as a pledge of safety, and Dubthach and Conchobor's son Cormac."

Then they went down with the messengers to the sea.

So they were brought back to Ireland. But Fergus was stopped through Conchobor's cunning. He was invited to a number of ale feasts and, by an old oath, couldn't refuse. The sons of Uisliu had sworn they would eat no food in Ireland until they ate Conchobor's food first, so they were bound to go on. Fiacha, Fergus's son, went on with them, while Fergus and Dubthach stayed behind. The sons of Uisliu came to the green at Emain. Eogan mac Durthacht, king of Fernmag, was there: he had come to make peace with Conchobor, with whom he had long been at enmity. He had been chosen to kill them. Conchobor's hired soldiers gathered around him so that the sons of Uisliu couldn't reach him. They stood in the middle of the green. The women settled on the ramparts of Emain.

7. This means Britain generally.

Eogan crossed the green with his men. Fergus's son came and stood at Noisiu's side. Eogan welcomed Noisiu with the hard thrust of a great spear that broke his back. Fergus's son grasped Noisiu in his two arms and pulled him down and threw himself across him, and Noisiu was finished off through Fergus's son's body. Then the slaughter broke out all over the green. No one left except by spike of spear or slash of sword. Derdriu was brought over to Conchobor and stood beside him with her hands bound at her back.

Fergus was told of this, and Dubthach and Cormac. They came at once and did mighty deeds. Dubthach killed Maine, Conchobor's son. Fiachna, son of Conchobor's daughter Fedelm, was killed with a single thrust. Fergus killed Traigthrén, Traiglethan's son, and his brother. Conchobor was outraged, and on a day soon afterward battle was joined between them, and three hundred among the men of Ulster fell. Before morning Dubthach had massacred the girls of Ulster and Fergus had burned Emain.

Then they went to Connacht, to Ailill and Medb—not that this was a home for Ulstermen, but that they knew these two would protect them. A full three thousand the exiles numbered. For sixteen years they made sure that weeping and trembling never died away in Ulster; there was weeping and trembling at their hands every single night. She was kept a year by Conchobor. In that time she never gave one smile, nor took enough food or sleep, nor lifted up her head from her knees. If they sent musicians to her, she would say this following poem:

> Sweet in your sight the fiery stride
> of raiding men returned to Emain.
> More nobly strode the three proud.
> sons of Uisliu toward their home:
>
> Noisiu bearing the best mead
> —I would wash him by the fire—
> Ardán, with a stag or a boar,
> Anle, shouldering his load.
>
> The son of Nes, battle-proud,
> drinks, you say, the choicest mead.
> Choicer still—a brimming sea—
> I have taken frequently.
>
> Modest Noisiu would prepare
> a cooking-pit in the forest floor.
> Sweeter then than any meat
> the son of Uisliu's, honey-sweet.
>
> Though for you the times are sweet
> with pipers and with trumpeters,
> I swear today I can't forget
> that I have known far sweeter airs.
>
> Conchobor your king may take delight
> in pipers and in trumpeters
> —I have known a sweeter thing,
> the three sons' triumphant song.

Noisiu's voice a wave roar,
a sweet sound to hear forever;
Ardán's bright baritone;
Anle, the hunter's, high tenor.

Noisiu: his grave-mound is made
and mournfully accompanied.
The highest hero—and I poured
the deadly potion when he died.

His cropped gold fleece I loved,
and fine form—a tall tree.
Alas, I needn't watch today,
nor wait for the son of Uisliu.

I loved the modest, mighty warrior,
loved his fitting, firm desire,
loved him at daybreak as he dressed
by the margin of the forest.

Those blue eyes that melted women,
and menaced enemies, I loved;
then, with our forest journey done,
his chanting through the dark woods.

I don't sleep now,
nor redden my fingernails.
What have I to do with welcomes?
The son of Indel[8] will not come.

I can't sleep,
lying there half the night.
These crowds—I am driven out of my mind.
I can neither eat nor smile.

What use for welcome have I now
with all these nobles crowding Emain?
Comfortless, no peace nor joy,
nor mansion nor pleasant ornament.

If Conchobor tried to soothe her, she would chant this following poem:

Conchobor, what are you thinking, you
that piled up sorrow over woe?
Truly, however long I live,
I cannot spare you much love.

The thing most dear to me in the world,
the very thing I most loved,
your harsh crime took from me.
I will not see him till I die.

8. The mother of the three sons.

I feel his lack, wearily,
the son of Uisliu. All I see—
black boulders on fair flesh
so bright once among the others.

Red-cheeked, sweet as the river-brink;
red-lipped; brows beetle-black;
pearly teeth gleaming bright
with a noble snowy light.

His figure easiest to find,
bright among Alba's fighting-men
—a border made of red gold
matched his handsome crimson cloak.

A soft multitude of jewels
in the satin tunic—itself a jewel:
for decoration, all told,
fifty ounces of light gold.

He carried a gold-hilted sword
and two javelins sharply tipped,
a shield rimmed with yellow gold
with a knob of silver at the middle.

Fergus did an injury
bringing us over the great sea.
How his deeds of valor shrank
when he sold honor for a drink!

If all Ulster's warriors
were gathered on this plain, Conchobor,
I would gladly give them all
for Noisiu, son of Uisliu.

Break my heart no more today.
In a short while I'll be no more.
Grief is heavier than the sea,
if you were but wise, Conchobor.

"What do you see that you hate most?" Conchobor said.

"You, surely," she said, "and Eogan mac Durthacht!"

"Go and live for a year with Eogan, then," Conchobor said.

Then he sent her over to Eogan.

They set out the next day for the fair of Macha. She was behind Eogan in
the chariot. She had sworn that two men alive in the world together would
never have her.

"This is good, Derdriu," Conchobor said. "Between me and Eogan you are
a sheep eyeing two rams."

A big block of stone was in front of her. She let her head be driven against
the stone, and made a mass of fragments of it, and she was dead.

LLUDD AND LLEUELYS

The Welsh tale of *Lludd and Lleuelys* is preserved in a collection of stories contained in two manuscripts, the English titles of which are the White Book of Rhydderch (written ca. 1300–25) and the Red Book of Hergest (ca. 1375–1425). The stories are thought to be much older, some dating back to the latter part of the eleventh century. The traditional but inaccurate title, given to the collection by its nineteenth-century translator, is *The Mabinogion*, a mistake for *Mabinogi*, which has been interpreted as a generic term for the youthful exploits of a hero but probably refers to a group of interconnected traditional stories. A group of the *Mabinogi* deals with characters who are related through crossovers between the human world and a supernatural other-world; *Lludd and Lleuelys*, however, is one of several independent tales. Lludd is among the kings of Britain mentioned by Geoffrey of Monmouth, where he appears (as in the tale below) as a restorer of the walls of London and builder of many towers in that city. Geoffrey says that the city's original name Trinovantum (New Troy), given to it by its eponymous founder Brutus (see pp. 116–18), was changed to Caer Lludd (Lludd's city or stronghold), which became Caer Llundein, and finally London. The tale here has the same etymology for London though nothing about a change of names. Geoffrey probably took the etymology from a Welsh source, and the redactor of *Lludd and Lleuelys* could have taken it from Geoffrey's *History*, which was translated into Welsh. Either way, the etymology is not convincing but typifies a characteristic of both Irish and Welsh literature to explain place names with stories. *Lludd and Lleuelys* gives us an idea of the kind of material Geoffrey of Monmouth must have been dealing with and what he may have chosen to omit. The three plagues of which King Lludd rids his land on the advice of his brother are the stuff of folktales, which Geoffrey may have regarded as too far-fetched to belong in a history book even though he did not draw that line at Merlin's magic.

Ll in Welsh represents a sound that does not exist in English and may be approximated by an aspirated *l* [hl] or simply pronounced as [1]. Welsh *u* may represent short or long *i*. The double consonant *dd* corresponds to *th* in see*the*. Thus Lludd in Welsh is pronounced something like *hleethe*, but when his name is anglicized, it is spelled and pronounced as Lud.

Lludd and Lleuelys[1]

Beli Mawr son of Mynogan had three sons: Lludd, Caswallawn, and Ninniaw; according to the lore about him, Lleuelys was a fourth son. After Beli died, the kingdom of the isle of Britain fell into the hands of Lludd, his eldest son, and Lludd ruled it successfully. He refurbished the walls of London, and surmounted them with countless towers. After that he ordered the citizens to build houses of such quality that no kingdom would have houses as splendid as were in London.

And besides that, he was a good warrior and generous, and he gave food and drink freely to all who sought it, and although he had many forts and cities, he loved this one more than any other, and dwelt there most of the year. For that reason it was called Caer Lludd, and finally Caer Llundein. After the foreign people came it was called Llundein or Londres.

Lludd loved Lleuelys best of all his brothers, for he was a wise and prudent

---

1. The translation is by Patrick K. Ford, *The Mabinogi and Other Medieval Welsh Tales* (1977).

man. When Lleuelys heard that the king of France had died leaving no heir save a daughter, and that he had left his realm in her hands, he came to his brother Lludd seeking counsel and encouragement from him. And not only for personal advantage, but to try to add honor, dignity, and merit to their race, if he could go to the kingdom of France to seek that woman for his wife. His brother agreed with him immediately, and he was pleased with that counsel. Without delay ships were made ready and filled with armed horsemen, and they set out for France. As soon as they disembarked, they sent messengers to announce to the nobles of France the nature of the business they had come to attempt. And by joint counsel of the nobles of France and her princes, the maiden was given to Lleuelys, and the realm's crown along with her. After that, he ruled the land wisely, prudently, and in good fortune, as long as he lived.

After some time had passed, three oppressions came upon the isle of Britain, such that none of the islands had ever seen before. The first of these was the advent of a people called the Coraniaid; so great was their knowledge that there was no utterance over the face of the land—however low it was spoken—that, if the wind met it, they didn't know. For that reason, one could do them no harm.

The second oppression was a cry that resounded every May Day eve above every hearth in Britain; it went through the hearts of men and terrified them so much that men lost their color and their strength, women miscarried, sons and daughters lost their senses and all animals, forests, earth and waters were left barren.

The third oppression was that despite how extensive the preparations and provisions were that were readied in the king's courts, even though it be a year's provision of food and drink, nothing was ever had of it except what could be consumed on the very first night.

The first oppression was evident and clear enough, but no one knew the meaning of the other two oppressions. There was greater hope, therefore, of deliverance from the first than from the second or third.

Lludd, the king, grew anxious and worried then, for he didn't know how he could get relief from those oppressions. He summoned all the nobles of his realm, and sought advice from them concerning what they could do against those oppressions. With the unanimous counsel of the nobles, Lludd son of Beli determined to go to his brother Lleuelys, king of France, for he was a man of great and wise counsel, from whom to seek advice. And they prepared a fleet—secretly and quietly, lest that people or anyone else know the meaning of their business except the king and his counselors. When they had been prepared, Lludd and those whom he had selected went to their ships and began to plough the seas toward France.

When news of that came to Lleuelys—since he did not know the reason for his brother's fleet—he came from the other side to meet him, with an enormous fleet. When Lludd saw that, he left all his ships out at sea except one, and in that he went to meet his brother. The other did the same. After they came together, each put his arms around the other's neck, and they greeted each other with brotherly affection. When Lludd had told his brother the purpose of his mission, Lleuelys said that he knew the meaning of his arrival in those lands. Then they conspired to conduct their business differently, in order that the wind might not carry their speech, lest the Coraniaid know what they said. So Lleuelys had a long brass horn made, and they talked through that. But whatever speech one of them uttered through the horn, only adverse, contrary speech was heard by the other. When Lleuelys saw that, and that a demon was obstructing them and creating turmoil in the horn, he had wine poured into the horn to cleanse it. By virtue of the wine, the demon was driven out.

When their speech was unobstructed, Lleuelys told his brother that he would give him some vermin, and that he should let some of them live to breed, in case by chance that sort of oppression came again. The others he should take and break up in water. That, he affirmed, would be good to destroy the race of Coraniaid, as follows: after he came home to his realm, he should summon all the people together—his people and the Coraniaid people in the same assembly, with the pretext of making peace between them. When they were all together, he should take that charged water and sprinkle it on everyone universally. And he affirmed that that water would poison the Coraniaid people, but that it would neither kill nor injure any of his own people.

"The second oppression in your realm," he said, "is a dragon. A dragon of foreign blood is fighting with him and seeking to overthrow him. Because of that, your dragon utters a horrible scream. This is how you shall be instructed regarding that: after you return home, have the length and width of the island measured. Where you discover the exact center, have that place dug up. Then, have a vatful of the best mead that can be made put into that hole, with a cover of silk brocade over the top of the vat. And then you yourself stand watch, and you will see the dragons fighting in the shape of horrible animals. Finally, they will assume the form of dragons in the air. Last of all, after they cease their violent and fierce battle, being tired, they will fall in the shape of two young pigs onto the coverlet. They will sink the sheet with them and draw it down to the bottom of the vat; they will drink all the mead, and after that they will sleep. Then immediately wrap the cover around them. In the strongest place you can find in your kingdom, deposit them in a stone chest, and hide it in the ground. And as long as they remain in that secure place, no oppression shall visit the isle of Britain from another place."

"The cause of the third oppression," he said, "is a powerful magician who carries off your food, your drink, and your provisions, and by his sorcery and his magic he puts everyone to sleep. And so you yourself must stand guard over your banquets and your feasts. And lest he induce sleep in you, have a vat of cold water at hand, and when sleep weighs you down, get into the vat."

Lludd returned to his country then, and without delay summoned every single one of his own people and the Coraniaid. He broke the vermin up in the water, as Lleuelys had taught him, and sprinkled it generally over everyone. All the Coraniaid folk were destroyed instantly without injury to any of the Britons.

Some time after that, Lludd had the island measured in length and breadth; the middle point was found to be in Oxford. There he had the earth dug up, and in that hole he put a vat full of the best mead that could be made, with a silk veil over the surface. He himself stood watch that night. As he was thus, he could see the dragons fighting. When they grew weary and exhausted, they fell onto the screen and dragged it down with them to the bottom of the vat. After they drank the mead they slept; as they slept, Lludd wrapped the veil about them. In the safest place he could find in Eryri, he secluded them in a stone chest. After that the place was called Dinas Emrys; before that it was known as Dinas Ffaraon Dandde. He was one of three stewards whose hearts broke from sorrow.

Thus was stopped the tempestuous scream that was in the realm.

When that was done, Lludd the king had a feast of great magnitude prepared. When it was ready, he put a vat full of cold water beside him and he personally stood guard. And as he stood there fully armed, about the third watch of the night, he heard much magnificent music and songs of different kinds, and drowsiness driving him to sleep. What he did then—lest his plan be thwarted and he be overcome by sleep—was to leap into the water frequently. At last a man of enormous stature, armed with powerful, heavy weapons, came in carrying a basket. As was his custom, he put all the preparations and the provisions of food and drink into the basket and started out with it. Nothing astounded Lludd more than such a quantity as that fitting into that basket. Thereupon, Lludd the King set out after him, and shouted; "Stop! Stop!" he said, "though you have committed many outrages and have been responsible for many losses before this, you'll do it no more—unless your prowess proves you stronger than I or more valiant."

Immediately, he set the basket on the floor and waited for him. They fought ferociously, until sparks flew from their weapons. Finally, Lludd took hold of him, and fate took care that the victory fell to Lludd, casting the tyrant to the ground beneath him. When he had conquered him through force and violence, the fellow sought protection from him.

"How could I give you protection," said the King, "after how much loss and injury you have perpetrated against me?"

"All the losses I have ever caused you," said the other, "I will restore to you, as well as I have carried them off, and I will not do the like from this moment on, but will be your faithful man henceforth."

And the King accepted that from him. Thus did Lludd ward off the three oppressions from the isle of Britain. From then until the end of his life, Lludd ruled the isle of Britain successfully and peacefully.

This tale is called the Adventure of Lludd and Lleuelys, and so it ends.

ANCRENE RIWLE (RULE FOR ANCHORESSES)

In the twelfth and thirteenth centuries, there was a movement toward a more solitary religious life and a more personal encounter with God. In the early days of Christianity, monasticism had originated with the desert fathers, men who withdrew to the wilderness in order to lead a life of prayer and meditation. The fifth and sixth centuries saw the growth and spread of religious orders, men and women living in religious communities, especially the Benedictine order, founded in Italy by St. Benedict. New orders founded in the eleventh and twelfth centuries—the Cistercians, for example— emphasized a more actively engaged and individual spirituality. The Dominican and

Franciscan orders were not confined to their houses but were preaching and teaching orders who staffed the newly founded universities.

Along with the new orders, a number of both men and women chose to become anchorites or hermits, living alone or in small groups. In his *Rule*, St. Benedict had described such solitaries with a military metaphor: "They have built up their strength and go from the battle line in the ranks of their brothers to the single combat of the desert. Self-reliant now, without the support of another, they are ready with God's help to grapple single-handed with the vices of body and mind." Benedict's battle imagery anticipates the affinities between this solitary kind of spirituality and the literary form of romance, both of which were developing in the twelfth and thirteenth centuries. The individual soul confined in its enclosure fights temptation as Sir Gawain rides out alone in the wilderness to seek the Green Chapel and encounters temptation along the way (see pp. 173–99). The wilderness in romance often contains hermits, who may be genuinely holy men, or they may be enchanters like Archimago, disguised as a holy hermit, in the *Faerie Queene*. The influence of romance on religion and of religion on romance is also strikingly seen in portrayals of Christ as a knight who jousts for the love and salvation of human souls, which is a motif common to *Ancrene Riwle*, William Herebert's poem *What is he, this lordling, that cometh from the fight* (pp. 352–53), and *Piers Plowman* (see pp. 336–38).

Anchoress (the feminine form of *anchorite*, from the Greek *anachoretes*, "one who lives apart") refers to a religious recluse who, unlike a hermit, lives in an enclosure, attached to a church, from which she never emerges. Anchoresses and anchorites might live singly, like Julian of Norwich (see pp. 355–56) or in small groups. *Ancrene Riwle* (ca. 1215) was originally written for three young sisters, who, the author says in an aside in one manuscript, come from a noble family with ample means to support them. The author of *Ancrene Riwle* addresses the sisters in a colloquial, urbane, and personal prose style that distinguishes the guide both as a book of religious instruction and as a literary achievement of Early Middle English.

The excerpt comes from Part 7, to which the author gave the title "Love."[1]

From Ancrene Riwle

[THE PARABLE OF THE CHRIST-KNIGHT]

A lady was completely surrounded by her enemies, her land laid waste, and she herself quite destitute, in a castle of clay. But a powerful king had fallen in love with her so inordinately that to win her love he sent her his messengers, one after another, often many together; he sent her many splendid presents of jewelry, provisions to support her, help from his noble army to hold her castle. She accepted everything as if it meant nothing to her, and was so hard-hearted that he could never come closer to gaining her love. What more do you want? At last he came himself; showed her his handsome face, as the most supremely handsome of men; spoke so very tenderly, and with words so beguiling that they could raise the dead to life; worked many wonders and did great feats before her eyes; showed her his power; told her about his kingdom; offered to make her queen of all that he owned. All this had no effect. Was not this scorn surprising?—for she was never fit to be his maidservant. But because of his gentle nature love had so overcome him that at last he said: "You are under attack, lady, and your enemies are so strong that without my help there is no way that you can escape falling into their

1. The translation is from *Medieval English Prose for Women*, edited by Bella Millett and Jocelyn Wogan-Browne (1990).

hands, and being put to a shameful death after all your troubles. For your love I am willing to take on that fight, and rescue you from those who are seeking your death. But I know for certain that in fighting them I shall receive a mortal wound; and I will accept it gladly in order to win your heart. Now, therefore, I beg you, for the love I am showing towards you, to love me at least when this is done, after my death, although you refused to during my life." This king did just as he had promised; he rescued her from all her enemies, and was himself shamefully ill-treated and at last put to death. But by a miracle he rose from death to life. Would not this lady have a base nature if she did not love him after this above all things?

This king is Jesus, Son of God, who in just this way wooed our soul, which devils had besieged. And he, like a noble suitor, after numerous messengers and many acts of kindness came to prove his love, and showed by feats of arms that he was worthy of love, as was the custom of knights once upon a time. He entered the tournament and, like a bold knight, had his shield pierced through and through in battle for love of his lady. His shield, which hid his divinity, was his dear body, which was stretched out on the cross: broad as a shield above in his extended arms, narrow below, where the one foot (as many people think) was fixed above the other. That this shield has no sides is to signify that his disciples, who should have stood by him and been his sides, all fled from him and abandoned him like strangers, as the Gospel says: *They all abandoned him and fled* [Matthew 26.56]. This shield is given to us against all temptations, as Jeremiah testifies: *You will give your labor as a shield for the heart* [Lamentations 3.65]. This shield not only protects us against all evils, but does still more: it crowns us in heaven. *With the shield of good will* [Psalms 5.12]—"Lord," says David, "you have crowned us with the shield of your good will." He says "shield of good will" because he suffered willingly all that he suffered. Isaiah says: *He was offered because he wished to be* [Isaiah 53.7].

"But, master," you say, "what was the point? Could he not have saved us without so much suffering?" Yes, indeed, very easily; but he did not wish to. Why? To deprive us of any excuse for denying him our love, since he had paid so dearly for it. You buy cheaply what you do not value highly. He bought us with his heart's blood—a higher price was never paid—to attract our love, which cost him so much suffering. In a shield there are three things: the wood, and the leather, and the painted design. So it was in this shield: the wood of the cross, the leather of God's body, the painting of the red blood which colored it so brightly. The third reason, then: after a brave knight's death, his shield is hung high in the church in his memory. Just so this shield—that is, the crucifix—is placed in church where it can be seen most easily, to be a reminder of the knightly prowess of Jesus Christ on the cross. His beloved should see in this how he bought her love: he let his shield be pierced, his side opened up, to show her his heart, to show her openly how deeply he loved her, and to attract her heart.

Middle English Literature in the Fourteenth and Fifteenth Centuries

SIR GAWAIN AND THE GREEN KNIGHT
ca. 1375–1400

The finest Arthurian romance in English survives in only one manuscript, which also contains three religious poems—*Pearl, Patience,* and *Purity*—generally believed to be by the same poet. Nothing is known about the author except what can be inferred from the works. The dialect of the poems locates them in a remote corner of the northwest midlands between Cheshire and Staffordshire, and details of Sir Gawain's journey north show that the author was familiar with the geography of that region. But if author and audience were provincials, *Sir Gawain* and the other poems in the manuscript reveal them to have been highly sophisticated and well acquainted both with the international culture of the high Middle Ages and with ancient native traditions.

Sir Gawain belongs to the so-called Alliterative Revival. After the Norman Conquest, alliterative verse doubtless continued to be recited by oral poets. At the beginning, the *Gawain* poet pretends that this romance is an oral poem and asks the audience to "listen" to a story, which he has "heard." Alliterative verse also continued to appear in Early Middle English texts. Layamon's *Brut* (see pp. 122–24) is the outstanding example. During the late fourteenth century there was a renewed flowering of alliterative poetry, especially in the north and west of Britain, which includes *Piers Plowman* and a splendid poem known as *The Alliterative Morte Darthur*.

The *Gawain* poet's audience evidently valued the kind of alliterative verse that Chaucer's Parson caricatures as "Rum-Ram-Ruf by lettre" (see p. 312, line 43). They would also have understood archaic poetic diction surviving from Old English poetry such as *athel* (noble) and words of Scandinavian origin such as *skete* (quickly) and *skifted* (alternated). They were well acquainted with French Arthurian romances and the latest fashions in clothing, armor, and castle building. In making Sir Gawain, Arthur's sister's son, the preeminent knight of the Round Table, the poet was faithful to an older tradition. The thirteenth-century French romances, which in the next century became the main sources of Sir Thomas Malory, had made Sir Lancelot the best of Arthur's knights and Lancelot's adultery with Queen Guinevere the central event on which the fate of Arthur's kingdom turns. In *Sir Gawain* Lancelot is only one name in a list of Arthur's knights. Arthur is still a youth, and the court is in its springtime. Sir Gawain epitomizes this first blooming of Arthurian chivalry, and the reputation of the court rests upon his shoulders.

Ostensibly, Gawain's head is what is at stake. The main plot belongs to a type folklorists classify as the "Beheading Game," in which a supernatural challenger offers to let his head be cut off in exchange for a return blow. The earliest written occurrence of this motif is in the Middle Irish tale of *Bricriu's Feast*. The *Gawain* poet could have encountered it in several French romances as well as in oral tradition. But the outcome of the game here does not turn only on the champion's courage as it does in

Bricriu's Feast. The *Gawain* poet has devised another series of tests for the hero that link the beheading with his truth, the emblem of which is the pentangle—a five-pointed star—displayed on Gawain's coat of arms and shield. The word *truth* in Middle English, as in Chaucer's ballade of that name (see p. 315), means not only what it still means now—a fact, belief, or idea held to be "true"—but what is conveyed by the old-fashioned variant from the same root: *troth*—that is, faith pledged by one's word and owed to a lord, a spouse, or anyone who puts someone else under an obligation. In this respect, Sir Gawain is being measured against a moral and Christian ideal of chivalry. Whether or not he succeeds in that contest is a question carefully left unresolved—perhaps as a challenge for the reader.

The poet has framed Gawain's adventure with references in the first and last stanzas to what are called the "Brutus books," the foundation stories that trace the origins of Rome and Britain back to the destruction of Troy. See, for example, the selection from Geoffrey of Monmouth's *History of the Kings of Britain* (p. 115). A cyclical sense of history as well as of the cycles of the seasons of the year, the generations of humankind, and of individual lives runs through *Sir Gawain and the Green Knight*.

The poem is written in stanzas that contain a group of alliterative lines (the number of lines in a stanza varies). The line is longer and does not contain a fixed number or pattern of stresses like the classical alliterative measure of Old English poetry. Each stanza closes with five short lines rhyming *a b a b a*. The first of these rhyming lines contains just two (rarely three) syllables and is called the "bob"; the four three-stress lines that follow are called the "wheel." For details on alliterative verse, see "Old and Middle English Prosody" (pp. 19–20). The opening stanza is printed below in Middle English with an interlinear translation. The alliterating sounds, which should be stressed, have been italicized.

Sithen the *sege* and the *assaut* was *sesed* at Troye,
After the siege and the assault was ceased at Troy,

The *borgh brittened* and *brent* to *brondes* and askes,
The city crumbled and burned to brands and ashes,

The *tulk* that the *trammes* of *tresoun* ther wroght
The man who the plots of treason there wrought

Was *tried* for his *tricherie*, the *trewest* on erthe.
Was tried for his treachery, the truest on earth.

Hit was *Ennias* the *athel* and his *highe* kynde,
It was Aeneas the noble and his high race,

That sithen *depreced provinces*, and *patrounes* bicome
Who after subjugated provinces, and lords became

Welneghe of al the *wele* in the *west* iles.
Wellnigh of all the wealth in the west isles.

Fro *riche* Romulus to Rome *ricchis* hym swythe,
Then noble Romulus to Rome proceeds quickly,

With gret *bobbaunce* that *burghe* he *biges* upon fyrst
With great pride that city he builds at first

And *nevenes* hit his aune *nome*, as hit *now* hat;
And names it his own name, as it now is called;

Ticius to Tuskan and *t*eldes bigynnes,
Ticius (goes) to Tuscany and houses begins,

Langaberde in Lumbardie *l*yftes up homes,
Longbeard in Lombardy raises up homes,

And *f*er over the French *f*lod, Felix Brutus
And far over the English Channel, Felix Brutus

On mony *b*onkkes ful *b*rode Bretayn he settes
On many banks very broad Brittain he sets

> Wyth wynne,
> With joy,

Where *w*erre and *w*rake and *w*onder
Where war and revenge and wondrous happenings

Bi sythes has wont therinne,
On occasions have dwelled therein

And oft *b*othe *b*lysse and *b*lunder
And often both joy and strife

Ful *s*kete has *s*kyfted *s*ynne.
Very swiftly have alternated since.

Sir Gawain and the Green Knight[1]

Part 1

Since the siege and the assault was ceased at Troy,
The walls breached and burnt down to brands and ashes,
The knight that had knotted the nets of deceit
Was impeached for his perfidy, proven most true,[2]
5   It was high-born Aeneas and his haughty race
That since prevailed over provinces, and proudly reigned
Over well-nigh all the wealth of the West Isles.[3]
Great Romulus[4] to Rome repairs in haste;
With boast and with bravery builds he that city
10   And names it with his own name, that it now bears.
Ticius to Tuscany, and towers raises,
Langobard[5] in Lombardy lays out homes,
And far over the French Sea, Felix Brutus[6]
On many broad hills and high Britain he sets,
15   most fair.

1. The Modern English translation is by Marie Borroff (1967), who has reproduced the alliterative meter of the original as well as the "bob" and "wheel," the five-line rhyming group that concludes each of the long irregular stanzas.
2. The treacherous knight is Aeneas, who was a traitor to his city, Troy, according to medieval tradition, but Aeneas was actually tried ("impeached") by the Greeks for his refusal to hand over to them his sister Polyxena.
3. Perhaps Western Europe.
4. The legendary founder of Rome is here given Trojan ancestry, like Aeneas.
5. The reputed founder of Lombardy. "Ticius": not otherwise known.
6. Great-grandson of Aeneas and legendary founder of Britain; not elsewhere given the name Felix (Latin "happy").

Where war and wrack and wonder
By shifts have sojourned there,
And bliss by turns with blunder
In that land's lot had share.

20 And since this Britain was built by this baron great,
Bold boys bred there, in broils delighting,
That did in their day many a deed most dire.
More marvels have happened in this merry land
Than in any other I know, since that olden time,
25 But of those that here built, of British kings,
King Arthur was counted most courteous of all,
Wherefore an adventure I aim to unfold,
That a marvel of might some men think it,
And one unmatched among Arthur's wonders.
30 If you will listen to my lay but a little while,
As I heard it in hall, I shall hasten to tell
                    anew.
                As it was fashioned featly
                In tale of derring-do,
35   And linked in measures meetly
                By letters tried and true.

This king lay at Camelot[7] at Christmastide;
Many good knights and gay his guests were there,
Arrayed of the Round Table[8] rightful brothers,
40 With feasting and fellowship and carefree mirth.
There true men contended in tournaments many,
Joined there in jousting these gentle knights,
Then came to the court for carol-dancing,
For the feast was in force full fifteen days,
45 With all the meat and the mirth that men could devise,
Such gaiety and glee, glorious to hear,
Brave din by day, dancing by night.
High were their hearts in halls and chambers,
These lords and these ladies, for life was sweet.
50 In peerless pleasures passed they their days,
The most noble knights known under Christ,
And the loveliest ladies that lived on earth ever,
And he the comeliest king, that that court holds,
For all this fair folk in their first age
55   were still.
                Happiest of mortal kind,
                King noblest famed of will;
                You would now go far to find
                So hardy a host on hill.

60 While the New Year was new, but yesternight come,
This fair folk at feast two-fold was served,

7. Capital of Arthur's kingdom, presumably located in southwest England or southern Wales.
8. According to legend, Merlin made the Round Table after a dispute broke out among Arthur's knights about precedence: it seated one hundred knights. The table described in the poem is not round.

When the king and his company were come in together,
The chanting in chapel achieved and ended.
Clerics and all the court acclaimed the glad season,
65 Cried Noel anew, good news to men;
Then gallants gather gaily, hand-gifts to make,
Called them out clearly, claimed them by hand,
Bickered long and busily about those gifts.
Ladies laughed aloud, though losers they were,
70 And he that won was not angered, as well you will know.[9]
All this mirth they made until meat was served;
When they had washed them worthily, they went to their seats,
The best seated above, as best it beseemed,
Guenevere the goodly queen gay in the midst
75 On a dais well-decked and duly arrayed
With costly silk curtains, a canopy over,
Of Toulouse and Turkestan tapestries rich,
All broidered and bordered with the best gems
Ever brought into Britain, with bright pennies
80   to pay.
                        Fair queen, without a flaw,
                        She glanced with eyes of grey.
                        A seemlier that once he saw,
                        In truth, no man could say.

85 But Arthur would not eat till all were served;
So light was his lordly heart, and a little boyish;
His life he liked lively—the less he cared
To be lying for long, or long to sit,
So busy his young blood, his brain so wild.
90 And also a point of pride pricked him in heart,
For he nobly had willed, he would never eat
On so high a holiday, till he had heard first
Of some fair feat or fray some far-borne tale,
Of some marvel of might, that he might trust,
95 By champions of chivalry achieved in arms,
Or some suppliant came seeking some single knight
To join with him in jousting, in jeopardy each
To lay life for life, and leave it to fortune
To afford him on field fair hap or other.
100 Such is the king's custom, when his court he holds
At each far-famed feast amid his fair host
                        so dear.
                        The stout king stands in state
                        Till a wonder shall appear;
105   He leads, with heart elate,
                        High mirth in the New Year.

So he stands there in state, the stout young king,
Talking before the high table of trifles fair.
There Gawain the good knight by Guenevere sits,

9. The dispensing of New Year's gifts seems to have involved kissing.

110 With Agravain à la dure main on his other side,
    Both knights of renown, and nephews of the king.
    Bishop Baldwin above begins the table,
    And Yvain, son of Urien, ate with him there.
    These few with the fair queen were fittingly served;
115 At the side-tables[1] sat many stalwart knights.
    Then the first course comes, with clamor of trumpets
    That were bravely bedecked with bannerets bright,
    With noise of new drums and the noble pipes.
    Wild were the warbles that wakened that day
120 In strains that stirred many strong men's hearts.
    There dainties were dealt out, dishes rare,
    Choice fare to choose, on chargers so many
    That scarce was there space to set before the people
    The service of silver, with sundry meats,
125   on cloth.
                Each fair guest freely there
                Partakes, and nothing loth;
                Twelve dishes before each pair;
                Good beer and bright wine both.

130 Of the service itself I need say no more,
    For well you will know no tittle was wanting.
    Another noise and a new was well-nigh at hand,
    That the lord might have leave his life to nourish;
    For scarce were the sweet strains still in the hall,
135 And the first course come to that company fair,
    There hurtles in at the hall-door an unknown rider,
    One the greatest on ground in growth of his frame:
    From broad neck to buttocks so bulky and thick,
    And his loins and his legs so long and so great,
140 Half a giant on earth I hold him to be,
    But believe him no less than the largest of men,
    And that the seemliest in his stature to see, as he rides,
    For in back and in breast though his body was grim,
    His waist in its width was worthily small,
145 And formed with every feature in fair accord
                          was he.
                Great wonder grew in hall
                At his hue most strange to see,
                For man and gear and all
150   Were green as green could be.

    And in guise all of green, the gear and the man:
    A coat cut close, that clung to his sides,
    And a mantle to match, made with a lining
    Of furs cut and fitted—the fabric was noble,
155 Embellished all with ermine, and his hood beside,
    That was loosed from his locks, and laid on his shoulders.

1. The side tables are on the main floor and run along the walls at a right angle with the high table, which
is on a dais.

With trim hose and tight, the same tint of green,
His great calves were girt, and gold spurs under
He bore on silk bands that embellished his heels,
160 And footgear well-fashioned, for riding most fit.
And all his vesture verily was verdant green;
Both the bosses on his belt and other bright gems
That were richly ranged on his raiment noble
About himself and his saddle, set upon silk,
165 That to tell half the trifles would tax my wits,
The butterflies and birds embroidered thereon
In green of the gayest, with many a gold thread.
The pendants of the breast-band, the princely crupper,
And the bars of the bit were brightly enameled;
170 The stout stirrups were green, that steadied his feet,
And the bows of the saddle and the side-panels both,
That gleamed all and glinted with green gems about.
The steed he bestrides of that same green
                so bright.
175   A green horse great and thick;
           A headstrong steed of might;
           In broidered bridle quick,
           Mount matched man aright.

Gay was this goodly man in guise all of green,
180 And the hair of his head to his horse suited;
Fair flowing tresses enfold his shoulders;
A beard big as a bush on his breast hangs,
That with his heavy hair, that from his head falls,
Was evened all about above both his elbows,
185 That half his arms thereunder were hid in the fashion
Of a king's cap-à-dos,[2] that covers his throat.
The mane of that mighty horse much to it like,
Well curled and becombed, and cunningly knotted
With filaments of fine gold amid the fair green,
190 Here a strand of the hair, here one of gold;
His tail and his foretop twin in their hue,
And bound both with a band of a bright green
That was decked adown the dock with dazzling stones
And tied tight at the top with a triple knot
195 Where many bells well burnished rang bright and clear.
Such a mount in his might, nor man on him riding,
None had seen, I dare swear, with sight in that hall
                so grand.
           As lightning quick and light
200   He looked to all at hand;
           It seemed that no man might
           His deadly dints withstand.

Yet had he no helm, nor hauberk neither,
Nor plate, nor appurtenance appending to arms,

---

2. The word *capados* occurs in this form in Middle English only in *Gawain*, here and in line 572. The translator has interpreted it, as the poet apparently did also, as *cap-à-dos*, i.e., a garment covering its wearer "from head to back," on the model of *cap-à-pie*, "from head to foot," referring to armor.

205   Nor shaft pointed sharp, nor shield for defense,
      But in his one hand he had a holly bob
      That is goodliest in green when groves are bare,
      And an ax in his other, a huge and immense,
      A wicked piece of work in words to expound:
210   The head on its haft was an ell long;
      The spike of green steel, resplendent with gold;
      The blade burnished bright, with a broad edge,
      As well shaped to shear as a sharp razor;
      Stout was the stave in the strong man's gripe,
215   That was wound all with iron to the weapon's end,
      With engravings in green of goodliest work.
      A lace lightly about, that led to a knot,
      Was looped in by lengths along the fair haft,
      And tassels thereto attached in a row,
220   With buttons of bright green, brave to behold.
      This horseman hurtles in, and the hall enters;
      Riding to the high dais, recked he no danger;
      Not a greeting he gave as the guests he o'erlooked,
      Nor wasted his words, but "Where is," he said,
225   "The captain of this crowd? Keenly I wish
      To see that sire with sight, and to himself say
                  my say."
             He swaggered all about
             To scan the host so gay;
230   He halted, as if in doubt
             Who in that hall held sway.

      There were stares on all sides as the stranger spoke,
      For much did they marvel what it might mean
      That a horseman and a horse should have such a hue,
235   Grow green as the grass, and greener, it seemed,
      Than green fused on gold more glorious by far.
      All the onlookers eyed him, and edged nearer,
      And awaited in wonder what he would do,
      For many sights had they seen, but such a one never,
240   So that phantom and faerie the folk there deemed it,
      Therefore chary of answer was many a champion bold,
      And stunned at his strong words stone-still they sat
      In a swooning silence in the stately hall.
      As all were slipped into sleep, so slackened their speech
245   apace.
             Not all, I think, for dread,
             But some of courteous grace
             Let him who was their head
             Be spokesman in that place.

250   Then Arthur before the high dais that entrance beholds,
      And hailed him, as behooved, for he had no fear,
      And said "Fellow, in faith you have found fair welcome;
      The head of this hostelry Arthur am I;
      Leap lightly down, and linger, I pray,
255   And the tale of your intent you shall tell us after."

"Nay, so help me," said the other, "He that on high sits,
To tarry here any time, 'twas not mine errand;
But as the praise of you, prince, is puffed up so high,
And your court and your company are counted the best,
260 Stoutest under steel-gear on steeds to ride,
Worthiest of their works the wide world over,
And peerless to prove in passages of arms,
And courtesy here is carried to its height,
And so at this season I have sought you out.
265 You may be certain by the branch that I bear in hand
That I pass here in peace, and would part friends,
For had I come to this court on combat bent,
I have a hauberk at home, and a helm beside,
A shield and a sharp spear, shining bright,
270 And other weapons to wield, I ween well, to boot,
But as I willed no war, I wore no metal.
But if you be so bold as all men believe,
You will graciously grant the game that I ask
                              by right."
275   Arthur answer gave
                 And said, "Sir courteous knight,
                 If contest bare you crave,
                 You shall not fail to fight."

"Nay, to fight, in good faith, is far from my thought;
280 There are about on these benches but beardless children,
Were I here in full arms on a haughty steed,
For measured against mine, their might is puny.
And so I call in this court for a Christmas game,
For 'tis Yule and New Year, and many young bloods about;
285 If any in this house such hardihood claims,
Be so bold in his blood, his brain so wild,
As stoutly to strike one stroke for another,
I shall give him as my gift this gisarme noble,
This ax, that is heavy enough, to handle as he likes,
290 And I shall bide the first blow, as bare as I sit.
If there be one so wilful my words to assay,
Let him leap hither lightly, lay hold of this weapon;
I quitclaim it forever, keep it as his own,
And I shall stand him a stroke, steady on this floor,
295 So you grant me the guerdon to give him another,
                              sans blame.
                 In a twelvemonth and a day
                 He shall have of me the same;
                 Now be it seen straightway
300   Who dares take up the game."

If he astonished them at first, stiller were then
All that household in hall, the high and the low;
The stranger on his green steed stirred in the saddle,
And roisterously his red eyes he rolled all about,
305 Bent his bristling brows, that were bright green,

Wagged his beard as he watched who would arise.
When the court kept its counsel he coughed aloud,
And cleared his throat coolly, the clearer to speak:
"What, is this Arthur's house," said that horseman then,
310 "Whose fame is so fair in far realms and wide?
Where is now your arrogance and your awesome deeds,
Your valor and your victories and your vaunting words?
Now are the revel and renown of the Round Table
Overwhelmed with a word of one man's speech,
315 For all cower and quake, and no cut felt!"
With this he laughs so loud that the lord grieved;
The blood for sheer shame shot to his face,
          and pride.
          With rage his face flushed red,
320   And so did all beside.
          Then the king as bold man bred
          Toward the stranger took a stride.

And said "Sir, now we see you will say but folly,
Which whoso has sought, it suits that he find.
325 No guest here is aghast of your great words.
Give to me your gisarme, in God's own name,
And the boon you have begged shall straight be granted."
He leaps to him lightly, lays hold of his weapon;
The green fellow on foot fiercely alights.
330 Now has Arthur his ax, and the haft grips,
And sternly stirs it about, on striking bent.
The stranger before him stood there erect,
Higher than any in the house by a head and more;
With stern look as he stood, he stroked his beard,
335 And with undaunted countenance drew down his coat,
No more moved nor dismayed for his mighty dints
Than any bold man on bench had brought him a drink
          of wine.
          Gawain by Guenevere
340   Toward the king doth now incline:
          "I beseech, before all here,
          That this melee may be mine."

"Would you grant me the grace," said Gawain to the king,
"To be gone from this bench and stand by you there,
345 If I without discourtesy might quit this board,
And if my liege lady misliked it not,
I would come to your counsel before your court noble.
For I find it not fit, as in faith it is known,
When such a boon is begged before all these knights,
350 Though you be tempted thereto, to take it on yourself
While so bold men about upon benches sit,
That no host under heaven is hardier of will,
Nor better brothers-in-arms where battle is joined;
I am the weakest, well I know, and of wit feeblest;
355 And the loss of my life would be least of any;

That I have you for uncle is my only praise;
My body, but for your blood, is barren of worth;
And for that this folly befits not a king,
And 'tis I that have asked it, it ought to be mine,
360 And if my claim be not comely let all this court judge,
in sight."
       The court assays the claim,
       And in counsel all unite
       To give Gawain the game
365   And release the king outright.

Then the king called the knight to come to his side,
And he rose up readily, and reached him with speed,
Bows low to his lord, lays hold of the weapon,
And he releases it lightly, and lifts up his hand,
370 And gives him God's blessing, and graciously prays
That his heart and his hand may be hardy both.
"Keep, cousin," said the king, "what you cut with this day,
And if you rule it aright, then readily, I know,
You shall stand the stroke it will strike after."
375 Gawain goes to the guest with gisarme in hand,
And boldly he bides there, abashed not a whit.
Then hails he Sir Gawain, the horseman in green:
"Recount we our contract, ere you come further.
First I ask and adjure you, how you are called
380 That you tell me true, so that trust it I may."
"In good faith," said the good knight, "Gawain am I
Whose buffet befalls you, what'er betide after,
And at this time twelvemonth take from you another
With what weapon you will, and with no man else
385   alive."
       The other nods assent:
       "Sir Gawain, as I may thrive,
       I am wondrous well content
       That you this dint shall drive."

390 "Sir Gawain," said the Green Knight, "By God, I rejoice
That your fist shall fetch this favor I seek,
And you have readily rehearsed, and in right terms,
Each clause of my covenant with the king your lord,
Save that you shall assure me, sir, upon oath,
395 That you shall seek me yourself, wheresoever you deem
My lodgings may lie, and look for such wages
As you have offered me here before all this host."
"What is the way there?" said Gawain. "Where do you dwell?
I heard never of your house, by him that made me,
400 Nor I know you not, knight, your name nor your court.
But tell me truly thereof, and teach me your name,
And I shall fare forth to find you, so far as I may,
And this I say in good certain, and swear upon oath."
"That is enough in New Year, you need say no more,"
405 Said the knight in the green to Gawain the noble,

"If I tell you true, when I have taken your knock,
And if you handily have hit, you shall hear straightway
Of my house and my home and my own name;
Then follow in my footsteps by faithful accord.
410 And if I spend no speech, you shall speed the better:
You can feast with your friends, nor further trace
                    my tracks.
            Now hold your grim tool steady
            And show us how it hacks."
415   "Gladly, sir; all ready,"
            Says Gawain; he strokes the ax.

The Green Knight upon ground girds him with care:
Bows a bit with his head, and bares his flesh:
His long lovely locks he laid over his crown,
420 Let the naked nape for the need be shown.
Gawain grips to his ax and gathers it aloft—
The left foot on the floor before him he set—
Brought it down deftly upon the bare neck,
That the shock of the sharp blow shivered the bones
425 And cut the flesh cleanly and clove it in twain,
That the blade of bright steel bit into the ground.
The head was hewn off and fell to the floor;
Many found it at their feet, as forth it rolled;
The blood gushed from the body, bright on the green,
430 Yet fell not the fellow, nor faltered a whit,
But stoutly he starts forth upon stiff shanks,
And as all stood staring he stretched forth his hand,
Laid hold of his head and heaved it aloft,
Then goes to the green steed, grasps the bridle,
435 Steps into the stirrup, bestrides his mount,
And his head by the hair in his hand holds,
And as steady he sits in the stately saddle
As he had met with no mishap, nor missing were
                    his head.
440   His bulk about he haled,
            That fearsome body that bled;
            There were many in the court that quailed
            Before all his say was said.

For the head in his hand he holds right up;
445 Toward the first on the dais directs he the face,
And it lifted up its lids, and looked with wide eyes,
And said as much with its mouth as now you may hear:
"Sir Gawain, forget not to go as agreed,
And cease not to seek till me, sir, you find,
450 As you promised in the presence of these proud knights.
To the Green Chapel come, I charge you, to take
Such a dint as you have dealt—you have well deserved
That your neck should have a knock on New Year's morn.
The Knight of the Green Chapel I am well-known to many,
455 Wherefore you cannot fail to find me at last;

Therefore come, or be counted a recreant knight."
With a roisterous rush he flings round the reins,
Hurtles out at the hall-door, his head in his hand,
That the flint-fire flew from the flashing hooves.
460 Which way he went, not one of them knew
Nor whence he was come in the wide world
                so fair.
          The king and Gawain gay
          Make game of the Green Knight there,
465   Yet all who saw it say
          'Twas a wonder past compare.

Though high-born Arthur at heart had wonder,
He let no sign be seen, but said aloud
To the comely queen, with courteous speech,
470 "Dear dame, on this day dismay you no whit;
Such crafts are becoming at Christmastide,
Laughing at interludes, light songs and mirth,
Amid dancing of damsels with doughty knights.
Nevertheless of my meat now let me partake,
475 For I have met with a marvel, I may not deny."
He glanced at Sir Gawain, and gaily he said,
"Now, sir, hang up your ax,[3] that has hewn enough,"
And over the high dais it was hung on the wall
That men in amazement might on it look,
480 And tell in true terms the tale of the wonder.
Then they turned toward the table, these two together,
The good king and Gawain, and made great feast,
With all dainties double, dishes rare,
With all manner of meat and minstrelsy both,
485 Such happiness wholly had they that day
                in hold.
          Now take care, Sir Gawain,
          That your courage wax not cold
          When you must turn again
490   To your enterprise foretold.

Part 2

This adventure had Arthur of handsels[4] first
When young was the year, for he yearned to hear tales;
Though they wanted for words when they went to sup,
Now are fierce deeds to follow, their fists stuffed full.
495 Gawain was glad to begin those games in hall,
But if the end be harsher, hold it no wonder,
For though men are merry in mind after much drink,
A year passes apace, and proves ever new:
First things and final conform but seldom.
500 And so this Yule to the young year yielded place,

3. A colloquial expression equivalent to "bury the hatchet," but here with an appropriate literal sense also.
4. New Year's presents.

And each season ensued at its set time;
After Christmas there came the cold cheer of Lent,
When with fish and plainer fare our flesh we reprove;
But then the world's weather with winter contends:
505   The keen cold lessens, the low clouds lift;
Fresh falls the rain in fostering showers
On the face of the fields; flowers appear.
The ground and the groves wear gowns of green;
Birds build their nests, and blithely sing
510   That solace of all sorrow with summer comes
                ere long.
           And blossoms day by day
           Bloom rich and rife in throng;
           Then every grove so gay
515   Of the greenwood rings with song.

And then the season of summer with the soft winds,
When Zephyr sighs low over seeds and shoots;
Glad is the green plant growing abroad,
When the dew at dawn drops from the leaves,
520   To get a gracious glance from the golden sun.
But harvest with harsher winds follows hard after,
Warns him to ripen well ere winter comes;
Drives forth the dust in the droughty season,
From the face of the fields to fly high in air.
525   Wroth winds in the welkin wrestle with the sun,
The leaves launch from the linden and light on the ground,
And the grass turns to gray, that once grew green.
Then all ripens and rots that rose up at first,
And so the year moves on in yesterdays many,
530   And winter once more, by the world's law,
                draws nigh.
           At Michaelmas° the moon   *September 29*
           Hangs wintry pale in sky;
           Sir Gawain girds him soon
535   For travails yet to try.

Till All-Hallows' Day[5] with Arthur he dwells,
And he held a high feast to honor that knight
With great revels and rich, of the Round Table.
Then ladies lovely and lords debonair
540   With sorrow for Sir Gawain were sore at heart;
Yet they covered their care with countenance glad:
Many a mournful man made mirth for his sake.
So after supper soberly he speaks to his uncle
Of the hard hour at hand, and openly says,
545   "Now, liege lord of my life, my leave I take;
The terms of this task too well you know—
To count the cost over concerns me nothing.
But I am bound forth betimes to bear a stroke

---

5. All Saints' Day, November 1.

From the grim man in green, as God may direct."
550 Then the first and foremost came forth in throng:
Yvain and Eric and others of note,
Sir Dodinal le Sauvage, the Duke of Clarence,
Lionel and Lancelot and Lucan the good,
Sir Bors and Sir Bedivere, big men both,
555 And many manly knights more, with Mador de la Porte.
All this courtly company comes to the king
To counsel their comrade, with care in their hearts;
There was much secret sorrow suffered that day
That one so good as Gawain must go in such wise
560 To bear a bitter blow, and his bright sword
                    lay by.
              He said, "Why should I tarry?"
              And smiled with tranquil eye;
              "In destinies sad or merry,
565   True men can but try."

He dwelt there all that day, and dressed in the morning;
Asked early for his arms, and all were brought.
First a carpet of rare cost was cast on the floor
Where much goodly gear gleamed golden bright;
570 He takes his place promptly and picks up the steel,
Attired in a tight coat of Turkestan silk
And a kingly cap-à-dos, closed at the throat,
That was lavishly lined with a lustrous fur.
Then they set the steel shoes on his sturdy feet
575 And clad his calves about with comely greaves,
And plate well-polished protected his knees,
Affixed with fastenings of the finest gold.
Fair cuisses enclosed, that were cunningly wrought,
His thick-thewed thighs, with thongs bound fast,
580 And massy chain-mail of many a steel ring
He bore on his body, above the best cloth,
With brace burnished bright upon both his arms,
Good couters and gay, and gloves of plate,
And all the goodly gear to grace him well
585   that tide.
              His surcoat blazoned bold;
              Sharp spurs to prick with pride;
              And a brave silk band to hold
              The broadsword at his side.

590 When he had on his arms, his harness was rich,
The least latchet or loop laden with gold;
So armored as he was, he heard a mass,
Honored God humbly at the high altar.
Then he comes to the king and his comrades-in-arms,
595 Takes his leave at last of lords and ladies,
And they clasped and kissed him, commending him to Christ.
By then Gringolet was girt with a great saddle
That was gaily agleam with fine gilt fringe,
New-furbished for the need with nail-heads bright;

600 The bridle and the bars bedecked all with gold;
The breast-plate, the saddlebow, the side-panels both,
The caparison and the crupper accorded in hue,
And all ranged on the red the resplendent studs
That glittered and glowed like the glorious sun.
605 His helm now he holds up and hastily kisses,
Well-closed with iron clinches, and cushioned within;
It was high on his head, with a hasp behind,
And a covering of cloth to encase the visor,
All bound and embroidered with the best gems
610 On broad bands of silk, and bordered with birds,
Parrots and popinjays preening their wings,
Lovebirds and love-knots as lavishly wrought
As many women had worked seven winters thereon,
                              entire.
615   The diadem costlier yet
                That crowned that comely sire,
                With diamonds richly set,
                That flashed as if on fire.

Then they showed forth the shield, that shone all red,
620 With the pentangle[6] portrayed in purest gold.
About his broad neck by the baldric he casts it,
That was meet for the man, and matched him well.
And why the pentangle is proper to that peerless prince
I intend now to tell, though detain me it must.
625 It is a sign by Solomon sagely devised
To be a token of truth, by its title of old,
For it is a figure formed of five points,
And each line is linked and locked with the next
For ever and ever, and hence it is called
630 In all England, as I hear, the endless knot.
And well may he wear it on his worthy arms,
For ever faithful five-fold in five-fold fashion
Was Gawain in good works, as gold unalloyed,
Devoid of all villainy, with virtues adorned
635   in sight.
                On shield and coat in view
                He bore that emblem bright,
                As to his word most true
                And in speech most courteous knight.

6. A five-pointed star, formed by five lines that are drawn without lifting the pencil from the paper, supposed to have mystical significance; as Solomon's sign (line 625) it was enclosed in a circle.

640   And first, he was faultless in his five senses,
      Nor found ever to fail in his five fingers,
      And all his fealty was fixed upon the five wounds
      That Christ got on the cross, as the creed tells;
      And wherever this man in melee took part,
645   His one thought was of this, past all things else,
      That all his force was founded on the five joys⁷
      That the high Queen of heaven had in her child.
      And therefore, as I find, he fittingly had
      On the inner part of his shield her image portrayed,
650   That when his look on it lighted, he never lost heart.
      The fifth of the five fives followed by this knight
      Were beneficence boundless and brotherly love
      And pure mind and manners, that none might impeach,
      And compassion most precious—these peerless five
655   Were forged and made fast in him, foremost of men.
      Now all these five fives were confirmed in this knight,
      And each linked in other, that end there was none,
      And fixed to five points, whose force never failed,
      Nor assembled all on a side, nor asunder either,
660   Nor anywhere at an end, but whole and entire
      However the pattern proceeded or played out its course.
      And so on his shining shield shaped was the knot
      Royally in red gold against red gules,
      That is the peerless pentangle, prized of old
665   in lore.
             Now armed is Gawain gay,
             And bears his lance before,
             And soberly said good day,
             He thought forevermore.

670   He struck his steed with the spurs and sped on his way
      So fast that the flint-fire flashed from the stones.
      When they saw him set forth they were sore aggrieved,
      And all sighed softly, and said to each other,
      Fearing for their fellow, "Ill fortune it is
675   That you, man, must be marred, that most are worthy!
      His equal on this earth can hardly be found;
      To have dealt more discreetly had done less harm,
      And have dubbed him a duke, with all due honor.
      A great leader of lords he was like to become,
680   And better so to have been than battered to bits,
      Beheaded by an elf-man,° for empty pride!   *supernatural being*
      Who would credit that a king could be counseled so,
      And caught in a cavil in a Christmas game?"
      Many were the warm tears they wept from their eyes
685   When goodly Sir Gawain was gone from the court
                   that day.
             No longer he abode,

---

7. Most commonly in Middle English literature, the Annunciation, Nativity, Resurrection, Ascension, and Assumption, although the list varies. These overlap but are not identical with the Five Joyful Mysteries of the Rosary, which were not formally established until the 16th century.

> But speedily went his way
> Over many a wandering road,
> 690   As I heard my author say.

Now he rides in his array through the realm of Logres,[8]
Sir Gawain, God knows, though it gave him small joy!
All alone must he lodge through many a long night
Where the food that he fancied was far from his plate;
695 He had no mate but his mount, over mountain and plain,
Nor man to say his mind to but almighty God,
Till he had wandered well-nigh into North Wales.
All the islands of Anglesey he holds on his left,
And follows, as he fares, the fords by the coast,
700 Comes over at Holy Head, and enters next
The Wilderness of Wirral[9]—few were within
That had great good will toward God or man.
And earnestly he asked of each mortal he met
If he had ever heard aught of a knight all green,
705 Or of a Green Chapel, on ground thereabouts,
And all said the same, and solemnly swore
They saw no such knight all solely green
                         in hue.
               Over country wild and strange
710   The knight sets off anew;
               Often his course must change
               Ere the Chapel comes in view.

Many a cliff must he climb in country wild;
Far off from all his friends, forlorn must he ride;
715 At each strand or stream where the stalwart passed
'Twere a marvel if he met not some monstrous foe,
And that so fierce and forbidding that fight he must.
So many were the wonders he wandered among
That to tell but the tenth part would tax my wits.
720 Now with serpents he wars, now with savage wolves,
Now with wild men of the woods, that watched from the rocks,
Both with bulls and with bears, and with boars besides,
And giants that came gibbering from the jagged steeps.
Had he not borne himself bravely, and been on God's side,
725 He had met with many mishaps and mortal harms.
And if the wars were unwelcome, the winter was worse,
When the cold clear rains rushed from the clouds
And froze before they could fall to the frosty earth.
Near slain by the sleet he sleeps in his irons
730 More nights than enough, among naked rocks,
Where clattering from the crest the cold stream ran
And hung in hard icicles high overhead.
Thus in peril and pain and predicaments dire
He rides across country till Christmas Eve,

8. One of the names for Arthur's kingdom.
9. Gawain went from Camelot north to the northern coast of Wales, opposite the islands of Anglesey; there he turned east across the Dee to the
forest of Wirral in Cheshire.

735   our knight.
       And at that holy tide
       He prays with all his might
       That Mary may be his guide
       Till a dwelling comes in sight.

740 By a mountain next morning he makes his way
     Into a forest fastness, fearsome and wild;
     High hills on either hand, with hoar woods below,
     Oaks old and huge by the hundred together.
     The hazel and the hawthorn were all intertwined
745 With rough raveled moss, that raggedly hung,
     With many birds unblithe upon bare twigs
     That peeped most piteously for pain of the cold.
     The good knight on Gringolet glides thereunder
     Through many a marsh and mire, a man all alone;
750 He feared for his default, should he fail to see
     The service of that Sire that on that same night
     Was born of a bright maid, to bring us his peace.
     And therefore sighing he said, "I beseech of Thee, Lord,
     And Mary, thou mildest mother so dear,
755 Some harborage where haply I might hear mass
     And Thy matins tomorrow—meekly I ask it,
     And thereto proffer and pray my pater and ave
                   and creed."
              He said his prayer with sighs,
760   Lamenting his misdeed;
              He crosses himself, and cries
              On Christ in his great need.

     No sooner had Sir Gawain signed himself thrice
     Than he was ware, in the wood, of a wondrous dwelling,
765 Within a moat, on a mound, bright amid boughs
     Of many a tree great of girth that grew by the water—
     A castle as comely as a knight could own,
     On grounds fair and green, in a goodly park
     With a palisade of palings planted about
770 For two miles and more, round many a fair tree.
     The stout knight stared at that stronghold great
     As it shimmered and shone amid shining leaves,
     Then with helmet in hand he offers his thanks
     To Jesus and Saint Julian,¹ that are gentle both,
775 That in courteous accord had inclined to his prayer;
     "Now fair harbor," said he, "I humbly beseech!"
     Then he pricks his proud steed with the plated spurs,
     And by chance he has chosen the chief path
     That brought the bold knight to the bridge's end
780   in haste.
              The bridge hung high in air;
              The gates were bolted fast;

---

1. Patron saint of hospitality.

The walls well-framed to bear
The fury of the blast.

785   The man on his mount remained on the bank
     Of the deep double moat that defended the place.
     The wall went in the water wondrous deep,
     And a long way aloft it loomed overhead.
     It was built of stone blocks to the battlements' height,
790   With corbels under cornices in comeliest style;
     Watch-towers trusty protected the gate,
     With many a lean loophole, to look from within:
     A better-made barbican the knight beheld never.
     And behind it there hoved a great hall and fair:
795   Turrets rising in tiers, with tines° at their tops,   *spikes*
     Spires set beside them, splendidly long,
     With finials° well-fashioned, as filigree fine.   *gable ornaments*
     Chalk-white chimneys over chambers high
     Gleamed in gay array upon gables and roofs;
800   The pinnacles in panoply, pointing in air,
     So vied there for his view that verily it seemed
     A castle cut of paper for a king's feast.[2]
     The good knight on Gringolet thought it great luck
     If he could but contrive to come there within
805   To keep the Christmas feast in that castle fair

and bright.
There answered to his call
A porter most polite;
From his station on the wall

810

He greets the errant knight.

     "Good sir," said Gawain, "Wouldst go to inquire
     If your lord would allow me to lodge here a space?"
     "Peter!" said the porter, "For my part, I think
     So noble a knight will not want for a welcome!"
815   Then he bustles off briskly, and comes back straight,
     And many servants beside, to receive him the better.
     They let down the drawbridge and duly went forth
     And kneeled down on their knees on the naked earth
     To welcome this warrior as best they were able.
820   They proffered him passage—the portals stood wide—
     And he beckoned them to rise, and rode over the bridge.
     Men steadied his saddle as he stepped to the ground,
     And there stabled his steed many stalwart folk.
     Now come the knights and the noble squires
825   To bring him with bliss into the bright hall.
     When his high helm was off, there hied forth a throng
     Of attendants to take it, and see to its care;
     They bore away his brand° and his blazoned shield;   *sword*
     Then graciously he greeted those gallants each one,
830   And many a noble drew near, to do the knight honor.

---

2. A common table decoration at feasts.

All in his armor into hall he was led,
Where fire on a fair hearth fiercely blazed.
And soon the lord himself descends from his chamber
To meet with good manners the man on his floor.
835 He said, "To this house you are heartily welcome:
What is here is wholly yours, to have in your power
                                   and sway."
                    "Many thanks," said Sir Gawain;
                    "May Christ your pains repay!"
840   The two embrace amain
                    As men well met that day.

Gawain gazed on the host that greeted him there,
And a lusty fellow he looked, the lord of that place:
A man of massive mold, and of middle age;
845 Broad, bright was his beard, of a beaver's hue,
Strong, steady his stance, upon stalwart shanks,
His face fierce as fire, fair-spoken withal,
And well-suited he seemed in Sir Gawain's sight
To be a master of men in a mighty keep.
850 They pass into a parlor, where promptly the host
Has a servant assigned him to see to his needs,
And there came upon his call many courteous folk
That brought him to a bower where bedding was noble,
With heavy silk hangings hemmed all in gold,
855 Coverlets and counterpanes curiously wrought,
A canopy over the couch, clad all with fur,
Curtains running on cords, caught to gold rings,
Woven rugs on the walls of eastern work,
And the floor, under foot, well-furnished with the same.
860 Amid light talk and laughter they loosed from him then
His war-dress of weight and his worthy clothes.
Robes richly wrought they brought him right soon,
To change there in chamber and choose what he would.
When he had found one he fancied, and flung it about,
865 Well-fashioned for his frame, with flowing skirts,
His face fair and fresh as the flowers of spring,
All the good folk agreed, that gazed on him then,
His limbs arrayed royally in radiant hues,
That so comely a mortal never Christ made
870   as he.
                    Whatever his place of birth,
                    It seemed he well might be
                    Without a peer on earth
                    In martial rivalry.

875 A couch before the fire, where fresh coals burned,
They spread for Sir Gawain splendidly now
With quilts quaintly stitched, and cushions beside,
And then a costly cloak they cast on his shoulders
Of bright silk, embroidered on borders and hems,
880 With furs of the finest well-furnished within,
And bound about with ermine, both mantle and hood;

And he sat at that fireside in sumptuous estate
And warmed himself well, and soon he waxed merry.
Then attendants set a table upon trestles broad,
885   And lustrous white linen they laid thereupon,
A saltcellar of silver, spoons of the same.
He washed himself well and went to his place,
Men set his fare before him in fashion most fit.
There were soups of all sorts, seasoned with skill,
890   Double-sized servings, and sundry fish,
Some baked, some breaded, some broiled on the coals,
Some simmered, some in stews, steaming with spice,
And with sauces to sup that suited his taste.
He confesses it a feast with free words and fair;
895   They requite him as kindly with courteous jests,
well-sped.
"Tonight you fast[3] and pray;
Tomorrow we'll see you fed."
The knight grows wondrous gay
900   As the wine goes to his head.

Then at times and by turns, as at table he sat,
They questioned him quietly, with queries discreet,
And he courteously confessed that he comes from the court,
And owns him of the brotherhood of high-famed Arthur,
905   The right royal ruler of the Round Table,
And the guest by their fireside is Gawain himself,
Who has happened on their house at that holy feast.
When the name of the knight was made known to the lord,
Then loudly he laughed, so elated he was,
910   And the men in that household made haste with joy
To appear in his presence promptly that day,
That of courage ever-constant, and customs pure,
Is pattern and paragon, and praised without end:
Of all knights on earth most honored is he.
915   Each said solemnly aside to his brother,
"Now displays of deportment shall dazzle our eyes
And the polished pearls of impeccable speech;
The high art of eloquence is ours to pursue
Since the father of fine manners is found in our midst.
920   Great is God's grace, and goodly indeed,
That a guest such as Gawain he guides to us here
When men sit and sing of their Savior's birth
in view.
With command of manners pure
925   He shall each heart imbue;
Who shares his converse, sure,
Shall learn love's language true."

When the knight had done dining and duly arose,
The dark was drawing on; the day nigh ended.

---

3. Gawain is said to be "fasting" because the meal, although elaborate, consisted only of fish dishes, appropriate to a fasting day.

930 Chaplains in chapels and churches about
Rang the bells aright, reminding all men
Of the holy evensong of the high feast.
The lord attends alone: his fair lady sits
In a comely closet, secluded from sight.
935 Gawain in gay attire goes thither soon;
The lord catches his coat, and calls him by name,
And has him sit beside him, and says in good faith
No guest on God's earth would he gladlier greet.
For that Gawain thanked him; the two then embraced
940 And sat together soberly the service through.
Then the lady, that longed to look on the knight,
Came forth from her closet with her comely maids.
The fair hues of her flesh, her face and her hair
And her body and her bearing were beyond praise,
945 And excelled the queen herself, as Sir Gawain thought.
He goes forth to greet her with gracious intent;
Another lady led her by the left hand
That was older than she—an ancient, it seemed,
And held in high honor by all men about.
950 But unlike to look upon, those ladies were,
For if the one was fresh, the other was faded:
Bedecked in bright red was the body of one;
Flesh hung in folds on the face of the other;
On one a high headdress, hung all with pearls;
955 Her bright throat and bosom fair to behold,
Fresh as the first snow fallen upon hills;
A wimple the other one wore round her throat;
Her swart chin well swaddled, swathed all in white;
Her forehead enfolded in flounces of silk
960 That framed a fair fillet, of fashion ornate,
And nothing bare beneath save the black brows,
The two eyes and the nose, the naked lips,
And they unsightly to see, and sorrily bleared.
A beldame, by God, she may well be deemed,
965   of pride!
            She was short and thick of waist,
               Her buttocks round and wide;
            More toothsome, to his taste,
               Was the beauty by her side.

970 When Gawain had gazed on that gay lady,
With leave of her lord, he politely approached;
To the elder in homage he humbly bows;
The lovelier he salutes with a light embrace.
He claims a comely kiss, and courteously he speaks;
975 They welcome him warmly, and straightway he asks
To be received as their servant, if they so desire.
They take him between them; with talking they bring him
Beside a bright fire; bade then that spices
Be freely fetched forth, to refresh them the better,
980 And the good wine therewith, to warm their hearts.

The lord leaps about in light-hearted mood;
Contrives entertainments and timely sports;
Takes his hood from his head and hangs it on a spear,
And offers him openly the honor thereof
985   Who should promote the most mirth at that Christmas feast;
"And I shall try for it, trust me—contend with the best,
Ere I go without my headgear by grace of my friends!"
Thus with light talk and laughter the lord makes merry
To gladden the guest he had greeted in hall
990   that day.
            At the last he called for light
            The company to convey;
            Gawain says goodnight
            And retires to bed straightway.

995   On the morn when each man is mindful in heart
That God's son was sent down to suffer our death,
No household but is blithe for his blessed sake;
So was it there on that day, with many delights.
Both at larger meals and less they were lavishly served
1000   By doughty lads on dais, with delicate fare;
The old ancient lady, highest she sits;
The lord at her left hand leaned, as I hear;
Sir Gawain in the center, beside the gay lady,
Where the food was brought first to that festive board,
1005   And thence throughout the hall, as they held most fit,
To each man was offered in order of rank.
There was meat, there was mirth, there was much joy,
That to tell all the tale would tax my wits,
Though I pained me, perchance, to paint it with care;
1010   But yet I know that our knight and the noble lady
Were accorded so closely in company there,
With the seemly solace of their secret words,
With speeches well-sped, spotless and pure,
That each prince's pastime their pleasures far
1015   outshone.
            Sweet pipes beguile their cares,
            And the trumpet of martial tone;
            Each tends his affairs
            And those two tend their own.

1020   That day and all the next, their disport was noble,
And the third day, I think, pleased them no less;
The joys of St. John's Day° were justly praised,   *December 27*
And were the last of their like for those lords and ladies;
Then guests were to go in the gray morning,
1025   Wherefore they whiled the night away with wine and with mirth,
Moved to the measures of many a blithe carol;
At last, when it was late, took leave of each other,
Each one of those worthies, to wend his way.
Gawain bids goodbye to his goodly host
1030   Who brings him to his chamber, the chimney beside,

And detains him in talk, and tenders his thanks
And holds it an honor to him and his people
That he has harbored in his house at that holy time
And embellished his abode with his inborn grace.
1035 "As long as I may live, my luck is the better
That Gawain was my guest at God's own feast!"
"Noble sir," said the knight, "I cannot but think
All the honor is your own—may heaven requite it!
And your man to command I account myself here
1040 As I am bound and beholden, and shall be, come
what may."
The lord with all his might
Entreats his guest to stay;
Brief answer makes the knight:
1045 Next morning he must away.

Then the lord of that land politely inquired
What dire affair had forced him, at that festive time,
So far from the king's court to fare forth alone
Ere the holidays wholly had ended in hall.
1050 "In good faith," said Gawain, "you have guessed the truth:
On a high errand and urgent I hastened away,
For I am summoned by myself to seek for a place—
I would I knew whither, or where it might be!
Far rather would I find it before the New Year
1055 Than own the land of Logres, so help me our Lord!
Wherefore, sir, in friendship this favor I ask,
That you say in sober earnest, if something you know
Of the Green Chapel, on ground far or near,
Or the lone knight that lives there, of like hue of green.
1060 A certain day was set by assent of us both
To meet at that landmark, if I might last,
And from now to the New Year is nothing too long,
And I would greet the Green Knight there, would God but allow,
More gladly, by God's Son, than gain the world's wealth!
1065 And I must set forth to search, as soon as I may;
To be about the business I have but three days
And would as soon sink down dead as desist from my errand."
Then smiling said the lord, "Your search, sir, is done,
For we shall see you to that site by the set time.
1070 Let Gawain grieve no more over the Green Chapel;
You shall be in your own bed, in blissful ease,
All the forenoon, and fare forth the first of the year,
And make the goal by midmorn, to mind your affairs,
no fear!
1075 Tarry till the fourth day
And ride on the first of the year.
We shall set you on your way;
It is not two miles from here."

Then Gawain was glad, and gleefully he laughed:
1080 "Now I thank you for this, past all things else!

Now my goal is here at hand! With a glad heart I shall
Both tarry, and undertake any task you devise."
Then the host seized his arm and seated him there;
Let the ladies be brought, to delight them the better,
1085 And in fellowship fair by the fireside they sit;
So gay waxed the good host, so giddy his words,
All waited in wonder what next he would say.
Then he stares on the stout knight, and sternly he speaks:
"You have bound yourself boldly my bidding to do—
1090 Will you stand by that boast, and obey me this once?"
"I shall do so indeed," said the doughty knight;
"While I lie in your lodging, your laws will I follow."
"As you have had," said the host, "many hardships abroad
And little sleep of late, you are lacking, I judge,
1095 Both in nourishment needful and nightly rest;
You shall lie abed late in your lofty chamber
Tomorrow until mass, and meet then to dine
When you will, with my wife, who will sit by your side
And talk with you at table, the better to cheer
1100   our guest.
                  A-hunting I will go
                  While you lie late and rest."
                  The knight, inclining low,
                  Assents to each behest.

1105 "And Gawain," said the good host, "agree now to this:
Whatever I win in the woods I will give you at eve,
And all you have earned you must offer to me;
Swear now, sweet friend, to swap as I say,
Whether hands, in the end, be empty or better."
1110 "By God," said Sir Gawain, "I grant it forthwith!
If you find the game good, I shall gladly take part."
"Let the bright wine be brought, and our bargain is done,"
Said the lord of that land—the two laughed together.
Then they drank and they dallied and doffed all constraint,
1115 These lords and these ladies, as late as they chose,
And then with gaiety and gallantries and graceful adieux
They talked in low tones, and tarried at parting.
With compliments comely they kiss at the last;
There were brisk lads about with blazing torches
1120 To see them safe to bed, for soft repose
                  long due.
                  Their covenants, yet awhile,
                  They repeat, and pledge anew;
                  That lord could well beguile
1125   Men's hearts, with mirth in view.

Part 3

Long before daylight they left their beds;
Guests that wished to go gave word to their grooms,
And they set about briskly to bind on saddles,

Tend to their tackle, tie up trunks.
1130 The proud lords appear, appareled to ride,
Leap lightly astride, lay hold of their bridles,
Each one on his way to his worthy house.
The liege lord of the land was not the last
Arrayed there to ride, with retainers many;
1135 He had a bite to eat when he had heard mass;
With horn to the hills he hastens amain.
By the dawn of that day over the dim earth,
Master and men were mounted and ready.
Then they harnessed in couples the keen-scented hounds,
1140 Cast wide the kennel-door and called them forth,
Blew upon their bugles bold blasts three;
The dogs began to bay with a deafening din,
And they quieted them quickly and called them to heel,
A hundred brave huntsmen, as I have heard tell,
1145   together.
            Men at stations meet;
            From the hounds they slip the tether;
            The echoing horns repeat,
            Clear in the merry weather.

1150 At the clamor of the quest, the quarry trembled;
Deer dashed through the dale, dazed with dread;
Hastened to the high ground, only to be
Turned back by the beaters, who boldly shouted.
They harmed not the harts, with their high heads,
1155 Let the bucks go by, with their broad antlers,
For it was counted a crime, in the close season,
If a man of that demesne should molest the male deer.
The hinds were headed up, with "Hey!" and "Ware!"
The does with great din were driven to the valleys.
1160 Then you were ware, as they went, of the whistling of arrows;
At each bend under boughs the bright shafts flew
That tore the tawny hide with their tapered heads.
Ah! they bray and they bleed, on banks they die,
And ever the pack pell-mell comes panting behind;
1165 Hunters with shrill horns hot on their heels—
Like the cracking of cliffs their cries resounded.
What game got away from the gallant archers
Was promptly picked off at the posts below
When they were harried on the heights and herded to the streams:
1170 The watchers were so wary at the waiting-stations,
And the greyhounds so huge, that eagerly snatched,
And finished them off as fast as folk could see
                    with sight.
            The lord, now here, now there,
1175   Spurs forth in sheer delight.
            And drives, with pleasures rare,
            The day to the dark night.

So the lord in the linden-wood leads the hunt
And Gawain the good knight in gay bed lies,

1180 Lingered late alone, till daylight gleamed,
Under coverlet costly, curtained about.
And as he slips into slumber, slyly there comes
A little din at his door, and the latch lifted,
And he holds up his heavy head out of the clothes;

1185 A corner of the curtain he caught back a little
And waited there warily, to see what befell.
Lo! it was the lady, loveliest to behold,
That drew the door behind her deftly and still
And was bound for his bed—abashed was the knight,

1190 And laid his head low again in likeness of sleep;
And she stepped stealthily, and stole to his bed,
Cast aside the curtain and came within,
And set herself softly on the bedside there,
And lingered at her leisure, to look on his waking.

1195 The fair knight lay feigning for a long while,
Conning in his conscience what his case might
Mean or amount to—a marvel he thought it.
But yet he said within himself, "More seemly it were
To try her intent by talking a little."

1200 So he started and stretched, as startled from sleep,
Lifts wide his lids in likeness of wonder,
And signs himself swiftly, as safer to be,
                                                with art.
                        Sweetly does she speak
1205   And kindling glances dart,
                        Blent white and red on cheek
                        And laughing lips apart.

"Good morning, Sir Gawain," said that gay lady,
"A slack sleeper you are, to let one slip in!

1210 Now you are taken in a trice—a truce we must make,
Or I shall bind you in your bed, of that be assured."
Thus laughing lightly that lady jested.
"Good morning, good lady," said Gawain the blithe,
"Be it with me as you will; I am well content!

1215 For I surrender myself, and sue for your grace,
And that is best, I believe, and behooves me now."
Thus jested in answer that gentle knight.
"But if, lovely lady, you misliked it not,
And were pleased to permit your prisoner to rise,

1220 I should quit this couch and accoutre me better,
And be clad in more comfort for converse here."
"Nay, not so, sweet sir," said the smiling lady;
"You shall not rise from your bed; I direct you better:
I shall hem and hold you on either hand,

1225 And keep company awhile with my captive knight.
For as certain as I sit here, Sir Gawain you are,
Whom all the world worships, whereso you ride;
Your honor, your courtesy are highest acclaimed
By lords and by ladies, by all living men;

1230 And lo! we are alone here, and left to ourselves:
My lord and his liegemen are long departed,

The household asleep, my handmaids too,
The door drawn, and held by a well-driven bolt,
And since I have in this house him whom all love,
1235   I shall while the time away with mirthful speech
                    at will.
                My body is here at hand,
                Your each wish to fulfill;
                Your servant to command
1240   I am, and shall be still."

"In good faith," said Gawain, "my gain is the greater,
Though I am not he of whom you have heard;
To arrive at such reverence as you recount here
I am one all unworthy, and well do I know it.
1245   By heaven, I would hold me the happiest of men
If by word or by work I once might aspire
To the prize of your praise—'twere a pure joy!"
"In good faith, Sir Gawain," said that gay lady,
"The well-proven prowess that pleases all others,
1250   Did I scant or scout it, 'twere scarce becoming.
But there are ladies, believe me, that had liefer far
Have thee here in their hold, as I have today,
To pass an hour in pastime with pleasant words,
Assuage all their sorrows and solace their hearts,
1255   Than much of the goodly gems and gold they possess.
But laud be to the Lord of the lofty skies,
For here in my hands all hearts' desire
                    doth lie."
                Great welcome got he there
1260   From the lady who sat him by;
                With fitting speech and fair
                The good knight makes reply.

"Madame," said the merry man, "Mary reward you!
For in good faith, I find your beneficence noble.
1265   And the fame of fair deeds runs far and wide,
But the praise you report pertains not to me,
But comes of your courtesy and kindness of heart."
"By the high Queen of heaven" (said she) "I count it not so,
For were I worth all the women in this world alive,
1270   And all wealth and all worship were in my hands,
And I should hunt high and low, a husband to take,
For the nurture I have noted in thee, knight, here,
The comeliness and courtesies and courtly mirth—
And so I had ever heard, and now hold it true—
1275   No other on this earth should have me for wife."
"You are bound to a better man," the bold knight said,
"Yet I prize the praise you have proffered me here,
And soberly your servant, my sovereign I hold you,
And acknowledge me your knight, in the name of Christ."
1280   So they talked of this and that until 'twas nigh noon,
And ever the lady languishing in likeness of love.

With feat words and fair he framed his defense,
For were she never so winsome, the warrior had
The less will to woo, for the wound that his bane

1285   must be.
        He must bear the blinding blow,
        For such is fate's decree:
        The lady asks leave to go;
        He grants it full and free.

1290 Then she gaily said goodbye, and glanced at him, laughing,
And as she stood, she astonished him with a stern speech:
"Now may the Giver of all good words these glad hours repay!
But our guest is not Gawain—forgot is that thought."
"How so?" said the other, and asks in some haste,
1295 For he feared he had been at fault in the forms of his speech.
But she held up her hand, and made answer thus:
"So good a knight as Gawain is given out to be,
And the model of fair demeanor and manners pure,
Had he lain so long at a lady's side,
1300 Would have claimed a kiss, by his courtesy,
Through some touch or trick of phrase at some tale's end."
Said Gawain, "Good lady, I grant it at once!
I shall kiss at your command, as becomes a knight,
And more, lest you mislike, so let be, I pray."
1305 With that she turns toward him, takes him in her arms,
Leans down her lovely head, and lo! he is kissed.
They commend each other to Christ with comely words,
He sees her forth safely, in silence they part,
And then he lies no later in his lofty bed,
1310 But calls to his chamberlain, chooses his clothes,
Goes in those garments gladly to mass,
Then takes his way to table, where attendants wait,
And made merry all day, till the moon rose
                  in view
1315   Was never knight beset
        'Twixt worthier ladies two:
        The crone and the coquette;
        Fair pastimes they pursue.

And the lord of the land rides late and long,
1320 Hunting the barren hind over the broad heath.
He had slain such a sum, when the sun sank low,
Of does and other deer, as would dizzy one's wits.
Then they trooped in together in triumph at last,
And the count of the quarry quickly they take.
1325 The lords lent a hand with their liegemen many,
Picked out the plumpest and put them together
And duly dressed the deer, as the deed requires.
Some were assigned the assay of the fat:
Two fingers' width fully they found on the leanest.
1330 Then they slit the slot open and searched out the paunch,
Trimmed it with trencher-knives and tied it up tight.

They flayed the fair hide from the legs and trunk,
Then broke open the belly and laid bare the bowels,
Deftly detaching and drawing them forth.
1335 And next at the neck they neatly parted
The weasand° from the windpipe, and cast away the guts.   *esophagus*
At the shoulders with sharp blades they showed their skill,
Boning them from beneath, lest the sides be marred;
They breached the broad breast and broke it in twain,
1340 And again at the gullet they begin with their knives,
Cleave down the carcass clear to the breach;
Two tender morsels they take from the throat,
Then round the inner ribs they rid off a layer
And carve out the kidney-fat, close to the spine,
1345 Hewing down to the haunch, that all hung together,
And held it up whole, and hacked it free,
And this they named the numbles,⁴ that knew such terms
                              of art.
                    They divide the crotch in two,
1350   And straightway then they start
                    To cut the backbone through
                    And cleave the trunk apart.

With hard strokes they hewed off the head and the neck,
Then swiftly from the sides they severed the chine,
1355 And the corbie's bone⁵ they cast on a branch.
Then they pierced the plump sides, impaled either one
With the hock of the hind foot, and hung it aloft,
To each person his portion most proper and fit.
On a hide of a hind the hounds they fed
1360 With the liver and the lights,° the leathery paunches,   *lungs*
And bread soaked in blood well blended therewith.
High horns and shrill set hounds a-baying,
Then merrily with their meat they make their way home,
Blowing on their bugles many a brave blast.
1365 Ere dark had descended, that doughty band
Was come within the walls where Gawain waits
                              at leisure.
                    Bliss and hearth-fire bright
                    Await the master's pleasure;
1370   When the two men met that night,
                    Joy surpassed all measure.

Then the host in the hall his household assembles,
With the dames of high degree and their damsels fair.
In the presence of the people, a party he sends
1375 To convey him his venison in view of the knight.
And in high good-humor he hails him then,
Counts over the kill, the cuts on the tallies,
Holds high the hewn ribs, heavy with fat.

4. The other internal organs.
5. A bit of gristle assigned to the ravens ("corbies").

"What think you, sir, of this? Have I thriven well?
1380   Have I won with my woodcraft a worthy prize?"
"In good earnest," said Gawain, "this game is the finest
I have seen in seven years in the season of winter."
"And I give it to you, Gawain," said the goodly host,
"For according to our convenant, you claim it as your own."
1385   "That is so," said Sir Gawain, "the same say I:
What I worthily have won within these fair walls,
Herewith I as willingly award it to you."
He embraces his broad neck with both his arms,
And confers on him a kiss in the comeliest style.
1390   "Have here my profit, it proved no better;
Ungrudging do I grant it, were it greater far."
"Such a gift," said the good host, "I gladly accept—
Yet it might be all the better, would you but say
Where you won this same award, by your wits alone."
1395   "That was no part of the pact; press me no further,
For you have had what behooves; all other claims
                      forbear."
               With jest and compliment
               They conversed, and cast off care;
1400   To the table soon they went;
               Fresh dainties wait them there.

And then by the chimney-side they chat at their ease;
The best wine was brought them, and bounteously served;
And after in their jesting they jointly accord
1405   To do on the second day the deeds of the first:
That the two men should trade, betide as it may,
What each had taken in, at eve when they met.
They seal the pact solemnly in sight of the court;
Their cups were filled afresh to confirm the jest;
1410   Then at last they took their leave, for late was the hour,
Each to his own bed hastening away.
Before the barnyard cock had crowed but thrice
The lord had leapt from his rest, his liegemen as well.
Both of mass and their meal they made short work:
1415   By the dim light of dawn they were deep in the woods
                    away.
               With huntsmen and with horns
               Over plains they pass that day;
               They release, amid the thorns,
1420   Swift hounds that run and bay.

Soon some were on a scent by the side of a marsh;
When the hounds opened cry, the head of the hunt
Rallied them with rough words, raised a great noise.
The hounds that had heard it came hurrying straight
1425   And followed along with their fellows, forty together.
Then such a clamor and cry of coursing hounds
Arose, that the rocks resounded again.
Hunters exhorted them with horn and with voice;

Then all in a body bore off together
1430 Between a mere in the marsh and a menacing crag,
To a rise where the rock stood rugged and steep,
And boulders lay about, that blocked their approach.
Then the company in consort closed on their prey:
They surrounded the rise and the rocks both,
1435 For well they were aware that it waited within,
The beast that the bloodhounds boldly proclaimed.
Then they beat on the bushes and bade him appear,
And he made a murderous rush in the midst of them all;
The best of all boars broke from his cover,
1440 That had ranged long unrivaled, a renegade old,
For of tough-brawned boars he was biggest far,
Most grim when he grunted—then grieved were many,
For three at the first thrust he threw to the earth,
And dashed away at once without more damage.
1445 With "Hi!" "Hi!" and "Hey!" "Hey!" the others followed,
Had horns at their lips, blew high and clear.
Merry was the music of men and of hounds
That were bound after this boar, his bloodthirsty heart
                    to quell.
1450   Often he stands at bay,
              Then scatters the pack pell-mell;
              He hurts the hounds, and they
              Most dolefully yowl and yell.

Men then with mighty bows moved in to shoot,
1455 Aimed at him with their arrows and often hit,
But the points had no power to pierce through his hide,
And the barbs were brushed aside by his bristly brow;
Though the shank of the shaft shivered in pieces,
The head hopped away, wheresoever it struck.
1460 But when their stubborn strokes had stung him at last,
Then, foaming in his frenzy, fiercely he charges,
Hies at them headlong that hindered his flight,
And many feared for their lives, and fell back a little.
But the lord on a lively horse leads the chase;
1465 As a high-mettled huntsman his horn he blows;
He sounds the assembly and sweeps through the brush,
Pursuing this wild swine till the sunlight slanted.
All day with this deed they drive forth the time
While our lone knight so lovesome lies in his bed,
1470 Sir Gawain safe at home, in silken bower
                    so gay.
              The lady, with guile in heart,
              Came early where he lay;
              She was at him with all her art
1475   To turn his mind her way.

She comes to the curtain and coyly peeps in;
Gawain thought it good to greet her at once,

And she richly repays him with her ready words,
Settles softly at his side, and suddenly she laughs,
1480 And with a gracious glance, she begins on him thus:
"Sir, if you be Gawain, it seems a great wonder—
A man so well-meaning, and mannerly disposed,
And cannot act in company as courtesy bids,
And if one takes the trouble to teach him, 'tis all in vain.
1485 That lesson learned lately is lightly forgot,
Though I painted it as plain as my poor wit allowed."
"What lesson, dear lady?" he asked all alarmed;
"I have been much to blame, if your story be true."
"Yet my counsel was of kissing," came her answer then,
1490 "Where favor has been found, freely to claim
As accords with the conduct of courteous knights."
"My dear," said the doughty man, "dismiss that thought;
Such freedom, I fear, might offend you much;
It were rude to request if the right were denied."
1495 "But none can deny you," said the noble dame,
"You are stout enough to constrain with strength, if you choose,
Were any so ungracious as to grudge you aught."
"By heaven," said he, "you have answered well,
But threats never throve among those of my land,
1500 Nor any gift not freely given, good though it be.
I am yours to command, to kiss when you please;
You may lay on as you like, and leave off at will."
                    With this,
          The lady lightly bends
1505   And graciously gives him a kiss;
          The two converse as friends
          Of true love's trials and bliss.

"I should like, by your leave," said the lovely lady,
"If it did not annoy you, to know for what cause
1510 So brisk and so bold a young blood as you,
And acclaimed for all courtesies becoming a knight—
And name what knight you will, they are noblest esteemed
For loyal faith in love, in life as in story;
For to tell the tribulations of these true hearts,
1515 Why, 'tis the very title and text of their deeds,
How bold knights for beauty have braved many a foe,
Suffered heavy sorrows out of secret love,
And then valorously avenged them on villainous churls
And made happy ever after the hearts of their ladies.
1520 And you are the noblest knight known in your time;
No household under heaven but has heard of your fame,
And here by your side I have sat for two days
Yet never has a fair phrase fallen from your lips
Of the language of love, not one little word!
1525 And you, that with sweet vows sway women's hearts,
Should show your winsome ways, and woo a young thing,
And teach by some tokens the craft of true love.

How! are you artless, whom all men praise?
Or do you deem me so dull, or deaf to such words?
1530   Fie! Fie!
                    In hope of pastimes new
                    I have come where none can spy;
                    Instruct me a little, do,
                    While my husband is not nearby."

1535 "God love you, gracious lady!" said Gawain then;
"It is a pleasure surpassing, and a peerless joy,
That one so worthy as you would willingly come
And take the time and trouble to talk with your knight
And content you with his company—it comforts my heart.
1540 But to take to myself the task of telling of love,
And touch upon its texts, and treat of its themes
To one that, I know well, wields more power
In that art, by a half, than a hundred such
As I am where I live, or am like to become,
1545 It were folly, fair dame, in the first degree!
In all that I am able, my aim is to please,
As in honor behooves me, and am evermore
Your servant heart and soul, so save me our Lord!"
Thus she tested his temper and tried many a time,
1550 Whatever her true intent, to entice him to sin,
But so fair was his defense that no fault appeared,
Nor evil on either hand, but only bliss
                         they knew.
                    They linger and laugh awhile;
1555   She kisses the knight so true,
                    Takes leave in comeliest style
                    And departs without more ado.

Then he rose from his rest and made ready for mass,
And then a meal was set and served, in sumptuous style;
1560 He dallied at home all day with the dear ladies,
But the lord lingered late at his lusty sport;
Pursued his sorry swine, that swerved as he fled,
And bit asunder the backs of the best of his hounds
When they brought him to bay, till the bowmen appeared
1565 And soon forced him forth, though he fought for dear life,
So sharp were the shafts they shot at him there.
But yet the boldest drew back from his battering head,
Till at last he was so tired he could travel no more,
But in as much haste as he might, he makes his retreat
1570 To a rise on rocky ground, by a rushing stream.
With the bank at his back he scrapes the bare earth,
The froth foams at his jaws, frightful to see.
He whets his white tusks—then weary were all
Those hunters so hardy that hoved round about
1575 Of aiming from afar, but ever they mistrust
                         his mood.
                    He had hurt so many by then

That none had hardihood
To be torn by his tusks again,
1580   That was brainsick, and out for blood.

Till the lord came at last on his lofty steed,
Beheld him there at bay before all his folk;
Lightly he leaps down, leaves his courser,
Bares his bright sword, and boldly advances;
1585   Straight into the stream he strides towards his foe.
The wild thing was wary of weapon and man;
His hackles rose high; so hotly he snorts
That many watched with alarm, lest the worst befall.
The boar makes for the man with a mighty bound
1590   So that he and his hunter came headlong together
Where the water ran wildest—the worse for the beast,
For the man, when they first met, marked him with care,
Sights well the slot, slips in the blade,
Shoves it home to the hilt, and the heart shattered,
1595   And he falls in his fury and floats down the water,
                    ill-sped.
            Hounds hasten by the score
            To maul him, hide and head;
            Men drag him in to shore
1600   And dogs pronounce him dead.

With many a brave blast they boast of their prize,
All hallooed in high glee, that had their wind;
The hounds bayed their best, as the bold men bade
That were charged with chief rank in that chase of renown.
1605   Then one wise in woodcraft, and worthily skilled,
Began to dress the boar in becoming style:
He severs the savage head and sets it aloft,
Then rends the body roughly right down the spine;
Takes the bowels from the belly, broils them on coals,
1610   Blends them well with bread to bestow on the hounds.
Then he breaks out the brawn in fair broad flitches,
And the innards to be eaten in order he takes.
The two sides, attached to each other all whole,
He suspended from a spar that was springy and tough;
1615   And so with this swine they set out for home;
The boar's head was borne before the same man
That had stabbed him in the stream with his strong arm,
                    right through.
            He thought it long indeed
1620   Till he had the knight in view;
            At his call, he comes with speed
            To claim his payment due.

The lord laughed aloud, with many a light word,
When he greeted Sir Gawain—with good cheer he speaks.
1625   They fetch the fair dames and the folk of the house;
He brings forth the brawn, and begins the tale

Of the great length and girth, the grim rage as well,
Of the battle of the boar they beset in the wood.
The other man meetly commended his deeds
1630 And praised well the prize of his princely sport,
For the brawn of that boar, the bold knight said,
And the sides of that swine surpassed all others.
Then they handled the huge head; he owns it a wonder,
And eyes it with abhorrence, to heighten his praise.
1635 "Now, Gawain," said the good man, "this game becomes yours
By those fair terms we fixed, as you know full well."
"That is true," returned the knight, "and trust me, fair friend,
All my gains, as agreed, I shall give you forthwith."
He clasps him and kisses him in courteous style,
1640 Then serves him with the same fare a second time.
"Now we are even," said he, "at this evening feast,
And clear is every claim incurred here to date,
                    and debt."
                "By Saint Giles!" the host replies,
1645   "You're the best I ever met!
                If your profits are all this size,
                We'll see you wealthy yet!"

Then attendants set tables on trestles about,
And laid them with linen; light shone forth,
1650 Wakened along the walls in waxen torches.
The service was set and the supper brought;
Royal were the revels that rose then in hall
At that feast by the fire, with many fair sports:
Amid the meal and after, melody sweet,
1655 Carol-dances comely and Christmas songs,
With all the mannerly mirth my tongue may describe.
And ever our gallant knight beside the gay lady;
So uncommonly kind and complaisant was she,
With sweet stolen glances, that stirred his stout heart,
1660 That he was at his wits' end, and wondrous vexed;
But he could not rebuff her, for courtesy forbade,
Yet took pains to please her, though the plan might
                    go wrong.
                When they to heart's delight
1665   Had reveled there in throng,
                To his chamber he calls the knight,
                And thither they go along.

And there they dallied and drank, and deemed it good sport
To enact their play anew on New Year's Eve,
1670 But Gawain asked again to go on the morrow,
For the time until his tryst was not two days.
The host hindered that, and urged him to stay,
And said, "On my honor, my oath here I take
That you shall get to the Green Chapel to begin your chores
1675 By dawn on New Year's Day, if you so desire.
Wherefore lie at your leisure in your lofty bed,

And I shall hunt hereabouts, and hold to our terms,
And we shall trade winnings when once more we meet,
For I have tested you twice, and true have I found you;
1680 Now think this tomorrow: the third pays for all;
Be we merry while we may, and mindful of joy,
For heaviness of heart can be had for the asking."
This is gravely agreed on and Gawain will stay.
They drink a last draught and with torches depart
1685   to rest.
        To bed Sir Gawain went:
        His sleep was of the best;
        The lord, on his craft intent,
        Was early up and dressed.

1690 After mass, with his men, a morsel he takes;
Clear and crisp the morning; he calls for his mount;
The folk that were to follow him afield that day
Were high astride their horses before the hall gates.
Wondrous fair were the fields, for the frost was light;
1695 The sun rises red amid radiant clouds,
Sails into the sky, and sends forth his beams.
They let loose the hounds by a leafy wood;
The rocks all around re-echo to their horns;
Soon some have set off in pursuit of the fox,
1700 Cast about with craft for a clearer scent;
A young dog yaps, and is yelled at in turn;
His fellows fall to sniffing, and follow his lead,
Running in a rabble on the right track,
And he scampers all before; they discover him soon,
1705 And when they see him with sight they pursue him the faster,
Railing at him rudely with a wrathful din.
Often he reverses over rough terrain,
Or loops back to listen in the lee of a hedge;
At last, by a little ditch, he leaps over the brush,
1710 Comes into a clearing at a cautious pace,
Then he thought through his wiles to have thrown off the hounds
Till he was ware, as he went, of a waiting-station
Where three athwart his path threatened him at once,
        all gray.
1715   Quick as a flash he wheels
        And darts off in dismay;
        With hard luck at his heels
        He is off to the wood away.

Then it was heaven on earth to hark to the hounds
1720 When they had come on their quarry, coursing together!
Such harsh cries and howls they hurled at his head
As all the cliffs with a crash had come down at once.
Here he was hailed, when huntsmen met him;
Yonder they yelled at him, yapping and snarling;
1725 There they cried "Thief!" and threatened his life,
And ever the harriers at his heels, that he had no rest.

Often he was menaced when he made for the open,
And often rushed in again, for Reynard was wily;
And so he leads them a merry chase, the lord and his men,
1730 In this manner on the mountains, till midday or near,
While our hero lies at home in wholesome sleep
Within the comely curtains on the cold morning.
But the lady, as love would allow her no rest,
And pursuing ever the purpose that pricked her heart,
1735 Was awake with the dawn, and went to his chamber
In a fair flowing mantle that fell to the earth,
All edged and embellished with ermines fine;
No hood on her head, but heavy with gems
Were her fillet and the fret° that confined her tresses;   ornamental net
1740 Her face and her fair throat freely displayed;
Her bosom all but bare, and her back as well.
She comes in at the chamber-door, and closes it with care,
Throws wide a window—then waits no longer,
But hails him thus airily with her artful words,
1745   with cheer:
           "Ah, man, how can you sleep?
           The morning is so clear!"
           Though dreams have drowned him deep,
           He cannot choose but hear.

1750 Deep in his dreams he darkly mutters
As a man may that mourns, with many grim thoughts
Of that day when destiny shall deal him his doom
When he greets his grim host at the Green Chapel
And must bow to his buffet, bating all strife.
1755 But when he sees her at his side he summons his wits,
Breaks from the black dreams, and blithely answers.
That lovely lady comes laughing sweet,
Sinks down at his side, and salutes him with a kiss.
He accords her fair welcome in courtliest style;
1760 He sees her so glorious, so gaily attired,
So faultless her features, so fair and so bright,
His heart swelled swiftly with surging joys.
They melt into mirth with many a fond smile,
Nor was fair language lacking, to further that hour's
1765   delight.
           Good were their words of greeting;
           Each joyed in other's sight;
           Great peril attends that meeting
           Should Mary forget her knight.

1770 For that high-born beauty so hemmed him about,
Made so plain her meaning, the man must needs
Either take her tendered love or distastefully refuse.
His courtesy concerned him, lest crass he appear,
But more his soul's mischief, should he commit sin
1775 And belie his loyal oath to the lord of that house.
"God forbid!" said the bold knight. "That shall not befall!"

With a little fond laughter he lightly let pass
All the words of special weight that were sped his way;
"I find you much at fault," the fair one said,
1780   "Who can be cold toward a creature so close by your side,
Of all women in this world most wounded in heart,
Unless you have a sweetheart, one you hold dearer,
And allegiance to that lady so loyally knit
That you will never love another, as now I believe.
1785   And, sir, if it be so, then say it, I beg you;
By all your heart holds dear, hide it no longer
               with guile."
        "Lady, by Saint John,"
        He answers with a smile,
1790   "Lover have I none,
        Nor will have, yet awhile."

"Those words," said the woman, "are the worst of all,
But I have had my answer, and hard do I find it!
Kiss me now kindly: I can but go hence
1795   To lament my life long like a maid lovelorn."
She inclines her head quickly and kisses the knight,
Then straightens with a sigh, and says as she stands,
"Now, dear, ere I depart, do me this pleasure:
Give me some little gift, your glove or the like,
1800   That I may think on you, man, and mourn the less."
"Now by heavens," said he, "I wish I had here
My most precious possession, to put it in your hands,
For your deeds, beyond doubt, have often deserved
A repayment far passing my power to bestow.
1805   But a love-token, lady, were of little avail;
It is not to your honor to have at this time
A glove as a guerdon from Gawain's hand,
And I am here on an errand in unknown realms
And have no bearers with baggage with becoming gifts,
1810   Which distresses me, madame, for your dear sake.
A man must keep within his compass: account it neither grief
               nor slight."
        "Nay, noblest knight alive,"
        Said that beauty of body white,
1815   "Though you be loath to give,
        Yet you shall take, by right."

She reached out a rich ring, wrought all of gold,
With a splendid stone displayed on the band
That flashed before his eyes like a fiery sun;
1820   It was worth a king's wealth, you may well believe.
But he waved it away with these ready words:
"Before God, good lady, I forgo all gifts;
None have I to offer, nor any will I take."
And she urged it on him eagerly, and ever he refused,
1825   And vowed in very earnest, prevail she would not.
And she sad to find it so, and said to him then,

"If my ring is refused for its rich cost—
You would not be my debtor for so dear a thing—
I shall give you my girdle; you gain less thereby."
1830 She released a knot lightly, and loosened a belt
That was caught about her kirtle, the bright cloak beneath,
Of a gay green silk, with gold overwrought,
And the borders all bound with embroidery fine,
And this she presses upon him, and pleads with a smile,
1835 Unworthy though it were, that it would not be scorned.
But the man still maintains that he means to accept
Neither gold nor any gift, till by God's grace
The fate that lay before him was fully achieved.
"And be not offended, fair lady, I beg,
1840 And give over your offer, for ever I must
                                decline.
                    I am grateful for favor shown
                    Past all deserts of mine,
                    And ever shall be your own
1845   True servant, rain or shine."

"Now does my present displease you," she promptly inquired,
"Because it seems in your sight so simple a thing?
And belike, as it is little, it is less to praise,
But if the virtue that invests it were verily known,
1850 It would be held, I hope, in higher esteem.
For the man that possesses this piece of silk,
If he bore it on his body, belted about,
There is no hand under heaven that could hew him down,
For he could not be killed by any craft on earth."
1855 Then the man began to muse, and mainly he thought
It was a pearl for his plight, the peril to come
When he gains the Green Chapel to get his reward:
Could he escape unscathed, the scheme were noble!
Then he bore with her words and withstood them no more,
1860 And she repeated her petition and pleaded anew,
And he granted it, and gladly she gave him the belt,
And besought him for her sake to conceal it well,
Lest the noble lord should know—and, the knight agrees
That not a soul save themselves shall see it thenceforth
1865   with sight.
                    He thanked her with fervent heart,
                    As often as ever he might;
                    Three times, before they part,
                    She has kissed the stalwart knight.

1870 Then the lady took her leave, and left him there,
For more mirth with that man she might not have.
When she was gone, Sir Gawain got from his bed,
Arose and arrayed him in his rich attire;
Tucked away the token the temptress had left,
1875 Laid it reliably where he looked for it after.
And then with good cheer to the chapel he goes,

Approached a priest in private, and prayed to be taught
To lead a better life and lift up his mind,
Lest he be among the lost when he must leave this world.
1880 And shamefaced at shrift he showed his misdeeds
From the largest to the least, and asked the Lord's mercy,
And called on his confessor to cleanse his soul,
And he absolved him of his sins as safe and as clean
As if the dread Day of Doom were to dawn on the morrow.
1885 And then he made merry amid the fine ladies
With deft-footed dances and dalliance light,
As never until now, while the afternoon wore
     away.
    He delighted all around him,
1890   And all agreed, that day,
    They never before had found him
    So gracious and so gay.

Now peaceful be his pasture, and love play him fair!
The host is on horseback, hunting afield;
1895 He has finished off this fox that he followed so long:
As he leapt a low hedge to look for the villain
Where he heard all the hounds in hot pursuit,
Reynard comes racing out of a rough thicket,
And all the rabble in a rush, right at his heels.
1900 The man beholds the beast, and bides his time,
And bares his bright sword, and brings it down hard,
And he blenches from the blade, and backward he starts;
A hound hurries up and hinders that move,
And before the horse's feet they fell on him at once
1905 And ripped the rascal's throat with a wrathful din.
The lord soon alighted and lifted him free,
Swiftly snatched him up from the snapping jaws,
Holds him over his head, halloos with a will,
And the dogs bayed the dirge, that had done him to death.
1910 Hunters hastened thither with horns at their lips,
Sounding the assembly till they saw him at last.
When that comely company was come in together,
All that bore bugles blew them at once,
And the others all hallooed, that had no horns.
1915 It was the merriest medley that ever a man heard,
The racket that they raised for Sir Reynard's soul
     that died.
    Their hounds they praised and fed,
    Fondling their heads with pride,
1920   And they took Reynard the Red
    And stripped away his hide.

And then they headed homeward, for evening had come,
Blowing many a blast on their bugles bright.
The lord at long last alights at his house,
1925 Finds fire on the hearth where the fair knight waits,
Sir Gawain the good, that was glad in heart.

With the ladies, that loved him, he lingered at ease;
He wore a rich robe of blue, that reached to the earth
And a surcoat lined softly with sumptuous furs;
1930 A hood of the same hue hung on his shoulders;
With bands of bright ermine embellished were both.
He comes to meet the man amid all the folk,
And greets him good-humoredly, and gaily he says,
"I shall follow forthwith the form of our pledge
1935 That we framed to good effect amid fresh-filled cups."
He clasps him accordingly and kisses him thrice,
As amiably and as earnestly as ever he could.
"By heaven," said the host, "you have had some luck
Since you took up this trade, if the terms were good."
1940 "Never trouble about the terms," he returned at once,
"Since all that I owe here is openly paid."
"Marry!" said the other man, "mine is much less,
For I have hunted all day, and nought have I got
But this foul fox pelt, the fiend take the goods!
1945 Which but poorly repays such precious things
That you have cordially conferred, such kisses three
                    so good."
                "Enough!" said Sir Gawain;
                "I thank you, by the rood!"
1950   And how the fox was slain
                He told him, as they stood.

With minstrelsy and mirth, with all manner of meats,
They made as much merriment as any men might
(Amid laughing of ladies and light hearted girls;
1955 So gay grew Sir Gawain and the goodly host)
Unless they had been besotted, or brainless fools.
The knight joined in jesting with that joyous folk,
Until at last it was late; ere long they must part,
And be off to their beds, as behooved them each one.
1960 Then politely his leave of the lord of the house
Our noble knight takes, and renews his thanks:
"The courtesies countless accorded me here,
Your kindness at this Christmas, may heaven's King repay!
Henceforth, if you will have me, I hold you my liege,
1965 And so, as I have said, I must set forth tomorrow,
If I may take some trusty man to teach, as you promised,
The way to the Green Chapel, that as God allows
I shall see my fate fulfilled on the first of the year."
"In good faith," said the good man, "with a good will
1970 Every promise on my part shall be fully performed."
He assigns him a servant to set him on the path,
To see him safe and sound over the snowy hills,
To follow the fastest way through forest green
                    and grove.
1975   Gawain thanks him again,
                So kind his favors prove,
                And of the ladies then
                He takes his leave, with love.

Courteously he kissed them, with care in his heart,
1980 And often wished them well, with warmest thanks,
Which they for their part were prompt to repay.
They commend him to Christ with disconsolate sighs;
And then in that hall with the household he parts—
Each man that he met, he remembered to thank
1985 For his deeds of devotion and diligent pains,
And the trouble he had taken to tend to his needs;
And each one as woeful, that watched him depart,
As he had lived with him loyally all his life long.
By lads bearing lights he was led to his chamber
1990 And blithely brought to his bed, to be at his rest.
How soundly he slept, I presume not to say,
For there were matters of moment his thoughts might well
　　　　　　　　pursue.
　　　　　　Let him lie and wait;
1995　　　　　He has little more to do,
　　　　　　Then listen, while I relate
　　　　　　How they kept their rendezvous.

Part 4

Now the New Year draws near, and the night passes,
The day dispels the dark, by the Lord's decree;
2000 But wild weather awoke in the world without:
The clouds in the cold sky cast down their snow
With great gusts from the north, grievous to bear.
Sleet showered aslant upon shivering beasts;
The wind warbled wild as it whipped from aloft,
2005 And drove the drifts deep in the dales below.
Long and well he listens, that lies in his bed;
Though he lifts not his eyelids, little he sleeps;
Each crow of the cock he counts without fail.
Readily from his rest he rose before dawn,
2010 For a lamp had been left him, that lighted his chamber.
He called to his chamberlain, who quickly appeared,
And bade him get him his gear, and gird his good steed,
And he sets about briskly to bring in his arms,
And makes ready his master in manner most fit.
2015 First he clad him in his clothes, to keep out the cold,
And then his other harness, made handsome anew,
His plate-armor of proof, polished with pains,
The rings of his rich mail rid of their rust,
And all was fresh as at first, and for this he gave thanks
2020　　　　　　　　indeed.
　　　　　　With pride he wears each piece,
　　　　　　New-furbished for his need:
　　　　　　No gayer from here to Greece;
　　　　　　He bids them bring his steed.

2025 In his richest raiment he robed himself then:
His crested coat-armor, close-stitched with craft,
With stones of strange virtue on silk velvet set;

All bound with embroidery on borders and seams
And lined warmly and well with furs of the best.
2030 Yet he left not his love-gift, the lady's girdle;
Gawain, for his own good, forgot not that:
When the bright sword was belted and bound on his haunches,
Then twice with that token he twined him about.
Sweetly did he swathe him in that swatch of silk,
2035 That girdle of green so goodly to see,
That against the gay red showed gorgeous bright.
Yet he wore not for its wealth that wondrous girdle,
Nor pride in its pendants, though polished they were,
Though glittering gold gleamed at the end,
2040 But to keep himself safe when consent he must
To endure a deadly dint, and all defense
                              denied.
                    And now the bold knight came
                    Into the courtyard wide;
2045   That folk of worthy fame
                    He thanks on every side.

Then was Gringolet girt, that was great and huge,
And had sojourned safe and sound, and savored his fare;
He pawed the earth in his pride, that princely steed.
2050 The good knight draws near him and notes well his look,
And says sagely to himself, and soberly swears,
"Here is a household in hall that upholds the right!
The man that maintains it, may happiness be his!
Likewise the dear lady, may love betide her!
2055 If thus they in charity cherish a guest
That are honored here on earth, may they have his reward
That reigns high in heaven—and also you all;
And might I live in this land but a little while,
I should willingly reward you, and well, if I might."
2060 Then he steps into the stirrup and bestrides his mount;
His shield is shown forth; on his shoulder he casts it;
Strikes the side of his steed with his steel spurs,
And he starts across the stones, nor stands any longer
                              to prance.
2065   On horseback was the swain
                    That bore his spear and lance;
                    "May Christ this house maintain
                    And guard it from mischance!"

The bridge was brought down, and the road gates
2070 Unbarred and carried back upon both sides;
He commended him to Christ, and crossed over the planks;
Praised the noble porter, who prayed on his knees
That God save Sir Gawain, and bade him good day,
And went on his way alone with the man
2075 That was to lead him ere long to that luckless place
Where the dolorous dint must be dealt him at last.
Under bare boughs they ride, where steep banks rise,

Over high cliffs they climb, where cold snow clings;
The heavens held aloof, but heavy thereunder
2080　Mist mantled the moors, moved on the slopes.
Each hill had a hat, a huge cape of cloud;
Brooks bubbled and broke over broken rocks,
Flashing in freshets that waterfalls fed.
Roundabout was the road that ran through the wood
2085　Till the sun at that season was soon to rise,
　　　　　　　　　　　　that day.
　　　　　　　　　They were on a hilltop high;
　　　　　　　　　The white snow round them lay;
　　　　　　　　　The man that rode nearby
2090　　　　　　　Now bade his master stay.

"For I have seen you here safe at the set time,
And now you are not far from that notable place
That you have sought for so long with such special pains.
But this I say for certain, since I know you, sir knight,
2095　And have your good at heart, and hold you dear—
Would you heed well my words, it were worth your while—
You are rushing into risks that you reck not of:
There is a villain in yon valley, the veriest on earth,
For he is rugged and rude, and ready with his fists,
2100　And most immense in his mold of mortals alive,
And his body bigger than the best four
That are in Arthur's house, Hector[6] or any.
He gets his grim way at the Green Chapel;
None passes by that place so proud in his arms
2105　That he does not dash him down with his deadly blows,
For he is heartless wholly, and heedless of right,
For be it chaplain or churl that by the Chapel rides,
Monk or mass-priest or any man else,
He would as soon strike him dead as stand on two feet.
2110　Wherefore I say, just as certain as you sit there astride,
You cannot but be killed, if his counsel holds,
For he would trounce you in a trice, had you twenty lives
　　　　　　　　　　　　for sale.
　　　　　　　　　He has lived long in this land
2115　　　　　　　And dealt out deadly bale;
　　　　　　　　　Against his heavy hand
　　　　　　　　　Your power cannot prevail.

"And so, good Sir Gawain, let the grim man be;
Go off by some other road, in God's own name!
2120　Leave by some other land, for the love of Christ,
And I shall get me home again, and give you my word
That I shall swear by God's self and the saints above,
By heaven and by my halidom[7] and other oaths more,
To conceal this day's deed, nor say to a soul

6. Either the Trojan hero or one of Arthur's　　7. Holiness or, more likely, patron saints.
knights.

2125 That ever you fled for fear from any that I knew."
"Many thanks!" said the other man—and demurring he speaks—
"Fair fortune befall you for your friendly words!
And conceal this day's deed I doubt not you would,
But though you never told the tale, if I turned back now,
2130 Forsook this place for fear, and fled, as you say,
I were a caitiff coward; I could not be excused.
But I must to the Chapel to chance my luck
And say to that same man such words as I please,
Befall what may befall through Fortune's will
2135   or whim.
    Though he be a quarrelsome knave
    With a cudgel great and grim,
    The Lord is strong to save:
    His servants trust in him."

2140 "Marry," said the man, "since you tell me so much,
And I see you are set to seek your own harm,
If you crave a quick death, let me keep you no longer!
Put your helm on your head, your hand on your lance,
And ride the narrow road down yon rocky slope
2145 Till it brings you to the bottom of the broad valley.
Then look a little ahead, on your left hand,
And you will soon see before you that self-same Chapel,
And the man of great might that is master there.
Now goodbye in God's name, Gawain the noble!
2150 For all the world's wealth I would not stay here,
Or go with you in this wood one footstep further!"
He tarried no more to talk, but turned his bridle,
Hit his horse with his heels as hard as he might,
Leaves the knight alone, and off like the wind
2155   goes leaping.
    "By God," said Gawain then,
    "I shall not give way to weeping;
    God's will be done, amen!
    I commend me to his keeping."

2160 He puts his heels to his horse, and picks up the path;
Goes in beside a grove where the ground is steep,
Rides down the rough slope right to the valley;
And then he looked a little about him—the landscape was wild,
And not a soul to be seen, nor sign of a dwelling,
2165 But high banks on either hand hemmed it about,
With many a ragged rock and rough-hewn crag;
The skies seemed scored by the scowling peaks.
Then he halted his horse, and hoved there a space,
And sought on every side for a sight of the Chapel,
2170 But no such place appeared, which puzzled him sore,
Yet he saw some way off what seemed like a mound,
A hillock high and broad, hard by the water,
Where the stream fell in foam down the face of the steep
And bubbled as if it boiled on its bed below.

2175 The knight urges his horse, and heads for the knoll;
Leaps lightly to earth; loops well the rein
Of his steed to a stout branch, and stations him there.
He strides straight to the mound, and strolls all about,
Much wondering what it was, but no whit the wiser;
2180 It had a hole at one end, and on either side,
And was covered with coarse grass in clumps all without,
And hollow all within, like some old cave,
Or a crevice of an old crag—he could not discern
aright.
2185   "Can this be the Chapel Green?
        Alack!" said the man, "here might
        The devil himself be seen
        Saying matins at black midnight!"

"Now by heaven," said he, "it is bleak hereabouts;
2190 This prayer-house is hideous, half-covered with grass!
Well may the grim man mantled in green
Hold here his orisons, in hell's own style!
Now I feel it is the Fiend, in my five wits,
That has tempted me to this tryst, to take my life;
2195 This is a Chapel of mischance, may the mischief take it!
As accursed a country church as I came upon ever!"
With his helm on his head, his lance in his hand,
He stalks toward the steep wall of that strange house.
Then he heard, on the hill, behind a hard rock,
2200 Beyond the brook, from the bank, a most barbarous din:
Lord! it clattered in the cliff fit to cleave it in two,
As one upon a grindstone ground a great scythe!
Lord! it whirred like a mill-wheel whirling about!
Lord! it echoed loud and long, lamentable to hear!
Then "By heaven," said the bold knight, "that business
2205   up there
Is arranged for my arrival, or else I am much
        misled.
        Let God work! Ah me!
        All hope of help has fled!
2210   Forfeit my life may be
        But noise I do not dread."

Then he listened no longer, but loudly he called,
"Who has power in this place, high parley to hold?
For none greets Sir Gawain, or gives him good day;
2215 If any would a word with him, let him walk forth
And speak now or never, to speed his affairs."
"Abide," said one on the bank above over his head,
"And what I promised you once shall straightway be given."
Yet he stayed not his grindstone, nor stinted its noise,
2220 But worked awhile at his whetting before he would rest,
And then he comes around a crag, from a cave in the rocks,
Hurtling out of hiding with a hateful weapon,
A Danish° ax devised for that day's deed,   *i.e., long-bladed*

With a broad blade and bright, bent in a curve,
2225 Filed to a fine edge—four feet it measured
By the length of the lace that was looped round the haft.
And in form as at first, the fellow all green,
His lordly face and his legs, his locks and his beard,
Save that firm upon two feet forward he strides,
2230 Sets a hand on the ax-head, the haft to the earth;
When he came to the cold stream, and cared not to wade,
He vaults over on his ax, and advances amain
On a broad bank of snow, overbearing and brisk
                    of mood.
2235   Little did the knight incline
               When face to face they stood;
               Said the other man, "Friend mine,
               It seems your word holds good!"

"God love you, Sir Gawain!" said the Green Knight then,
2240 "And well met this morning, man, at my place!
And you have followed me faithfully and found me betimes,
And on the business between us we both are agreed:
Twelve months ago today you took what was yours,
And you at this New Year must yield me the same.
2245 And we have met in these mountains, remote from all eyes:
There is none here to halt us or hinder our sport;
Unhasp your high helm, and have here your wages;
Make no more demur than I did myself
When you hacked off my head with one hard blow."
2250 "No, by God," said Sir Gawain, "that granted me life,
I shall grudge not the guerdon, grim though it prove;
Bestow but one stroke, and I shall stand still,
And you may lay on as you like till the last of my part
                    be paid."
2255   He proffered, with good grace,
               His bare neck to the blade,
               And feigned a cheerful face:
               He scorned to seem afraid.

Then the grim man in green gathers his strength,
2260 Heaves high the heavy ax to hit him the blow.
With all the force in his frame he fetches it aloft,
With a grimace as grim as he would grind him to bits;
Had the blow he bestowed been as big as he threatened,
A good knight and gallant had gone to his grave.
2265 But Gawain at the great ax glanced up aside.
As down it descended with death-dealing force,
And his shoulders shrank a little from the sharp iron.
Abruptly the brawny man breaks off the stroke,
And then reproved with proud words that prince among knights.
2270 "You are not Gawain the glorious," the green man said,
"That never fell back on field in the face of the foe,
And now you flee for fear, and have felt no harm:
Such news of that knight I never heard yet!

I moved not a muscle when you made to strike,
2275 Nor caviled at the cut in King Arthur's house;
My head fell to my feet, yet steadfast I stood,
And you, all unharmed, are wholly dismayed—
Wherefore the better man I, by all odds,
                    must be."
2280   Said Gawain, "Strike once more;
                I shall neither flinch nor flee;
                But if my head falls to the floor
                There is no mending me!"

"But go on, man, in God's name, and get to the point!
2285 Deliver me my destiny, and do it out of hand,
For I shall stand to the stroke and stir not an inch
Till your ax has hit home—on my honor I swear it!"
"Have at thee then!" said the other, and heaves it aloft,
And glares down as grimly as he had gone mad.
2290 He made a mighty feint, but marred not his hide;
Withdrew the ax adroitly before it did damage.
Gawain gave no ground, nor glanced up aside,
But stood still as a stone, or else a stout stump
That is held in hard earth by a hundred roots.
2295 Then merrily does he mock him, the man all in green:
"So now you have your nerve again, I needs must strike;
Uphold the high knighthood that Arthur bestowed,
And keep your neck-bone clear, if this cut allows!"
Then was Gawain gripped with rage, and grimly he said,
2300 "Why, thrash away, tyrant, I tire of your threats;
You make such a scene, you must frighten yourself."
Said the green fellow, "In faith, so fiercely you speak
That I shall finish this affair, nor further grace
                    allow."
2305   He stands prepared to strike
                And scowls with both lip and brow;
                No marvel if the man mislike
                Who can hope no rescue now.

He gathered up the grim ax and guided it well:
2310 Let the barb at the blade's end brush the bare throat;
He hammered down hard, yet harmed him no whit
Save a scratch on one side, that severed the skin;
The end of the hooked edge entered the flesh,
And a little blood lightly leapt to the earth.
2315 And when the man beheld his own blood bright on the snow,
He sprang a spear's length with feet spread wide,
Seized his high helm, and set it on his head,
Shoved before his shoulders the shield at his back,
Bares his trusty blade, and boldly he speaks—
2320 Not since he was a babe born of his mother
Was he once in this world one-half so blithe—
"Have done with your hacking—harry me no more!
I have borne, as behooved, one blow in this place;

If you make another move I shall meet it midway
2325 And promptly, I promise you, pay back each blow
      with brand.
     One stroke acquits me here;
     So did our covenant stand
     In Arthur's court last year—
2330   Wherefore, sir, hold your hand!"

He lowers the long ax and leans on it there,
Sets his arms on the head, the haft on the earth,
And beholds the bold knight that bides there afoot,
How he faces him fearless, fierce in full arms,
2335 And plies him with proud words—it pleases him well.
Then once again gaily to Gawain he calls,
And in a loud voice and lusty, delivers these words:
"Bold fellow, on this field your anger forbear!
No man has made demands here in manner uncouth,
2340 Nor done, save as duly determined at court.
I owed you a hit and you have it; be happy therewith!
The rest of my rights here I freely resign.
Had I been a bit busier, a buffet, perhaps,
I could have dealt more directly, and done you some harm.
2345 First I flourished with a feint, in frolicsome mood,
And left your hide unhurt—and here I did well
By the fair terms we fixed on the first night;
And fully and faithfully you followed accord:
Gave over all your gains as a good man should.
2350 A second feint, sir, I assigned for the morning
You kissed my comely wife—each kiss you restored.
For both of these there behooved two feigned blows
      by right.
     True men pay what they owe;
2355   No danger then in sight.
     You failed at the third throw,
     So take my tap, sir knight.

"For that is my belt about you, that same braided girdle,
My wife it was that wore it; I know well the tale,
2360 And the count of your kisses and your conduct too,
And the wooing of my wife—it was all my scheme!
She made trial of a man most faultless by far
Of all that ever walked over the wide earth;
As pearls to white peas, more precious and prized,
2365 So is Gawain, in good faith, to other gay knights.
Yet you lacked, sir, a little in loyalty there,
But the cause was not cunning, nor courtship either,
But that you loved your own life; the less, then, to blame."
The other stout knight in a study stood a long while,
2370 So gripped with grim rage that his great heart shook.
All the blood of his body burned in his face
As he shrank back in shame from the man's sharp speech.
The first words that fell from the fair knight's lips:

"Accursed be a cowardly and covetous heart!
2375 In you is villainy and vice, and virtue laid low!"
Then he grasps the green girdle and lets go the knot,
Hands it over in haste, and hotly he says:
"Behold there my falsehood, ill hap betide it!
Your cut taught me cowardice, care for my life,
2380 And coveting came after, contrary both
To largesse and loyalty belonging to knights.
Now am I faulty and false, that fearful was ever
Of disloyalty and lies, bad luck to them both!
              and greed.
2385   I confess, knight, in this place,
          Most dire is my misdeed;
          Let me gain back your good grace,
          And thereafter I shall take heed."

Then the other laughed aloud, and lightly he said,
2390 "Such harm as I have had, I hold it quite healed.
You are so fully confessed, your failings made known,
And bear the plain penance of the point of my blade,
I hold you polished as a pearl, as pure and as bright
As you had lived free of fault since first you were born.
2395 And I give you, sir, this girdle that is gold-hemmed
And green as my garments, that, Gawain, you may
Be mindful of this meeting when you mingle in throng
With nobles of renown—and known by this token
How it chanced at the Green Chapel, to chivalrous knights.
2400 And you shall in this New Year come yet again
And we shall finish out our feast in my fair hall,
             with cheer."
          He urged the knight to stay,
          And said, "With my wife so dear
2405   We shall see you friends this day,
          Whose enmity touched you near."

"Indeed," said the doughty knight, and doffed his high helm,
And held it in his hands as he offered his thanks,
"I have lingered long enough—may good luck be yours,
2410 And he reward you well that all worship bestows!
And commend me to that comely one, your courteous wife,
Both herself and that other, my honoured ladies,
That have trapped their true knight in their trammels so quaint.
But if a dullard should dote, deem it no wonder,
2415 And through the wiles of a woman be wooed into sorrow,
For so was Adam by one, when the world began,
And Solomon by many more, and Samson the mighty—
Delilah was his doom, and David thereafter
Was beguiled by Bathsheba, and bore much distress;
2420 Now these were vexed by their devices—'twere a very joy
Could one but learn to love, and believe them not.
For these were proud princes, most prosperous of old,
Past all lovers lucky, that languished under heaven,

bemused.
2425 And one and all fell prey
To women that they had used;
If I be led astray,
Methinks I may be excused.

"But your girdle, God love you! I gladly shall take
2430 And be pleased to possess, not for the pure gold,
Nor the bright belt itself, nor the beauteous pendants,
Nor for wealth, nor worldly state, nor workmanship fine,
But a sign of excess it shall seem oftentimes
When I ride in renown, and remember with shame
2435 The faults and the frailty of the flesh perverse,
How its tenderness entices the foul taint of sin;
And so when praise and high prowess have pleased my heart,
A look at this love-lace will lower my pride.
But one thing would I learn, if you were not loath,
2440 Since you are lord of yonder land where I have long sojourned
With honor in your house—may you have His reward
That upholds all the heavens, highest on throne!
How runs your right name?—and let the rest go."
"That shall I give you gladly," said the Green Knight then;
2445 "Bertilak de Hautdesert, this barony I hold.
Through the might of Morgan le Faye,[8] that lodges at my house,
By subtleties of science and sorcerers' arts,
The mistress of Merlin,[9] she has caught many a man,
For sweet love in secret she shared sometime
2450 With that wizard, that knows well each one of your knights
and you.
Morgan the Goddess, she,
So styled by title true;
None holds so high degree
2455 That her arts cannot subdue.

"She guided me in this guise to your glorious hall,
To assay, if such it were, the surfeit of pride
That is rumored of the retinue of the Round Table.
She put this shape upon me to puzzle your wits,
2460 To afflict the fair queen, and frighten her to death
With awe of that elvish man that eerily spoke
With his head in his hand before the high table.
She was with my wife at home, that old withered lady,
Your own aunt[1] is she, Arthur's half-sister,
2465 The Duchess' daughter of Tintagel, that dear King Uther
Got Arthur on after, that honored is now.
And therefore, good friend, come feast with your aunt;
Make merry in my house; my men hold you dear,

8. Arthur's half-sister, an enchantress who sometimes abetted him, sometimes made trouble for
him.
9. The wise magician who had helped Arthur
become king.

1. Morgan was the daughter of Igraine, duchess
of Tintagel, and her husband the duke; Igraine
conceived Arthur when his father, Uther, lay with
her through one of Merlin's trickeries.

And I wish you as well, sir, with all my heart,
2470 As any man God ever made, for your great good faith."
But the knight said him nay, that he might by no means.
They clasped then and kissed, and commended each other
To the Prince of Paradise, and parted with one
          assent.
2475   Gawain sets out anew;
       Toward the court his course is bent;
       And the knight all green in hue,
       Wheresoever he wished, he went.

Wild ways in the world our worthy knight rides
2480 On Gringolet, that by grace had been granted his life.
He harbored often in houses, and often abroad,
And with many valiant adventures verily he met
That I shall not take time to tell in this story.
The hurt was whole that he had had in his neck,
2485 And the bright green belt on his body he bore,
Oblique, like a baldric, bound at his side,
Below his left shoulder, laced in a knot,
In betokening of the blame he had borne for his fault;
And so to court in due course he comes safe and sound.
2490 Bliss abounded in hall when the high-born heard
That good Gawain was come; glad tidings they thought it.
The king kisses the knight, and the queen as well,
And many a comrade came to clasp him in arms,
And eagerly they asked, and awesomely he told,
2495 Confessed all his cares and discomfitures many,
How it chanced at the Chapel, what cheer made the knight,
The love of the lady, the green lace at last.
The nick on his neck he naked displayed
That he got in his disgrace at the Green Knight's hands,
2500   alone.
       With rage in heart he speaks,
       And grieves with many a groan;
       The blood burns in his cheeks
       For shame at what must be shown.

2505 "Behold, sir," said he, and handles the belt,
"This is the blazon of the blemish that I bear on my neck;
This is the sign of sore loss that I have suffered there
For the cowardice and coveting that I came to there;
This is the badge of false faith that I was found in there,
2510 And I must bear it on my body till I breathe my last.
For one may keep a deed dark, but undo it no whit,
For where a fault is made fast, it is fixed evermore."
The king comforts the knight, and the court all together
Agree with gay laughter and gracious intent
2515 That the lords and the ladies belonging to the Table,
Each brother of that band, a baldric should have,
A belt borne oblique, of a bright green,
To be worn with one accord for that worthy's sake.

So that was taken as a token by the Table Round,
2520 And he honored that had it, evermore after,
As the best book of knighthood bids it be known.
In the old days of Arthur this happening befell;
The books of Brutus' deeds bear witness thereto
Since Brutus, the bold knight, embarked for this land
2525 After the siege ceased at Troy and the city fared
                                        amiss.
            Many such, ere we were born,
            Have befallen here, ere this.
            May He that was crowned with thorn
2530   Bring all men to His bliss! Amen.

Honi Soit Qui Mal Pense[2]

2. "Shame be to the man who has evil in his mind." This is the motto of the Order of the Garter, founded ca. 1350: apparently a copyist of the poem associated this order with the one founded to honor Gawain.

GEOFFREY CHAUCER
ca. 1343–1400

Medieval social theory held that society was made up of three "estates": the nobility, composed of a small hereditary aristocracy, whose mission on earth was to rule over and defend the body politic; the church, whose duty was to look after the spiritual welfare of that body; and everyone else, the large mass of commoners who were supposed to do the work that provided for its physical needs. By the late fourteenth century, however, these basic categories were layered into complex, interrelated, and unstable social strata among which birth, wealth, profession, and personal ability all played a part in determining one's status in a world that was rapidly changing economically, politically, and socially. Chaucer's life and his works, especially *The Canterbury Tales*, were profoundly influenced by these forces. A growing and prosperous middle class was beginning to play increasingly important roles in church and state, blurring the traditional class boundaries, and it was into this middle class that Chaucer was born.

Chaucer was the son of a prosperous wine merchant and probably spent his boyhood in the mercantile atmosphere of London's Vintry, where ships docked with wines from France and Spain. Here he would have mixed daily with people of all sorts, heard several languages spoken, become fluent in French, and received schooling in Latin. Instead of apprenticing Chaucer to the family business, however, his father was apparently able to place him, in his early teens, as a page in one of the great aristocratic households of England, that of the countess of Ulster who was married to Prince Lionel, the second son of Edward III. There Chaucer would have acquired the manners and skills required for a career in the service of the ruling class, not only in the role of personal attendant in royal households but in a series of administrative posts.

We can trace Chaucer's official and personal life in a considerable number of surviving historical documents, beginning with a reference, in Elizabeth of Ulster's household accounts, to an outfit he received as a page (1357). He was captured by the French and ransomed in one of Edward III's campaigns during the Hundred Years

War (1359). He was a member of King Edward's personal household (1367) and took part in several diplomatic missions to Spain (1366), France (1368), and Italy (1372). As controller of customs on wool, sheepskins, and leather for the port of London (1374–85), Chaucer audited and kept books on the export taxes, which were one of the Crown's main sources of revenue. During this period he was living in a rent-free apartment over one of the gates in the city wall, probably as a perquisite of the customs job. He served as a justice of the peace and knight of the shire (the title given to members of Parliament) for the county of Kent (1385–86) where he moved after giving up the controllership. As clerk of the king's works (1389–91), Chaucer was responsible for the maintenance of numerous royal residences, parks, and other holdings; his duties included supervision of the construction of the nave of Westminster Abbey and of stands and lists for a celebrated tournament staged by Richard II. While the records show Chaucer receiving many grants and annuities in addition to his salary for these services, they also show that at times he was being pressed by creditors and obliged to borrow money.

These activities brought Chaucer into association with the ruling nobility of the kingdom, with Prince Lionel and his younger brother John of Gaunt, duke of Lancaster, England's most powerful baron during much of Chaucer's lifetime; with their father, King Edward; and with Edward's grandson, who succeeded to the throne as Richard II. Near the end of his life Chaucer addressed a comic *Complaint to His Purse* to Henry IV—John of Gaunt's son, who had usurped the crown from his cousin Richard—as a reminder that the treasury owed Chaucer his annuity. Chaucer's wife, Philippa, served in the households of Edward's queen and of John of Gaunt's second wife, Constance, daughter of the king of Castile. A Thomas Chaucer, who was probably Chaucer's son, was an eminent man in the next generation, and Thomas's daughter Alice was married successively to the earl of Salisbury and the duke of Suffolk. The gap between the commoners and the aristocracy would thus have been bridged by Chaucer's family in the course of three generations.

None of these documents contains any hint that this hardworking civil servant wrote poetry, although poetry would certainly have been among the diversions cultivated at English courts in Chaucer's youth. That poetry, however, would have been in French, which still remained the fashionable language and literature of the English aristocracy, whose culture in many ways had more in common with that of the French nobles with whom they warred than with that of their English subjects. Chaucer's earliest models, works by Guillaume de Machaut (1300?–1377) and Jean Froissart (1333?–1400?), the leading French poets of the day, were lyrics and narratives about courtly love, often cast in the form of a dream in which the poet acted as a protagonist or participant in some aristocratic love affair. The poetry of Machaut and Froissart derives from the thirteenth-century *Romance of the Rose*, a long dream allegory in which the dreamer suffers many agonies and trials for the love of a symbolic rosebud. Chaucer's apprentice work may well have been a partial translation of the twenty-one-thousand-line *Romance*. His first important original poem is *The Book of the Duchess*, an elegy in the form of a dream vision commemorating John of Gaunt's first wife, the young duchess of Lancaster, who died in 1368.

The diplomatic mission that sent Chaucer to Italy in 1372 was in all likelihood a milestone in his literary development. Although he may have acquired some knowledge of the language and literature from Italian merchants and bankers posted in London, this visit and a subsequent one to Florence (1378) brought him into direct contact with the Italian Renaissance. Probably he acquired manuscripts of works by Dante, Petrarch, and Boccaccio—the last two still alive at the time of Chaucer's visit, although he probably did not meet them. These writers provided him with models of new verse forms, new subject matter, and new modes of representation. *The House of Fame*, still a dream vision, takes the poet on a journey in the talons of a gigantic eagle to the celestial palace of the goddess Fame, a trip that at many points affectionately parodies Dante's journey in the *Divine Comedy*. In his dream vision *The*

Parliament of Fowls, all the birds meet on St. Valentine's Day to choose their mates; their "parliament" humorously depicts the ways in which different classes in human society think and talk about love. Boccaccio provided sources for two of Chaucer's finest poems—although Chaucer never mentions his name. *The Knight's Tale,* the first of *The Canterbury Tales,* is based on Boccaccio's romance *Il Teseida* (The Story of Theseus). His longest completed poem, *Troilus and Criseyde* (ca. 1385), which tells the story of how Trojan Prince Troilus loved and finally lost Criseyde to the Greek warrior Diomede, is an adaptation of Boccaccio's *Il Filostrato* (The Love-Stricken). Chaucer reworked the latter into one of the greatest love poems in any language. Even if he had never written *The Canterbury Tales, Troilus* would have secured Chaucer a place among the major English poets.

A final dream vision provides the frame for Chaucer's first experiment with a series of tales, the unfinished *Legend of Good Women.* In the dream, Chaucer is accused of heresy and antifeminism by Cupid, the god of love himself, and ordered to do penance by writing a series of "legends," i.e., saints' lives, women who were betrayed by false men and died for love. Perhaps a noble patron, possibly Queen Anne, asked the poet to write something to make up for telling about Criseyde's betrayal of Troilus.

Throughout his life Chaucer also wrote moral and religious works, chiefly translations. Besides French, which was a second language for him, and Italian, Chaucer also read Latin. He made a prose translation of the Latin *Consolation of Philosophy,* written by the sixth-century Roman statesman Boethius while in prison awaiting execution for crimes for which he had been unjustly condemned. The *Consolation* became a favorite book for the Middle Ages, providing inspiration and comfort through its lesson that worldly fortune is deceitful and ephemeral and through the platonic doctrine that the body itself is only a prison house for the soul that aspires to eternal things. The influence of Boethius is deeply ingrained in *The Knight's Tale* and *Troilus.* The ballade *Truth* compresses the Boethian and Christian teaching into three stanzas of homely moral advice.

Thus long before Chaucer conceived of *The Canterbury Tales,* his writings were many faceted: they embrace prose and poetry; human and divine love; French, Italian, and Latin sources; secular and religious influences; comedy and philosophy. Moreover, different elements are likely to mix in the same work, often making it difficult to extract from Chaucer simple, direct, and certain meanings.

This Chaucerian complexity owes much to the wide range of Chaucer's learning and his exposure to new literary currents on the Continent but perhaps also to the special social position he occupied as a member of a new class of civil servants. Born into the urban middle class, Chaucer, through his association with the court and service of the Crown, had attained the rank of "esquire," roughly equivalent to what would later be termed a "gentleman." His career brought him into contact with overlapping bourgeois and aristocratic social worlds, without his being securely anchored in either. Although he was born a commoner and continued to associate with commoners in his official life, he did not live as a commoner; and although his training and service at court, his wife's connections, and probably his poetry brought him into contact with the nobility, he must always have been conscious of the fact that he did not really belong to that society of which birth alone could make one a true member. Situated at the intersection of these social worlds, Chaucer had the gift of being able to view with both sympathy and humor the behaviors, beliefs, and pretensions of the diverse people who comprised the levels of society. Chaucer's art of being at once involved in and detached from a given situation is peculiarly his own, but that art would have been appreciated by a small group of friends close to Chaucer's social position—men like Sir Philip de la Vache, to whom Chaucer addressed the humorous envoy to *Truth.* Chaucer belongs to an age when poetry was read aloud. A beautiful frontispiece to a manuscript of *Troilus* pictures the poet's public performance before a magnificently dressed royal audience, and he may well have been invited at times to read his poems at court. But besides addressing a listening audience, to whose allegedly superior taste and sensibility the poet often ironically defers (for example, *The General Prologue,* lines 745–48), Chaucer has in mind discriminating readers whom he might expect to share his sense of humor and his complex attitudes toward the company of "sondry folk" who make the pilgrimage to Canterbury.

The text given here is from E. T. Donaldson's *Chaucer's Poetry: An Anthology for the Modern Reader* (1958, 1975) with some modifications. For *The Canterbury Tales* the Hengwrt Manuscript has provided the textual basis. The spelling has been altered to improve consistency and has been modernized in so far as is possible without distorting the phonological values of the Middle English. A discussion of Middle English pronunciation, grammar, and prosody is included in the introduction to "The Middle Ages" (pp. 14–20).

The Canterbury Tales   Chaucer's original plan for *The Canterbury Tales*—if we assume it to be the same as that which the fictional Host proposes at the end of *The General Prologue*—projected about one hundred twenty stories, two for each pilgrim to tell on the way to Canterbury and two more on the way back. Chaucer actually completed only twenty-two and the beginnings of two others. He did write an ending, for the Host says to the Parson, who tells the last tale, that everyone except him has told "his tale." Indeed, the pilgrims never even get to Canterbury. The work was probably first conceived in 1386, when Chaucer was living in Greenwich, some miles east of London. From his house he might have been able to see the pilgrim road that led toward the shrine of the famous English saint, Thomas à Becket, the archbishop of Canterbury who was murdered in his cathedral in 1170. Medieval pilgrims were notorious tale tellers, and the sight and sound of the bands riding toward Canterbury may well have suggested to Chaucer the idea of using a fictitious pilgrimage as a framing device for a number of stories. Collections of stories linked by such a device were common in the later Middle Ages. Chaucer's contemporary John Gower had used one in his *Confessio Amantis.* The most famous medieval framing tale besides Chaucer's is Boccaccio's *Decameron,* in which ten different narrators each tell a tale a day for ten days. Chaucer could have known the *Decameron,* which contains tales with plots analogous to plots found also in *The Canterbury Tales,* but these stories were widespread, and there is no proof that Chaucer got them from Boccaccio.

Chaucer's artistic exploitation of the device is, in any case, altogether his own. Whereas in Gower a single speaker relates all the stories, and in Boccaccio the ten speakers—three young gentlemen and seven young ladies—all belong to the same sophisticated social elite, Chaucer's pilgrim narrators represent a wide spectrum of ranks and occupations. This device, however, should not be mistaken for "realism." It is highly unlikely that a group like Chaucer's pilgrims would ever have joined together and communicated on such seemingly equal terms. That is part of the fiction, as is the tacit assumption that a group so large could have ridden along listening to one another tell tales in verse. The variety of tellers is matched by the diversity of their tales: tales are assigned to appropriate narrators and juxtaposed to bring out contrasts in genre, style, tone, and values. Thus the Knight's courtly romance about the rivalry of two noble lovers for a lady is followed by the Miller's fabliau of the seduction of an old carpenter's young wife by a student. In several of *The Canterbury Tales* there is a fascinating accord between the narrators and their stories, so that the story takes on rich overtones from what we have learned of its teller in *The General Prologue* and elsewhere, and the character itself grows and is revealed by the story. Chaucer conducts two fictions simultaneously—that of the individual tale and that of the pilgrim to whom he has assigned it. He develops the second fiction not only through *The General Prologue* but also through the "links," the interchanges among pilgrims connecting the stories. These interchanges sometimes lead to quarrels. Thus *The Miller's Tale* offends the Reeve, who takes the figure of the Miller's foolish, cuckolded carpenter as directed personally at himself, and he retaliates with a story satirizing an arrogant miller very much like the pilgrim Miller. The antagonism of the two tellers provides comedy in the links and enhances the comedy of their tales. The links also offer interesting literary commentary on the tales by members of the pilgrim audience, especially the Host, whom the pilgrims have declared "governour" and "juge" of the storytelling. Further dramatic interest is created by the fact that several tales respond to topics taken up by previous tellers. The Wife of Bath's thesis that women should have sovereignty over men in marriage gets a reply from the Clerk, which in turn elicits responses from the Merchant and the Franklin. The tales have their own logic and interest quite apart from the framing fiction; no other medieval framing fiction, however, has such varied and lively interaction between the frame and the individual stories.

The composition of none of the tales can be accurately dated; most of them were written during the last fourteen years of Chaucer's life, although a few were probably written earlier and inserted into *The Canterbury Tales*. The popularity of the poem in late medieval England is attested by the number of surviving manuscripts: more than eighty, none from Chaucer's lifetime. It was also twice printed by William Caxton, who introduced printing to England in 1476, and often reprinted by Caxton's early successors. The manuscripts reflect the unfinished state of the poem—the fact that when he died Chaucer had not made up his mind about a number of details and hence left many inconsistencies. The poem appears in the manuscripts as nine or ten "fragments" or blocks of tales; the order of the poems within each fragment is generally the same, but the order of the fragments themselves varies widely. The fragment containing *The General Prologue;* the Knight's, Miller's, and Reeve's tales; and the Cook's unfinished tale, always comes first, and the fragment consisting of *The Parson's Tale* and *The Retraction* always comes last. But the others, such as that containing the Wife of Bath, the Friar, and the Summoner or that consisting of the Physician and Pardoner or the longest fragment, consisting of six tales concluding with the Nun's Priest's, are by no means stable in relation to one another. The order followed here, that of the Ellesmere manuscript, has been adopted as the most nearly satisfactory.

THE GENERAL PROLOGUE

Chaucer did not need to make a pilgrimage himself to meet the types of people that his fictitious pilgrimage includes, because most of them had long inhabited literature as well as life: the ideal Knight, who had taken part in all the major expeditions and battles of the crusades during the last half-century; his fashionably dressed son, the Squire, a typical young lover; the lady Prioress, the hunting Monk, and the flattering Friar, who practice the little vanities and larger vices for which such ecclesiastics were conventionally attacked; the prosperous Franklin; the fraudulent Doctor; the lusty and domineering Wife of Bath; the austere Parson; and so on down through the lower orders to that spellbinding preacher and mercenary, the Pardoner, peddling his paper indulgences and phony relics. One meets all these types throughout medieval literature, but particularly in a genre called estates satire, which sets out to expose and pillory typical examples of corruption at all levels of society. A remarkable number of details in *The General Prologue* could have been taken straight out of books as well as drawn from life. Although it has been argued that some of the pilgrims are portraits of actual people, the impression that they are drawn from life is more likely to be a function of Chaucer's art, which is able to endow types with a reality we generally associate only with people we know. The salient features of each pilgrim leap out randomly at the reader, as they might to an observer concerned only with what meets the eye. This imitation of the way our minds actually perceive reality may make us fail to notice the care with which Chaucer has selected his details to give an integrated sketch of the person being described. Most of these details give something more than mere verisimilitude to the description. The pilgrims' facial features, the clothes they wear, the foods they like to eat, the things they say, the work they do are all clues not only to their social rank but to their moral and spiritual condition and, through the accumulation of detail, to the condition of late-medieval society, of which, collectively, they are representative. What uniquely distinguishes Chaucer's prologue from more conventional estates satire, such as the *Prologue* to *Piers Plowman*, is the suppression in all but a few flagrant instances of overt moral judgment. The narrator, in fact, seems to be expressing chiefly admiration and praise at the superlative skills and accomplishments of this particular group, even such dubious ones as the Friar's begging techniques or the Manciple's success in cheating the learned lawyers who employ him. The reader is left free to draw out the ironic implications of details presented with such seeming artlessness, even while falling in with the easygoing mood of "felaweship" that pervades Chaucer's prologue to the pilgrimage.

FROM THE CANTERBURY TALES

The General Prologue

Whan that April with his° showres soote°   *its/fresh*
The droughte of March hath perced to the roote,
And bathed every veine[1] in swich° licour,°   *such/liquid*
Of which vertu[2] engendred is the flowr;
5 Whan Zephyrus eek° with his sweete breeth   *also*
Inspired[3] hath in every holt° and heeth°   *grove/field*
The tendre croppes,° and the yonge sonne[4]   *shoots*
Hath in the Ram his halve cours yronne,
And smale fowles° maken melodye   *birds*
10 That sleepen al the night with open yë°—   *eye*
So priketh hem° Nature in hir corages[5]—   *them*
Thanne longen folk to goon° on pilgrimages,   *go*
And palmeres for to seeken straunge strondes
To ferne halwes,[6] couthe° in sondry° londes; *known/various*
15 And specially from every shires ende
Of Engelond to Canterbury they wende,
The holy blisful martyr[7] for to seeke
That hem hath holpen° whan that they were seke.° *helped/sick*
  Bifel° that in that seson on a day,   *It happened*
20 In Southwerk[8] at the Tabard as I lay,
Redy to wenden on my pilgrimage
To Canterbury with ful° devout corage,   *very*
At night was come into that hostelrye

1. I.e., in plants.
2. By the power of which.
3. Breathed into. "Zephyrus": the west wind.
4. The sun is young because it has run only halfway through its course in Aries, the Ram—the first sign of the zodiac in the solar year.
5. Their hearts.
6. Far-off shrines. "Palmeres": palmers, wide-ranging pilgrims—especially those who sought out the "straunge strondes" (foreign shores) of the Holy Land.
7. St. Thomas à Becket, murdered in Canterbury Cathedral in 1170.
8. Southwark, site of the Tabard Inn, was then a suburb of London, south of the Thames River.

Wel nine and twenty in a compaignye
25   Of sondry folk, by aventure° yfalle   *chance*
In felaweshipe, and pilgrimes were they alle
That toward Canterbury wolden° ride.   *would*
The chambres and the stables weren wide,
And wel we weren esed° at the beste.⁹   *accommodated*
30   And shortly,° whan the sonne was to reste,¹   *in brief*
So hadde I spoken with hem everichoon°   *every one*
That I was of hir felaweshipe anoon,°   *at once*
And made forward² erly for to rise,
To take oure way ther as³ I you devise.°   *describe*
35   But nathelees,° whil I have time and space,⁴   *nevertheless*
Er° that I ferther in this tale pace,°   *before/proceed*
Me thinketh it accordant to resoun⁵
To telle you al the condicioun
Of eech of hem, so as it seemed me,
40   And whiche they were, and of what degree,°   *social rank*
And eek° in what array that they were inne: *also*
And at a knight thanne° wol I first biginne.   *then*
    A Knight ther was, and that a worthy man,
That fro the time that he first bigan
45   To riden out, he loved chivalrye,
Trouthe and honour, freedom and curteisye.⁶
Ful worthy was he in his lordes werre,°   *war*
And therto hadde he riden, no man ferre,°   *farther*
As wel in Cristendom as hethenesse,°   *heathen lands*
50   And⁷ evere honoured for his worthinesse.
    At Alisandre⁸ he was whan it was wonne;
Ful ofte time he hadde the boord bigonne⁹
Aboven alle nacions in Pruce;
In Lettou had he reised,° and in Ruce,   *campaigned*
55   No Cristen man so ofte of his degree;
In Gernade° at the sege eek hadde he be   *Granada*
Of Algezir, and riden in Belmarye;
At Lyeis was he, and at Satalye,
Whan they were wonne; and in the Grete See¹
60   At many a noble arivee° hadde he be.   *military landing*
    At mortal batailes² hadde he been fifteene,
And foughten for oure faith at Tramissene
In listes³ thries,° and ay° slain his fo.   *thrice/always*
    This ilke° worthy Knight hadde been also   *same*
65   Sometime with the lord of Palatye⁴

---

9. In the best possible way.
1. Had set.
2. I.e., (we) made an agreement.
3. Where.
4. I.e., opportunity.
5. It seems to me according to reason.
6. Courtesy. "Trouthe": integrity. "Freedom": generosity of spirit.
7. I.e., and he was.
8. The Knight has taken part in campaigns fought against three groups who threatened Christian Europe during the 14th century: the Moslems in the Near East, from whom Alexandria was seized

after a famous siege; the northern barbarians in Prussia, Lithuania, and Russia; and the Moors in North Africa. The place names in the following lines refer to battlegrounds in these continuing wars.
9. Sat in the seat of honor at military feasts.
1. The Mediterranean.
2. Tournaments fought to the death.
3. Lists, tournament grounds.
4. A Moslem: alliances of convenience were often made during the Crusades between Christians and Moslems.

Again° another hethen in Turkye;   *against*
And everemore he hadde a soverein pris.°   *reputation*
And though that he were worthy, he was wis,[5]
And of his port° as meeke as is a maide.   *demeanor*
70 He nevere yit no vilainye° ne saide   *rudeness*
In al his lif unto no manere wight:[6]
He was a verray,° parfit,° gentil° knight.   *true / perfect / noble*
But for to tellen you of his array,
His hors° were goode, but he was nat gay.[7]   *horses*
75 Of fustian° he wered° a gipoun[8]   *thick cloth / wore*
Al bismotered with his haubergeoun,[9]
For he was late° come from his viage,°   *lately / expedition*
And wente for to doon his pilgrimage.
    With him ther was his sone, a yong Squier,[1]
80 A lovere and a lusty bacheler,
With lokkes crulle° as° they were laid in presse.   *curly / as if*
Of twenty yeer of age he was, I gesse.
Of his stature he was of evene° lengthe,   *moderate*
And wonderly delivere,° and of greet° strengthe.   *agile / great*
85 And he hadde been som time in chivachye[2]
In Flandres, in Artois, and Picardye,
And born him wel as of so litel space,[3]
In hope to stonden in his lady° grace.   *lady's*
Embrouded° was he as it were a mede,[4]   *embroidered*
90 Al ful of fresshe flowres, white and rede;°   *red*
Singing he was, or floiting,° al the day: *whistling*
He was as fressh as is the month of May.
Short was his gowne, with sleeves longe and wide.
Wel coude he sitte on hors, and faire ride;
95 He coude songes make, and wel endite,°   *compose verse*
Juste[5] and eek° daunce, and wel portraye° and write.   *also / sketch*
So hote° he loved that by nightertale[6]   *hotly*
He slepte namore than dooth a nightingale.
Curteis he was, lowely,° and servisable,   *humble*
100 And carf biforn his fader at the table.[7]
    A Yeman hadde he[8] and servants namo°   *no more*
At that time, for him liste[9] ride so;
And he[1] was clad in cote and hood of greene.
A sheef of pecok arwes,° bright and keene,   *arrows*
105 Under his belt he bar° ful thriftily;°   *bore / properly*
Wel coude he dresse° his takel° yemanly:[2]   *tend to / gear*
His arwes drouped nought with fetheres lowe.

---

5. I.e., he was wise as well as bold.
6. Any sort of person. In Middle English, negatives are multiplied for emphasis, as in these two lines: "nevere," "no," "ne," "no."
7. I.e., gaily dressed.
8. Tunic worn underneath the coat of mail.
9. All rust-stained from his hauberk (coat of mail).
1. The vague term "Squier" (Squire) here seems to be the equivalent of "bacheler" (line 80), a young knight still in the service of an older one.
2. On cavalry expeditions. The places in the next line are sites of skirmishes in the constant warfare between the English and the French.

3. I.e., considering the little time he had been in service.
4. Mead, meadow.
5. Joust, fight in a tournament.
6. At night.
7. It was a squire's duty to carve his lord's meat.
8. I.e., the Knight. The "Yeman" (Yeoman) is an independent commoner who acts as the Knight's military servant.
9. It pleased him to.
1. I.e., the Yeoman.
2. In a workmanlike way.

And in his hand he bar a mighty bowe.
A not-heed° hadde he with a brown visage.   close-cut head
110 Of wodecraft wel coude° he al the usage.   knew
Upon his arm he bar a gay bracer,[3]
And by his side a swerd° and a bokeler,[4]   sword
And on that other side a gay daggere,
Harneised° wel and sharp as point of spere;   mounted
115 A Cristophre[5] on his brest of silver sheene;°   bright
An horn he bar, the baudrik[6] was of greene.
A forster° was he soothly,° as I gesse.   forester/truly
    Ther was also a Nonne, a Prioresse,
That of hir smiling was ful simple and coy.[7]
120 Hir gretteste ooth was but by sainte Loy!°   Eloi
And she was cleped° Madame Eglantine.   named
Ful wel she soong° the service divine,   sang
Entuned° in hir nose ful semely;[8]   chanted
And Frenssh she spak ful faire and fetisly,°   elegantly
125 After the scole° of Stratford at the Bowe[9]—   school
For Frenssh of Paris was to hire unknowe.
At mete° wel ytaught was she withalle:°   meals/besides
She leet° no morsel from hir lippes falle,   let
Ne wette hir fingres in hir sauce deepe;
130 Wel coude she carye a morsel, and wel keepe°   take care
That no drope ne fille° upon hir brest.   should fall
In curteisye was set ful muchel hir lest.[1]
Hir over-lippe° wiped she so clene   upper lip
That in hir coppe° ther was no ferthing° seene   cup/bit
135 Of grece,° whan she dronken hadde hir draughte;   grease
Ful semely after hir mete she raughte.°   reached
And sikerly° she was of greet disport,[2]   certainly
And ful plesant, and amiable of port,°   mien
And pained hire to countrefete cheere[3]
140 Of court, and to been statlich° of manere,   dignified
And to been holden digne[4] of reverence.
But, for to speken of hir conscience,
She was so charitable and so pitous°   merciful
She wolde weepe if that she saw a mous
145 Caught in a trappe, if it were deed° or bledde.   dead
Of[5] smale houndes hadde she that she fedde
With rosted flessh, or milk and wastelbreed;°   fine white bread
But sore wepte she if oon of hem were deed,
Or if men smoot it with a yerde smerte;[6]
150 And al was conscience and tendre herte.
Ful semely hir wimpel° pinched° was,   headdress/pleated
Hir nose tretis,° hir yën° greye as glas,   well-formed/eyes

3. Wrist guard for archers.
4. Buckler (a small shield).
5. St. Christopher medal.
6. Baldric (a supporting strap).
7. Sincere and shy. The Prioress is the mother superior of her nunnery.
8. In a seemly, proper manner.
9. The French learned in a convent school in

Stratford-at-the-Bow, a suburb of London, was evidently not up to the Parisian standard.
1. I.e., her chief delight lay in good manners.
2. Of great good cheer.
3. And took pains to imitate the behavior.
4. And to be considered worthy.
5. I.e., some.
6. If someone struck it with a rod sharply.

Hir mouth ful smal, and therto° softe and reed,°   *moreover/red*
But sikerly° she hadde a fair forheed: *certainly*
155 It was almost a spanne brood,[7] I trowe,°   *believe*
For hardily,° she was nat undergrowe.   *assuredly*
Ful fetis° was hir cloke, as I was war;°   *becoming/aware*
Of smal° coral aboute hir arm she bar   *dainty*
A paire of bedes, gauded all with greene,[8]
160 And theron heeng° a brooch of gold ful sheene,°   *hung/bright*
On which ther was first writen a crowned A,[9]
And after, *Amor vincit omnia.*[1]
Another Nonne with hire hadde she
That was hir chapelaine,° and preestes three.[2]   *secretary*
165 A Monk ther was, a fair for the maistrye,[3]
An outridere[4] that loved venerye,°   *hunting*
A manly man, to been an abbot able.°   *worthy*
Ful many a daintee° hors hadde he in stable,   *fine*
And whan he rood,° men mighte his bridel heere   *rode*
170 Ginglen° in a whistling wind as clere   *jingle*
And eek° as loude as dooth the chapel belle   *also*
Ther as this lord was kepere of the celle.[5]
The rule of Saint Maure or of Saint Beneit,
By cause that it was old and somdeel strait[6]—
175 This ilke° Monk leet olde thinges pace,°   *same/pass away*
And heeld° after the newe world the space.°   *held/course*
He yaf° nought of that text a pulled hen[7]   *gave*
That saith that hunteres been° nought holy men,   *are*
Ne that a monk, whan he is recchelees,[8]
180 Is likned til° a fissh that is waterlees—   *to*
This is to sayn, a monk out of his cloistre;
But thilke° text heeld he nat worth an oystre.   *that same*
And I saide his opinion was good:
What° sholde he studye and make himselven wood°   *why/crazy*
185 Upon a book in cloistre alway to poure,°   *pore*
Or swinke° with his handes and laboure,   *work*
As Austin bit?[9] How shal the world be served?
Lat Austin have his swink to him reserved!
Therefore he was a prikasour° aright.   *hard rider*
190 Grehoundes he hadde as swift as fowl in flight.
Of priking° and of hunting for the hare   *riding*
Was al his lust,° for no cost wolde he spare.   *pleasure*
I sawgh his sleeves purfiled° at the hand   *fur lined*
With gris,° and that the fineste of a land;   *gray fur*
195 And for to festne his hood under his chin
He hadde of gold wrought a ful curious[1] pin:

---

7. A handsbreadth wide.
8. Provided with green beads to mark certain prayers. "A paire": string (i.e., a rosary).
9. An *A* with an ornamental crown on it.
1. "Love conquers all."
2. The three get reduced to just one nun's priest.
3. I.e., a superlatively fine one.
4. A monk charged with supervising property distant from the monastery. Monasteries obtained income from large landholdings.

5. Prior of an outlying cell (branch) of the monastery.
6. Somewhat strict. St. Maurus and St. Benedict were authors of monastic rules.
7. He didn't give a plucked hen for that text.
8. Reckless, careless of rule.
9. I.e., as St. Augustine bids. St. Augustine had written that monks should perform manual labor.
1. Of careful workmanship.

A love-knotte in the grettere° ende ther was.   *greater*
His heed was balled,° that shoon as any glas,   *bald*
And eek his face, as he hadde been anoint:
200 He was a lord ful fat and in good point;[2]
His yën steepe,° and rolling in his heed,   *protruding*
That stemed as a furnais of a leed,[3]
His bootes souple,° his hors in greet estat°   *supple/condition*
Now certainly he was a fair prelat.[4]
205 He was nat pale as a forpined° gost: *wasted away*
A fat swan loved he best of any rost.
His palfrey° was as brown as is a berye.   *saddle horse*
    A Frere ther was, a wantoune° and a merye,   *jovial*
A limitour,[5] a ful solempne° man.   *ceremonious*
210 In alle the ordres foure is noon that can°   *knows*
So muche of daliaunce° and fair langage: *sociability*
He hadde maad ful many a mariage
Of yonge wommen at his owene cost;
Unto his ordre he was a noble post.[6]
215 Ful wel biloved and familier was he
With frankelains over al[7] in his contree,
And with worthy wommen of the town—
For he hadde power of confessioun,
As saide himself, more than a curat,°   *parish priest*
220 For of° his ordre he was licenciat.[8]   *by*
Ful swetely herde he confessioun,
And plesant was his absolucioun.
He was an esy man to yive penaunce
Ther as he wiste to have[9] a good pitaunce;°   *donation*
225 For unto a poore ordre for to yive
Is signe that a man is wel yshrive,[1]
For if he yaf, he dorste make avaunt°   *boast*
He wiste° that a man was repentaunt;   *knew*
For many a man so hard is of his herte
230 He may nat weepe though him sore smerte:[2]
Therfore, in stede of weeping and prayeres,
Men mote° yive silver to the poore freres.[3]   *may*
    His tipet° was ay farsed° ful of knives   *hood/stuffed*
And pinnes, for to yiven faire wives;
235 And certainly he hadde a merye note;
Wel coude he singe and playen on a rote;°   *fiddle*
Of yeddinges he bar outrely the pris.[4]
His nekke whit was as the flowr-de-lis;°   *lily*
Therto he strong was as a champioun.

2. In good shape, plump.
3. That glowed like a furnace with a pot in it.
4. Prelate (an important churchman).
5. The "Frere" (Friar) is a member of one of the four religious orders whose members live by begging; as a "limitour" he has been granted by his order exclusive begging rights within a certain limited area.
6. I.e., pillar, a staunch supporter.
7. I.e., with franklins everywhere. Franklins were well-to-do country men.

8. I.e., licensed to hear confessions.
9. Where he knew he would have.
1. Shriven, absolved.
2. Although he is sorely grieved.
3. Before granting absolution, the confessor must be sure the sinner is contrite; moreover, the absolution is contingent on the sinner's performance of an act of satisfaction. In the case of Chaucer's Friar, a liberal contribution served both as proof of contrition and as satisfaction.
4. He absolutely took the prize for ballads.

240 He knew the tavernes wel in every town,
And every hostiler° and tappestere,° *innkeeper/barmaid*
Bet° than a lazar or a beggestere.⁵ *better*
For unto swich a worthy man as he
Accorded nat, as by his facultee,⁶
245 To have with sike° lazars aquaintaunce: *sick*
It is nat honeste,° it may nought avaunce,° *dignified/profit*
For to delen with no swich poraile,⁷
But al with riche, and selleres of vitaile;° *foodstuffs*
And over al ther as⁸ profit sholde arise,
250 Curteis he was, and lowely of servise.
Ther was no man nowher so vertuous:° *effective*
He was the beste beggere in his hous.° *friary*
And yaf a certain ferme for the graunt:⁹
Noon of his bretheren cam ther in his haunt.¹
255 For though a widwe° hadde nought a sho,° *widow/shoe*
So plesant was his *In principio*²
Yit wolde he have a ferthing° er he wente; *small coin*
His purchas was wel bettre than his rente.³
And rage he coude as it were right a whelpe;⁴
260 In love-dayes⁵ ther coude he muchel° helpe, *much*
For ther he was nat lik a cloisterer,
With a thredbare cope, as is a poore scoler,
But he was lik a maister⁶ or a pope.
Of double worstede was his semicope,° *short robe*
265 And rounded as a belle out of the presse.° *bell mold*
Somwhat he lipsed° for his wantounesse° *lisped/affectation*
To make his Englissh sweete upon his tonge;
And in his harping, whan he hadde songe,° *sung*
His yën twinkled in his heed aright
270 As doon the sterres° in the frosty night. *stars*
This worthy limitour was cleped Huberd.

   A Marchant was ther with a forked beerd,
In motelee,⁷ and hye on hors he sat,
Upon his heed a Flandrissh° bevere hat, *Flemish*
275 His bootes clasped faire and fetisly.° *elegantly*
His resons° he spak ful solempnely, *opinions*
Souning° alway th' encrees of his winning.° *implying/profit*
He wolde the see were kept for any thing⁸
Bitwixen Middelburgh and Orewelle.
280 Wel coude he in eschaunge sheeldes⁹ selle.

---

5. "Beggestere": female beggar. "Lazar:" leper.
6. It was not suitable because of his position.
7. I.e., poor trash. The oldest order of friars had been founded by St. Francis to administer to the spiritual needs of precisely those classes the Friar avoids.
8. Everywhere.
9. And he paid a certain rent for the privilege of begging.
1. Assigned territory.
2. A friar's usual salutation: "In the beginning [was the Word]" (John 1.1).
3. I.e., the money he got through such activity was more than his proper income.

4. And he could flirt wantonly, as if he were a puppy.
5. Days appointed for the settlement of lawsuits out of court.
6. A man of recognized learning.
7. Motley, a cloth of mixed color.
8. I.e., he wished the sea to be guarded at all costs. The sea route between Middelburgh (in the Netherlands) and Orwell (in Suffolk) was vital to the Merchant's export and import of wool—the basis of England's chief trade at the time.
9. Shields were units of transfer in international credit, which he exchanged at a profit.

This worthy man ful wel his wit bisette:°   *employed*
Ther wiste° no wight° that he was in dette,   *knew / person*
So statly° was he of his governaunce,[1]   *dignified*
With his bargaines,° and with his chevissaunce.° *bargainings / borrowing*
285   Forsoothe° he was a worthy man withalle;   *in truth*
But, sooth to sayn, I noot° how men him calle.   *don't know*
    A Clerk[2] ther was of Oxenforde also
That unto logik hadde longe ygo.[3]
As lene was his hors as is a rake,
290   And he was nought right fat, I undertake,
But looked holwe,° and therto sobrely.   *hollow*
Ful thredbare was his overeste courtepy,
For he hadde geten him yit no benefice,[4]
Ne was so worldly for to have office.°   *secular employment*
295   For him was levere[5] have at his beddes heed
Twenty bookes, clad in blak or reed,
Of Aristotle and his philosophye,
Than robes riche, or fithele,° or gay sautrye.[6]   *fiddle*
But al be that he was a philosophre[7]
300   Yit hadde he but litel gold in cofre;°   *coffer*
But al that he mighte of his freendes hente,°   *take*
On bookes and on lerning he it spente,
And bisily gan for the soules praye
Of hem that yaf him wherwith to scoleye.°   *study*
305   Of studye took he most cure° and most heede.   *care*
Nought oo° word spak he more than was neede,   *one*
And that was said in forme[8] and reverence,
And short and quik,° and ful of heigh sentence:[9]   *lively*
Souning° in moral vertu was his speeche,   *resounding*
310   And gladly wolde he lerne, and gladly teche.
    A Sergeant of the Lawe, war and wis,[1]
That often hadde been at the Parvis[2]
Ther was also, ful riche of excellence.
Discreet he was, and of greet reverence—
315   He seemed swich, his wordes weren so wise.
Justice he was ful often in assise°   *circuit courts*
By patente[3] and by plein° commissioun.   *full*
For his science° and for his heigh renown   *knowledge*
Of fees and robes hadde he many oon.
320   So greet a purchasour° was nowher noon;   *speculator in land*
Al was fee simple[4] to him in effect—
His purchasing mighte nat been infect.[5]

---

1. The management of his affairs.
2. The Clerk is a student at Oxford; to become a student, he would have had to signify his intention of becoming a cleric, but he was not bound to proceed to a position of responsibility in the church.
3. Who had long since matriculated in philosophy.
4. Ecclesiastical living, such as the income a parish priest receives. "Courtepy": outer cloak.
5. He would rather.
6. Psaltery (a kind of harp).
7. The word may also mean alchemist, someone who tries to turn base metals into gold. The Clerk's

"philosophy" does not pay either way.
8. With decorum.
9. Elevated thought.
1. Wary and wise. The Sergeant is not only a practicing lawyer but one of the high justices of the nation.
2. The Paradise, the porch of St. Paul's Cathedral, a meeting place for lawyers and their clients.
3. Royal warrant.
4. Owned outright without legal impediments.
5. Invalidated on a legal technicality.

Nowher so bisy a man as he ther nas;°   *was not*
And yit he seemed bisier than he was.
325 In termes hadde he caas and doomes⁶ alle
That from the time of King William⁷ were falle.
Therto he coude endite and make a thing,⁸
Ther coude no wight pinchen° at his writing;   *cavil*
And every statut coude° he plein° by rote.⁹   *knew/entire*
330 He rood but hoomly° in a medlee cote,¹   *unpretentiously*
Girt with a ceint° of silk, with barres² smale.   *belt*
Of his array telle I no lenger tale.
    A Frankelain³ was in his compaignye:
Whit was his beerd as is the dayesye;°   *daisy*
335 Of his complexion he was sanguin.⁴
Wel loved he by the morwe a sop in win.⁵
To liven in delit° was evere his wone,°   *sensual delight/wont*
For he was Epicurus⁶ owene sone,
That heeld opinion that plein° delit   *full*
340 Was verray° felicitee parfit.°   *true/perfect*
An housholdere and that a greet was he:
Saint Julian⁷ he was in his contree.
His breed, his ale, was always after oon;⁸
A bettre envined° man was nevere noon.   *wine-stocked*
345 Withouten bake mete was nevere his hous,
Of fissh and flessh, and that so plentevous°   *plenteous*
It snewed° in his hous of mete° and drinke,   *snowed/food*
Of alle daintees that men coude thinke.
After° the sondry sesons of the yeer   *according to*
350 So chaunged he his mete° and his soper.°   *dinner/supper*
Ful many a fat partrich hadde he in mewe,°   *cage*
And many a breem,° and many a luce° in stewe.⁹   *carp/pike*
Wo was his cook but if his sauce were
Poinant° and sharp, and redy all his gere.   *spicy*
355 His table dormant in his halle alway
Stood redy covered all the longe day.¹
At sessions ther was he lord and sire.
Ful ofte time he was Knight of the Shire.²
An anlaas° and a gipser° al of silk   *dagger/purse*
360 Heeng at his girdel,³ whit as morne° milk.   *morning*
A shirreve° hadde he been, and countour.⁴   *sheriff*
Was nowhere swich a worthy vavasour.⁵

6. Law cases and decisions. "By termes": i.e., by heart.
7. I.e., the Conqueror (reigned 1066–87).
8. Compose and draw up a deed.
9. By heart.
1. A coat of mixed color.
2. Transverse stripes.
3. The "Frankelain" (Franklin) is a prosperous country man, whose lower-class ancestry is no impediment to the importance he has attained in his county.
4. A reference to the fact that the Franklin's temperament, "humor," is dominated by blood as well as to his red face (see p. 225, n.8).
5. I.e., in the morning he was very fond of a piece of bread soaked in wine.

6. The Greek philosopher whose teaching is popularly believed to make pleasure the chief goal of life.
7. The patron saint of hospitality.
8. Always of the same high quality.
9. Fishpond.
1. Tables were usually dismounted when not in use, but the Franklin kept his mounted and set ("covered"), hence "dormant."
2. County representative in Parliament. "Sessions": i.e., sessions of the justices of the peace.
3. Hung at his belt.
4. Auditor of county finances.
5. Feudal landholder of lowest rank; a provincial gentleman.

An Haberdasshere and a Carpenter,
A Webbe,° a Dyere, and a Tapicer°—   *weaver / tapestry maker*
365 And they were clothed alle in oo liveree[6]
Of a solempne and greet fraternitee.
Ful fresshe and newe hir gere apiked° was;   *trimmed*
Hir knives were chaped° nought with bras,   *mounted*
But al with silver; wrought ful clene and weel
370 Hir girdles and hir pouches everydeel.°   *altogether*
Wel seemed eech of hem a fair burgeis°   *burgher*
To sitten in a yeldehalle° on a dais.   *guildhall*
Everich, for the wisdom that he can,[7]
Was shaply° for to been an alderman.   *suitable*
375 For catel° hadde they ynough and rente,°   *property / income*
And eek hir wives wolde it wel assente—
And elles certain were they to blame:
It is ful fair to been ycleped° "Madame,"   *called*
And goon to vigilies all bifore,[8]
380 And have a mantel royalliche ybore.[9]
    A Cook they hadde with hem for the nones,[1]
To boile the chiknes with the marybones,°   *marrowbones*
And powdre-marchant tart and galingale.[2]
Wel coude he knowe° a draughte of London ale.   *recognize*
385 He coude roste, and seethe,° and broile, and frye,   *boil*
Maken mortreux,° and wel bake a pie.   *stews*
But greet harm was it, as it thoughte° me,   *seemed to*
That on his shine a mormal° hadde he,   *ulcer*
For blankmanger,[3] that made he with the beste.
390   A Shipman was ther, woning° fer by weste—°   *dwelling / in the west*
For ought I woot,° he was of Dertemouthe.[4]   *know*
He rood upon a rouncy° as he couthe,[5]   *large nag*
In a gowne of falding° to the knee.   *heavy wool*
A daggere hanging on a laas° hadde he   *strap*
395 Aboute his nekke, under his arm adown.
The hote somer hadde maad his hewe° al brown;   *color*
And certainly he was a good felawe.
Ful many a draughte of win hadde he drawe[6]
Fro Burdeuxward, whil that the chapman sleep:[7]
400 Of nice° conscience took he no keep;°   *fastidious / heed*
If that he faught and hadde the hyer° hand,   *upper*
By water he sente hem hoom to every land.[8]
But of his craft, to rekene wel his tides,
His stremes° and his daungers° him bisides,[9]   *currents / hazards*
405 His herberwe° and his moone, his lodemenage,[1]   *anchorage*

6. In one livery, i.e., the uniform of their "frater-nitee" or guild, a partly religious, partly social organization.
7. Was capable of.
8. I.e., at the head of the procession. "Vigiles": feasts held on the eve of saints' days.
9. Royally carried.
1. For the occasion.
2. "Powdre-marchant" and "galingale" are flavoring materials.

3. A white stew or mousse.
4. Dartmouth, a port in the southwest of England.
5. As best he could.
6. Drawn, i.e., stolen.
7. Merchant slept. "Fro Burdeauxward": from Bordeaux; i.e., while carrying wine from Bordeaux (the wine center of France).
8. He drowned his prisoners.
9. Around him.
1. Pilotage, art of navigation.

There was noon swich from Hulle to Cartage.[2]
Hardy he was and wis to undertake;[3]
With many a tempest hadde his beerd been shake;
He knew alle the havenes° as they were   *harbors*
410   Fro Gotlond to the Cape of Finistere,[4]
And every crike° in Britaine° and in Spaine.   *inlet/Brittany*
His barge ycleped was the Maudelaine.°   *Magdalene*
    With us ther was a Doctour of Physik:°   *medicine*
In al this world ne was ther noon him lik
415   To speken of physik and of surgerye.
For° he was grounded in astronomye,°   *because/astrology*
He kepte° his pacient a ful greet deel[5]   *tended to*
In houres by his magik naturel.[6]
Wel coude he fortunen the ascendent
420   Of his images[7] for his pacient.
He knew the cause of every maladye,
Were it of hoot or cold or moiste or drye,
And where engendred and of what humour:[8]
He was a verray parfit praktisour.[9]
425   The cause yknowe,° and of his° harm the roote,   *known/its*
Anoon he yaf the sike man his boote.°   *remedy*
    Ful redy hadde he his apothecaries
To senden him drogges° and his letuaries,°   *drugs/medicines*
For eech of hem made other for to winne:
430   Hir frendshipe was nought newe to biginne.
Wel knew he the olde Esculapius,[1]
And Deiscorides and eek Rufus,
Olde Ipocras, Hali, and Galien,
Serapion, Razis, and Avicen,
435   Averrois, Damascien, and Constantin,
Bernard, and Gatesden, and Gilbertin.
Of his diete mesurable° was he,   *moderate*
For it was of no superfluitee,
But of greet norissing° and digestible.   *nourishment*
440   His studye was but litel on the Bible.
In sanguin° and in pers° he clad was al,   *blood red/blue*
Lined with taffata and with sendal;°   *silk*
And yit he was but esy of dispence;°   *expenditure*

2. From Hull (in northern England) to Cartagena
(in Spain).
3. Shrewd in his undertakings.
4. From Gotland (an island in the Baltic) to Fin-
isterre (the westernmost point in Spain).
5. Closely.
6. Natural—as opposed to black—magic. "In
houres": i.e., the astrologically important hours
(when conjunctions of the planets might help his
recovery).
7. Assign the propitious time, according to the
position of stars, for using talismanic images. Such
images, representing either the patient himself or
points in the zodiac, were thought to be influential
on the course of the disease.
8. Diseases were thought to be caused by a dis-
turbance of one or another of the four bodily
"humors," each of which, like the four elements,
was a compound of two of the elementary qualities

mentioned in line 422: the melancholy humor,
seated in the black bile, was cold and dry (like
earth); the sanguine, seated in the blood, hot and
moist (like air); the choleric, seated in the yellow
bile, hot and dry (like fire); the phlegmatic, seated
in the phlegm, cold and moist (like water).
9. True perfect practitioner.
1. The Doctor is familiar with the treatises that
the Middle Ages attributed to the "great names" of
medical history, whom Chaucer names: the purely
legendary Greek demigod Aesculapius; the Greeks
Dioscorides, Rufus, Hippocrates, Galen, and Serapion; the Persians Hali and Rhazes; the Arabians
Avicenna and Averroës; the early Christians John
(?) of Damascus and Constantine Afer; the Scots-
man Bernard Gordon; the Englishmen John of
Gatesden and Gilbert, the former an early contemporary of Chaucer.

He kepte that he wan in pestilence.[2]

445 For° gold in physik is a cordial,[3]   *because*
   Therfore he loved gold in special.
      A good Wif was ther of biside Bathe,
   But she was somdeel deef,° and that was scathe.°   *a bit deaf/a pity*
   Of cloth-making she hadde swich an haunt,°   *skill*
450 She passed° hem of Ypres and of Gaunt.[4]   *surpassed*
   In al the parissh wif ne was ther noon
   That to the offring[5] bifore hire sholde goon,
   And if ther dide, certain so wroth° was she   *angry*
   That she was out of alle charitee.
455 Hir coverchiefs° ful fine were of ground°—   *headcovers/texture*
   I dorste° swere they weyeden° ten pound   *dare/weighed*
   That on a Sonday weren° upon hir heed.   *were*
   Hir hosen° weren of fin scarlet reed,°   *leggings/red*
   Ful straite yteyd,[6] and shoes ful moiste° and newe.   *supple*
460 Bold was hir face and fair and reed of hewe.
   She was a worthy womman al hir live:
   Housbondes at chirche dore[7] she hadde five,
   Withouten° other compaignye in youthe—   *not counting*
   But therof needeth nought to speke as nouthe.°   *now*
465 And thries hadde she been at Jerusalem;
   She hadde passed many a straunge° streem;   *foreign*
   At Rome she hadde been, and at Boloigne,
   In Galice at Saint Jame, and at Coloigne:[8]
   She coude° muchel of wandring by the waye: *knew*
470 Gat-toothed[9] was she, soothly for to saye.
   Upon an amblere[1] esily she sat,
   Ywimpled° wel, and on hir heed an hat   *veiled*
   As brood as is a bokeler or a targe,[2]
   A foot-mantel° aboute hir hipes large,   *riding skirt*
475 And on hir feet a paire of spores° sharpe.   *spurs*
   In felaweshipe wel coude she laughe and carpe:°   *talk*
   Of remedies of love she knew parchaunce,°   *as it happened*
   For she coude of that art the olde daunce.[3]
      A good man was ther of religioun,
480 And was a poore Person° of a town,   *parson*
   But riche he was of holy thought and werk.
   He was also a lerned man, a clerk,
   That Cristes gospel trewely° wolde preche;   *faithfully*
   His parisshens° devoutly wolde he teche.   *parishioners*
485 Benigne he was, and wonder° diligent,   *wonderfully*
   And in adversitee ful pacient,

---

2. He saved the money he made during the plague time.
3. A stimulant. Gold was thought to have some medicinal properties.
4. Ypres and Ghent ("Gaunt") were Flemish cloth-making centers.
5. The offering in church, when the congregation brought its gifts forward.
6. Tightly laced.
7. In medieval times, weddings were performed at the church door.
8. Rome, Boulogne (in France), St. James (of Compostella) in Galicia (Spain), and Cologne (in Germany) were all sites of shrines much visited by pilgrims.
9. Gap-toothed, thought to be a sign of amorousness.
1. Horse with an easy gait.
2. "Bokeler" and "targe": small shields.
3. I.e., she knew all the tricks of that trade.

And swich he was preved° ofte sithes.°   *proved/times*
Ful loth were him to cursen for his tithes,[4]
But rather wolde he yiven, out of doute,[5]
490   Unto his poore parisshens aboute
Of his offring[6] and eek of his substaunce:°   *property*
He coude in litel thing have suffisaunce.°   *sufficiency*
Wid was his parissh, and houses fer asonder,
But he ne lafte° nought for rain ne thonder,   *neglected*
495   In siknesse nor in meschief,° to visite   *misfortune*
The ferreste° in his parissh, muche and lite,[7]   *farthest*
Upon his feet, and in his hand a staf.
This noble ensample° to his sheep he yaf   *example*
That first he wroughte,[8] and afterward he taughte.
500   Out of the Gospel he tho° wordes caughte,°   *those/took*
And this figure° he added eek therto: *metaphor*
That if gold ruste, what shal iren do?
For if a preest be foul, on whom we truste,
No wonder is a lewed° man to ruste.   *uneducated*
505   And shame it is, if a preest take keep,°   *heed*
A shiten° shepherde and a clene sheep.   *befouled*
Wel oughte a preest ensample for to yive
By his clennesse how that his sheep sholde live.
He sette nought his benefice[9] to hire
510   And leet° his sheep encombred in the mire   *left*
And ran to London, unto Sainte Poules,[1]
To seeken him a chaunterye[2] for soules,
Or with a bretherhede to been withholde,[3]
But dwelte at hoom and kepte wel his folde,
515   So that the wolf ne made it nought miscarye:
He was a shepherde and nought a mercenarye.
And though he holy were and vertuous,
He was to sinful men nought despitous,°   *scornful*
Ne of his speeche daungerous° ne digne,°   *disdainful/haughty*
520   But in his teching discreet and benigne,
To drawen folk to hevene by fairnesse
By good ensample—this was his bisinesse.
But it° were any persone obstinat,   *if there*
What so he were, of heigh or lowe estat,
525   Him wolde he snibben° sharply for the nones:[4]   *scold*
A bettre preest I trowe° ther nowher noon is.   *believe*
He waited after[5] no pompe and reverence,
Ne maked him a spiced conscience,[6]

4. He would be most reluctant to invoke excommunication in order to collect his tithes.
5. Without doubt.
6. The offering made by the congregation of his church was at the Parson's disposal.
7. Great and small.
8. I.e., he practiced what he preached.
9. I.e., his parish. A priest might rent his parish to another and take a more profitable position.
1. St. Paul's Cathedral.
2. Chantry, i.e., a foundation that employed

priests for the sole duty of saying masses for the souls of wealthy persons. St. Paul's had many of them.
3. Or to be employed by a brotherhood; i.e., to take a lucrative and fairly easy position as chaplain with a parish guild (see p. 224, 1st n. 6).
4. On the spot, promptly.
5. I.e., expected.
6. Nor did he assume an overfastidious conscience, a holier-than-thou attitude.

	But Cristes lore° and his Apostles twelve	*teaching*
530	He taughte, but first he folwed it himselve.	
	With him ther was a Plowman, was his brother,	
	That hadde ylad° of dong° ful many a fother.[7]	*carried/dung*
	A trewe swinkere° and a good was he,	*worker*
	Living in pees° and parfit charitee.	*peace*
535	God loved he best with al his hoole° herte	*whole*
	At alle times, though him gamed or smerte,[8]	
	And thanne his neighebor right as himselve.	
	He wolde thresshe, and therto dike° and delve,°	*work hard/dig*
	For Cristes sake, for every poore wight,	
540	Withouten hire, if it laye in his might.	
	His tithes payed he ful faire and wel,	
	Bothe of his propre swink[9] and his catel.°	*property*
	In a tabard° he rood upon a mere.°	*workman's smock/mare*
	Ther was also a Reeve° and a Millere,	*estate manager*
545	A Somnour, and a Pardoner[1] also,	
	A Manciple,° and myself—ther were namo.	*steward*
	The Millere was a stout carl° for the nones.	*fellow*
	Ful big he was of brawn° and eek of bones—	*muscle*
	That preved[2] wel, for overal ther he cam	
550	At wrastling he wolde have alway the ram.[3]	
	He was short-shuldred, brood,° a thikke knarre.[4]	*broad*
	Ther was no dore that he nolde heve of harre,[5]	
	Or breke it at a renning° with his heed.°	*running/head*
	His beerd as any sowe or fox was reed,°	*red*
555	And therto brood, as though it were a spade;	
	Upon the cop right[6] of his nose he hade	
	A werte,° and theron stood a tuft of heres,	*wart*
	Rede as the bristles of a sowes eres;°	*ears*
	His nosethirles° blake were and wide.	*nostrils*
560	A swerd and a bokeler° bar° he by his side.	*shield/bore*
	His mouth as greet was as a greet furnais.°	*furnace*
	He was a janglere° and a Goliardais,[7]	*chatterer*
	And that was most of sinne and harlotries.°	*obscenities*
	Wel coude he stelen corn and tollen thries[8]—	
565	And yit he hadde a thombe[9] of gold, pardee.°	*by heaven*
	A whit cote and a blew hood wered° he.	*wore*
	A baggepipe wel coude he blowe and soune,°	*sound*
	And therwithal° he broughte us out of towne.	*therewith*
	A gentil Manciple[1] was ther of a temple,	
570	Of which achatours° mighte take exemple	*buyers of food*
	For to been wise in bying of vitaile;°	*victuals*
	For wheither that he paide or took by taile,[2]	

---

7. Load.
8. Whether he was pleased or grieved.
9. His own work.
1. "Somnour" (Summoner): server of summonses to the ecclesiastical court. "Pardoner": dispenser of papal pardons (see p. 230, 1st n. 8, and p. 231, n. 5).
2. Proved, i.e., was evident.
3. A ram was frequently offered as the prize in wrestling, a village sport.
4. Sturdy fellow.

5. He would not heave off (its) hinge.
6. Right on the tip.
7. Goliard, teller of ribald stories.
8. Take toll thrice—i.e., deduct from the grain far more than the lawful percentage.
9. Thumb. Ironic allusion to a proverb: "An honest miller has a golden thumb."
1. The Manciple is the business agent of a community of lawyers in London (a "temple").
2. By talley, i.e., on credit.

Algate he waited so in his achat[3]
That he was ay biforn and in good stat.[4]
575 Now is nat that of God a ful fair grace
That swich a lewed° mannes wit shal pace°   *uneducated/surpass*
The wisdom of an heep of lerned men?
Of maistres° hadde he mo than thries ten   *masters*
That weren of lawe expert and curious,°   *cunning*
580 Of whiche ther were a dozeine in that hous
Worthy to been stiwardes of rente° and lond   *income*
Of any lord that is in Engelond,
To make him live by his propre good[5]
In honour dettelees but if he were wood,[6]
585 Or live as scarsly° as him list° desire,   *economically/it pleases*
And able for to helpen al a shire
In any caas° that mighte falle° or happe,   *event/befall*
And yit this Manciple sette hir aller cappe![7]
       The Reeve was a sclendre° colerik[8] man;   *slender*
590 His beerd was shave as neigh° as evere he can;   *close*
His heer was by his eres ful round yshorn;
His top was dokked[9] lik a preest biforn;°   *in front*
Ful longe were his legges and ful lene,
Ylik a staf, ther was no calf yseene.°   *visible*
595 Wel coude he keepe° a gerner° and a binne—   *guard/granary*
Ther was noon auditour coude on him winne.[1]
Wel wiste° he by the droughte and by the rain   *knew*
The yeelding of his seed and of his grain.
His lordes sheep, his neet,° his dayerye,°   *cattle/dairy herd*
600 His swin, his hors, his stoor,° and his pultrye   *stock*
Was hoolly° in this Reeves governinge,   *wholly*
And by his covenant yaf[2] the rekeninge,
Sin° that his lord was twenty-yeer of age.   *since*
There coude no man bringe him in arrerage.[3]
605 Ther nas baillif, hierde, nor other hine,
That he ne knew his sleighte and his covine[4]—
They were adrad° of him as of the deeth.°   *afraid/plague*
His woning° was ful faire upon an heeth;°   *dwelling/meadow*
With greene trees shadwed was his place.
610 He coude bettre than his lord purchace.°   *acquire goods*
Ful riche he was astored° prively.°   *stocked/secretly*
His lord wel coude he plesen subtilly,
To yive and lene° him of his owene good,°   *lend/property*
And have a thank, and yit a cote and hood.
615 In youthe he hadde lerned a good mister:°   *occupation*
He was a wel good wrighte, a carpenter.
This Reeve sat upon a ful good stot°   *stallion*

3. Always he was on the watch in his purchasing.
4. Financial condition. "Ay biforn": i.e., ahead of the game.
5. His own money.
6. Out of debt unless he were crazy.
7. This Manciple made fools of them all.
8. Choleric describes a person whose dominant humor is yellow bile (choler)—i.e., a hot-tempered person. The Reeve is the superintendent of a large farming estate.
9. Cut short; the clergy wore the head partially shaved.
1. I.e., find him in default.
2. And according to his contract he gave.
3. Convict him of being in arrears financially.
4. There was no bailiff (i.e., foreman), shepherd, or other farm laborer whose craftiness and plots he didn't know.

That was a pomely° grey and highte° Scot.   *dapple / was named*
A long surcote° of pers° upon he hade,[5]   *overcoat / blue*
620 And by his side he bar° a rusty blade.   *bore*
Of Northfolk was this Reeve of which I telle,
Biside a town men clepen Baldeswelle.°   *Bawdswell*
Tukked[6] he was as is a frere aboute,
And evere he rood the hindreste of oure route.[7]

625   A Somnour[8] was ther with us in that place
That hadde a fir-reed° cherubinnes[9] face,   *fire-red*
For saucefleem° he was, with yën narwe,   *pimply*
And hoot° he was, and lecherous as a sparwe,°   *hot / sparrow*
With scaled° browes blake and piled[1] beerd: *scabby*
630 Of his visage children were aferd.°   *afraid*
Ther nas quiksilver, litarge, ne brimstoon,
Boras, ceruce, ne oile of tartre noon,[2]
Ne oinement that wolde clense and bite,
That him mighte helpen of his whelkes° white,   *pimples*
635 Nor of the knobbes° sitting on his cheekes.   *lumps*
Wel loved he garlek, oinons, and eek leekes,
And for to drinke strong win reed as blood.
Thanne wolde he speke and crye as he were wood;°   *mad*
And whan that he wel dronken hadde the win,
640 Thanne wolde he speke no word but Latin:
A fewe termes hadde he, two or three,
That he hadde lerned out of som decree;
No wonder is—he herde it al the day,
And eek ye knowe wel how that a jay°   *parrot*
645 Can clepen "Watte"[3] as wel as can the Pope—
But whoso coude in other thing him grope,°   *examine*
Thanne hadde he spent all his philosophye;[4]
Ay *Questio quid juris*[5] wolde he crye.

    He was a gentil harlot° and a kinde;   *rascal*
650 A bettre felawe sholde men nought finde:
He wolde suffre,° for a quart of win,   *permit*
A good felawe to have his concubin
A twelfmonth, and excusen him at the fulle;[6]
Ful prively° a finch eek coude he pulle.[7]   *secretly*
655 And if he foond° owher° a good felawe   *found / anywhere*
He wolde techen him to have noon awe
In swich caas of the Ercedekenes curs,[8]
But if[9] a mannes soule were in his purs,

5. He had on.
6. With clothing tucked up like a friar.
7. Hindmost of our group.
8. The "Somnour" (Summoner) is an employee of the ecclesiastical court, whose duty is to bring to court persons whom the archdeacon—the justice of the court—suspects of offenses against canon law. By this time, however, summoners had generally transformed themselves into corrupt detectives who spied out offenders and blackmailed them by threats of summonses.
9. Cherubs, often depicted in art with red faces.
1. Uneven, partly hairless.
2. These are all ointments for diseases affecting the skin, probably diseases of venereal origin.
3. Call out: "Walter"—like modern parrots' "Polly."
4. I.e., learning.
5. "What point of law does this investigation involve?" A phrase frequently used in ecclesiastical courts.
6. Fully. Ecclesiastical courts had jurisdiction over many offenses that today would come under civil law, including sexual offenses.
7. "To pull a finch" (pluck a bird) is to have sexual relations with a woman.
8. Archdeacon's sentence of excommunication.
9. Unless.

For in his purs he sholde ypunisshed be.
660 "Purs is the Ercedekenes helle," saide he.
　　　But wel I woot he lied right in deede:
　　　Of cursing° oughte eech gilty man him drede,   *excommunication*
　　　For curs wol slee° right as assoiling° savith—   *slay/absolution*
　　　And also war him of a *significavit*.[1]
665 　　In daunger[2] hadde he at his owene gise°   *disposal*
　　　The yonge girles of the diocise,
　　　And knew hir conseil,° and was al hir reed.[3]   *secrets*
　　　A gerland hadde he set upon his heed
　　　As greet as it were for an ale-stake,[4]
670 A bokeler hadde he maad him of a cake.
　　　With him ther rood a gentil Pardoner[5]
　　　Of Rouncival, his freend and his compeer,°   *comrade*
　　　That straight was comen fro the Court of Rome.[6]
　　　Ful loude he soong,° "Com hider, love, to me."   *sang*
675 This Somnour bar to him a stif burdoun:[7]
　　　Was nevere trompe° of half so greet a soun.   *trumpet*
　　　　This Pardoner hadde heer as yelow as wex,
　　　But smoothe it heeng° as dooth a strike° of flex;°   *hung/hank/flax*
　　　By ounces[8] heenge his lokkes that he hadde,
680 And therwith he his shuldres overspradde,°   *overspread*
　　　But thinne it lay, by colpons,° oon by oon;   *strands*
　　　But hood for jolitee° wered° he noon,   *nonchalance/wore*
　　　For it was trussed up in his walet:°   *pack*
　　　Him thoughte he rood al of the newe jet.°   *fashion*
685 Dischevelee° save his cappe he rood al bare.   *with hair down*
　　　Swiche glaring yën hadde he as an hare.
　　　A vernicle[9] hadde he sowed upon his cappe,
　　　His walet biforn him in his lappe,
　　　Bretful° of pardon, come from Rome al hoot.°   *brimful/hot*
690 A vois he hadde as smal° as hath a goot;°   *high-pitched/goat*
　　　No beerd hadde he, ne nevere sholde have;
　　　As smoothe it was as it were late yshave:
　　　I trowe° he were a gelding[1] or a mare.   *believe*
　　　But of his craft, fro Berwik into Ware,[2]
695 Ne was ther swich another pardoner;
　　　For in his male° he hadde a pilwe-beer°   *bag/pillowcase*
　　　Which that he saide was Oure Lady veil;
　　　He saide he hadde a gobet° of the sail   *piece*
　　　That Sainte Peter hadde whan that he wente
700 Upon the see, til Jesu Crist him hente.°   *seized*

---

1. And also one should be careful of a *significavit* (the writ that transferred the guilty offender from the ecclesiastical to the civil arm for punishment).
2. Under his domination.
3. Was their chief source of advice.
4. A tavern was signalized by a pole ("ale-stake"), rather like a modern flagpole, projecting from its front wall; on this hung a garland, or "bush."
5. A Pardoner dispensed papal pardon for sins to those who contributed to the charitable institution that he was licensed to represent; this Pardoner purported to be collecting for the hospital of Roncesvalles ("Rouncival") in Spain, which had a London branch.
6. The papal court.
7. I.e., provided him with a strong bass accompaniment.
8. I.e., thin strands.
9. Portrait of Christ's face as it was said to have been impressed on St. Veronica's handkerchief, i.e., a souvenir reproduction of a famous relic in Rome.
1. A neutered stallion, i.e., a eunuch.
2. I.e., from one end of England to the other.

He hadde a crois° of laton,° ful of stones,   *cross / brassy metal*
And in a glas he hadde pigges bones,
But with thise relikes[3] whan that he foond°   *found*
A poore person° dwelling upon lond,[4]   *parson*
705   Upon° a day he gat° him more moneye   *in / got*
Than that the person gat in monthes twaye;
And thus with feined° flaterye and japes°   *false / tricks*
He made the person and the peple his apes.°   *dupes*
But trewely to tellen at the laste,
710   He was in chirche a noble ecclesiaste;
Wel coude he rede a lesson and a storye,°   *liturgical narrative*
But alderbest° he soong an offertorye,[5]   *best of all*
For wel he wiste° whan that song was songe,   *knew*
He moste° preche and wel affile° his tonge   *must / sharpen*
715   To winne silver, as he ful wel coude—
Therefore he soong the merierly° and loude.   *more merrily*
    Now have I told you soothly in a clause[6]
Th'estaat, th'array, the nombre, and eek the cause
Why that assembled was this compaignye
720   In Southwerk at this gentil hostelrye
That highte the Tabard, faste° by the Belle;[7]   *close*
But now is time to you for to telle
How that we baren us[8] that ilke° night   *same*
Whan we were in that hostelrye alight;
725   And after wol I telle of oure viage,°   *trip*
And al the remenant of oure pilgrimage.
But first I praye you of youre curteisye
That ye n'arette it nought my vilainye[9]
Though that I plainly speke in this matere
730   To telle you hir wordes and hir cheere,°   *behavior*
Ne though I speke hir wordes proprely;°   *accurately*
For this ye knowen also wel as I:
Who so shal telle a tale after a man
He moot° reherce,° as neigh as evere he can,   *must / repeat*
735   Everich a word, if it be in his charge,°   *responsibility*
Al speke he[1] nevere so rudeliche and large,°   *broadly*
Or elles he moot telle his tale untrewe,
Or feine° thing, or finde° wordes newe;   *make up / devise*
He may nought spare[2] although he were his brother:
740   He moot as wel saye oo word as another.
Crist spak himself ful brode° in Holy Writ,   *broadly*
And wel ye woot no vilainye° is it;   *rudeness*
Eek Plato saith, who so can him rede,
The wordes mote be cosin to the deede.
745   Also I praye you to foryive it me
Al° have I nat set folk in hir degree   *although*
Here in this tale as that they sholde stonde:

---

3. Relics, i.e., the pigs' bones that the Pardoner represented as saints' bones.
4. Upcountry.
5. Part of the mass sung before the offering of alms.
6. I.e., in a short space.
7. Another tavern in Southwark.
8. Bore ourselves.
9. That you do not attribute it to my boorishness.
1. Although he speak.
2. I.e., spare anyone.

My wit is short, ye may wel understonde.
  Greet cheere made oure Host[3] us everichoon,
750 And to the soper sette he us anoon.°   *at once*
He served us with vitaile° at the beste.   *food*
Strong was the win, and wel to drinke us leste.° *it pleased*
A semely man oure Hoste was withalle
For to been a marchal[4] in an halle;
755 A large man he was, with yën steepe,°   *prominent*
A fairer burgeis° was ther noon in Chepe[5]— *burgher*
Bold of his speeche, and wis, and wel ytaught,
And of manhood him lakkede right naught.
Eek therto he was right a merye man,
760 And after soper playen he bigan,
And spak of mirthe amonges othere thinges—
Whan that we hadde maad oure rekeninges[6]—
And saide thus, "Now, lordinges, trewely,
Ye been to me right welcome, hertely.°   *heartily*
765 For by my trouthe, if that I shal nat lie,
I sawgh nat this yeer so merye a compaignye
At ones in this herberwe° as is now.   *inn*
Fain° wolde I doon you mirthe, wiste I[7] how. *gladly*
And of a mirthe I am right now bithought,
770 To doon you ese, and it shal coste nought.
  "Ye goon to Canterbury—God you speede;
The blisful martyr quite you youre meede.[8]
And wel I woot as ye goon by the waye
Ye shapen you[9] to talen° and to playe,   *converse*
775 For trewely, confort ne mirthe is noon
To ride by the waye domb as stoon;°   *stone*
And therefore wol I maken you disport
As I saide erst,° and doon you som confort; *before*
And if you liketh alle, by oon assent,
780 For to stonden at[1] my juggement,
And for to werken as I shall you saye,
Tomorwe whan ye riden by the waye—
Now by my fader° soule that is deed,   *father's*
But° ye be merye I wol yive you myn heed!° *unless / head*
785 Holde up youre handes withouten more speeche."
  Oure counseil was nat longe for to seeche;° *seek*
Us thought it was not worth to make it wis,[2]
And graunted him withouten more avis,°   *deliberation*
And bade him saye his voirdit° as him leste.[3] *verdict*
790 "Lordinges," quod he, "now herkneth for the beste;
But taketh it nought, I praye you, in desdain.
This is the point, to speken short and plain,
That eech of you, to shorte° with oure waye *shorten*
In this viage, shal tellen tales twaye°—   *two*

3. The landlord of the Tabard Inn.
4. Marshal, one who was in charge of feasts.
5. Cheapside, business center of London.
6. Had paid our bills.
7. If I knew.
8. Pay you your reward.

9. Intend.
1. Abide by.
2. We didn't think it worthwhile to make an issue of it.
3. It pleased.

795 To Canterburyward, I mene it so,
And hoomward he shal tellen othere two,
Of aventures that whilom° have bifalle;   *once upon a time*
And which of you that bereth him best of alle—
That is to sayn, that telleth in this cas
800 Tales of best sentence° and most solas°—   *meaning / delight*
Shal have a soper at oure aller cost,[4]
Here in this place, sitting by this post,
Whan that we come again fro Canterbury.
And for to make you the more mury°   *merry*
805 I wol myself goodly° with you ride—   *kindly*
Right at myn owene cost—and be youre gide.
And who so wol my juggement withsaye°   *contradict*
Shal paye al that we spende by the waye.
And if ye vouche sauf that it be so,
810 Telle me anoon, withouten wordes mo,°   *more*
And I wol erly shape me[5] therefore."
      This thing was graunted and oure othes swore
With ful glad herte, and prayden[6] him also
That he wolde vouche sauf for to do so,
815 And that he wolde been oure governour,
And of oure tales juge and reportour,°   *accountant*
And sette a soper at a certain pris,°   *price*
And we wol ruled been at his devis,°   *disposal*
In heigh and lowe; and thus by oon assent
820 We been accorded to his juggement.
And therupon the win was fet° anoon;   *fetched*
We dronken and to reste wente eechoon°   *each one*
Withouten any lenger° taryinge.   *longer*
      Amorwe° whan that day bigan to springe   *in the morning*
825 Up roos oure Host and was oure aller cok,[7]
And gadred us togidres in a flok,
And forth we riden, a litel more than pas,°   *walking pace*
Unto the watering of Saint Thomas;[8]
And ther oure Host bigan his hors arreste,°   *halt*
830 And saide, "Lordes, herkneth if you leste:°   *it please*
Ye woot youre forward° and it you recorde:[9]   *agreement*
If evensong and morwesong° accorde,°   *morning song / agree*
Lat see now who shal telle the firste tale.
As evere mote° I drinken win or ale,   *may*
835 Who so be rebel to my juggement
Shal paye for al that by the way is spent.
Now draweth cut er that we ferrer twinne:[1]
He which that hath the shorteste shal biginne.
      "Sire Knight," quod he, "my maister and my lord,
840 Now draweth cut, for that is myn accord.°   *will*
Cometh neer," quod he, "my lady Prioresse,
And ye, sire Clerk, lat be youre shamefastnesse°—   *modesty*

---

4. At the cost of us all.
5. Prepare myself.
6. I.e., we prayed.
7. Was rooster for us all.

8. A watering place near Southwark.
9. You recall it.
1. Go farther. "Draweth cut": i.e., draw straws.

Ne studieth nought. Lay hand to, every man!"
Anoon to drawen every wight bigan,
845   And shortly for to tellen as it was
Were it by aventure, or sort, or cas,[2]
The soothe° is this, the cut fil° to the Knight;   *truth/fell*
Of which ful blithe and glad was every wight,
And telle he moste° his tale, as was resoun,   *must*
850   By forward and by composicioun,[3]
As ye han herd. What needeth wordes mo?
And whan this goode man sawgh that it was so,
As he that wis was and obedient
To keepe his forward by his free assent,
855   He saide, "Sin° I shal biginne the game,   *since*
What, welcome be the cut, in Goddes name!
Now lat us ride, and herkneth what I saye."
And with that word we riden forth oure waye,
And he bigan with right a merye cheere°   *countenance*
860   His tale anoon, and saide as ye may heere.

---

2. Whether it was luck, fate, or chance.   3. By agreement and compact.

[*The Knight's Tale* is a romance of 2,350 lines, which Chaucer had written before beginning *The Canterbury Tales*—one of several works assumed to be earlier that he inserted into the collection. It is probably the same story, with only minor revisions, that Chaucer referred to in *The Legend of Good Women* as "al the love of Palamon and Arcite." These are the names of the two heroes of *The Knight's Tale*, kinsmen and best friends who are taken prisoner at the siege and destruction of ancient Thebes by Theseus, the ruler of Athens. Gazing out from their prison cell in a tower, they fall in love at first sight and almost at the same moment with Theseus's sister-in-law, Emily, who is taking an early-morning walk in a garden below their window. After a bitter rivalry, they are at last reconciled through a tournament in which Emily is the prize. Arcite wins the tournament but, as he lies dying after being thrown by his horse, he makes a noble speech encouraging Palamon and Emily to marry. The tale is an ambitious combination of classical setting and mythology, romance plot, and themes of fortune and destiny.]

The Miller's Prologue and Tale

The Miller's Tale belongs to a genre known as the "fabliau": a short story in verse that deals satirically, often grossly and fantastically as well as hilariously, with intrigues and deceptions about sex or money (and often both these elements in the same story). These are the tales Chaucer is anticipating in *The General Prologue* when he warns his presumably genteel audience that they must expect some rude speaking (see lines 727–44). An even more pointed apology follows at the end of *The Miller's Prologue*. Fabliau tales exist everywhere in oral literature; as a literary form they flourished in France, especially in the thirteenth century. By having Robin the Miller tell a fabliau to "quit" (to requite or pay back) the Knight's aristocratic romance, Chaucer sets up a dialectic between classes, genres, and styles that he exploits throughout *The Canterbury Tales*.

The Prologue

group/was not

recall
especially

laughed
pouch

can
repay

with difficulty
would not/take off

know

dear

with propriety

public affirmation
tone of voice
speak or say wrongly

saint's life

ignorant/obscenity
also
injure
reputation

dear
cuckold

Whan that the Knight hadde thus his tale ytold,
In al the route° nas° ther yong ne old
That he ne saide it was a noble storye,
And worthy for to drawen° to memorye,
5   And namely° the gentils everichoon.
    Oure Hoste lough° and swoor, "So mote I goon,[1]
This gooth aright: unbokeled is the male.°
Lat see now who shal telle another tale.
For trewely the game is wel bigonne.
10 Now telleth ye, sire Monk, if that ye conne,°
Somwhat to quite° with the Knightes tale."
    The Millere, that for dronken[2] was al pale,
So that unnethe° upon his hors he sat,
He nolde° avalen° neither hood ne hat,
15 Ne abiden no man for his curteisye,
But in Pilates vois[3] he gan to crye,
And swoor, "By armes[4] and by blood and bones,
I can° a noble tale for the nones,
With which I wol now quite the Knightes tale."
20 Oure Hoste sawgh that he was dronke of ale,
And saide, "Abide, Robin, leve° brother,
Som bettre man shal telle us first another.
Abide, and lat us werken thriftily."°
    "By Goddes soule," quod he, "that wol nat I,
25 For I wol speke or elles go my way."
    Oure Host answerde, "Tel on, a devele way![5]
Thou art a fool; thy wit is overcome."
    "Now herkneth," quod the Millere, "alle and some.[6]
But first I make a protestacioun°
30 That I am dronke: I knowe it by my soun.°
And therfore if that I misspeke° or saye,
Wite it[7] the ale of Southwerk, I you praye;
For I wol telle a legende° and a lif
Bothe of a carpenter and of his wif,
35 How that a clerk hath set the wrightes cappe."[8]
    The Reeve answerde and saide, "Stint thy clappe![9]
Lat be thy lewed° dronken harlotrye.°
It is a sinne and eek° a greet folye
To apairen° any man or him defame,
40 And eek to bringen wives in swich fame.°
Thou maist ynough of othere thinges sayn."
    This dronken Millere spak ful soone again,
And saide, "Leve° brother Osewold,
Who hath no wif, he is no cokewold.°
45 But I saye nat therfore that thou art oon.

---

1. So might I walk—an oath.
2. I.e., drunkenness.
3. The harsh voice usually associated with the character of Pontius Pilate in the mystery plays.
4. I.e., by God's arms, a blasphemous oath.

5. I.e., in the devil's name.
6. Each and every one.
7. Blame it on.
8 I.e., how a clerk made a fool of a carpenter.
9. Stop your chatter.

Ther ben ful goode wives many oon,°   *a one*
And evere a thousand goode ayains oon badde.
That knowestou wel thyself but if thou madde.°   *rave*
Why artou angry with my tale now?
50   I have a wif, pardee,° as wel as thou,   *by God*
Yit nolde° I, for the oxen in my plough,   *would not*
Take upon me more than ynough°   *enough*
As deemen of myself that I were oon:[1]
I wol bileve wel that I am noon.
55   An housbonde shal nought been inquisitif
Of Goddes privetee,° nor of his wif.   *secrets*
So[2] he may finde Goddes foison° there,   *plenty*
Of the remenant° needeth nought enquere."°   *rest/inquire*
     What sholde I more sayn but this Millere
60   He nolde his wordes for no man forbere,
But tolde his cherles tale in his manere.
M'athinketh° that I shal reherce° it here,   *I regret/repeat*
And therefore every gentil wight I praye,
Deemeth nought, for Goddes love, that I saye
65   Of yvel entente, but for° I moot reherse   *because*
Hir tales alle, be they bet° or werse,   *better*
Or elles falsen° som of my matere.   *falsify*
And therfore, whoso list it nought yheere°   *hear*
Turne over the leef,° and chese° another tale,   *page/choose*
70   For he shal finde ynowe,° grete and smale,   *enough*
Of storial[3] thing that toucheth gentilesse,°   *gentility*
And eek moralitee and holinesse:
Blameth nought me if that ye chese amis.
The Millere is a cherl, ye knowe wel this,
75   So was the Reeve eek, and othere mo,
And harlotrye° they tolden bothe two.   *ribaldry*
Aviseth you,[4] and putte me out of blame:
And eek men shal nought maken ernest of game.

The Tale

     Whilom° ther was dwelling at Oxenforde   *once upon a time*
80   A riche gnof° that gestes heeld to boorde,[5]   *churl*
And of his craft he was a carpenter.
With him ther was dwelling a poore scoler,
Hadde lerned art,[6] but al his fantasye°   *desire*
Was turned for to lere° astrologye,   *learn*
85   And coude a certain of conclusiouns,
To deemen by interrogaciouns,[7]
If that men axed° him in certain houres   *asked*
Whan that men sholde have droughte or elles showres,
Or if men axed him what shal bifalle

---

1. To think that I were one (a cuckold).
2. Provided that.
3. Historical, i.e., true.
4. Take heed.
5. I.e., took in boarders.

6. Who had completed the first stage of university education (the trivium).
7. I.e., and he knew a number of propositions on which to base astrological analyses (which would reveal the matters in the next three lines).

90 Of every thing—I may nat rekene hem alle.
        This clerk was cleped° hende[8] Nicholas.   called
    Of derne love he coude, and of solas,[9]
    And therto he was sly and ful privee,°   secretive
    And lik a maide meeke for to see.
95 A chambre hadde he in that hostelrye
    Allone, withouten any compaignye,
    Ful fetisly ydight[1] with herbes swoote,°   sweet
    And he himself as sweete as is the roote
    Of licoris or any setewale.[2]
100 His Almageste[3] and bookes grete and smale,
    His astrelabye, longing for[4] his art,
    His augrim stones,[5] layen faire apart
    On shelves couched° at his beddes heed;   set
    His presse° ycovered with a falding reed;[6]   storage chest
105 And al above ther lay a gay sautrye,°   psaltery (harp)
    On which he made a-nightes melodye
    So swetely that al the chambre roong,°   rang
    And Angelus ad Virginem[7] he soong,
    And after that he soong the Kinges Note:[8]
110 Ful often blessed was his merye throte.
    And thus this sweete clerk his time spente
    After his freendes finding and his rente.[9]
        This carpenter hadde wedded newe° a wif   lately
    Which that he loved more than his lif.
115 Of eighteteene yeer she was of age;
    Jalous he was, and heeld hire narwe in cage,
    For she was wilde and yong, and he was old,
    And deemed himself been lik a cokewold.[1]
    He knew nat Caton,[2] for his wit was rude,
120 That bad men sholde wedde his similitude:[3]
    Men sholde wedden after hir estat,[4]
    For youthe and elde° is often at debat.   age
    But sith that he was fallen in the snare,
    He moste endure, as other folk, his care.
125   Fair was this yonge wif, and therwithal
    As any wesele° hir body gent and smal.[5]   weasel
    A ceint she wered, barred[6] al of silk;
    A barmcloth° as whit as morne° milk   apron / morning
    Upon hir lendes,° ful of many a gore;°   loins / flounce
130 Whit was hir smok,° and broiden° al bifore   undergarment / embroidered
    And eek bihinde, on hir coler° aboute,   collar

8. Courteous, handy, attractive.
9. I.e., he knew about secret love and pleasurable practices.
1. Elegantly furnished.
2. Setwall, a spice.
3. The 2nd-century treatise by Ptolemy, still the standard astronomy textbook.
4. Belonging to. "Astrelabye": astrolabe, an astronomical instrument.
5. Counters used in arithmetic.
6. Red coarse woolen cloth.
7. "The Angel to the Virgin," an Annunciation

hymn.
8. Probably a popular song of the time.
9. In accordance with his friends' provision and his own income.
1. I.e., suspected of himself that he was like a cuckold.
2. Dionysius Cato, the supposed author of a book of maxims used in elementary education.
3. Commanded that one should wed his equal.
4. Men should marry according to their condition.
5. Slender and delicate.
6. A belt she wore, with transverse stripes.

Of° col-blak silk, withinne and eek withoute;   *with*
The tapes° of hir white voluper°   *ribbons/cap*
Were of the same suite of⁷ hir coler;
135 Hir filet° brood° of silk and set ful hye;   *headband/broad*
And sikerly° she hadde a likerous° yë;   *certainly/wanton*
Ful smale ypulled⁸ were hir browes two,
And tho were bent,° and blake as any slo.°   *arching/sloeberry*
She was ful more blisful on to see
140 Than is the newe perejonette° tree,   *pear*
And softer than the wolle° is of a wether;°   *wool/ram*
And by hir girdel° heeng° a purs of lether,   *belt/hung*
Tasseled with silk and perled with latoun.⁹
In al this world, to seeken up and down,
145 Ther nis no man so wis that coude thenche°   *imagine*
So gay a popelote° or swich° a wenche.   *doll/such*
Ful brighter was the shining of hir hewe
Than in the Towr¹ the noble° yforged newe.   *gold coin*
But of hir song, it was as loud and yerne°   *lively*
150 As any swalwe° sitting on a berne.°   *swallow/barn*
Therto she coude skippe and make game°   *play*
As any kide or calf folwing his dame.°   *mother*
Hir mouth was sweete as bragot or the meeth,²
Or hoord of apples laid in hay or heeth.°   *heather*
155 Winsing° she was as is a joly° colt,   *skittish/high-spirited*
Long as a mast, and upright° as a bolt.°   *straight/arrow*
A brooch she bar upon hir lowe coler
As brood as is the boos° of a bokeler;°   *boss/shield*
Hir shoes were laced on hir legges hye.
160 She was a primerole,° a piggesnye,³   *primrose*
For any lord to leggen° in his bedde,   *lay*
Or yit for any good yeman to wedde.
  Now sire, and eft° sire, so bifel the cas   *again*
That on a day this hende Nicholas
165 Fil° with this yonge wif to rage° and playe,   *happened/flirt*
Whil that hir housbonde was at Oseneye⁴
(As clerkes been ful subtil and ful quainte),°   *clever*
And prively he caughte hire by the queinte,⁵
And saide, "Ywis,° but° if ich° have my wille,   *truly/unless/I*
170 For derne° love of thee, lemman, I spille,"°   *secret/die*
And heeld hire harde by the haunche-bones,°   *thighs*
And saide, "Lemman,° love me al atones,⁶   *sweetheart*
Or I wol dien, also° God me save."   *so*
And she sproong° as a colt dooth in a trave,⁷   *sprang*
175 And with hir heed she wried° faste away;   *twisted*
She saide, "I wol nat kisse thee, by my fay.°   *faith*
Why, lat be," quod she, "lat be, Nicholas!
Or I wol crye 'Out, harrow,° and allas!'   *help*

---

7. The same kind as, i.e., black.
8. Delicately plucked.
9. I.e., with brassy spangles on it.
1. The Tower of London, the Mint.
2. "Bragot" and "meeth" are honey drinks.
3. A pig's eye, a name for a common flower.

4. A town near Oxford.
5. Elegant (thing); a euphemism for the female genitals.
6. Right now.
7. Frame for holding a horse to be shod.

Do way youre handes, for your curteisye!"
180   This Nicholas gan mercy for to crye,
And spak so faire, and profred him so faste,[8]
That she hir love him graunted atte laste,
And swoor hir ooth by Saint Thomas of Kent[9]
That she wolde been at his comandement,
185   Whan that she may hir leiser[1] wel espye.
"Myn housbonde is so ful of jalousye
That but ye waite° wel and been privee   *be on guard*
I woot right wel I nam but deed,"[2] quod she.
"Ye moste been ful derne° as in this cas."   *secret*
190   "Nay, therof care thee nought," quod Nicholas.
"A clerk hadde litherly biset his while,[3]
But if he coude a carpenter bigile."
And thus they been accorded and ysworn
To waite° a time, as I have told biforn.   *watch for*
195   Whan Nicholas hadde doon this everydeel,°   *every bit*
And thakked° hire upon the lendes° weel,   *patted / loins*
He kiste hire sweete, and taketh his sautrye,
And playeth faste, and maketh melodye.
      Thanne fil° it thus, that to the parissh chirche,   *befell*
200   Cristes owene werkes for to wirche,°   *perform*
This goode wif wente on an haliday:°   *holy day*
Hir forheed shoon as bright as any day,
So was it wasshen whan she leet° hir werk.   *left*
      Now was ther of that chirche a parissh clerk,[4]
205   The which that was ycleped° Absolon: *called*
Crul° was his heer, and as the gold it shoon,   *curly*
And strouted° as a fanne[5] large and brode;   *spread out*
Ful straight and evene lay his joly shode.[6]
His rode° was reed, his yën greye as goos.°   *complexion / goose*
210   With Poules window corven[7] on his shoos,
In hoses° rede he wente fetisly.°   *stockings / elegantly*
Yclad he was ful smale° and proprely,   *finely*
Al in a kirtel° of a light waget°—   *tunic / blue*
Ful faire and thikke been the pointes[8] set—
215   And therupon he hadde a gay surplis,°   *surplice*
As whit as is the blosme upon the ris.°   *bough*
A merye child° he was, so God me save.   *young man*
Wel coude he laten blood, and clippe,[9] and shave,
And maken a chartre of land, or acquitaunce;[1]
220   In twenty manere° coude he trippe and daunce   *ways*
After the scole of Oxenforde tho,°   *then*
And with his legges casten° to and fro,   *prance*
And playen songes on a smal rubible;°   *fiddle*
Therto he soong somtime a loud quinible,[2]

8. I.e., made such vigorous advances.
9. Thomas à Becket.
1. I.e., opportunity.
2. I am no more than dead, I am done for.
3. Poorly employed his time.
4. Assistant to the parish priest, not a cleric or student.
5. Wide-mouthed basket for separating grain from chaff.

6. Parting of the hair.
7. Carved with intricate designs, like the tracery in the windows of St. Paul's.
8. Laces for fastening the tunic and holding up the hose.
9. Let blood and give haircuts. Bleeding was a medical treatment performed by barbers.
1. Legal release. "Chartre": deed.
2. Part requiring a very high voice.

225 And as wel coude he playe on a giterne:°   *guitar*
     In al the town nas brewhous ne taverne
     That he ne visited with his solas,°   *entertainment*
     Ther any gailard tappestere[3] was.
     But sooth to sayn, he was somdeel squaimous°   *a bit squeamish*
230 Of° farting, and of speeche daungerous.[4]   *about*
        This Absolon, that joly° was and gay,   *pretty, amorous*
     Gooth with a cencer° on the haliday,   *incense burner*
     Cencing the wives of the parissh faste,
     And many a lovely look on hem he caste,
235 And namely° on this carpenteres wif: *especially*
     To looke on hire him thoughte a merye lif.
     She was so propre° and sweete and likerous,[5]   *neat*
     I dar wel sayn, if she hadde been a mous,
     And he a cat, he wolde hire hente° anoon.   *pounce on*
240 This parissh clerk, this joly Absolon,
     Hath in his herte swich a love-longinge°   *lovesickness*
     That of no wif ne took he noon offringe—
     For curteisye he saide he wolde noon.
     The moone, whan it was night, ful brighte shoon,°   *shone*
245 And Absolon his giterne° hath ytake—   *guitar*
     For paramours° he thoughte for to wake—   *love*
     And forth he gooth, jolif° and amorous,   *pretty*
     Til he cam to the carpenteres hous,
     A litel after cokkes hadde ycrowe,
250 And dressed him up by a shot-windowe[6]
     That was upon the carpenteres wal.
     He singeth in his vois gentil and smal,°   *dainty*
     "Now dere lady, if thy wille be,
     I praye you that ye wol rewe° on me,"   *have pity*
255 Ful wel accordant to his giterninge.[7]
     This carpenter awook and herde him singe,
     And spak unto his wif, and saide anoon,
     "What, Alison, heerestou nought Absolon
     That chaunteth thus under oure bowres° wal?"   *bedroom's*
260 And she answerde hir housbonde therwithal,
     "Yis, God woot, John, I heere it everydeel."°   *every bit*
        This passeth forth. What wol ye bet than weel?[8]
     Fro day to day this joly Absolon
     So woweth° hire that him is wo-bigoon: *woos*
265 He waketh° al the night and al the day;   *stays awake*
     He kembed° his lokkes brode[9] and made him gay;   *combed*
     He woweth hire by menes and brocage,[1]
     And swoor he wolde been hir owene page°   *personal servant*
     He singeth, brokking° as a nightingale;   *trilling*
270 He sente hire piment,° meeth,° and spiced ale,   *spiced wine / mead*
     And wafres° piping hoot out of the gleede;°   *pastries / coals*
     And for she was of towne,[2] he profred meede°—   *money*

3. Gay barmaid.   8. Better than well.
4. Prudish about (vulgar) talk.   9. I.e., wide-spreading.
5. Wanton, appetizing.   1. By go-betweens and agents.
6. Took his position by a hinged window.   2. Because she was a town woman.
7. In harmony with his guitar playing.

For som folk wol be wonnen for richesse,
And som for strokes,° and som for gentilesse.   blows (force)
275   Somtime to shewe his lightnesse and maistrye,³
He playeth Herodes⁴ upon a scaffold° hye.   platform, stage
But what availeth him as in this cas?
She loveth so this hende Nicholas
That Absolon may blowe the bukkes horn;⁵
280   He ne hadde for his labour but a scorn.
And thus she maketh Absolon hir ape,⁶
And al his ernest turneth til° a jape.°   to/joke
Ful sooth is this proverbe, it is no lie;
Men saith right thus: "Alway the nye slye
285   Maketh the ferre leve to be loth."⁷
For though that Absolon be wood° or wroth,   furious
By cause that he fer was from hir sighte,
This nye° Nicholas stood in his lighte.   nearby
Now beer° thee wel, thou hende Nicholas,   bear
290   For Absolon may waile and singe allas.
        And so bifel it on a Saterday
This carpenter was goon til Oseney,
And hende Nicholas and Alisoun
Accorded been to this conclusioun,
295   That Nicholas shal shapen° hem a wile°   arrange/trick
This sely⁸ jalous housbonde to bigile,
And if so be this game wente aright,
She sholden sleepen in his arm al night—
For this was his desir and hire° also.   hers
300   And right anoon, withouten wordes mo,
This Nicholas no lenger wolde tarye,
But dooth ful softe unto his chambre carye
Bothe mete and drinke for a day or twaye,
And to hir housbonde bad hire for to saye,
305   If that he axed after Nicholas,
She sholde saye she niste° wher he was—   didn't know
Of al that day she sawgh him nought with yë:
She trowed° that he was in maladye,   believed
For for no cry hir maide coude him calle,
310   He nolde answere for no thing that mighte falle.°   happen
        This passeth forth al thilke° Saterday   this
That Nicholas stille in his chambre lay,
And eet,° and sleep,° or dide what him leste,⁹   ate/slept
Til Sonday that the sonne gooth to reste.
315   This sely carpenter hath greet mervaile
Of Nicholas, or what thing mighte him aile,
And saide, "I am adrad,° by Saint Thomas,   afraid
It stondeth nat aright with Nicholas.
God shilde° that he deide sodeinly!   forbid

---

3. Facility and virtuosity.
4. Herod, a role traditionally played as a bully in the mystery plays.
5. Blow the buck's horn, i.e., go whistle, waste his time.

6. I.e., thus she makes a monkey out of Absolon.
7. Always the sly man at hand makes the distant dear one hated.
8. Poor innocent.
9. He wanted.

320 This world is now ful tikel,° sikerly: *precarious*
    I sawgh today a corps yborn to chirche
    That now a° Monday last I sawgh him wirche.°   *on/work*
    Go up," quod he unto his knave° anoon,   *manservant*
    "Clepe° at his dore or knokke with a stoon.°   *call/stone*
325 Looke how it is and tel me boldely."
        This knave gooth him up ful sturdily,
    And at the chambre dore whil that he stood
    He cride and knokked as that he were wood,°   *mad*
    "What? How? What do ye, maister Nicholay?
330 How may ye sleepen al the longe day?"
    But al for nought: he herde nat a word.
    An hole he foond ful lowe upon a boord,
    Ther as the cat was wont in for to creepe,
    And at that hole he looked in ful deepe,
335 And atte laste he hadde of him a sighte.
        This Nicholas sat evere caping° uprighte   *gaping*
    As he hadde kiked° on the newe moone.   *gazed*
    Adown he gooth and tolde his maister soone
    In what array° he saw this ilke° man.   *condition/same*
340 This carpenter to blessen him¹ bigan,
    And saide, "Help us, Sainte Frideswide!
    A man woot litel what him shal bitide.
    This man is falle, with his astromye,°   *astronomy*
    In som woodnesse° or in som agonye.   *madness*
345 I thoughte ay° wel how that it sholde be: *always*
    Men sholde nought knowe of Goddes privetee.
    Ye, blessed be alway a lewed° man   *ignorant*
    That nought but only his bileve° can.°   *creed/knows*
    So ferde° another clerk with astromye: *fared*
350 He walked in the feeldes for to prye°   *gaze*
    Upon the sterres,° what ther sholde bifalle,   *stars*
    Til he was in a marle-pit² yfalle—
    He saw nat that. But yit, by Saint Thomas,
    Me reweth sore³ for hende Nicholas.
355 He shal be rated of⁴ his studying,
    If that I may, by Jesus, hevene king!
    Get me a staf that I may underspore,°   *pry up*
    Whil that thou, Robin, hevest° up the dore.   *heave*
    He shal⁵ out of his studying, as I gesse."
360 And to the chambre dore he gan him dresse.⁶
    His knave was a strong carl° for the nones,°   *fellow/purpose*
    And by the haspe he haaf° it up atones: *heaved*
    Into° the floor the dore fil° anoon.   *on/fell*
    This Nicholas sat ay as stille as stoon,
365 And evere caped up into the air.
    This carpenter wende° he were in despair,   *thought*
    And hente° him by the shuldres mightily,   *seized*
    And shook him harde, and cride spitously,°   *vehemently*

1. Cross himself.   4. Scolded for.
2. Pit from which a fertilizing clay is dug.   5. I.e., shall come.
3. I sorely pity.   6. Took his stand.

"What, Nicholay, what, how! What! Looke adown!
370 Awaak and thenk on Cristes passioun![7]
I crouche[8] thee from elves and fro wightes."°   wicked creatures
Therwith the nightspel saide he anoonrightes[9]
On foure halves° of the hous aboute,   sides
And on the thresshfold° on the dore withoute: threshold
375 "Jesu Crist and Sainte Benedight,°   Benedict
Blesse this hous from every wikked wight!
For nightes nerye the White Pater Noster.[1]
Where wentestou,° thou Sainte Petres soster?°   did you go/sister
And at the laste this hende Nicholas
380 Gan for to sike° sore, and saide, "Allas,   sigh
Shal al the world be lost eftsoones° now?"   again
    This carpenter answerde, "What saistou?
What, thenk on God as we doon, men that swinke."°   work
    This Nicholas answerde, "Fecche me drinke,
385 And after wol I speke in privetee
Of certain thing that toucheth me and thee.
I wol telle it noon other man, certain."
    This carpenter gooth down and comth again,
And broughte of mighty° ale a large quart,   strong
390 And when that eech of hem hadde dronke his part,
This Nicholas his dore faste shette,°   shut
And down the carpenter by him he sette,
And saide, "John, myn hoste lief° and dere,   beloved
Thou shalt upon thy trouthe° swere me here   word of honor
395 That to no wight thou shalt this conseil° wraye;°   secret/disclose
For it is Cristes conseil that I saye,
And if thou telle it man,[2] thou art forlore,°   lost
For this vengeance thou shalt have therfore,
That if thou wraye me, thou shalt be wood."[3]
400   "Nay, Crist forbede it, for his holy blood,"
Quod tho this sely° man. "I nam no labbe,°   innocent/tell-tale
And though I saye, I nam nat lief to gabbe.[4]
Say what thou wilt, I shal it nevere telle
To child ne wif, by him that harwed helle."[5]
405   "Now John," quod Nicholas, "I wol nought lie.
I have yfounde in myn astrologye,
As I have looked in the moone bright,
That now a Monday next, at quarter night,[6]
Shal falle a rain, and that so wilde and wood,°   furious
410 That half so greet was nevere Noees° flood.   Noah's
This world," he saide, "in lasse° than an hour   less
Shal al be dreint,° so hidous is the showr.   drowned
Thus shal mankinde drenche° and lese° hir lif."   drown/lose

---

7. I.e., the Crucifixion.
8. Make the sign of the cross on.
9. The night-charm he said right away (to ward off
evil spirits).
1. Pater Noster is Latin for "Our Father," the
beginning of the Lord's Prayer. The line is obscure,
but a conjectural reading would be, "May the
White 'Our Father' (or 'Our White Father') [either
a prayer or the personification of a protecting

power] defend [nerye] (us) against nights." The
"nightspel" is a jumble of Christian references and
pagan superstition.
2. To anyone.
3. Go mad.
4. And though I say it myself, I don't like to gossip.
5. By Him that despoiled hell—i.e., Christ.
6. I.e., shortly before dawn.

This carpenter answerde, "Allas, my wif!
415 And shal she drenche? Allas, myn Alisoun!"
For sorwe of this he fil almost⁷ adown,
And saide, "Is there no remedye in this cas?"
"Why yis, for⁸ Gode," quod hende Nicholas,
"If thou wolt werken after lore and reed⁹—
420 Thou maist nought werken after thyn owene heed;°   head
For thus saith Salomon that was ful trewe,
'Werk al by conseil and thou shalt nought rewe.'°   be sorry
And if thou werken wolt by good conseil,
I undertake, withouten mast or sail,
425 Yit shal I save hire and thee and me.
Hastou nat herd how saved was Noee
Whan that oure Lord hadde warned him biforn
That al the world with water sholde be lorn?"°   lost
"Yis," quod this carpenter, "ful yore° ago."   long
430 "Hastou nat herd," quod Nicholas, "also
The sorwe of Noee with his felaweshipe?
Er° that he mighte gete his wif to shipe,   before
Him hadde levere,¹ I dar wel undertake,
At thilke time than alle his wetheres² blake
435 That she hadde had a ship hirself allone.³
And therfore woostou° what is best to doone?   do you know
This axeth° haste, and of an hastif° thing   requires / urgent
Men may nought preche or maken tarying.
Anoon go gete us faste into this in°   lodging
440 A kneeding trough or elles a kimelin°   brewing tub
For eech of us, but looke that they be large,°   wide
In whiche we mowen swimme as in a barge,⁴
And han therinne vitaile suffisaunt⁵
But for a day—fy° on the remenaunt!   fie
445 The water shal aslake° and goon away   diminish
Aboute prime⁶ upon the nexte day.
But Robin may nat wite° of this, thy knave,   know
Ne eek thy maide Gille I may nat save.
Axe nought why, for though thou axe me,
450 I wol nought tellen Goddes privetee.°   secrets
Suffiseth thee, but if thy wittes madde,°   go mad
To han° as greet a grace as Noee hadde.   have
Thy wif shal I wel saven, out of doute.
Go now thy way, and speed thee heraboute.
455 But whan thou hast for hire° and thee and me   her
Ygeten us thise kneeding-tubbes three,
Thanne shaltou hangen hem in the roof ful hye,
That no man of oure purveyance° espye.   preparations
And whan thou thus hast doon as I have said,
460 And hast oure vitaile faire in hem ylaid,

---

7. Almost fell.
8. I.e., by.
9. Act according to learning and advice.
1. He had rather.
2. Rams. I.e., he'd have given all the black rams he had.

3. The reluctance of Noah's wife to board the ark is a traditional comic theme in the mystery plays.
4. In which we can float as in a vessel.
5. Sufficient food.
6. 9 A.M.

And eek an ax to smite the corde atwo,
Whan that the water comth that we may go,
And broke an hole an heigh⁷ upon the gable
Unto the gardinward,⁸ over the stable,
465 That we may freely passen forth oure way,
Whan that the grete showr is goon away,
Thanne shaltou swimme as merye, I undertake,
As dooth the white doke° after hir drake.   duck
Thanne wol I clepe,° 'How, Alison? How, John?   call
470 Be merye, for the flood wol passe anoon.'
And thou wolt sayn, 'Hail, maister Nicholay!
Good morwe, I see thee wel, for it is day!'
And thanne shal we be lordes al oure lif
Of al the world, as Noee and his wif.
475 But of oo thing I warne thee ful right:
Be wel avised° on that ilke night   warned
That we been entred into shippes boord
That noon of us ne speke nought a word,
Ne clepe, ne crye, but been in his prayere,
480 For it is Goddes owene heeste dere.⁹
Thy wif and thou mote hange fer atwinne,¹
For that bitwixe you shal be no sinne—
Namore in looking than ther shal in deede.
This ordinance is said: go, God thee speede.
485 Tomorwe at night whan men been alle asleepe,
Into oure kneeding-tubbes wol we creepe,
And sitten there, abiding Goddes grace.
Go now thy way, I have no lenger space°   time
To make of this no lenger sermoning.
490 Men sayn thus: 'Send the wise and say no thing.'
Thou art so wis it needeth thee nat teche:
Go save oure lif, and that I thee biseeche."
    This sely carpenter gooth forth his way:
Ful ofte he saide allas and wailaway,
495 And to his wif he tolde his privetee,
And she was war,° and knew it bet° than he,   aware / better
What al this quaint cast was for to saye.²
But nathelees she ferde° as she wolde deye,   acted
And saide, "Allas, go forth thy way anoon.
500 Help us to scape,° or we been dede eechoon.   escape
I am thy trewe verray wedded wif:
Go, dere spouse, and help to save oure lif."
    Lo, which a greet thing is affeccioun!°   emotion
Men may dien of imaginacioun,
505 So deepe° may impression be take.   deeply
This sely carpenter biginneth quake;
Him thinketh verrailiche° that he may see   truly
Noees flood come walwing° as the see   rolling

7. On high.
8. Toward the garden.
9. Precious commandment.
1. Far apart.
2. What all this clever plan meant.

To drenchen° Alison, his hony dere.   *drown*
510 He weepeth, waileth, maketh sory cheere;
He siketh° with ful many a sory swough,°   *sighs/groan*
And gooth and geteth him a kneeding-trough,
And after a tubbe and a kimelin,
And prively he sente hem to his in,°   *dwelling*
515 And heeng° hem in the roof in privetee;   *hung*
His° owene hand he made laddres three,   *with his*
To climben by the ronges° and the stalkes°   *rungs/uprights*
Unto the tubbes hanging in the balkes,°   *rafters*
And hem vitailed,° bothe trough and tubbe,   *victualed*
520 With breed and cheese and good ale in a jubbe,° *jug*
Suffising right ynough as for a day.
But er° that he hadde maad al this array,   *before*
He sente his knave, and eek his wenche also,
Upon his neede[3] to London for to go.
525 And on the Monday whan it drow to[4] nighte,
He shette° his dore withouten candel-lighte,   *shut*
And dressed° alle thing as it sholde be,   *arranged*
And shortly up they clomben° alle three.   *climbed*
They seten° stille wel a furlong way.[5]   *sat*
530 "Now, Pater Noster, clum,"[6] saide Nicholay,
And "Clum" quod John, and "Clum" saide Alisoun.
This carpenter saide his devocioun,
And stille he sit° and biddeth° his prayere,   *sits/prays*
Awaiting on the rain, if he it heere.°   *might hear*
535 The dede sleep, for wery bisinesse,
Fil° on this carpenter right as I gesse   *fell*
Aboute corfew time,[7] or litel more.
For travailing of his gost[8] he groneth sore,
And eft° he routeth,° for his heed mislay.[9]   *then/snores*
540 Down of the laddre stalketh Nicholay,
And Alison ful softe adown she spedde:
Withouten wordes mo they goon to bedde
Ther as the carpenter is wont to lie.
Ther was the revel and the melodye,
545 And thus lith° Alison and Nicholas   *lies*
In bisinesse of mirthe and of solas,°   *pleasure*
Til that the belle of Laudes[1] gan to ringe,
And freres° in the chauncel° gonne singe.   *friars/chancel*
This parissh clerk, this amorous Absolon,
550 That is for love alway so wo-bigoon,
Upon the Monday was at Oseneye,
With compaignye him to disporte and playe,
And axed upon caas a cloisterer[2]
Ful prively after John the carpenter;

---

3. On an errand for him.
4. Drew toward.
5. The time it takes to go a furlong (i.e., a few minutes).
6. Hush (?). "Pater Noster": Our Father.
7. Probably about 8 P.M.

8. Affliction of his spirit.
9. Lay in the wrong position.
1. The first church service of the day, before daybreak.
2. Here a member of the religious order of Osney Abbey. "Upon caas": by chance.

555 And he drow him apart out of the chirche,
And saide, "I noot:[3] I sawgh him here nought wirche°   work
Sith Saterday. I trowe that he be went
For timber ther oure abbot hath him sent.
For he is wont for timber for to go,
560 And dwellen atte grange[4] a day or two.
Or elles he is at his hous, certain.
Where that he be I can nought soothly sayn."
    This Absolon ful jolif was and light,[5]
And thoughte, "Now is time to wake al night,
565 For sikerly,° I sawgh him nought stiringe   certainly
Aboute his dore sin day bigan to springe.
So mote° I thrive, I shal at cokkes crowe   may
Ful prively knokken at his windowe
That stant° ful lowe upon his bowres° wal.   stands/bedroom's
570 To Alison now wol I tellen al
My love-longing,° for yet I shal nat misse   lovesickness
That at the leeste way[6] I shal hire kisse.
Som manere confort shal I have, parfay.°   in faith
My mouth hath icched al this longe day:
575 That is a signe of kissing at the leeste.
Al night me mette[7] eek I was at a feeste.
Therfore I wol go sleepe an hour or twaye,
And al the night thanne wol I wake and playe."
    Whan that the firste cok hath crowe, anoon
580 Up rist° this joly lovere Absolon,   rises
And him arrayeth gay at point devis.[8]
But first he cheweth grain[9] and licoris,
To smellen sweete, er he hadde kembd° his heer.   combed
Under his tonge a trewe-love[1] he beer,°   bore
585 For therby wende° he to be gracious.°   supposed/pleasing
He rometh° to the carpenteres hous,   strolls
And stille he stant° under the shot-windowe—   stands
Unto his brest it raughte,° it was so lowe—   reached
And ofte he cougheth with a semisoun.°   small sound
590 "What do ye, hony-comb, sweete Alisoun,
My faire brid,[2] my sweete cinamome?°   cinnamon
Awaketh, lemman° myn, and speketh to me.   sweetheart
Wel litel thinken ye upon my wo
That for your love I swete° ther I go.   sweat
595 No wonder is though that I swelte° and swete: melt
I moorne as doth a lamb after the tete.°   teat
Ywis, lemman, I have swich love-longinge,
That lik a turtle° trewe is my moorninge: dove
I may nat ete namore than a maide."
600 "Go fro the windowe, Jakke fool," she saide.
"As help me God, it wol nat be com-pa-me.°   come-kiss-me

3. Don't know.
4. The outlying farm belonging to the abbey.
5. Was very amorous and cheerful.
6. I.e., at least.
7. I dreamed.
8. To perfection.
9. Grain of paradise; a spice.
1. Sprig of a cloverlike plant.
2. Bird or bride.

I love another, and elles I were to blame,
Wel bet° than thee, by Jesu, Absolon.   *better*
Go forth thy way or I wol caste a stoon,
605   And lat me sleepe, a twenty devele way."³
"Allas," quod Absolon, "and wailaway,
That trewe love was evere so yvele biset.⁴
Thanne kis me, sin that it may be no bet,
For Jesus love and for the love of me."
610   "Woltou thanne go thy way therwith?" quod she.
"Ye, certes, lemman," quod this Absolon.
"Thanne maak thee redy," quod she. "I come anoon."
And unto Nicholas she saide stille,°   *quietly*
"Now hust,° and thou shalt laughen al thy fille."   *hush*
615   This Absolon down sette him on his knees,
And said, "I am a lord at alle degrees,⁵
For after this I hope ther cometh more.
Lemman, thy grace, and sweete brid, thyn ore!"°   *mercy*
The windowe she undooth, and that in haste.
620   "Have do," quod she, "come of and speed thee faste,
Lest that oure neighebores thee espye."
This Absolon gan wipe his mouth ful drye:
Derk was the night as pich or as the cole,
And at the windowe out she putte hir hole,
625   And Absolon, him fil no bet ne wers,⁶
But with his mouth he kiste hir naked ers,
Ful savourly,° er he were war of this.   *with relish*
Abak he sterte,° and thoughte it was amis,   *started*
For wel he wiste a womman hath no beerd.°   *beard*
630   He felte a thing al rough and longe yherd,°   *haired*
And saide, "Fy, allas, what have I do?"
"Teehee," quod she, and clapte the windowe to.
And Absolon gooth forth a sory pas.⁷
"A beerd, a beerd!"⁸ quod hende Nicholas,
635   "By Goddes corpus,° this gooth faire and weel."   *body*
This sely Absolon herde everydeel,°   *every bit*
And on his lippe he gan for anger bite,
And to himself he saide, "I shal thee quite."°   *repay*
Who rubbeth now, who froteth° now his lippes   *wipes*
640   With dust, with sond,° with straw, with cloth, with chippes,   *sand*
But Absolon, that saith ful ofte allas?
"My soule bitake° I unto Satanas,°   *commit/Satan*
But me were levere⁹ than all this town," quod he,
"Of this despit° awroken° for to be.   *insult/avenged*
645   Allas," quod he, "allas I ne hadde ybleint!"°   *turned aside*
His hote love was cold and al yqueint,°   *quenched*
For fro that time that he hadde kist hir ers
Of paramours he sette nought a kers,¹
For he was heled° of his maladye.   *cured*

---

3. In the name of twenty devils.
4. Ill-used.
5. In every way.
6. It befell him neither better nor worse.

7. I.e., walking sadly.
8. A trick (slang), but with a play on line 629.
9. I had rather.
1. He didn't care a piece of cress for woman's love.

650 Ful ofte paramours he gan defye,°   *renounce*
    And weep° as dooth a child that is ybete.   *wept*
    A softe paas² he wente over the streete
    Until° a smith men clepen daun Gervais,³   *to*
    That in his forge smithed plough harneis:°   *equipment*
655 He sharpeth shaar and cultour⁴ bisily.
    This Absolon knokketh al esily,°   *quietly*
    And saide, "Undo, Gervais, and that anoon."°   *at once*
    "What, who artou?" "It am I, Absolon."
    "What, Absolon? What, Cristes sweete tree!°   *cross*
660 Why rise ye so rathe?° Ey, benedicite,°   *early/bless me*
    What aileth you? Som gay girl, God it woot,
    Hath brought you thus upon the viritoot.⁵
    By Sainte Note, ye woot wel what I mene."
    This Absolon ne roughte nat a bene⁶
665 Of al his play. No word again he yaf:
    He hadde more tow on his distaf⁷
    Than Gervais knew, and saide, "Freend so dere,
    This hote cultour in the chimenee° here,   *fireplace*
    As lene⁸ it me: I have therwith to doone.
670 I wol bringe it thee again ful soone."
    Gervais answerde, "Certes, were it gold,
    Or in a poke nobles alle untold,⁹
    Thou sholdest have, as I am trewe smith.
    Ey, Cristes fo,¹ what wol ye do therwith?"
675   "Therof," quod Absolon, "be as be may.
    I shal wel telle it thee another day."
    And caughte the cultour by the colde stele.°   *handle*
    Ful softe out at the dore he gan to stele,
    And wente unto the carpenteres wal:
680 He cougheth first and knokketh therwithal
    Upon the windowe, right as he dide er.°   *before*
    This Alison answerde, "Who is ther
    That knokketh so? I warante² it a thief."
    "Why, nay," quod he, "God woot, my sweete lief,°   *dear*
685 I am thyn Absolon, my dereling.°   *darling*
    Of gold," quod he, "I have thee brought a ring—
    My moder yaf it me, so God me save;
    Ful fin it is and therto wel ygrave:°   *engraved*
    This wol I yiven thee if thou me kisse."
690 This Nicholas was risen for to pisse,
    And thoughte he wolde amenden³ al the jape:°   *joke*
    He sholde kisse his ers er that he scape.
    And up the windowe dide he hastily,
    And out his ers he putteth prively,
695 Over the buttok to the haunche-boon.
    And therwith spak this clerk, this Absolon,

---

2. I.e., quiet walk.
3. Master Gervais.
4. He sharpens plowshare and coulter (the turf cutter on a plow).
5. I.e., on the prowl.
6. Didn't care a bean.

7. I.e., more on his mind.
8. I.e., please lend.
9. Or gold coins all uncounted in a bag.
1. Foe, i.e., Satan.
2. I.e., wager.
3. Improve on.

"Speek, sweete brid, I noot nought wher thou art."
This Nicholas anoon leet flee[4] a fart
As greet as it hadde been a thonder-dent°   *thunderbolt*
700 That with the strook he was almost yblent,°   *blinded*
And he was redy with his iren hoot,°   *hot*
And Nicholas amidde the ers he smoot:°   *smote*
Of° gooth the skin an hande-brede° aboute;   *off/handsbreadth*
The hote cultour brende so his toute°   *buttocks*
705 That for the smert° he wende for to[5] die;   *pain*
As he were wood° for wo he gan to crye,   *crazy*
"Help! Water! Water! Help, for Goddes herte!"
    This carpenter out of his slomber sterte,
And herde oon cryen "Water!" as he were wood,
710 And thoughte, "Allas, now cometh Noweles[6] flood!"
He sette him up[7] withoute wordes mo,
And with his ax he smoot the corde atwo,
And down gooth al: he foond neither to selle
Ne breed ne ale til he cam to the celle,[8]
715 Upon the floor, and ther aswoune° he lay.   *in a faint*
    Up sterte hire[9] Alison and Nicholay,
And criden "Out" and "Harrow" in the streete.
The neighebores, bothe smale and grete,
In ronnen for to gauren° on this man   *gape*
720 That aswoune lay bothe pale and wan,
For with the fal he brosten° hadde his arm;   *broken*
But stonde he moste° unto his owene harm,   *must*
For whan he spak he was anoon bore down[1]
With° hende Nicholas and Alisoun: *by*
725 They tolden every man that he was wood—
He was agast so of Noweles flood,
Thurgh fantasye, that of his vanitee°   *folly*
He hadde ybought him kneeding-tubbes three,
And hadde hem hanged in the roof above,
730 And that he prayed hem, for Goddes love,
To sitten in the roof, *par compaignye*.[2]
    The folk gan laughen at his fantasye.
Into the roof they kiken° and they cape,°   *peer/gape*
And turned al his harm unto a jape,°   *joke*
735 For what so that this carpenter answerde,
It was for nought: no man his reson° herde;   *argument*
With othes grete he was so sworn adown,
That he was holden° wood in al the town,   *considered*
For every clerk anoonright heeld with other:
740 They saide, "The man was wood, my leve brother,"
And every wight gan laughen at this strif.°   *fuss*
Thus swived[3] was the carpenteres wif
For al his keeping° and his jalousye,   *guarding*

4. Let fly.
5. Thought he would.
6. The carpenter is confusing Noah and Noel (Christmas).
7. Got up.
8. He found time to sell neither bread nor ale until

he arrived at the foundation, i.e., he did not take time out.
9. Started.
1. Refuted.
2. For company's sake.
3. The vulgar verb for having sexual intercourse.

And Absolon hath kist hir nether° yë,   *lower*
745 And Nicholas is scalded in the toute:
This tale is doon, and God save al the route!°   *company*

The Man of Law's Epilogue

The Reeve has taken *The Miller's Tale* personally and retaliates with a fabliau about
a miller whose wife and daughter are seduced by two clerks. Next the Cook begins
yet another fabliau, which breaks off after fifty-five lines, thereby closing Fragment I
of *The Canterbury Tales*. Chaucer may never have settled on a final order for the tales
he completed, but all modern editors, following many manuscripts, agree in putting
The Man of Law's Tale next. The Man of Law tells a long moralistic tale about the
many trials of a heroine called Constance for the virtue she personifies. This tale is
finished, but Fragment II shows that *The Canterbury Tales* reaches us as a work in
progress, which Chaucer kept revising, creating many problems for its scribes and
editors. In the link that introduces him, the Man of Law says he will tell a tale in
prose, but the story of Constance turns out to be in a seven-line stanza called rhyme
royal. That inconsistency has led to speculation that at one time the Man of Law was
assigned a long prose allegory, which Chaucer later reassigned to his own pilgrim
persona. In thirty-five manuscripts *The Man of Law's Tale* is followed by an *Epilogue*
omitted in twenty-two of the manuscripts that contain more or less complete versions
of *The Canterbury Tales*. The often-missing link begins with the Host praising the
Man of Law's Tale and calling upon the Parson to tell another uplifting tale. The
Parson, however, rebukes the Host for swearing. The Host angrily accuses the Parson
of being a "Lollard," a derogatory term for followers of the reformist preacher John
Wycliffe. This is Chaucer's only overt reference to an important religious and political
controversy that anticipates the sixteenth-century English Reformation.

A third speaker, about whose identity the manuscripts disagree (six read "Summoner"; twenty-eight, "Squire"; one, "Shipman"), interrupts with the promise to tell
a merry tale. Several modern editions, including the standard one used by scholars,
print *The Man of Law's Epilogue* at the end of Fragment II, and begin Fragment III
with *The Wife of Bath's Prologue*. Because the third speaker in the former *sounds* like
the Wife, an argument has been made that she is the pilgrim who refers to "My joly
body" (line 23), who at one time told a fabliau tale in which the narrator speaks of
married women in the first person plural ("we," "us," "our"). Chaucer, so the argument
goes, later gave that story to the Shipman. If in fact the Wife of Bath did once tell
what is now *The Shipman's Tale*, that would be an indication of the exciting new
possibilities he discovered in the literary form he had invented.

    Oure Host upon his stiropes stood anoon
    And saide, "Goode men, herkneth everichoon,
    This was a thrifty° tale for the nones,°   *proper / occasion*
    Sire parissh Preest," quod he, "for Goddes bones,
5   Tel us a tale as was thy forward° yore.°   *agreement / earlier*
    I see wel that ye lerned men in lore°   *teaching*
    Can° muche good, by Goddes dignitee."   *know*
    The Person him answerde, "Benedicite,°   *bless me*
    What aileth the man so sinfully to swere?"
10 Oure Host answerede, "O Jankin, be ye there?"[1]
    I smelle a lollere[2] in the wind," quod he.

---

1. Is that where you're coming from? "Jankin": Johnny; derogatory name for a priest.

2. Contemptuous term for a religious reformer considered radical; a heretic.

"Now, goode men," quod oure Hoste, "herkneth me:
Abideth, for Goddes digne° passioun,   *worthy*
For we shal have a predicacioun.°   *sermon*
15 This lollere here wol prechen us somwhat."
"Nay, by my fader soule, that shal he nat,"
Saide the [Wif of Bathe],³ "here shal he nat preche:
He shal no gospel glosen⁴ here ne teche.
We leven° alle in the grete God," quod [she].   *believe*
20 He wolde sowen som difficultee
Or sprengen cokkel in oure clene corn.⁵
And therfore, Host, I warne thee biforn,
My joly body shal a tale telle
And I shal clinken you so merye a belle
25 That I shal waken al this compaignye.
But it shal nat been of philosophye,
Ne physlias,⁶ ne termes quainte of lawe:
There is but litel Latin in my mawe."°   *stomach*

The Wife of Bath's Prologue and Tale

In creating the Wife of Bath, Chaucer drew upon a centuries-old tradition of antifeminist writings that was particularly nurtured by the medieval church. In their
conviction that the rational, intellectual, spiritual, and, therefore, higher side of
human nature predominated in men, whereas the irrational, material, earthly, and,
therefore, lower side of human nature predominated in women, St. Paul and the early
Church fathers exalted celibacy and virginity above marriage, although they were also
obliged to concede the necessity and sanctity of matrimony. In the fourth century, a
monk called Jovinian wrote a tract in which he apparently presented marriage as a
positive good rather than as a necessary evil. That tract is known only through St.
Jerome's extreme attack upon it. Jerome's diatribe and other antifeminist and anti-
matrimonial literature provided Chaucer with a rich body of bookish male "auctoritee"
(authority) against which the Wife of Bath asserts her female "experience" and
defends her rights and justifies her life as a five-time married woman. In her polemical
wars with medieval clerks and her matrimonial wars with her five husbands, the last
of whom was once a clerk of Oxenford, the Wife of Bath seems ironically to confirm
the accusations of the clerks, but at the same time she succeeds in satirizing the
shallowness of the stereotypes of women and marriage in antifeminist writings and
in demonstrating how much the largeness and complexity of her own character rise
above that stereotype.

The Prologue

Experience, though noon auctoritee
Were in this world, is right ynough for me
To speke of wo that is in mariage:
For lordinges,° sith I twelf yeer was of age—   *gentlemen*
5 Thanked be God that is eterne on live—
Housbondes at chirche dore¹ I have had five

---

3. On the speaker here, see discussion in headnote.
4. Gloss, with the sense of distorting the meaning
of scripture.
5. Sow tares (impure doctrine) in our pure wheat.

6. No such word exists. The speaker is coining a
professional-sounding term in philosophy, law, or
medicine.
1. The actual wedding ceremony was celebrated
at the church door, not in the chancel.

(If I so ofte mighte han wedded be),
And alle were worthy men in hir degree.
But me was told, certain, nat longe agoon is,
10   That sith that Crist ne wente nevere but ones°   once
To wedding in the Cane[2] of Galilee,
That by the same ensample° taughte he me   example
That I ne sholde wedded be but ones.
Herke eek,° lo, which° a sharp word for the nones,[3]   also/what
15   Biside a welle, Jesus, God and man,
Spak in repreve° of the Samaritan: reproof
"Thou hast yhad five housbondes," quod he,
"And that ilke° man that now hath thee   same
Is nat thyn housbonde." Thus saide he certain.
20   What that he mente therby I can nat sayn,
But that I axe° why the fifthe man   ask
Was noon housbonde to the Samaritan?[4]
How manye mighte she han in mariage?
Yit herde I nevere tellen in myn age
25   Upon this nombre diffinicioun.°   definition
Men may divine° and glosen° up and down,   guess/interpret
But wel I woot,° expres,° withouten lie,   know/expressly
God bad us for to wexe[5] and multiplye:
That gentil text can I wel understonde.
30   Eek wel I woot° he saide that myn housbonde   know
Sholde lete° fader and moder and take to me,[6]   leave
But of no nombre mencion made he—
Of bigamye or of octogamye:[7]
Why sholde men thanne speke of it vilainye?
35   Lo, here the wise king daun° Salomon: master
I trowe° he hadde wives many oon,[8]   believe
As wolde God it leveful° were to me   permissible
To be refresshed half so ofte as he.
Which yifte[9] of God hadde he for alle his wives!
40   No man hath swich° that in this world alive is.   such
God woot this noble king, as to my wit,°   knowledge
The firste night hadde many a merye fit°   bout
With eech of hem, so wel was him on live.[1]
Blessed be God that I have wedded five,
45   Of whiche I have piked out the beste,[2]
Bothe of hir nether purs[3] and of hir cheste.°   money box
Diverse scoles maken parfit° clerkes,   perfect
And diverse practikes[4] in sondry werkes
Maken the werkman parfit sikerly:°   certainly
50   Of five housbondes scoleying° am I.   schooling

---

2. Cana (see John 2.1).
3. To the purpose.
4. Christ was actually referring to a sixth man who was not married to the Samaritan woman (cf. John 4.6 ff.).
5. I.e., increase (see Genesis 1.28).
6. See Matthew 19.5.
7. I.e., of two or even eight marriages. The Wife of Bath is referring to successive, rather than

simultaneous, marriages.
8. Solomon had seven hundred wives and three hundred concubines (1 Kings 11.3).
9. What a gift.
1. I.e., so pleasant a life he had.
2. Whom I have cleaned out of everything worthwhile.
3. Lower purse, i.e., testicles.
4. Practical experiences.

Welcome the sixte whan that evere he shal![5]
For sith I wol nat kepe me chast in al,
Whan my housbonde is fro the world agoon,
Som Cristen man shal wedde me anoon.°   right away
55   For thanne th'Apostle[6] saith that I am free
To wedde, a Goddes half, where it liketh me.[7]
He saide that to be wedded is no sinne:
Bet is to be wedded than to brinne.[8]
What rekketh me[9] though folk saye vilainye
60   Of shrewed° Lamech[1] and his bigamye?   cursed
I woot wel Abraham was an holy man,
And Jacob eek, as fer as evere I can,°   know
And eech of hem hadde wives mo than two,
And many another holy man also.
65   Where can ye saye in any manere age
That hye God defended° mariage   prohibited
By expres word? I praye you, telleth me.
Or where comanded he virginitee?
I woot as wel as ye, it is no drede,°   doubt
70   Th'Apostle, whan he speketh of maidenhede,°   virginity
He saide that precept therof hadde he noon:
Men may conseile a womman to be oon,°   single
But conseiling nis° no comandement.   is not
He putte it in oure owene juggement.
75   For hadde God comanded maidenhede,
Thanne hadde he dampned° wedding with the deede;[2]   condemned
And certes, if there were no seed ysowe,
Virginitee, thanne wherof sholde it growe?
Paul dorste nat comanden at the leeste
80   A thing of which his maister yaf° no heeste.°   gave / command
The dart[3] is set up for virginitee:
Cacche whoso may, who renneth° best lat see.   runs
But this word is nought take of[4] every wight,°   person
But ther as[5] God list° yive it of his might.   it pleases
85   I woot wel that th'Apostle was a maide,°   virgin
But nathelees, though that he wroot and saide
He wolde that every wight were swich° as he,   such
Al nis but conseil to virginitee;
And for to been a wif he yaf me leve
90   Of indulgence; so nis it no repreve°   disgrace
To wedde me[6] if that my make° die,   mate
Withouten excepcion of bigamye[7]—
Al° were it good no womman for to touche[8]   although
(He mente as in his bed or in his couche,

---

5. I.e., shall come along.
6. St. Paul.
7. I please. "A Goddes half": on God's behalf.
8. "It is better to marry than to burn" (1 Corinthians 7.9). Many of the Wife's citations of St. Paul are from this chapter, often secondhand from St. Jerome's tract Against Jovinian.
9. What do I care.
1. The first man whom the Bible mentions as having two wives (Genesis 4.19–24); he is cursed,

however, not for his marriages but for murder.
2. I.e., at the same time.
3. I.e., prize in a race.
4. Understood for, i.e., applicable to.
5. Where.
6. For me to marry.
7. I.e., without there being any legal objection on the score of remarriage.
8. "It is good for a man not to touch a woman" (1 Corinthians 7.1).

95   For peril is bothe fir° and tow° t'assemble—   *fire/flax*
      Ye knowe what this ensample may resemble).⁹
      This al and som,¹ he heeld virginitee
      More parfit than wedding in freletee.°   *frailty*
      (Freletee clepe I but if² that he and she
100   Wolde leden al hir lif in chastitee.)
      I graunte it wel, I have noon envye
      Though maidenhede preferre° bigamye:°   *excel/remarriage*
      It liketh hem to be clene in body and gost.°   *spirit*
      Of myn estaat ne wol I make no boost;
105   For wel ye knowe, a lord in his houshold
      Ne hath nat every vessel al of gold:
      Some been of tree,° and doon hir lord servise.   *wood*
      God clepeth° folk to him in sondry wise,   *calls*
      And everich hath of God a propre³ yifte,
110   Som this, som that, as him liketh shifte.°   *ordain*
      Virginitee is greet perfeccioun,
      And continence eek with devocioun,
      But Crist, that of perfeccion is welle,°   *source*
      Bad nat every wight he sholde go selle
115   Al that he hadde and yive it to the poore,
      And in swich wise folwe him and his fore:°⁴   *footsteps*
      He spak to hem that wolde live parfitly°—   *perfectly*
      And lordinges, by youre leve, that am nat I.
      I wol bistowe the flour of al myn age
120   In th'actes and in fruit of mariage.
          Telle me also, to what conclusioun°   *end*
      Were membres maad of generacioun
      And of so parfit wis a wrighte ywrought?⁵
          Trusteth right wel, they were nat maad for nought.
125   Glose° whoso wol, and saye bothe up and down   *interpret*
      That they were maked for purgacioun
      Of urine, and oure bothe thinges smale
      Was eek° to knowe a femele from a male,   *also*
      And for noon other cause—saye ye no?
130   Th'experience woot it is nought so.
      So that the clerkes be nat with me wrothe,
      I saye this, that they been maad for bothe—
      That is to sayn, for office° and for ese°   *use/pleasure*
      Of engendrure,° ther we nat God displese.   *procreation*
135   Why sholde men elles in hir bookes sette
      That man shal yeelde⁶ to his wif hir dette?°   *(marital) debt*
      Now wherwith sholde he make his payement
      If he ne used his sely° instrument?   *innocent*
      Thanne were they maad upon a creature
140   To purge urine, and eek for engendrure.
          But I saye nought that every wight is holde,°   *bound*
      That hath swich harneis° as I to you tolde,   *equipment*

---

9. I.e., what this metaphor may apply to.   4. Matthew 19.21.
1. This is all there is to it.   5. And wrought by so perfectly wise a maker.
2. Frailty I call it unless.   6. I.e., pay.
3. I.e., his own.

To goon and usen hem in engendrure:
Thanne sholde men take of chastitee no cure.°   *heed*
145 Crist was a maide° and shapen as a man,   *virgin*
And many a saint sith that the world bigan,
Yit lived they evere in parfit chastitee.
I nil° envye no virginitee: *will not*
Lat hem be breed° of pured° whete seed,   *bread / refined*
150 And lat us wives hote° barly breed—   *be called*
And yit with barly breed, Mark telle can,
Oure Lord Jesu refresshed many a man.[7]
In swich estaat as God hath cleped us
I wol persevere: I nam nat precious.°   *fastidious*
155 In wifhood wol I use myn instrument
As freely° as my Makere hath it sent.   *generously*
If I be daungerous,[8] God yive me sorwe:
Myn housbonde shal it han bothe eve and morwe,°   *morning*
    Whan that him list[9] come forth and paye his dette.
160 An housbonde wol I have, I wol nat lette,[1]
Which shal be bothe my dettour° and my thral,°   *debtor / slave*
And have his tribulacion withal°   *as well*
Upon his flessh whil that I am his wif.
I have the power during al my lif
165 Upon his propre° body, and nat he: *own*
Right thus th'Apostle tolde it unto me,
And bad oure housbondes for to love us weel.
Al this sentence° me liketh everydeel.°   *sense / entirely*

[AN INTERLUDE]

Up sterte° the Pardoner and that anoon: *started*
170 "Now dame," quod he, "by God and by Saint John,
Ye been a noble prechour in this cas.
I was aboute to wedde a wif: allas,
What° sholde I bye° it on my flessh so dere?   *why / purchase*
Yit hadde I levere° wedde no wif toyere."°   *rather / this year*
175 "Abid," quod she, "my tale is nat bigonne.
Nay, thou shalt drinken of another tonne,°   *tun, barrel*
Er° that I go, shal savoure wors than ale.   *before*
And whan that I have told thee forth my tale
Of tribulacion in mariage,
180 Of which I am expert in al myn age—
This is to saye, myself hath been the whippe—
Thanne maistou chese° wheither thou wolt sippe   *choose*
Of thilke° tonne that I shal abroche;°   *this same / open*
Be war of it, er thou too neigh approche,
185 For I shal telle ensamples mo than ten.
'Whoso that nil° be war by othere men,   *will not*
By him shal othere men corrected be.'

---

7. In the descriptions of the miracle of the loaves and fishes, it is actually John, not Mark, who mentions barley bread (6.9).
8. In romance *dangerous* is a term for disdainfulness with which a woman rejects a lover. The Wife means she will not withhold sexual favors, in emulation of God's generosity (line 156).
9. When he wishes to.
1. I will not leave off, desist.

Thise same wordes writeth Ptolomee:
Rede in his *Almageste* and take it there."[2]
190   "Dame, I wolde praye you if youre wil it were,"
Saide this Pardoner, "as ye bigan,
Telle forth youre tale; spareth for no man,
And teche us yonge men of youre practike."°   *mode of operation*
   "Gladly," quod she, "sith it may you like;°   *please*
195 But that I praye to al this compaignye,
If that I speke after my fantasye,[3]
As taketh nat agrief° of that I saye,   *amiss*
For myn entente nis but for to playe."

[THE WIFE CONTINUES]

  Now sire, thanne wol I telle you forth my tale.
200 As evere mote I drinke win or ale,
I shal saye sooth: tho° housbondes that I hadde,   *those*
As three of hem were goode, and two were badde.
The three men were goode, and riche, and olde;
Unnethe° mighte they the statut holde   *scarcely*
205 In which they were bounden unto me—
Ye woot wel what I mene of this, pardee.
As help me God, I laughe whan I thinke
How pitously anight I made hem swinke;°   *work*
And by my fay,° I tolde of it no stoor:[4]   *faith*
210 They hadde me yiven hir land and hir tresor;
Me needed nat do lenger diligence
To winne hir love or doon hem reverence.
They loved me so wel, by God above,
That I ne tolde no daintee of[5] hir love.
215 A wis womman wol bisye hire evere in oon[6]
To gete hire love, ye, ther as she hath noon.
But sith I hadde hem hoolly in myn hand,
And sith that they hadde yiven me al hir land,
What° sholde I take keep° hem for to plese,   *why/care*
220 But it were for my profit and myn ese?
I sette hem so awerke,° by my fay,   *awork*
That many a night they songen° wailaway.   *sang*
The bacon was nat fet° for hem, I trowe,   *brought back*
That some men han in Essexe at Dunmowe.[7]
225 I governed hem so wel after° my lawe   *according to*
That eech of hem ful blisful was and fawe°   *glad*
To bringe me gaye thinges fro the faire;
They were ful glade whan I spak hem faire,
For God it woot, I chidde° hem spitously.°   *chided/cruelly*
230   Now herkneth how I bar me[8] proprely:

2. "He who will not be warned by the example of others shall become an example to others." The *Almagest*, an astronomical work by the Greek astronomer and mathematician Ptolemy (2nd century C.E.), contains no such aphorism.
3. If I speak according to my fancy.
4. I set no store by it.

5. Set no value on.
6. Busy herself constantly.
7. At Dunmow, a side of bacon was awarded to the couple who after a year of marriage could claim no quarrels, no regrets, and the desire, if freed, to remarry one another.
8. Bore myself, behaved.

Ye wise wives, that conne understonde,
Thus sholde ye speke and bere him wrong on honde[9]—
For half so boldely can ther no man
Swere and lie as a woman can.
235 I saye nat this by wives that been wise,
But if it be whan they hem misavise.[1]
A wis wif, if that she can hir good,[2]
Shal bere him on hande the cow is wood,[3]
And take witnesse of hir owene maide
240 Of hir assent.[4] But herkneth how I saide:
 "Sire olde cainard,° is this thyn array?[5]   *sluggard*
Why is my neighebores wif so gay?
She is honoured overal° ther she gooth: *wherever*
I sitte at hoom; I have no thrifty° cloth.   *decent*
245 What doostou at my neighebores hous?
Is she so fair? Artou so amorous?
What roune° ye with oure maide, benedicite?[6]   *whisper*
Sire olde lechour, lat thy japes° be.   *tricks, intrigues*
And if I have a gossib° or a freend   *confidant*
250 Withouten gilt, ye chiden as a feend,
If that I walke or playe unto his hous.
Thou comest hoom as dronken as a mous,
And prechest on thy bench, with yvel preef.[7]
Thou saist to me, it is a greet meschief°   *misfortune*
255 To wedde a poore womman for costage.[8]
And if that she be riche, of heigh parage,°   *descent*
Thanne saistou that it is a tormentrye
To suffre hir pride and hir malencolye.°   *bad humor*
And if that she be fair, thou verray knave,
260 Thou saist that every holour° wol hire have: *lecher*
She may no while in chastitee abide
That is assailed upon eech a side.
 "Thou saist som folk desiren us for richesse,
Som[9] for oure shap, and som for oure fairnesse,
265 And som for she can outher° singe or daunce,   *either*
And som for gentilesse and daliaunce,°   *flirtatiousness*
Som for hir handes and hir armes smale°—   *slender*
Thus gooth al to the devel by thy tale![1]
Thou saist men may nat keepe[2] a castel wal,
270 It may so longe assailed been overal.°   *everywhere*
And if that she be foul,° thou saist that she   *ugly*
Coveiteth° every man that she may see;   *desires*
For as a spaniel she wol on him lepe,
Til that she finde som man hire to chepe.°   *bargain for*
275 Ne noon so grey goos gooth ther in the lake,

9. Accuse him falsely.
1. Unless it happens that they make a mistake.
2. If she knows what's good for her.
3. Shall persuade him the chough has gone crazy. The chough, a talking bird, was popularly supposed to tell husbands of their wives' infidelity.
4. And call as a witness her maid, who is on her side.

5. I.e., is this how you behave?
6. Bless me.
7. I.e., (may you have) bad luck.
8. Because of the expense.
9. "Som," in this and the following lines, means "one."
1. I.e., according to your story.
2. I.e., keep safe.

	As, saistou, wol be withoute make;°	*mate*
	And saist it is an hard thing for to weelde°	*possess*
	A thing that no man wol, his thankes, heelde.[3]	
	Thus saistou, lorel,° whan thou goost to bedde,	*wretch*
280	And that no wis man needeth for to wedde,	
	Ne no man that entendeth° unto hevene—	*aims*
	With wilde thonder-dint° and firy levene°	*thunderbolt / lightning*
	Mote thy welked nekke be tobroke![4]	
	Thou saist that dropping° houses and eek smoke	*leaking*
285	And chiding wives maken men to flee	
	Out of hir owene hous: a, benedicite,	
	What aileth swich an old man for to chide?	
	Thou saist we wives wil oure vices hide	
	Til we be fast,[5] and thanne we wol hem shewe—	
290	Wel may that be a proverbe of a shrewe!°	*rascal*
	Thou saist that oxen, asses, hors,° and houndes,	*horses*
	They been assayed° at diverse stoundes;°	*tried out / times*
	Bacins, lavours,° er that men hem bye,°	*washbowls / buy*
	Spoones, stooles, and al swich housbondrye,°	*household goods*
295	And so be° pottes, clothes, and array°—	*are / clothing*
	But folk of wives maken noon assay	
	Til they be wedded—olde dotard shrewe!	
	And thanne, saistou, we wil oure vices shewe.	
	Thou saist also that it displeseth me	
300	But if° that thou wolt praise my beautee,	*unless*
	And but thou poure° alway upon my face,	*gaze*
	And clepe me 'Faire Dame' in every place,	
	And but thou make a feeste on thilke day	
	That I was born, and make me fressh and gay,	
305	And but thou do to my norice° honour,	*nurse*
	And to my chamberere within my bowr,[6]	
	And to my fadres folk, and his allies[7]—	
	Thus saistou, olde barel-ful of lies.	
	And yit of our apprentice Janekin,	
310	For his crispe° heer, shining as gold so fin,	*curly*
	And for° he squiereth me bothe up and down,	*because*
	Yit hastou caught a fals suspecioun;	
	I wil° him nat though thou were deed° tomorwe.	*want / dead*
	"But tel me this, why hidestou with sorwe[8]	
315	The keyes of thy cheste° away fro me?	*money box*
	It is my good° as wel as thyn, pardee.	*property*
	What, weenestou° make an idiot of oure dame?[9]	*do you think to*
	Now by that lord that called is Saint Jame,	
	Thou shalt nought bothe, though thou were wood,°	*furious*
320	Be maister of my body and of my good:	
	That oon thou shalt forgo, maugree thine yën.[1]	
	"What helpeth it of me enquere° and spyen?	*inquire*

3. No man would willingly hold.
4. May thy withered neck be broken!
5. I.e., married.
6. And to my chambermaid within my bedroom.
7. Relatives by marriage.
8. I.e., with sorrow to you.
9. I.e., me, the mistress of the house.
1. Despite your eyes, i.e., despite anything you can do about it.

I trowe thou woldest loke° me in thy cheste.   *lock*
Thou sholdest saye, 'Wif, go wher thee leste.°   *it may please*
325 Taak youre disport.² I nil leve° no tales: *believe*
I knowe you for a trewe wif, dame Alis.'
We love no man that taketh keep or charge³
Wher that we goon: we wol been at oure large.⁴
Of alle men yblessed mote he be
330 The wise astrologen° daun Ptolomee,   *astronomer*
That saith this proverbe in his *Almageste*:
'Of alle men his wisdom is the hyeste
That rekketh° nat who hath the world in honde.'⁵   *cares*
By this proverbe thou shalt understonde,
335 Have thou⁶ ynough, what thar° thee rekke or care   *need*
How merily that othere folkes fare?
For certes, olde dotard, by youre leve,
Ye shal han queinte⁷ right ynough at eve:
He is too greet a nigard that wil werne°   *refuse*
340 A man to lighte a candle at his lanterne;
He shal han nevere the lasse° lighte, pardee.   *less*
Have thou ynough, thee thar nat plaine thee.⁸
    "Thou saist also that if we make us gay
With clothing and with precious array,
345 That it is peril of oure chastitee,
And yit, with sorwe, thou moste enforce thee,⁹
And saye thise wordes in th' Apostles¹ name:
'In habit° maad with chastitee and shame   *clothing*
Ye wommen shal apparaile you,' quod he,
350 'And nat in tressed heer² and gay perree,°   *jewelry*
As perles, ne with gold ne clothes riche.'³
After thy text, ne after thy rubriche,⁴
I wol nat werke as muchel as a gnat.
Thou saidest this, that I was lik a cat:
355 For whoso wolde senge° a cattes skin,   *singe*
Thanne wolde the cat wel dwellen in his in;°   *lodging*
And if the cattes skin be slik° and gay,   *sleek*
She wol nat dwelle in house half a day,
But forth she wol, er any day be dawed,⁵
360 To shewe her skin and goon a-caterwawed.°   *caterwauling*
This is to saye, if I be gay, sire shrewe,
I wol renne° out, my borel° for to shewe.   *run/clothing*
Sir olde fool, what helpeth⁶ thee t'espyen?
Though thou praye Argus with his hundred yën⁷
365 To be my wardecors,° as he can best,   *bodyguard*
In faith, he shal nat keepe° me but me lest:⁸   *guard*

2. Enjoy yourself.
3. Notice or interest.
4. I.e., liberty.
5. Who rules the world.
6. If you have.
7. Elegant, pleasing thing; a euphemism for sexual enjoyment.
8. I.e., you need not complain.
9. Strengthen your position.
1. I.e., St. Paul's.

2. I.e., elaborate hairdo.
3. See 1 Timothy 2.9.
4. Rubric, i.e., direction.
5. Has dawned.
6. What does it help.
7. Argus was a monster whom Juno set to watch over one of Jupiter's mistresses. Mercury put all one hundred of his eyes to sleep and slew him.
8. Unless I please.

Yit coude I make his beerd,[9] so mote I thee.°   *prosper*
    "Thou saidest eek that ther been thinges three,
    The whiche thinges troublen al this erthe,
370 And that no wight may endure the ferthe.°   *fourth*
    O leve° sire shrewe, Jesu shorte° thy lif!   *dear / shorten*
    Yit prechestou and saist an hateful wif
    Yrekened° is for oon of thise meschaunces.[1]   *is counted*
    Been ther nat none othere resemblaunces
375 That ye may likne youre parables to,[2]
    But if° a sely° wif be oon of tho?   *unless / innocent*
    "Thou liknest eek wommanes love to helle,
    To bareine° land ther water may nat dwelle;   *barren*
    Thou liknest it also to wilde fir—
380 The more it brenneth,° the more it hath desir   *burns*
    To consumen every thing that brent° wol be;   *burned*
    Thou saist right° as wormes shende° a tree,   *just / destroy*
    Right so a wif destroyeth hir housbonde—
    This knowen they that been to wives bonde."°   *bound*
385   Lordinges, right thus, as ye han understonde,
    Bar I stifly mine olde housbondes on honde[3]
    That thus they saiden in hir dronkenesse—
    And al was fals, but that I took witnesse
    On Janekin and on my nece also.
390 O Lord, the paine I dide hem and the wo,
    Ful gilteles, by Goddes sweete pine!°   *suffering*
    For as an hors I coude bite and whine;°   *whinny*
    I coude plaine° and° I was in the gilt,   *complain / if*
    Or elles often time I hadde been spilt.°   *ruined*
395 Whoso that first to mille comth first grint.°   *grinds*
    I plained first: so was oure werre stint.[4]
    They were ful glade to excusen hem ful blive°   *quickly*
    Of thing of which they nevere agilte hir live.[5]
    Of wenches wolde I beren hem on honde,[6]
400 Whan that for sik[7] they mighte unnethe° stonde,   *scarcely*
    Yit tikled I his herte for that he
    Wende° I hadde had of him so greet cheertee.°   *thought / affection*
    I swoor that al my walking out by nighte
    Was for to espye wenches that he dighte.[8]
405 Under that colour[9] hadde I many a mirthe.
    For al swich wit is yiven us in oure birthe:
    Deceite, weeping, spinning God hath yive
    To wommen kindely° whil they may live.   *naturally*
    And thus of oo thing I avaunte me:[1]
410 At ende I hadde the bet° in eech degree,   *better*
    By sleighte or force, or by som manere thing,
    As by continuel murmur° or grucching;°   *complaint / grumbling*

---

9. I.e., deceive him.
1. For the other three misfortunes see Proverbs 30.21–23.
2. Are there no other (appropriate) similitudes to which you might draw analogies?
3. I rigorously accused my old husbands.
4. Our war brought to an end.

5. Of which they were never guilty in their lives.
6. Falsely accuse them.
7. I.e., sickness.
8. Had intercourse with.
9. I.e., pretense.
1. Boast.

Namely° abedde hadden they meschaunce: *especially*
Ther wolde I chide and do hem no plesaunce;[2]
415   I wolde no lenger in the bed abide
If that I felte his arm over my side,
Til he hadde maad his raunson° unto me;   *ransom*
Thanne wolde I suffre him do his nicetee.°   *foolishness (sex)*
And therfore every man this tale I telle:
420   Winne whoso may, for al is for to selle;
With empty hand men may no hawkes lure.
For winning° wolde I al his lust endure,   *profit*
And make me a feined° appetit—   *pretended*
And yit in bacon[3] hadde I nevere delit.
425   That made me that evere I wolde hem chide;
For though the Pope hadde seten° hem biside,   *sat*
I wolde nought spare hem at hir owene boord.°   *table*
For by my trouthe, I quitte° hem word for word.   *repaid*
As help me verray God omnipotent,
430   Though I right now sholde make my testament,
I ne owe hem nat a word that it nis quit.
I broughte it so aboute by my wit
That they moste yive it up as for the beste,
Or elles hadde we nevere been in reste;
435   For though he looked as a wood° leoun,   *furious*
Yit sholde he faile of his conclusioun.°   *object*
        Thanne wolde I saye, "Goodelief, taak keep,[4]
How mekely looketh Wilekin,[5] oure sheep!
Com neer my spouse, lat me ba° thy cheeke—   *kiss*
440   Ye sholden be al pacient and meeke,
And han a sweete-spiced° conscience,   *mild*
Sith ye so preche of Jobes pacience;
Suffreth alway, sin ye so wel can preche;
And but ye do, certain, we shal you teche
445   That it is fair to han a wif in pees.
Oon of us two moste bowen, doutelees,
And sith a man is more resonable
Than womman is, ye mosten been suffrable.°   *patient*
What aileth you to grucche° thus and grone?   *grumble*
450   Is it for ye wolde have my queinte° allone?   *sexual organ*
Why, taak it al—lo, have it everydeel.°   *all of it*
Peter,[6] I shrewe° you but ye° love it weel.   *curse / if you don't*
For if I wolde selle my bele chose,[7]
I coude walke as fressh as is a rose;
455   But I wol keepe it for youre owene tooth.°   *taste*
Ye be to blame. By God, I saye you sooth!"°   *the truth*
Swiche manere° wordes hadde we on honde.   *kind of*
Now wol I speke of my ferthe° housbonde.   *fourth*
        My ferthe housbonde was a revelour°   *reveler*
460   This is to sayn, he hadde a paramour°   *mistress*

---

2. Give them no pleasure.   6. By St. Peter.
3. I.e., old meat.   7. French for "beautiful thing"; a euphemism for
4. Good friend, take notice.   sexual organs.
5. I.e., Willie.

And I was yong and ful of ragerye,°   *passion*
Stibourne° and strong and joly as a pie:°   *untamable/magpie*
How coude I daunce to an harpe smale,°   *gracefully*
And singe, ywis,° as any nightingale,   *indeed*
465   Whan I hadde dronke a draughte of sweete win.
Metellius, the foule cherl, the swin,
That with a staf birafte° his wif hir lif   *deprived*
For° she drank win, though I hadde been his wif,   *because*
Ne sholde nat han daunted° me fro drinke;   *frightened*
470   And after win on Venus moste° I thinke,   *must*
For also siker° as cold engendreth hail,   *sure*
A likerous° mouth moste han a likerous° tail: *greedy/lecherous*
In womman vinolent° is no defence—   *who drinks*
This knowen lechours by experience.
475   But Lord Crist, whan that it remembreth me[8]
Upon my youthe and on my jolitee,
It tikleth me aboute myn herte roote—
Unto this day it dooth myn herte boote°   *good*
That I have had my world as in my time.
480   But age, allas, that al wol envenime,°   *poison*
Hath me biraft[9] my beautee and my pith°—   *vigor*
Lat go, farewel, the devel go therwith!
The flour is goon, ther is namore to telle:
The bren° as I best can now moste I selle;   *bran*
485   But yit to be right merye wol I fonde.°   *strive*
Now wol I tellen of my ferthe housbonde.
    I saye I hadde in herte greet despit
That he of any other hadde delit,
But he was quit,° by God and by Saint Joce: *paid back*
490   I made him of the same wode a croce[1]—
Nat of my body in no foul manere—
But, certainly, I made folk swich cheere[2]
That in his owene grece I made him frye,
For angre and for verray jalousye.
495   By God, in erthe I was his purgatorye,
For which I hope his soule be in glorye.
For God it woot, he sat ful ofte and soong°   *sang*
Whan that his sho ful bitterly him wroong.°   *pinched*
Ther was no wight save God and he that wiste°   *knew*
500   In many wise how sore I him twiste.
He deide whan I cam fro Jerusalem,
And lith ygrave under the roode-beem,[3]
Al° is his tombe nought so curious[4]   *although*
As was the sepulcre of him Darius,
505   Which that Apelles wroughte subtilly:[5]
It nis but wast to burye him preciously.°   *expensively*
Lat him fare wel, God yive his soule reste;

---

8. When I look back.
9. Has taken away from me.
1. I made him a cross of the same wood. The proverb has much the same sense as the one quoted in line 493.
2. Pretended to be in love with others.

3. And lies buried under the rood beam (the crucifix beam running between nave and chancel).
4. Carefully wrought.
5. Accordingly to medieval legend, the artist Apelles decorated the tomb of Darius, king of the Persians.

He is now in his grave and in his cheste.°   *coffin*
    Now of my fifthe housbonde wol I telle—
510 God lete his soule nevere come in helle—
And yit he was to me the moste shrewe:[6]
That feele I on my ribbes al by rewe,[7]
And evere shal unto myn ending day.
But in oure bed he was so fressh and gay,
515 And therwithal so wel coulde he me glose°   *flatter, coax*
Whan that he wolde han my bele chose,
That though he hadde me bet° on every boon,°   *beaten/bone*
He coude winne again my love anoon.°   *immediately*
I trowe I loved him best for that he
520 Was of his love daungerous[8] to me.
We wommen han, if that I shal nat lie,
In this matere a quainte fantasye:[9]
Waite what[1] thing we may nat lightly° have,   *easily*
Therafter wol we crye al day and crave;
525 Forbede us thing, and that desiren we;
Preesse on us faste, and thanne wol we flee.
With daunger oute we al oure chaffare:[2]
Greet prees° at market maketh dere° ware,   *crowd/expensive*
And too greet chepe is holden at litel pris.[3]
530 This knoweth every womman that is wis.
    My fifthe housbonde—God his soule blesse!—
Which that I took for love and no richesse,
He somtime was a clerk at Oxenforde,
And hadde laft° scole and wente at hoom to boorde   *left*
535 With my gossib,° dwelling in oure town   *confidante*
God have hir soule!—hir name was Alisoun;
She knew myn herte and eek my privetee°   *secrets*
Bet° than oure parissh preest, as mote I thee.° *better/prosper*
To hire biwrayed° I my conseil° al,   *disclosed/secrets*
540 For hadde myn housbonde pissed on a wal,
Or doon a thing that sholde han cost his lif,
To hire,° and to another worthy wif,   *her*
And to my nece which I loved weel,
I wolde han told his conseil everydeel;°   *entirely*
545 And so I dide ful often, God it woot,
That made his face often reed° and hoot°   *red/hot*
For verray shame, and blamed himself for he
Hadde told to me so greet a privetee.
    And so bifel that ones° in a Lente—   *once*
550 So often times I to my gossib wente,
For evere yit I loved to be gay,
And for to walke in March, Averil, and May,
From hous to hous, to heere sondry tales—
That Janekin clerk and my gossib dame Alis
555 And I myself into the feeldes wente.

---

6. Worst rascal.
7. In a row.
8. I.e., he played hard to get.
9. Strange fancy.

1. Whatever.
2. (Meeting) with reserve, we spread out our merchandise.
3. Too good a bargain is held at little value.

Myn housbonde was at London al that Lente:
I hadde the better leiser for to playe,
And for to see, and eek for to be seye°   seen
Of lusty folk—what wiste I wher my grace°   luck
560   Was shapen° for to be, or in what place?   destined
Therfore I made my visitaciouns
To vigilies[4] and to processiouns,
To preching eek, and to thise pilgrimages,
To playes of miracles and to mariages,
565   And wered upon[5] my gaye scarlet gites°—   gowns
Thise wormes ne thise motthes ne thise mites,
Upon my peril,[6] frete° hem neveradeel: ate
And woostou why? For they were used weel.
        Now wol I tellen forth what happed me.
570   I saye that in the feeldes walked we,
Til trewely we hadde swich daliaunce,°   flirtation
This clerk and I, that of my purveyaunce°   foresight
I spak to him and saide him how that he,
If I were widwe, sholde wedde me.
575   For certainly, I saye for no bobaunce,°   boast
Yit was I nevere withouten purveyaunce
Of mariage n'of othere thinges eek:
I holde a mouses herte nought worth a leek
That hath but oon hole for to sterte° to,   run
580   And if that faile thanne is al ydo.[7]
I bar him on hand[8] he hadde enchaunted me
(My dame° taughte me that subtiltee);   mother
And eek I saide I mette° of him al night: dreamed
He wolde han slain me as I lay upright,°   on my back
585   And al my bed was ful of verray blood—
"But yit I hope that ye shul do me good;
For blood bitokeneth° gold, as me was taught."   signifies
And al was fals, I dremed of it right naught,
But as I folwed ay my dames° lore°   mother's / teaching
590   As wel of that as othere thinges more.
But now sire—lat me see, what shal I sayn?
Aha, by God, I have my tale again.
        Whan that my ferthe housbonde was on beere,°   funeral bier
I weep,° algate,° and made sory cheere,   wept / anyhow
595   As wives moten,° for it is usage,°   must / custom
And with my coverchief covered my visage;
But for I was purveyed° of a make.°   provided / mate
I wepte but smale, and that I undertake.°   guarantee
        To chirche was myn housbonde born amorwe;[9]
600   With neighebores that for him maden sorwe,
And Janekin oure clerk was oon of tho.
As help me God, whan that I saw him go
After the beere, me thoughte he hadde a paire
Of legges and of feet so clene[1] and faire,

4. Evening service before a religious holiday.
5. Wore.
6. On peril (to my soul), an oath.
7. I.e., the game is up.
8. I pretended to him.
9. In the morning.
1. I.e., neat.

605 That al myn herte I yaf unto his hold.°   *possession*
 He was, I trowe,° twenty winter old,   *believe*
 And I was fourty, if I shal saye sooth—
 But yit I hadde alway a coltes tooth:[2]
 Gat-toothed[3] was I, and that bicam me weel;
610 I hadde the prente[4] of Sainte Venus seel.°   *seal*
 As help me God, I was a lusty oon,
 And fair and riche and yong and wel-bigoon,°   *well-situated*
 And trewely, as mine housbondes tolde me,
 I hadde the beste quoniam[5] mighte be.
615 For certes I am al Venerien
 In feeling, and myn herte is Marcien:[6]
 Venus me yaf my lust, my likerousnesse,°   *amorousness*
 And Mars yaf me my sturdy hardinesse.
 Myn ascendent was Taur[7] and Mars therinne—
620 Allas, allas, that evere love was sinne!
 I folwed ay° my inclinacioun   *ever*
 By vertu of my constellacioun;[8]
 That made me I coude nought withdrawe
 My chambre of Venus from a good felawe.
625 Yit have I Martes° merk upon my face,   *Mars's*
 And also in another privee place.
 For God so wis° be my savacioun,°   *surely/salvation*
 I loved nevere by no discrecioun,°   *moderation*
 But evere folwede myn appetit,
630 Al were he short or long or blak or whit;
 I took no keep,° so that he liked° me,   *heed/pleased*
 How poore he was, ne eek of what degree.
  What sholde I saye but at the monthes ende
 This joly clerk Janekin that was so hende°   *courteous, nice*
635 Hath wedded me with greet solempnitee,°   *splendor*
 And to him yaf I al the land and fee°   *property*
 That evere was me yiven therbifore—
 But afterward repented me ful sore:
 He nolde suffre no thing of my list.°   *wish*
640 By God, he smoot° me ones on the list°   *struck/ear*
 For that I rente° out of his book a leef,   *tore*
 That of the strook° myn ere weex° al deef.   *blow/grew*
 Stibourne° I was as is a leonesse,   *stubborn*
 And of my tonge a verray jangleresse,°   *chatterbox*
645 And walke I wolde, as I hadde doon biforn,
 From hous to hous, although he hadde it[9] sworn;
 For which he often times wolde preche,
 And me of olde Romain geestes° teche,   *stories*
 How he Simplicius Gallus lafte° his wif,   *left*
650 And hire forsook for terme of al his lif,
 Nought but for open-heveded he hire sey[1]

2. I.e., youthful appetites.
3. Gap-toothed women were considered to be amorous.
4. Print, i.e., a birthmark.
5. Latin for "because"; another euphemism for a sexual organ.
6. Influenced by Mars. "Venerien": astrologically influenced by Venus.
7. My birth sign was the constellation Taurus, a sign in which Venus is dominant.
8. I.e., horoscope.
9. I.e., the contrary.
1. Just because he saw her bareheaded.

Looking out at his dore upon a day.
　　Another Romain tolde he me by name
That, for his wif was at a someres° game　　*summer's*
655　Withouten his witing,° he forsook hire eke;　　*knowledge*
And thanne wolde he upon his Bible seeke
That ilke proverbe of Ecclesiaste[2]
Where he comandeth and forbedeth faste°　　*strictly*
Man shal nat suffre his wif go roule° aboute;　　*roam*
660　Thanne wolde he saye right thus withouten doute:
"Whoso that buildeth his hous al of salwes,°　　*willow sticks*
And priketh° his blinde hors over the falwes,[3]　　*rides*
And suffreth° his wif to go seeken halwes,°　　*allows/shrines*
Is worthy to be hanged on the galwes."°　　*gallows*
665　But al for nought—I sette nought an hawe[4]
Of his proverbes n'of his olde sawe;
N' I wolde nat of him corrected be:
I hate him that my vices telleth me,
And so doon mo, God woot, of us than I.
670　This made him with me wood al outrely:°　　*entirely*
I nolde nought forbere° him in no cas.　　*submit to*
　　Now wol I saye you sooth, by Saint Thomas,
Why that I rente° out of his book a leef,　　*tore*
For which he smoot me so that I was deef.
675　He hadde a book that gladly night and day
For his disport° he wolde rede alway.　　*entertainment*
He cleped it *Valerie*[5] *and Theofraste,*
At which book he lough° alway ful faste;　　*laughed*
And eek ther was somtime a clerk at Rome,
680　A cardinal, that highte Saint Jerome,
That made a book[6] again° Jovinian;　　*against*
In which book eek ther was Tertulan,
Crysippus, Trotula, and Helouis,[7]
That was abbesse nat fer fro Paris;
685　And eek the Parables of Salomon,
Ovides *Art,*[8] and bookes many oon—
And alle thise were bounden in oo volume.
And every night and day was his custume,
Whan he hadde leiser and vacacioun°　　*free time*
690　From other worldly occupacioun,
To reden in this book of wikked wives.
He knew of hem mo legendes and lives
Than been of goode wives in the Bible.
For trusteth wel, it is an impossible°　　*impossibility*
695　That any clerk wol speke good of wives,
But if it be of holy saintes lives,

2. Ecclesiasticus (25.25).
3. Plowed land.
4. I did not rate at the value of a hawthorn berry.
5. *"Valerie":* i.e., the *Letter of Valerius Concerning Not Marrying,* by Walter Map; *"Theofraste":* Theophrastus's *Book Concerning Marriage.* Medieval manuscripts often contained a number of different works, sometimes, as here, dealing with the same subject.

6. St. Jerome's antifeminist *Against Jovinian.*
7. "Tertulan": i.e., Tertullian, author of treatises on sexual modesty. "Crysippus": mentioned by Jerome as an antifeminist. "Trotula": a female doctor whose presence here is unexplained. "Helouis": i.e., Eloise, whose love affair with the great scholar Abelard was a medieval scandal.
8. Ovid's *Art of Love.* "Parables of Salomon": the biblical Book of Proverbs.

N'of noon other womman nevere the mo—
Who painted the leon, tel me who?[9]
By God, if wommen hadden writen stories,
700   As clerkes han within hir oratories,°   *chapels*
They wolde han writen of men more wikkednesse
Than al the merk[1] of Adam may redresse.
The children of Mercurye and Venus[2]
Been in hir werking° ful contrarious:°   *operation/opposed*
705   Mercurye loveth wisdom and science,
And Venus loveth riot° and dispence;°   *revelry/spending*
And for hir diverse disposicioun
Each falleth in otheres exaltacioun,[3]
And thus, God woot, Mercurye is desolat
710   In Pisces wher Venus is exaltat,[4]
And Venus falleth ther Mercurye is raised:
Therfore no womman of no clerk is praised.
The clerk, whan he is old and may nought do
Of Venus werkes worth his olde sho,°   *shoe*
715   Thanne sit° he down and writ° in his dotage   *sits/writes*
That wommen can nat keepe hir mariage.
    But now to purpose why I tolde thee
That I was beten for a book, pardee:
Upon a night Janekin, that was our sire,[5]
720   Redde on his book as he sat by the fire
Of Eva first, that for hir wikkednesse
Was al mankinde brought to wrecchednesse,
For which that Jesu Crist himself was slain
That boughte° us with his herte blood again—   *redeemed*
725   Lo, heer expres of wommen may ye finde
That womman was the los° of al mankinde.[6]   *ruin*
    Tho° redde he me how Sampson loste his heres: *then*
Sleeping his lemman° kitte° it with hir sheres,   *lover/cut*
Thurgh which treson loste he both his yën.
730   Tho redde he me, if that I shal nat lien,
Of Ercules and of his Dianire,[7]
That caused him to sette himself afire.
    No thing forgat he the sorwe and wo
That Socrates hadde with his wives two—
735   How Xantippa caste pisse upon his heed:
This sely° man sat stille as he were deed;   *poor, hapless*
He wiped his heed, namore dorste° he sayn   *dared*
But "Er that thonder stinte,° comth a rain."   *stops*
    Of Pasipha[8] that was the queene of Crete—
740   For shrewednesse° him thoughte the tale sweete—   *malice*

9. In one of Aesop's fables, the lion, shown a picture of a man killing a lion, asked who painted the picture. Had a lion been the artist, of course, the roles would have been reversed.
1. Mark, sex.
2. I.e., clerks and women, astrologically ruled by Mercury and Venus, respectively.
3. Because of their contrary positions (as planets), each one descends (in the belt of the zodiac) as the other rises, hence one loses its power as the other

becomes dominant.
4. I.e., Mercury is deprived of power in Pisces (the sign of the Fish), where Venus is most powerful.
5. My husband.
6. The stories of wicked women Chaucer drew mainly from St. Jerome and Walter Map.
7. Dejanira unwittingly gave Hercules a poisoned shirt, which hurt him so much that he committed suicide by fire.
8. Pasiphaë, who had intercourse with a bull.

Fy, speek namore, it is a grisly thing
Of hir horrible lust and hir liking.°   *pleasure*
  Of Clytermistra⁹ for hir lecherye
That falsly made hir housbonde for to die,
745 He redde it with ful good devocioun.
  He tolde me eek for what occasioun
Amphiorax¹ at Thebes loste his lif:
Myn housbonde hadde a legende of his wif
Eriphylem, that for an ouche° of gold   *trinket*
750 Hath prively unto the Greekes told
Wher that hir housbonde hidde him in a place,
For which he hadde at Thebes sory grace.
  Of Livia tolde he me and of Lucie:²
They bothe made hir housbondes for to die,
755 That oon for love, that other was for hate;
Livia hir housbonde on an even late
Empoisoned hath for that she was his fo;
Lucia likerous° loved hir housbonde so   *lecherous*
That for° he sholde alway upon hire thinke, *in order that*
760 She yaf him swich a manere love-drinke
That he was deed er it were by the morwe.³
And thus algates° housbondes han sorwe.   *in every way*
  Thanne tolde he me how oon Latumius
Complained unto his felawe Arrius
765 That in his garden growed swich a tree,
On which he saide how that his wives three
Hanged hemself for herte despitous.⁴
  "O leve° brother," quod this Arrius,   *dear*
"Yif me a plante of thilke blessed tree,
770 And in my gardin planted shal it be."
  Of latter date of wives hath he red
That some han slain hir housbondes in hir bed
And lete hir lechour dighte⁵ hire al the night,
Whan that the cors° lay in the floor upright;° *corpse/on his back*
775 And some han driven nailes in hir brain
Whil that they sleepe, and thus they han hem slain;
Some han hem yiven poison in hir drinke.
He spak more harm than herte may bithinke,° *imagine*
And therwithal he knew of mo proverbes
780 Than in this world ther growen gras or herbes:
"Bet° is," quod he, "thyn habitacioun   *better*
Be with a leon or a foul dragoun
Than with a womman using° for to chide." *accustomed*
"Bet is," quod he, "hye in the roof abide
785 Than with an angry wif down in the hous:
They been so wikked° and contrarious,   *perverse*

9. Clytemnestra, who, with her lover, Aegisthus, slew her husband, Agamemnon.
1. Amphiaraus, betrayed by his wife, Eriphyle, and forced to go to the war against Thebes.
2. Livia murdered her husband in behalf of her lover, Sejanus. "Lucie": i.e., Lucilla, who was said

to have poisoned her husband, the poet Lucretius, with a potion designed to keep him faithful.
3. He was dead before it was near morning.
4. For malice of heart.
5. Have intercourse with.

They haten that hir housbondes loveth ay."
He saide, "A womman cast° hir shame away   *casts*
When she cast of° hir smok,"⁶ and ferthermo,   *off*
790   "A fair womman, but she be chast also,
Is like a gold ring in a sowes nose."
Who wolde weene,° or who wolde suppose   *think*
The wo that in myn herte was and pine?°   *suffering*
     And whan I sawgh he wolde nevere fine°   *end*
795   To reden on this cursed book al night,
Al sodeinly three leves have I plight°   *snatched*
Out of his book right as he redde, and eke
I with my fist so took⁷ him on the cheeke
That in oure fir he fil° bakward adown.   *fell*
800   And up he sterte as dooth a wood° leoun,   *raging*
And with his fist he smoot me on the heed°   *head*
That in the floor I lay as I were deed.°   *dead*
And whan he sawgh how stille that I lay,
He was agast, and wolde have fled his way,
805   Til atte laste out of my swough° I braide:°   *swoon/started*
"O hastou slain me, false thief?" I saide,
"And for my land thus hastou mordred° me?   *murdered*
Er I be deed yit wol I kisse thee."
And neer he cam and kneeled faire adown,
810   And saide, "Dere suster Alisoun,
As help me God, I shal thee nevere smite.
That I have doon, it is thyself to wite.°   *blame*
Foryif it me, and that I thee biseeke."°   *beseech*
And yit eftsoones° I hitte him on the cheeke,   *another time*
815   And saide, "Thief, thus muchel am I wreke.°   *avenged*
Now wol I die: I may no lenger speke."
     But at the laste with muchel care and wo
We fille⁸ accorded by us selven two.
He yaf me al the bridel° in myn hand,   *bridle*
820   To han the governance of hous and land,
And of his tonge and his hand also;
And made⁹ him brenne° his book anoonright tho.   *burn*
And whan that I hadde geten unto me
By maistrye° al the sovereinetee,°   *skill/dominion*
825   And that he saide, "Myn owene trewe wif,
Do as thee lust° the terme of al thy lif;   *it pleases*
Keep thyn honour, and keep eek myn estat,"
After that day we hadde nevere debat.
God help me so, I was to him as kinde
830   As any wif from Denmark unto Inde,°   *India*
And also trewe, and so was he to me.
I praye to God that sit° in majestee,   *sits*
So blesse his soule for his mercy dere.
Now wol I saye my tale if ye wol heere.

6. Undergarment.   8. I.e., became.
7. I.e., hit.   9. I.e., I made.

[ANOTHER INTERRUPTION]

835   The Frere lough° whan he hadde herd all this: *laughed*
"Now dame," quod he, "so have I joye or blis,
This is a long preamble of a tale."
And whan the Somnour herde the Frere gale,°   *exclaim*
"Lo," quod the Somnour, "Goddes armes two,
840 A frere wol entremette him¹ everemo!
Lo, goode men, a flye and eek a frere
Wol falle in every dissh and eek matere.
What spekestou of preambulacioun?
What, amble or trotte or pisse or go sitte down!
845 Thou lettest° oure disport in this manere."   *hinder*
    "Ye, woltou so, sire Somnour?" quod the Frere.
"Now by my faith, I shal er that I go
Telle of a somnour swich a tale or two
That al the folk shal laughen in this place."
850   "Now elles, Frere, I wol bishrewe° thy face,"   *curse*
Quod this Somnour, "and I bishrewe me,
But if I telle tales two or three
Of freres, er I come to Sidingborne,²
That I shal make thyn herte for to moorne°—   *mourn*
855 For wel I woot thy pacience is goon."
    Oure Hoste cride, "Pees, and that anoon!"
And saide, "Lat the womman telle hir tale:
Ye fare as folk that dronken been of ale.
Do, dame, tel forth youre tale, and that is best."
860   "Al redy, sire," quod she, "right as you lest°—   *it pleases*
If I have licence of this worthy Frere."
"Yis, dame," quod he, "tel forth and I wol heere."

The Tale

As was suggested in the headnote to *The Man of Law's Epilogue,* Chaucer may have originally written the fabliau that became *The Shipman's Tale* for the Wife of Bath. If so, then he replaced it with a tale that is not simply appropriate to her character but that develops it even beyond the complexity already revealed in her *Prologue.* The story survives in two other versions in which the hero is Sir Gawain, whose courtesy contrasts sharply with the behavior of the knight in the Wife's tale. As Chaucer has the Wife tell it, the tale expresses her views about the relations of the sexes, her wit and humor, and her fantasies. Like Marie de France's lay *Lanval* (see pp. 126–40), the Wife's tale is about a fairy bride who seeks out and tests a mortal lover.

    In th'olde dayes of the King Arthour,
Of which that Britouns speken greet honour,
865 Al was this land fulfild of faïrye:³
The elf-queene° with hir joly compaignye   *queen of the fairies*
Daunced ful ofte in many a greene mede°—   *meadow*
This was the olde opinion as I rede;
I speke of many hundred yeres ago.

---

1. Intrude himself.
2. Sittingbourne (a town forty miles from London).
3. I.e., filled full of supernatural creatures.

870 But now can no man see none elves mo,
For now the grete charitee and prayeres
Of limitours,[4] and othere holy freres,
That serchen every land and every streem,
As thikke as motes° in the sonne-beem,   *dust particles*
875 Blessing halles, chambres, kichenes, bowres,
Citees, burghes,° castels, hye towres,   *townships*
Thropes, bernes, shipnes,[5] dayeries—
This maketh that ther been no faïries.
For ther as wont to walken was an elf
880 Ther walketh now the limitour himself,
In undermeles° and in morweninges,°   *afternoons/mornings*
And saith his Matins and his holy thinges,
As he gooth in his limitacioun.[6]
Wommen may go saufly° up and down: *safely*
885 In every bussh or under every tree
Ther is noon other incubus[7] but he,
And he ne wol doon hem but[8] dishonour.
      And so bifel it that this King Arthour
Hadde in his hous a lusty bacheler,°   *young knight*
890 That on a day cam riding fro river,[9]
And happed° that, allone as he was born,   *it happened*
He sawgh a maide walking him biforn;
Of which maide anoon, maugree hir heed,[1]
By verray force he rafte° hir maidenheed;   *deprived her of*
895 For which oppression° was swich clamour,   *rape*
And swich pursuite° unto the King Arthour,   *petitioning*
That dampned was this knight for to be deed[2]
By cours of lawe, and sholde han lost his heed—
Paraventure° swich was the statut tho—   *perchance*
900 But that the queene and othere ladies mo
So longe prayeden the king of grace,
Til he his lif him graunted in the place,
And yaf him to the queene, al at hir wille,
To chese° wheither she wolde him save or spille.[3]   *choose*
905 The queene thanked the king with al hir might,
And after this thus spak she to the knight,
Whan that she saw hir time upon a day:
"Thou standest yit," quod she, "in swich array°   *condition*
That of thy lif yit hastou no suretee.°   *guarantee*
910 I graunte thee lif if thou canst tellen me
What thing it is that wommen most desiren:
Be war and keep thy nekke boon° from iren.   *bone*
And if thou canst nat tellen me anoon,°   *right away*
Yit wol I yive thee leve for to goon
915 A twelfmonth and a day to seeche° and lere°   *search/learn*
An answere suffisant° in this matere,   *satisfactory*

---

4. Friars licensed to beg in a certain territory.
5. Thorps (villages), barns, stables.
6. I.e., the friar's assigned area. His "holy thinges" are prayers.
7. An evil spirit that seduces mortal women.
8. "Ne . . . but": only.

9. Hawking, usually carried out on the banks of a stream.
1. Despite her head, i.e., despite anything she could do.
2. This knight was condemned to death.
3. Put to death.

And suretee wol I han er that thou pace,°   *pass*
Thy body for to yeelden in this place."
    Wo was this knight, and sorwefully he siketh.°   *sighs*
920 But what, he may nat doon al as him liketh,
And atte laste he chees° him for to wende,   *chose*
And come again right at the yeres ende,
With swich answere as God wolde him purveye,°   *provide*
And taketh his leve and wendeth forth his waye.
925 He seeketh every hous and every place
Wher as he hopeth for to finde grace,
To lerne what thing wommen love most.
But he ne coude arriven in no coost⁴
Wher as he mighte finde in this matere
930 Two creatures according in fere.⁵
    Some saiden wommen loven best richesse;
Some saide honour, some saide jolinesse;°   *pleasure*
Some riche array, some saiden lust abedde,
And ofte time to be widwe and wedde.
935 Some saide that oure herte is most esed
Whan that we been yflatered and yplesed—
He gooth ful neigh the soothe, I wol nat lie:
A man shal winne us best with flaterye,
And with attendance° and with bisinesse°   *attention/solicitude*
940 Been we ylimed,° bothe more and lesse.   *ensnared*
    And some sayen that we loven best
For to be free, and do right as us lest,°   *it pleases*
And that no man repreve° us of oure vice,   *reprove*
But saye that we be wise and no thing nice.°   *foolish*
945 For trewely, ther is noon of us alle,
If any wight wol clawe° us on the galle,°   *rub/sore spot*
That we nil kike° for° he saith us sooth: *kick/because*
Assaye° and he shal finde it that so dooth.   *try*
For be we nevere so vicious withinne,
950 We wol be holden° wise and clene of sinne.   *considered*
    And some sayn that greet delit han we
For to be holden stable and eek secree,⁶
And in oo° purpos stedefastly to dwelle,   *one*
And nat biwraye° thing that men us telle—   *disclose*
955 But that tale is nat worth a rake-stele.°   *rake handle*
Pardee,° we wommen conne no thing hele:°   *by God/conceal*
Witnesse on Mida.° Wol ye heere the tale?   *Midas*
    Ovide, amonges othere thinges smale,
Saide Mida hadde under his longe heres,
960 Growing upon his heed, two asses eres,
The whiche vice° he hidde as he best mighte   *defect*
Ful subtilly from every mannes sighte,
That save his wif ther wiste° of it namo.   *knew*
He loved hire most and trusted hire also.
965 He prayed hire that to no creature
She sholde tellen of his disfigure.°   *deformity*

4. I.e., country.
5. Agreeing together.
6. Reliable and also closemouthed.

She swoor him nay, for al this world to winne,
She nolde do that vilainye or sinne
To make hir housbonde han so foul a name:
970 She nolde nat telle it for hir owene shame.
But nathelees, hir thoughte that she dyde°   would die
That she so longe sholde a conseil° hide;   secret
Hire thoughte it swal° so sore about hir herte   swelled
That nedely som word hire moste asterte,[7]
975 And sith she dorste nat telle it to no man,
Down to a mareis° faste° by she ran—   marsh / close
Til she cam there hir herte was afire—
And as a bitore bombleth[8] in the mire,
She laide hir mouth unto the water down:
980 "Biwray° me nat, thou water, with thy soun,"°   betray / sound
Quod she. "To thee I telle it and namo:°   to no one else
Myn housbonde hath longe asses eres two.
Now is myn herte al hool,[9] now is it oute.
I mighte no lenger keep it, out of doute."
985 Here may ye see, though we a time abide,
Yit oute it moot:° we can no conseil hide.   must
The remenant of the tale if ye wol heere,
Redeth Ovide, and ther ye may it lere.[1]
    This knight of which my tale is specially,
990 Whan that he sawgh he mighte nat come thereby—
This is to saye what wommen loven most—
Within his brest ful sorweful was his gost,°   spirit
But hoom he gooth, he mighte nat sojourne:°   delay
The day was come that hoomward moste° he turne.   must
995 And in his way it happed him to ride
In al this care under° a forest side,   by
Wher as he sawgh upon a daunce go
Of ladies foure and twenty and yit mo;
Toward the whiche daunce he drow ful yerne,[2]
1000 In hope that som wisdom sholde he lerne.
But certainly, er he cam fully there,
Vanisshed was this daunce, he niste° where.   knew not
No creature sawgh he that bar° lif,   bore
Save on the greene he sawgh sitting a wif°—   woman
1005 A fouler wight ther may no man devise.°   imagine
Again[3] the knight this olde wif gan rise,
And saide, "Sire knight, heer forth lith° no way.°   lies / road
Telle me what ye seeken, by youre fay.°   faith
Paraventure it may the better be:
1010 Thise olde folk conne° muchel thing," quod she.   know
    "My leve moder,"° quod this knight, "certain,   mother
I nam but deed but if that I can sayn
What thing it is that wommen most desire.
Coude ye me wisse,° I wolde wel quite youre hire."[4]   teach

---

7. Of necessity some word must escape her.
8. Makes a booming noise. "Bittore": bittern, a heron.
9. I.e., sound.
1. Learn. The reeds disclosed the secret by whis-
pering "aures aselli" (ass's ears).
2. Drew very quickly.
3. I.e., to meet.
4. Repay your trouble.

1015   "Plight° me thy trouthe here in myn hand," quod she,   *pledge*
    "The nexte thing that I requere° thee,   *require of*
    Thou shalt it do, if it lie in thy might,
    And I wol telle it you er it be night."
      "Have heer my trouthe," quod the knight. "I graunte."
1020   "Thanne," quod she, "I dar me wel avaunte°   *boast*
    Thy lif is sauf,° for I wol stande therby.   *safe*
    Upon my lif the queene wol saye as I.
    Lat see which is the pruddeste° of hem alle   *proudest*
    That wereth on⁵ a coverchief or a calle°   *headdress*
1025   That dar saye nay of that I shal thee teche.
    Lat us go forth withouten lenger speeche."
    Tho rouned° she a pistel° in his ere,   *whispered/message*
    And bad him to be glad and have no fere.
      Whan they be comen to the court, this knight
1030   Saide he hadde holde his day as he hadde hight,°   *promised*
    And redy was his answere, as he saide.
    Ful many a noble wif, and many a maide,
    And many a widwe—for that they been wise—
    The queene hirself sitting as justise,
1035   Assembled been this answere for to heere,
    And afterward this knight was bode° appere.   *bidden to*
    To every wight comanded was silence,
    And that the knight sholde telle in audience°   *open hearing*
    What thing that worldly wommen loven best.
1040   This knight ne stood nat stille as dooth a best,°   *beast*
    But to his question anoon answerde
    With manly vois that al the court it herde.
      "My lige° lady, generally," quod he,   *liege*
    "Wommen desire to have sovereinetee°   *dominion*
1045   As wel over hir housbonde as hir love,
    And for to been in maistrye him above.
    This is youre moste desir though ye me kille.
    Dooth as you list:° I am here at youre wille."   *please*
      In al the court ne was ther wif ne maide
1050   Ne widwe that contraried° that he saide,   *contradicted*
    But saiden he was worthy han° his lif.   *to have*
      And with that word up sterte° that olde wif,   *started*
    Which that the knight sawgh sitting on the greene;
    "Mercy," quod she, "my soverein lady queene,
1055   Er that youre court departe, do me right.
    I taughte this answere unto the knight,
    For which he plighte me his trouthe there
    The firste thing I wolde him requere°   *require*
    He wolde it do, if it laye in his might.
1060   Bifore the court thanne praye I thee, sire knight,"
    Quod she, "that thou me take unto thy wif,
    For wel thou woost that I have kept° thy lif.   *saved*
    If I saye fals, say nay, upon thy fay."
      This knight answerde, "Allas and wailaway,
1065   I woot right wel that swich was my biheeste.°   *promise*

5. That wears.

For Goddes love, as chees° a newe requeste: *choose*
Taak al my good and lat my body go."
    "Nay thanne," quod she, "I shrewe° us bothe two.   *curse*
For though that I be foul and old and poore,
1070 I nolde for al the metal ne for ore
That under erthe is grave° or lith° above,   *buried/lies*
But if thy wif I were and eek thy love."
    "My love," quod he. "Nay, my dampnacioun!°   *damnation*
Allas, that any of my nacioun[6]
1075 Sholde evere so foule disparaged° be."   *degraded*
But al for nought, th'ende is this, that he
Constrained was: he needes moste hire wedde,
And taketh his olde wif and gooth to bedde.
    Now wolden some men saye, paraventure,
1080 That for my necligence I do no cure[7]
To tellen you the joye and al th'array
That at the feeste was that ilke day.
To which thing shortly answere I shal:
I saye ther nas no joye ne feeste at al;
1085 Ther nas but hevinesse and muche sorwe.
For prively he wedded hire on morwe,[8]
And al day after hidde him as an owle,
So wo was him, his wif looked so foule.
    Greet was the wo the knight hadde in his thought:
1090 Whan he was with his wif abedde brought,
He walweth° and he turneth to and fro.   *tosses*
His olde wif lay smiling everemo,
And saide, "O dere housbonde, benedicite,°   *bless me*
Fareth° every knight thus with his wif as ye?   *behaves*
1095 Is this the lawe of King Arthures hous?
Is every knight of his thus daungerous?°   *standoffish*
I am youre owene love and youre wif;
I am she which that saved hath youre lif;
And certes yit ne dide I you nevere unright.
1100 Why fare ye thus with me this firste night?
Ye faren like a man hadde lost his wit.
What is my gilt? For Goddes love, telle it,
And it shal been amended if I may."
    "Amended!" quod this knight. "Allas, nay, nay,
1105 It wol nat been amended neveremo.
Thou art so lothly° and so old also,   *hideous*
And therto comen of so lowe a kinde,°   *lineage*
That litel wonder is though I walwe and winde.°   *turn*
So wolde God myn herte wolde breste!"°   *break*
1110   "Is this," quod she, "the cause of youre unreste?"
"Ye, certainly," quod he. "No wonder is."
    "Now sire," quod she, "I coude amende al this,
If that me liste, er it were dayes three,
So° wel ye mighte bere you[9] unto me.   *provided that*
1115   "But for ye speken of swich gentilesse°   *nobility*

---

6. I.e., family.   8. In the morning.
7. I do not take the trouble.   9. Behave.

As is descended out of old richesse—
That therfore sholden ye be gentilmen—
Swich arrogance is nat worth an hen.
Looke who that is most vertuous alway,
1120 Privee and apert,[1] and most entendeth° ay°   *tries/always*
To do the gentil deedes that he can,
Taak him for the gretteste° gentilman.   *greatest*
Crist wol° we claime of him oure gentilesse,   *desires that*
Nat of oure eldres for hir 'old richesse.'
1125 For though they yive us al hir heritage,
For which we claime to been of heigh parage,°   *descent*
Yit may they nat biquethe for no thing
To noon of us hir vertuous living,
That made hem gentilmen ycalled be,
1130 And bad[2] us folwen hem in swich degree.
      "Wel can the wise poete of Florence,
That highte Dant,[3] speken in this sentence;°   *topic*
Lo, in swich manere rym is Dantes tale:
'Ful selde° up riseth by his braunches[4] smale   *seldom*
1135 Prowesse° of man, for God of his prowesse   *excellence*
Wol that of him we claime oure gentilesse.'
For of oure eldres may we no thing claime
But temporel thing that man may hurte and maime.
Eek every wight woot this as wel as I,
1140 If gentilesse were planted natureelly
Unto a certain linage down the line,
Privee and apert, thanne wolde they nevere fine°   *cease*
To doon of gentilesse the faire office°—   *function*
They mighte do no vilainye or vice.
1145 "Taak fir and beer° it in the derkeste hous   *bear*
Bitwixe this and the Mount of Caucasus,
And lat men shette° the dores and go thenne,°   *shut/thence*
Yit wol the fir as faire lye° and brenne°   *blaze/burn*
As twenty thousand men mighte it biholde:
1150 His° office natureel ay wol it holde,   *its*
Up° peril of my lif, til that it die.   *upon*
Heer may ye see wel how that genterye°   *gentility*
Is nat annexed° to possessioun,[5]   *related*
Sith folk ne doon hir operacioun
1155 Alway, as dooth the fir, lo, in his kinde.°   *nature*
For God it woot, men may wel often finde
A lordes sone do shame and vilainye;
And he that wol han pris of his gentrye,[6]
For he was boren° of a gentil° hous,   *born/noble*
1160 And hadde his eldres noble and vertuous,
And nil himselven do no gentil deedes,
Ne folwen his gentil auncestre that deed° is,   *dead*
He nis nat gentil, be he duc or erl—
For vilaines sinful deedes maken a cherl.

---

1. Privately and publicly.
2. I.e., they bade.
3. Dante (see his *Convivio*).
4. I.e., by the branches of a man's family tree.
5. I.e., inheritable property.
6. Have credit for his noble birth.

1165	Thy gentilesse[7] nis but renomee°	*renown*
	Of thine auncestres for hir heigh bountee,°	*magnanimity*
	Which is a straunge° thing for thy persone.	*external*
	For gentilesse[8] cometh fro God allone.	
	Thanne comth oure verray gentilesse of grace:	
1170	It was no thing biquethe us with oure place.	
	Thenketh how noble, as saith Valerius,[9]	
	Was thilke Tullius Hostilius	
	That out of poverte° roos to heigh noblesse.	*poverty*
	Redeth Senek° and redeth eek Boece:°	*Seneca/Boethius*
1175	Ther shul ye seen expres that no drede° is	*doubt*
	That he is gentil that dooth gentil deedes.	
	And therfore, leve housbonde, I thus conclude:	
	Al° were it that mine auncestres weren rude,[1]	*although*
	Yit may the hye God—and so hope I—	
1180	Graunte me grace to liven vertuously.	
	Thanne am I gentil whan that I biginne	
	To liven vertuously and waive° sinne.	*avoid*
	"And ther as ye of poverte me repreve,°	*reprove*
	The hye God, on whom that we bileve,	
1185	In wilful° poverte chees° to live his lif;	*voluntary/chose*
	And certes every man, maiden, or wif	
	May understonde that Jesus, hevene king,	
	Ne wolde nat chese° a vicious living.	*choose*
	Glad poverte is an honeste° thing, certain;	*honorable*
1190	This wol Senek and othere clerkes sayn.	
	Whoso that halt him paid of[2] his poverte,	
	I holde him riche al hadde he nat a sherte.°	*shirt*
	He that coveiteth[3] is a poore wight,	
	For he wolde han that is nat in his might;	
1195	But he that nought hath, ne coveiteth° have,	*desires to*
	Is riche, although we holde him but a knave.	
	Verray° poverte it singeth proprely.°	*true/appropriately*
	Juvenal saith of poverte, 'Merily	
	The poore man, whan he gooth by the waye,	
1200	Biforn the theves he may singe and playe.'	
	Poverte is hateful good, and as I gesse,	
	A ful greet bringere out of bisinesse;[4]	
	A greet amendere eek of sapience°	*wisdom*
	To him that taketh it in pacience;	
1205	Poverte is thing, although it seeme elenge,°	*wretched*
	Possession that no wight wol chalenge;[5]	
	Poverte ful often, whan a man is lowe,	
	Maketh[6] his God and eek himself to knowe;	
	Poverte a spectacle° is, as thinketh me,	*pair of spectacles*
1210	Thurgh which he may his verray° freendes see.	*true*
	And therfore, sire, sin that I nought you greve,	

7. I.e., the gentility you claim.
8. I.e., true gentility.
9. A Roman historian.
1. I.e., low born.
2. Considers himself satisfied with.

3. I.e., suffers desires.
4. I.e., remover of cares.
5. Claim as his property.
6. I.e., makes him.

Of my poverte namore ye me repreve.°   *reproach*
    "Now sire, of elde° ye repreve me: *old age*
And certes sire, though noon auctoritee
1215 Were in no book, ye gentils of honour
Sayn that men sholde an old wight doon favour,
And clepe him fader for youre gentilesse—
And auctours[7] shal I finde, as I gesse.
    "Now ther ye saye that I am foul and old:
1220 Thanne drede you nought to been a cokewold,°   *cuckold*
For filthe and elde, also mote I thee,[8]
Been grete wardeins° upon chastitee.   *guardians*
But nathelees, sin I knowe your delit,
I shal fulfille youre worldly appetit.
1225   "Chees° now," quod she, "oon of thise thinges twaye: *choose*
To han me foul and old til that I deye
And be to you a trewe humble wif,
And nevere you displese in al my lif,
Or elles ye wol han me yong and fair,
1230 And take youre aventure° of the repair[9]   *chance*
That shal be to youre hous by cause of me—
Or in some other place, wel may be.
Now chees youreselven wheither° that you liketh."   *whichever*
    This knight aviseth him[1] and sore siketh;°   *sighs*
1235 But atte laste he saide in this manere:
"My lady and my love, and wif so dere,
I putte me in youre wise governaunce:
Cheseth° youreself which may be most plesaunce°   *choose/pleasure*
And most honour to you and me also.
1240 I do no fors the wheither[2] of the two,
For as you liketh it suffiseth° me."   *satisfies*
    "Thanne have I gete° of you maistrye," quod she,   *got*
"Sin I may chese and governe as me lest?"°   *it pleases*
    "Ye, certes, wif," quod he. "I holde it best."
1245   "Kisse me," quod she. "We be no lenger wrothe.
For by my trouthe, I wol be to you bothe—
This is to sayn, ye, bothe fair and good.
I praye to God that I mote sterven wood,[3]
But° I to you be al so good and trewe   *unless*
1250 As evere was wif sin that the world was newe.
And but I be tomorn° as fair to seene   *tomorrow morning*
As any lady, emperisse, or queene,
That is bitwixe the eest and eek the west,
Do with my lif and deeth right as you lest:
1255 Caste up the curtin,[4] looke how that it is."
    And whan the knight sawgh verraily al this,
That she so fair was and so yong therto,
For joye he hente° hire in his armes two;   *took*
His herte bathed in a bath of blisse;

---

7. I.e., authorities.
8. So may I prosper.
9. I.e., visits.
1. Considers.

2. I do not care whichever.
3. Die mad.
4. The curtain around the bed.

1260	A thousand time arewe° he gan hire kisse,	*in a row*
	And she obeyed him in every thing	
	That mighte do him plesance or liking.°	*pleasure*
	And thus they live unto hir lives ende	
	In parfit° joye. And Jesu Crist us sende	*perfect*
1265	Housbondes meeke, yonge, and fresshe abedde—	
	And grace t'overbide° hem that we wedde.	*outlive*
	And eek I praye Jesu shorte° hir lives	*shorten*
	That nought wol be governed by hir wives,	
	And olde and angry nigardes of dispence°—	*spending*
1270	God sende hem soone a verray° pestilence!	*veritable*

The Pardoner's Prologue and Tale

As with *The Wife of Bath's Prologue* and *Tale*, *The Pardoner's Prologue* and *Tale*
develop in profound and surprising ways the portrait sketched in *The General Prologue*. In his *Prologue* the Pardoner boasts to his fellow pilgrims about his own deprav-
ity and the ingenuity with which he abuses his office and extracts money from poor
and ignorant people.

The medieval pardoner's job was to collect money for the charitable enterprises,
such as hospitals, supported by the church. In return for donations he was licensed
by the pope to award token remission of sins that the donor should have repented
and confessed. By canon law pardoners were permitted to work only in a prescribed
area; within that area they might visit churches during Sunday service, briefly explain
their mission, receive contributions, and in the pope's name issue indulgence, which
was not considered to be a sale but a gift from the infinite treasury of Christ's mercy
made in return for a gift of money. In practice, pardoners ignored the restrictions on
their office, made their way into churches at will, preached emotional sermons, and
claimed extraordinary power for their pardons.

The Pardoner's Tale is a bombastic sermon against gluttony, gambling, and swearing, which he preaches to the pilgrims to show off his professional skills. The sermon
is framed by a narrative that is supposed to function as an *exemplum* (that is, an
illustration) of the scriptural text, the one on which the Pardoner, as he tells the
pilgrims, always preaches: "*Radix malorum est cupiditas*" (Avarice is the root of evil).

The Introduction

	Oure Hoste gan to swere as he were wood°	*insane*
	"Harrow,"° quod he, "by nailes and by blood,[1]	*help*
	This was a fals cherl and a fals justise.[2]	
	As shameful deeth as herte may devise	
5	Come to thise juges and hir advocats.	
	Algate° this sely° maide is slain, allas!	*at any rate / innocent*
	Allas, too dere boughte she beautee!	
	Wherfore I saye alday° that men may see	*always*
	The yiftes of Fortune and of Nature	
10	Been cause of deeth to many a creature.	

1. I.e., God's nails and blood.
2. The Host has been affected by the Physicians's
sad tale of the Roman maiden Virginia, whose
great beauty caused a judge to attempt to obtain

her person by means of a trumped-up lawsuit in
which he connived with a "churl" who claimed her
as his slave; in order to preserve her chastity, her
father killed her.

As bothe yiftes that I speke of now,
Men han ful ofte more for harm than prow.°   *benefit*
    "But trewely, myn owene maister dere,
This is a pitous tale for to heere.
15 But nathelees, passe over, is no fors:[3]
I praye to God to save thy gentil cors,°   *body*
And eek thine urinals and thy jurdones,[4]
Thyn ipocras and eek thy galiones,[5]
And every boiste° ful of thy letuarye°—   *box/medicine*
20 God blesse hem, and oure lady Sainte Marye.
So mote I theen,[6] thou art a propre man,
And lik a prelat, by Saint Ronian![7]
Saide I nat wel? I can nat speke in terme.[8]
But wel I woot, thou doost° myn herte to erme°   *make/grieve*
25 That I almost have caught a cardinacle.[9]
By corpus bones,[1] but if° I have triacle,°   *unless/medicine*
Or elles a draughte of moiste° and corny° ale,   *fresh/malty*
Or but I here anoon° a merye tale,   *at once*
Myn herte is lost for pitee of this maide.
30 "Thou bel ami,[2] thou Pardoner," he saide,
"Tel us som mirthe or japes° right anoon."   *jokes*
    "It shal be doon," quod he, "by Saint Ronion.
But first," quod he, "here at this ale-stake[3]
I wol bothe drinke and eten of a cake."°   *flat loaf of bread*
35   And right anoon thise gentils gan to crye,
"Nay, lat him telle us of no ribaudye.°   *ribaldry*
Tel us som moral thing that we may lere,°   *learn*
Som wit,[4] and thanne wol we gladly heere."
    "I graunte, ywis,"° quod he, "but I moot thinke   *certainly*
40 Upon som honeste° thing whil that I drinke."   *decent*

The Prologue

Lordinges—quod he—in chirches whan I preche,
I paine me[5] to han° an hautein° speeche,   *have/loud*
And ringe it out as round as gooth a belle,
For I can al by rote[6] that I telle.
45 My theme is alway oon,[7] and evere was:
Radix malorum est cupiditas.[8]
First I pronounce whennes° that I come,   *whence*
And thanne my bulles shewe I alle and some:[9]
Oure lige lordes seel on my patente,[1]

3. I.e., never mind.
4. Jordans (chamber pots): the Host is somewhat confused in his endeavor to use technical medical terms. "Urinals": vessels for examining urine.
5. A medicine, probably invented on the spot by the Host, named after Galen. "Ipocras": a medicinal drink named after Hippocrates.
6. So might I prosper.
7. St. Ronan or St. Ninian, with a possible play on "runnion" (sexual organ).
8. Speak in technical idiom.
9. Apparently a cardiac condition, confused in the Host's mind with a cardinal.
1. An illiterate oath, mixing "God's bones" with

corpus dei ("God's body").
2. Fair friend.
3. Sign of a tavern.
4. I.e., something with significance.
5. Take pains.
6. I know all by heart.
7. I.e., the same. "Theme": biblical text on which the sermon is based.
8. Avarice is the root of evil (1 Timothy 6.10).
9. Each and every one. "Bulles": papal bulls, official documents.
1. I.e., the pope's or bishop's seal on my papal license.

50	That shewe I first, my body to warente,°	keep safe
	That no man be so bold, ne preest ne clerk,	
	Me to destourbe of Cristes holy werk.	
	And after that thanne telle I forth my tales²—	
	Bulles of popes and of cardinales,	
55	Of patriarkes and bisshopes I shewe,	
	And in Latin I speke a wordes fewe,	
	To saffron with³ my predicacioun,°	preaching
	And for to stire hem to devocioun.	
	Thanne shewe I forth my longe crystal stones,°	jars
60	Ycrammed ful of cloutes° and of bones	rags
	Relikes been they, as weenen° they eechoon.	suppose
	Thanne have I in laton° a shulder-boon	brass
	Which that was of an holy Jewes sheep.	
	"Goode men," I saye, "take of my wordes keep:°	notice
65	If that this boon be wasshe in any welle,	
	If cow, or calf, or sheep, or oxe swelle,	
	That any worm hath ete or worm ystonge,⁴	
	Take water of that welle and wassh his tonge,	
	And it is hool⁵ anoon. And ferthermoor,	
70	Of pokkes° and of scabbe and every soor°	pox, pustules / sore
	Shal every sheep be hool that of this welle	
	Drinketh a draughte. Take keep eek° that I telle:	also
	If that the goode man that the beestes oweth°	owns
	Wol every wike,° er° that the cok him croweth,	week / before
75	Fasting drinken of this welle a draughte—	
	As thilke° holy Jew oure eldres taughte—	that same
	His beestes and his stoor° shal multiplye.	stock
	"And sire, also it heleth jalousye:	
	For though a man be falle in jalous rage,	
80	Lat maken with this water his potage,°	soup
	And nevere shal he more his wif mistriste,°	mistrust
	Though he the soothe of hir defaute wiste,⁶	
	Al hadde she⁷ taken preestes two or three.	
	"Here is a mitein° eek that ye may see:	mitten
85	He that his hand wol putte in this mitein	
	He shal have multiplying of his grain,	
	Whan he hath sowen, be it whete or otes—	
	So that he offre pens or elles grotes.⁸	
	"Goode men and wommen, oo thing warne I you:	
90	If any wight be in this chirche now	
	That hath doon sinne horrible, that he	
	Dar nat for shame of it yshriven° be,	confessed
	Or any womman, be she yong or old,	
	That hath ymaked hir housbonde cokewold,°	cuckold
95	Swich° folk shal have no power ne no grace	such
	To offren to⁹ my relikes in this place;	

2. I go on with my yarn.
3. To add spice to.
4. That has eaten any worm or been bitten by any snake.
5. I.e., sound.
6. Knew the truth of her infidelity.
7. Even if she had.
8. Pennies, groats, coins.
9. To make gifts in reverence of.

And whoso findeth him out of swich blame,
He wol come up and offre in Goddes name,
And I assoile° him by the auctoritee   absolve
100 Which that by bulle ygraunted was to me."
    By this gaude° have I wonne, yeer by yeer,   trick
An hundred mark[1] sith° I was pardoner.   since
I stonde lik a clerk in my pulpet,
And whan the lewed° peple is down yset,   ignorant
105 I preche so as ye han herd bifore,
And telle an hundred false japes° more.   tricks
Thanne paine I me[2] to strecche forth the nekke,
And eest and west upon the peple I bekke°   nod
As dooth a douve,° sitting on a berne;°   dove/barn
110 Mine handes and my tonge goon so yerne°   fast
That it is joye to see my bisinesse.
Of avarice and of swich cursednesse°   sin
Is al my preching, for to make hem free°   generous
To yiven hir pens, and namely° unto me,   especially
115 For myn entente is nat but for to winne,[3]
And no thing for correccion of sinne:
I rekke° nevere whan that they been beried°   care/buried
Though that hir soules goon a-blakeberied.[4]
For certes, many a predicacioun°   sermon
120 Comth ofte time of yvel entencioun:
Som for plesance of folk and flaterye,
To been avaunced° by ypocrisye,   promoted
And som for vaine glorye, and som for hate;
For whan I dar noon otherways debate,°   fight
125 Thanne wol I stinge him[5] with my tonge smerte°   sharply
In preching, so that he shal nat asterte°   escape
To been defamed falsly, if that he
Hath trespassed to my bretheren[6] or to me.
For though I telle nought his propre name,
130 Men shal wel knowe that it is the same
By signes and by othere circumstaunces.
Thus quite° I folk that doon us displesaunces;[7]   pay back
Thus spete° I out my venim under hewe°   spit/false colors
Of holinesse, to seeme holy and trewe.
135 But shortly myn entente I wol devise:°   explain
I preche of no thing but for coveitise;°   covetousness
Therfore my theme is yit and evere was
Radix malorum est cupiditas.
    Thus can I preche again that same vice
140 Which that I use, and that is avarice.
But though myself be gilty in that sinne,
Yit can I make other folk to twinne°   separate
From avarice, and sore to repente—
But that is nat my principal entente:

---

1. Marks (pecuniary units).
2. I take pains.
3. My intent is only to make money.
4. Go blackberrying, i.e., go to hell.

5. An adversary critical of pardoners.
6. Injured my fellow pardoners.
7. Make trouble for us.

145	I preche no thing but for coveitise.	
	Of this matere it oughte ynough suffise.	
	Thanne telle I hem ensamples[8] many oon	
	Of olde stories longe time agoon,	
	For lewed° peple loven tales olde—	*ignorant*
150	Swiche° thinges can they wel reporte and holde.[9]	*such*
	What, trowe° ye that whiles I may preche,	*believe*
	And winne gold and silver for° I teche,	*because*
	That I wol live in poverte wilfully?°	*voluntarily*
	Nay, nay, I thoughte° it nevere, trewely,	*intended*
155	For I wol preche and begge in sondry landes;	
	I wol nat do no labour with mine handes,	
	Ne make baskettes and live therby,	
	By cause I wol nat beggen idelly.[1]	
	I wol none of the Apostles countrefete:°	*imitate*
160	I wol have moneye, wolle,° cheese, and whete,	*wool*
	Al were it[2] yiven of the pooreste page,	
	Or of the pooreste widwe in a village—	
	Al sholde hir children sterve[3] for famine.	
	Nay, I wol drinke licour of the vine	
165	And have a joly wenche in every town.	
	But herkneth, lordinges, in conclusioun,	
	Youre liking° is that I shal telle a tale:	*pleasure*
	Now have I dronke a draughte of corny ale,	
	By God, I hope I shal you telle a thing	
170	That shal by reson been at youre liking;	
	For though myself be a ful vicious man,	
	A moral tale yit I you telle can,	
	Which I am wont to preche for to winne.	
	Now holde youre pees, my tale I wol biginne.	

The Tale

175	In Flandres whilom° was a compaignye	*once*
	Of yonge folk that haunteden° folye—	*practiced*
	As riot, hasard, stewes,[4] and tavernes,	
	Wher as with harpes, lutes, and giternes°	*guitars*
	They daunce and playen at dees° bothe day and night,	*dice*
180	And ete also and drinke over hir might,[5]	
	Thurgh which they doon the devel sacrifise	
	Within that develes temple in cursed wise	
	By superfluitee° abhominable.	*overindulgence*
	Hir othes been so grete and so dampnable	
185	That it is grisly for to heere hem swere:	
	Oure blessed Lordes body they totere[6]—	
	Hem thoughte that Jewes rente° him nought ynough.	*tore*
	And eech of hem at otheres sinne lough.°	*laughed*

---

8. Exempla (stories illustrating moral principles).
9. Repeat and remember.
1. I.e., without profit.
2. Even though it were.
3. Even though her children should die.

4. Wild parties, gambling, brothels.
5. Beyond their capacity.
6. Tear apart (a reference to oaths sworn by parts of His body, such as "God's bones!" or "God's teeth!").

And right anoon thanne comen tombesteres,°   *dancing girls*
190   Fetis° and smale,° and yonge frutesteres,[7]   *shapely/slender*
Singeres with harpes, bawdes,° wafereres[8]—   *pimps*
Whiche been the verray develes officeres,
To kindle and blowe the fir of lecherye
That is annexed unto glotonye:[9]
195   The Holy Writ take I to my witnesse
That luxure° is in win and dronkenesse.   *lechery*
Lo, how that dronken Lot[1] unkindely°   *unnaturally*
Lay by his doughtres two unwitingly:
So dronke he was he niste° what he wroughte.°   *didn't know/did*
200   Herodes, who so wel the stories soughte,[2]
Whan he of win was repleet° at his feeste,   *filled*
Right at his owene table he yaf his heeste°   *command*
To sleen° the Baptist John, ful giltelees.   *slay*
    Senek[3] saith a good word doutelees:
205   He saith he can no difference finde
Bitwixe a man that is out of his minde
And a man which that is dronkelewe,°   *drunken*
But that woodnesse, yfallen in a shrewe,[4]
Persevereth lenger than dooth dronkenesse.
210   O glotonye, ful of cursednesse!°   *wickedness*
O cause first of oure confusioun!°   *downfall*
O original of oure dampnacioun,°   *damnation*
Til Crist hadde bought° us with his blood again!   *redeemed*
Lo, how dere, shortly for to sayn,
215   Abought° was thilke° cursed vilainye;   *paid for/that same*
Corrupt was al this world for glotonye:
Adam oure fader and his wif also
Fro Paradis to labour and to wo
Were driven for that vice, it is no drede.°   *doubt*
220   For whil that Adam fasted, as I rede,
He was in Paradis; and whan that he
Eet° of the fruit defended° on a tree,   *ate/forbidden*
Anoon he was out cast to wo and paine.
O glotonye, on thee wel oughte us plaine!°   *complain*
225   O, wiste a man[5] how manye maladies
Folwen of excesse and of glotonies,
He wolde been the more mesurable°   *moderate*
Of his diete, sitting at his table.
Allas, the shorte throte, the tendre mouth,
230   Maketh that eest and west and north and south,
In erthe, in air, in water, men to swinke,°   *work*
To gete a gloton daintee mete° and drinke.   *food*
Of this matere, O Paul, wel canstou trete:
"Mete unto wombe,° and wombe eek unto mete,   *belly*
235   Shal God destroyen bothe," as Paulus saith.[6]

7. Fruit-selling girls.
8. Girl cake vendors.
9. I.e., closely related to gluttony.
1. See Genesis 19.30–36.
2. For the story of Herod and St. John the Baptist, see Mark 6.17–29. "Who so . . . soughte": i.e.,

whoever looked it up in the Gospel would find.
3. Seneca, the Roman Stoic philosopher.
4. But that madness, occurring in a wicked man.
5. If a man knew.
6. See 1 Corinthians 6.13.

Allas, a foul thing is it, by my faith,
To saye this word, and fouler is the deede
Whan man so drinketh of the white and rede[7]
That of his throte he maketh his privee°   *toilet*
240 Thurgh thilke cursed superfluitee.°   *overindulgence*
     The Apostle[8] weeping saith ful pitously,
"Ther walken manye of which you told have I—
I saye it now weeping with pitous vois—
They been enemies of Cristes crois,°   *cross*
245 Of whiche the ende is deeth—wombe is hir god!"[9]
O wombe, O bely, O stinking cod,°   *bag*
Fulfilled° of dong° and of corrupcioun!   *filled full / dung*
At either ende of thee foul is the soun.°   *sound*
How greet labour and cost is thee to finde!°   *provide for*
250 Thise cookes, how they stampe° and straine and grinde,   *pound*
And turnen substance into accident[1]
To fulfillen al thy likerous° talent!°   *greedy / appetite*
Out of the harde bones knokke they
The mary,° for they caste nought away   *marrow*
255 That may go thurgh the golet[2] softe and soote.°   *sweetly*
Of spicerye° of leef and bark and roote   *spices*
Shal been his sauce ymaked by delit,
To make him yit a newer appetit.
But certes, he that haunteth swiche delices°   *pleasures*
260 Is deed° whil that he liveth in tho° vices.   *dead / those*
     A lecherous thing is win, and dronkenesse
Is ful of striving° and of wrecchednesse.   *quarreling*
O dronke man, disfigured is thy face!
Sour is thy breeth, foul artou to embrace!
265 And thurgh thy dronke nose seemeth the soun
As though thou saidest ay,° "Sampsoun, Sampsoun."   *always*
And yit, God woot,° Sampson drank nevere win.[3]   *knows*
Thou fallest as it were a stiked swin;°   *stuck pig*
Thy tonge is lost, and al thyn honeste cure,[4]
270 For dronkenesse is verray sepulture°   *burial*
Of mannes wit° and his discrecioun.   *intelligence*
In whom that drinke hath dominacioun
He can no conseil° keepe, it is no drede.°   *secrets / doubt*
Now keepe you fro the white and fro the rede—
275 And namely° fro the white win of Lepe[5]   *particularly*
That is to selle in Fisshstreete or in Chepe:[6]
The win of Spaine creepeth subtilly
In othere wines growing faste° by,   *close*
Of which ther riseth swich fumositee°   *heady fumes*
280 That whan a man hath dronken draughtes three
And weeneth° that he be at hoom in Chepe,   *supposes*

---

7. I.e., white and red wines.
8. I.e., St. Paul.
9. See Philippians 3.18.
1. A philosophic joke, depending on the distinction between inner reality (substance) and outward appearance (accident).
2. Through the gullet.

3. Before Samson's birth an angel told his mother that he would be a Nazarite throughout his life; members of this sect took no strong drink.
4. Care for self-respect.
5. A town in Spain.
6. Fishstreet and Cheapside in the London market district.

He is in Spaine, right at the town of Lepe,
Nat at The Rochele ne at Burdeux town;[7]
And thanne wol he sayn, "Sampsoun, Sampsoun."
285 But herkneth, lordinges, oo° word I you praye,   *one*
That alle the soverein actes,[8] dar I saye,
Of victories in the Olde Testament,
Thurgh verray God that is omnipotent,
Were doon in abstinence and in prayere:
290 Looketh° the Bible and ther ye may it lere.°   *behold / learn*
        Looke Attila, the grete conquerour,[9]
Deide° in his sleep with shame and dishonour,   *died*
Bleeding at his nose in dronkenesse:
A capitain sholde live in sobrenesse.
295 And overal this, aviseth you[1] right wel
What was comanded unto Lamuel[2]—
Nat Samuel, but Lamuel, saye I—
Redeth the Bible and finde it expresly,
Of win-yiving° to hem that han[3] justise: *wine-serving*
300 Namore of this, for it may wel suffise.
        And now that I have spoken of glotonye,
Now wol I you defende° hasardrye:°   *prohibit / gambling*
Hasard is verray moder° of lesinges,°   *mother / lies*
And of deceite and cursed forsweringes,°   *perjuries*
305 Blaspheme of Crist, manslaughtre, and wast° also   *waste*
Of catel° and of time; and ferthermo,   *property*
It is repreve° and contrarye of honour   *disgrace*
For to been holden a commune hasardour,°   *gambler*
And evere the hyer he is of estat
310 The more is he holden desolat.[4]
If that a prince useth hasardrye,
In alle governance and policye
He is, as by commune opinioun,
Yholde the lasse° in reputacioun.   *less*
315 Stilbon, that was a wis embassadour,
Was sent to Corinthe in ful greet honour
Fro Lacedomye° to make hir alliaunce,   *Sparta*
And whan he cam him happede° parchaunce   *it happened*
That alle the gretteste° that were of that lond   *greatest*
320 Playing at the hasard he hem foond,°   *found*
For which as soone as it mighte be
He stal him[5] hoom again to his contree,
And saide, "Ther wol I nat lese° my name,   *lose*
N'I wol nat take on me so greet defame°   *dishonor*
325 You to allye unto none hasardours:
Sendeth othere wise embassadours,
For by my trouthe, me were levere[6] die
Than I you sholde to hasardours allye.

---

7. The Pardoner is joking about the illegal custom of adulterating fine wines of Bordeaux and La Rochelle with strong Spanish wine.
8. Distinguished deeds.
9. Attila was the leader of the Huns who almost captured Rome in the 5th century.
1. Consider.

2. Lemuel's mother told him that kings should not drink (Proverbs 31.4–5).
3. I.e., administer.
4. I.e. dissolute.
5. He stole away.
6. I had rather.

For ye that been so glorious in honours
330 Shal nat allye you with hasardours
As by my wil, ne as by my tretee."°   *treaty*
This wise philosophre, thus saide he.
    Looke eek that to the king Demetrius
The King of Parthes,° as the book[7] saith us,   *Parthians*
335 Sente him a paire of dees° of gold in scorn,   *dice*
For he hadde used hasard therbiforn,
For which he heeld his glorye or his renown
At no value or reputacioun.
Lordes may finden other manere play
340 Honeste° ynough to drive the day away.   *honorable*
    Now wol I speke of othes false and grete
A word or two, as olde bookes trete:
    Greet swering is a thing abhominable,
And fals swering is yit more reprevable.°   *reprehensible*
345 The hye God forbad swering at al—
Witnesse on Mathew.[8] But in special
Of swering saith the holy Jeremie,[9]
"Thou shalt swere sooth thine othes and nat lie,
And swere in doom° and eek in rightwisnesse,°   *equity/righteousness*
350 But idel swering is a cursednesse."°   *wickedness*
    Biholde and see that in the firste Table[1]
Of hye Goddes heestes° honorable   *commandments*
How that the seconde heeste of him is this:
"Take nat my name in idel or amis."
355 Lo, rather° he forbedeth swich swering   *sooner*
Than homicide, or many a cursed thing.
I saye that as by ordre thus it stondeth—
This knoweth that[2] his heestes understondeth
How that the seconde heeste of God is that.
360 And fertherover,° I wol thee telle al plat°   *moreover/plain*
That vengeance shal nat parten° from his hous   *depart*
That of his othes is too outrageous.
"By Goddes precious herte!" and "By his nailes!"°   *fingernails*
And "By the blood of Crist that is in Hailes,[3]
365 Sevene is my chaunce,° and thyn is cink and traye!"[4]   *winning number*
"By Goddes armes, if thou falsly playe
This daggere shal thurghout thyn herte go!"
This fruit cometh of the bicche bones[5] two—
Forswering, ire, falsnesse, homicide.
370 Now for the love of Crist that for us dyde,°   *died*
Lete° youre othes bothe grete and smale.   *leave*
But sires, now wol I telle forth my tale.
    Thise riotoures° three of whiche I telle,   *revelers*
Longe erst er prime[6] ronge of any belle,
375 Were set hem in a taverne to drinke,

---

7. The book that relates this and the previous incident is the *Policraticus* of the 12th-century Latin writer John of Salisbury.
8. "But I say unto you, Swear not at all" (Matthew 5.34).
9. Jeremiah 4.2.
1. I.e., the first three of the Ten Commandments.

2. I.e., he that.
3. An abbey in Gloucestershire supposed to possess some of Christ's blood.
4. Five and three.
5. I.e., damned dice.
6. Long before 9 A.M.

And as they sat they herde a belle clinke
Biforn a cors° was caried to his grave.   *corpse*
That oon of hem gan callen to his knave:°   *servant*
Go bet,"[7] quod he, "and axe° redily°   *ask/promptly*
380   What cors is this that passeth heer forby,
And looke° that thou reporte his name weel."°   *be sure/well*
      "Sire," quod this boy, "it needeth neveradeel:[8]
It was me told er ye cam heer two houres.
He was, pardee,° an old felawe of youres,   *by God*
385   And sodeinly he was yslain tonight,°   *last night*
Fordronke° as he sat on his bench upright;   *very drunk*
Ther cam a privee° thief men clepeth° Deeth,   *stealthy/call*
That in this contree al the peple sleeth,°   *slays*
And with his spere he smoot his herte atwo,
390   And wente his way withouten wordes mo.
He hath a thousand slain this° pestilence.   *during this*
And maister, er ye come in his presence,
Me thinketh that it were necessarye
For to be war of swich an adversarye;
395   Beeth redy for to meete him everemore:
Thus taughte me my dame.° I saye namore."   *mother*
      "By Sainte Marye," saide this taverner,
"The child saith sooth, for he hath slain this yeer,
Henne° over a mile, within a greet village,   *hence*
400   Bothe man and womman, child and hine[9] and page.
I trowe° his habitacion be there.   *believe*
To been avised° greet wisdom it were   *wary*
Er that he dide a man a dishonour."
      "Ye, Goddes armes," quod this riotour,
405   "Is it swich peril with him for to meete?
I shal him seeke by way and eek by streete,[1]
I make avow to Goddes digne° bones.   *worthy*
Herkneth, felawes, we three been alle ones:°   *of one mind*
Lat eech of us holde up his hand to other
410   And eech of us bicome otheres brother,
And we wol sleen this false traitour Deeth.
He shal be slain, he that so manye sleeth,
By Goddes dignitee, er it be night."
      Togidres han thise three hir trouthes plight[2]
415   To live and dien eech of hem with other,
As though he were his owene ybore° brother.   *born*
And up they sterte,° al dronken in this rage,   *started*
And forth they goon towardes that village
Of which the taverner hadde spoke biforn,
420   And many a grisly ooth thanne han they sworn,
And Cristes blessed body they torente:°   *tore apart*
Deeth shal be deed° if that they may him hente.°   *dead/catch*
      Whan they han goon nat fully half a mile,
Right as they wolde han treden° over a stile,   *stepped*

---

7. Better, i.e., quick.
8. It isn't a bit necessary.
9. Farm laborer.

1. By highway and byway.
2. Pledged their words of honor.

425 An old man and a poore with hem mette;
This olde man ful mekely hem grette,°   greeted
And saide thus, "Now lordes, God you see."³
    The pruddeste° of thise riotoures three   proudest
Answerde again, "What, carl° with sory grace,   fellow
430 Why artou al forwrapped° save thy face?   muffled up
Why livestou so longe in so greet age?"
    This olde man gan looke in his visage,
And saide thus, "For° I ne can nat finde   because
A man, though that I walked into Inde,°   India
435 Neither in citee ne in no village,
That wolde chaunge his youthe for myn age;
And therefore moot° I han myn age stille,   must
As longe time as it is Goddes wille.
    "Ne Deeth, allas, ne wol nat have my lif.
440 Thus walke I lik a restelees caitif,°   wretch
And on the ground which is my modres° gate   mother's
I knokke with my staf bothe erly and late,
And saye, 'Leve° moder, leet me in: dear
Lo, how I vanisshe, flessh and blood and skin.
445 Allas, whan shal my bones been at reste?
Moder, with you wolde I chaunge° my cheste⁴   exchange
That in my chambre longe time hath be,
Ye, for an haire-clout⁵ to wrappe me.'
But yit to me she wol nat do that grace,
450 For which ful pale and welked° is my face.   withered
But sires, to you it is no curteisye
To speken to an old man vilainye,°   rudeness
But° he trespasse° in word or elles in deede.   unless/offend
In Holy Writ ye may yourself wel rede,
455 'Agains⁶ an old man, hoor° upon his heed,   hoar
Ye shall arise.'⁷ Wherfore I yive you reed,°   advice
Ne dooth unto an old man noon harm now,
Namore than that ye wolde men dide to you
In age, if that ye so longe abide.⁸
460 And God be with you wher ye go° or ride: walk
I moot go thider as I have to go."
    "Nay, olde cherl, by God thou shalt nat so,"
Saide this other hasardour anoon.
"Thou partest nat so lightly,° by Saint John!   easily
465 Thou speke° right now of thilke traitour Deeth,   spoke
That in this contree alle oure freendes sleeth:
Have here my trouthe, as thou art his espye,°   spy
Tel wher he is, or thou shalt it abye,°   pay for
By God and by the holy sacrament!
470 For soothly thou art oon of his assent⁹
To sleen us yonge folk, thou false thief."
    "Now sires," quod he, "if that ye be so lief°   anxious

3. May God protect you.
4. Chest for one's belongings, used here as the
symbol for life—or perhaps a coffin.
5. Haircloth, for a winding sheet.

6. In the presence of.
7. Cf. Leviticus 19.32.
8. I.e., if you live so long.
9. I.e., one of his party.

To finde Deeth, turne up this crooked way,
For in that grove I lafte° him, by my fay,°   *left/faith*
475   Under a tree, and ther he wol abide:
Nat for youre boost° he wol him no thing hide.   *boast*
See ye that ook?° Right ther ye shal him finde.   *oak*
God save you, that boughte again[1] mankinde,
And you amende." Thus saide this olde man.
480   And everich of thise riotoures ran
Til he cam to that tree, and ther they founde
Of florins° fine of gold ycoined rounde   *coins*
Wel neigh an eighte busshels as hem thoughte—
Ne lenger thanne after Deeth they soughte,
485   But eech of hem so glad was of the sighte,
For that the florins been so faire and brighte,
That down they sette hem by this precious hoord.
The worste of hem he spak the firste word:
     "Bretheren," quod he, "take keep° what that I saye: *heed*
490   My wit is greet though that I bourde° and playe.   *joke*
This tresor hath Fortune unto us yiven
In mirthe and jolitee oure lif to liven,
And lightly° as it cometh so wol we spende.   *easily*
Ey, Goddes precious dignitee, who wende[2]
495   Today that we sholde han so fair a grace?
But mighte this gold be caried fro this place
Hoom to myn hous—or elles unto youres—
For wel ye woot that al this gold is oures—
Thanne were we in heigh felicitee.
500   But trewely, by daye it mighte nat be:
Men wolde sayn that we were theves stronge,°   *flagrant*
And for oure owene tresor doon us honge.[3]
This tresor moste ycaried be by nighte,
As wisely and as slyly as it mighte.
505   Therefore I rede° that cut° amonges us alle   *advise/straws*
Be drawe, and lat see wher the cut wol falle;
And he that hath the cut with herte blithe
Shal renne° to the town, and that ful swithe,°   *run/quickly*
And bringe us breed and win ful prively;
510   And two of us shal keepen° subtilly   *guard*
This tresor wel, and if he wol nat tarye,
Whan it is night we wol this tresor carye
By oon assent wher as us thinketh best."
That oon of hem the cut broughte in his fest°   *fist*
515   And bad hem drawe and looke wher it wol falle;
And it fil° on the yongeste of hem alle,   *fell*
And forth toward the town he wente anoon.
And also° soone as that he was agoon,°   *as/gone away*
That oon of hem spak thus unto that other:
520   "Thou knowest wel thou art my sworen brother;
Thy profit wol I telle thee anoon:
Thou woost wel that oure felawe is agoon,

1. Redeemed.
2. Who would have supposed.
3. Have us hanged.

And here is gold, and that ful greet plentee,
That shall departed° been among us three.   *divided*
525 But nathelees, if I can shape° it so   *arrange*
That it departed were among us two,
Hadde I nat doon a freendes turn to thee?"
    That other answerde, "I noot[4] how that may be:
He woot that the gold is with us twaye.
530 What shal we doon? What shal we to him saye?"
    "Shal it be conseil?"[5] saide the firste shrewe.°   *villain*
"And I shal telle in a wordes fewe
What we shul doon, and bringe it wel aboute."
    "I graunte," quod that other, "out of doute,
535 That by my trouthe I wol thee nat biwraye."°   *expose*
    "Now," quod the firste, "thou woost wel we be twaye,
And two of us shal strenger° be than oon: *stronger*
Looke whan that he is set that right anoon
Aris as though thou woldest with him playe,
540 And I shal rive° him thurgh the sides twaye,   *pierce*
Whil that thou strugelest with him as in game,
And with thy daggere looke thou do the same;
And thanne shal al this gold departed be,
My dere freend, bitwixe thee and me.
545 Thanne we may bothe oure lustes° al fulfille,   *desires*
And playe at dees° right at oure owene wille."   *dice*
And thus accorded been thise shrewes twaye
To sleen the thridde, as ye han herd me saye.
    This yongeste, which that wente to the town,
550 Ful ofte in herte he rolleth up and down
The beautee of thise florins newe and brighte.
"O Lord," quod he, "if so were that I mighte
Have al this tresor to myself allone,
Ther is no man that liveth under the trone°   *throne*
555 Of God that sholde live so merye as I."
And at the laste the feend oure enemy
Putte in his thought that he sholde poison beye,°   *buy*
With which he mighte sleen his felawes twaye—
Forwhy° the feend° foond him in swich livinge   *because/devil*
560 That he hadde leve° him to sorwe bringe:[6]   *permission*
For this was outrely° his fulle entente,   *plainly*
To sleen hem bothe, and nevere to repente.
    And forth he gooth—no lenger wolde he tarye—
Into the town unto a pothecarye,°   *apothecary*
565 And prayed him that he him wolde selle
Som poison that he mighte his rattes quelle,°   *kill*
And eek ther was a polcat[7] in his hawe°   *yard*
That, as he saide, his capons hadde yslawe,°   *slain*
And fain he wolde wreke him[8] if he mighte
570 On vermin that destroyed him[9] by nighte.
    The pothecarye answerde, "And thou shalt have

---

4. Don't know.
5. A secret.
6. Christian doctrine teaches that the devil may not tempt people except with God's permission.

7. A weasellike animal.
8. He would gladly avenge himself.
9. I.e., were ruining his farming.

A thing that, also° God my soule save,   *as*
In al this world there is no creature
That ete or dronke hath of this confiture°   *mixture*
575   Nat but the mountance° of a corn° of whete—   *amount/grain*
That he ne shal his lif anoon forlete.°   *lose*
Ye, sterve° he shal, and that in lasse° while   *die/less*
Than thou wolt goon a paas[1] nat but a mile,
The poison is so strong and violent."
580   This cursed man hath in his hand yhent°   *taken*
This poison in a box and sith° he ran   *then*
Into the nexte streete unto a man
And borwed of him large botels three,
And in the two his poison poured he—
585   The thridde he kepte clene for his drinke,
For al the night he shoop him[2] for to swinke°   *work*
In carying of the gold out of that place.
And whan this riotour with sory grace
Hadde filled with win his grete botels three,
590   To his felawes again repaireth he.
         What needeth it to sermone of it more?
For right as they had cast° his deeth bifore,   *plotted*
Right so they han him slain, and that anoon.
And whan that this was doon, thus spak that oon:
595   "Now lat us sitte and drinke and make us merye,
And afterward we wol his body berye."°   *bury*
And with that word it happed him par cas[3]
To take the botel ther the poison was,
And drank, and yaf his felawe drinke also,
600   For which anoon they storven° bothe two.   *died*
         But certes I suppose that Avicen
Wroot nevere in no canon ne in no *fen*[4]
Mo wonder signes[5] of empoisoning
Than hadde thise wrecches two er hir ending:
605   Thus ended been thise homicides two,
And eek the false empoisonere also.
         O cursed sinne of alle cursednesse!
O traitours homicide, O wikkednesse!
O glotonye, luxure,° and hasardrye!   *lechery*
610   Thou blasphemour of Crist with vilainye
And othes grete of usage° and of pride!   *habit*
Allas, mankinde, how may it bitide
That to thy Creatour which that thee wroughte,
And with his precious herte blood thee boughte,°   *redeemed*
615   Thou art so fals and so unkinde,° allas?   *unnatural*
         Now goode men, God foryive you youre trespas,
And ware° you fro the sinne of avarice: *guard*
Myn holy pardon may you alle warice°—   *save*
So that ye offre nobles or sterlinges,[6]

---

1. Take a walk.
2. He was preparing.
3. By chance.
4. The *Canon of Medicine*, by Avicenna, an 11th-

century Arabic philosopher, was divided into sections called "fens."
5. More wonderful symptoms.
6. "Nobles" and "sterlinges" were valuable coins.

620 Or elles silver brooches, spoones, ringes.
   Boweth your heed under this holy bulle!
   Cometh up, ye wives, offreth of youre wolle!°   *wool*
   Youre name I entre here in my rolle: anoon
   Into the blisse of hevene shul ye goon.
625 I you assoile° by myn heigh power—   *absolve*
   Ye that wol offre—as clene and eek as cleer
   As ye were born.—And lo, sires, thus I preche.
   And Jesu Crist that is oure soules leeche°   *physician*
   So graunte you his pardon to receive,
630 For that is best—I wol you nat deceive.

The Epilogue

   "But sires, oo word forgat I in my tale:
   I have relikes and pardon in my male°   *bag*
   As faire as any man in Engelond,
   Whiche were me yiven by the Popes hond.
635 If any of you wol of devocioun
   Offren and han myn absolucioun,
   Come forth anoon, and kneeleth here adown,
   And mekely receiveth my pardoun,
   Or elles taketh pardon as ye wende,°   *ride along*
640 Al newe and fressh at every miles ende—
   So that ye offre alway newe and newe[7]
   Nobles or pens whiche that be goode and trewe.
   It is an honour to everich° that is heer   *everyone*
   That ye have a suffisant° pardoner   *competent*
645 T'assoile you in contrees as ye ride,
   For aventures° whiche that may bitide: *accidents*
   Paraventure ther may falle oon or two
   Down of his hors and breke his nekke atwo;
   Looke which a suretee° is it to you alle   *safeguard*
650 That I am in youre felaweshipe yfalle
   That may assoile you, bothe more and lasse,[8]
   Whan that the soule shal fro the body passe.
   I rede° that oure Hoste shal biginne,   *advise*
   For he is most envoluped° in sinne.   *involved*
655 Com forth, sire Host, and offre first anoon,
   And thou shalt kisse the relikes everichoon,°   *each one*
   Ye, for a grote: unbokele° anoon thy purs."   *unbuckle*
   "Nay, nay," quod he, "thanne have I Cristes curs!
   Lat be," quod he, "it shal nat be, so theech!°   *may I prosper*
660 Thou woldest make me kisse thyn olde breech°   *breeches*
   And swere it were a relik of a saint,
   Though it were with thy fundament° depeint.°   *anus/stained*
   But, by the crois which that Sainte Elaine foond,[9]
   I wolde I hadde thy coilons° in myn hond,   *testicles*
665 In stede of relikes or of saintuarye.°   *relic-box*

7. Over and over.
8. Both high and low (i.e., everybody).
9. I.e., by the cross that St. Helena found. Helena, mother of Constantine the Great, was reputed to have found the True Cross.

Lat cutte hem of: I wol thee helpe hem carye.
They shal be shrined in an hogges tord."°   *turd*
    This Pardoner answerde nat a word:
So wroth he was no word ne wolde he saye.
670 "Now," quod oure Host, "I wol no lenger playe
With thee, ne with noon other angry man."
    But right anoon the worthy Knight bigan,
Whan that he sawgh that al the peple lough,°   *laughed*
"Namore of this, for it is right ynough.
675 Sire Pardoner, be glad and merye of cheere,
And ye, sire Host that been to me so dere,
I praye you that ye kisse the Pardoner,
And Pardoner, I praye thee, draw thee neer,
And as we diden lat us laughe and playe."
680 Anoon they kiste and riden forth hir waye.

The Nun's Priest's Tale

In the framing story, *The Nun's Priest's Tale* is linked to a dramatic exchange that
follows *The Monk's Tale*. The latter consists of brief tragedies, the common theme of
which is the fall of famous men and one woman, most of whom are rulers, through
the reversals of Fortune. Like *The Knight's Tale*, this was probably an earlier work of
Chaucer's, one that he never finished. As the Monk's tragedies promise to go on and
on monotonously, the Knight interrupts and politely tells the Monk that his tragedies
are too painful. The Host chimes in to say that the tragedies are "nat worth a bot-
terflye" and asks the Monk to try another subject, but the Monk is offended and
refuses. The Host then turns to the Nun's Priest, that is, the priest who is accom-
panying the Prioress. The three priests said in *The General Prologue* to have been
traveling with her have apparently been reduced to one.

The Nun's Priest's Tale is an example of the literary genre known as the "beast
fable," familiar from the fables of Aesop in which animals, behaving like human
beings, point a moral. In the Middle Ages fables often functioned as elementary texts
to teach boys Latin. Marie de France's fables in French are the earliest known vernacular translations (see pp. 140–41). This particular fable derives from an episode
in the French *Roman de Renard*, a "beast epic," which satirically represents a feudal
animal society ruled over by Noble the Lion. Reynard the Fox is a wily trickster hero
who is constantly preying upon and outwitting the other animals, although sometimes
Reynard himself is outwitted by one of his victims.

In *The Nun's Priest's Tale*, morals proliferate: both the priest-narrator and his hero,
Chauntecleer the rooster, spout examples, learned allusions, proverbs, and senten-
tious generalizations, often in highly inflated rhetoric. The simple beast fable is thus
inflated into a delightful satire of learning and moralizing and of the pretentious
rhetoric by which medieval writers sometimes sought to elevate their works. Among
them, we we may include Chaucer himself who in this tale seems to be making
affectionate fun of some of his own works like the tragedies which became *The Monk's
Tale*.

A poore widwe somdeel stape° in age   *advanced*
Was whilom° dwelling in a narwe¹ cotage,   *once upon a time*

1. I.e., small.

Biside a grove, stonding in a dale:
This widwe of which I telle you my tale,
5 Sin thilke° day that she was last a wif,   *that same*
In pacience ladde° a ful simple lif.   *led*
For litel was hir catel° and hir rente,°   *property/income*
By housbondrye° of swich as God hire sente   *economy*
She foond° hirself and eek hir doughtren two.   *provided for*
10 Three large sowes hadde she and namo,
Three kin,° and eek a sheep that highte° Malle.   *cows/was called*
Ful sooty was hir bowr° and eek hir halle.   *bedroom*
In which she eet ful many a sclendre° meel;   *scanty*
Of poinant° sauce hire needed neveradeel:°   *pungent/not a bit*
15 No daintee morsel passed thurgh hir throte—
Hir diete was accordant to hir cote.°   *cottage*
Repleccioun° ne made hire nevere sik: *overeating*
Attempre° diete was al hir physik,°   *moderate/medicine*
And exercise and hertes suffisaunce.°   *contentment*
20 The goute lette hire nothing for to daunce,²
N'apoplexye shente° nat hir heed.°   *hurt/head*
No win ne drank she, neither whit ne reed:°   *red*
Hir boord° was served most with whit and blak,³   *table*
Milk and brown breed, in which she foond no lak;⁴
25 Seind bacon, and somtime an ey° or twaye,   *egg*
For she was as it were a manere daye.⁵
A yeerd° she hadde, enclosed al withoute   *yard*
With stikkes, and a drye dich aboute,
In which she hadde a cok heet° Chauntecleer: *named*
30 In al the land of crowing nas° his peer.   *was not*
His vois was merier than the merye orgon
On massedayes that in the chirche goon;⁶
Wel sikerer⁷ was his crowing in his logge°   *dwelling*
Than is a clok or an abbeye orlogge;°   *timepiece*
35 By nature he knew eech ascensioun
Of th'equinoxial⁸ in thilke town:
For whan degrees fifteene were ascended,
Thanne crew° he that it mighte nat been amended.°   *crowed/improved*
His comb was redder than the fin coral,
40 And batailed° as it were a castel wal;   *battlemented*
His bile° was blak, and as the jeet° it shoon;   *bill/jet*
Like asure⁹ were his legges and his toon;°   *toes*
His nailes whitter° than the lilye flowr,   *whiter*
And lik the burned° gold was his colour.   *burnished*
45 This gentil° cok hadde in his governaunce   *noble*
Sevene hennes for to doon al his plesaunce,°   *pleasure*
Whiche were his sustres and his paramours,¹

---

2. The gout didn't hinder her at all from dancing.
3. I.e., milk and bread.
4. Found no fault.
5. I.e., a kind of dairywoman. "Seind": scorched (i.e., broiled).
6. I.e., is played.
7. More reliable.
8. I.e., he knew by instinct each step in the pro-

gression of the celestial equator. The celestial equator was thought to make a 360° rotation around the earth every twenty-four hours; therefore, a progression of 15° would be equal to the passage of an hour (line 37).
9. Blue (lapis lazuli).
1. His sisters and his mistresses.

And wonder like to him as of colours;
Of whiche the faireste hewed° on hir throte   *colored*
50   Was cleped° faire damoisele Pertelote: *called*
Curteis she was, discreet, and debonaire,°   *meek*
And compaignable,° and bar° hirself so faire,   *companionable / bore*
Sin thilke day that she was seven night old,
That trewely she hath the herte in hold
55   Of Chauntecleer, loken° in every lith.°   *locked / limb*
He loved hire so that wel was him therwith.[2]
But swich a joye was it to heere hem singe,
Whan that the brighte sonne gan to springe,
In sweete accord *My Lief is Faren in Londe*[3]—
60   For thilke time, as I have understonde,
Beestes and briddes couden speke and singe.
     And so bifel that in a daweninge,
As Chauntecleer among his wives alle
Sat on his perche that was in the halle,
65   And next him sat this faire Pertelote,
This Chauntecleer gan gronen in his throte,
As man that in his dreem is drecched° sore.   *troubled*
     And whan that Pertelote thus herde him rore,°   *roar*
She was agast, and saide, "Herte dere,
70   What aileth you to grone in this manere?
Ye been a verray slepere,[4] fy, for shame!"
     And he answerde and saide thus, "Madame,
I praye you that ye take it nat agrief.°   *amiss*
By God, me mette I was in swich meschief[5]
75   Right now, that yit myn herte is sore afright.
Now God," quod he, "my swevene recche aright,[6]
And keepe my body out of foul prisoun!
Me mette° how that I romed up and down   *dreamed*
Within oure yeerd, wher as I sawgh a beest,
80   Was lik an hound and wolde han maad arrest[7]
Upon my body, and han had me deed.[8]
His colour was bitwixe yelow and reed,
And tipped was his tail and bothe his eres
With blak, unlik the remenant° of his heres;°   *rest / hairs*
85   His snoute smal, with glowing yën twaye.
Yit of his look for fere almost I deye:°   *die*
This caused me my groning, doutelees."
     "Avoi,"° quod she, "fy on you, hertelees!°   *fie / coward*
Allas," quod she, "for by that God above,
90   Now han ye lost myn herte and al my love!
I can nat love a coward, by my faith.
For certes, what so any womman saith,
We alle desiren, if it mighte be,
To han housbondes hardy, wise, and free,°   *generous*

[handwritten marginal note: what women want]

---

2. That he was well contented.
3. "My Love Has Gone Away," a popular song of the time. See p. 352.
4. Sound sleeper.
5. I dreamed that I was in such misfortune.

6. Interpret my dream correctly (i.e., in an auspicious manner).
7. Would have laid hold.
8. I.e., killed me.

95	And secree,° and no nigard, ne no fool,	*discreet*
	Ne him that is agast of every tool,°	*weapon*
	Ne noon avauntour.° By that God above,	*boaster*
	How dorste° ye sayn for shame unto youre love	*dare*
	That any thing mighte make you aferd?	
100	Have ye no mannes herte and han a beerd?°	*beard*
	Allas, and conne° ye been agast of swevenes?°	*can/dreams*
	No thing, God woot, but vanitee⁹ in swevene is!	
	Swevenes engendren of replexiouns,¹	
	And ofte of fume° and of complexiouns,°	*gas/bodily humors*
105	Whan humours been too habundant in a wight.²	
	Certes, this dreem which ye han met° tonight	*dreamed*
	Comth of the grete superfluitee	
	Of youre rede colera,³ pardee,	
	Which causeth folk to dreden° in hir dremes	*fear*
110	Of arwes,° and of fir with rede lemes,°	*arrows/flames*
	Of rede beestes, that they wol hem bite,	
	Of contek,° and of whelpes grete and lite⁴—	*strife*
	Right° as the humour of malencolye⁵	*just*
	Causeth ful many a man in sleep to crye	
115	For fere of blake beres° or boles° blake,	*bears/bulls*
	Or elles blake develes wol hem take.	
	Of othere humours coude I tell also	
	That werken many a man in sleep ful wo,	
	But I wol passe as lightly° as I can.	*quickly*
120	Lo, Caton,⁶ which that was so wis a man,	
	Saide he nat thus? 'Ne do no fors of⁷ dremes.'	
	Now, sire," quod she, "whan we flee fro the bemes,⁸	
	For Goddes love, as take som laxatif.	
	Up° peril of my soule and of my lif,	*upon*
125	I conseile you the beste, I wol nat lie,	
	That bothe of colere and of malencolye	
	Ye purge you; and for° ye shal nat tarye,	*in order that*
	Though in this town is noon apothecarye,	
	I shal myself to herbes techen you,	
130	That shal been for youre hele° and for youre prow,°	*health/benefit*
	And in oure yeerd tho° herbes shal I finde,	*those*
	The whiche han of hir propretee by kinde°	*nature*
	To purge you binethe and eek above.	
	Foryet° nat this, for Goddes owene love.	*forget*
135	Ye been ful colerik° of complexioun;	*bilious*
	Ware° the sonne in his ascencioun	*beware that*
	Ne finde you nat repleet° of humours hote;°	*filled/hot*
	And if it do, I dar wel laye° a grote	*bet*
	That ye shul have a fevere terciane,⁹	

9. I.e., empty illusion.
1. Dreams have their origin in overeating.
2. I.e., when humors (bodily fluids) are too abundant in a person. Pertelote's diagnosis is based on the familiar concept that an excess of one of the bodily humors in a person affected his or her temperament (see p. 225, n. 8).
3. Red bile.

4. And of big and little dogs.
5. I.e., black bile.
6. Dionysius Cato, supposed author of a book of maxims used in elementary education.
7. Pay no attention to.
8. Fly down from the rafters.
9. Tertian (recurring every other day).

140 Or an agu° that may be youre bane.°   *ague / death*
  A day or two ye shul han digestives
  Of wormes, er° ye take youre laxatives   *before*
  Of lauriol, centaure, and fumetere,[1]
  Or elles of ellebor° that groweth there,   *hellebore*
145 Of catapuce, or of gaitres beries,[2]
  Of herb-ive° growing in oure yeerd ther merye is[3]—   *herb ivy*
  Pekke hem right up as they growe and ete hem in.
  Be merye, housbonde, for youre fader° kin!   *father's*
  Dredeth no dreem: I can saye you namore."
150   "Madame," quod he, "graunt mercy of youre lore,[4]
  But nathelees, as touching daun° Catoun,   *master*
  That hath of wisdom swich a greet renown,
  Though that he bad no dremes for to drede,
  By God, men may in olde bookes rede
155 Of many a man more of auctoritee°   *authority*
  Than evere Caton was, so mote I thee,°   *prosper*
  That al the revers sayn of his sentence,°   *opinion*
  And han wel founden by experience
  That dremes been significaciouns
160 As wel of joye as tribulaciouns
  That folk enduren in this lif present.
  Ther needeth make of this noon argument:
  The verray preve[5] sheweth it in deede.
   "Oon of the gretteste auctour[6] that men rede
165 Saith thus, that whilom two felawes wente
  On pilgrimage in a ful good entente,
  And happed so they comen in a town,
  Wher as ther was swich congregacioun
  Of peple, and eek so strait of herbergage,[7]
170 That they ne founde as muche as oo cotage
  In which they bothe mighte ylogged° be;   *lodged*
  Wherfore they mosten° of necessitee   *must*
  As for that night departe° compaignye.   *part*
  And eech of hem gooth to his hostelrye,
175 And took his logging as it wolde falle.°   *befall*
  That oon of hem was logged in a stalle,
  Fer° in a yeerd, with oxen of the plough;   *far away*
  That other man was logged wel ynough,
  As was his aventure° or his fortune,   *lot*
180 That us governeth alle as in commune.
  And so bifel that longe er it were day,
  This man mette° in his bed, ther as he lay,   *dreamed*
  How that his felawe gan upon him calle,
  And saide, 'Allas, for in an oxes stalle
185 This night I shal be mordred° ther I lie!   *murdered*
  Now help me, dere brother, or I die!

---

1. Of laureole, centaury, and fumitory. These, and the herbs mentioned in the next lines, were all common medieval medicines used as cathartics.
2. Of caper berry or of gaiter berry.
3. Where it is pleasant.
4. Many thanks for your instruction.
5. Actual experience.
6. I.e., one of the greatest authors (perhaps Cicero or Valerius Maximus).
7. And also such a shortage of lodging.

In alle haste com to me,' he saide.
    "This man out of his sleep for fere abraide,°   *started up*
But whan that he was wakened of his sleep,
190 He turned him and took of this no keep:°   *heed*
Him thoughte his dreem nas but a vanitee.°   *illusion*
Thus twies in his sleeping dremed he,
And atte thridde time yit his felawe
Cam, as him thoughte, and saide, 'I am now slawe:°   *slain*
195 Bihold my bloody woundes deepe and wide.
Aris up erly in the morwe tide,[8]
And atte west gate of the town,' quod he,
'A carte ful of dong° ther shaltou see,   *dung*
In which my body is hid ful prively:
200 Do thilke carte arresten boldely.[9]
My gold caused my mordre, sooth to sayn'
—And tolde him every point how he was slain,
With a ful pitous face, pale of hewe.
And truste wel, his dreem he foond° ful trewe,   *found*
205 For on the morwe° as soone as it was day,   *morning*
To his felawes in° he took the way,   *lodging*
And whan that he cam to this oxes stalle,
After his felawe he bigan to calle.
    "The hostiler° answerde him anoon,   *innkeeper*
210 And saide, 'Sire, youre felawe is agoon:°   *gone away*
As soone as day he wente out of the town.'
    "This man gan fallen in suspecioun,
Remembring on his dremes that he mette;°   *dreamed*
And forth he gooth, no lenger wolde he lette,°   *tarry*
215 Unto the west gate of the town, and foond
A dong carte, wente as it were to donge° lond,   *put manure on*
That was arrayed in that same wise
As ye han herd the dede° man devise;   *dead*
And with an hardy herte he gan to crye,
220 'Vengeance and justice of this felonye!
My felawe mordred is this same night,
And in this carte he lith° gaping upright!°   *lies / on his back*
I crye out on the ministres,' quod he,
'That sholde keepe and rulen this citee.
225 Harrow,° allas, here lith my felawe slain!'   *help*
What sholde I more unto this tale sayn?
The peple up sterte° and caste the carte to grounde,   *started*
And in the middel of the dong they founde
The dede man that mordred was al newe.[1]
230   "O blisful God that art so just and trewe,
Lo, how that thou biwrayest° mordre alway!   *disclose*
Mordre wol out, that see we day by day:
Mordre is so wlatsom° and abhominable   *loathsome*
To God that is so just and resonable,
235 That he ne wol nat suffre it heled° be,   *concealed*

8. In the morning.   1. Recently.
9. Boldly have this same cart seized.

Though it abide a yeer or two or three.
Mordre wol out: this my conclusioun.
And right anoon ministres of that town
Han hent° the cartere and so sore him pined,[2]   seized
240 And eek the hostiler so sore engined,°   racked
That they biknewe° hir wikkednesse anoon,   confessed
And were anhanged° by the nekke boon.   hanged
Here may men seen that dremes been to drede.[3]
"And certes, in the same book I rede—
245 Right in the nexte chapitre after this—
I gabbe° nat, so have I joye or blis—   lie
Two men that wolde han passed over see
For certain cause into a fer contree,
If that the wind ne hadde been contrarye
250 That made hem in a citee for to tarye,
That stood ful merye upon an haven° side—   harbor's
But on a day again° the even-tide   toward
The wind gan chaunge, and blewe right as hem leste:[4]
Jolif° and glad they wenten unto reste,   merry
255 And casten° hem ful erly for to saile.   determined
"But to that oo man fil° a greet mervaile;   befell
That oon of hem, in sleeping as he lay,
Him mette[5] a wonder dreem again the day:
Him thoughte a man stood by his beddes side,
260 And him comanded that he sholde abide,
And saide him thus, 'If thou tomorwe wende,
Thou shalt be dreint:° my tale is at an ende.'   drowned
"He wook and tolde his felawe what he mette,
And prayed him his viage° to lette;°   voyage / delay
265 As for that day he prayed him to bide.
"His felawe that lay by his beddes side
Gan for to laughe, and scorned him ful faste.°   hard
'No dreem,' quod he, 'may so myn herte agaste°   terrify
That I wol lette for to do my thinges.°   business
270 I sette nat a straw by thy dreminges,[6]
For swevenes been but vanitees and japes:[7]
Men dreme alday° of owles or of apes,[8]   constantly
And of many a maze° therwithal—   delusion
Men dreme of thing that nevere was ne shal.[9]
275 But sith I see that thou wolt here abide,
And thus forsleuthen° wilfully thy tide,°   waste / time
God woot, it reweth me;[1] and have good day.'
And thus he took his leve and wente his way.
But er that he hadde half his cours ysailed—
280 Noot I nat why ne what meschaunce it ailed—
But casuelly the shippes botme rente,[2]

2. Tortured.
3. Worthy of being feared.
4. Just as they wished.
5. He dreamed.
6. I don't care a straw for your dreamings.
7. Dreams are but illusions and frauds.

8. I.e., of absurdities.
9. I.e., shall be.
1. I'm sorry.
2. I don't know why nor what was the trouble with it—but accidentally the ship's bottom split.

And ship and man under the water wente,
In sighte of othere shippes it biside,
That with hem sailed at the same tide.
285 And therfore, faire Pertelote so dere,
By swiche ensamples olde maistou lere°   learn
That no man sholde been too recchelees°   careless
Of dremes, for I saye thee doutelees
That many a dreem ful sore is for to drede.
290   "Lo, in the lif of Saint Kenelm[3] I rede—
That was Kenulphus sone, the noble king
Of Mercenrike°—how Kenelm mette a thing   Mercia
A lite° er he was mordred on a day.   little
His mordre in his avision° he sey.°   dream / saw
295 His norice° him expounded everydeel°   nurse / every bit
His swevene, and bad him for to keepe him[4] weel
For traison, but he nas but seven yeer old,
And therfore litel tale hath he told
Of any dreem,[5] so holy was his herte.
300 By God, I hadde levere than my sherte[6]
That ye hadde rad° his legende as have I.   read
    "Dame Pertelote, I saye you trewely,
Macrobeus,[7] that writ the Avisioun
In Affrike of the worthy Scipioun,
305 Affermeth° dremes, and saith that they been   confirms
Warning of thinges that men after seen.
    "And ferthermore, I praye you looketh wel
In the Olde Testament of Daniel,
If he heeld° dremes any vanitee.[8]   considered
310   "Rede eek of Joseph[9] and ther shul ye see
Wher° dremes be somtime—I saye nat alle—   whether
Warning of thinges that shul after falle.
    "Looke of Egypte the king daun Pharao,
His bakere and his botelere° also,   butler
315 Wher they ne felte noon effect in dremes.[1]
Whoso wol seeke actes of sondry remes°   realms
May rede of dremes many a wonder thing.
    "Lo Cresus, which that was of Lyde° king,   Lydia
Mette° he nat that he sat upon a tree,   dreamed
320 Which signified he sholde anhanged° be?   hanged
    "Lo here Andromacha, Ectores° wif,   Hector's
That day that Ector sholde lese° his lif,   lose
She dremed on the same night biforn
How that the lif of Ector sholde be lorn,°   lost
325 If thilke° day he wente into bataile;   that same
She warned him, but it mighte nat availe:°   do any good

---

3. Kenelm succeeded his father as king of Mercia
at the age of seven, but was slain by his aunt (in
821).
4. Guard himself.
5. Therefore he has set little store by any dream.
6. I.e., I'd give my shirt.
7. Macrobius wrote a famous commentary on Cic-

ero's account in De Republica of the dream of
Scipio Africanus Minor; the commentary came to
be regarded as a standard authority on dream lore.
8. See Daniel 7.
9. See Genesis 37.
1. See Genesis 39–41.

He wente for to fighte nathelees,
But he was slain anoon° of Achilles.   right away
But thilke tale is al too long to telle,
330 And eek it is neigh day, I may nat dwelle.
Shortly I saye, as for conclusioun,
That I shal han of this avisioun[2]
Adversitee, and I saye ferthermoor
That I ne telle of[3] laxatives no stoor,
335 For they been venimes,° I woot it weel: poisons
I hem defye, I love hem neveradeel.°   not a bit
  "Now lat us speke of mirthe and stinte° al this.   stop
Madame Pertelote, so have I blis,
Of oo thing God hath sente me large grace:
340 For whan I see the beautee of youre face—
Ye been so scarlet reed° aboute youre yën—   red
It maketh al my drede for to dien.
For also siker° as In principio,[4] } rooster   certain
Mulier est hominis confusio.[5]   } quotes Genesis
345 Madame, the sentence° of this Latin is,   meaning
'Womman is mannes joye and al his blis.'
For whan I feele anight youre softe side—
Al be it that I may nat on you ride,
For that oure perche is maad so narwe, allas—
350 I am so ful of joye and of solas°   delight
That I defye bothe swevene and dreem."
And with that word he fleigh° down fro the beem,   flew
For it was day, and eek his hennes alle,
And with a "chuk" he gan hem for to calle,
355 For he hadde founde a corn lay in the yeerd.
Real° he was, he was namore aferd:°   regal/afraid
He fethered[6] Pertelote twenty time,
And trad hire as ofte er it was prime.[7]
He looketh as it were a grim leoun,
360 And on his toes he rometh up and down:
Him deined[8] nat to sette his foot to grounde.
He chukketh whan he hath a corn yfounde,
And to him rennen° thanne his wives alle.   run
Thus royal, as a prince is in his halle,
365 Leve I this Chauntecleer in his pasture,
And after wol I telle his aventure.
    Whan that the month in which the world bigan,
That highte° March, whan God first maked man,   is called
Was compleet, and passed were also,
370 Sin March biran,° thritty days and two,[9]   passed by
Bifel that Chauntecleer in al his pride,
His sevene wives walking him biside,

---

2. Divinely inspired dream (as opposed to the more ordinary "swevene" or "dreem").
3. Set by.
4. Beginning of the Gospel of St. John that gives the essential premises of Christianity: "In the beginning was the Word."
5. Woman is man's ruination.
6. I.e., embraced.
7. 9 A.M. "Trad": trod, copulated with.
8. He deigned.
9. The rhetorical time telling yields the date May 3.

Caste up his yën to the brighte sonne,
That in the signe of Taurus hadde yronne
375 Twenty degrees and oon and somwhat more,
And knew by kinde,° and by noon other lore,   *nature*
That it was prime, and crew with blisful stevene.°   *voice*
"The sonne," he saide, "is clomben[1] up on hevene
Fourty degrees and oon and more, ywis.°   *indeed*
380 Madame Pertelote, my worldes blis,
Herkneth thise blisful briddes° how they singe,   *birds*
And see the fresshe flowers how they springe:
Ful is myn herte of revel and solas."
But sodeinly him fil° a sorweful cas,°   *befell/chance*
385 For evere the latter ende of joye is wo—
God woot that worldly joye is soone ago,
And if a rethor° coude faire endite,   *rhetorician*
He in a cronicle saufly° mighte it write,   *safely*
As for a soverein notabilitee.[2]
390 Now every wis man lat him herkne me:
This storye is also° trewe, I undertake,   *as*
As is the book of *Launcelot de Lake*,[3]
That wommen holde in ful greet reverence.
Now wol I turne again to my sentence.°   *main point*
395   A colfox[4] ful of sly iniquitee,
That in the grove hadde woned° yeres three,   *dwelled*
By heigh imaginacion forncast,[5]
The same night thurghout the hegges° brast°   *hedges/burst*
Into the yeerd ther Chauntecleer the faire
400 Was wont, and eek his wives, to repaire;
And in a bed of wortes° stille he lay   *cabbages*
Til it was passed undren° of the day,   *midmorning*
Waiting his time on Chauntecleer to falle,
As gladly doon thise homicides alle,
405 That in await liggen to mordre[6] men.
O false mordrour, lurking in thy den!
O newe Scariot! Newe Geniloun![7]
False dissimilour!° O Greek Sinoun,[8]   *dissembler*
That broughtest Troye al outrely° to sorwe!   *utterly*
410 O Chauntecleer, accursed be that morwe°   *morning*
That thou into the yeerd flaugh° fro the bemes!   *flew*
Thou were ful wel ywarned by thy dremes
That thilke day was perilous to thee;
But what that God forwoot° moot° needes be,   *foreknows/must*
415 After° the opinion of certain clerkes: *according to*
Witnesse on him that any parfit° clerk is   *perfect*
That in scole is greet altercacioun

1. Has climbed.
2. Indisputable fact.
3. Romances of the courteous knight Lancelot of the Lake were very popular.
4. Fox with black markings.
5. Predestined by divine planning.
6. That lie in ambush to murder.

7. I.e., Ganelon, who betrayed Roland to the Saracens (in the medieval French epic *The Song of Roland*). "Scariot": Judas Iscariot.
8. Sinon, who persuaded the Trojans to take the Greeks' wooden horse into their city—with, of course, the result that the city was destroyed.

In this matere, and greet disputisoun,°   *disputation*
And hath been of an hundred thousand men.
420 But I ne can nat bulte it to the bren,[9]
As can the holy doctour Augustin,
Or Boece, or the bisshop Bradwardin[1]—
Wheither that Goddes worthy forwiting°   *foreknowledge*
Straineth me nedely[2] for to doon a thing
425 ("Nedely" clepe I simple necessitee),
Or elles if free chois be graunted me
To do that same thing or do it naught,
Though God forwoot° it er that I was wrought;   *foreknew*
Or if his witing° straineth neveradeel,   *knowledge*
430 But by necessitee condicionel[3]—
I wol nat han to do of swich matere:
My tale is of a cok, as ye may heere,
That took his conseil of his wif with sorwe,
To walken in the yeerd upon that morwe
435 That he hadde met° the dreem that I you tolde.   *dreamed*
Wommenes conseils been ful ofte colde,[4]
Wommanes conseil broughte us first to wo,
And made Adam fro Paradis to go,
Ther as he was ful merye and wel at ese.
440 But for I noot° to whom it mighte displese   *don't know*
If I conseil of wommen wolde blame,
Passe over, for I saide it in my game°—   *sport*
Rede auctours where they trete of swich matere,
And what they sayn of wommen ye may heere—
445 Thise been the cokkes wordes and nat mine:
I can noon harm of no womman divine.°   *guess*
    Faire in the sond° to bathe hire merily   *sand*
Lith° Pertelote, and alle hir sustres by,   *lies*
Again° the sonne, and Chauntecleer so free°   *in/noble*
450 Soong° merier than the mermaide in the see—   *sang*
For Physiologus[5] saith sikerly
How that they singen wel and merily.
    And so bifel that as he caste his yë
Among the wortes on a boterflye,°   *butterfly*
455 He was war of this fox that lay ful lowe.
No thing ne liste him[6] thanne for to crowe,
But cride anoon "Cok cok!" and up he sterte,°   *started*
As man that[7] was affrayed in his herte—
For naturelly a beest desireth flee
460 Fro his contrarye[8] if he may it see,

---

9. Sift it to the bran, i.e., get to the bottom of it.
1. St. Augustine, Boethius (6th-century Roman philosopher, whose *Consolation of Philosophy* was translated by Chaucer), and Thomas Bradwardine (archbishop of Canterbury, d. 1349) were all concerned with the interrelationship between people's free will and God's foreknowledge.
2. Constrains me necessarily.
3. Boethius's "conditional necessity" permitted a

large measure of free will.
4. I.e., baneful.
5. Supposed author of a bestiary, a book of moralized zoology describing both natural and supernatural animals (including mermaids).
6. He wished.
7. Like one who.
8. I.e., his natural enemy.

Though he nevere erst° hadde seen it with his yë.   *before*
This Chauntecleer, whan he gan him espye,
He wolde han fled, but that the fox anoon
Saide, "Gentil sire, allas, wher wol ye goon?
465   Be ye afraid of me that am youre freend?
Now certes, I were worse than a feend
If I to you wolde° harm or vilainye.   *meant*
I am nat come youre conseil° for t'espye,   *secrets*
But trewely the cause of my cominge
470   Was only for to herkne how ye singe:
For trewely, ye han as merye a stevene°   *voice*
As any angel hath that is in hevene.
Therwith ye han in musik more feelinge
Than hadde Boece,[9] or any that can singe.
475   My lord your fader—God his soule blesse!—
And eek youre moder, of hir gentilesse,°   *gentility*
Han in myn hous ybeen, to my grete ese.
And certes sire, ful fain° wolde I you plese.   *gladly*
      "But for men speke of singing, I wol saye,
480   So mote I brouke[1] wel mine yën twaye,
Save ye, I herde nevere man to singe
As dide youre fader in the morweninge.
Certes, it was of herte° al that he soong.°   *heartfelt/sang*
And for to make his vois the more strong,
485   He wolde so paine him[2] that with bothe his yën
He moste winke,[3] so loude wolde he cryen;
And stonden on his tiptoon therwithal,
And strecche forth his nekke long and smal;
And eek he was of swich discrecioun
490   That ther nas no man in no regioun
That him in song or wisdom mighte passe.
I have wel rad° in *Daun Burnel the Asse*[4]   *read*
Among his vers how that ther was a cok,
For a preestes sone yaf him a knok[5]
495   Upon his leg whil he was yong and nice,°   *foolish*
He made him for to lese° his benefice.[6]   *lose*
But certain, ther nis no comparisoun
Bitwixe the wisdom and discrecioun
Of youre fader and of his subtiltee.[7]
500   Now singeth, sire, for sainte° charitee!   *holy*
Lat see, conne° ye youre fader countrefete?"°   *can/imitate*
      This Chauntecleer his winges gan to bete,
As man that coude his traison nat espye,
So was he ravisshed with his flaterye.
505   Allas, ye lordes, many a fals flatour°   *flatterer*
Is in youre court, and many a losengeour°   *deceiver*

9. Boethius also wrote a treatise on music.
1. So might I enjoy the use of.
2. Take pains.
3. He had to shut his eyes.
4. Master Brunellus, a discontented donkey, was
the hero of a 12th-century satirical poem by Nigel

Wireker.
5. Because a priest's son gave him a knock.
6. The offended cock neglected to crow so that his
master, now grown to manhood, overslept, missing
his ordination and losing his benefice.
7. His (the cock in the story) cleverness.

That plesen you wel more, by my faith,
Than he that soothfastnesse° unto you saith!   *truth*
Redeth Ecclesiaste[8] of flaterye.
510 Beeth war, ye lordes, of hir trecherye.
    This Chauntecleer stood hye upon his toos,
Strecching his nekke, and heeld his yën cloos,
And gan to crowe loude for the nones;°   *occasion*
And daun Russel the fox sterte° up atones,   *jumped*
515 And by the gargat° hente° Chauntecleer,   *throat / seized*
And on his bak toward the wode him beer,°   *bore*
For yit ne was ther no man that him sued.°   *followed*
    O destinee that maist nat been eschued!°   *eschewed*
Allas that Chauntecleer fleigh° fro the bemes!   *flew*
520 Allas his wif ne roughte nat of[9] dremes!
And on a Friday fil° al this meschaunce!   *befell*
    O Venus that art goddesse of plesaunce,
Sin that thy servant was this Chauntecleer,
And in thy service dide al his power—
525 More for delit than world[1] to multiplye—
Why woldestou suffre him on thy day[2] to die?
    O Gaufred,[3] dere maister soverein,
That, whan thy worthy king Richard was slain
With shot,[4] complainedest his deeth so sore,
530 Why ne hadde I now thy sentence and thy lore,[5]
The Friday for to chide as diden ye?
For on a Friday soothly slain was he.
Thanne wolde I shewe you how that I coude plaine°   *lament*
For Chauntecleres drede and for his paine.
535   Certes, swich cry ne lamentacioun
Was nevere of ladies maad when Ilioun°   *Ilium, Troy*
Was wonne, and Pyrrus[6] with his straite° swerd,   *drawn*
Whan he hadde hent° King Priam by the beerd   *seized*
And slain him, as saith us *Eneidos*,[7]
540 As maden alle the hennes in the cloos,°   *yard*
Whan they hadde seen of Chauntecleer the sighte.
But sovereinly° Dame Pertelote shrighte°   *supremely / shrieked*
Ful louder than dide Hasdrubales[8] wif
Whan that hir housbonde hadde lost his lif,
545 And that the Romains hadden brend° Cartage: *burned*
She was so ful of torment and of rage°   *madness*
That wilfully unto the fir she sterte,°   *jumped*
And brende hirselven with a stedefast herte.
    O woful hennes, right so criden ye
550 As, whan that Nero brende the citee
Of Rome, criden senatoures wives

8. The Book of Ecclesiasticus, in the Apocrypha.
9. Didn't care for.
1. I.e., population.
2. Friday is Venus's day.
3. Geoffrey of Vinsauf, a famous medieval rhetorician, who wrote a lament on the death of Richard I in which he scolded Friday, the day on which the king died.

4. I.e., a missile.
5. Thy wisdom and thy learning.
6. Pyrrhus was the Greek who slew Priam, king of Troy.
7. As the *Aeneid* tells us.
8. Hasdrubal was king of Carthage when it was destroyed by the Romans.

For that hir housbondes losten alle hir lives:[9]
Withouten gilt this Nero hath hem slain.
Now wol I turne to my tale again.
555 The sely° widwe and eek hir doughtres two   *innocent*
Herden thise hennes crye and maken wo,
And out at dores sterten° they anoon,   *leapt*
And sien° the fox toward the grove goon,   *saw*
And bar upon his bak the cok away,
560 And criden, "Out, harrow,° and wailaway,   *help*
Ha, ha, the fox," and after him they ran,
And eek with staves many another man;
Ran Colle oure dogge, and Talbot and Gerland,[1]
And Malkin with a distaf in hir hand,
565 Ran cow and calf, and eek the verray hogges,
Sore aferd° for berking of the dogges   *frightened*
And shouting of the men and wommen eke.
They ronne° so hem thoughte hir herte breke;[2]   *ran*
They yelleden as feendes doon in helle;
570 The dokes° criden as men wolde hem quelle;°   *ducks/kill*
The gees for fere flowen° over the trees;   *flew*
Out of the hive cam the swarm of bees;
So hidous was the noise, a, benedicite,°   *bless me*
Certes, he Jakke Straw[3] and his meinee°   *company*
575 Ne made nevere shoutes half so shrille
Whan that they wolden any Fleming kille,
As thilke day was maad upon the fox:
Of bras they broughten bemes° and of box,°   *trumpets/boxwood*
Of horn, of boon,° in whiche they blewe and pouped,°   *bone/tooted*
580 And therwithal they skriked° and they houped°—   *shrieked/whooped*
It seemed as that hevene sholde falle.
    Now goode men, I praye you herkneth alle:
Lo, how Fortune turneth° sodeinly   *reverses, overturns*
The hope and pride eek of hir enemy.
585 This cok that lay upon the foxes bak,
In al his drede unto the fox he spak,
And saide, "Sire, if that I were as ye,
Yit sholde I sayn, as wis° God helpe me,   *surely*
'Turneth ayain, ye proude cherles alle!
590 A verray pestilence upon you falle!
Now am I come unto this wodes side,
Maugree your heed,[4] the cok shal here abide.
I wol him ete, in faith, and that anoon.' "
    The fox answerde, "In faith, it shal be doon."
595 And as he spak that word, al sodeinly
The cok brak from his mouth deliverly,°   *nimbly*
And hye upon a tree he fleigh° anoon.   *flew*
    And whan the fox sawgh that he was agoon,

---

9. According to the legend, Nero not only set fire
to Rome (in 64 C.E.) but also put many senators to
death.
1. Two other dogs.
2. Would break.

3. One of the leaders of the Uprising of 1381,
which was partially directed against the Flemings
living in London.
4. Despite your head—i.e., despite anything you
can do.

"Allas," quod he, "O Chauntecleer, allas!
600   I have to you," quod he, "ydoon trespas,
In as muche as I maked you aferd
When I you hente° and broughte out of the yeerd.   seized
But sire, I dide it in no wikke° entente: wicked
Come down, and I shal telle you what I mente.
605   I shal saye sooth to you, God help me so."
        "Nay thanne," quod he, "I shrewe° us bothe two: curse
But first I shrewe myself, bothe blood and bones,
If thou bigile me ofter than ones;
Thou shalt namore thurgh thy flaterye
610   Do° me to singe and winken with myn yëe.   cause
For he that winketh whan he sholde see,
Al wilfully, God lat him nevere thee."°   prosper
        "Nay," quod the fox, "but God yive him meschaunce
That is so undiscreet of governaunce°   self-control
615   That jangleth° whan he sholde holde his pees."   chatters
        Lo, swich it is for to be reccheless°   careless
And necligent and truste on flaterye.
But ye that holden this tale a folye
As of a fox, or of a cok and hen,
620   Taketh the moralitee, goode men.
For Saint Paul saith that al that writen is
To oure doctrine it is ywrit, ywis:[5]
Taketh the fruit, and lat the chaf be stille.[6]
Now goode God, if that it be thy wille,
625   As saith my lord, so make us alle goode men,
And bringe us to his hye blisse. Amen.

Close of *Canterbury Tales*

Close of *Canterbury Tales*   At the end of *The Canterbury Tales*, Chaucer invokes a common allegorical theme, that life on earth is a pilgrimage. As Chaucer puts it in his moral ballade *Truth* (p. 315), "Here in noon home . . . / Forth, pilgrim, forth!" In the final fragment, he makes explicit a metaphor that has been implicit all along in the journey to Canterbury. The pilgrims never arrive at the shrine of St. Thomas, but in *The Parson's Tale*, and in its short introduction and in the "Retraction" that follows it, Chaucer seems to be making an end for two pilgrimages that had become one, that of his fiction and that of his life.

In the introduction to the tale we find the twenty-nine pilgrims moving through a nameless little village as the sun sinks to within twenty-nine degrees of the horizon. The atmosphere contains something of both the chill and the urgency of a late autumn afternoon, and we are surprised to find that the pilgrimage is almost over, that there is need for haste to make that "good end" that every medieval Christian hoped for. This delicately suggestive passage, rich with allegorical overtones, introduces an extremely long penitential treatise, translated by Chaucer from Latin or French sources. Although often assumed to be an earlier work, it may well have been written by Chaucer to provide the ending for *The Canterbury Tales*.

In the "Retraction" that follows *The Parson's Tale*, Chaucer acknowledges, lists,

5. See Romans 15.4.
6. The "fruit" refers to the kernel of moral or doctrinal meaning; the "chaf," or husk, is the narrative
containing that meaning. The metaphor was commonly applied to scriptural interpretation.

revokes, and asks forgiveness for his "giltes" (that is, his sins), which consist of having written most of the works on which his reputation as a great poet depends. He thanks Christ and Mary for his religious and moral works. One need not take this as evidence of a spiritual crisis or conversion at the end of his life. The "Retraction" seems to have been written to appear at the end of *The Canterbury Tales*, without censoring any of the tales deemed to be sinful. At the same time, one need not question Chaucer's sincerity. A readiness to deny his own reality before the reality of his God is implicit in many of Chaucer's works, and the placement of the "Retraction" within or just outside the border of the fictional pilgrimage suggests that although Chaucer finally rejected his fictions, he recognized that he and they were inseparable.

From The Parson's Tale

The Introduction

By that[1] the Manciple hadde his tale al ended,
The sonne fro the south line[2] was descended
So lowe, that he has nat to my sighte
Degrees nine and twenty as in highte.
5 Four of the clokke it was, so as I gesse,
For elevene foot, or litel more or lesse,
My shadwe was at thilke time as there,
Of swich feet as° my lengthe parted° were   *as if/divided*
In sixe feet equal of proporcioun.[3]
10 Therwith the moones exaltacioun[4]—
I mene Libra—always gan ascende,
As we were entring at a thropes° ende.   *village's*
For which oure Host, as he was wont to gie°   *lead*
As in this caas oure joly compaignye,
15 Saide in this wise, "Lordinges everichoon,
Now lakketh us no tales mo than oon:
Fulfild is my sentence° and my decree;   *purpose*
I trowe° that we han herd of ech degree;   *believe*
Almost fulfild is al myn ordinaunce.
20 I praye to God, so yive him right good chaunce
That telleth this tale to us lustily.
Sire preest," quod he, "artou a vicary,°   *vicar*
Or arte a Person? Say sooth, by thy fay.°   *faith*
Be what thou be, ne breek° thou nat oure play,   *break*
25 For every man save thou hath told his tale.
Unbokele and shew us what is in thy male!°   *bag*
For trewely, me thinketh by thy cheere°   *expression*
Thou sholdest knitte up wel a greet matere.
Tel us a fable anoon, for cokkes bones!"[5]
30   This Person answerde al atones,°   *immediately*
"Thou getest fable noon ytold for me,
For Paul, that writeth unto Timothee,
Repreveth° hem that waiven soothfastnesse,[6]   *reproves*

---

1. By the time that.
2. I.e., the line that runs some 28° to the south of the celestial equator and parallel to it.
3. This detailed analysis merely says that the shadows are lengthening.
4. I.e., the astrological sign in which the moon's influence was dominant.
5. Cock's bones, a euphemism for God's bones.
6. Depart from truth (see 1 Timothy 1.4).

And tellen fables and swich wrecchednesse.
35 Why sholde I sowen draf° out of my fest,°   *chaff/fist*
Whan I may sowen whete if that me lest?[7]
For which I saye that if you list to heere
Moralitee and vertuous matere,
And thanne that ye wol yive me audience,
40 I wol ful fain,° at Cristes reverence,   *gladly*
Do you plesance leveful° as I can.   *lawful*
But trusteth wel, I am a southren man:
I can nat geeste Rum-Ram-Ruf by lettre[8]—
Ne, God woot, rym holde° I but litel bettre.   *consider*
45 And therfore, if you list—I wol nat glose[9]—
I wol you telle a merye tale in prose
To knitte up al this feeste and make an ende.
And Jesu for his grace wit me sende
To shewe you the way in this viage°   *journey*
50 Of thilke parfit glorious pilgrimage
That highte° Jerusalem celestial.   *is called*
And if ye vouche sauf, anoon I shal
Biginne upon my tale, for which I praye
Telle youre avis:° I can no bettre saye.   *opinion*
55 But nathelees, this meditacioun
I putte it ay under correccioun
Of clerkes, for I am nat textuel:[1]
I take but the sentence,° trusteth wel.   *meaning*
Therefore I make protestacioun°   *public acknowledgment*
60 That I wol stonde to correccioun."
    Upon this word we han assented soone,
For, as it seemed, it was for to doone[2]
To enden in som vertuous sentence,°   *doctrine*
And for to yive him space° and audience;   *time*
65 And bede[3] oure Host he sholde to him saye
That alle we to telle his tale him praye.
    Oure Hoste hadde the wordes for us alle:
"Sire preest," quod he, "now faire you bifalle:
Telleth," quod he, "youre meditacioun.
70 But hasteth you; the sonne wol adown.
Beeth fructuous,° and that in litel space,°   *fruitful/time*
And to do wel God sende you his grace.
Saye what you list, and we wol gladly heere."
And with that word he saide in this manere.

---

7. It pleases me.
8. I.e., I cannot tell stories in the alliterative measure (without rhyme): this form of poetry was not
common in southeastern England.

9. I.e., speak in order to please.
1. Literal, faithful to the letter.
2. Necessary to be done.
3. I.e., we bade.

Chaucer's Retraction

Here taketh the makere of this book his leve[4]

Now praye I to hem alle that herkne this litel tretis[5] or rede, that if ther
be any thing in it that liketh[6] hem, that therof they thanken oure Lord Jesu
Crist, of whom proceedeth al wit[7] and al goodnesse. And if ther be any thing
that displese hem, I praye hem also that they arrette it to the defaute of myn
unconning,[8] and nat to my wil, that wolde ful fain have said bettre if I hadde
had conning. For oure book saith, "Al that is writen is writen for oure doctrine,"[9] and that is myn entente. Wherfore I biseeke[1] you mekely, for the
mercy of God, that ye praye for me that Crist have mercy on me and foryive
me my giltes, and namely of my translacions and enditinges[2] of worldly vanitees, the whiche I revoke in my retraccions: as is the *Book of Troilus;* the
Book also of *Fame;* the *Book of the Five and Twenty Ladies;*[3] the *Book of the
Duchesse;* the *Book of Saint Valentines Day of the Parlement of Briddes;* the
Tales of Canterbury, thilke that sounen into[4] sinne; the *Book of the Leon;*[5]
and many another book, if they were in my remembrance, and many a song
and many a leccherous lay: that Crist for his grete mercy foryive me the
sinne. But of the translacion of Boece[6] *De Consolatione,* and othere bookes
of legendes of saintes, and omelies,[7] and moralitee, and devocion, that
thanke I oure Lord Jesu Crist and his blisful Moder and alle the saintes of
hevene, biseeking hem that they from hennes[8] forth unto my lives ende sende
me grace to biwaile my giltes and to studye to the salvacion of my soule, and
graunte me grace of verray penitence, confession, and satisfaccion to doon
in this present lif, thurgh the benigne grace of him that is king of kinges and
preest over alle preestes, that boughte[9] us with the precious blood of his
herte, so that I may been oon of hem at the day of doom that shulle be saved.
Qui cum patre et Spiritu Sancto vivit et regnas Deus per omnia saecula.[1]
Amen.

1386–1400

LYRICS AND OCCASIONAL VERSE

In addition to his narrative verse, Chaucer wrote lyric poetry on the models of famous
French and Italian poets who made lyric into a medieval art form aimed at learned
and aristocratic audiences, an audience that included fellow poets. Chaucer also
embedded lyric in narrative poetry. As an example of courtly lyric, we print a "song"
that Troilus, the hero of Chaucer's romance *Troilus and Criseyde,* makes up about
his violent and puzzling emotions after falling in love. The "song" is actually Chaucer's

4. "Chaucer's Retraction" is the title given to this
passage by modern editors. The heading, "Here . . .
leve," which does appear in all manuscripts, may
be by Chaucer himself or by a scribe.
5. Hear this little treatise, i.e., *The Parson's Tale.*
6. Pleases.
7. Understanding.
8. Ascribe it to the defect of my lack of skill.
9. Romans 15.4.
1. Beseech.

2. Compositions. "Namely": especially.
3. I.e., the *Legend of Good Women.*
4. Those that tend toward.
5. The *Book of the Lion* has not been preserved.
6. Boethius.
7. Homilies.
8. Hence.
9. Redeemed.
1. Who with the Father and the Holy Spirit livest
and reignest God forever.

translation into rhyme royal of one of Petrarch's sonnets, more than a century before Sir Thomas Wyatt introduced the sonnet form itself to England. In the fifteenth century, Troilus's song was sometimes excerpted and included in anthologies of lyric poetry.

Chaucer also wrote homiletic ballades, one of which is entitled *Truth* by modern editors and called "ballade de bon conseil" (ballade of good advice) in some manuscripts. A ballade is a verse form of three or more stanzas, each with an identical rhyme scheme and the same last line, the refrain. Often a ballade ends with a shorter final stanza called an *envoy* in which the poem is addressed or sent to a friend or patron, or, conventionally, to a "prince" or "princes" in general. The good advice of *Truth* is to abandon worldly pursuits of wealth and power and to concentrate on the pilgrimage that leads to our true home in heaven. There are many copies of *Truth* with only this heartfelt advice. The one printed below contains a unique humorous *envoy*, addressed to a "Vache" (French for "cow"), who is probably a Sir Philip de la Vache.

A single stanza *To His Scribe Adam* comically conveys Chaucer's exasperation at the sloppy work of a professional copyist. The *Complaint to His Purse* is a parody of a lover's complaint to his lady: Ladies, like coins, should be golden, and, like purses, they should not be "light" (i.e., fickle). *Purse* survives both without and with an *envoy*. The addressee in the latter case is the recently crowned Henry IV, who is being wittily implored to restore payment of Chaucer's annuity, which had been interrupted by the new king's deposition of Richard II.

Troilus's Song[1]

If no love is, O God, what feele I so?
And if love, is, what thing and which is he?
If love be good, from whennes cometh my wo?
If it be wikke,° a wonder thinketh° me,   *miserable/it seems to*
5 Whan every torment and adversitee
That cometh of him may to me savory° thinke,°   *pleasant/seem*
For ay° thurste I, the more that ich° drinke.   *always/I*

And if that at myn owene lust° I brenne,°   *desire/burn*
From whennes cometh my wailing and my plainte?°   *complaint*
10 If harm agree° me, wherto plaine° I thenne?   *agrees with/complain*
I noot,° ne why unwery° that I fainte.   *know not/not weary*
O quikke° deeth, O sweete harm so quainte,°   *living/strange*
How may° of thee in me swich quantitee,   *can there be*
But if that I consente that it be?

15 And if that I consente, I wrongfully
Complaine: ywis,° thus possed° to and fro   *indeed/tossed*
All stereles° within a boot° am I   *rudderless/boat*
Amidde the see, bitwixen windes two,
That in contrarye stonden everemo.
20 Allas, what is this wonder maladye?
For hoot° of cold, for cold of hoot I die.   *hot*

---

1. *Troilus and Criseyde*, Book 1, lines 400–420. A translation of Petrarch's Sonnet 88, "S'amor non è."

Truth[1]

Flee fro the prees° and dwelle with soothfastnesse;   *crowd*
Suffise unto° thy thing, though it be smal;   *be content with*
For hoord hath[2] hate, and climbing tikelnesse;°   *insecurity*
Prees hath envye, and wele° blent° overal.   *prosperity/blinds*
5   Savoure° no more than thee bihoove shal;   *relish*
Rule wel thyself that other folk canst rede:°   *advise*
And Trouthe shal delivere,[3] it is no drede.°   *doubt*

Tempest thee nought al crooked to redresse[4]
In trust of hire[5] that turneth as a bal;
10   Muche wele stant in litel bisinesse;[6]
Be war therfore to spurne ayains an al.[7]
Strive nat as dooth the crokke° with the wal.   *pot*
Daunte° thyself that dauntest otheres deede: *master*
And Trouthe shal delivere, it is no drede.

15   That° thee is sent, receive in buxomnesse;°   *what/obedience*
The wrastling for the world axeth° a fal;   *asks for*
Here is noon hoom, here nis° but wildernesse: *is not*
Forth, pilgrim, forth! Forth, beest, out of thy stal!
Know thy countree, looke up, thank God of al.
20   Hold the heigh way and lat thy gost° thee lede: *spirit*
And Trouthe shal delivere, it is no drede.

Envoy

Therfore, thou Vache,[8] leve thyn olde wrecchednesse
Unto the world; leve° now to be thral.   *i.e., cease*
Crye him mercy° that of his heigh goodnesse   *thank him*
25   Made thee of nought, and in especial
Draw unto him, and pray in general,
For thee and eek for othere, hevenelich meede:[9]
And Trouthe shal delivere, it is no drede.

To His Scribe Adam[1]

Adam scrivain,° if evere it thee bifalle   *scribe*
Boece or *Troilus*[2] for to writen newe,

---

1. Taking as his theme Christ's words to his disciples (in John 8.32), "And ye shall know the truth, and the truth shall make you free," Chaucer plays on the triple meaning that the Middle English word *trouthe* seems to have had for him: the religious truth of Christianity, the moral virtue of integrity, and the philosophical idea of reality. By maintaining one's faith and one's integrity, one rises superior to the vicissitudes of this world and comes eventually to know reality—which is not, however, of this world.
2. Hoarding causes.
3. I.e., truth shall make you free.
4. Do not disturb yourself to straighten all that's crooked.

5. Fortune, who turns like a ball in that she is always presenting a different aspect to people.
6. Peace of mind stands in little anxiety.
7. Awl, i.e., "don't kick against the pricks," wound yourself by kicking a sharp instrument.
8. Probably Sir Philip de la Vache, with a pun on the French for "cow."
9. Reward, with a pun on *meadow*.
1. Chaucer had fair copies of longer works made by a professional scribe. This humorous complaint about Adam's sloppy work is written in the verse form of Chaucer's great poem *Troilus and Criseyde*.
2. *Troilus and Criseyde*. "Boece": i.e., Chaucer's translation of Boethius's *De Consolatione*.

Under thy longe lokkes thou moste[3] have the scalle,°   scurf
But after my making thou write more trewe,[4]
5 So ofte a day I moot° thy werk renewe,   must
It to correcte, and eek to rubbe and scrape:
And al is thurgh thy necligence and rape.°   haste

Complaint to His Purse

To you, my purs, and to noon other wight,°   person
Complaine I, for ye be my lady dere.
I am so sory, now that ye be light,
For certes, but if° ye make me hevy cheere,   unless
5 Me were as lief[1] be laid upon my beere;°   bier
For which unto youre mercy thus I crye:
Beeth hevy again, or elles moot° I die.   must

Now voucheth sauf° this day er° it be night   grant / before
That I of you the blisful soun may heere,
10 Or see youre colour, lik the sonne bright,
That of yelownesse hadde nevere peere.°   equal
Ye be my life, ye be myn hertes steere,°   rudder, guide
Queene of confort and of good compaignye:
Beeth hevy again, or elles moot I die.

15 Ye purs, that been to me my lives light
And saviour, as in this world down here,
Out of this towne[2] helpe me thurgh your might,
Sith that ye wol nat be my tresorere;°   treasurer
For I am shave as neigh as any frere.[3]
20 But yit I praye unto youre curteisye:
Beeth hevy again, or elles moot I die.

Envoy to Henry IV

O conquerour of Brutus Albioun,[4]
Which that by line° and free eleccioun   lineage
Been verray° king, this song to you I sende: true
25 And ye, that mowen° alle oure harmes amende,   may
Have minde upon my supplicacioun.

---

3. I.e., may you.
4. Unless you write more accurately what I've
composed.
1. I'd just as soon.
2. Probably Westminster, where Chaucer had
rented a house.

3. Shaved as close as any (tonsured) friar, an
expression for being broke.
4. Britain (Albion) was supposed to have been
founded by Brutus, the grandson of Aeneas, the
founder of Rome.

WILLIAM LANGLAND
ca. 1330–1387

William Langland is agreed by most scholars to be the sole author of a long religious allegory in alliterative verse known as *The Vision of Piers Plowman* or more simply *Piers Plowman*, which survives in three distinct versions that scholars refer to as the A-, B-, and C-texts. The first, about twenty-four hundred lines long, breaks off at a rather inconclusive point in the action; the second is a revision of the first plus an extension of more than four thousand lines; and the third is a revision of the second. About Langland we know hardly anything except what can be inferred from the poem itself. He came from the west of England and was probably a native of the Malvern Hills area in which the opening of the poem is set. We can never identify the persona of the narrator of a medieval text positively or precisely with its author, especially when we are dealing with allegory. Nevertheless, a passage that was added to the C-text, the last of the selections printed here, gives the strong impression of being at one and the same time an allegory in which the narrator represents willful Mankind and a poignantly ironic self-portrait of the stubborn-willed poet who occasionally plays on his own name: "I have lived in *land* . . . my name is *Long Will*" (15.152). In this new episode the narrator tries to defend his shiftless way of life against Conscience and Reason, presumably his own conscience and reason. Conscience dismisses his specious argument that a clerical education has left him no "tools" to support himself with except for his prayer book and the Psalms with which he prays for the souls of those from whom he begs alms. The entire work conforms well with the notion that its author was a man who was educated to enter the church but who, through marriage and lack of preferment, was reduced to poverty and may well have wandered in his youth like those "hermits" he scornfully describes in the prologue.

Piers Plowman has the form of a dream vision, a common medieval type in which the author presents the story under the guise of having dreamed it. The dream vision generally involves allegory, not only because one expects from a dream the unrealistic, the fanciful, but also because people have always suspected that dreams relate the truth in disguised form—that they are natural allegories. Through a series of such visions it traces the Dreamer-narrator's tough-minded, persistent, and passionate search for answers to his many questions, especially the question he puts early in the poem to Lady Holy Church: "How I may save my soul." Langland's theme is nothing less than the history of Christianity as it unfolds both in the world of the Old and New Testaments and in the life and heart of an individual fourteenth-century Christian—two seemingly distinct realms between which the poet's allegory moves with dizzying rapidity.

The first selection, from the prologue to the poem, introduces the famous vision of the Field of Folk. The poet describes fourteenth-century English society in terms of its failure to represent an ideal society living in accord with Christian principles; hence the satirical poetry for which Langland is noted. Society's failure, of course, is attributable in part to the corruption of the church and ecclesiastics, and whenever he considers clerical corruption, he pours out savagely indignant satire. But he is equally angry with the failure of the wealthy laity—untaught by the church to practice charity—to alleviate the sufferings of the poor.

After his vision of the Field of Folk, the Dreamer in *Passus 1* (*Passus*, Latin for "step," is the word the poet uses for the sections of his poem) is approached by Lady Holy Church, who explains to him the fundamental principles of Christianity with which, presumably, he has been familiar since childhood. But mere knowledge is not enough for him: he must learn by experience and feel in his heart what he learns—a process that takes up the rest of the poem. The departure of Lady Holy Church is followed by the vision of Lady Meed whose name has the basically neutral meaning of "reward" or "pay" but who in Langland's often scathing satire represents "bribery" or "graft" in state and church. Lady Meed is about to be married to a figure named False over the protests of Conscience. The episode presents Langland's mordant view of a country being bled by a swarm of greedy and corrupt officials but holds out some hope that the king with the counsel of Conscience and Reason may yet bring about reforms.

At the beginning of *Passus* 5 the Dreamer awakes for the first time, but after a very short interval he falls asleep again and dreams that Reason preaches a sermon to the whole kingdom, causing the people to confess their sins. Langland describes the confession by personifying the seven deadly sins and having each one relate to the personified figure Repentance how badly he behaves in society. The confessions of Envy and Gluttony, included in the second selection, display most clearly Langland's social realism.

In the third and fourth selections, which comprise the conclusion of *Passus* 5 and most of *Passus* 6, the prayer of Repentance inspires Hope (personified as a trumpeter) to move the people to set out blindly in search of Truth, a figure for God or Christ, but there is no one to show them the way. At this point Piers Plowman, the titular hero, makes his first appearance. Piers explains that the "way" to Saint Truth leads through the two "great" commandments of Matthew 22.37–39 (to love God and thy neighbor) and the Ten Commandments, and he offers himself as the people's guide. First, however, all must help Piers plow his half acre. The episode is a brilliant allegory of how people in the ideal community should work together for the common good but how the actual society breaks down, especially in times of plenty. The only effective enforcer of social order is not the knight, who represents the ruling class, but Hunger, a grim figure that graphically portrays the ravages of famine during the fourteenth century.

Passus 18 describes the central event of Christianity, Christ's crucifixion, followed by an account of the descent into hell, traditionally called the "Harrowing of Hell." The Dreamer has come a long way in his personal search for Truth, and this vision is the most immediate and fulfilling answer to the questions he addressed to Lady Holy Church, although not a final answer, for in Langland's poem the search has no end in this life. Piers, who in earlier appearances had assumed aspects of Adam, Moses, and the Good Samaritan, is now partially identified with Christ. With this development his farm produce is no longer simple foodstuffs, but becomes the souls of the patriarchs and prophets, and of all humankind, which must be redeemed from the devil's power by Christ's sacrifice on the cross. In lines 20 and 33 these souls are referred to as the "fruit" of Piers Plowman, which Christ, having assumed Piers's human nature, will win back from hell, where it has been since Adam's sin. Langland describes the crucifixion as a literal, historical event, yet at the same time he speaks of it as if it were a medieval joust between the Christ-knight and an adversary. After Christ dies on the cross, the Dreamer hears an argument among the "Four Daughters of God" (personifications taken from Psalm 85.10) about the validity and efficacy of Christ's sacrifice: Righteousness and Truth maintain that the Old Law condemns mankind irredeemably, while Mercy and Peace prophesy that by Christ's New Law man will be saved. Christ appears before hell's gates as a great light, the devils are thrown into confusion, and the souls of the righteous are released from hell's power. The four Daughters of God are reconciled as the New Law fulfills the Old, and the Dreamer wakes to celebrate Easter with his family.

A large number of manuscripts and two sixteenth-century editions show that *Piers Plowman* was avidly read and studied by a great many people from the end of the fourteenth century to the reign of Elizabeth I. Some of these readers have left a record of their engagement with the poem in marginal comments. Almost from the first, it was a controversial text. Within four years of the writing of the second version— which scholars have good evidence to date 1377, the year of Edward III's death and Richard II's accession to the throne—it had become so well known that the leaders of the Uprising of 1381 used phrases borrowed from it as part of the rhetoric of the rebellion. Langland's sympathy with the sufferings of the poor and his indignant satire of official corruption undoubtedly made his poem popular with the rebels, although he himself, despite his interest in social reform, remained a fundamentally conservative and orthodox thinker. The passionate sympathy for the commoner, idealized in *Piers Plowman,* also appealed to reformers who felt that true religion was best represented not by the ecclesiastical hierarchy but by the humblest orders of society. Many persons reading his poem in the sixteenth century (it was first printed in 1550) saw in *Piers Plowman* a prophecy and forerunner of the English Reformation. Immersed as it is in thorny political and theological controversies of its own day, *Piers Plowman* is arguably the most difficult and, at times, even the most frustrating of Middle English texts, but its poetic, intellectual, and moral complexity and integrity also make it one of the most rewarding.

From The Vision of Piers Plowman[1]

From *The Prologue*

[THE FIELD OF FOLK]

In a summer season when the sun was mild
I clad myself in clothes as I'd become a sheep;
In the habit of a hermit unholy of works,[2]
Walked wide in this world, watching for wonders.
5   And on a May morning, on Malvern Hills,
There befell me as by magic a marvelous thing:
I was weary of wandering and went to rest
At the bottom of a broad bank by a brook's side,
And as I lay lazily looking in the water
10 I slipped into a slumber, it sounded so pleasant.
There came to me reclining there a most curious dream
That I was in a wilderness, nowhere that I knew;
But as I looked into the east, up high toward the sun,
I saw a tower on a hill-top, trimly built,
15 A deep dale beneath, a dungeon tower in it,
With ditches deep and dark and dreadful to look at.
A fair field full of folk I found between them,
Of human beings of all sorts, the high and the low,
Working and wandering as the world requires.
20   Some applied themselves to plowing, played very rarely,
Sowing seeds and setting plants worked very hard;
Won what wasters gluttonously consume.
And some pursued pride, put on proud clothing,
Came all got up in garments garish to see.
25 To prayers and penance many put themselves,
All for love of our Lord lived hard lives,
Hoping thereafter to have Heaven's bliss—
Such as hermits and anchorites that hold to their cells,

---

1. The translation is by E. T. Donaldson (1990) and is based on *Piers Plowman: The B Version,* edited by George Kane and E. T. Donaldson (1975).

2. For Langland's opinion of hermits, see lines 28–30 and 53–57. The sheep's clothing may suggest the habit's physical resemblance to sheep's wool as well as a false appearance of innocence.

Don't care to go cavorting about the countryside,
30   With some lush livelihood delighting their bodies.
And some made themselves merchants—they managed better,
As it seems to our sight that such men prosper.
And some make mirth as minstrels can
And get gold for their music, guiltless, I think.
35   But jokers and word jugglers, Judas' children,[3]
Invent fantasies to tell about and make fools of themselves,
And have whatever wits they need to work if they wanted.
What Paul preaches of them I don't dare repeat here:
Qui loquitur turpiloquium[4] is Lucifer's henchman.
40   Beadsmen[5] and beggars bustled about
Till both their bellies and their bags were crammed to the brim;
Staged flytings[6] for their food, fought over beer.
In gluttony, God knows, they go to bed
And rise up with ribaldry, those Robert's boys.°   i.e., robbers
45   Sleep and sloth pursue them always.
      Pilgrims and palmers[7] made pacts with each other
To seek Saint James[8] and saints at Rome.
They went on their way with many wise stories,
And had leave to lie all their lives after.
50   I saw some that said they'd sought after saints:
In every tale they told their tongues were tuned to lie
More than to tell the truth—such talk was theirs.
A heap of hermits with hooked staffs
Went off to Walsingham,[9] with their wenches behind them.
55   Great long lubbers that don't like to work
Dressed up in cleric's dress to look different from other men
And behaved as they were hermits, to have an easy life.
I found friars there—all four of the orders[1]—
Preaching to the people for their own paunches' welfare,
60   Making glosses° of the Gospel that would look good for   interpretations
      themselves;
Coveting copes,[2] they construed it as they pleased.
Many of these Masters[3] may clothe themselves richly,
For their money and their merchandise[4] march hand in hand.
Since Charity[5] has proved a peddler and principally shrives lords,
65   Many marvels have been manifest within a few years.
Unless Holy Church and friars' orders hold together better,
The worst misfortune in the world will be welling up soon.

---

3. Minstrels who entertain with jokes and fantastic stories are regarded as descendants of Christ's betrayer, Judas.

4. Who speaks filthy language. Not Paul, though cf. Ephesians 5.3–4.

5. Prayer sayers, i.e., people who offered to say prayers, sometimes counted on the beads of the rosary, for the souls of those who gave them alms.

6. Contests in which the participants took turns insulting each other, preferably in verse.

7. Virtually professional pilgrims who took advantage of the hospitality offered them to go on traveling year after year (see p. 215, n. 6).

8. I.e., his shrine at Compostela in Spain.

9. English town, site of a famous shrine to the Virgin Mary.

1. In Langland's day there were four orders of friars in England: Franciscans, Dominicans, Carmelites, and Augustinians.

2. Monks', friars', and hermits' capes.

3. I.e., masters of divinity.

4. The "merchandise" sold by the friars for money is shrift, that is, confession and remission of sins, which by canon law cannot be sold.

5. The ideal of the friars, as stated by St. Francis, was simply love, i.e., charity.

A pardoner[6] preached there as if he had priest's rights,
Brought out a bull[7] with bishop's seals,
70 And said he himself could absolve them all
Of failure to fast, of vows they'd broken.
Unlearned men believed him and liked his words,
Came crowding up on knees to kiss his bulls.
He banged them with his brevet and bleared their eyes,[8]
75 And raked in with his parchment-roll rings and brooches.
Thus you give your gold for gluttons' well-being,
And squander it on scoundrels schooled in lechery.
If the bishop were blessed and worth both his ears,
His seal should not be sent out to deceive the people.
80 —It's nothing to the bishop that the blackguard preaches,
And the parish priest and the pardoner split the money
That the poor people of the parish would have but for them.
  Parsons and parish priests complained to the bishop
That their parishes were poor since the pestilence-time,[9]
85 Asked for license and leave to live in London,
And sing Masses there for simony,[1] for silver is sweet.

* * *

  Yet scores of men stood there in silken coifs
Who seemed to be law-sergeants[2] that served at the bar,
Pleaded cases for pennies and impounded[3] the law,
And not for love of our Lord once unloosed their lips:
215 You might better measure mist on Malvern Hills
Than get a "mum" from their mouths till money's on the table.
Barons and burgesses[4] and bondmen also
I saw in this assemblage, as you shall hear later;
Bakers and brewers and butchers aplenty.
220 Weavers of wool and weavers of linen,
Tailors, tinkers, tax-collectors in markets,
Masons, miners, many other craftsmen.
Of all living laborers there leapt forth some,
Such as diggers of ditches that do their jobs badly,
225 And dawdle away the long day with *"Dieu save dame Emme."*[5]
Cooks and their kitchen-boys crying, "Hot pies, hot!
Good geese and pork! Let's go and dine!"
Tavern-keepers told them a tale of the same sort:
"White wine of Alsace and wine of Gascony,

---

6. An official empowered to pass on from the pope temporal indulgence for the sins of people who contributed to charitable enterprises—a function frequently abused.
7. Papal license to act as a pardoner, endorsed with the local bishop's seals.
8. I.e., pulled the wool over their eyes. "Brevet": pardoner's license.
9. Since 1349 England had suffered a number of epidemics of the plague, the Black Death, which had caused famine and depopulated the countryside.
1. Buying and selling the functions, spiritual powers, or offices of the church. Wealthy persons, especially in London, set up foundations to pay

priests to sing masses for their souls and those of their relatives (see the portrait of Chaucer's Parson, p. 227, lines 509–12).
2. Important lawyers (see *The General Prologue* to *The Canterbury Tales*, p. 222, lines 311ff.). "Coifs": a silk scarf was a lawyer's badge of office.
3. Detained in legal custody. Pennies were fairly valuable coins in medieval England.
4. Town dwellers who had full rights as the citizens of a municipality. In contrast, barons were members of the upper nobility, and bondmen were peasants who held their land from a lord in return for customary services or rent.
5. "God save Dame Emma," presumably a popular song.

230   Of the Rhine and of La Rochelle, to wash the roast down with."
All this I saw sleeping, and seven times more.

From *Passus* 5

[THE CONFESSION OF ENVY]

75   Envy with heavy heart asked for shrift
And grieving for his guilt began his confession.
He was pale as a sheep's pelt, appeared to have the palsy.
He was clothed in a coarse cloth—I couldn't describe it—
A tabard[6] and a tunic, a knife tied to his side,
80   Like those of a friar's frock were the foresleeves.
Like a leek that had lain long in the sun
So he looked with lean cheeks, louring foully.
His body was so blown up for anger that he bit his lips
And shook his fist fiercely, he wanted to avenge himself
85   With acts or with words when he saw his chance.
Every syllable he spat out was of a serpent's tongue;
From chiding and bringing charges was his chief livelihood,
With backbiting and bitter scorn and bearing false witness.
This was all his courtesy wherever he showed himself.
90   "I'd like to be shriven," said this scoundrel, "if shame would let me.
By God, I'd be gladder that Gib had bad luck
Than if I'd won this week a wey[7] of Essex cheese.
I've a neighbor dwelling next door, I've done him harm often
And blamed him behind his back to blacken his name.
95   I've done my best to damage him day after day
And lied to lords about him to make him lose money,
And turned his friends into his foes with my false tongue.
His good luck and his glad lot grieve me greatly.
Between household and household I often start disputes
100   So that both life and limb are lost for my speech.
When I met the man in market that I most hated,
I fondled him affectionately as if I were a friend of his:
He is stronger than I am—I don't dare harm him.
But if I had might and mastery I'd murder him once for all.
105   When I come to kirk° and kneel before Christ's Cross   *church*
To pray for the people as the priest teaches,
For pilgrims, for palmers, for all the people after,
Then crouching there I call on Christ to give him sorrow
That took away my tankard and my torn sheet.[8]
110   Away from the altar I turn my eyes
And notice how Heinie has a new coat;
Then I wish it were mine and all the web[9] it came from.
And when he loses I laugh—that lightens my heart,
But when he wins I weep and wail the time.
115   I condemn men when they do evil, yet I do much worse;

---

6. A loose sleeveless jacket, worn over the tunic.
7. A very large measure.
8. The loss of Envy's tankard and torn sheet, and

his fury at it, have not been explained.
9. I.e., bolt of cloth.

Whoever upbraids me for that, I hate him deadly after.
I wish that every one were my servant,
And if any man has more than I, that angers my heart.
So I live loveless like a loathsome dog
120 So that all my breast is blown up for bitterness of spirit.
For many years I might not eat as a man ought
For envy and ill will are hard to digest.
Is there any sugar or sweet thing to assuage my swelling
Or any *diapenidion*[1] that will drive it from my heart,
125 Or any shrift or shame, unless I have my stomach scraped?"
     "Yes, readily," said Repentance, directing him to live better;
"Sorrow for sins is salvation for souls."
"I am sorry," said Envy. "I'm seldom anything else,
And that makes me so miserable, since I may not avenge myself.
130 I've been among burgesses buying at London
And made Backbiting a broker to blame men's wares.
When he sold and I didn't, then I was ready
To lie and lour at my neighbor and belittle his merchandise.
I will amend this if I may, by might of God almighty."

* * *

[THE CONFESSION OF GLUTTONY]

     Now Glutton begins to go to shrift
And takes his way towards the Church to tell his sins.
But Betty the brewer bade him good morning
And she asked him where he was going.
300 "To Holy Church," he said, "to hear Mass,
And then I shall be shriven and sin no more."
"I've got good ale, old friend," she said. "Glutton, will you try it?"
"Have you," he asked, "any hot spices?"
"I have pepper and peony and a pound of garlic,
305 A farthingworth of fennel seed[2] for fasting days."
Then Glutton goes in, and great oaths after.
Cissy the seamstress was sitting on the bench,
Wat the warren-keeper° and his wife too,   *game warden*
Tim the tinker and two of his servants,
310 Hick the hackneyman and Hugh the needle-seller,
Clarice of Cock's Lane and the clerk of the church,
Sir Piers of Pridie and Parnel[3] of Flanders,
Dave the ditch-digger and a dozen others,
A rebeck-player, a rat-catcher, a street-raker of Cheapside,
315 A rope-maker, a redingking,[4] and Rose the dish vendor,
Godfrey of Garlickhithe and Griffin the Welshman,
A heap of old-clothesmen early in the morning
Gladly treated Glutton to drinks of good ale.

1. A twist of medicinal sugar.
2. This herb was considered good for one drinking on an empty stomach. "Peony": considered a spice in the Middle Ages.
3. Parnel and Clarice are prostitutes.

4. What a "redingking" was is not known. "Rebeck-player": fiddler. "Street-raker": scavenger, hence street cleaner. "Cheapside": a section of London.

Clement the cobbler took the coat off his back
320 And put it up as a prize for a player of "New Fair."⁵
Then Hick the ostler⁶ took off his hood
And bade Bart the butcher to be on his side.
Then peddlers were appointed to appraise the goods:
For his cloak Clement should get the hood plus compensation.
325 They went to work quickly and whispered together
And appraised these prize items apart by themselves.
There were heaps of oaths for any one to hear.
They couldn't in conscience come to an agreement
Till Robin the roper was requested to rise
330 And named as an umpire so no quarrel should break out.
Then Hick the ostler had the cloak
In covenant that Clement should have the cup filled
And have Hick the ostler's hood, and call it a deal;
The first to regret the agreement should get up straightway
335 And greet Sir Glutton with a gallon of ale.
There was laughing and louring and "Let go the cup!"
They began to make bets and bought more rounds
And sat so till evensong⁷ and sang sometimes
Till Glutton had gulped down a gallon and a gill.°   quarter pint
340 His guts began to grumble like two greedy sows;
He pissed four pints in a Paternoster's length,⁸
And on the bugle of his backside he blew a fanfare
So that all that heard that horn held their noses after
And wished it had been waxed up with a wisp of gorse.⁹
345 He had no strength to stand before he had his staff in hand,
And then he made off moving like a minstrel's bitch,¹
Some times sideways and some times backwards,
Like some one laying lines to lime birds with.²
But as he started to step to the door his sight grew dim;
350 He fumbled for the threshold and fell on the ground.
Clement the cobbler caught him by the waist
To lift him aloft and laid him on his knees.
But Glutton was a large lout and a load to lift,
And he coughed up a custard in Clement's lap.
355 There's no hound so hungry in Hertfordshire
That would dare lap up that leaving, so unlovely the taste.
    With all the woe of this world his wife and his maid
Brought him to his bed and bundled him in it.

---

5. This was a game in which two participants exchanged items in their possession that were not of equal value and hence involved a cash payment by the player who put up the less valuable object. Clement puts up his cloak and Hick, his hood; each chooses an agent to represent him in the evaluation of the objects, which is conducted by peddlers. Hick is represented by Bart, but because the evaluators are unable to agree, Robin is named as an umpire. It is decided that Hick should have Clement's cloak and Clement Hick's hood but that Clement should receive a cup of ale as well or perhaps the money for a cup of ale, which he would then share with all the participants. A fine of fur-ther ale would be placed on either of the men who grumbled at the exchange.
6. I.e., a stableman (called "hackneyman" above, implying that he keeps horses for hire).
7. Vespers, the evening prayer service said just before sunset.
8. I.e., the time it takes to say the Lord's Prayer.
9. A spiny shrub. "Waxed up": i.e., sealed.
1. I.e., a trained dog performing some feat (probably walking on her hind legs) with difficulty.
2. Birds were caught by smearing a sticky substance ("lime") on strings laid out on the ground. A bird catcher "laying lines" would move systematically right and left or forward and backward.

And after all this excess he had a fit of sloth
360 So that he slept Saturday and Sunday till the sun set.
When he was awake and had wiped his eyes,
The first word he spoke was, "Where is the bowl?"
His spouse scolded him for his sin and wickedness,
And right so Repentance rebuked him at that time.
365 "As with words as well as with deeds you've done evil in your life,
Shrive yourself and be ashamed, and show it with your mouth."
"I, Glutton," he began, "admit I'm guilty of this:
That I've trespassed with my tongue, I can't tell how often;
Sworn by God's soul and his sides and 'So God help me!'
370 When there was no need for it nine hundred times.
And over-stuffed myself at supper and sometimes at midday,
So that I, Glutton, got rid of it before I'd gone a mile,
And spoiled what might have been saved and dispensed to the hungry;
Over-indulgently on feast days I've drunk and eaten both;
375 And sometimes sat so long there that I slept and ate at once;
To hear tales in taverns I've taken more drink;
Fed myself before noon on fasting days."
"This full confession," said Repentance, "will gain favor for you."
Then Glutton began to groan and to make great lament
380 For the life he had lived in so loathsome a way,
And vowed he would fast, what for hunger or for thirst:
"Shall never fish on Friday be fed to my belly
Till Abstinence my aunt has given me leave,
And yet I have hated her all my lifetime."

[PIERS PLOWMAN SHOWS THE WAY TO SAINT TRUTH]

Then Hope took hold of a horn of *Deus tu conversus vivificabis nos*[3]
And blew it with *Beati quorum remissae sunt iniquitates,*[4]
So that all the saints sang for sinners at once,
*"Men and animals thou shalt save inasmuch as thou hast multiplied
thy mercy, O God."*[5]
510 A thousand men then thronged together,
Cried upward to Christ and to his clean mother
To have grace to go to Truth—God grant they might!
But there was no one so wise as to know the way thither,
But they blundered forth like beasts over banks and hills
515 Till they met a man, many hours later,
Appareled like a pagan[6] in pilgrims' manner.
He bore a stout staff with a broad strap around it,
In the way of woodbine wound all about.
A bowl and a bag he bore by his side.
520 A hundred holy water phials were set on his hat,
Souvenirs of Sinai and shells of Galicia,
And many a Cross on his cloak and keys of Rome,
And the vernicle in front so folk should know

---

3. O God, you will turn and give us life (from the Mass).
4. Blessed [are they] whose transgressions are forgiven (Psalms 32.1).
5. Psalms 36.6–7.
6. I.e., outlandishly. (Langland's word *paynym* was especially associated with Saracens, i.e., Arabs.)

By seeing his signs what shrines he'd been to.[7]
525 These folk asked him fairly from whence he came.
"From Sinai," he said, "and from the Holy Sepulchre.
Bethlehem, Babylon, I've been to both;
In Armenia, in Alexandria,[8] in many other places.
You can tell by the tokens attached to my hat
530 That I've walked far and wide in wet and in dry
And sought out good saints for my soul's health."
"Did you ever see a saint," said they, "that men call Truth?
Could you point out a path to where that person lives?"
"No, so God save me," said the fellow then.
535 "I've never known a palmer with knapsack or staff
To ask after him ere now in this place."
    "Peter!"[9] said a plowman, and put forth his head.
"We're as closely acquainted as a clerk and his books.
Conscience and Kind Wit[1] coached me to his place
540 And persuaded me to swear to him I'd serve him forever,
Both to sow and set plants so long as I can work.
I have been his follower all these forty winters,
Both sowed his seed and overseen his cattle,
Indoors and outdoors taken heed for his profit,
545 Made ditches and dikes, done what he bids.
Sometimes I sow and sometimes I thresh,
In tailor's craft and tinker's, whatever Truth can devise.
I weave wool and wind it and do what Truth says.
For though I say it myself, I serve him to his satisfaction.
550 I get good pay from him, and now and again more.
He's the promptest payer that poor men know.
He withholds no worker's wages so he's without them by evening.
He's as lowly as a lamb and lovely of speech.
And if you'd like to learn where that lord dwells,
555 I'll direct you on the road right to his palace."
"Yes, friend Piers,"[2] said these pilgrims, and proffered him pay.
"No, by the peril of my soul!" said Piers, and swore on oath:
"I wouldn't take a farthing's fee for Saint Thomas's shrine.[3]
Truth would love me the less a long time after.
560   But you that are anxious to be off, here's how you go:
You must go through Meekness, both men and women,
Till you come into Conscience[4] that Christ knows the truth

---

7. A pilgrim to Canterbury collected a phial of holy water from St. Thomas's shrine; collecting another every time one passed through Canterbury was a mark of a professional pilgrim. "Sinai": souvenirs from the Convent of St. Katharine on Sinai. "Shells": the emblem of St. James at Compostela, in Galicia. "Many a cross": commemorating trips to the Holy Land. "Keys": the sign of St. Peter's keys, from Rome. "Vernicle": a copy of the image of Christ's face preserved on a cloth, another famous relic from Rome. It was believed to have appeared after Veronica gave her head cloth to Christ, as he was going to execution, to wipe his face on.
8. "Babylon": near Cairo, where there was a church on the site where Mary lived during the Flight into Egypt. "Armenia": presumably to visit Mt. Ararat, where the Ark is said to have landed. "Alexandria": the site of the martyrdom of St. Catherine and St. Mark.
9. I.e., an oath "By St. Peter!"
1. Moral sense and natural intelligence (common sense).
2. I.e., Peter, hence the particular appropriateness of his swearing by St. Peter (line 537), a connection that Langland will exploit in a variety of ways.
3. The shrine of St. Thomas at Canterbury was famous for the gold and jewels offered by important pilgrims.
4. Consciousness, moral awareness, related to but not identical with the moral sense personified in line 539.

That you love our Lord God of all loves the most,
And next to him your neighbors—in no way harm them,
565 Otherwise than you'd have them behave to you.
And so follow along a brook's bank, Be-Modest-Of-Speech,
Until you find a ford, Do-Your-Fathers-Honor;
    Honor thy father and thy mother, etc.[5]
Wade in that water and wash yourselves well there
And you'll leap the lighter all your lifetime.
570 So you shall see Swear-Not-Unless-It-Is-For-Need-
And-Namely-Never-Take-In-Vain-The-Name-Of-God-Almighty.
Then you'll come to a croft,[6] but don't come into it:
The croft is called Covet-Not-Men's-Cattle-Nor-Their-Wives
And-None-Of-Your-Neighbor's-Serving-Men-So-As-To-Harm-Them.
575 See that you break no boughs there unless they belong to you.
Two wooden statues stand there, but don't stop for them:
They're called Steal-Not and Slay-Not: stay away from both;
Leave them on your left hand and don't look back.
And hold well your holiday until the high evening.[7]
580 Then you shall blench at a barrow,[8] Bear-No-False-Witness:
It's fenced in with florins and other fees aplenty.
See that you pluck no plant there for peril of your soul.
Then you shall see Speak-The-Truth-So-It-Must-Be-Done-
And-Not-In-Any-Other-Way-Not-For-Any-Man's-Asking.
585 Then you shall come to a castle shining clear as the sun.
The moat is made of mercy, all about the manor;
And all the walls are of wit° to hold will out.   *reason*
The crenelations are of Christendom to save Christiankind,
Buttressed with Believe-So-Or-You-Won't-Be-Saved;
590 And all the houses are roofed, halls and chambers,
Not with lead but with Love-And-Lowness-As-Brothers-Of-One-
    Womb.
The bridge is of Pray-Properly-You-Will-Prosper-The-More.
Every pillar is of penance, of prayers to saints;
The hooks are of almsdeeds that the gates are hanging on.
595 The gate-keeper's name is Grace, a good man indeed;
His man is called Amend-Yourself, for he knows many men.
Say this sentence to him: 'Truth sees what's true;
I performed the penance the priest gave me to do
And I'm sorry for my sins and shall be so always
600 When I think thereon, though I were a pope.'
Pray Amend-Yourself mildly to ask his master once
To open wide the wicket-gate that the woman shut
When Adam and Eve ate unroasted apples.

5. Exodus 20.12. Beginning in lines 563–64 with the two "great" commandments (Matthew 22.37–39), Piers's directions include most of the commandments of Exodus 20. The line numbering is that of the edition on which the translation is based. The indented lines printed in italics are translated from the Latin of the original and are generally quotations from the Bible, the liturgy, or the fathers of the church. Hence they are given the status of "a-lines" because they are not composed by Langland. Thus this line is numbered 567a.
6. A small enclosed field, or a small agricultural holding worked by a tenant.
7. A holiday (i.e., a holy day) lasted until sunset ("high evening"); it was not supposed to be used for work, and drinking and games were forbidden, at least until after attendance at church services.
8. A low hillock or a burial mound.

Through Eve it was closed to all and through the Virgin
Mary it was opened again.[9]

605 For he keeps the latchkey though the king sleep.
And if Grace grants you to go in in this way
You shall see in yourself Truth sitting in your heart
In a chain of charity as though you were a child again,[1]
To suffer your sire's will and say nothing against it."

* * *

630 "By Christ," cried a pickpocket, "I have no kin there."
"Nor I," said an ape-trainer, "for anything I know."
"God knows," said a cake-seller, "if I were sure of this,
I wouldn't go a foot further for any friar's preaching."
"Yes!" said Piers Plowman, and prodded him for his good.
635 "Mercy is a maiden there that has dominion over them all,
And she is sib to all sinners, and her son as well,
And through the help of these two—think nothing else—
You might get grace there if you go in time."
"By Saint Paul!" said a pardoner, "possibly I'm not known there;
640 I'll go fetch my box with my brevets and a bull with bishop's letters."
"By Christ!" said a common woman,[2] "I'll keep you company.
You shall say I am your sister." I don't know what became of them.

Passus 6

[THE PLOWING OF PIERS'S HALF-ACRE]

"This would be a bewildering way unless we had a guide
Who could trace our way foot by foot": thus these folk complained.
Said Perkin[3] the Plowman, "By Saint Peter of Rome!
I have a half-acre to plow by the highway;
5 If I had plowed this half-acre and afterwards sowed it,
I would walk along with you and show you the way to go."
"That would be a long delay," said a lady in a veil.
"What ought we women to work at meanwhile?"
"Some shall sew sacks to stop the wheat from spilling.
10 And you lovely ladies, with your long fingers,
See that you have silk and sendal to sew when you've time
Chasubles[4] for chaplains for the Church's honor.
Wives and widows, spin wool and flax;
Make cloth, I counsel you, and teach the craft to your daughters.
15 The needy and the naked, take note how they fare:
Keep them from cold with clothing, for so Truth wishes.
For I shall supply their sustenance unless the soil fails
As long as I live, for the Lord's love in Heaven.

9. From a service commemorating the Virgin Mary.
1. Cf. Mark 10.15: "whosoever shall not receive the kingdom of God as a little child, he shall not enter therein." This childlike quality is here envisaged as total submissiveness (line 608). "In a chain of charity": either Truth is bound by (that is, con-strained by) *caritas* (love) or Truth is enthroned, adorned with *caritas* like a chain of office.
2. Prostitute. "Brevets": pardoner's credentials.
3. A nickname for Piers, or Peter.
4. Garments worn by priests to celebrate Mass. "Sendal": a thin, rich form of silk.

And all sorts of folk that feed on farm products,
20   Busily abet him who brings forth your food."
      "By Christ!" exclaimed a knight then, "your counsel is the best.
But truly, how to drive a team has never been taught me.
But show me," said the knight, "and I shall study plowing."
"By Saint Paul," said Perkin, "since you proffer help so humbly,
25   I shall sweat and strain and sow for us both,
And also labor for your love all my lifetime,
In exchange for your championing Holy Church and me
Against wasters and wicked men who would destroy me.
And go hunt hardily hares and foxes,
30   Boars and bucks that break down my hedges,
And have falcons at hand to hunt down the birds
That come to my croft[5] and crop my wheat."
Thoughtfully the knight then spoke these words:
"By my power, Piers, I pledge you my word
35   To uphold this obligation though I have to fight.
As long as I live I shall look after you."
"Yes, and yet another point," said Piers, "I pray you further:
See that you trouble no tenant unless Truth approves,
And though you may amerce[6] him, let Mercy set the fine,
40   And Meekness be your master no matter what Meed° does.   *bribery*
And though poor men proffer you presents and gifts,
Don't accept them for it's uncertain that you deserve to have them.
For at some set time you'll have to restore them
In a most perilous place called purgatory.
45   And treat no bondman badly—you'll be the better for it;
Though here he is your underling, it could happen in Heaven
That he'll be awarded a worthier place, one with more bliss:
      Friend, go up higher.[7]
For in the charnelhouse[8] at church churls are hard to distinguish,
Or a knight from a knave: know this in your heart.
50   And see that you're true of your tongue, and as for tales—hate them
Unless they have wisdom and wit for your workmen's instruction.
Avoid foul-mouthed fellows and don't be friendly to their stories,
And especially at your repasts shun people like them,
For they tell the Fiend's fables—be very sure of that."
55   "I assent, by Saint James," said the knight then,
"To work by your word while my life lasts."
"And I shall apparel myself," said Perkin, "in pilgrims' fashion
And walk along the way with you till we find Truth."
He donned his working-dress, some darned, some whole,
60   His gaiters and his gloves to guard his limbs from cold,
And hung his seed-holder behind his back instead of a knapsack:
"Bring a bushel of bread-wheat for me to put in it,
For I shall sow it myself and set out afterwards
On a pilgrimage as palmers do to procure pardon.
65   And whoever helps me plow or work in any way
Shall have leave, by our Lord, to glean my land in harvest-time,

5. A small enclosed field.
6. Punish with a fine the amount of which is at the discretion of the judge.

7. Luke 14.10.
8. A crypt for dead bodies.

And make merry with what he gets, no matter who grumbles.
And all kinds of craftsmen that can live in truth,
I shall provide food for those that faithfully live,
70 Except for Jack the juggler and Jonette from the brothel,
And Daniel the dice-player and Denot the pimp,
And Friar Faker and folk of his order,
And Robin the ribald for his rotten speech.
Truth told me once and bade me tell it abroad:
75 *Deleantur de libro viventium:*[9] I should have no dealings with them,
For Holy Church is under orders to ask no tithes[1] of them.
    For let them not be written with the righteous.[2]
Their good luck has left them, the Lord amend them now."
    Dame-Work-When-It's-Time-To was Piers's wife's name;
His daughter was called Do-Just-So-Or-Your-Dame-Will-Beat-You;
80 His son was named Suffer-Your-Sovereigns-To-Have-Their-Will-
Condemn-Them-Not-For-If-You-Do-You'll-Pay-A-Dear-Price-
Let-God-Have-His-Way-With-All-Things-For-So-His-Word-Teaches.
"For now I am old and hoary and have something of my own,
To penance and to pilgrimage I'll depart with these others;
85 Therefore I will, before I go away, have my will written:
'*In Dei nomine, amen,*[3] I make this myself.
He shall have my soul that has deserved it best,
And defend it from the Fiend—for so I believe—
Till I come to his accounting, as my Creed teaches me—
90 To have release and remission I trust in his rent book.
The kirk° shall have my corpse and keep my bones,   church
For of my corn and cattle it craved the tithe:
I paid it promptly for peril of my soul;
It is obligated, I hope, to have me in mind
95 And commemorate me in its prayers among all Christians.
My wife shall have what I won with truth, and nothing else,
And parcel it out among my friends and my dear children.
For though I die today, my debts are paid;
I took back what I borrowed before I went to bed.'
100 As for the residue and the remnant, by the Rood of Lucca,[4]
I will worship Truth with it all my lifetime,
And be his pilgrim at the plow for poor men's sake.
My plowstaff shall be my pikestaff and push at the roots
And help my coulter to cut and cleanse the furrows."
105   Now Perkin and the pilgrims have put themselves to plowing.
Many there helped him to plow his half-acre.
Ditchers and diggers dug up the ridges;
Perkin was pleased by this and praised them warmly.
There were other workmen who worked very hard:
110 Each man in his manner made himself a laborer,

---

9. Let them be blotted out of the book of the living (Psalms 69.28).
1. Because the money they make is not legitimate income or increase derived from the earth; therefore, they do not owe the tithes, or 10 percent taxes, due the church.
2. Psalms 69.28.
3. "In the name of God, amen," customary beginning of a will.

4. An ornate crucifix at Lucca in Italy was a popular object of pilgrimage. "Residue and remnant": land had to be left to one's natural heirs, although up to one-third of personal property (the "residue and remnant") could be left to the church for Masses for the testator or other purposes; the other two-thirds had to go to the family, one to the widow and the other to the children. Piers's arrangements seem to leave the wife considerably more latitude.

And some to please Perkin pulled up the weeds.
At high prime[5] Piers let the plow stand
To oversee them himself; whoever worked best
Should be hired afterward, when harvest-time came.
115 Then some sat down and sang over ale
And helped plow the half-acre with "Ho! trolly-lolly!"[6]
"Now by the peril of my soul!" said Piers in pure wrath,
"Unless you get up again and begin working now,
No grain that grows here will gladden you at need,
120 And though once off the dole you die let the Devil care!"
Then fakers were afraid and feigned to be blind;
Some set their legs askew as such loafers can
And made their moan to Piers, how they might not work:
"We have no limbs to labor with, Lord, we thank you;
125 But we pray for you, Piers, and for your plow as well,
That God of his grace make your grain multiply,
And reward you for whatever alms you will give us here,
For we can't strain and sweat, such sickness afflicts us."
     "If what you say is so," said Piers, "I'll soon find out.
130 I know you're ne'er-do-wells, and Truth knows what's right,
And I'm his sworn servant and so should warn him
Which ones they are in this world that do his workmen harm.
You waste what men win with toil and trouble.
But Truth shall teach you how his team should be driven,
135 Or you'll eat barley bread and use the brook for drink;
Unless you're blind or broken-legged, or bolted° with iron—   braced
Those shall eat as well as I do, so God help me,
Till God of his goodness gives them strength to arise.
But you could work as Truth wants you to and earn wages and bread
140 By keeping cows in the field, the corn from the cattle,
Making ditches or dikes or dinging on sheaves,
Or helping make mortar, or spreading muck afield.
You live in lies and lechery and in sloth too,
And it's only for suffrance that vengeance has not fallen on you.
145 But anchorites and hermits that eat only at noon
And nothing more before the morrow, they shall have my alms,
And buy copes at my cost—those that have cloisters and churches.
But Robert Runabout shall have no rag from me,
Nor 'Apostles' unless they can preach and have the bishop's permission.
150 They shall have bread and boiled greens and a bit extra besides,
For it's an unreasonable religious life that has no regular meals."
     Then Waster waxed angry and wanted to fight;
To Piers the Plowman he proffered his glove.
A Breton, a braggart, he bullied Piers too,
155 And told him to go piss with his plow, peevish wretch.
"Whether you're willing or unwilling, we will have our will
With your flour and your flesh, fetch it when we please,
And make merry with it, no matter what you do."
Then Piers the Plowman complained to the knight

---

5. 9 A.M., or after a substantial part of the day's work has been done, because laborers start so early.

6. Presumably the refrain of a popular song (note similarly musical loafers in the *Prologue*, lines 224–25).

160 To keep him safe, as their covenant was, from cursed rogues,
"And from these wolfish wasters that lay waste the world,
For they waste and win nothing, and there will never be
Plenty among the people while my plow stands idle."
Because he was born a courteous man the knight spoke kindly to
Waster
165 And warned him he would have to behave himself better:
"Or you'll pay the penalty at law, I promise, by my order!"
"It's not my way to work," said Waster, "I won't begin now!"
And made light of the law and lighter of the knight,
And said Piers wasn't worth a pea or his plow either,
170 And menaced him and his men if they met again.
    "Now by the peril of my soul!" said Piers, "I'll punish you all."
And he whooped after Hunger who heard him at once.
"Avenge me on these vagabonds," said he, "that vex the whole world."
Then Hunger in haste took hold of Waster by the belly
175 And gripped him so about the guts that his eyes gushed water.
He buffeted the Breton about the cheeks
That he looked like a lantern all his life after.
He beat them both so that he almost broke their guts.
Had not Piers with a pease loaf[7] prayed him to leave off
180 They'd have been dead and buried deep, have no doubt about it.
"Let them live," he said, "and let them feed with hogs,
Or else on beans and bran baked together."
Fakers for fear fled into barns
And flogged sheaves with flails from morning till evening,
185 So that Hunger wouldn't be eager to cast his eye on them.
For a potful of peas that Piers had cooked
A heap of hermits laid hands on spades
And cut off their copes and made short coats of them
And went like workmen to weed and to mow,
190 And dug dirt and dung to drive off Hunger.
Blind and bedridden got better by the thousand;
Those who sat to beg silver were soon healed,
For what had been baked for Bayard[8] was boon to many hungry,
And many a beggar for beans obediently labored,
195 And every poor man was well pleased to have peas for his wages,
And what Piers prayed them to do they did as sprightly as
sparrowhawks.
And Piers was proud of this and put them to work,
And gave them meals and money as they might deserve.
    Then Piers had pity and prayed Hunger to take his way
200 Off to his own home and hold there forever.
"I'm well avenged on vagabonds by virtue of you.
But I pray you, before you part," said Piers to Hunger,
"With beggars and street-beadsmen[9] what's best to be done?
For well I know that once you're away, they will work badly;
205 Misfortune makes them so meek now,

7. The cheapest and coarsest grade of bread, the food of those who cannot get better.
8. Generic name for a horse; a bread made of beans and bran, the coarsest category of bread, was used to feed horses and hounds, but was eaten by people when need was great.
9. Paid prayer sayers.

And it's for lack of food that these folk obey me.
And they're my blood brothers, for God bought° us all.　　　　　*redeemed*
Truth taught me once to love them every one
And help them with everything after their needs.
210　Now I'd like to learn, if you know, what line I should take
And how I might overmaster them and make them work."
"Hear now," said Hunger, "and hold it for wisdom:
Big bold beggars that can earn their bread,
With hounds' bread and horses' bread hold up their hearts,
215　And keep their bellies from swelling by stuffing them with beans—
And if they begin to grumble, tell them to get to work,
And they'll have sweeter suppers once they've deserved them.
And if you find any fellow-man that fortune has harmed
Through fire or through false men, befriend him if you can.
220　Comfort such at your own cost, for the love of Christ in Heaven;
Love them and relieve them—so the law of Kind° directs.　　　　*Nature*
　　　Bear ye one another's burdens.[1]
And all manner of men that you may find
That are needy or naked and have nothing to spend,
With meals or with money make them the better.
225　Love them and don't malign them; let God take vengeance.
Though they behave ill, leave it all up to God
　　　Vengeance is mine and I will repay.[2]
And if you want to gratify God, do as the Gospel teaches,
And get yourself loved by lowly men: so you'll unloose his grace."
　　　Make to yourselves friends of the mammon of unrighteousness.[3]
"I would not grieve God," said Piers, "for all the goods on earth!
230　Might I do as you say without sin?" said Piers then.
"Yes, I give you my oath," said Hunger, "or else the Bible lies:
Go to Genesis the giant, engenderer of us all:[4]
In sudore[5] and slaving you shall bring forth your food
And labor for your livelihood, and so our Lord commanded.
235　And Sapience says the same—I saw it in the Bible.
Piger propter frigus[6] would plow no field;
He shall be a beggar and none abate his hunger.
Matthew with man's face[7] mouths these words:
'Entrusted with a talent, *servus nequam*[8] didn't try to use it,
240　And earned his master's ill-will for evermore after,
And he took away his talent who was too lazy to work,
And gave it to him in haste that had ten already;
And after he said so that his servants heard it,
He that has shall have, and help when he needs it,
245　And he that nothing has shall nothing have and no man help him,

---

1. Galatians 6.2.
2. Romans 12.19.
3. Luke 16.9.
4. This puzzling epithet has been explained on the grounds that Genesis is the longest book (except for Psalms) in the Bible and that it recounts the creation of humankind.
5. In the sweat [of thy face shalt thou eat bread] (Genesis 3.19).
6. The sluggard [will not plow] by reason of the cold (Proverbs 20.4). "Sapience": the biblical "Wis-

dom Books" attributed to Solomon.
7. Each of the four Evangelists had his traditional pictorial image, derived partly from the faces of the four creatures in Ezekiel's vision (Ezekiel 1.5–12) and partly from those of the four beasts of the Apocalypse (Revelation 4.7): Matthew was represented as a winged man; Mark, a lion; Luke, a winged ox; and John, an eagle.
8. The wicked servant (Luke 19.22; see 17–27). "Talent": a unit of money.

And what he trusts he's entitled to I shall take away.'
Kind Wit wants each one to work,
Either in teaching or tallying or toiling with his hands,
Contemplative life or active life; Christ wants it too.
250 The Psalter says in the Psalm of *Beati omnes*,[9]
The fellow that feeds himself with his faithful labor,
He is blessed by the Book in body and in soul."
    The labors of thy hands, etc.[1]
    "Yet I pray you," said Piers, *"pour charité,*° if you know   *for charity*
Any modicum of medicine, teach me it, dear sir.
255 For some of my servants and myself as well
For a whole week do no work, we've such aches in our stomachs."
"I'm certain," said Hunger, "what sickness ails you.
You've munched down too much: that's what makes you groan,
But I assure you," said Hunger, "if you'd preserve your health,
260 You must not drink any day before you've dined on something.
Never eat, I urge you, ere Hunger comes upon you
And sends you some of his sauce to add savor to the food;
And keep some till suppertime, and don't sit too long;
Arise up ere Appetite has eaten his fill.
265 Let not Sir Surfeit sit at your table;
Love him not for he's a lecher whose delight is his tongue,
And for all sorts of seasoned stuff his stomach yearns.
And if you adopt this diet, I dare bet my arms
That Physic for his food will sell his furred hood
270 And his Calabrian[2] cloak with its clasps of gold,
And be content, by my troth, to retire from medicine
And learn to labor on the land lest livelihood fail him.
There are fewer physicians than frauds—reform them, Lord!—
Their drinks make men die before destiny ordains."
275 "By Saint Parnel,"[3] said Piers, "these are profitable words.
This is a lovely lesson; the Lord reward you for it!
Take your way when you will—may things be well with you always!"
    "My oath to God!" said Hunger, "I will not go away
Till I've dined this day and drunk as well."
280 "I've no penny," said Piers, "to purchase pullets,
And I can't get goose or pork; but I've got two green cheeses,
A few curds and cream and a cake of oatmeal,
A loaf of beans and bran baked for my children.
And yet I say, by my soul, I have no salt bacon
285 Nor any hen's egg, by Christ, to make ham and eggs,
But scallions aren't scarce, nor parsley, and I've scores of cabbages,
And also a cow and a calf, and a cart-mare
To draw dung to the field while the dry weather lasts.
By this livelihood I must live till Lammass[4] time
290 When I hope to have harvest in my garden.

---

9. Blessed [are] all [who] (Psalms 128.1).
1. Psalms 128.2.
2. Of gray fur (a special imported squirrel fur).
3. Who St. Pernelle was is obscure; other manuscripts and editions read "By Saint Paul."

4. The harvest festival, August 1 (the name derived from Old English *hlaf*, "loaf"), when a loaf made from the first wheat of the season was offered at Mass.

Then I can manage a meal that will make you happy."
All the poor people fetched peasepods;[5]
Beans and baked apples they brought in their skirts,
Chives and chervils and ripe cherries aplenty,
295 And offered Piers this present to please Hunger with.
Hunger ate this in haste and asked for more.
Then poor folk for fear fed Hunger fast,
Proffering leeks and peas, thinking to appease him.
And now harvest drew near and new grain came to market.[6]
300 Then poor people were pleased and plied Hunger with the best;
With good ale as Glutton taught they got him to sleep.
Then Waster wouldn't work but wandered about,
And no beggar would eat bread that had beans in it,
But the best bread or the next best, or baked from pure wheat,
305 Nor drink any half-penny ale[7] in any circumstances,
But of the best and the brownest that barmaids sell.
Laborers that have no land to live on but their hands
Deign not to dine today on last night's cabbage.
No penny-ale can please them, nor any piece of bacon,
310 But it must be fresh flesh or else fried fish,
And that *chaud* or *plus chaud*[8] so it won't chill their bellies.
Unless he's hired at high wages he will otherwise complain;
That he was born to be a workman he'll blame the time.
Against Cato's counsel he commences to murmur:
315 *Remember to bear your burden of poverty patiently.*[9]
He grows angry at God and grumbles against Reason,
And then curses the king and all the council after
Because they legislate laws that punish laboring men.[1]
But while Hunger was their master there would none of them complain
320 Or strive against the statute,[2] so sternly he looked.
But I warn you workmen, earn wages while you may,
For Hunger is hurrying hitherward fast.
With waters he'll awaken Waster's chastisement;
Before five years are fulfilled such famine shall arise.
325 Through flood and foul weather fruits shall fail,
And so Saturn[3] says and has sent to warn you:
When you see the moon amiss and two monks' heads,
And a maid have the mastery, and multiply by eight,[4]
Then shall Death withdraw and Dearth be justice,
330 And Daw the diker[5] die for hunger,
Unless God of his goodness grants us a truce.

5. Peas in the pod. These, like most foods in the next lines, are early crops.
6. Presumably as the new harvest approaches, merchants who have been holding grain for the highest prices release it for sale, because prices are about to tumble.
7. Weak ale diluted with water; in line 309, laborers are too fussy and will no longer accept even penny ale.
8. "Hot" or "very hot."
9. From Cato's *Distichs*, a collection of pithy phrases used to teach Latin to beginning students.
1. Like so many governments, late-14th-century England responded to inflation and the bargaining power of the relatively scarce laborers with wage and price freezes, which had their usual lack of effect. One way landowners, desperate to obtain enough laborers, tried to get around the wage laws was by offering food as well as cash.
2. I.e., anti-inflationary legislation.
3. Planet thought to influence the weather, generally perceived as hostile.
4. This cryptic prophecy has never been satisfactorily explained; the basic point is that it is Apocalyptic.
5. A laborer who digs dikes and ditches.

Passus 18

[THE HARROWING OF HELL]

Wool-chafed[6] and wet-shoed I went forth after
Like a careless creature unconscious of woe,
And trudged forth like a tramp, all the time of my life,
Till I grew weary of the world and wished to sleep again,
5   And lay down till Lent, and slept a long time,
Rested there, snoring roundly, till *Ramis-Palmarum*.[7]
      I dreamed chiefly of children and cheers of "*Gloria, laus!*"
And how old folk to an organ sang "*Hosanna!*"
And of Christ's passion and pain for the people he had reached for.
10   One resembling the Samaritan[8] and somewhat Piers the Plowman
Barefoot on an ass's back bootless came riding
Without spurs or spear: sprightly was his look,
As is the nature of a knight that draws near to be dubbed,
To get himself gilt spurs and engraved jousting shoes.
15   Then was Faith watching from a window and cried, "*A, fili David!*"
As does a herald of arms when armed men come to joust.
Old Jews of Jerusalem joyfully sang,
      "*Blessed is he who cometh in the name of the Lord.*"
And I asked Faith to reveal what all this affair meant,
20   And who was to joust in Jerusalem. "Jesus," he said,
"And fetch what the Fiend claims, the fruit of Piers the Plowman."
"Is Piers in this place?" said I; and he pierced me with his look:
"This Jesus for his gentleness will joust in Piers's arms,
In his helmet and in his hauberk, *humana natura*,[9]
25   So that Christ be not disclosed here as *consummatus Deus*.[1]
In the plate armor of Piers the Plowman this jouster will ride,
For no dint will do him injury as *in deitate Patris*.[2]
"Who shall joust with Jesus," said I, "Jews or Scribes?"[3]
"No," said Faith, "but the Fiend and False-Doom°-To-Die.   *sentence*
30   Death says he will undo and drag down low
All that live or look upon land or water.
Life says that he lies, and lays his life in pledge
That for all that Death can do, within three days he'll walk
And fetch from the Fiend the fruit of Piers the Plowman,
35   And place it where he pleases, and put Lucifer in bonds,
And beat and bring down burning death forever.
      O death, I will be thy death."[4]

---

6. Scratchy wool was worn next to the body as an act of penance.
7. Palm Sunday (literally, "branches of palms"): the background of this part of the poem is the biblical account of Christ's entry into Jerusalem on this day, when the crowds greeted him crying, "Hosanna [line 8] to the son of David [line 15]: Blessed is he that cometh in the name of the Lord [line 17a]; Hosanna in the highest" (see Matthew 21.9). "*Gloria, laus*" [line 7] are the first words of an anthem, "Glory, praise, and honor," that was sung by children in medieval religious processions on Palm Sunday.
8. In the previous vision, the Dreamer has

encountered Abraham, or Faith (mentioned in lines 15, 18, 28, and 92); Moses, or Hope; and the Good Samaritan, or Charity, who was riding toward a "jousting in Jerusalem" and who now appears as an aspect of Christ.
9. Human nature, which Christ assumed in order to redeem humanity. "Hauberk": coat of mail.
1. The perfect (three-personed) God.
2. In the godhead of the Father: as God, Christ could not suffer but as man, he could.
3. People who made a very strict, literal interpretation of the Old Law and hence rejected Christ's teaching of the New.
4. Cf. Hosea 13.14.

Then Pilate came with many people, *sedens pro tribunali*,[5]
To see how doughtily Death should do, and judge the rights of both.
40 The Jews and the justice were joined against Jesus,
And all the court cried upon him, "*Crucifige!*"[6] loud.
Then a plaintiff appeared before Pilate and said,
"This Jesus made jokes about Jerusalem's temple,
To have it down in one day and in three days after
45 Put it up again all new—here he stands who said it—
And yet build it every bit as big in all dimensions,
As long and as broad both, above and below."
"*Crucifige!*" said a sergeant, "he knows sorcerer's tricks."
"*Tolle! tolle!*"[7] said another, and took sharp thorns
50 And began to make a garland out of green thorn,
And set it sorely on his head and spoke in hatred,
"*Ave, Rabbi*," said that wretch, and shot reeds[8] at him;
They nailed him with three nails naked on a Cross,
And with a pole put a potion up to his lips
55 And bade him drink to delay his death and lengthen his days,
And said, "If you're subtle, let's see you help yourself.
If you are Christ and a king's son, come down from the Cross!
Then we'll believe that Life loves you and will not let you die."
"*Consummatum est*,"[9] said Christ and started to swoon,
60 Piteously and pale like a prisoner dying.
The Lord of Life and of Light then laid his eyelids together.
The day withdrew for dread and darkness covered the sun;
The wall wavered and split and the whole world quaked.
Dead men for that din came out of deep graves
65 And spoke of why that storm lasted so long:
"For a bitter battle," the dead body said;
"Life and Death in this darkness, one destroys the other.
No one will surely know which shall have the victory
Before Sunday about sunrise"; and sank with that to earth.
70 Some said that he was God's son that died so fairly:
Truly this was the Son of God.[1]
And some said he was a sorcerer: "We should see first
Whether he's dead or not dead before we dare take him down."
Two thieves were there that suffered death that time
75 Upon crosses beside Christ; such was the common law.
A constable came forth and cracked both their legs
And the arms afterward of each of those thieves.
But no bastard was so bold as to touch God's body there;
Because he was a knight and a king's son, Nature decreed that time
80 That no knave should have the hardiness to lay hand on him.
But a knight with a sharp spear was sent forth there
Named Longeus[2] as the legend tells, who had long since lost his
sight;

5. Sitting as a judge (cf. Matthew 27.19).
6. Crucify him! (John 19.15).
7. Away with him, away with him! (John 19.15).
8. Arrows, probably small ones intended to hurt rather than to kill. "*Ave, Rabbi*": "Hail, master" (Matthew 26.49): these are actually Judas's words when he kissed Christ in order to identify him to the arresting officers.
9. It is finished (John 19.30).
1. Matthew 27.54.
2. Longeus (usually Longinus) appears in the apocryphal Gospel of Nicodemus, which provided Langland with the material for much of his account of Christ's despoiling of hell.

Before Pilate and the other people in that place he waited on his
    horse.
For all that he might demur, he was made that time
85   To joust with Jesus, that blind Jew Longeus.
For all who watched there were unwilling, whether mounted or afoot,
To touch him or tamper with him or take him down from the Cross,
Except this blind bachelor that bore him through the heart.
The blood sprang down the spear and unsparred[3] his eyes.
90   The knight knelt down on his knees and begged Jesus for mercy.
"It was against my will, Lord, to wound you so sorely."
He sighed and said, "Sorely I repent it.
For what I here have done, I ask only your grace.
Have mercy on me, rightful Jesu!" and thus lamenting wept.
95   Then Faith began fiercely to scorn the false Jews,[4]
Called them cowards, accursed forever.
"For this foul villainy, may vengeance fall on you!
To make the blind beat the dead, it was a bully's thought.
Cursed cowards, no kind of knighthood was it
100   To beat a dead body with any bright weapon.
Yet he's won the victory in the fight for all his vast wound,
For your champion jouster, the chief knight of you all,
Weeping admits himself worsted and at the will of Jesus.
For when this darkness is done, Death will be vanquished,
105   And you louts have lost, for Life shall have the victory;
And your unfettered freedom has fallen into servitude;
And you churls and your children shall achieve no prosperity,
Nor have lordship over land or have land to till,
But be all barren and live by usury,
110   Which is a life that every law of our Lord curses.
Now your good days are done as Daniel prophesied;
When Christ came their kingdom's crown should be lost:
      When the Holy of Holies comes your anointing shall cease."[5]
What for fear of this adventure and of the false Jews
115   I withdrew in that darkness to *Descendit-ad-Inferna*,[6]
And there I saw surely *Secundum Scripturas*[7]
Where out of the west a wench,[8] as I thought,
Came walking on the way—she looked toward hell.
Mercy was that maid's name, a meek thing withal,
120   A most gracious girl, and goodly of speech.
Her sister as it seemed came softly walking
Out of the east, opposite, and she looked westward,
A comely creature and cleanly: Truth was her name.
Because of the virtue that followed her, she was afraid of nothing.
125   When these maidens met, Mercy and Truth,

---

3. Opened; in the original there is a play on words with "spear." "Bachelor": knight.

4. The references in this passage (lines 92–110) and in lines 258–60 appear to reflect a blind anti-Semitism all too prevalent in late-medieval art and literature, brought out especially in portrayals of the Passion. Elsewhere Langland exhibits a more enlightened attitude—for instance, in a passage in which he holds up Jewish charity as an example to Christians. In the present passage he may intend a distinction between those who betrayed and condemned Jesus and the "old Jews of Jerusalem" who welcomed him in the Palm Sunday procession (lines 7–17).

5. Daniel 9.24.

6. He descended into hell (from the Apostles' Creed).

7. According to the Scriptures.

8. The word is Langland's and had much the same connotations in his time as it has in ours.

Each of them asked the other about this great wonder,
And of the din and of the darkness, and how the day lowered,
And what a gleam and a glint glowed before hell.
"I marvel at this matter, by my faith," said Truth,
130   "And am coming to discover what this queer affair means."
"Do not marvel," said Mercy, "it means only mirth.
A maiden named Mary, and mother without touching
By any kind of creature, conceived through speech
And grace of the Holy Ghost; grew great with child;
135   With no blemish to her woman's body brought him into this world.
And that my tale is true, I take God to witness,
Since this baby was born it has been thirty winters,
Who died and suffered death this day about midday.
And that is the cause of this eclipse that is closing off the sun,
140   In meaning that man shall be removed from darkness
While this gleam and this glow go to blind Lucifer.
For patriarchs and prophets have preached of this often
That man shall save man through a maiden's help,
And what a tree took away a tree shall restore,[9]
145   And what Death brought down a death shall raise up."
"What you're telling," said Truth, "is just a tale of nonsense.
For Adam and Eve and Abraham and the rest,
Patriarchs and prophets imprisoned in pain,
Never believe that yonder light will lift them up,
150   Or have them out of hell—hold your tongue, Mercy!
Your talk is mere trifling. I, Truth, know the truth,
For whatever is once in hell, it comes out never.
Job the perfect patriarch disproves what you say:
Since in hell there is no redemption."[1]
155   Then Mercy most mildly uttered these words:
"From observation," she said, "I suppose they shall be saved,
Because venom destroys venom, and in that I find evidence
That Adam and Eve shall have relief.
For of all venoms the foulest is the scorpion's:
160   No medicine may amend the place where it stings
Till it's dead and placed upon it—the poison is destroyed,
The first effect of the venom, through the virtue it possesses.
So shall this death destroy—I dare bet my life—
All that Death did first through the Devil's tempting.
165   And just as the beguiler with guile beguiled man first,
So shall grace that began everything make a good end
And beguile the beguiler—and that's a good trick:
A trick by which to trick trickery."[2]
"Now let's be silent," said Truth. "It seems to me I see
170   Out of the nip[3] of the north, not far from here,
Righteousness come running—let's wait right here,
For she knows far more than we—she was here before us both."

---

9. The first tree bore the fruit that Adam and Eve
ate, thereby damning humankind; the second tree
is the cross on which Christ was crucified, thereby
redeeming humankind.
1. Cf. Job 7.9.

2. From a medieval Latin hymn.
3. The word is Langland's and the sense obscure;
it probably meant "coldness" to him, although an
Old English word similar to *nip* meant "gloom."

"That is so," said Mercy, "and I see here to the south
Where Peace clothed in patience[4] comes sportively this way.
175 Love has desired her long: I believe surely
That Love has sent her some letter, what this light means
That hangs over hell thus: she will tell us what it means."
When Peace clothed in patience approached near them both,
Righteousness did her reverence for her rich clothing
180 And prayed Peace to tell her to what place she was going,
And whom she was going to greet in her gay garments.
    "My wish is to take my way," said she, "and welcome them all
Whom many a day I might not see for murk of sin.
Adam and Eve and the many others in hell,
185 Moses and many more will merrily sing,
And I shall dance to their song: sister, do the same.
Because Jesus jousted well, joy begins to dawn.
        *Weeping may endure for a night, but joy cometh in the
            morning.*[5]
Love who is my lover sent letters to tell me
190 That my sister Mercy and I shall save mankind,
And that God has forgiven and granted me, Peace, and Mercy
To make bail for mankind for evermore after.
Look, here's the patent," said Peace: "*In pace in idipsum:*
And that this deed shall endure, *dormiam et requiescam.*"[6]
195   "What? You're raving," said Righteousness. "You must be really
            drunk.
Do you believe that yonder light might unlock hell
And save man's soul? Sister, don't suppose it.
At the beginning God gave the judgment himself
That Adam and Eve and all that followed them
200 Should die downright and dwell in torment after
If they touched a tree and ate the tree's fruit.
Adam afterwards against his forbidding
Fed on that fruit and forsook as it were
The love of our Lord and his lore too,
205 And followed what the Fiend taught and his flesh's will
Against Reason. I, Righteousness, record this with Truth,
That their pain should be perpetual and no prayer should help them,
Therefore let them chew as they chose, and let us not chide, sisters,
For it's misery without amendment, the morsel they ate."
210   "And I shall prove," said Peace, "that their pain must end,
And in time trouble must turn into well-being;
For had they known no woe, they'd not have known well-being;
For no one knows what well-being is who was never in woe,
Nor what is hot hunger who has never lacked food.
215 If there were no night, no man, I believe,
Could be really well aware of what day means.
Never should a really rich man who lives in rest and ease

---

4. What Langland envisioned clothes of patience to look like, aside from their "richness" (line 173), it is impossible to say; to him any abstraction could become a concrete allegory without visual identification.

5. Psalm 30.5.
6. The "patent" or "deed" is a document conferring authority: this one consists of phrases from Psalm 4.8: "In peace in the selfsame"; "I will sleep and find rest."

Know what woe is if it weren't for natural death.
So God, who began everything, of his good will
220 Became man by a maid for mankind's salvation
And allowed himself to be sold to see the sorrow of dying.
And that cures all care and is the first cause of rest,
For until we meet *modicum*,° I may well avow it,   small quantity
No man knows, I suppose, what 'enough' means.
225 Therefore God of his goodness gave the first man Adam
A place of supreme ease and of perfect joy,
And then he suffered him to sin so that he might know sorrow,
And thus know what well-being is—to be aware of it naturally.
And afterward God offered himself, and took Adam's nature,
230 To see what he had suffered in three separate places,
Both in Heaven and on earth, and now he heads for hell,
To learn what all woe is like who has learned of all joy.
So it shall fare with these folk: their folly and their sin
Shall show them what sickness is—and succor from all pain.
235 No one knows what war is where peace prevails,
Nor what is true well-being till 'Woe, alas!' teaches him."
    Then was there a wight with two broad eyes:
Book was that beaupere's[7] name, a bold man of speech.
"By God's body," said this Book, "I will bear witness
240 That when this baby was born there blazed a star
So that all the wise men in the world agreed with one opinion
That such a baby was born in Bethlehem city
Who should save man's soul and destroy sin.
And all the elements," said the Book, "hereof bore witness.
245 The sky first revealed that he was God who formed all things:
The hosts in Heaven took *stella comata*[8]
And tended her like a torch to reverence his birth.
The light followed the Lord into the low earth.
The water witnessed that he was God for he walked on it;
250 Peter the Apostle perceived his walking
And as he went on the water knew him well and said,
    'Bid me come unto thee on the water.'[9]
And lo, how the sun locked her light in herself
When she saw him suffer that made sun and sea.
255 The earth for heavy heart because he would suffer
Quaked like a quick° thing and the rock cracked all to pieces.   *living*
Lo, hell might not hold, but opened when God suffered,
And let out Simeon's sons[1] to see him hang on Cross.
And now shall Lucifer believe it, loath though he is,
260 For Jesus like a giant with an engine[2] comes yonder
To break and beat down all that may be against him,
And to have out of hell every one he pleases.

---

7. Fine fellow. The book's two broad eyes suggest the Old and New Testaments. "Wight": creature, person.
8. Hairy star, i.e., comet.
9. Matthew 14.28.
1. Simeon, who was present at the presentation of the infant Jesus in the temple, had been told by the Holy Ghost that "he should not see death"

before he had seen "the Lord's Christ" (Luke 2.26). The Apocryphal Gospel of Nicodemus echoes the incident in reporting that Simeon's sons were raised from death at the time of Jesus's crucifixion.
2. A device, probably thought of as a gigantic slingshot, although, of course, Christ needs nothing to break down his enemies but his own authority.

And I, Book, will be burnt unless Jesus rises to life
In all the mights of a man and brings his mother joy,
265 And comforts all his kin, and takes their cares away,
And all the joy of the Jews disjoins and disperses;
And unless they reverence his Rood and his resurrection
And believe on a new law be lost body and soul."
"Let's be silent," said Truth, "I hear and see both
270 A spirit speaks to hell and bids the portals be opened."
        Lift up your gates.[3]
    A voice loud in that light cried to Lucifer,
"Princes of this place, unpin and unlock,
For he comes here with crown who is King of Glory."
275 Then Satan[4] sighed and said to hell,
"Without our leave such a light fetched Lazarus away:[5]
Care and calamity have come upon us all.
If this King comes in he will carry off mankind
And lead it to where Lazarus is, and with small labor bind me.
280 Patriarchs and prophets have long prated of this,
That such a lord and a light should lead them all hence."
    "Listen," said Lucifer, "for this lord is one I know;
Both this lord and this light, it's long ago I knew him.
No death may do this lord harm, nor any devil's trickery,
285 And his way is where he wishes—but let him beware of the perils.
If he bereaves me of my right he robs me by force.
For by right and by reason the race that is here
Body and soul belongs to me, both good and evil.
For he himself said it who is Sire of Heaven,
290 If Adam ate the apple, all should die
And dwell with us devils: the Lord laid down that threat.
And since he who is Truth himself said these words,
And since I've possessed them seven thousand winters,
I don't believe law will allow him the least of them."
295 "That is so," said Satan, "but I'm sore afraid
Because you took them by trickery and trespassed in his garden,
And in the semblance of a serpent sat upon the apple tree
And egged them to eat, Eve by herself,
And told her a tale with treasonous words;
300 And so you had them out, and hither at the last."
"It's an ill-gotten gain where guile is at the root,
For God will not be beguiled," said Goblin, "nor tricked.
We have no true title to them, for it was by treason they were damned."
    "Certainly I fear," said the Fiend,[6] "lest Truth fetch them out.
305 These thirty winters, as I think, he's gone here and there and preached.

---

3. The first words of Psalm 24.9, which reads in the Latin version, "Lift up your gates, O princes, and be ye lift up, ye everlasting doors, and the King of Glory shall come in."
4. Langland, following a tradition also reflected in Milton's *Paradise Lost*, pictures hell as populated by a number of devils: Satan; Lucifer (line 273 ff.), who began the war in heaven and tempted Eve; Goblin (line 293); Belial (line 321); and Ashtoreth (line 404). Lucifer the rebel angel naturally

became identified with Satan, a word that in the Old Testament had originally meant an evil adversary; many of the other devils are displaced gods of pagan religions.
5. For Christ's raising of Lazarus from the dead, cf. John 11.
6. Here and in line 309 "the Fiend" is presumably Lucifer's most articulate critic, Satan, whom Christ names as his tempter in Matthew 4.10.

I've assailed him with sin, and sometimes asked
Whether he was God or God's son: he gave me short answer.
And thus he's traveled about like a true man these two and thirty
    winters.
And when I saw it was so, while she slept I went
310 To warn Pilate's wife what sort of man was Jesus,[7]
For some hated him and have put him to death.
I would have lengthened his life, for I believed if he died
That his soul would suffer no sin in his sight.
For the body, while it walked on its bones, was busy always
315 To save men from sin if they themselves wished.
And now I see where a soul comes descending hitherward
With glory and with great light; God it is, I'm sure.
My advice is we all flee," said the Fiend, "fast away from here.
For we had better not be at all than abide in his sight.
320 For your lies, Lucifer, we've lost all our prey.
Through you we fell first from Heaven so high:
Because we believed your lies we all leapt out.
And now for your latest lie we have lost Adam,
And all our lordship, I believe, on land and in hell."
325   *Now shall the prince of this world be cast out.*[8]
    Again the light bade them unlock, and Lucifer answered,
        "Who is that?[9]
What lord are you?" said Lucifer. The light at once replied,
    "The King of Glory.
The Lord of might and of main and all manner of powers:
    The Lord of Powers.
Dukes of this dim place, at once undo these gates
330 That Christ may come in, the Heaven-King's son."
And with that breath hell broke along with Belial's bars;
For° any warrior or watchman the gates wide opened.   *in spite of*
Patriarchs and prophets, *populus in tenebris,*[1]
Sang Saint John's song, *Ecce agnus Dei.*[2]
335 Lucifer could not look, the light so blinded him.
And those that the Lord loved his light caught away,
And he said to Satan, "Lo, here's my soul in payment
For all sinful souls, to save those that are worthy.
Mine they are and of me—I may the better claim them.
340 Although Reason records, and right of myself,
That if they ate the apple all should die,
I did not hold out to them hell here forever.
For the deed that they did, your deceit caused it;
You got them with guile against all reason.
345 For in my palace Paradise, in the person of an adder,

7. In Matthew 27.19 Pilate's wife warns Pilate to "have nothing to do with that just man [Jesus]," for she has been troubled by a dream about him. Langland has the Fiend admit to having caused the dream so that Pilate's wife should persuade her husband not to harm Jesus and thus keep him safe on earth and not come to visit hell and despoil it.
8. John 12.31. "Prince of this world" is a title for the devil.
9. This and the next two phrases translated from the Latin are from Psalm 24.8, following immediately on the words quoted in line 262a.
1. "People in darkness," the phrase is from Matthew 4.16, citing Isaiah 9.2, "The people that walked in darkness have seen a great light."
2. Behold the Lamb of God (John 1.36).

You stole by stealth something I loved.
Thus like a lizard with a lady's face[3]
Falsely you filched from me; the Old Law confirms
That guilers be beguiled, and that is good logic:
350   *A tooth for a tooth and an eye for an eye.*[4]
Ergo[5] soul shall requite soul and sin revert to sin,
And all that man has done amiss, I, man, will amend.
Member for member was amends in the Old Law,
And life for life also, and by that law I claim
355   Adam and all his issue at my will hereafter.
And what Death destroyed in them, my death shall restore
And both quicken° and requite what was quenched through   *revitalize*
    sin.
And that grace destroy guile is what good faith requires.
So don't believe it, Lucifer, against the law I fetch them,
360   But by right and by reason here ransom my liegemen.
       I have not come to destroy the law but to fulfill it.[6]
You fetched mine in my place unmindful of all reason
Falsely and feloniously; good faith taught me
To recover them by reason and rely on nothing else.
365   So what you got with guile through grace is won back.
You, Lucifer, in likeness of a loathsome adder
Got by guile those whom God loved;
And I, in likeness of a mortal man, who am master of Heaven,
Have graciously requited your guile: let guile go against guile!
370   And as Adam and all died through a tree
Adam and all through a tree return to life,
And guile is beguiled and grief has come to his guile:
    And he is fallen into the ditch which he made.[7]
And now your guile begins to turn against you,
375   And my grace to grow ever greater and wider.
The bitterness that you have brewed, imbibe it yourself
Who are doctor[8] of death, the drink you made.
    For I who am Lord of Life, love is my drink
And for that drink today I died upon earth.
380   I struggled so I'm thirsty still for man's soul's sake.
No drink may moisten me or slake my thirst
Till vintage time befall in the Vale of Jehoshaphat,[9]
When I shall drink really ripe wine, *Resurrectio mortuorum.*[1]
And then I shall come as a king crowned with angels
385   And have out of hell all men's souls.
Fiends and fiendkins shall stand before me
And be at my bidding, where best it pleases me.
But to be merciful to man then, my nature requires it.
For we are brothers of one blood, but not in baptism all.

---

3. In medieval art the devil tempting Eve was sometimes represented as a snake (see the "serpent" of line 288) and sometimes as a lizard with a female human face and standing upright.
4. See Matthew 5.38 citing Exodus 21.24.
5. Therefore. The Latin conjunction was used in formal debate to introduce the conclusion derived from a number of propositions.
6. See Matthew 5.17.

7. Psalm 7.15.
8. The ironical use of the word carries the sense both of "physician" and of "one learned in a discipline."
9. On the evidence of Joel 3.2, 12, the site of the Last Judgment was thought to be the Vale of Jehoshaphat.
1. The resurrection of the dead (from the Nicene Creed).

390 And all that are both in blood and in baptism my whole brothers
Shall not be damned to the death that endures without end.
Against thee only have I sinned, etc.[2]
It is not the custom on earth to hang a felon
Oftener than once, even though he were a traitor.
395 And if the king of the kingdom comes at that time
When a felon should suffer death or other such punishment,
Law would he give him life if he looks upon him.[3]
And I who am King of Kings shall come in such a time
Where doom to death damns all wicked,
400 And if law wills I look on them, it lies in my grace
Whether they die or do not die because they did evil.
And if it be any bit paid for, the boldness of their sins,
I may grant mercy through my righteousness and all my true words;
And though Holy Writ wills that I wreak vengeance on those
that wrought evil,
405 *No evil unpunished, etc.*[4]
They shall be cleansed and made clear and cured of their sins,
In my prison purgatory till *Parce!*° says 'Stop!'   *Spare!*
And my mercy shall be shown to many of my half-brothers,
For blood-kin may see blood-kin both hungry and cold,
410 But blood-kin may not see blood-kin bleed without his pity:
*I heard unspeakable words which it is not lawful for a man to
utter.*[5]
But my righteousness and right shall rule all hell
And mercy rule all mankind before me in Heaven.
For I'd be an unkind king unless I gave my kin help,
415 And particularly at such a time when help was truly needed.
Enter not into judgment with thy servant.[6]
Thus by law," said our Lord, "I will lead from here
Those I looked on with love who believed in my coming;
And for your lie, Lucifer, that you lied to Eve,
420 You shall buy it back in bitterness"—and bound him with chains.
Ashtoreth and all the gang hid themselves in corners;
They dared not look at our Lord, the least of them all,
But let him lead away what he liked and leave what he wished.
Many hundreds of angels harped and sang,
425 *Flesh sins, flesh redeems, flesh reigns as God of God.*[7]
Then Peace piped a note of poetry:
*As a rule the sun is brighter after the biggest clouds; After
hostilities love is brighter.*
"After sharp showers," said Peace, "the sun shines brightest;

2. Psalm 51.4. The psalm is understood to assign the sole power of judging the sinner to God, because it is only against God that the sinner has acted.
3. I.e., "Law dictates that the king pardon the felon if the king sees him."
4. [He is a just judge who leaves] no evil unpunished [and no good unrewarded]. Not from the Bible but from Pope Innocent III's tract *Of Contempt for the World* (1195).
5. In 2 Corinthians 12.4, St. Paul tells how in a vision he was snatched up to heaven where he heard things that may not be repeated among men.

Langland is apparently invoking a similar mystic experience when he puts into Christ's mouth a promise to spare many of his half-brothers, the unbaptized. The orthodox theology of the time taught that all the unbaptized were irredeemably damned, a proposition Langland refused to accept: in his vision he has heard words to the contrary that might not be repeated among men, because they would be held heretical.
6. Psalm 143.2.
7. From a medieval Latin hymn. The source of the two Latin verses immediately below is Alain of Lisle, a late 12th-century poet and philosopher.

No weather is warmer than after watery clouds;
430 Nor any love lovelier, or more loving friends,
Than after war and woe when Love and peace are masters.
There was never war in this world nor wickedness so sharp
That Love, if he liked, might not make a laughing matter.
And peace through patience puts an end to all perils."
435 "Truce!" said Truth, "you tell the truth, by Jesus!
Let's kiss in covenant, and each of us clasp other."
"And let no people," said Peace, "perceive that we argued;
For nothing is impossible to him that is almighty."
"You speak the truth," said Righteousness, and reverently kissed her,
440 Peace, and Peace her, *per saecula saeculorum:* [8]
    Mercy and Truth have met together; Righteousness and Peace
        have kissed each other. [9]
Truth sounded a trumpet then and sang *Te Deum Laudamus,* [1]
And then Love strummed a lute with a loud note:
    Behold how good and how pleasant, etc. [2]
445 Till the day dawned these damsels caroled.
When bells rang for the Resurrection, and right then I awoke
And called Kit my wife and Calote my daughter:
"Arise and go reverence God's resurrection,
And creep to the Cross on knees, and kiss it as a jewel,
450 For God's blessed body it bore for our good,
And it frightens the Fiend, for such is its power
That no grisly ghost may glide in its shadow."

From *The C-Text*

[THE DREAMER MEETS CONSCIENCE AND REASON] [3]

Thus I awoke, as God's my witness, when I lived in Cornhill, [4]
Kit and I in a cottage, clothed like a loller, [5]
And little beloved, believe you me,
Among lollers of London and illiterate hermits.
5 For I wrote rhymes of those men as Reason taught me.
For as I came by Conscience I met with Reason,
In a hot harvest time when I had my health,
And limbs to labor with, and loved good living,
And to do no deed but to drink and sleep.
10 My body sound, my mind sane, a certain one accosted me;
Roaming in remembrance, thus Reason upbraided me:

---

8. For ever and ever (the liturgical formula).
9. Psalm 85.10.
1. We praise thee, O Lord.
2. Psalm 133.1. The verse continues, "it is for brothers to dwell together in unity."
3. In the C-text, the last of the three versions of *Piers Plowman,* Langland prefixed to the "Confession of the Seven Deadly Sins" (*Passus* 5 of the B-text) an apology by the Dreamer, "Long Will," who is at once long (or tall) and long on willing (or, arguably, willful). Although there is no conclusive historical evidence for doing so, readers of *Piers Plowman* have generally regarded this passage as a source of information about the real author, about

whom we otherwise know so little.
4. An area of London associated with vagabonds, seedy clerics, and people at loose ends.
5. Idler, vagabond. The term was eventually applied to the proto-Protestant followers of John Wycliffe. "Kit": refers to "Kit my wife and Calote [i.e., Colette] my daughter" (B-text, 18.426). The Dreamer seems to be someone with clerical training who has received consecration into minor clerical orders (such as that of deacon) but who is not a priest. Lesser clerics could marry, although marriage blocked their further advancement in the church.

"Can you serve," he said, "or sing in a church?
Or cock hay with my hay-makers, or heap it on the cart,
Mow it or stack what's mown or make binding for sheaves?
15 Or have a horn and be a hedge-guard and lie outdoors at night,
And keep my corn in my field from cattle and thieves?
Or cut cloth or shoe-leather, or keep sheep and cattle,
Mend hedges, or harrow, or herd pigs or geese,
Or any other kind of craft that the commons needs,
20 So that you might be of benefit to your bread-providers?"
"Certainly!" I said, "and so God help me,
I am too weak to work with sickle or with scythe,
And too long,[6] believe me, for any low stooping,
Or laboring as a laborer to last any while."
"Then have you lands to live by," said Reason, "or relations with
25   money
To provide you with food? For you seem an idle man,
A spendthrift who thrives on spending, and throws time away.
Or else you get what food men give you going door to door,
Or beg like a fraud on Fridays[7] and feastdays in churches.
30 And that's a loller's life that earns little praise
Where Rightfulness rewards men as they really deserve.
        He shall reward every man according to his works.[8]
Or are you perhaps lame in your legs or other limbs of your body,
Or maimed through some misadventure, so that you might be
        excused?"
"When I was young, many years ago,
35 My father and my friends provided me with schooling,
Till I understood surely what Holy Scripture meant,
And what is best for the body as the Book tells,
And most certain for the soul, if so I may continue.
And, in faith, I never found, since my friends died,
40 Life that I liked save in these long clothes.[9]
And if I must live by labor and earn my livelihood,
The labor I should live by is the one I learned best.
        [Abide] in the same calling wherein you were called.[1]
And so I live in London and upland[2] as well.
The tools that I toil with to sustain myself
45 Are Paternoster and my primer, *Placebo* and *Dirige*,[3]
And sometimes my Psalter and my seven Psalms.
These I say for the souls of such as help me.
And those who provide my food vouchsafe, I think,
To welcome me when I come, once a month or so,
50 Now with him, now with her, and in this way I beg
Without bag or bottle but my belly alone.
        And also, moreover, it seems to me, sir Reason,

---

6. I.e., tall, perhaps a pun on "willfulness." The Dreamer is called "Long Will" in B-text, 15.152.
7. Fast days, because Christ was crucified on a Friday.
8. Matthew 16.27; cf. Psalm 62.12.
9. The long dress of a cleric, not limited to actual priests.
1. 1 Corinthians 7.20, with variations.
2. North of London, in rural country.

3. "I will please [the Lord]" and "Make straight [my way]" (Psalm 116.9 and 5.8, respectively). *Placebo* and *Dirige* are the first words of hymns based on two of the seven "penitential" Psalms that were part of the regular order of personal prayer. "Paternoster": the Lord's Prayer ("Our father"). The "primer" was the basic collection of private prayers for laypeople.

No clerk should be constrained to do lower-class work.
For by the law of Leviticus[4] that our Lord ordained
55 Clerks with tonsured crowns should, by common understanding,
Neither strain nor sweat nor swear at inquests,
Nor fight in a vanguard and defeat an enemy:
    Do not render evil for evil.[5]
For they are heirs of Heaven, all that have the tonsure,
And in choir and in churches they are Christ's ministers.
    The Lord is the portion of my inheritance. And elsewhere,
        Mercy does not constrain.[6]
60 It is becoming for clerks to perform Christ's service,
And untonsured boys be burdened with bodily labor.
For none should acquire clerk's tonsure unless he claims descent
From franklins[7] and free men and folk properly wedded.
Bondmen and bastards and beggars' children—
65 These belong to labor; and lords' kin should serve
God and good men as their degree requires,
Some to sing Masses or sit and write,
Read and receive what Reason ought to spend.
But since bondmen's boys have been made bishops,
70 And bastards' boys have been archdeacons,
And shoemakers and their sons have through silver become knights,
And lords' sons their laborers whose lands are mortgaged to them—
And thus for the right of this realm they ride against our enemies
To the comfort of the commons and to the king's honor—
75 And monks and nuns on whom mendicants must depend
Have had their kin named knights and bought knight's-fees,[8]
And popes and patrons have shunned poor gentle blood
And taken the sons of Simon Magus[9] to keep the sanctuary,
Life-holiness and love have gone a long way hence,
80 And will be so till this is all worn out or otherwise changed.
Therefore proffer me no reproach, Reason, I pray you,
For in my conscience I conceive what Christ wants me to do.
Prayers of a perfect man and appropriate penance
Are the labor that our Lord loves most of all.
85   "*Non de solo,*" I said, "forsooth *vivit homo,*
Nec in pane et in pabulo;[1] the Paternoster witnesses
Fiat voluntas Dei[2]—that provides us with everything."
    Said Conscience, "By Christ, I can't see that this lies;°   *is pertinent*
But it seems no serious perfectness to be a city-beggar,
90 Unless you're licensed to collect for prior or monastery."

4. Leviticus 21 sets restrictions on members of the priesthood.
5. 1 Thessalonians 5.15, with variations.
6. I.e., "mercy is not restricted," source unknown. The quotation above is from Psalm 16.5.
7. Freemen. By this date, the term did not just mean nonserfs but designated landowners who were becoming members of the gentry class yet were not knights. The distinction Langland seems to make in this line between franklins and freemen may reflect the rising status of certain families of "freedmen," the original meaning of the word *franklins.*
8. The estate a knight held from his overlord in

return for military service was called his "fee."
9. Priests who obtained office through bribery or "simony," a term derived from Simon Magus, a magician who offered the apostles money for their power to perform miracles through the Holy Spirit (see Acts 8).
1. "Not solely [by bread] doth man live, neither by bread nor by food"; the verse continues, "but by every word that proceedeth out of the mouth of God": Matthew 4.4, with variations; cf. Deuteronomy 8.3.
2. "God's will be done." The Lord's Prayer reads, "Thy will be done" (Matthew 6.10).

"That is so," I said, "and so I admit
That at times I've lost time and at times misspent it;
And yet I hope, like him who has often bargained
And always lost and lost, and at the last it happened
95   He bought such a bargain he was the better ever,
That all his looked paltry in the long run,
Such a winning was his through what grace decreed.
     The kingdom of Heaven is like unto treasure hidden in a field.
     The woman who found the piece of silver, etc.[3]
So I hope to have of him that is almighty
A gobbet of his grace, and begin a time
100 That all times of my time shall turn into profit."
     "And I counsel you," said Reason, "quickly to begin
The life that is laudable and reliable for the soul."
"Yes, and continue," said Conscience, and I came to the church."[4]

3. Matthew 13.44, Luke 15.9–10. Both passages come from parables that compare finding the kingdom of heaven to risking everything you have to get the one thing that matters most.
4. The four lines that follow this passage connect it to the beginning of the second dream (B-text, 5): "And to the church I set off, to honor God; before the Cross, on my knees, I beat my breast, sighing for my sins, saying my Paternoster, weeping and wailing until I fell asleep."

MIDDLE ENGLISH LYRICS

It was only late in the fourteenth century that English began to develop the kinds of aristocratic, formal, learned, and literary types of lyric that had long been cultivated on the Continent by the Troubador poets in the south of France, the Minnesänger in Germany (German *Minne* corresponds to French *fine amour*—that is, refined or aristocratic love), or the Italian poets whose works Dante characterized as the *dolce stil nuovo* (the sweet new style). Chaucer, under the influence of French poets, wrote lovers' complaints, homiletic poetry, and verse letters in the form of ballades, roundels, and other highly stylized lyric types (see pp. 313–16). In the fifteenth century, John Lydgate, Thomas Hoccleve, and others following Chaucer wrote lyrics of this sort, which were praised for embellishing the English language, and these along with Chaucer's were collected in manuscript anthologies that were produced commercially for well-to-do buyers.

Chaucer, his courtly predecessors, and their followers were of course familiar with and influenced by an ancient tradition of popular song from which only a small fraction survives. With one exception, the Middle English lyrics included in this section are the work of anonymous poets and are difficult to date with any precision. Some of these survive in a single manuscript, especially in anthologies of religious poetry and prose. The topics and language in these poems are highly conventional, yet the lyrics often seem remarkably fresh and spontaneous. Many are marked by strong accentual rhythms with a good deal of alliteration. Their pleasure does not come from originality or lived experience but from variations of expected themes and images. Some were undoubtedly set to music, and in a few cases the music has survived. Perhaps the earliest of those printed here, *The Cuckoo Song*, is a canon or round in which the voices follow one another and join together echoing the joyous cry, "Cuckou." The rooster and hen in *The Nun's Priest's Tale* sing *My Lief Is Faren in Londe* in "sweet accord." *I Am of Ireland* was undoubtedly accompanied by dancing as well as music.

A frequent topic that lyric shares with narrative is the itemization of the beloved's beauties. The Alisoun of the lyric and Alisoun of *The Miller's Tale* are both dark eyed, a quality that suggests a sexuality supressed in the conventional gray- or blue-eyed heroines of courtly romance. The lover in the lyric protests, as Nicholas does in *The Miller's Tale,* that he will die if he cannot obtain her love.

The joyous return of spring (the *reverdie,* spring song, or, literally, "regreening") is the subject of many lyrics. In love lyrics the mating of birds and animals in wild nature often contrasts with the melancholy of unrequited or forsaken lovers. These lovers are usually male. We know that some women wrote troubador and court poetry, but we do not know whether women composed popular lyrics; women certainly sang popular songs, just as they are portrayed doing in narrative poetry.

Many more religious lyrics were written down and preserved. These were mostly written by anonymous clerics, but in rare instances we know at least the name of an author. Seventeen poems by the Franciscan William Herebert are collected in a single manuscript. In his dramatic lyric printed here, the main speaker is the Christ-knight, returning from the Crucifixion, which is treated as a battle the way it is in *Dream of the Rood* and in Passus 18 of *Piers Plowman.* Christ in his bloodstained garments is compared in a famous image from Isaiah 63.2 to one who treads grapes in a winepress, a passage that is also the source of Julia Ward Howe's "grapes of wrath" in *The Battle Hymn of the Republic.*

The religious lyrics are for the most part devotional poems that depend on the Latin Bible and liturgy of the church. The passage from Isaiah adapted by Herebert was part of a lesson in a mass performed during Holy Week. But the diction of that poem, though there are a few French loan words, is predominantly of native English origin. Many of the poems, like Herebert's, contain an element of drama: *Ye that Pasen by the Weye* is spoken by Christ from the Cross to all wayfarers; similar verses are spoken by the crucified Christ to the crowd (as well as to the audience) in the mystery plays of the Crucifixion.

Among the most beautiful and tender lyrics are those about the Virgin Mary, who is the greatest of all queens and ladies. They celebrate Mary's joys, sorrows, and the mystery of her virgin motherhood. *Sunset on Calvary,* a tableau of Mary at the foot of the Cross, contains an implicit play upon English "sun," which is setting, and the "son," who is dying but, like the sun, will rise again. Like love songs the Marian lyrics often celebrate the mysteries of the natural world and thus defy any simple division of medieval lyric into "secular" or "religious" poetry. *I Sing of a Maiden* visualizes the conception of Jesus in terms of the falling dew, and he steals silently to her bower like a lover. *Adam Lay Bound* cheerfully treats the original sin as though it were a child's theft of an apple, which had the happy result of making Mary the Queen of Heaven. *The Corpus Christi Carol* has the form of a lullaby but penetrates by stages to the heart of a mystery similar to the Holy Grail, the chalice that contained Christ's blood, which continues to flow, as it does in this carol, for humanity's salvation.

The Cuckoo Song

> Sumer is ycomen in,
> Loude sing cuckou!
> Groweth seed and bloweth meed,[1]
> And springth the wode° now.   *wood*
> 5 Sing cuckou!
>
> Ewe bleteth after lamb,
> Loweth after calve cow,

---

1. The meadow blossoms.

Bulloc sterteth,° bucke verteth,°   *leaps/farts*
Merye sing cuckou!
10   Cuckou, cuckou,
Wel singest thou cuckou:
Ne swik° thou never now!   *cease*

Alison

Bitweene° Merch and Averil,   *in the seasons of*
When spray biginneth to springe,
The litel fowl hath hire wil°   *pleasure*
On hire leod[1] to singe.
5   Ich° libbe° in love-longinge   *I/live*
For semlokest° of alle thinge.   *seemliest, fairest*
Heo° may me blisse bringe: *she*
Ich am in hire baundoun.°   *power*
An hendy hap ich habbe yhent,[2]
10   Ichoot° from hevene it is me sent: *I know*
From alle[3] wommen my love is lent,°   *removed*
And light° on Alisoun.   *alights*

On hew° hire heer° is fair ynough,   *hue/hair*
Hire browe browne, hire yë° blake;   *eye*
15   With lossum cheere heo on me lough;[4]
With middel smal and wel ymake.
But° heo me wolle to hire take   *unless*
For to been hire owen make,°   *mate*
Longe to liven ichulle° forsake,   *I will*
20   And feye° fallen adown.   *dead*
An hendy hap, etc.

Nightes when I wende° and wake,   *turn*
Forthy° mine wonges° waxeth wan: *therefore/cheeks*
Levedy,° al for thine sake   *lady*
25   Longinge is ylent me on.[5]
In world nis noon so witer° man   *clever*
That al hire bountee° telle can;   *excellence*
Hire swire° is whittere° than the swan,   *neck/whiter*
And fairest may° in town.   *maid*
30   An hendy, etc.

Ich am for wowing° al forwake,°   *wooing/worn out from waking*
Wery so° water in wore.[6]   *as*
Lest any reve me[7] my make
Ich habbe y-yerned yore.[8]
35   Bettere is tholien° while° sore   *endure/for a time*
Than mournen evermore.
Geinest under gore,[9]

---

1. In her language.
2. A gracious chance I have received.
3. I.e., all other.
4. With lovely face she on me smiled.
5. Longing has come upon me.

6. Perhaps "millpond."
7. Deprive me.
8. I have been worrying long since.
9. Fairest beneath clothing.

Herkne to my roun:°   *song*
An hendy, etc.

My Lief Is Faren in Londe

My lief is faren in londe[1]—
Allas, why is she so?
And I am so sore bonde°   *bound*
I may nat come her to.
5   She hath myn herte in holde
Wherever she ride or go°—   *walk*
With trewe love a thousand folde.

Western Wind

Westron wind, when will thou blow?
The small rain down can rain.
Christ, that my love were in my arms,
And I in my bed again.

I Am of Ireland

Ich am of Irlonde,
And of the holy londe
    Of Irlonde.
Goode sire, praye ich thee,
5   For of° sainte charitee,   *sake of*
Com and dance with me
    In Irlonde.

What is he, this lordling, that cometh from the fight[1]

"What is he, this lordling,[2] that cometh from the fight
With blood-rede wede so grislich ydight,[3]
So faire ycointised,° so semelich in sight,[4]   *appareled*
So stiflich he gangeth,[5] so doughty° a knight?"   *valiant*

5   "Ich° it am, ich it am, that ne speke but right,[6]   *I*
Champioun to helen° mankinde in fight."   *save*

"Why then is thy shroud rede, with blood al ymeind,
As troddares in wringe with must al bespreind?"[7]

1. My beloved has gone away.
1. The poem, by William Herebert (d. 1333), par-
aphrases Isaiah 63.1–7, in which the "lordling"
(lord's son) is a messianic figure returning from
battle against the Edomites.
2. Who is this lord's son?
3. With blood-red garment, so terribly arrayed.

4. So fair to behold.
5. So boldly he goes.
6. Who speaks only what is right.
7. Why then is thy garment red, all stained with
blood, like treaders in the winepress all spattered
with must (the juice of the grapes).

"The wring ich have ytrodded al myself one°   *alone*
10 And of° al mankinde was none other wone.°   *for/hope*
Ich hem[8] have ytrodded in wrathe and in grame,°   *anger*
And al my wede is bespreind with here blood ysame,[9]
And al my robe yfouled° to here grete shame.   *soiled*
The day of th'ilke wreche[1] liveth in my thought;
15 The yeer of medes yelding ne foryet ich nought.[2]
Ich looked al aboute some helping mon;[3]
Ich soughte al the route,[4] but help nas ther non.
It was mine owne strengthe that this bote° wrought,   *remedy*
Mine owne doughtinesse that help ther me brought."[5]
20 Ich have ytrodded the folk in wrathe and in grame,
Adreint al with shennesse, ydrawe down with shame."[6]

"On Godes milsfulnesse° ich wil bethenche me,[7]   *mercy*
And herien° him in alle thing that he yeldeth° me."   *praise/gives*

Ye That Pasen by the Weye

Ye that pasen by the weye,
Abidet a little stounde.°   *while*
Beholdet, all my felawes,
Yif° any me lik is founde.   *if*
5 To the tre with nailes thre
Wol° fast I hange bounde;   *very*
With a spere all thoru my side
To mine herte is made a wounde.

Sunset on Calvary

Now gooth sunne under wode:[1]
Me reweth,[2] Marye, thy faire rode.°   *face*
Now gooth sunne under tree:
Me reweth, Marye, thy sone and thee.

I Sing of a Maiden

I sing of a maiden
    That is makelees:[1]
King of alle kinges
    To° her sone she chees.°   *as/chose*

8. Them, i.e., humankind symbolized by the grapes in the press. Cf. line 20.
9. And my garment is all spattered with their blood together.
1. That same vengeance (perhaps Judgment Day).
2. I do not forget the year of paying wages.
3. I looked all around for some man to help (me).
4. I searched the whole crowd.

5. My own valor brought help to me there.
6. All drowned with ignominy, pulled down with shame.
7. I will bethink myself.
1. Both the woods and the wooden Cross.
2. I pity.
1. Spotless, matchless, and mateless—a triple pun.

5   He cam also° stille   *as*
       Ther° his moder° was   *where/mother*
       As dewe in Aprille
       That falleth on the gras.

       He cam also stille
10   To his modres bowr
       As dewe in Aprille
       That falleth on the flowr.

       He cam also stille
       Ther his moder lay
15   As dewe in Aprille
       That falleth on the spray.

       Moder and maiden
       Was nevere noon but she:
       Wel may swich° a lady   *such*
20   Godes moder be.

Adam Lay Bound

Adam lay ybounden, bounden in a bond,
Four thousand winter thoughte he not too long;
And al was for an apple, an apple that he took,
As clerkes finden writen, writen in hire book.
5 Ne hadde[1] the apple taken been, the apple taken been,
Ne hadde nevere Oure Lady ybeen hevene Queen.
Blessed be the time that apple taken was:
Therfore we mown° singen *Deo Gratias.*[2]   *may*

The Corpus Christi Carol

Lully, lullay, lully, lullay,
The faucon° hath borne my make° away.   *falcon/mate*

He bare him up, he bare him down,
He bare him into an orchard brown.

5 In that orchard ther was an hall
That was hanged with purple and pall.°   *black velvet*

And in that hall ther was a bed:
It was hanged with gold so red.

And in that bed ther lith° a knight,   *lies*
10 His woundes bleeding by day and night.

---

1. Had not.   2. Thanks be to God.

By that beddes side ther kneeleth a may,°   *maid*
And she weepeth both night and day.

And by that beddes side ther standeth a stoon°   *stone*
Corpus Christi[1] writen thereon.

1. Body of Christ.

JULIAN OF NORWICH
1342–ca.1416

The "Showings," or "Revelations" as they are also called, were sixteen mystical visions received by the woman known as Julian of Norwich. The name may be one that she adopted when she became an anchoress in a cell attached to the church of St. Julian that still stands in that town on the northeast coast of England. An anchorite (m.) or anchoress (f.) is a religious recluse confined to an enclosure, which he or she has vowed never to leave. At the time of such an enclosing the burial service was performed, signifying that the enclosed person was dead to the world and that the enclosure corresponded to a grave. The point of this confinement was, of course, to pursue more actively the contemplative or spiritual life.

Julian may well have belonged to a religious order at the time that her visions led her to choose the life of an anchoress. We know very little about her except what she tells us in her writings. She is, however, very precise about the date of her visions. They occurred, she tells us, at the age of thirty and a half on May 13, 1373. Four extant wills bequeath sums for Julian's maintenance in her anchorage. The most important document witnessing her life is *The Book of Margery Kempe* (see the headnote for Margery Kempe, p. 367). Kempe sought out Julian's advice whether there might be any deception in Kempe's own visions, "for the anchoress," she says, "was expert in such things." Kempe's description of Julian's conversation accords well with the doctrines and personality that emerge from Julian's own book.

A Book of Showings survives in a short and a long version. The longer text, from which the following excerpts are taken, was the product of fifteen and more years of meditation on the meaning of the visions in which much had been obscure to Julian. Apparently the mystical experiences were never repeated, but through constant study and contemplation the showings acquired a greater clarity, richness, and profundity as they continued to be turned over in a mind both gifted with spiritual insight and learned in theology. Her editors document her extensive use of the Bible and her familiarity with medieval religious writings in both English and Latin.

Julian's showings are, in her words, both "ghostly" (that is, spiritual) and "bodily." They embrace powerful visual phenomena such as blood drops running from the crown of thorns and revelations that take place in pure mind. The years of meditation on these showings led her ultimately to a personal, profound, and difficult understanding of the Trinity—the one God in the three persons of the father, the son, and the Holy Spirit—and humanity's participation in that oneness. For Julian, God the father generates the human soul (conceived of as immortal "substance," co-eternal with God); God the son is the mother who bears, nourishes, and redeems (through his own incarnation) sensual human nature; God the Holy Spirit binds deity and humanity in eternal love and grace. Julian expresses such sophisticated theological concepts in language that can be intricate in its logic yet at other times transparently simple. She herself is amazed that God, who is so great and awe inspiring, can be so "homely" (so direct, intimate, and familial) with "a sinful creature." The blood of Christ reminds her of water dripping from the eaves of a house and of the scales of herring. Her concept of Jesus as mother has antecedents in both the Old and New Testaments, in medieval theology, and in the writings of medieval mystics (both men and women). The idea is integral to Julian's complex metaphysical reasoning about the Trinity; she also vividly realizes it by analogy with the emotional experiences of mother and child: a sinner is like a frightened child running to its mother for comfort and help.

Julian is an accomplished prose stylist, inheriting a tradition of English religious prose that goes back to the Old English period. Her book is one of many distinguished devotional and mystical works, both English and Continental, composed during the late Middle Ages, such as the *Dialogue* of Catherine of Siena (translated into Middle English as *The Orchard of Syon*) or the anonymous *Cloud of Unknowing*. Julian wrote and rewrote *A Book of Showings* to come to terms with her visions, but, like other visionaries, she felt the visions were not only a personal gift but an obligation. "We are all one," she says, "and I am sure I saw it for the profit of many other."

From A Book of Showings to the Anchoress Julian of Norwich[1]

[THE FIRST REVELATION]

Chapter 3

And when I was thirty year old and a half, God sent me a bodily sickness in the which I lay three days and three nights; and on the fourth night I took all my rites of holy church, and went[2] not to have liven till day. And after this I lay two days and two nights; and on the third night I weened[3] oftentimes to have passed, and so weened they that were with me. And yet in this I felt a great loathsomeness[4] to die, but for nothing that was on earth that me liketh to live for, ne[5] for no pain that I was afraid of, for I trusted in God of his mercy. But it was for I would have lived to have loved God better and longer time, that I might by the grace of that living have the more knowing and loving of God in the bliss of heaven. For me thought[6] all that time that I had lived here so little and so short in regard of[7] that endless bliss, I thought: Good Lord, may my living no longer be to thy worship?[8] And I understood by my reason and by the feeling of my pains that I should die; and I assented fully with all the will of my heart to be at God's will.

Thus I endured till day, and by then was my body dead from the middes downward, as to my feeling.[9] Then was I holpen[1] to be set upright, underset[2] with help, for to have the more freedom of my heart to be at God's will, and thinking on God while my life lasted. My curate was sent for to be at my ending, and before he came I had set up my eyen[3] and might not speak. He

1. The text is based on that given by Edmund Colledge, O.S.A., and James Walsh, S. J., for the Pontifical Institute of Mediaeval Studies, Toronto (1978), but it has been freely edited and modern spelling has been used where possible.
2. Thought.
3. Supposed.
4. Reluctance.
5. Nor.
6. I thought, [it] thought me.
7. In comparison with.
8. Glory.
9. As it felt to me.
1. Helped.
2. Supported.
3. Eyes.

set the cross before my face and said: "I have brought the image of thy savior; look thereupon and comfort thee therewith." Me thought I was well, for my eyen was set upright into heaven, where I trusted to come by the mercy of God; but nevertheless I assented to set my eyen in the face of the crucifix, if I might, and so I did, for me thought I might longer dure to look even forth than right up.[4] After this my sight began to fail. It waxed as dark about me in the chamber as if it had been night, save in the image of the cross, wherein held a common light; and I wist[5] not how. All that was beside the cross was ugly and fearful to me as[6] it had been much occupied with fiends.

After this the over[7] part of my body began to die so farforth that unneth[8] I had any feeling. My most pain was shortness of breath and failing of life. Then went[9] I verily to have passed. And in this suddenly all my pain was taken from me, and I was as whole, and namely in the over part of my body, as ever I was before. I marvelled of this sudden change, for me thought that it was a privy working of God, and not of kind;[1] and yet by feeling of this ease I trusted never more to have lived, ne the feeling of this ease was no full ease to me, for me thought I had liever[2] have been delivered of this world, for my heart was willfully set thereto.

Then came suddenly to my mind that I should desire the second wound of our Lord's gift and of his grace, that my body might be fulfilled with mind and feeling of his blessed passion, as I had before prayed,[3] for I would that his pains were my pains, with compassion and afterward longing to God. Thus thought me that I might with his grace have the wounds that I had before desired; but in this I desired never no bodily sight ne no manner showing of God, but compassion as me thought that a kind soul might have with our Lord Jesu, that for love would become a deadly[4] man. With him I desired to suffer, living in my deadly body, as God would give me grace.

Chapter 4

And in this suddenly I saw the red blood running down from under the garland, hot and freshly, plenteously and lively, right as it was in the time that the garland of thorns was pressed on his blessed head. Right so, both God and man, the same that suffered for me, I conceived truly and mightily that it was himself that shewed it me without any mean.[5]

And in the same showing suddenly the Trinity fulfilled my heart most of joy, and so I understood it shall be in heaven without end to all that shall come there. For the Trinity is God, God is the Trinity. The Trinity is our maker, the Trinity is our keeper, the Trinity is our everlasting lover, the Trinity is endless joy and our bliss, by our Lord Jesu Christ, and in our Lord Jesu Christ. And this was showed in the first sight and in all, for where Jesu appeareth, the blessed Trinity is understand, as to my sight.[6] And I said, "Benedicite dominus."[7] This I said for reverence in my meaning,[8] with a

4. Endure to look straight ahead than straight up.
5. Knew.
6. As if.
7. Upper.
8. To the extent that scarcely.
9. Thought.
1. Nature.
2. Rather.
3. Julian had prayed for three gifts: direct experi-

ence of Christ's passion, mortal sickness, and the wounds of true contrition, loving compassion, and a willed desire for God.
4. Mortal.
5. Intermediary.
6. Is understood, as I see it.
7. Blessed be the Lord.
8. Intention.

mighty voice, and full greatly was I astoned[9] for wonder and marvel that I had, that he that is so reverend and so dreadful[1] will be so homely[2] with a sinful creature living in this wretched flesh.

Thus I took it for that time that our Lord Jesu of his courteous love would show me comfort before the time of my temptation; for me thought it might well be that I should by the sufferance of God and with his keeping be tempted of[3] fiends before I should die. With this sight of his blessed passion, with the godhead that I saw in my understanding, I knew well that it was strength enough to me, yea, and to all creatures living that should be saved, against all the fiends of hell, and against all ghostly[4] enemies.

In this he brought our Lady Saint Mary to my understanding; I saw her ghostly in bodily likeness, a simple maiden and a meek, young of age, a little waxen above a child,[5] in the stature as she was when she conceived. Also God showed me in part the wisdom and the truth of her soul, wherein I understood the reverend beholding, that she beheld her God, that is her maker, marvelling with great reverence that he would be born of her that was a simple creature of his making. And this wisdom and truth, knowing the greatness of her maker and the littlehead[6] of herself that is made, made her to say full meekly to Gabriel: "Lo me here, God's handmaiden."[7] In this sight I did understand verily that she is more than all that God made beneath her in worthiness and in fullhead;[8] for above her is nothing that is made but the blessed manhood of Christ, as to my sight.

Chapter 5

In this same time that I saw this sight of the head bleeding, our good Lord showed a ghostly sight of his homely loving. I saw that he is to us all thing that is good and comfortable to our help. He is our clothing that for love wrappeth us and windeth us, halseth us[9] and all becloses us, hangeth about us for tender love that[1] he may never leave us. And so in this sight I saw that he is all thing that is good, as to my understanding.

And in this he showed a little thing, the quantity of an hazelnut, lying in the palm of my hand, as me seemed, and it was as round as a ball. I looked thereon with the eye of my understanding, and thought: What may this be? And it was answered generally thus: It is all that is made. I marvelled how it might last, for me thought it might suddenly have fallen to nought for[2] littleness. And I was answered in my understanding: It lasteth and ever shall, for God loveth it; and so hath all thing being by the love of God.

In this little thing I saw three properties. The first is that God made it, the second that God loveth it, the third that God keepeth[3] it. But what beheld I therein? Verily, the maker, the keeper, the lover. For till I am substantially united to him[4] I may never have full rest ne very[5] bliss; that is to say that I be so fastened to him that there be right nought that is made between my God and me.

---

9. Astonished.
1. Awe-inspiring.
2. Familiar, intimate (the quality of being "at home").
3. By.
4. Spiritual.
5. Grown a little older than a child.
6. Littleness.
7. See Luke 1.38.

8. Perfection.
9. Envelops us and embraces us.
1. So that.
2. Because of.
3. Looks after.
4. Joined to him in "substance," which Julian regards as the eternal essence of being.
5. True.

This little thing that is made, me thought it might have fallen to nought for littleness. Of this needeth us to have knowledge, that us liketh nought all thing that is made, for to love and have God that is unmade.[6] For this is the cause why we be not all in ease of heart and of soul, for we seek here rest in this thing that is so little, where no rest is in, and we know not our God, that is almighty, all wise and all good, for he is very rest. God will be known, and him liketh that we rest us in him; for all that is beneath him suffiseth not to us. And this is the cause why that no soul is in rest till it is noughted of all things that is made.[7] When she is wilfully[8] noughted for love, to have him that is all, then is she able to receive ghostly rest.

And also our good Lord showed that it is full great pleasance to him that a sely[9] soul come to him naked, plainly and homely. For this is the kind[1] yearning of the soul by the touching of the Holy Ghost, as by the understanding that I have in this showing: God of thy goodness gave me thyself, for thou art enough to me, and I may ask nothing that is less that may be full worship to thee. And if I ask any thing that is less, ever me wanteth;[2] but only in thee I have all.

And these words of the goodness of God be full lovesome to the soul and full near touching the will of our Lord, for his goodness fulfilleth all his creatures and all his blessed works and overpasseth[3] without end. For he is the endlesshead and he made us only to himself and restored us by his precious passion, and ever keepeth us in his blessed love; and all this is of his goodness.

* * *

From *Chapter 7*

And in all that time that he showed this that I have now said in ghostly sight, I saw the bodily sight lasting of the plenteous bleeding of the head. The great drops of blood fell down fro under the garland like pellets, seeming as it had come out of the veins. And in the coming out they were brown red, for the blood was full thick; and in the spreading abroad they were bright red. And when it came at the brows, there they vanished; and not withstanding the bleeding continued till many things were seen and understood. Nevertheless the fairhead and livelihead continued in the same beauty and liveliness.

The plenteoushead is like to the drops of water that fall of the evesing[4] of an house after a great shower of rain, that fall so thick that no man may number them with no bodily wit.[5] And for the roundness they were like to the scale of herring in the spreading of the forehead.

These three things came to my mind in the time: pellets for the roundhead[6] in the coming out of the blood, the scale of the herring for the roundhead in the spreading, the drops of the evesing of a house for the plenteoushead unnumerable. This showing was quick[7] and lively and hideous and dreadful and sweet and lovely; and of all the sight that I saw this was most comfort

6. I.e., we need to know that we should not be attracted to earthly things, which are made, to love and possess God, who is not made, who exists eternally.
7. Emptied of (its attachment to) all created things.
8. Of its free will.
9. Innocent.

1. Natural.
2. I am forever lacking.
3. Surpasses.
4. Eaves.
5. Intelligence.
6. Roundness.
7. Vivid.

to me, that our good Lord, that is so reverend and dreadful, is so homely and so courteous, and this most fulfilled me with liking and sickerness[8] in soule.

And to the understanding of this he showed this open example. It is the most worship[9] that a solemn king or a great lord may do to a poor servant if he will be homely with him; and namely if he show it himself of a full true meaning[1] and with a glad cheer both in private and openly. Then thinketh this poor creature thus: "Lo, what might this noble lord do more worship and joy to me than to show to me that am so little this marvelous homeliness? Verily, it is more joy and liking to me than if he gave me great gifts and were himself strange in manner." This bodily example was showed so high that this man's heart might be ravished and almost forget himself for joy of this great homeliness.

Thus it fareth by our Lord Jesu and by us, for verily it is the most joy that may be, as to my sight, that he that is highest and mightiest, noblest and worthiest, is lowest and meekest, homeliest and courteousest. And truly and verily this marvelous joy shall be show us all when we shall see him. And this will our good Lord that we believe and trust, joy and like, comfort us and make solace as we may with his grace and with his help, into[2] the time that we see it verily. For the most fullhead of joy that we shall have, as to my sight, is this marvelous courtesy and homeliness of our fader, that is our maker, in our Lord Jesu Christ, that is our brother and oure saviour. But this marvelous homeliness may no man know in this life, but if he have it by special showing of our Lord, or of great plenty of grace inwardly given of the Holy Ghost. But faith and belief with charity deserve the meed,[3] and so it is had by grace. For in faith with hope and charity our life is grounded. The showing is made to whom that God will, plainly teacheth the same opened and declared, with many privy points belonging to our faith and belief which be worshipful to be known. And when the showing which is given for a time is passed and hid, then faith keepeth it by grace of the Holy Ghost into our life's end. And thus by the showing it is none other than the faith, ne less ne more, as it may be seen by our Lord's meaning in the same matter, by then[4] it come to the last end.

Chapter 27

And after this our Lord brought to my mind the longing that I had to him before; and I saw nothing letted[5] me but sin, and so I beheld generally in us all, and me thought that if sin had not been, we should all have been clean[6] and like to our Lord as he made us. And thus in my folly before this time often I wondered why, by the great foreseeing wisdom of God, the beginning of sin was not letted.[7] For then thought me that all should have been well.

This stering[8] was much to be forsaken; and nevertheless mourning and sorrow I made therefore without reason and discretion. But Jesu that in this vision informed me of all that me needed answered by this word and said: "Sin is behovely,[9] but all shall be well, and all manner of thing shall be

8. Security.
9. Honor.
1. Intent.
2. Until.
3. Reward. "Charity": love. See 1 Corinthians 13.13.

4. By the time that.
5. Hindered.
6. Pure.
7. Prevented.
8. Fretting.
9. Necessary.

well."[1] In this naked word "Sin," our Lord brought to my mind generally all that is not good, and the shameful despite[2] and the uttermost tribulation that he bore for us in this life, and his dying and all his pains, and passion[3] of all his creatures ghostly and bodily. For we be all in part troubled, and we shall be troubled, following our master Jesu, till we be fully purged of our deadly[4] flesh which be not very good.

And with the beholding of this, with all the pains that ever were or ever shall be, I understood the passion of Christ for the most pain and over-passing.[5] And with all, this was showed in a touch, readily passed over into comfort. For our good Lord would not that the soul were afeared of this ugly sight. But I saw not sin, for I believe it had no manner of substance, ne no part of being,[6] ne it might not be known but by the pain that is caused thereof. And this pain is something, as to my sight, for a time, for it purgeth and maketh us to know ourself and ask mercy; for the passion of our Lord is comfort to us against all this, and so is his blessed will. And for the tender love that our good Lord hath to all that shall be saved, he comforteth readily and sweetly, meaning thus: It is true that sin is cause of all this pain, but all shall be well, and all manner of thing shall be well.

These words were showed full tenderly, showing no manner of blame to me ne to none that shall be safe.[7] Then were it great unkindness of me to blame or wonder on God of my sin, sithen[8] he blameth not me for sin. And in these same words I saw an high marvelous privity[9] hid in God, which privity he shall openly make and shall be known to us in heaven. In which knowing we shall verily see the cause why he suffered sin to come, in which sight we shall endlessly have joy.

[JESUS AS MOTHER]

From *Chapter 58*

God the blessedful Trinity, which is everlasting being, right as he is endless fro without beginning,[1] right so it was in his purpose endless to make mankind,[2] which fair kind[3] first was dight to[4] for his own son, the second person; and when he would,[5] by full accord of all the Trinity he made us all at once.[6] And in our making he knit us and oned[7] us to himself, by which oneing we be kept as clean[8] and as noble as we were made. By the virtue of that ilke[9] precious oneing we love our maker and like[1] him, praise and thank him, and endlessly enjoy[2] in him. And this is the working which is wrought continually in each soul that shall be saved, which is the godly will before said.

And thus in our making God almighty is our kindly[3] father, and god all

---

1. T. S. Eliot quotes this statement, versions of which appear several times in the *Showings*, in the last movement of his *Four Quartets*.
2. Spite.
3. Suffering.
4. Mortal.
5. Exceeding (pain).
6. On "substance" and "being," see chapter 5, p. 358, n. 4.
7. Saved.
8. Since.
9. Secret.
1. I.e., eternal.

2. I.e., his purpose to make humankind is also eternal.
3. Nature.
4. Prepared for.
5. Wanted to.
6. All of us at one and the same time.
7. United. Julian sustains the idea of oneness in the verb *oned* and the noun *oneing*.
8. Pure.
9. Same.
1. Please.
2. Rejoice.
3. Both "kind" and "natural."

wisdom is our kindly mother, with the love and the goodness of the Holy
Ghost, which is all one God, one Lord. And in the knitting and in the oneing
he is our very true spouse and we his loved wife[4] and his fair maiden, with
which wife he was never displeased. For he sayeth: "I love thee and thou
lovest me, and our love shall never part in two."

I beheld the working of all the blessed Trinity, in which beholding I saw
and understood these three properties: The property of the fatherhood, and
the property of the motherhood, and the property of the lordship in one God.
In our father almighty we have our keeping[5] and our bliss as anemptis[6] our
kindly substance which is to us by our making fro without beginning.[7] And
in the second person in wit[8] and wisdom we have our keeping as anemptis
our sensuality[9] our restoring and our saving, for he is our mother, brother
and savior And in our good lord the Holy Ghost we have our rewarding and
our yielding[1] for our living and our travail,[2] and endlessly overpassing[3] all
that we desire in his marvelous courtesy of his high plenteous grace. For all
our life is in three: in the first we have our being, and in the second we have
our increasing, and in the third we have our fulfilling. The first is kind,[4] the
second is mercy, the third is grace.

For the first[5] I saw and understood that the high might of the Trinity is
our father, and the deep wisdom of the Trinity is our mother, and the great
love of the Trinity is our lord; and all these have we in kind and in our
substantial making. And furthermore I saw that the second person, which is
our mother, substantially the same dearworthy person,[6] is now become our
mother sensual,[7] for we be double of God's making, that is to say substantial
and sensual. Our substance is the higher part, which we have in our father
God almighty; and the second person of the Trinity is our mother in kind in
our substantial making, in whom we be grounded and rooted, and he is our
mother of mercy in our sensual taking.[8]

* * *

From *Chapter 59*

* * *

And thus is Jesu our very[9] mother in kind of our first making, and he is
our very mother in grace by taking of our kind made. All the fair working
and all the sweet kindly offices of dearworthy motherhood is impropered to[1]
the second person, for in him we have this goodly will, whole and safe without end, both in kind and in grace, of his own proper goodness.

I understood three manner of beholdings of motherhood in God. The first
is ground of our kind making, the second is taking of our kind, and there
beginneth the motherhood of grace, the third is motherhood in working.[2]

4. The relationship between God and humanity is also conceived as a mystical marriage in which Christ is the bridegroom and the human soul his spouse.
5. Protection.
6. With regard to.
7. I.e., our natural created being, which is eternal. On *substance* see chapter 5, p. 358, n. 4.
8. Intelligence.
9. With regard to the nature of our sensual being (as opposed to substance).
1. Payment.

2. Life and labor.
3. Surpassing.
4. Nature.
5. For the first time.
6. The same beloved person with regard to our eternal being.
7. Mother of our physical being.
8. Taking on of sensuality.
9. True.
1. Appropriated to.
2. At work.

And therein is a forthspreading[3] by the same grace of length and breadth, of high and of deepness without end. And all is one love.

Chapter 60

But now me behooveth to say a little more of this forthspreading, as I understood, in the meaning of our Lord: how that we be brought again by the motherhood of mercy and grace into our kindly stead, where that we were in,[4] made by the motherhood of kind love, which kind love never leaveth us.

Our kind mother, our gracious mother (for he would[5] all wholly become our mother in all thing) he took the ground of his work full low[6] and full mildly in the maiden's womb. And that showed he first, where he brought that meek maiden before the eye of my understanding, in the simple stature as she was when she conceived;[7] that is to say our high god, the sovereign wisdom of all, in this low place he arrayed him and dight him[8] all ready in our poor flesh, himself to do the service, he and the office of motherhood in all thing. The mother's service is nearest, readiest, and surest: nearest for it is most of kind, readiest for it is most of love, and sikerest[9] for it is most of truth. This office ne might nor could never none doon to the full but he alone. We wit[1] that all our mothers bear us to pain and to dying. Ah, what is that? But our very Mother Jesu, he alone beareth us to joy and to endless living, blessed moot[2] he be. Thus he sustaineth us within him in love and travail, into the full time that he would suffer the sharpest thorns and grievous pains that ever were or ever shall be, and died at the last. And when he had done, and so borne us to bliss, yet might not all this make aseeth[3] to his marvelous love. And that showed he in these high overpassing words of love: "If I might suffer more I would suffer more."[4] He might no more die, but he would not stint[5] working.

Wherefore him behooveth to find[6] us, for the dearworthy love of motherhood hath made him debtor to us.[7] The mother may give her child sucken her milk, but our precious mother Jesu, he may feed us with himself, and doth full courteously and full tenderly with the blessed sacrament, that is precious food of very life; and with all the sweet sacraments he sustaineth us full mercifully and graciously, and so meant he in these blessed words, where he said: "I it am that holy church preacheth thee and teacheth thee." That is to say: All the health and the life of sacraments, all the virtue and the grace of my word, all the goodness that is ordained in holy church to thee, I it am.

The mother may lay her child tenderly to her breast, but our tender mother Jesu, he may homely lead us into his blessed breast by his sweet open side,[8] and show us therein in party of[9] the godhead and the joys of heaven with

---

3. (Infinite) spreading out, expansion.
4. The natural condition, i.e., the state of grace, that we were in originally.
5. Because he wanted to.
6. I.e., he laid the groundwork for his mission in a very humble place.
7. The appearance of the Virgin in Julian's first vision. See chapter 4, p. 358.
8. Arrayed and dressed himself.
9. Surest.
1. Know.

2. May.
3. Bring satisfaction.
4. These and other quotations refer back to Julian's earlier revelations.
5. Stop.
6. Nourish, feed.
7. As any mother is obligated to look after her child.
8. The wound inflicted by a soldier in John 19.34.
9. A part of.

ghostly sureness of endless bliss. And that showed he in the tenth revelation, giving the same understanding in this sweet word where he sayeth: "Lo, how I love thee." * * *

This fair lovely word "Mother," it is so sweet and so kind in itself that it may not verily be said of none ne to none but of him and to him[1] that is very mother of life and of all. To the property of motherhood longeth[2] kind love, wisdom, and knowing, and it is God. For though it be so that our bodily forthbringing be but little, low, and simple in regard[3] of our ghostly forth-bringing, yet it is he that doth it in the creatures by whom that it is done. The kind loving mother that woot and knoweth the need of her child, she keepeth it full tenderly as the kind and condition of motherhood will. And ever as it waxeth[4] in age and in stature, she changeth her works but not her love. And when it is waxed of more age, she suffereth it that it be chastised in breaking down of vices to make the child receive virtues and grace. This working with all that be fair and good, our Lord doth it in hem by whom it is done. Thus he is our mother in kind by the working of grace in the lower party for love of the higher. And he will[5] that we know it, for he will have all our love fastened to him; and in this I saw that all debt that we owe by God's bidding to fatherhood and motherhood is fulfilled in true loving of God, which blessed love Christ worketh in us. And this was showed in all, and namely in the words where he sayeth: "I it am that thou lovest."

Chapter 61

And in our ghostly forthbringing he useth more tenderness in keeping without any comparison, by as much as our soul is of more price in his sight. He kindleth our understanding, he prepareth our ways, he easeth our con-science, he comforteth our soul, he lighteth our heart and giveth us in party knowing and loving in his blessedful godhead, with gracious mind in his sweet manhood and his blessed passion, with courteous marveling in his high overpassing goodness, and maketh us to love all that he loveth for his love, and to be well apaid[6] with him and with all his works. And when we fall, hastily he raiseth us by his lovely becleping[7] and his gracious touching. And when we be strengthened by his sweet working, then we wilfully[8] choose him by his grace to be his servants and his lovers, lastingly without end.

And yet after this he suffereth some of us to fall more hard and more grievously than ever we did before, as us thinketh. And then ween[9] we (that be not all wise) that all were nought that we have begun. But it is not so, for it needeth us to fall, and it needeth us to see it; for if we fell not, we should not know how feeble and how wretched we be of ourself, nor also we should not so fulsomely[1] know the marvelous love of our maker.

For we shall verily see in heaven without end that we have grievously sinned in this life; and notwithstanding this we shall verily see that we were never hurt in his love, nor we were never the less of price in his sight. And by the assay of this falling we shall have an high and a marvelous knowing

1. Other manuscripts read "her," with reference to the Virgin.
2. Belongs.
3. In comparison with.
4. Grows.
5. Wants.
6. Pleased.
7. Calling (to us).
8. Gladly.
9. Suppose.
1. Fully.

of love in God without an end. For hard and marvelous is that love which may not nor will not be broken for[2] trespass.

And this was one understanding of profit; and other[3] is the lowness and meekness that we shall get by the sight of our falling, for thereby we shall highly be raised in heaven, to which rising we might never have come without that meekness. And therefore it needed us to see it; and if we see it not, though we fell it should not profit us. And commonly first we fall and sithen[4] we see it; and both is of the mercy of God.

The mother may suffer the child to fall sometime and be diseased[5] in diverse manner of peril come to her child for love. And though our earthly mother may suffer her child to perish, our heavenly mother Jesu may never suffer us that be his children to perish, for he is all mighty, all wisdom, and all love, and so is none but he, blessed mote he be.

But oft times when our falling and our wretchedness is showed to us, we be so sore adread and so greatly ashamed of ourself that unnethes[6] we wit where that we may hold us. But then will not our courteous mother that we flee away, for him were nothing loather;[7] for then he will that we use[8] the condition of a child. For when it is diseased and afeared, it runneth hastily to the mother; and if it may do no more, it crieth on the mother for help with all the might. So will he that we do as the meek child, saying thus: "My kind mother, my gracious mother, my dearworthy mother, have mercy on me. I have made myself foul and unlike to thee, and I may not nor can amend it but with thine help and grace."

And if we feel us not then eased, as soon be we sure that he useth[9] the condition of a wise mother. For if he see that it be for profit to us to mourn and to weep, he suffereth with ruth[1] and pity, into the best time,[2] for love. And he will then that we use the property of a child that ever more kindly trusteth to the love of the mother in weal and in woe. And he will that we take us mightily to the faith of holy church and find there our dearworthy mother in solace and true understanding with all the blessed common.[3] For one singular person may oftentimes be broken, as it seemeth to the self, but the whole body of holy church was never broken, nor never shall be without end. And therefore a sure thing it is, a good and a gracious, to willen meekly and mightily been fastened and oned to our mother holy church, that is Christ Jesu. For the flood of his mercy that is his dearworthy blood and precious water is plenteous to make us fair and clean. The blessed wounds of our savior be open and enjoy[4] to heal us. The sweet gracious hands of our mother be ready and diligent about us; for he in all this working useth the very office of a kind nurse that hath not else to do but to entend[5] the salvation of her child.

It is his office to save us, it is his worship to do it, and it is his will we know it; for he will we love him sweetly and trust in him meekly and mightily. And this showed he in these gracious words: "I keep thee full surely."

---

2. Because of.
3. Another.
4. Then.
5. Unhappy.
6. Scarcely.
7. Nothing would be more hateful to him.
8. He wants us to experience.

9. Right away we are sure he is practicing.
1. Compassion.
2. Until the right time.
3. Community.
4. Rejoice.
5. Be busy about.

[CONCLUSION]

Chapter 86

This book is begun by God's gift and his grace, but it is not yet performed,[6] as to my sight. For charity, pray we all together with God's working, thanking, trusting, enjoying, for thus will our good Lord be prayed, but the understanding that I took in all his own meaning, and in the sweet words where he sayeth full merrily: "I am ground of thy beseeching." For truly I saw and understood in our Lord's meaning that he showed it for he will have it known more than it is. In which knowing he will give us grace to love him and cleave to him, for he beheld his heavenly treasure with so great love on earth that he will give us more light, and solace in heavenly joy, in drawing of our hearts fro sorrow and darkness which we are in.

And fro the time that it was showed, I desired oftentimes to wit[7] in what was our Lord's meaning. And fifteen year after and more, I was answered in ghostly understanding, saying thus: "What, wouldst thou wit thy Lord's meaning in this thing? Wit it well, love was his meaning. Who showeth it thee? Love. What showed he thee? Love. Wherefore showeth he it thee? For love. Hold thee therein, thou shalt wit more in the same. But thou shalt never wit therein other withouten end."

Thus was I learned,[8] that love is our Lord's meaning. And I saw full surely in this and in all, that ere God made us he loved us, which love was never slaked[9] ne never shall. And in this love he hath done all his works, and in this love he hath made all things profitable to us, and in this love our life is everlasting. In our making we had beginning, but the love wherein he made us was in him fro without beginning. In which love we have our beginning, and all this shall we see in God withouten end.

Deo gracias. Explicit liber revelacionum Julyane anacorite Norwyche, cuius anime propicietur deus.[1]

ca. 1390

6. Completed.
7. Know.
8. Taught.
9. Abated.

1. Thanks be to God. Here ends the book of revelations of Julian, anchorite of Norwich, on whose soul may god have mercy.

MARGERY KEMPE
ca. 1373–1438

The Book of Margery Kempe is the spiritual autobiography of a medieval laywoman, telling of her struggles to carry out instructions for a holy life that she claimed to have received in personal visions from Christ and the Virgin Mary. The assertion of such a mission by a married woman, the mother of fourteen children, was in itself sufficient grounds for controversy; in addition, Kempe's outspoken defense of her visions as well as her highly emotional style of religious expression embroiled her with fellow citizens and pilgrims and with the church, although she also won both lay and clerical supporters. Ordered by the archbishop of York to swear not to teach in his diocese, she courageously stood up for her freedom to speak her conscience.

Margery Kempe was the daughter of John Burnham, five-time mayor of King's Lynn, a thriving commercial town in Norfolk. At about the age of twenty she married John Kempe, a well-to-do fellow townsman. After the traumatic delivery of her first child—the rate of maternal mortality in childbirth was high—she sought to confess to a priest whose harsh, censorious response precipitated a mental breakdown, from which she eventually recovered through the first of her visions. Her subsequent conversion and strict religious observances generated a good deal of domestic strife, but she continued to share her husband's bed until, around the age of forty, she negotiated a vow of celibacy with him, which was confirmed before the bishop and left her free to undertake a pilgrimage to the Holy Land. There she experienced visions of Christ's passion and of the sufferings of the Virgin. These visions recurred during the rest of her life, and her noisy weeping at such times made her the object of much scorn and hostility. Her orthodoxy was several times examined, as in her encounter with the archbishop of York, but her unquestioning acceptance of the church's doctrines and authority, and perhaps also her status as a former mayor's daughter, shielded her against charges of heresy.

Like the Wife of Bath in *The Canterbury Tales*, Kempe was unable to read or write but acquired her command of Scripture and theology from sermons and other oral sources. Late in her life, she dictated her story in two parts to two different scribes; the latter of these was a priest who revised the whole text. Nevertheless, it seems likely that the work retains much of the characteristic form and expression of its author.

Kempe was an exceptional woman and was regarded by many of her contemporaries as an eccentric and even a heretic. The generally accepted way for a woman to follow a religious vocation was for her to enter a convent or to become a recluse like Julian of Norwich, author of a profound mystical treatise *A Book of Showings* (p. 355). Kempe tells of her visit to the famous anchoress; the two women talked, and Julian seems to have understood and approved of Kempe's way of life. Modern scholars have linked that way of life to patterns of late medieval religious experience. In particular, she exemplifies the affective piety advocated by the Franciscans, which emphasized the importance of love through a direct experiential knowledge of Christ by every Christian. *The Book of Margery Kempe* is a remarkable record of the powerful and potentially liberating effect this doctrine exercised on the fifteenth-century laity and on women in particular.

From The Book of Margery Kempe[1]

[THE BIRTH OF HER FIRST CHILD AND HER FIRST VISION]

When this creature[2] was twenty year of age or somedeal more, she was married to a worshipful burgess and was with child within short time, as kind[3] would. And after that she had conceived, she was labored with great accesses[4] till the child was born, and then, what for labor she had in childing and for sickness going before, she despaired of her life, weening[5] she might not live. And then she sent for her ghostly father,[6] for she had a thing in

---

1. The text is based on the unique manuscript, first discovered in 1934, edited by Sanford B. Meech and Hope Emily Allen, but has been freely edited. Spelling has been modernized. The selections here given are from Chapters 1, 2, 11, 18, 28, 52, and 76.
2. Throughout the book Kempe refers to herself in the third person as "this creature," a standard way of saying "this person, a being created by God."
3. Nature.
4. Fits of pain.
5. Supposing.
6. Spiritual father, i.e., a priest.

conscience which she had never showed before that time in all her life. For she was ever letted[7] by her enemy, the Devil, evermore saying to her while she was in good heal[8] her needed no confession but [to] do penance by herself alone, and all should be forgiven, for God is merciful enow. And therefore this creature oftentimes did great penance in fasting bread and water and other deeds of alms with devout prayers, save she would not show it in confession. And when she was any time sick or diseased, the Devil said in her mind that she should be damned for she was not shriven of that default.[9] Wherefore after that her child was born she, not trusting her life, sent for her ghostly father, as said before, in full will to be shriven of all her lifetime as near as she could. And, when she came to the point for to say that thing which she had so long concealed, her confessor was a little too hasty and gan sharply to undernim[1] her ere that she had fully said her intent, and so she would no more say for nought he might do.

And anon for dread she had of damnation on that one side and his sharp reproving on that other side, this creature went out of her mind and was wonderly vexed and labored with spirits half year eight weeks and odd days. And in this time she saw, as her thought, devils open their mouths all inflamed with burning lows[2] of fire as they should 'a swallowed her in, sometime ramping[3] at her, sometime threating her, sometime pulling her and hauling her both night and day during the foresaid time. And also the devils cried upon her with great threatings and bade her she should forsake her Christendom, her faith, and deny her God, his Mother, and all the saints in Heaven, her good works and all good virtues, her father, her mother, and all her friends. And so she did. She slandered her husband, her friends, and her own self; she spoke many a reprevous word and many a shrewd[4] word; she knew no virtue nor goodness; she desired all wickedness; like as the spirits tempted her to say and do so she said and did. She would 'a fordone[5] herself many a time at their steering[6] and 'a been damned with them in Hell, and into witness thereof she bit her own hand so violently that it was seen all her life after. And also she rived[7] her skin on her body again her heart with her nails spiteously,[8] for she had none other instruments, and worse she would 'a done save she was bound and kept with strength both day and night that she might not have her will.

And when she had long been labored in this and many other temptations that men weened she should never 'a scaped[9] or lived, then on a time as she lay alone and her keepers were from her, our merciful Lord Christ Jesu, ever to be trusted (worshiped be his name) never forsaking his servant in time of need, appeared to his creature, which had forsaken him, in likeness of a man, most seemly, most beauteous, and most amiable that ever might be seen with man's eye, clad in a mantle of purple silk, sitting upon her bed's side, looking upon her with so blessed a cheer[1] that she was strengthened in all her spirits, said to her these words: "Daughter, why hast thou forsaken

7. Prevented.
8. Health.
9. Sin.
1. Rebuke. "Gan": began.
2. Blazes.
3. Raising their arms.
4. Wicked. "Reprevous": reproachful.

5. Destroyed.
6. Direction.
7. Tore.
8. Cruelly.
9. Escaped.
1. Expression.

me, and I forsook never thee?" And anon as he had said these words she saw verily how the air opened as bright as any levin,[2] and he sty[3] up into the air, not right hastily and quickly, but fair and easily that she might well behold him in the air till it was closed again. And anon the creature was stabled[4] in her wits and in her reason as well as ever she was before, and prayed her husband as so soon as he came to her that she might have the keys of the buttery[5] to take her meat and drink as she had done before.

[HER PRIDE AND ATTEMPTS TO START A BUSINESS]

And when this creature was thus graciously come again to her mind, she thought she was bound to God and that she would be his servant. Nevertheless, she would not leave her pride nor her pompous array that she had used beforetime, neither for her husband nor for none other man's counsel. And yet she wist full well that men said her full much villainy, for she wore gold pipes on her head and her hoods with the tippets were dagged.[6] Her cloaks also were dagged and laid with divers colors between the dags that it should be the more staring[7] to men's sight and herself the more be worshiped. And when her husband would speak to her for to leave her pride she answered shrewdly and shortly and said that she was come of worthy kindred—him seemed never for to 'a wedded her[8]—for her father was sometime mayor of the town N and sithen[9] he was alderman of the high Gild of the Trinity in N.[1] And therefore she would save[2] the worship of her kindred whatsoever any man said. She had full great envy at her neighbors that they should be arrayed as well as she. All her desire was for to be worshiped of the people. She would not beware by one's chastening nor be content with the good that God had sent her, as her husband was, but ever desired more and more.

And then, for pure covetise[3] and for to maintain her pride, she gan to brew and was one of the greatest brewers in the town N a three year or four till she lost much good,[4] for she had never ure[5] thereto. For though she had never so good servants and cunning[6] in brewing, yet it would never prove[7] with them. For when the ale was as fair standing under barm[8] as any man might see, suddenly the barm would fall down[9] that all the ale was lost every brewing after other, that her servants were ashamed and would not dwell with her. Then this creature thought how God had punished her beforetime and she could not beware, and now eftsoons[1] by losing of her goods, and then she left and brewed no more. And then she asked her husband mercy for she would not follow his counsel aforetime, and she said that her pride was cause of all her punishing and she would amend that she had trespassed with good will.

---

2. Flash of lightning.
3. Ascended.
4. Made stable.
5. Pantry.
6. I.e., her hoods were ornamented with loose bands of cloth ("tippets") and slashed according to high fashion of the time. "Pipes": tubular head ornaments.
7. Obtrusive.
8. It never became him to have married her.
9. Afterward.

1. The merchant guild of Lynn was the Guild of the Holy Trinity.
2. Maintain.
3. Avarice.
4. Wealth.
5. Experience [in brewing].
6. Skill.
7. Turn out well.
8. The froth or head.
9. I.e., go flat.
1. Again.

[MARGERY AND HER HUSBAND REACH A SETTLEMENT][2]

It befell upon a Friday on Midsummer Even in right hot weather, as this creature was coming from York-ward[3] bearing a bottle with beer in her hand and her husband a cake in his bosom, he asked his wife this question: "Margery, if there came a man with a sword and would smite off my head unless that I should commune kindly[4] with you as I have done before, say me truth of your conscience—for ye say ye will not lie—whether would ye suffer my head to be smit off or else suffer me to meddle with you again as I did sometime?" "Alas, sir," she said, "why move[5] ye this matter and have we been chaste this eight weeks?" "For I will wit[6] the truth of your heart." And then she said with great sorrow, "Forsooth, I had liefer[7] see you be slain than we should turn again to our uncleanness." And he said again, "Ye are no good wife."

And then she asked her husband what was the cause that he had not meddled with her eight weeks before, sithen[8] she lay with him every night in his bed. And he said he was so made afeared when he would 'a touched her that he durst no more do. "Now, good sir, amend you and ask God mercy, for I told you near three year sithen that ye should be slain suddenly, and now is this the third year, and yet I hope I shall have my desire. Good sir, I pray you grant me that I shall ask, and I shall pray for you that ye shall be saved through the mercy of our Lord Jesu Christ, and ye shall have more meed[9] in Heaven than if ye wore a hair or a habergeon.[1] I pray you, suffer me to make a vow of chastity in what bishop's hand that God will." "Nay," he said, "that will I not grant you, for now I may use you without deadly sin and then might I not so." Then she said again, "If it be the will of the Holy Ghost to fulfill that I have said, I pray God ye might consent thereto; and if it be not the will of the Holy Ghost, I pray God ye never consent thereto."

Then went they forth to-Bridlington-ward[2] in right hot weather, the foresaid creature having great sorrow and great dread for her chastity. And as they came by a cross, her husband set him down under the cross, cleping[3] his wife unto him and saying these words unto her, "Margery, grant me my desire, and I shall grant you your desire. My first desire is that we shall lie still together in one bed as we have done before; the second that ye shall pay my debts ere ye go to Jerusalem; and the third that ye shall eat and drink with me on the Friday as ye were wont to do."[4] "Nay, sir," she said, "to break the Friday I will never grant you while I live." "Well," he said, "then shall I meddle with you again."

She prayed him that he would give her leave to make her prayers, and he granted it goodly. Then she knelt down beside a cross in the field and prayed in this manner with great abundance of tears, "Lord God, thou knowest all

2. Despite her resolution, Kempe made one more attempt to run a profitable business: she set up a horse mill to grind grain, but the horses refused to draw, and the enterprise was as disastrous as her brewing had been. After that she did indeed reform.
3. The direction of York.
4. In the way of nature.
5. Bring up.
6. Learn.

7. Rather.
8. Since.
9. Reward.
1. Hair shirt or mail shirt.
2. In the direction of Bridlington.
3. Calling.
4. Christ had told her that keeping a strict Friday fast would allow her to have her wish to end further sexual relations with her husband.

thing; thou knowest what sorrow I have had to be chaste in my body to thee all this three year, and now might I have my will and I dare not for love of thee. For if I would break that manner of fasting which thou commandest me to keep on the Friday without meat[5] or drink, I should now have my desire. But, blessed Lord, thou knowest I will not contrary thy will, and mickle[6] now is my sorrow unless that I find comfort in thee. Now, blessed Jesu, make thy will known to me unworthy that I may follow thereafter and fulfil it with all my might." And then our Lord Jesu Christ with great sweetness spoke to this creature, commanding her to go again to her husband and pray him to grant her that she desired, "And he shall have that he desireth. For, my dearworthy daughter, this was the cause that I bade thee fast for thou shouldest the sooner obtain and get thy desire, and now it is granted thee. I will no longer thou fast, therefore I bid thee in the name of Jesu eat and drink as thy husband doth."

Then this creature thanked our Lord Jesu Christ of his grace and his goodness, sithen[7] rose up and went to her husband, saying unto him, "Sir, if it like[8] you, ye shall grant me my desire and ye shall have your desire. Granteth me that ye shall not come in my bed, and I grant you to quit your debts ere I go to Jerusalem. And maketh my body free to God so that ye never make no challenging in me[9] to ask no debt of matrimony after this day while ye live, and I shall eat and drink on the Friday at your bidding." Then said her husband again to her, "As free may your body be to God as it hath been to me." This creature thanked God greatly, enjoying that she had her desire, praying her husband that they should say three Pater Noster[1] in the worship of the Trinity for the great grace that he had granted them. And so they did, kneeling under a cross, and sithen they ate and drank together in great gladness of spirit. This was on a Friday on Midsummer Even.

[A VISIT WITH JULIAN OF NORWICH][2]

And then she was bidden by our Lord for to go to an anchoress in the same city, which hight[3] Dame Julian. And so she did and showed her the grace that God put in her soul of compunction, contrition, sweetness and devotion, compassion with holy meditation and high contemplation, and ful many holy speeches and dalliance[4] that our Lord spoke to her soul, and many wonderful revelations which she showed to the anchoress to wit[5] if there were any deceit in them, for the anchoress was expert in such things and good counsel could give.

The anchoress, hearing the marvelous goodness of our Lord, highly thanked God with all her heart for his visitation, counseling this creature to be obedient to the will of our Lord God and fulfill with all her mights whatever he put in her soul if it were not again[6] the worship of God and profit of her even-Christians,[7] for, if it were, then it were not the moving of a good

---

5. Food.
6. Much.
7. Afterward.
8. Please.
9. Make my body free to [be possessed by] God so that you never call me to account. Kempe uses legal terminology.

1. "Our Father," i.e, the Lord's Prayer.
2. See the headnote for Julian of Norwich (p. 355).
3. Who was called.
4. Conversation.
5. Know.
6. Against.
7. Fellow Christians.

spirit but rather of an evil spirit: "The Holy Ghost moveth never a thing again charity,[8] and, if he did, he were contrarious to his own self, for he is all charity. Also he moveth a soul to all chasteness, for chaste livers be cleped[9] the temple of the Holy Ghost, and the Holy Ghost maketh a soul stable and steadfast in the right faith and the right belief. And a double man in soul is ever unstable and unsteadfast in all his ways. He that is evermore doubting is like to the flood of the sea, the which is moved and borne about with the wind, and that man is not like to receive the gifts of God. What creature that hath these tokens, he must steadfastly believe that the Holy Ghost dwelleth in his soul. And much more, when God visiteth a creature with tears of contrition, devotion, or compassion, he may and ought to leve[1] that the Holy Ghost is in his soul. Saint Paul saith that the Holy Ghost asketh for us with mournings and weepings unspeakable,[2] that is to say, he maketh us to ask and pray with mournings and weepings so plentivously[3] that the tears may not be numbered. There may no evil spirit give these tokens, for Jerome saith that tears torment more the Devil than do the pains of Hell. God and the Devil been evermore contrarious, and they shall never dwell together in one place, and the Devil hath no power in a man's soul. Holy Writ saith that the soul of a rightful man is the seat of God, and so I trust sister that ye been. I pray God grant you perseverance. Set all your trust in God and fear not the language of the world, for the more despite, shame, and reproof that ye have in the world, the more is your merit in the sight of God. Patience is necessary unto you, for in that shall ye keep your soul."

Much was the holy dalliance that the anchoress and this creature had by communing in the lof[4] of our Lord Jesu Christ many days that they were together.

[PILGRIMAGE TO JERUSALEM]

* * * And so they[5] went forth into the Holy Land till they might see Jerusalem. And when this creature saw Jerusalem, riding on an ass, she thanked God with all her heart, praying him for his mercy that like as he had brought her to see this earthly city Jerusalem, he would grant her grace to see the blissful city Jerusalem above, the city of Heaven. Our Lord Jesu Christ, answering to her thought, granted her to have her desire. Then for joy that she had and the sweetness that she felt in the dalliance[6] of our Lord, she was in point to 'a fallen off her ass, for she might not bear the sweetness and grace that God wrought in her soul. Then twain[7] pilgrims of Dutchmen went to her and kept her from falling, of which the one was a priest. And he put spices in her mouth to comfort her, weening[8] she had been sick. And so they helped her forth to Jerusalem. And when she came there, she said, "Sirs, I pray you be not displeased though I weep sore in this holy place where our Lord Jesu Christ was quick[9] and dead."

Then went they to the Temple in Jerusalem, and they were let in that one day at evensong time and they abide there till the next day at evensong time.

8. Love.
9. Called (see 1 Corinthians 6.19).
1. Believe.
2. Inarticulate (Romans 8.26).
3. Plentifully.
4. Praise.

5. The company of pilgrims.
6. Conversation.
7. Two.
8. Thinking.
9. Living.

Then the friars lifted up a cross and led the pilgrims about from one place to another where our Lord had suffered his pains and his passions, every man and woman bearing a wax candle in their hand. And the friars always as they went about told them what our Lord suffered in every place.[1] And the foresaid creature wept and sobbed so plentiously[2] as though she had seen our Lord with her bodily eye suffering his Passion at that time. Before her in her soul she saw him verily by contemplation, and that caused her to have compassion. And when they came up onto the Mount of Calvary she fell down that she might not stand nor kneel but wallowed and wrested[3] with her body, spreading her arms abroad, and cried with a loud voice as though her heart should 'a burst asunder, for in the city of her soul she saw verily and freshly how our Lord was crucified. Before her face she heard and saw in her ghostly sight the mourning of our Lady, of St. John and of Mary Magdalene,[4] and of many other that loved our Lord. And she had so great compassion and so great pain to see our Lord's pain that she might not keep herself from crying and roaring though she should 'a been dead therefore.

And this was the first cry that ever she cried in any contemplation. And this manner of crying endured many years after this time for aught that any man might do, and therefore suffered she much despite and much reproof. The crying was so loud and so wonderful that it made the people astoned[5] unless that they had heard it before or else that they knew the cause of the crying. And she had them so oftentimes that they made her right[6] weak in her bodily mights, and namely if she heard of our Lord's Passion. And sometime when she saw the Crucifix, or if she saw a man had a wound or a beast, whether[7] it were, or if a man beat a child before her or smote a horse or another beast with a whip, if she might see it or hear it, her thought she saw our Lord be beaten or wounded like as she saw in the man or in the beast, as well in the field as in the town, and by herself alone as well as among the people. First when she had her cryings at Jerusalem, she had them oftentimes, and in Rome also. And when she came home into England, first at her coming home it came but seldom as it were once in a month, sithen[8] once in the week, afterward quotidianly,[9] and once she had fourteen on one day, and another day she had seven, and so as God would visit her, sometime in the church, sometime in the street, sometime in the chamber, sometime in the field when God would send them, for she knew never time nor hour when they should come. And they came never without passing[1] great sweetness of devotion and high contemplation. And as soon as she perceived that she should cry, she would keep it in as much as she might that the people should not 'a heard it for noying[2] of them. For some said it was a wicked spirit vexed her; some said it was a sickness; some said she had drunken too much wine; some banned[3] her; some wished she had been in the haven;[4] some would she had been in the sea in a bottomless boat; and so each man as him thought. Other ghostly[5] men loved her and favored her the more.

---

1. I.e., in Jerusalem.
2. Plentifully.
3. Twisted and turned.
4. Mary, St. John, and Mary Magdalene are traditionally portrayed at the foot of the Cross in medieval art. See John 19.25.
5. Astonished.
6. Especially.

7. Whichever.
8. After.
9. Daily.
1. Surpassing.
2. Annoying.
3. Cursed.
4. Harbor.
5. Spiritual.

Some great clerks[6] said our Lady cried never so, nor no saint in Heaven, but they knew full little what she felt, nor they would not believe but that she might 'a abstained her from crying if she had wished.

[EXAMINATION BEFORE THE ARCHBISHOP]

There was a monk should preach in York, the which had heard much slander and much evil language of the said creature. And when he should preach, there was much multitude of people to hear him, and she present with them. And so when he was in his sermon, he rehearsed[7] many matters so openly that the people conceived well that it was for cause of her, wherefore her friends that loved her well were full sorry and heavy thereof, and she was much the more merry, for she had matter to prove her patience and her charity wherethrough she trusted to please our Lord Christ Jesu. When the sermon was done, a doctor of divinity which loved her well with many other also came to her and said, "Margery, how have ye done this day?" "Sir," she said, "right well, blessed be God. I have cause to be right merry and glad in my soul that I may anything suffer for his love, for he suffered much more for me."

Anon after came a man which loved her right well of good will with his wife and other more and led her seven mile thence to the Archbishop of York,[8] and brought her into a fair chamber, where came a good clerk, saying to the good man which had brought her thither, "Sir, why have ye and your wife brought this woman hither? She shall steal away from you, and then shall ye have a villainy[9] of her." The good man said, "I dare well say she will abide and be at her answer[1] with good will."

On the next day she was brought into the Archbishop's Chapel, and there came many of the Archbishop's meinie, despising her, calling her "loller"[2] and "heretic," and swore many an horrible oath that she should be burnt. And she through the strength of Jesu said again to them, "Sirs, I dread me ye shall be burnt in hell without end, unless that ye amend you of your oaths-swearing, for ye keep not the commandments of God. I would not swear as ye do for all the good[3] of this world." Then they went away as they had been ashamed. She then, making her prayer in her mind, asked grace so to be demeaned[4] that day as was most pleasance[5] to God and profit to her own soul and good example to her even-Christians.[6] Our Lord, answering her, said it should be right well.

At the last the said Archbishop came into the Chapel with his clerks and sharply he said to her, "Why goest thou in white? Art thou a maiden?" She, kneeling on her knees before him, said, "Nay, sir, I am no maiden; I am a wife." He commanded his men to fetch a pair of fetters and said she should be fettered, for she was a false heretic. And then she said, "I am none heretic, nor ye shall none prove me." The Archbishop went away and let her stand alone. Then she made her prayers to our Lord God almighty for to help her

---

6. Clerics.
7. Repeated.
8. The archbishop was at this time residing not in York but at his palace in Cawood.
9. Slander.
1. Answer charges against her.

2. Lollard: a follower of the reformer John Wycliffe. "Meinie": household.
3. Property.
4. Treated.
5. Pleasing.
6. Fellow Christians.

and succor her against all her enemies, ghostly and bodily, a long while, and her flesh trembled and quaked wonderly that she was fain[7] to put her hands under her clothes that it should not be espied.

Sithen[8] the Archbishop came again into the Chapel with many worthy clerks, amongst which was the same doctor[9] which had examined her before and the monk that had preached again her a little time before in York. Some of the people asked whether she were a Christian woman or a Jew; some said she was a good woman, and some said nay. Then the Archbishop took his see,[1] and his clerks also, each of them in his degree, much people being present. And in the time while the people was gathering together and the Archbishop taking his see, the said creature stood all behind, making her prayers for help and succor against her enemies with high devotion so long that she melted all into tears. And at the last she cried loud therewith that the Archbishop and his clerks and much people had great wonder of her, for they had not heard such crying before.

When her crying was passed, she came before the Archbishop and fell down on her knees, the Archbishop saying full boistously[2] unto her, "Why weepest thou so, woman?" She answering said, "Sir, ye shall will some day that ye had wept as sore as I." And then anon after the Archbishop put to her the Articles of our Faith,[3] to the which God gave her grace to answer well and truly and readily without any great study so that he might not blame her, then he said to the clerks, "She knoweth her Faith well enough. What shall I do with her?" The clerks said, "We know well that she can[4] the Articles of the Faith, but we will not suffer her to dwell among us, for the people hath great faith in her dalliance, and peradventure[5] she might pervert some of them." Then the Archbishop said unto her, "I am evil informed of thee; I hear say thou art a right wicked woman." And she said again, "Sir, so I hear say that ye are a wicked man. And if ye be as wicked as men say, ye shall never come in Heaven unless that ye amend you while ye be here." Then said he full boistously, "Why, thou wretch, what say men of me?" She answered, "Other men, sir, can tell you well enow." Then said a great clerk with a furred hood, "Peace, thou speak of thyself and let him be."

Sithen said the Archbishop to her, "Lay thine hand on the book here before me and swear that thou shalt go out of my diocese as soon as thou may." "Nay, sir," she said, "I pray you, give me leave to go again into York to take my leave of my friends." Then he gave her leave for one day or two. She thought it was too short a time, wherefore she said again, "Sir, I may not go out of this diocese so hastily, for I must tarry and speak with good men ere I go, and I must, sir, with your leave, go to Bridlington and speak with my confessor, a good man, the which was the good Prior's confessor that is now canonized."[6] Then said the Archbishop to her, "Thou shalt swear that thou shalt not teach nor challenge the people in my diocese." "Nay, sir, I shall not swear," she said, "for I shall speak of God and undernim[7] them that swear great oaths wheresoever I go unto the time that the Pope and Holy Church

---

7. Glad.
8. Then.
9. Doctor of theology.
1. Throne.
2. Coarsely.
3. The twelve separate statements of the Apostles'

Creed.
4. Knows.
5. Perhaps. "Dalliance": conversation.
6. St. John of Bridlington, recently canonized.
7. Reprove.

hath ordained that no man shall be so hardy to speak of God, for God almighty forbids not, sir, that we shall speak of him. And also the Gospel maketh mention that when the woman had heard our Lord preach, she came before him with a loud voice and said, 'Blessed be the womb that thee bore and the teats that gave thee suck.' Then our Lord said again to her, 'Forsooth so are they blessed that hear the word of God and keep it.' And therefore, sir, me thinketh that the Gospel giveth me leave to speak of God." "Ah, sir," said the clerks, "here woot[8] we well that she hath a devil within her, for she speaks of the Gospel." As swithe[9] a great clerk brought forth a book and laid Saint Paul for his party[1] against her that no woman should preach. She answering thereto said, "I preach not, sir, I come in no pulpit. I use but communication and good words, and that will I do while I live." Then said a doctor which had examined her beforetime, "Sir, she told me the worst tales of priests that ever I heard." The Bishop commanded her to tell that tale.

"Sir, with your reverence, I spoke but of one priest by the manner of example, the which, as I have learned, went wil[2] in a wood through the sufferance of God for the profit of his soul till the night came upon him. He, destitute of his harbor,[3] found a fair arbor in the which he rested that night, having a fair pear tree in the midst, all flourished and belished,[4] and blooms full delectable to his sight, where came a bear, great and boisteous,[5] ugly to behold, shaking the pear tree and felling down the flowers. Greedily this grievous beast ate and devoured those fair flowers. And, when he had eaten 'em, turning his tail-end in the priest's presence, voided 'em out again at the hinder part. The priest having great abomination at that loathly sight, conceiving great heaviness[6] for doubt what it might mean, on the next day he wandered forth in his way, all heavy and pensive, whom it fortuned to meet with a seemly aged man like to a palmer or a pilgrim, the which inquired of the priest the cause of his heaviness. The priest, rehearsing the matter before-written, said he conceived great dread and heaviness when he beheld that loathly beast defoul and devour so fair flowers and blooms and afterward so horribly to devoid 'em before him at his tail-end, and he not understanding what this might mean. Then the palmer, showing himself the messenger of God, thus areasoned[7] him: 'Priest, thou thyself art the pear tree, somedeal[8] flourishing and flowering through thy service-saying and the sacraments-ministering, though thou do undevoutly, for thou takest full little heed how thou sayest thy matins and thy service, so it be[9] blabbered to an end. Then goest thou to thy mass without devotion, and for thy sin hast thou full little contrition. Thou receivest there the fruit of everlasting life, the sacrament of the altar, in full feeble disposition. Sithen[1] al the day after thou misspendest thy time, thou givest thee to buying and selling, chopping and changing[2] as it were a man of the world. Thou sittest at the ale, giving thee to gluttony and excess, to lust of thy body through lechery and uncleanness. Thou breakest the commandments of God through swearing, lying, detraction, and back-

---

8. Know.
9. At once.
1. Side of the argument.
2. Erring.
3. Lacking a place to put up.
4. Blossoming and embellished.
5. Rough.

6. Depression.
7. Addressed.
8. Somewhat.
9. As long as it is.
1. Then.
2. Bargaining and exchanging.

biting, and such other sins using. Thus be thy misgovernance, like unto the loathly bear: thou devourest and destroyest the flowers and blooms of virtuous living to thine endless damnation and many men's hindering, less than[3] thou have grace of repentance and amending.' "

Then the Archbishop liked well the tale and commended it, saying it was a good tale. And the clerk which had examined her beforetime in the absence of the Archbishop said, "Sir, this tale smiteth me to the heart." The foresaid creature said to the clerk, "Ah, worshipful doctor, sir, in place where my dwelling is most is a worthy clerk, a good preacher, which boldly speaketh again the misgovernance[4] of the people and will flatter no man. He sayeth many times in the pulpit, 'If any man be evil-pleased with my preaching, note him well, for he is guilty.' And right so, sir," said she to the clerk, "fare ye by me,[5] God forgive it you." The clerk wist not well what he might say to her. Afterward the same clerk came to her and prayed her of forgiveness that he had so been again her. Also he prayed her specially to pray for him.

And then anon[6] after the Archbishop said, "Where shall I have a man that might lead this woman from me?" As swithe there started up many young men, and every man said of them, "My Lord, I will go with her." The Archbishop answered, "Ye be too young; I will not have you." Then a good sad[7] man of the Archbishop's meinie asked his Lord what he would give him and[8] he should lead her. The Archbishop proffered him five shillings, and the man asked a noble.[9] The Archbishop answering said, "I will not ware[1] so much on her body." "Yes, good sir," said the said creature, "our Lord shall reward you right well again." Then the Archbishop said to the man, "See, here is five shillings, and lead her fast out of this country." She kneeling down on her knees asked his blessing. He, praying her to pray for him, blessed her and let her go. Then she going again to York was received of much people and of full worthy clerks, which enjoyed[2] in our Lord that had given her, not lettered, wit and wisdom to answer so many learned men without villainy or blame, thanking be to God.

[MARGERY NURSES HER HUSBAND IN HIS OLD AGE]

It happed on a time that the husband of the said creature, a man in great age passing three score year,[3] as he would 'a come down of his chamber barefoot and barelegged, he sledered[4] or else failed of his footing and fell down to the ground fro the greses,[5] and his head under him grievously broken and bruised, in so much that he had in his head five tents[6] many days while his head was in healing. And, as God would, it was known to some of his neighbors how he was fallen down of the greses, peradventure[7] through the din and the lushing[8] of his falling. And so they came to him and found him lying with his head under him, half alive, all rowed[9] with blood, never like to 'a spoken with priest ne with clerk but through high grace and miracle.[1]

3. Unless.
4. Against the misconduct.
5. You behave with me.
6. Straightway.
7. Sober.
8. If.
9. A coin worth six shillings and eight pence.
1. Spend.
2. Rejoiced.

3. Sixty years.
4. Slipped.
5. Steps.
6. Swabs for probing wounds.
7. Perchance.
8. Rushing.
9. Streaked.
1. I.e., unlikely to have confessed to a priest and received last rites except by grace.

Then the said creature, his wife, was sent for, and so she came to him. Then was he taken up and his head was sewed, and he was sick a long time after that[2] men weened[3] that he should be dead. And then the people said, if he died, his wife was worthy to be hanged for his death, forasmuch as she might 'a kept him and did not. They dwelled not together, ne they lay not together, for, as is written before, the both with one assent and with free will of their either[4] had made a vow to live chaste. And therefore to enchewen[5] all perils they dwelled and sojourned in diverse places where no suspicion should be had of their incontinence, for first they dwelled together after that they had made their vow, and then the people slandered 'em and said they used their lust and their liking as they did before their vow-making. And when they went out on pilgrimage or to see and speak with other ghostly creatures, many evil folk whose tongues were their own hurt, failing the dread and love of our Lord Jesu Christ,[6] deemed and said that they went rather to woods, groves, or valeys to use[7] the lust of their bodies that the people should not aspie it ne wit it. They, having knowledge of how prone the people was to deem evil of 'em, desiring to avoid all occasion, in as much as they might goodly, by their good will and their both consenting, they parted asunder as touching to their board and their chambers, and weened to board in diverse places. And this was the cause that she was not with him and also that she should not be letted[8] fro her contemplation. And therefore when he had fallen and grievously was hurt, as is said before, the people said if he died, it was worthy that she should[9] answer for his death.

Then she prayed to our Lord that her husband might live a year and she to be delivered out [of] slander if it were His pleasance.[1] Our Lord said to her mind, "Daughter, thou shalt have thy boon, for he shall live, and I have wrought a great miracle for thee that he was not dead. And I bid thee take him home and keep him for my love."

She said, "Nay, good Lord, for I shall then not tend to thee as I do now."

"Yes, daughter," said our Lord, "thou shalt have as much meed[2] for to keep him and help him in his need at home as if thou were in church to make thy prayers. And thou hast said many times that thou wouldst fain keep me. I pray thee now keep him for the love of me, for he hath sometime fulfilled thy will and my will both, and he hath made thy body free to me that thou shouldst serve me and live chaste and clean, and therfore I will that thou be free to help him at his need in my name."

"A, Lord," said she, "for thy mercy grant me grace to obey Thy will and fulfill Thy will and let never my ghostly enemies have no power to let me fro fulfilling of Thy will." Then she took home her husband to her and kept him years after as long as he lived and had full much labor with him, for in his last days he turned childish again and lacked reason, that[3] he could not do his own easement to go to a sege[4] or else he would not, but as a child voided his natural digestion in his linen clothes there he sat by the fire or at the table, whether it were,[5] he would spare no place. And therefore was her labor

---

2. So that.
3. Thought.
4. Each of them.
5. Avoid.
6. I.e., their gossip hurt themselves, [because] lacking in fear and love of Christ.
7. Practice.

8. Prevented.
9. She deserved to.
1. If he pleased.
2. Reward.
3. So that.
4. Stool.
5. Wherever it might be.

much the more in washing and wringing and her costage in firing[6] and letted her full much fro her contemplation that many times she should 'a irked[7] her labor save she bethought her how she in her young age had full many delectable thoughts, fleshly lusts, and inordinate loves to his person.[8] And therefore she was glad to be punished with the same person and took it much the more easily and served him and helped him, as her thought, as she would 'a done Christ himself.

1436–38

6. Expense in firewood.   8. Body.
7. Have resented.

MYSTERY PLAYS

The word *mystery*, as applied to medieval drama, refers to the spiritual mystery of Christ's redemption of humankind, and mystery plays are dramatizations of the Old Testament, which foretells that redemption, and of the New, which recounts it. In England the mysteries were generally composed in cycles containing as many as forty-eight individual plays: a typical cycle would begin with the Creation, continue with the Fall of Man, and proceed through the most significant events of the Old Testament, such as the Flood, to the New Testament, which provided plays on the Nativity, the chief events of Christ's life, the Crucifixion, the Harrowing of Hell (based on sources now deemed apocryphal), and the Last Judgment.

The church had its own drama in Latin, dating back to the tenth century, which developed through the dramatization and elaboration of the liturgy—the regular service—for certain holidays, the Easter morning service in particular. The vernacular drama was once thought to have evolved from the liturgical, passing by stages from the church into the streets of the town. However, even though the vernacular plays at times echo their Latin counterparts and although their authors may have been clerics, the mysteries represent an old and largely independent tradition of vernacular religious drama. As early as the twelfth century a *Play of Adam* in Anglo-Norman French was performed in England, a dramatization of the Fall with highly sophisticated dialogue, characterization, and stagecraft.

During the late fourteenth and the fifteenth centuries the great English mystery cycles, four of which have survived complete, were formed in the towns that, in spite of war and plague, became increasingly prosperous and independent. Most of our knowledge of the plays, apart from the texts themselves, comes through municipal and guild records. Every trade in urban society had its guild, an organization combining the functions of a modern trade union, club, religious society, and political action group. The guilds, which played a major role in the governance of the towns, produced the plays; each guild was responsible for putting on a traditional play during the holidays when the cycles were presented.

The town and guild documents tell us a great deal about the evolution, staging, and all aspects of the production of the cycles. In some of the towns each company had a wagon that served as a stage. The wagon would proceed from one strategic point in the city to another, and the play would be performed a number of times on the same day. The spectators gathered at any one place would never be without a play before them and might see the whole cycle without moving. In other towns, plays were probably acted out in sequence on a platform erected at a single location such as the main city square.

The cycles were performed every year at the time of one of two great early summer festivals—Whitsuntide, the week following the seventh Sunday after Easter, or Corpus Christi, a week later. They served as both religious instruction and entertainment for wide audiences, including unlearned folk like the carpenter in *The Miller's Tale* (lines 405–74), who recalls from them the trouble Noah had getting his wife aboard the ark, but also educated laypeople and clerics, who besides enjoying the sometimes boisterous comedy would find the plays acting out traditional interpretations of Scripture such as the ark as a type, or prefiguration, of the church.

Thus the cycles were public spectacles watched by every layer of society, and they paved the way for the professional theater in the age of Elizabeth I. The rainbow in *Noah's Flood* and the Angel's *Gloria* in the *Shepherds' Play*, with their messages of mercy and hope, unite actors and audience in a common faith. Yet the first shepherd's opening speech, complaining of taxation and the insolent exploitation of farmers by "gentlery-men," shows how the plays also served as vehicles of social criticism and reveal many of the rifts and tensions in the late-medieval social fabric.

The Chester Play of Noah's Flood   The most durable of the four surviving English mystery cycles was that of Chester, which was still occasionally performed when Shakespeare was a boy and was produced for the last time in 1575. The plays, however, remained of great interest to antiquarians and were a source of municipal pride. The five surviving manuscripts are all later than the final performance. Because the cycle had been extensively revised during the sixteenth century, we cannot know what it was like during the medieval period. The text we have is certainly very late. God's lengthy instructions to Noah concerning "clean" and "unclean" beasts reflect a new, probably Protestant, interest in Jewish law, also seen in other plays of the Chester cycle. But the revisers were also concerned to preserve what they felt to be traditional medieval features and, in the case of *Noah's Flood*, to introduce such a feature when it was missing. Thus the entertaining scene in which Noah and his wife quarrel and she gives him a box on the ear is an interpolation based on an old comic tradition that is well attested in the other cycle plays and in Chaucer's *The Miller's Tale*. The Chester play is a typical example of the composite authorship so characteristic of many medieval works, by which a text, passing through many hands and generations, carries with it traces of its past that blend in a rich, although not always smooth mixture. An interesting feature of the play is its stage directions, which show how such business as the animals on the ark was managed. A few additional stage directions are provided in braces.

Noah's Flood[1].

The Waterleaders and Drawers of Dee[2]

CAST OF CHARACTERS

GOD	NOAH'S WIFE
NOAH	SHEM'S WIFE
SHEM	HAM'S WIFE
HAM	JAPHET'S WIFE
JAPHETH	GOSSIPS

*And first in some high place—or in the clouds, if it may be—God speaketh to
Noah, standing without the ark[3] with all his family.*

GOD   I, God, that[4] all this world hath wrought,
    Heaven and earth, and all of nought,
    I see my people in deed and thought
       Are set foully° in sin.   *are mired*
5   My ghost shall not leng in mon,
    That through flesh-liking is my fon,
    But till six score years be comen and gone,
       To look if they will blin.[5]

    Man that I made will I destroy,
10   Beast, worm, and fowl to fly;[6]
    For on earth they do me noy,°   *harm*
       The folk that are thereon.
    It harmes me so hurtfully,°   *grievously*
    The malice that doth now multiply,
15   That sore it grieves me inwardly
       That ever I made mon.

    Therefore Noah, my servant free,°   *noble*
    That righteous man art as I see,
    A ship soon thou shalt make thee
20   Of trees dry and light.
    Little chambers therein thou make
    And binding slitch also thou take;

1. The text is based on that of R. M. Lumiansky and David Mills in *The Chester Mystery Cycle* (1974), but has been freely edited. Spelling has been normalized except in some cases for the sake of rhyme and meter. Stage directions are original except for a few added in braces.
2. The guild responsible for the production of the play, the Waterleaders and Drawers, carted and sold water, a trade appropriate for the producers of Noah's flood.
3. Outside the ark. Evidently the ark is already on stage, although Noah and his family will simulate its building.
4. Who. *That* is used throughout as the relative pronoun.
5. My spirit shall remain with mankind, who through fleshly lust are my foes, only till six score [120] years be come and gone, to see if they will stop [sinning]. I.e., God allows the human race a probationary period to reform (cf. lines 149–50), probably a misunderstanding of Genesis 6.3, where God limits the human life span to 120 years. "Mon": man. In the West-Midland dialect, *a* is rounded before a nasal and rhymes with the vowel of *gone* and *on*. Both spellings *mon* and *man* occur in the manuscripts.
6. Animal, reptile, and bird flying.

Within and without thou ne slake
To annoint it through all thy might.[7]

25   Three hundred cubits it shall be long
And fifty broad to make it strong;
Of height sixty. The meet thou fong;[8]
     Thus measure thou it about.
One window work through thy wit;
30   A cubit of length and breadth make it.
Upon the side a door shall shut,
     For to come in and out.

Eating-places thou make also,
Three roofed chambers on a row,[9]
35   For with water I think to flow°   *drown*
     Man that I can° make.   *did*
Destroyed all the world shall be—
Save thou, thy wife, thy sonnes three,
And their wives also with thee—
40   Shall saved be for thy sake.

NOAH   A, Lord, I thank thee loud and still[1]
That to me art in such will
And spares me and my household to spill.[2]
     As now I soothly° find.   *truly*
45   Thy bidding, Lord, I shall fulfill
Nor never more Thee grieve ne grill,°   *offend*
That such grace has sent me till°   *to me*
     Amonges all mankind.

Have done, you men and women all,
50   Hie° you, lest this water fall,   *haste*
To work this ship, chamber and hall,
     As God hath bidden us do.
SHEM   Father, I am already boun:°   *prepared*
An ax I have, by my crown,[3]
55   As sharp as any in all this town,
     For to go thereto.

HAM   I have a hatchet wonder keen
To bite well, as may be seen;
A better ground,° as I ween,°   *sharpened/think*
60   Is not in all this town.
JAPHETH   And I can well make a pin°   *peg*
And with this hammer knock it in.

---

7. Do not slacken to smear it [to make it water-tight], inside and out, with all your might. "Slitch": mud (for caulking).
8. Take thou the measurement.
9. May refer to three decks, but the text is obscure.
1. Aloud and silent, i.e., at all times.
2. Who are so minded toward me and refrain from destroying me and my household.
3. By my head (an oath).

Go we work but° more din,°   *without/fuss*
And I am ready boun.

65   NOAH'S WIFE   And we shall bring timber to,°   *thereto*
For we mun° nothing else do—   *may*
Woman been weak to underfo°   *undertake*
Any great travail.°   *labor*
SHEM'S WIFE   Here is a good hackestock;°   *chopping block*
70   On this you may hewe and knock,
Shall none be idle in this flock,
Ne now may no man fail.

HAM'S WIFE   And I will go gather slitch,°   *pitch*
The ship for to cleam° and pitch.   *caulk*
75   Annoint° it must be every stitch—   *smeared*
Board, tree,° and pin.   *mast*
JAPHETH'S WIFE   And I will gather chippes here
To make a fire for you in fere,°   *together*
And for to dighte° your dinner   *prepare*
80   Against° you come in.   *before*

[*Then they make signs as if they were working with different tools.*]

NOAH   Now in the name of God I begin
To make the ship that we shall in,°   *go in*
That we may be ready for to swim°   *float*
At the coming of the flood.
85   These boards I pin here together
To bear us safe from the weather
That we may row both hither and thither
And safe be from this flood.

Of this tree will I make a mast
90   Tied with cables that will last,
With a sail-yard° for each blast,   *spar*
And each thing in their kind.
With topcastle[4] and bowsprit,
Both cords and ropes I have all meet°   *suitable*
95   To sail forth at the nexte wet;°   *rain*
This ship is at an end.

⟨Wife, in this vessel we shall be kept;
My children and thou, I would in ye leapt.[5]

4. An armed platform at the masthead. "And each thing in their kind": and each kind of thing (required).
5. I would like you to jump aboard. The behavior of Noah's Wife in the next two stanzas and in lines 193–252, both enclosed in angle brackets, is inconsistent with her cooperation and meek words in lines 65–68 and elsewhere. Nor does it make

sense that Noah orders her to board the ark before God tells him to take his family inside. Stylistic evidence strongly suggests that these comic exchanges were added, probably in the early 16th century, to bring the Chester play in line with the tradition of the shrewish and recalcitrant Wife of the other mystery cycles.

NOAH'S WIFE   In faith, Noah, I had as lief thou slept.
100   For all thy frankish fare,
   I will not do after thy rede.⁶
NOAH   Good wife, do now as I thee bid.
NOAH'S WIFE   By Christ, not ere I see more need,
   Though thou stand all day and stare.

105   NOAH   Lord, that° women been crabbed ay,°   *how/always*
   And none are meek, I dare well say.
   That is well seen by me today
      In witness of you each one.⁷
   Good wife, let be all this bear°   *behavior*
110   That thou makest in this place here,
   For all they ween° that thou art master—   *think*
      And so thou art, by Saint John.)

   GOD   Noah, take thou thy meinie,°   *household*
   And in the ship hie° that ye be;   *hasten*
115   For none so righteous man to me
      Is now on earth living.
   Of clean beasts with thee thou take
   Seven and seven ere then thou slake;⁸
   He and she, make to make,°   *mate with mate*
120   Belive in that thou bring.⁹

   Of beasts unclean two and two,
   Male and female, but mo;°   *no more*
   Of clean fowls seven also
      The he and she together;
125   Of fowls unclean, twain and no more,
   As I of beasts said before,
   That shall be saved through my lore,°   *teaching*
      Against° I send this weather.   *before*

   Of meats° that may be eaten,   *foods*
130   Into the ship look they be gotten,
   For that may be no way forgotten.
      And do this al bedene.°   *at once*
   To sustain man and beasts therein.
   Ay till the water cease and blin.°   *stop*
135   This world is filled full of sin,
      And that is now well seen.

   Seven days been yet coming;°   *are yet to come*
   You shall have space° them in to bring.   *time*

After that it is my liking
140   Mankind to annoy.°   *afflict*
Forty days and forty nights
Rain shall fall for their unrights,°   *sins*
And that I have made through mights[1]
Now think I to destroy.

145 NOAH   Lord, at Your bidding I am bain.°   *ready*
Sithen° no other grace will gain,°   *since/avail*
It will I fulfill fain,°   *gladly*
For gracious I Thee find.
An hundred winters and twenty
150 This ship-making tarried° have I,   *delayed*
If through amendment Thy mercy
Would fall to mankind.[2]

Have done, ye men and women all;
Hie you lest this water fall,
155 That each beast were in his stall
And into the ship brought.
Of clean beastes seven shall be,
Of unclean two; thus God bade me.
The flood is nigh, you may well see;
160   Therefore tarry you nought.

[*Then* NOAH *shall go into the ark with all his family, his wife except, and the ark must be boarded[3] round about. And on the boards all the beasts and fowls hereafter rehearsed must be painted, that their words may agree with the pictures.*]

SHEM   Sir, here are lions, leopards in;
Horses, mares, oxen, and swine,
Goats, calves, sheep, and kine
Here sitten thou may see.
165 HAM   Camels, asses, man may find,
Buck and doe, hart and hind.
All beasts of all manner kind
Here been, as thinketh me.

JAPHETH   Take here cattes, dogges too,
170   Otters and foxes, fulmarts° also;   *polecats*
Hares hopping gaily can go
Here have cole° for to eat.   *cabbage*
NOAH'S WIFE   And here are bears, wolves set,
Apes, owls, marmoset,
175   Weasels, squirrels, and ferret;
Here they eat their meat.°   *food*

---

1. That [which] I have made through [my] power.
2. If through reform mankind would obtain Thy
mercy (cf. lines 7–8).
3. Supplied with boards.

SHEM'S WIFE   Here are beasts in this house;
    Here cats maken it crouse;[4]
    Here a raton,° here a mouse   *rat*
180   That standen near together.
    HAM'S WIFE   And here are fowles less and more—
    Herons, cranes, and bittor,°   *bittern*
    Swanes, peacocks—and them before,
    Meat for this weather.

185   JAPHETH'S WIFE   Here are cockes, kites, crowes,
    Rookes, ravens, many rowes,
    Duckes, curlews, whoever knowes,
       Each one in this kind.
    And here are doves, digges,° drakes,   *ducks*
190   Redshanks running through the lakes;
    And each fowl that leden° makes   *song*
       In this ship man may find.

    ⟨NOAH   Wife, come in. Why stands thou there?
    Thou art ever froward;[5] that dare I swear.
195   Come, in God's name! Time it were,
       For fear lest that we drown!
    NOAH'S WIFE   Yea, sir, set up your sail
    And row forth with evil hail;°   *ill luck*
    For withouten any fail°   *doubt*
200   I will not out of this town.

    But° I have my gossips° every one,   *unless/friends*
    One foot further I will not gone.°   *go*
    They shall not drown, by Saint John,
       And° I may save their life.   *if*
205   They loved me full well, by Christ.
    But thou wilt let them into thy chist,° *ark (chest)*
    Else row forth, Noah, when thee list° *you please*
       And get thee a new wife.

    NOAH   Shem, son, lo thy mother is wrow;° *angry*
210   By God, such another I do not know.
    SHEM   Father, I shall fetch her in, I trow,° *trust*
    Withouten any fail.
    Mother, my father after thee send
    And bids thee into yonder ship wend.° *go*
215   Look up and see the wind,
       For we been ready to sail.

    NOAH'S WIFE   Son, go again to him and say
    I will not come therein today.
    NOAH   Come in, Wife, in twenty devils way,[6]

---

4. Have a merry time.   6. In the name of twenty devils.
5. Bold, presumptuous.

220   Or else stand there without.°   *outside*
   HAM   Shall we all fetch her in?
   NOAH   Yea, son, in Christ's blessing and mine,
     I would ye hied you betime,
       For of this flood I stand in doubt.[7]

Song

225   THE GOOD GOSSIPS   The flood comes fleeting in full fast,[8]
     On every side that spreadeth full far.
     For fear of drowning I am aghast;
     Good gossip, let us draw near.

     And let us drink ere we depart,
230   For oftentimes we have done so.
     For at one draught thou drink a quart,
     And so will I do ere I go.

   NOAH'S WIFE   Here is a pottle of Malmsey[9] good and strong;
     It will rejoice both heart and tongue.
235   Though Noah think us never so long,
     Yet we will drink atyte.°   *at once*

   JAPHETH   Mother, we pray you all together—
     For we are here, your own childer°—   *children*
     Come into the ship for fear of the weather,
240   For his love that you bought![1]
   NOAH'S WIFE   That will I not for all your call
     But° I have my gossips all.   *unless*
   SHEM   I° faith, mother, yet thou shall,   *in*
     Whether thou will or nought.   {*Drags her aboard.*}

245   NOAH   Welcome, wife, into this boat.
   NOAH'S WIFE   {*slaps him*} Have thou that for thy note!°   *trouble*
   NOAH   Aha, Mary,[2] this is hot!
     It is good for to be still.
     Ah, children, methinks my boat removes.°   *moves off*
250   Our tarrying here me highly grieves.
     Over the land the water spreads;
       God do as He will.)

  [*Then they sing and* NOAH *shall speak again.*[3]]

   NOAH   Ah, great God that art so good,
     That° workes not thy will is wood.°   *whoever/crazy*

---

7. I want you to hurry before it's too late because I'm afraid of the flood.
8. The flood comes flowing in very fast.
9. A sweet wine. "Pottle": two-quart measure.
1. For the love of him who redeemed you (i.e., Christ).
2. [By] Mary (an oath).
3. The manuscripts do not indicate what song Noah and his family sing. A song might originally have followed after line 192.

255   Now all this world is on a flood,
            As we see well in sight.
        The windows I will shut anon,
        And into my chamber I will gone.
        Till this water, so great one,
260   Is slaked° through Thy might.   *diminished*

[*Then shall* NOAH *shut the window of the ark, and for a little space within the boards he shall be silent; and afterward opening the window and looking round about saying:*]

        Now forty days are fully gone.
        Send a raven I will anon,
        If aughtwhere° earth, tree, or stone   *anywhere*
            Be dry in any place.
265   And if this fowl come not again,
        It is a sign, sooth to sayn,°   *truth to say*
        That dry it is on hill or plain,
            And God hath done some grace.

[*Then he shall send forth a raven, and taking a dove in his hands, let him say:*]

        Ah, Lord, wherever this raven be,
270   Somewhere is dry, well I see;
        But yet a dove, by my lewty,°   *faith*
            After I will send.
        Thou wilt turn again to me,
        For of all fowls that may fle°   *fly*
275   Thou art most meek and hend.°   *gentle*

[*Then he shall send forth the dove; and there shall be another dove in the ship, bearing an olive branch in its mouth, which someone shall let down from the mast into* NOAH's *hands with a rope; and then let* NOAH *say:*]

        Ah, Lord, blessed be thou ay,
        That me hast comfort° thus today.   *comforted*
        By this sight I may well say
            This flood begins to cease.
280   My sweet dove to me brought has
        A branch of olive from some place,
        This betokeneth God has done us some grace,
            And is a sign of peace.

        Ah, Lord, honored must Thou be;
285   All earth dries now I see.
        But yet till thou command me,
            Hence I will not hie.
        All this water is away;

Therefore, as soon as I may,
290 Sacrifice I shall do in fay°   *faith*
    To Thee devoutly.

GOD Noah, take thy wife anon,
    And thy children every one;
    Out of the ship thou shalt gone,
295   And they all with thee.
    Beasts and all that can fly,
    Out anon they shall hie.
    On earth to grow and multiply.
        I will that it so be.

300 NOAH Lord, I thank Thee through Thy might;
    Thy bidding shall be done in hight,°   *haste*
    And, as fast as I may dight,°   *get ready*
        I will do Thee honor.
    And to Thee offer sacrifice
305 Therefore comes in all wise,[4]
    For of these beasts that been His,
        Offer I will this store.°   *great number*

[*Then, going out of the ark with his whole family he shall take his animals
and birds and offer and sacrifice them.*]

    Lord God in majesty,
    That such grace has granted me,
310 Where all was lorn,° safe to be,   *lost*
        Therefore now am I boun,°   *ready*
    My wife, my children, and my meinie,°   *household*
    With sacrifice to honor Thee
    Of beasts, fowls, as Thou mayst see,
315   And full devotioun.

GOD Noah, to me thou art full able°   *very worthy*
    And thy sacrifice acceptable,
    For I have found thee true and stable,
        On thee now must I min.[5]
320 Wary° earth I will no more   *curse*
    For man's sins that grieve me sore;
    For of youth man full yore
        Has been inclined to sin.[6]

    Ye shall now grow and multiply
325 And earth again to edify.°   *replenish*
    Each beast, and fowl that may fly,
        Shall be feared° of you;   *afraid*

4. Is, therefore, becoming in every way.
5. I must now be mindful of you.
6. Because for a very long time man, from his youth, has been inclined to sin.

And fish in sea, all that may flete,°   swim
Shall sustain you, I thee beheet;°   promise
330   To eat of them ye ne let
        That clean been you may know.[7]

Thereas° ye have eaten before   whereas
Trees and roots since ye were bore,°   born
Of clean beasts now, less and more,
335   I give you leave to eat—
Save blood and flesh both in fere.[8]
Of wrong dead carrion that is here,
Eat ye not of that in no manner,
        For that ay ye shall let.[9]

340   Manslaughter also ay ye shall flee,
For that is not pleasant unto me.
They that shed blood, he or she,
        Aughtwhere° amongst mankin,°   anywhere / mankind
That blood foully shed shall be
345   And vengeance have, that men shall see.
Therefore beware now all ye,
        Ye fall not into that sin.

A forward,° Noah, with thee I make   covenant
And all thy seed for thy sake,
350   Of such vengeance for to slake,[1]
        For now I have my will.
Here I beheet thee an hest[2]
That man, woman, fowl, ne beast,
With water while this world shall last
355   I will no more spill.°   destroy

My bow° between you and me   rainbow
In the firmament shall be
By very° tokening that you may see   true
        That such vengeance shall cease.
360   That man ne woman shall never more
Be wasted by water as hath before;[3]
But for sin that grieveth me sore,
        Therefore this vengeance was.

Where cloudes in the welkin° been,   sky
365   That ilke° bow shall be seen,   same
In tokening that my wrath and teen°   anger

7. Do not abstain from eating those you know to be clean (Genesis 9.1–3). The eating of meat will henceforth be permissible so long as the dietary laws are observed. "Ye": God speaks not just to Noah but to all the human race.
8. Except for blood and flesh both together (Genesis 9.4).

9. Of wrongly dead carrion (i.e., meat not killed according to dietary law), which is here, of that do not eat at all, for you must always leave that alone.
1. To give over such vengeance (as the flood).
2. Here I make you a promise.
3. Be destroyed by water as has happened.

Shall never thus wroken° be.   *avenged*
The string is turned towards you,
And towards me is bent the bow,[4]
370   That such weather shall never show;[5]
And this beheet° I thee.   *promise*

My blessing now I give thee here,
To thee, Noah, my servant dear,
For vengeance shall no more appear;
375   And now farewell, my darling dear.

The Wakefield Second Shepherds' Play

The Wakefield Second Shepherds' Play   In putting on the stage biblical shepherds and soldiers, medieval playwrights inevitably and often quite deliberately gave them the appearance and characters of contemporary men and women. No play better illustrates this aspect of the drama than the *Second Shepherds' Play*, so called because it is the second of two Nativity plays that are part of the cycle believed to have been performed at Wakefield in Yorkshire. As the play opens, the shepherds complain about the cold, the taxes, and the high-handed treatment they get from the gentry—evils closer to shepherds on the Yorkshire moors than to those keeping their flocks near Bethlehem. The sophisticated dramatic intelligence at work in this and several other of the Wakefield plays belonged undoubtedly to one individual, who probably revised older, more traditional plays some time during the last quarter of the fifteenth century. His identity is not known, but because of his achievement scholars refer to him as the Wakefield Master. He was probably a highly educated cleric stationed in the vicinity of Wakefield, perhaps a friar of a nearby priory. The Wakefield Master had a genius for combining comedy, including broad farce, with religion in ways that make them enhance one another. In the *Second Shepherds' Play*, by linking the comic subplot of Mak and Gill with the solemn story of Christ's nativity, the Wakefield Master has produced a dramatic parable of what the Nativity means in Christian history and in Christian hearts. No one will fail to observe the parallelism between the stolen sheep, ludicrously disguised as Mak's latest heir, lying in the cradle, and the real Lamb of God, born in the stable among beasts. A complex of relationships based on this relationship suggests itself. But perhaps the most important point is that the charity twice shown by the shepherds—in the first instance to the supposed son of Mak and in the second instance to Mak and Gill when they decide to let them off with only the mildest of punishments—is rewarded when they are invited to visit the Christ Child, the embodiment of charity. The bleak beginning of the play, with its series of individual complaints, is ultimately balanced by the optimistic ending, which sees the shepherds once again singing together in harmony.

The *Second Shepherds' Play* is exceptional among the mystery plays in its development of plot and character. There is no parallel to its elaboration of the comic subplot and no character quite like Mak, who has doubtless been imported into religious drama from popular farce. Mak is perhaps the best humorous character outside of Chaucer's works in this period. A braggart of the worst kind, he has something of Falstaff's charm; and he resembles Falstaff also in his grotesque attempts to maintain the last shreds of his dignity when he is caught in a lie. Most readers will be glad that the shepherds do not carry out their threat to have the death penalty invoked for his crime.

Following the 1994 edition of the Early English Text Society, the stanza, tradition-

---

4. The rainbow is visualized as a bow aimed away from the earth at the sky.

5. [A sign] that such a flood shall never appear.

ally printed as nine lines (with an opening quatrain of four long lines, the first halves of which rhyme with one another) is rendered here as "thirteeners," rhyming *a b a b a b a b c d d d c.*

The Second Shepherds' Play[1]

CAST OF CHARACTERS

COLL	GILL
GIB	ANGEL
DAW	MARY
MAK	

[*A field.*]

[*Enter* COLL]

COLL	Lord, what° these weathers are cold,	*how*
	And I am ill happed;°	*badly covered*
	I am nearhand dold,°	*numb*
	So long have I napped;	
5	My legs they fold,°	*give way*
	My fingers are chapped.	
	It is not as I wold,°	*would (wish)*
	For I am all lapped°	*wrapped*
	In sorrow:	
10	In storms and tempest,	
	Now in the east, now in the west,	
	Woe is him that has never rest	
	Midday nor morrow.	
	But we sely° husbands[2]	*hapless*
15	That walks on the moor,	
	In faith we are nearhands°	*nearly*
	Out of the door.°	*homeless*
	No wonder, as it stands	
	If we be poor,	
20	For the tilth of our lands	
	Lies fallow as the floor,[3]	
	As ye ken.°	*know*
	We are so hammed,	
	Fortaxed, and rammed,	

1. The text is based on the (1994) edition by A. C. Cawley and Martin Stevens, but has been freely edited. Spelling has been normalized except where rhyme makes changes impossible. Because the original text has no indications of scenes and only four stage directions, written in Latin, appropriate scenes of action and additional stage directions have been added; the four original stage directions are identified in the notes.
2. Farmers. The shepherds are also tenant farmers.
3. The arable part of our land lies fallow (as flat) as the floor. Landowners were converting farmland to pasture for sheep.

25   We are made hand-tamed
      With these gentlery-men.[4]

    Thus they reave° us our rest—   *rob*
    Our Lady them wary!°   *curse*
    These men that are lord-fest,°   *attached to lords*
30   They cause the plow tarry.[5]
    That, men say, is for the best—
    We find it contrary.
    Thus are husbands oppressed
    In point to miscarry.
35   On live.[6]
    Thus hold they us under,
    Thus they bring us in blunder,°   *trouble*
    It were a great wonder
      And° ever should we thrive.   *if*

40   There shall come a swain°   *fellow*
    As proud as a po:°   *peacock*
    He must borrow my wain,°   *wagon*
    My plow also;
    Then I am full fain°   *glad*
45   To grant ere he go.
    Thus live we in pain,
    Anger, and woe,
      By night and by day.
    He must have if he lang° it,   *wants*
50   If I should forgang it.[7]
    I were better be hanged
      Than once say him nay.[8]

    For may he get a paint-sleeve[9]
    Or brooch nowadays,
55   Woe is him that him grieve
    Or once again-says.°   *gainsays*
    Dare no man him reprieve,°   *reprove*
    What mastery he maes.[1]
    And yet may no man lieve°   *believe*
60   One word that he says,
      No letter.
    He can make purveyance[2]
    With boast and bragance,°   *bragging*

4. We are so hamstrung, overtaxed, and beaten down [that] we are made to obey these gentry folk. Coll is complaining about the peasants' hard lot, at the mercy of retainers of the wealthy landowners.
5. Hold up the plow, i.e., interfere with the farm work.
6. In life. "In point to miscarry": to the point of ruin.
7. Even if I have to do without it.
8. In the manuscript, this stanza follows the next.
9. An embroidered sleeve, part of the livery worn by the landlord's officers as a badge of authority.
1. No matter what force he uses.
2. Requisition (of private property).

And all is through maintenance[3]
65   Of men that are greater.

It does me good, as I walk
Thus by mine one,°   *self*
Of this world for to talk
In manner of moan.
70   To my sheep I will stalk,
And hearken anon,
There abide on a balk,[4]
Or sit on a stone,
     Full soon;
75   For I trow,° pardie,°   *think/by God*
True men if they be,
We get more company
Ere it be noon.[5]

[*Enter* GIB, *who at first does not see* COLL.]

GIB   Benste and Dominus,[6]
80   What may this bemean?°   *mean*
Why fares this world thus?
Such have we not seen.
Lord, these weathers are spiteous°   *cruel*
And the winds full keen,
85   And the frosts so hideous
They water mine een,°   *eyes*
     No lie.
Now in dry, now in wet,
Now in snow, now in sleet,
90   When my shoon° freeze to my feet   *shoes*
     It is not all easy.

But as far as I ken,°   *see*
Or yet as I go,°   *walk*
We sely° wedmen°   *hapless/married men*
95   Dree° mickle° woe;   *suffer/much*
We have sorrow then and then°—   *constantly*
It falls oft so.
Sely Copple, our hen,[7]
Both to and fro
100   She cackles;
But begin she to croak,
To groan or to cluck,

---

3. Practice of retaining servants under a nobleman's protection with the power to lord it over his
tenants.
4. A raised strip of grassland dividing parts of a
field.

5. I.e., if the other shepherds keep their promise
to meet Coll.
6. Bless us and Lord.
7. Silly Copple, our hen, i.e., Gib's wife, who hen-
pecks him.

Woe is him is our cock,
   For he is in the shackles.

105 These men that are wed
Have not all their will:
When they are full hard stead°   *beset*
They sigh full still;°   *constantly*
God wot° they are led   *knows*
110 Full hard and full ill;
In bower nor in bed
They say nought theretill.°   *against that*
   This tide°   *time*
My part have I fun;°   *found, learned*
115 I know my lesson:
Woe is him that is bun,°   *bound (in wedlock)*
   For he must abide.

But now late in our lives—
A marvel to me,
120 That I think my heart rives°   *splits*
Such wonders to see;
What that destiny drives
It should so be[8]—
Some men will have two wives,
125 And some men three
   In store.[9]
Some are woe° that has any,   *miserable*
But so far can° I,   *know*
Woe is him that has many,
130   For he feels sore.

But young men a-wooing,
For God that you bought,°   *redeemed*
Be well ware of wedding
And think in your thought:
135 "Had I wist"° is a thing   *known*
That serves of nought.
Mickle° still° mourning   *much/continual*
Has wedding home brought,
   And griefs,
140 With many a sharp shower,°   *fight*
For thou may catch in an hour
That° shall sow° thee full sour°   *that which/vex/bitterly*
   As long as thou lives.

For as ever read I 'pistle,[1]
145 I have one to my fere[2]

8. What destiny causes must occur.
9. I.e., by remarrying after being widowed.

1. Epistle, i.e., part of the church service.
2. As my mate.

As sharp as a thistle,
As rough as a brere;°   *briar*
She is browed like a bristle,
With a sour-loten cheer;³
150   Had she once wet her whistle
She could sing full clear
     Her Pater Noster.⁴
She is great as a whale;
She has a gallon of gall:
155   By him that died for us all,
     I would I had run to° I lost her.   *till*

COLL   God look over the raw!⁵
     [*to* GIB] Full deafly ye stand!
GIB   Yea, the devil in thy maw°   *guts*
160   So tariand!⁶
Saw thou awhere° of Daw?   *anywhere*
COLL   Yea, on a lea-land°   *pasture land*
Heard I him blaw.°   *blow (his horn)*
He comes here at hand,
165   Not far.
Stand still.
GIB   Why?
COLL   For he comes, hope° I.   *think*
GIB   He will make us both a lie
     But if° we be ware.   *unless*

[*Enter* DAW,⁷ *who does not see the others.*]

170   DAW   Christ's cross me speed
And Saint Nicholas!⁸
Thereof had I need:
It is worse than it was.
Whoso could take heed
175   And let the world pass,
It is ever in dread°   *doubt*
And brickle° as glass,   *brittle*
     And slithes.°   *slips away*
This world foor° never so,   *behaved*
180   With marvels mo° and mo,   *more*
Now in weal, now in woe,
And all thing writhes.°   *changes*

Was never sin° Noah's flood   *since*
Such floods seen,

---

3. She has brows like pig's bristles and a sour-looking face.
4. "Our Father," or The Lord's Prayer.
5. I.e., God watch over the audience! Coll has been trying to get Gib's attention as the latter harangues the audience.
6. For being so late.
7. Daw (Davy) is a boy working for the older shepherds.
8. May Christ's cross and St. Nicholas help me.

185   Winds and rains so rude
    And storms so keen:
    Some stammered, some stood
    In doubt,[9] as I ween.°   *suppose*
    Now God turn all to good!
190   I say as I mean.
      For ponder: *consider (this)*
    These floods so they drown
    Both in fields and in town,
    And bears all down,
195   And that is a wonder.

    We that walk on the nights
    Our cattle to keep,°   *keep watch over*
    We see sudden° sights   *startling*
    When other men sleep.
200   Yet methink my heart lights:°   *feels lighter*
    I see shrews peep.[1]

    [*He sees the others, but does not hail them.*]

    Ye are two tall wights.°   *creatures*
    I will give my sheep
      A turn.
205   But full ill have I meant:[2]
    As I walk on this bent°   *field*
    I may lightly° repent,   *quickly*
      My toes if I spurn.°   *stub*

    Ah, sir, God you save,
210   And master mine!
    A drink fain° would I have,   *gladly*
    And somewhat to dine.
      COLL   Christ's curse, my knave,
    Thou art a lither° hine!°   *lazy/servant*
215   GIB What, the boy list rave!
    Abide unto sine.[3]
      We have made it.°   *had dinner*
    Ill thrift on thy pate![4]
    Though the shrew° came late   *rascal*
220   Yet is he in state
      To dine—if he had it.

    DAW   Such servants as I,
    That° sweats and swinks,°   *who/toil*

---

9. Probably refers to people's consternation at the time of Noah's Flood.
1. I see rascals peeping. Daw is relieved to recognize the other shepherds aren't monstrous apparitions.

2. But that's a very poor idea (to give the sheep a turn).
3. The boy must be crazy! Wait till later.
4. Bad luck on thy head!

Eats our bread full dry,
225   And that me forthinks.°   *angers*
We are oft wet and weary
When master-men winks,°   *sleep*
Yet comes full lately°   *tardily*
Both dinners and drinks.
230   But nately°   *profitably*
Both our dame and our sire,⁵
When we have run in the mire,
They can nip at our hire,⁶
And pay us full lately.

235   But here my troth, master,
For the fare° that ye make°   *food/provide*
I shall do thereafter:
Work as I take.⁷
I shall do a little, sir,
240   And among° ever lake,°   *betweentimes/play*
For yet lay my supper
Never on my stomach⁸
In fields.
Whereto should I threap?°   *haggle*
245   With my staff can I leap,°   *run away*
And men say, "Light cheap
Litherly foryields."⁹

COLL   Thou were an ill lad
To ride a-wooing
250   With a man that had
But little of spending.¹
GIB   Peace, boy, I bade—
No more jangling,
Or I shall make thee full rad,°   *quickly (stop)*
255   By the heaven's King!
With thy gauds°—   *tricks*
Where are our sheep, boy?—we scorn.²
DAW   Sir, this same day at morn
I left them in the corn°   *wheat*
260   When they rang Lauds.³

They have pasture good,
They cannot go wrong.
COLL   That is right. By the rood,°   *cross*
These nights are long!
265   Yet I would, ere we yode,°   *went*

5. I.e., mistress and master.
6. They can deduct from our wages.
7. I.e., work (as little) as I am paid.
8. I.e., a full stomach has never weighed me down.
9. A cheap bargain repays badly (a proverb).

1. You would be a bad servant to take wooing for a man with little money to spend.
2. We scorn (your tricks).
3. The first church service of the day (morn) but performed while it is still dark.

One° gave us a song.   someone
GIB   So I thought as I stood,
   To mirth° us among.°   cheer/meanwhile
DAW   I grant.
270 COLL   Let me sing the tenory.°   tenor
GIB   And I the treble so hee.°   high
DAW   Then the mean° falls to me.   middle part
   Let see how you chant.   [*They sing.*]

[*Enter* MAK *with a cloak over his clothes.*][4]

MAK   Now, Lord, for thy names seven,
275   That made both moon and starns°   stars
   Well mo than I can neven,°   name
   Thy will, Lord, of me tharns.[5]
   I am all uneven°—   at odds
   That moves oft my harns.[6]
280   Now would God I were in heaven,
   For there weep no barns.°   children
    So still.°   continually
COLL   Who is that pipes so poor?
MAK   [*aside*] Would God ye wist° how I foor!°   knew/fared
285   [*aloud*] Lo, a man that walks on the moor
   And has not all his will.

GIB   Mak, where has thou gane?°   gone
   Tell us tiding.
DAW.   Is he come? Then ilkane
290   Take heed to his thing.[7]

[*Snatches the cloak from him.*]

MAK   What! Ich[8] be a yeoman,
   I tell you, of the king,
   The self and the same,
   Sond° from a great lording   messenger
295   And sich.°   suchlike
   Fie on you! Goth° hence   go
   Out of my presence:
   I must have reverence.
    Why, who be ich?

300 COLL   Why make ye it so quaint?[9]
   Mak, ye do wrang.°   wrong
GIB   But, Mak, list ye saint?
   I trow that ye lang.[1]

---

4. Stage direction in the original manuscript.
5. Thy will, Lord, falls short in regard to me.
6. That often disturbs my brains.
7. Each one look to his possessions (lest Mak steal them). The stage direction below is in the manuscript.
8. I (a southern dialect form in contrast with the northern dialect spoken by the Yorkshire shepherds). Mak pretends to be an important person from the south.
9. Why are you putting on such airs?
1. Do you want to play the saint? I guess you long (to do so).

DAW I trow the shrew can paint²—

305   The devil might him hang!

MAK Ich shall make complaint

And make you all to thwang°   *be flogged*

At a word,

And tell even° how ye doth.   *exactly*

310 COLL But Mak, is that sooth?

Now take out that Southern tooth,³

And set in a turd!⁴

GIB Mak, the devil in your ee!°   *eye*

A stroke would I lean° you!   *give*

315 DAW Mak, know ye not me?

By God, I could teen° you.   *vex*

MAK God look° you all three: *guard*

Methought I had seen you.

Ye are a fair company.

320 COLL Can ye now mean you?⁵

GIB Shrew, peep!⁶

Thus late as thou goes,

What will men suppose?

And thou has an ill nose⁷

325   Of stealing sheep.

MAK And I am true as steel,

All men wate.°   *know*

But a sickness I feel

That holds me full hate:°   *hot, feverish*

330 My belly fares not weel,

It is out of estate.

DAW Seldom lies the de'el°   *devil*

Dead by the gate.⁸

MAK Therefore⁹

335 Full sore am I and ill

If I stand stone-still,

I eat not a needill¹

This month and more.

COLL How fares thy wife? By my hood,

340 How fares sho?°   *she*

MAK Lies waltering,° by the rood,   *sprawling*

By the fire, lo!

And a house full of brood.°   *children*

---

2. I think the rascal knows how to put on false colors.

3. I.e., now stop pretending to speak like a southerner.

4. I.e., shut up!

5. Can you now remember (who you are)?

6. Rascal, watch out.

7. Noise, i.e., reputation.

8. Road, i.e., the devil is always on the move.

9. Mak ignores Daw and continues his speech from line 331.

1. As sure as I'm standing here as still as a stone, I haven't eaten a needle (i.e., a tiny bit).

She drinks well, too:
345 Ill speed other good
That she will do!²
    But sho
Eats as fast as she can;
And ilk° year that comes to man   *every*
350 She brings forth a lakan°—   *baby*
    And some years two.

But were I now more gracious°   *prosperous*
And richer by far,
I were eaten out of house
355 And of harbar.°   *home*
Yet is she a foul douce,°   *sweetheart*
If ye come nar:³
There is none that trows°   *imagines*
Nor knows a war°   *worse*
360   Than ken° I.   *know*
Now will ye see what I proffer:
To give all in my coffer
Tomorn at next° to offer   *tomorrow*
    Her head-masspenny.⁴

365 GIB   I wot° so forwaked⁵   *know*
    Is none in this shire.
    I would sleep if° I taked   *even if*
    Less to my hire.⁶
    DAW   I am cold and naked
370   And would have a fire.
    COLL   I am weary forraked°   *from walking*
    And run in the mire.
        Wake thou.⁷   [*Lies down.*]
    GIB   Nay, I will lie down by,
375   For I must sleep, truly.   [*Lies down beside him.*]
    DAW   As good a man's son was I
        As any of you.

[*Lies down and motions to* MAK *to lie between them.*]

But Mak, come hither, between
Shall thou lie down.
380 MAK   Then might I let you bedeen
    Of that ye would rown,⁸

2. I.e., that (drinking) is the only good she does.
3. I.e., near the truth.
4. The penny paid to sing a mass for her soul; i.e., I wish she were dead.
5. Exhausted from lack of sleep.
6. I should take a cut in wages.
7. Keep watch.
8. Then I might be in the way if you wanted to whisper together.

No dread.°   doubt
From my top to my toe,   [*Lies down and prays.*]
Manus tuas commendo
385   Pontio Pilato.⁹
        Christ's cross me speed!°   help

[*He gets up as the others sleep and speaks.*]¹

Now were time for a man
That lacks what he wold°   would, wants
To stalk privily than°   then
390   Unto a fold,°   sheepfold
And nimbly to work than,
And be not too bold,
For he might abuy° the bargan°   pay for/bargain
    At the ending.
395   Now were time for to reel:°   move fast
But he needs good counseel°   counsel
That fain would fare weel°   well
    And has but little spending.°   money

[*He draws a magic circle around the shepherds and recites a spell.*]

But about you a circill,°   circle
400   As round as a moon,
To° I have done that° I will,   until/what
Till that it be noon,
That ye lie stone-still
To° that I have done;   until
405   And I shall say theretill°   thereto
Of good words a foon:°   few
    "On hight,
Over your heads my hand I lift.
Out go your eyes! Fordo your sight!"²
410   But yet I must make better shift
    And it be right.³

Lord, what° they sleep hard—   how
That may ye all hear.
Was I never a shephard,
415   But now will I lear.°   learn
If the flock be scar'd,
Yet shall I nip near.⁴
How! Draws hitherward!⁵   [*He catches one.*]
Now mends our cheer

9. "Thy hands I commend to Pontius Pilate." A
parody of Luke 23.46, "Into thy hands I commend
my spirit."
1. One of the original stage directions.
2. May your sight be rendered powerless.

3. If it is to turn out all right.
4. Even if the flock is alarmed, yet shall I grip (a
sheep) close.
5. Stop! come this way.

420   From sorrow.
   A fat sheep, I dare say!
   A good fleece, dare I lay!°   *bet*
   Eft-quit° when I may,   *repay*
    But this will I borrow.

[Moves with the sheep to his cottage and calls from outside.]

425   How, Gill, art thou in?
   Get us some light.
   GILL *[inside]* Who makes such a din
   This time of the night?
   I am set for to spin;
430   I hope not I might
   Rise a penny to win[6]—
   I shrew° them on height!   *curse*
    So fares
   A housewife that has been
435   To be raised thus between:
   Here may no note be seen
    For such small chares.[7]

   MAK Good wife, open the hek!°   *door*
   Sees thou not what I bring?
440   GILL I may thole thee draw the sneck.[8]
   Ah, come in, my sweeting.°   *sweetheart*
   MAK Yea, thou thar not reck
   Of my long standing.[9]

[She opens the door.]

   GILL By the naked neck
445   Art thou like for to hing.°   *hang*
   MAK Do way!°   *let it be*
   I am worthy° my meat,   *worthy of*
   For in a strait° I can get   *pinch*
   More than they that swink° and sweat *work*
450   All the long day.

   Thus it fell to my lot,
   Gill, I had such grace.°   *luck*
   GILL It were a foul blot
   To be hanged for the case.°   *deed*
455   MAK I have 'scaped,° Jelot,°   *escaped/Gill*
   Of as hard a glase.°   *blow*
   GILL But "So long goes the pot

6. I don't think I can earn a penny by getting up (from my work).
7. So it goes with anyone who has been a house-wife—to be interrupted like this: no work gets done here because of such petty chores.
8. I'll let you draw the latch.
9. Sure, you needn't care about keeping me standing a long time.

To the water," men says,
　　　"At last
460　　Comes it home broken."
　　MAK　Well know I the token,°　　　　　　　　　*saying*
　　　　But let it never be spoken!
　　　　But come and help fast.

　　　　I would he were flain,°　　　　　　　　　*skinned*
465　　I list° well eat:　　　　　　　　　　　　*wish*
　　　　This twelvemonth was I not so fain
　　　　Of one sheep-meat.
　　GILL　Come they ere he be slain,
　　　　And hear the sheep bleat—
470　　MAK　Then might I be ta'en°—　　　　　　*taken*
　　　　That were a cold sweat!
　　　　　Go spar°　　　　　　　　　　　　　　*fasten*
　　　　The gate-door.°　　　　　　　　　　　*street door*
　　GIL　　　　　　Yes, Mak,
　　　　For and° they come at thy back—　　　　　*if*
475　　MAK　Then might I buy, for all the pack,
　　　　The devil of the war.[1]

　　GILL　A good bourd° have I spied,　　　　　*trick*
　　　　Sin° thou can° none.　　　　　　　　　*since/know*
　　　　Here shall we him hide
480　　To° they be gone,　　　　　　　　　　*until*
　　　　In my cradle. Abide!
　　　　Let me alone,
　　　　And I shall lie beside
　　　　In childbed and groan.
485　　MAK　Thou red,°　　　　　　　　　　*get ready*
　　　　And I shall say thou was light°　　　　*delivered*
　　　　Of a knave-child° this night.　　　　*boy child*
　　GILL　Now well is me day bright
　　　　That ever I was bred.[2]

490　　This is a good guise°　　　　　　　　　*method*
　　　　And a far-cast:°　　　　　　　　　　*clever trick*
　　　　Yet a woman's advice
　　　　Helps at the last.
　　　　I wot° never who spies:　　　　　　　*know*
495　　Again° go thou fast.　　　　　　　　　*back*
　　MAK　But° I come ere they rise,　　　　　*unless*
　　　　Else blows a cold blast.
　　　　I will go sleep.
　　　　Yet sleeps all this meny,°　　　　　*company*
500　　And I shall go stalk privily,

1. Then I might have to pay the devil the worse on　　　2. Now lucky for me the bright day I was born.
account of the whole pack of them.

As it had never been I
　That carried their sheep.　　　　　*[Lies down among them.]*

[The shepherds are waking.]

COLL　*Resurrex a mortruus!*[3]
　Have hold my hand!
505　*Judas carnas dominus!*[4]
　I may not well stand.
　My foot sleeps, by Jesus,
　And I walter° fastand.°　　　　　　　　*stagger/(from) fasting*
　I thought we had laid us
510　Full near England.
　GIB　Ah, yea?
　Lord, what° I have slept weel!°　　　　*how/well*
　As fresh as an eel,
　As light I me feel
515　　As leaf on a tree.

DAW　Benste° be herein!　　　　　　　　*(God's) blessing*
　So my body quakes,
　My heart is out of skin,
　What-so° it makes.°　　　　　　　　　*whatever/causes*
520　Who makes all this din?
　So my brows blakes,[5]
　To the door will I win.[6]
　Hark, fellows, wakes!
　　We were four:
525　See ye aywhere of Mak now?
　COLL　We were up ere thou.
　GIB　Man, I give God avow
　　Yet yede he naw're.[7]

DAW　Methought he was lapped°　　　　　*covered*
530　In a wolfskin.
　COLL　So are many happed°　　　　　　*clad*
　Now, namely° within.　　　　　　　　*especially*
　DAW　When we had long napped,
　Methought with a gin°　　　　　　　　*snare*
535　A fat sheep he trapped,
　But he made no din.
　GIB　Be still!
　Thy dream makes thee wood.°　　　　　*crazy*
　It is but phantom, by the rood.°　　　*cross*
540　COLL　Now God turn all to good,
　　If it be his will.

---

3. A garbled form of "resurrexit a mortuis" (he
arose from the dead) from the Creed.
4. Judas, (in?)carnate lord.
5. My brow turns pale (with fear).

6. I'll head for the door. Still half-asleep, Daw
thinks he's inside.
7. He's gone nowhere yet.

[They wake up MAK *who pretends to have been asleep.]*

GIB   Rise, Mak, for shame!
    Thou lies right lang.°   *long*
  MAK   Now Christ's holy name
545   Be us amang!°   *among*
    What is this? For Saint Jame,
    I may not well gang.°   *walk*
    I trow° I be the same.   *think*
    Ah, my neck has lain wrang.°   *wrong*
    [One of them twists his neck.]
550   Enough!
    Mickle° thank! Sin° yestereven   *much/since*
    Now, by Saint Stephen,
    I was flayed with a sweven—
      My heart out of slough.[8]

555   I thought Gill began to croak
    And travail° full sad,°   *labor/hard*
    Well-near at the first cock,[9]
    Of a young lad,
    For to mend° our flock—   *increase*
560   Then be I never glad:
    I have tow on my rock[1]
    More than ever I had.
      Ah, my head!
    A house full of young tharms!°   *bellies*
565   The devil knock out their harns!°   *brains*
    Woe is him has many barns,°   *children*
      And thereto little bread.

    I must go home, by your leave,
    To Gill, as I thought.°   *intended*
570   I pray you look° my sleeve,   *examine*
    That I steal nought.
    I am loath you to grieve
    Or from you take aught.
  DAW   Go forth! Ill might thou chieve!°   *prosper*
575   Now would I we sought
      This morn,
    That we had all our store.[2]
  COLL   But I will go before.
    Let us meet.
  GIB   Whore?°   *where*
580   DAW   At the crooked thorn.

---

8. I was terrified by a dream—my heart [jumped] out of [my] skin.
9. First cockcrow, i.e., midnight.
1. Flax on my distaff (i.e., trouble, mouths to feed).
2. Now I want us to make sure . . . we have all our stock.

[MAK's *house.* MAK *at the door.*]

MAK Undo this door!

GILL   Who is here?

MAK How long shall I stand?

GILL Who makes such a bere?°   *clamor*

    Now walk in the weniand!³

585 MAK Ah, Gill, what cheer?

    It is I, Mak, your husband.

GILL Then may we see here

    The devil in a band,⁴

      Sir Guile!

590 Lo, he comes with a lote°   *sound*

    As° he were holden in° the throat: *as if/by*

    I may not sit at my note°   *work*

      A hand-long° while.   *short*

MAK Will ye hear what fare° she makes   *fuss*

595 To get her a glose?°   *excuse*

    And does nought but lakes°   *plays*

    And claws° her toes?   *scratches*

GILL Why, who wanders? Who wakes?

    Who comes? Who goes?

600 Who brews? Who bakes?

    What makes me thus hose?⁵

      And than°   *then*

    It is ruth° to behold,   *pity*

    Now in hot, now in cold,

605 Full woeful is the household

      That wants° a woman.   *lacks*

    But what end has thou made

    With the herds,° Mak?   *shepherds*

MAK The last word that they said

610 When I turned my back,

    They would look that they had

    Their sheep all the pack.

    I hope they will not be well paid⁶

    When they their sheep lack.

615   Pardie!°   *by God*

    But how-so the game goes,

    To me they will suppose,⁷

    And make a foul nose,°   *noise*

      And cry out upon me.

3. Waning of the moon (an unlucky time), i.e., "Go with bad luck!"

4. In a noose (?) Gill perhaps continues to remind Mak that sheep stealing is a hanging offense.

5. Hoarse (from shouting at her husband and children).

6. I expect they won't be well pleased.

7. They will suspect me.

620 But thou must do as thou hight.° *promised*
GILL I accord me theretill.[8]
I shall swaddle him right
In my cradill.

[*She wraps up the sheep and puts it in the cradle.*]

If it were a greater sleight,
625 Yet could I help till.[9]
I will lie down straight.° *immediately*
Come hap° me. *cover*
MAK I will. [*Covers her.*]
GILL Behind
Come Coll and his marrow;[1]
630 They will nip° us full narrow.° *pinch/closely*
MAK But I may cry "Out, harrow,"[2]
The sheep if they find.

GILL Hearken ay when they call—
They will come anon.
635 Come and make ready all,
And sing by thine one.° *self*
Sing "lullay"° thou shall, *lullaby*
For I must groan
And cry out by the wall
640 On Mary and John
For sore.° *pain*
Sing "lullay" on fast
When thou hears at the last,[3]
And but I play a false cast,[4]
645 Trust me no more.

[*The shepherds meet again.*]

DAW Ah, Coll, good morn.
Why sleeps thou not?
COLL Alas, that ever I was born!
We have a foul blot:
650 A fat wether° have we lorn.° *ram/lost*
DAW Marry, God's forbot!° *God forbid*
GIB Who should do us that scorn?
That were a foul spot!° *disgrace*
COLL Some shrew.° *rascal*
655 I have sought with my dogs
All Horbury[5] shrogs,° *thickets*

8. I agree to that.
9. Even if it were a greater trick, I could still help with it.
1. Coll and his mate are coming on your tracks.

2. A cry of distress.
3. When at last you hear (them coming).
4. Unless I play a false trick.
5. A village near Wakefield.

And of fifteen hogs
Found I but one ewe.[6]

DAW   Now trow° me, if ye will,   *believe*
660   By Saint Thomas of Kent,
Either Mak or Gill
Was at that assent.[7]
COLL   Peace, man, be still!
I saw when he went.
665   Thou slanders him ill—
Thou ought to repent
Good speed.°   *speedily*
GIB   Now as ever might I thee,°   *thrive*
If I should even here dee,°   *die*
670   I would say it were he
That did that same deed.

DAW   Go we thither, I read,°   *advise*
And run on our feet.
Shall I never eat bread
675   The sooth to I weet.[8]
COLL   Nor drink in my head,
With him till I meet.[9]
GIB   I will rest in no stead°   *place*
Till that I him greet,
680   My brother.
One I will hight:[1]
Till I see him in sight
Shall I never sleep one night
There I do another.[2]

[*The shepherds approach* MAK's *house.* MAK *and* GILL *within, she in
bed, groaning, he singing a lullaby.*]

685   DAW   Will ye hear how they hack?[3]
Our sire list° croon.   *wants to*
COLL   Heard I never none crack°   *sing loudly*
So clear out of tune.
Call on him.
GIB   Mak!
690   Undo your door soon!°   *at once*
MAK   Who is that spake,
As° it were noon,   *as if*
On loft?°   *loudly*

6. And with fifteen lambs I found only a ewe (i.e.,
the wether [ram] was missing).
7. Was a party to it.
8. Until I know the truth.
9. Nor take a drink till I meet with him.

1. One thing will I promise.
2. I'll never sleep in the same place two nights in
a row.
3. Trill; a musical term used sarcastically, as also
"crack" below.

Who is that, I say?
695 DAW Good fellows, were it day.[4]
MAK As far as ye may,
[opening] Good,° speaks soft   *good men*

Over a sick woman's head
That is at malease.[5]
700 I had liefer° be dead   *rather*
Ere she had any disease.°   *distress*
GILL Go to another stead!°   *place*
I may not well wheeze:°   *breathe*
Each foot that ye tread
705 Goes through my nese.°   *nose*
So, hee![6]
COLL Tell us, Mak, if you may,
How fare ye, I say?
MAK But are ye in this town today?[7]
710 Now how fare ye?

Ye have run in the mire
And are wet yit.
I shall make you a fire
If you will sit.
715 A nurse would I hire.
Think ye on yit?[8]
Well quit is my hire—
My dream this is it—
A season.[9]
720 I have barns,° if ye knew,   *children*
Wel mo° than enew:°   *more/enough*
But we must drink as we brew,
And that is but reason.

I would ye dined ere ye yode.°   *went*
725 Methink that ye sweat.
GIB Nay, neither mends our mood,
Drink nor meat.[1]
MAK Why sir, ails you aught but good?[2]
DAW Yea, our sheep that we get°   *tend*
730 Are stolen as they yode:°   *wandered*
Our loss is great.
MAK Sirs, drinks!
Had I been thore,°   *there*

---

4. Good friends, if it were daylight (i.e., not friends, since it's still night).
5. Who feels badly.
6. So loudly, i.e., your tramping goes right through my head.
7. I.e., what brings you to this neighborhood today?

8. Do you still remember (my dream)?
9. Ironic: my season's wages are well paid—my dream (that Gill was giving birth) has come true.
1. Neither food nor drink will improve our mood.
2. Does anything other than good trouble you? I.e., what's wrong?

Some should have bought° it full sore.   *paid for*
735 COLL   Marry, some men trows° that ye wore,°   *think/were*
And that us forthinks.°   *displeases*

GIB   Mak, some men trows,
That it should be ye.
DAW   Either ye or your spouse,
740 So say we.
MAK   Now if you have suspouse°   *suspicion*
To Gill or to me,
Come and ripe° the house   *ransack*
And then may ye see
745 Who had her³—
If I any sheep fot,°   *fetched, stole*
Either cow or stot⁴—
And Gill my wife rose not
Here sin she laid her.°   *lay down*

750 As I am true and leal,°   *honest*
To God here I pray
That this be the first meal
That I shall eat this day.
COLL   Mak, as I have sele,⁵
755 Advise thee, I say:
He learned timely to steal
That could not say nay.⁶   [*They begin to search.*]
GILL   I swelt!°   *die*
Out, thieves, from my wones!°   *dwelling*
760 Ye come to rob us for the nones.⁷
MAK   Hear ye not how she groans?
Your hearts should melt.

GILL   Out, thieves, from my barn!°   *child*
Nigh him not thore!⁸
765 MAK   Wist ye how she had farn,⁹
Your hearts would be sore.
You do wrong, I you warn,
That thus comes before°   *in the presence*
To a woman that has farn°—   *been in labor*
770 But I say no more.
GILL   Ah, my middill!°   *middle*
I pray to God so mild,
If ever I you beguiled,
That I eat this child
775 That lies in this cradill.

3. I.e., the sheep.
4. Either female or male.
5. As I hope to have salvation.
6. He learned early to steal who could not say no

(proverbial).
7. You come for the purpose of robbing us.
8. Don't come close to him there.
9. If you knew how she had fared (in labor).

MAK   Peace, woman, for God's pain,
    And cry not so!
      Thou spills° thy brain   *harm*
    And makes me full woe.
780 GIB   I trow our sheep be slain.
    What find ye two?
  DAW   All work we in vain;
    As well may we go.
      But hatters!¹
785   I can find no flesh,
    Hard nor nesh,°   *soft*
    Salt nor fresh,
      But two tome° platters.   *empty*

    Quick cattle but this,²
790   Tame nor wild,
    None, as I have bliss,
      As loud as he smiled.³   *[Approaches the cradle.]*
  GILL   No, so God me bliss,°   *bless*
    And give me joy of my child!
795 COLL   We have marked° amiss—   *aimed*
    I hold° us beguiled.   *consider*
  GIB   Sir, don!°   *totally*
    [*to* MAK]   Sir—Our Lady him save!—
    Is your child a knave?⁴
800 MAK   Any lord might him have,
    This child, to° his son.   *as*

    When he wakens he kips,°   *snatches, grabs*
    That joy is to see.
  DAW   In good time to his hips,
805   And in sely.⁵
    But who were his gossips,°   *godparents*
    So soon ready?
  MAK   So fair fall their lips⁶—
  COLL   Hark, now, a lee,°   *lie*
810 MAK   So God them thank,
    Perkin, and Gibbon Waller, I say,
    And gentle John Horne, in good fay°—   *faith*
    He made all the garray°   *quarrel*
    With the great shank.⁷

815 GIB   Mak, friends will we be,
    For we are all one.°   *in accord*

---

1. An expression of consternation.
2. Livestock other than this (the baby).
3. Smelled as strongly as he (the missing ram).
4. Boy (although Mak takes the alternate meaning of "rascal").

5. Good luck and happiness to him.
6. May good luck befall them.
7. An allusion to a dispute among the shepherds in the author's *First Shepherds' Play.*

MAK   We? Now I hold for me,
     For mends get I none.[8]
     Farewell all three,
820   All glad[9] were ye gone.
DAW   Fair words may there be,
     But love is there none
       This year.   [They go out the door.]
COLL   Gave ye the child anything?
825 GIB   I trow not one farthing.
DAW   Fast again will I fling.°   dash
     Abide ye me there.   [He runs back.]

     Mak, take it no grief
     If I come to thy barn.°   child
830 MAK   Nay, thou does me great reprief,°   shame
     And foul has thou farn.°   behaved
DAW   The child it will not grief,
     That little day-starn.°   day star
     Mak, with your leaf,°   permission
835   Let me give your barn
       But sixpence.
MAK   Nay, do way! He sleeps.
DAW   Methinks he peeps.°   opens his eyes
MAK   When he wakens he weeps.
840   I pray you go hence.

     [The other shepherds reenter.]

DAW   Give me leave him to kiss,
     And lift up the clout.°   cover
     [lifts the cover]
     What the devil is this?
     He has a long snout!
845 COLL   He is marked amiss.
     We wot ill about.[1]
GIB   Ill-spun weft, ywis,
     Ay comes foul out.[2]
       Aye, so!
850   He is like to our sheep.
DAW   How, Gib, may I peep?
COLL   I trow kind will creep
     Where it may not go.[3]

GIB   This was a quaint gaud
855   And a far-cast.[4]

---

8. I'll look out for myself, for I'll get no compensation.
9. I.e., I would be glad.
1. He is deformed. We know something fishy is going on around here.
2. An ill-spun web, indeed, always comes out

badly (proverbial), i.e., ill work always comes to a bad end.
3. Nature will creep where it can't walk (proverbial), i.e., nature will reveal itself by hook or crook.
4. This was a cunning trick and a clever ruse.

It was high fraud.
DAW Yea, sirs, was't.°   *it was*
Let bren° this bawd   *burn*
And bind her fast.
860   A false scaud°   *scold*
Hang at the last:[5]
   So shall thou.
Will you see how they swaddle
His four feet in the middle?
865   Saw I never in the cradle
   A horned lad ere now.

MAK   Peace bid I! What,
Let be your fare!°   *fuss*
I am he that him gat.°   *begot*
870   And yond woman him bare.
COLL   What devil shall he hat?[6]
Lo, God, Mak's heir!
GIB   Let be all that!
Now God give him care°—   *sorrow*
875   I sawgh!°   *saw*
GILL   A pretty child is he
As sits on a woman's knee,
A dillydown,° pardie,°   *darling/by God*
   To gar° a man laugh.   *make*

880   DAW   I know him by the earmark—
That is a good token.
MAK   I tell you, sirs, hark,
His nose was broken.
Sithen° told me a clerk   *later*
885   That he was forspoken.°   *bewitched*
COLL   This is a false wark.°   *work*
I would fain be wroken.°   *avenged*
   Get wapen.°   *weapon*
GILL   He was taken with an elf[7]
890   I saw it myself—
When the clock struck twelf
   Was he forshapen.°   *transformed*

GIB   Ye two are well feft
Sam in a stead.[8]
895   DAW   Sin° they maintain their theft,   *since*
Let do° them to dead.°   *put/death*
MAK   If I trespass eft,°   *again*

5. Will hang in the end.
6. What the devil shall he be named?
7. He was stolen by a fairy, i.e., the baby is a
changeling.
8. You two are well endowed in the same place,
i.e., you are two of a kind.

   Gird° off my head.   *chop*
   With you will I be left.[9]
900 COLL Sirs, do my read:°   *advice*
   For this trespass
   We will neither ban° ne flite,°   *curse / quarrel*
   Fight nor chite,°   *chide*
   But have done as tite,°   *quickly*
905   And cast him in canvas.

   [*They toss* MAK *in a blanket.*]

      [*The fields*]
  COLL Lord, what° I am sore,   *how*
   In point for to brist!°   *burst*
   In faith, I may no more—
   Therefore will I rist.°   *rest*
910 GIB As a sheep of seven score[1]
   He weighed in my fist:
   For to sleep aywhore°   *anywhere*
   Methink that I list.°   *want*
  DAW Now I pray you
915   Lie down on this green.
  COLL On the thieves yet I mean.° *think*
  DAW Whereto should ye teen?° *be angry*
   Do as I say you.   [*They lie down.*]

  [*An* ANGEL *sings* Gloria in Excelsis *and then speaks.*][2]

  ANGEL Rise, herdmen hend,°   *gracious*
920 For now is he born
   That shall take fro the fiend° *devil*
   That Adam had lorn;[3]
   That warlock° to shend,°   *devil / destroy*
   This night is he born.
925 God is made your friend
   Now at this morn,
   He behestys.°   *promises*
   At Bedlem° go see: *Bethlehem*
   There lies that free,°   *noble one*
930 In a crib full poorly,
   Betwixt two bestys.°   *beasts*

  [*The* ANGEL *withdraws.*]

  COLL This was a quaint° steven° *marvelous / voice*
   That ever yet I hard.°   *heard*
   It is a marvel to neven°   *tell of*

---

9. I put myself at your mercy.   God] in the highest" (see Luke 2.14).
1. I.e., 140 pounds.   3. That [which] Adam had brought to ruin.
2. This is an original stage direction; "Glory [to

935   Thus to be scar'd.°   *scared*
       GIB Of God's Son of heaven
            He spake upward.°   *on high*
            All the wood on a leven
            Methought that he gard
940   Appear.⁴
       DAW He spake of a barn°   *child*
            In Bedlem, I you warn.°   *tell*
       COLL That betokens yond starn.⁵
            Let us seek him there.

945   GIB Say, what was his song?
            Heard ye not how he cracked it?⁶
            Three breves° to a long?   *short notes*
       DAW Yea, marry, he hacked it.
            Was no crochet° wrong,   *note*
950   Nor nothing that lacked it.⁷
       COLL For to sing us among,
            Right as he knacked it,
            I can.°   *know how*
       GIB Let see how ye croon!
955   Can ye bark at the moon?
       DAW Hold your tongues! Have done!
       COLL Hark after, than!   [*Sings.*]

       GIB To Bedlem he bade
            That we should gang:°   *go*
960   I am full fard°   *afraid*
       That we tarry too lang.°   *long*
       DAW Be merry and not sad;
            Of mirth is our sang:
            Everlasting glad°   *joy*
965   To meed° may we fang.°   *reward/get*
       COLL Without nose°   *noise*
            Hie we thither forthy°   *therefore*
            To that child and that lady;
            If° we be wet and weary,   *though*
970   We have it not to lose.⁸

       GIB We find by the prophecy—
            Let be your din!—
            Of David and Isay,
            And mo than I min,⁹
975   That prophesied by clergy°   *learning*
       That in a virgin

---

4. I thought he made the whole woods appear in a flash of light.
5. That's what yonder star means.
6. Trilled it; a technical musical term, close in meaning to *hacked* and *knacked*: to break (notes), to sing in a lively or ornate manner (cf. lines 685

and 687).
7. That it lacked.
8. We must not neglect it.
9. Of David and Isaiah and more than I remember.

Should he light° and lie,   *alight*
To sloken° our sin   *quench*
   And slake° it,   *relieve*
980 Our kind,° from woe,   *humankind*
For Isay said so:
Ecce virgo
   Concipiet[1] a child that is naked.

DAW   Full glad may we be
985 And° we abide that day   *if*
That lovely to see,
That all mights may.[2]
Lord, well were me
For once and for ay
990 Might I kneel on my knee,
Some word for to say
   To that child.
But the angel said
In a crib was he laid,
995 He was poorly arrayed,
   Both meaner° and mild.   *very humbly*

COLL   Patriarchs that has been,
And prophets beforn,°   *before (our time)*
That desired to have seen
1000 This child that is born,
They are gone full clean—
That have they lorn.[3]
We shall see him, I ween,°   *think*
Ere it be morn,
1005   To token.[4]
When I see him and feel,
Then wot° I full weel°   *know/well*
It is true as steel
   That° prophets have spoken: *what*

1010 To so poor as we are
That he would appear,
First find and declare[5]
   By his messenger.
GIB   Go we now, let us fare,
1015   The place is us near.
DAW   I am ready and yare;°   *eager*
Go we in fere°   *together*
   To that bright.°   *glorious one*
Lord, if thy wills be—

1. Behold, a virgin shall conceive (Isaiah 7.14).
2. I.e., when we see that lovely one who is all-powerful.
3. That (sight) have they lost.
4. As a sign.
5. Find (us) first (of all), and make known (his birth).

1020   We are lewd° all three—   *ignorant*
        Thou grant us some kins glee⁶
        To comfort thy wight.°   *child*

[*They go to Bethlehem and enter the stable.*]

COLL   Hail, comely and clean!°   *pure*
        Hail, young child!
1025   Hail Maker, as I mean,°   *believe*
        Of° a maiden so mild!   *born of*
        Thou has waried,° I ween,°   *cursed / think*
        The warlock° so wild.   *devil*
        The false guiler of teen,⁷
1030   Now goes he beguiled.
          Lo, he merries!°   *is merry*
        Lo, he laughs, my sweeting!
        A well fair meeting!
        I have holden my heting:°   *promise*
1035   Have a bob° of cherries.   *bunch*

GIB   Hail, sovereign Saviour,
        For thou has us sought!
        Hail freely food° and flour,°   *noble child / flower*
        That all thing has wrought!
1040   Hail, full of favour,
        That made all of nought!
        Hail! I kneel and I cower.°   *crouch*
        A bird have I brought
          To my barn.°   *child*
1045   Hail, little tiny mop!°   *baby*
        Of our creed thou art crop.°   *head*
        I would drink on thy cup,
        Little day-starn.   *day star*

DAW   Hail, darling dear,
1050   Full of Godhead!
        I pray thee be near
        When that I have need.
        Hail, sweet is thy cheer°—   *face*
        My heart would bleed
1055   To see thee sit here
        In so poor weed,°   *clothing*
          With no pennies.
        Hail, put forth thy dall!°   *hand*
        I bring thee but a ball:
1060   Have and play thee withal,
        And go to the tennis.

6. Some kind of cheer.   7. The false grievous deceiver, i.e., the devil.

MARY The Father of heaven,
    God omnipotent,
    That set all on seven,[8]
1065   His Son has he sent.
    My name could he neven,
    And light ere he went.[9]
    I conceived him full even
    Through might as he meant.[1]
1070   And now is he born.
    He° keep you from woe!   *(may)* he
    I shall pray him so.
    Tell forth as ye go,
    And min on° this morn.   *remember*

1075 COLL Farewell, lady,
    So fair to behold,
    With thy child on thy knee.
  GIB But he lies full cold.
    Lord, well is me.
1080   Now we go, thou behold.
  DAW Forsooth, already
    It seems to be told
    Full oft.
  COLL What grace we have fun!°   *received*
1085 GIB Come forth, now are we won!°   *redeemed*
  DAW To sing are we bun:°   *bound*
    Let take on loft.[2]
    [*They sing.*]

8. Who created everything in seven (days).
9. My name did he name, and alighted (in me) before he went (see Luke 1.28).

1. I conceived him, indeed, through his power, just as he intended.
2. Let's raise our voices.

SIR THOMAS MALORY
ca. 1405–1471

Morte Darthur (Death of Arthur) is the title that William Caxton, the first English printer, gave to Malory's volume, which Caxton described more accurately in his Preface as "the noble histories of * * * King Arthur and of certain of his knights." The volume begins with the mythical story of Arthur's birth. King Uther Pendragon falls in love with the wife of one of his barons. Merlin's magic transforms Uther into the likeness of her husband, and Arthur is born of this union. The volume ends with the destruction of the Round Table and the deaths of Arthur, Queen Guinevere, and Sir Lancelot, who is Arthur's best knight and the queen's lover. The bulk of the work is taken up with the separate adventures of the knights of the Round Table.

On the evolution of the Arthurian saga, see the headnote to *Legendary Histories of Britain*, p. 115. During the thirteenth century the stories about Arthur and his knights had been turned into a series of enormously long prose romances in French, and it was these, as Caxton informed his readers, "Sir Thomas Malory did take out of certain books of French and reduced into English."

Little was known about the author until the early twentieth century when scholars began to unearth the criminal record of a Sir Thomas Malory of Newbold Revell in Warwickshire. In 1451 he was arrested for the first time to prevent his doing injury— presumably further injury—to a priory in Lincolnshire, and shortly thereafter he was accused of a number of criminal acts. These included escaping from prison after his first arrest, twice breaking into and plundering the Abbey of Coombe, extorting money from various persons, and committing rape. Malory pleaded innocent of all charges. The Wars of the Roses—in which Malory, like the formidable earl of Warwick (the "kingmaker"), whom he seems to have followed, switched sides from Lancaster to York and back again—may account for some of his troubles with the law. After a failed Lancastrian revolt, the Yorkist king, Edward IV, specifically excluded Malory from four amnesties he granted to the Lancastrians.

The identification of this Sir Thomas Malory (there is another candidate with the same name) as the author of the Morte was strengthened by the discovery in 1934 of a manuscript that differed from Caxton's text, the only version previously known. The manuscript contained eight separate romances. Caxton, in order to give the impression of a continuous narrative, had welded these together into twenty-one books, subdivided into short chapters with summary chapter headings. Caxton suppressed all but the last of the personal remarks the author had appended to individual tales in the manuscript. At the very end of the book Malory asks "all gentlemen and gentlewomen that readeth this book * * * pray for me while I am alive that God send me good deliverance." The discovery of the manuscript revealed that at the close of the first tale he had written: "this was drawyn by a knight presoner Sir Thomas Malleoré, that God sende him good recover." There is strong circumstantial evidence, therefore, that the book from which the Arthurian legends were passed on to future generations to be adapted in literature, art, and film was written in prison by a man whose violent career might seem at odds with the chivalric ideals he professes.

Such a contradiction—if it really is one—should not be surprising. Nostalgia for an ideal past that never truly existed is typical of much historical romance. Like the slave-owning plantation society of Margaret Mitchell's Gone with the Wind, whose southern gentlemen cultivate chivalrous manners and respect for gentlewomen, Malory's Arthurian world is a fiction. In our terms, it cannot even be labeled "historical," although the distinction between romance and history is not one that Malory would have made. Only rarely does he voice skepticism about the historicity of his tale; one such example is his questioning of the myth of Arthur's return. Much of the tragic power of his romance lies in his sense of the irretrievability of past glory in comparison with the sordidness of his own age.

The success of Malory's retelling owes much to his development of a terse and direct prose style, especially the naturalistic dialogue that keeps his narrative close to earth. And both he and many of his characters are masters of understatement who express themselves, in moments of great emotional tension, with a bare minimum of words.

In spite of its professed dedication to service of women, Malory's chivalry is primarily devoted to the fellowship and competitions of aristocratic men. Fighting consists mainly of single combats in tournaments, chance encounters, and battles, which Malory never tires of describing in professional detail. Commoners rarely come into view; when they do, the effect can be chilling—as when pillagers by moonlight plunder the corpses of the knights left on the field of Arthur's last battle. Above all, Malory cherishes an aristocratic male code of honor for which his favorite word is "worship." Men win or lose "worship" through their actions in war and love.

The most "worshipful" of Arthur's knights is Sir Lancelot, the "head of all Christian knights," as he is called in a moving eulogy by his brother, Sir Ector. But Lancelot is compromised by his fatal liaison with Arthur's queen and torn between the incompatible loyalties that bind him as an honorable knight, on the one hand, to his lord Arthur and, on the other, to his lady Guinevere. Malory loves his character Lancelot even to the point of indulging in the fleeting speculation, after Lancelot has been admitted to the queen's chamber, that their activities might have been innocent, "for love that time was not as love is nowadays." But when the jealousy and malice of two wicked knights forces the affair into the open, nothing can avert the breaking up of the fellowship of the Round Table and the death of Arthur himself, which Malory relates with somber magnificence as the passing of a great era.

From Morte Darthur[1]

[THE CONSPIRACY AGAINST LANCELOT AND GUINEVERE]

In May, when every lusty[2] heart flourisheth and burgeoneth, for as the season is lusty to behold and comfortable,[3] so man and woman rejoiceth and gladdeth of summer coming with his fresh flowers, for winter with his rough winds and blasts causeth lusty men and women to cower and to sit fast by the fire—so this season it befell in the month of May a great anger and unhap that stinted not[4] till the flower of chivalry of all the world was destroyed and slain. And all was long upon two unhappy[5] knights which were named Sir Agravain and Sir Mordred that were brethren unto Sir Gawain.[6] For this Sir Agravain and Sir Mordred had ever a privy[7] hate unto the Queen, Dame Guinevere, and to Sir Lancelot, and daily and nightly they ever watched upon Sir Lancelot.

So it misfortuned Sir Gawain and all his brethren were in King Arthur's chamber, and then Sir Agravain said thus openly, and not in no counsel,[8] that many knights might hear: "I marvel that we all be not ashamed both to see and to know how Sir Lancelot lieth daily and nightly by the Queen. And all we know well that it is so, and it is shamefully suffered of us all[9] that we should suffer so noble a king as King Arthur is to be shamed."

Then spoke Sir Gawain and said, "Brother, Sir Agravain, I pray you and charge you, move no such matters no more afore[1] me, for wit you well, I will not be of your counsel."[2]

"So God me help," said Sir Gaheris and Sir Gareth,[3] "we will not be known of your deeds."[4]

"Then will I!" said Sir Mordred.

"I lieve[5] you well," said Sir Gawain, "for ever unto all unhappiness, sir, ye will grant.[6] And I would that ye left all this and make you not so busy, for I know," said Sir Gawain, "what will fall of it."[7]

---

1. The selections given here are from the section that Caxton called book 20, chaps. 1–4, 8–10, and book 21, chaps. 3–7, 10–12, with omissions. In the Winchester manuscript this section is titled "The Most Piteous Tale of the Morte Arthur Saunz Guerdon" (i.e., the death of Arthur without reward or compensation). The text has been based on Winchester, with some readings introduced from the Caxton edition; spelling has been modernized and modern punctuation added.
2. Merry.
3. Pleasant.
4. Misfortune that ceased not.
5. On account of two ill-fated.
6. Gawain and Agravain are sons of King Lot of

Orkney and his wife, Arthur's half-sister Morgause. Mordred is the illegitimate son of Arthur and Morgause.
7. Secret.
8. Secret manner.
9. Put up with by all of us.
1. Before. "Move": propose.
2. On your side. "Wit you well": know well, i.e., give you to understand.
3. Sons of King Lot and Gawain's brothers.
4. A party to your doings.
5. Believe.
6. You will consent to all mischief.
7. Come of it.

"Fall whatsoever fall may," said Sir Agravain, "I will disclose it to the King."

"Not by my counsel," said Sir Gawain, "for and[8] there arise war and wrack betwixt[9] Sir Lancelot and us, wit you well, brother, there will many kings and great lords hold with Sir Lancelot. Also, brother, Sir Agravain," said Sir Gawain, "ye must remember how often times Sir Lancelot hath rescued the King and the Queen. And the best of us all had been full cold at the heartroot[1] had not Sir Lancelot been better than we, and that has he proved himself full oft. And as for my part," said Sir Gawain, "I will never be against Sir Lancelot for[2] one day's deed, when he rescued me from King Carados of the Dolorous Tower and slew him and saved my life. Also, brother, Sir Agravain and Sir Mordred, in like wise Sir Lancelot rescued you both and three score and two[3] from Sir Tarquin. And therefore, brother, methinks such noble deeds and kindness should be remembered."

"Do as ye list,"[4] said Sir Agravain, "for I will layne[5] it no longer."

So with these words came in Sir Arthur.

"Now, brother," said Sir Gawain, "stint your noise."[6]

"That will I not," said Sir Agravain and Sir Mordred.

"Well, will ye so?" said Sir Gawain. "Then God speed you, for I will not hear of your tales, neither be of your counsel."

"No more will I," said Sir Gaheris.

"Neither I," said Sir Gareth, "for I shall never say evil by[7] that man that made me knight." And therewithal they three departed making great dole.[8]

"Alas!" said Sir Gawain and Sir Gareth, "now is this realm wholly destroyed and mischieved,[9] and the noble fellowship of the Round Table shall be disparbeled."[1]

So they departed, and then King Arthur asked them what noise they made. "My lord," said Sir Agravain, "I shall tell you, for I may keep[2] it no longer. Here is I and my brother Sir Mordred broke[3] unto my brother Sir Gawain, Sir Gaheris, and to Sir Gareth—for this is all, to make it short—how that we know all that Sir Lancelot holdeth your queen, and hath done long; and we be your sister[4] sons, we may suffer it no longer. And all we woot[5] that ye should be above Sir Lancelot, and ye are the king that made him knight, and therefore we will prove it that he is a traitor to your person."

"If it be so," said the King, "wit[6] you well, he is none other. But I would be loath to begin such a thing but[7] I might have proofs of it, for Sir Lancelot is an hardy knight, and all ye know that he is the best knight among us all. And but if he be taken with the deed,[8] he will fight with him that bringeth up the noise, and I know no knight that is able to match him. Therefore, and[9] it be sooth as ye say, I would that he were taken with the deed."

For, as the French book saith, the King was full loath that such a noise

---

8. If.
9. Strife between.
1. Would have been dead.
2. On account of.
3. I.e., sixty-two.
4. You please.
5. Conceal.
6. Stop making scandal.
7. About.
8. Lamentation.

9. Put to shame.
1. Dispersed.
2. Conceal.
3. Revealed.
4. Sister's.
5. Know.
6. Know.
7. Unless.
8. Unless he is caught in the act.
9. If.

should be upon Sir Lancelot and his queen. For the King had a deeming[1] of it, but he would not hear of it, for Sir Lancelot had done so much for him and for the Queen so many times that, wit you well, the King loved him passingly[2] well.

"My lord," said Sir Agravain, "ye shall ride tomorn[3] on hunting, and doubt ye not, Sir Lancelot will not go with you. And so when it draweth toward night, ye may send the Queen word that ye will lie out all that night, and so may ye send for your cooks. And then, upon pain of death, that night we shall take him with the Queen, and we shall bring him unto you, quick[4] or dead."

"I will well,"[5] said the King. "Then I counsel you to take with you sure fellowship."

"Sir," said Sir Agravain, "my brother, Sir Mordred, and I will take with us twelve knights of the Round Table."

"Beware," said King Arthur, "for I warn you, ye shall find him wight."[6]

"Let us deal!"[7] said Sir Agravain and Sir Mordred.

So on the morn King Arthur rode on hunting and sent word to the Queen that he would be out all that night. Then Sir Agravain and Sir Mordred got to them[8] twelve knights and hid themself in a chamber in the castle of Carlisle. And these were their names: Sir Colgrevance, Sir Mador de la Porte, Sir Guingalen, Sir Meliot de Logres, Sir Petipace of Winchelsea, Sir Galeron of Galway, Sir Melion de la Mountain, Sir Ascamore, Sir Gromore Somyr Jour, Sir Curselayne, Sir Florence, and Sir Lovell. So these twelve knights were with Sir Mordred and Sir Agravain, and all they were of Scotland, or else of Sir Gawain's kin, or well-willers[9] to his brother.

So when the night came, Sir Lancelot told Sir Bors[1] how he would go that night and speak with the Queen.

"Sir," said Sir Bors, "ye shall not go this night by my counsel."

"Why?" said Sir Lancelot.

"Sir," said Sir Bors, "I dread me[2] ever of Sir Agravain that waiteth upon[3] you daily to do you shame and us all. And never gave my heart against no going that ever ye went[4] to the queen so much as now, for I mistrust[5] that the King is out this night from the Queen because peradventure he hath lain[6] some watch for you and the Queen. Therefore, I dread me sore of some treason."

"Have ye no dread," said Sir Lancelot, "for I shall go and come again and make no tarrying."

"Sir," said Sir Bors, "that me repents,[7] for I dread me sore that your going this night shall wrath[8] us all."

"Fair nephew," said Sir Lancelot, "I marvel me much why ye say thus, sithen[9] the Queen hath sent for me. And wit you well, I will not be so much a coward, but she shall understand I will[1] see her good grace."

---

1. Suspicion.
2. Exceedingly.
3. Tomorrow.
4. Alive.
5. Readily agree.
6. Strong.
7. Leave it to us.
8. Gathered to themselves.
9. Partisans.
1. Nephew and confidant of Sir Lancelot.

2. I am afraid.
3. Lies in wait.
4. Never misgave my heart against any visit you made.
5. Suspect.
6. Perhaps he has set.
7. I regret.
8. Cause injury to.
9. Since.
1. Wish to.

"God speed you well," said Sir Bors, "and send you sound and safe again!"

So Sir Lancelot departed and took his sword under his arm, and so he walked in his mantel,[2] that noble knight, and put himself in great jeopardy. And so he passed on till he came to the Queen's chamber, and so lightly he was had[3] into the chamber. And then, as the French book saith, the Queen and Sir Lancelot were together. And whether they were abed or at other manner of disports, me list[4] not thereof make no mention, for love that time[5] was not as love is nowadays.

But thus as they were together there came Sir Agravain and Sir Mordred with twelve knights with them of the Round Table, and they said with great crying and scaring[6] voice: "Thou traitor, Sir Lancelot, now are thou taken!" And thus they cried with a loud voice that all the court might hear it. And these fourteen knights all were armed at all points, as[7] they should fight in a battle.

"Alas!" said Queen Guinevere, "now are we mischieved[8] both!"

"Madam," said Sir Lancelot, "is there here any armor within your chamber that I might cover my body withal? And if there be any, give it me, and I shall soon stint[9] their malice, by the grace of God!"

"Now, truly," said the Queen, "I have none armor neither helm, shield, sword, neither spear, wherefore I dread me sore our long love is come to a mischievous end. For I hear by their noise there be many noble knights, and well I woot they be surely[1] armed, and against them ye may make no resistance. Wherefore ye are likely to be slain, and then shall I be burned! For and[2] ye might escape them," said the Queen, "I would not doubt but that ye would rescue me in what danger that ever I stood in."

"Alas!" said Sir Lancelot, "in all my life thus was I never bestead[3] that I should be thus shamefully slain for lack of mine armor."

But ever in one[4] Sir Agravain and Sir Mordred cried: "Traitor knight, come out of the Queen's chamber! For wit thou well thou art beset so that thou shalt not escape."

"Ah, Jesu mercy!" said Sir Lancelot, "this shameful cry and noise I may not suffer, for better were death at once than thus to endure this pain." Then he took the Queen in his arms and kissed her and said, "Most noblest Christian queen, I beseech you, as ye have been ever my special good lady, and I at all times your poor knight and true unto[5] my power, and as I never failed you in right nor in wrong sithen the first day King Arthur made me knight, that ye will pray for my soul if that I be slain. For well I am assured that Sir Bors, my nephew, and all the remnant of my kin, with Sir Lavain and Sir Urry,[6] that they will not fail you to rescue you from the fire. And therefore, mine own lady, recomfort yourself,[7] whatsoever come of me, that ye go with Sir Bors, my nephew, and Sir Urry and they all will do you all the pleasure that they may, and ye shall live like a queen upon my lands."

2. Cloak. Lancelot goes without armor.
3. Quickly he was received.
4. I care. "Disports": pastimes.
5. At that time.
6. Terrifying.
7. Completely, as if.
8. Come to grief.
9. Stop.
1. Securely.

2. If.
3. Beset.
4. In unison.
5. To the utmost of.
6. The brother of Elaine, the Fair Maid of Astolat, and a knight miraculously healed of his wound by Sir Lancelot. "Remnant": rest.
7. Take heart again.

"Nay, Sir Lancelot, nay!" said the Queen. "Wit thou well that I will not live long after thy days. But and[8] ye be slain I will take my death as meekly as ever did martyr take his death for Jesu Christ's sake."

"Well, Madam," said Sir Lancelot, "sith it is so that the day is come that our love must depart,[9] wit you well I shall sell my life as dear as I may. And a thousandfold," said Sir Lancelot, "I am more heavier[1] for you than for myself! And now I had liefer[2] than to be lord of all Christendom that I had sure armor upon me, that men might speak of my deeds ere ever I were slain."

"Truly," said the Queen, "and[3] it might please God, I would that they would take me and slay me and suffer[4] you to escape."

"That shall never be," said Sir Lancelot. "God defend me from such a shame! But, Jesu Christ, be Thou my shield and mine armor!" And therewith Sir Lancelot wrapped his mantel about his arm well and surely; and by then they had gotten a great form[5] out of the hall, and therewith they all rushed at the door. "Now, fair lords," said Sir Lancelot, "leave[6] your noise and your rushing, and I shall set open this door, and then may ye do with me what it liketh you."[7]

"Come off,[8] then," said they all, "and do it, for it availeth thee not to strive against us all. And therefore let us into this chamber, and we shall save thy life until thou come to King Arthur."

Then Sir Lancelot unbarred the door, and with his left hand he held it open a little, that but one man might come in at once. And so there came striding a good knight, a much[9] man and a large, and his name was called Sir Colgrevance of Gore. And he with a sword struck at Sir Lancelot mightily. And he put aside[1] the stroke and gave him such a buffet[2] upon the helmet that he fell groveling dead within the chamber door. Then Sir Lancelot with great might drew the knight within[3] the chamber door. And then Sir Lancelot, with help of the Queen and her ladies, he was lightly[4] armed in Colgrevance's armor. And ever stood Sir Agravain and Sir Mordred, crying, "Traitor knight! Come forth out of the Queen's chamber!"

"Sirs, leave[5] your noise," said Sir Lancelot, "for wit you well, Sir Agravain, ye shall not prison me this night. And therefore, and[6] ye do by my counsel, go ye all from this chamber door and make you no such crying and such manner of slander as ye do. For I promise you by my knighthood, and ye will depart and make no more noise, I shall as tomorn appear afore you all and before the King, and then let it be seen which of you all, other else ye all,[7] that will deprove[8] me of treason. And there shall I answer you, as a knight should, that hither I came to the Queen for no manner of mal engine,[9] and that will I prove and make it good upon you with my hands."

"Fie upon thee, traitor," said Sir Agravain and Sir Mordred, "for we will

8. If.
9. Come to an end.
1. More grieved.
2. Rather.
3. If.
4. Allow.
5. Bench.
6. Stop.
7. Pleases you.
8. Go ahead.

9. Big.
1. Fended off.
2. Blow.
3. Inside.
4. Quickly.
5. Stop.
6. If.
7. Or else all of you.
8. Accuse.
9. Evil design.

have thee malgré thine head[1] and slay thee, and we list. For we let thee wit we have the choice of[2] King Arthur to save thee other slay thee."

"Ah, sirs," said Sir Lancelot, "is there none other grace with you? Then keep[3] yourself!" And then Sir Lancelot set all open the chamber door and mightily and knightly he strode in among them. And anon[4] at the first stroke he slew Sir Agravain, and after twelve of his fellows. Within a little while he had laid them down cold to the earth, for there was none of the twelve knights might stand Sir Lancelot one buffet.[5] And also he wounded Sir Mordred, and therewithal he fled with all his might.

And then Sir Lancelot returned again unto the Queen and said, "Madam, now wit you well, all our true love is brought to an end, for now will King Arthur ever be my foe. And therefore, Madam, and it like you[6] that I may have you with me, I shall save you from all manner adventurous[7] dangers."

"Sir, that is not best," said the Queen, "me seemeth, for[8] now ye have done so much harm, it will be best that ye hold you still with this. And if ye see that as tomorn they will put me unto death, then may ye rescue me as ye think best."

"I will well,"[9] said Sir Lancelot, "for have ye no doubt, while I am a man living I shall rescue you." And then he kissed her, and either of them gave other a ring, and so there he left the Queen and went until[1] his lodging.

[WAR BREAKS OUT BETWEEN ARTHUR AND LANCELOT][2]

Then said King Arthur unto Sir Gawain, "Dear nephew, I pray you make ready in your best armor with your brethren, Sir Gaheris and Sir Gareth, to bring my Queen to the fire, there to have her judgment and receive the death."

"Nay, my most noble king," said Sir Gawain, "that will I never do, for wit you well I will never be in that place where so noble a queen as is my lady Dame Guinevere shall take such a shameful end. For wit you well," said Sir Gawain, "my heart will not serve me for to see her die, and it shall never be said that ever I was of your counsel for her death."

"Then," said the King unto Sir Gawain, "suffer[3] your brethren Sir Gaheris and Sir Gareth to be there."

"My lord," said Sir Gawain, "wit you well they will be loath to be there present because of many adventures[4] that is like to fall, but they are young and full unable to say you nay."

Then spake Sir Gaheris and the good knight Sir Gareth unto King Arthur: "Sir, ye may well command us to be there, but wit you well it shall be sore against our will. But and[5] we be there by your straight commandment, ye shall plainly[6] hold us there excused—we will be there in peaceable wise and bear none harness of war upon us."

1. In spite of you.
2. From.
3. Defend.
4. Right away.
5. Withstand Sir Lancelot one blow.
6. If it please you.
7. Perilous.
8. Because.
9. Agree.
1. To.
2. Lancelot and Sir Bors mobilize their friends for the rescue of Guinevere. In the morning Mordred reports the events of the night to Arthur who, against Gawain's strong opposition, condemns the queen to be burned, for "the law was such in those days that whatsoever they were, of what estate or degree, if they were found guilty of treason there should be none other remedy but death."
3. Allow.
4. Chance occurrences.
5. If.
6. Openly. "Straight": strict.

"In the name of God," said the King, "then make you ready, for she shall have soon[7] her judgment."

"Alas," said Sir Gawain, "that ever I should endure[8] to see this woeful day." So Sir Gawain turned him and wept heartily, and so he went into his chamber.

And then the Queen was led forth without[9] Carlisle, and anon she was dispoiled into[1] her smock. And then her ghostly father[2] was brought to her to be shriven of her misdeeds.[3] Then was there weeping and wailing and wringing of hands of many lords and ladies, but there were but few in comparison that would bear any armor for to strengthen[4] the death of the Queen.

Then was there one that Sir Lancelot had sent unto that place, which went to espy what time the Queen should go unto her death. And anon as[5] he saw the Queen dispoiled into her smock and shriven, then he gave Sir Lancelot warning. Then was there but spurring and plucking up[6] of horses, and right so they came unto the fire. And who[7] that stood against them, there were they slain—there might none withstand Sir Lancelot. So all that bore arms and withstood them, there were they slain, full many a noble knight. * * * And so in this rushing and hurling, as Sir Lancelot thrang[8] here and there, it misfortuned him[9] to slay Sir Gaheris and Sir Gareth, the noble knight, for they were unarmed and unwares.[1] As the French book saith, Sir Lancelot smote Sir Gaheris and Sir Gareth upon the brain-pans, wherethrough[2] that they were slain in the field, howbeit[3] Sir Lancelot saw them not. And so were they found dead among the thickest of the press.

Then when Sir Lancelot had thus done, and slain and put to flight all that would withstand him, then he rode straight unto Queen Guinevere and made a kirtle[4] and a gown to be cast upon her, and then he made her to be set behind him and prayed her to be of good cheer. Now wit you well the Queen was glad that she was escaped from death, and then she thanked God and Sir Lancelot.

And so he rode his way with the Queen, as the French book saith, unto Joyous Garde,[5] and there he kept her as a noble knight should. And many great lords and many good knights were sent him, and many full noble knights drew unto him. When they heard that King Arthur and Sir Lancelot were at debate,[6] many knights were glad, and many were sorry of their debate.

Now turn we again unto King Arthur, that when it was told him how and in what manner the Queen was taken away from the fire, and when he heard of the death of his noble knights, and in especial Sir Gaheris and Sir Gareth, then he swooned for very pure[7] sorrow. And when he awoke of his swoon, then he said: "Alas, that ever I bore crown upon my head! For now have I lost the fairest fellowship of noble knights that ever held Christian king[8] together. Alas, my good knights be slain and gone away from me. Now within these two days I have lost nigh forty knights and also the noble fellowship

---

7. Right away.
8. Live.
9. Outside.
1. Undressed down to.
2. Spiritual father, i.e., her priest.
3. For her to be confessed of her sins.
4. Secure.
5. As soon as.
6. Urging forward.
7. Whoever.

8. Pressed. "Hurling": turmoil.
9. He had the misfortune.
1. Unaware.
2. Through which.
3. Although.
4. Petticoat.
5. Lancelot's castle in England.
6. Strife.
7. Sheer.
8. That Christian king ever held.

of Sir Lancelot and his blood,[9] for now I may nevermore hold them together with my worship.[1] Alas, that ever this war began!

"Now, fair fellows," said the King, "I charge you that no man tell Sir Gawain of the death of his two brethren, for I am sure," said the King, "when he heareth tell that Sir Gareth is dead, he will go nigh out of his mind. Mercy Jesu," said the King, "why slew he Sir Gaheris and Sir Gareth? For I dare say, as for Sir Gareth, he loved Sir Lancelot above all men earthly."[2]

"That is truth," said some knights, "but they were slain in the hurling,[3] as Sir Lancelot thrang in the thickest of the press. And as they were unarmed, he smote them and wist[4] not whom that he smote, and so unhappily[5] they were slain."

"Well," said Arthur, "the death of them will cause the greatest mortal war that ever was, for I am sure that when Sir Gawain knoweth hereof that Sir Gareth is slain, I shall never have rest of him[6] till I have destroyed Sir Lancelot's kin and himself both, other else he to destroy me. And therefore," said the King, "wit you well, my heart was never so heavy as it is now. And much more I am sorrier for my good knights' loss[7] than for the loss of my fair queen; for queens I might have enough, but such a fellowship of good knights shall never be together in no company. And now I dare say," said King Arthur, "there was never Christian king that ever held such a fellowship together. And alas, that ever Sir Lancelot and I should be at debate. Ah, Agravain, Agravain!" said the King, "Jesu forgive it thy soul, for thine evil will that thou and thy brother Sir Mordred haddest unto Sir Lancelot hath caused all this sorrow." And ever among these complaints the King wept and swooned.

Then came there one to Sir Gawain and told him how the Queen was led away with[8] Sir Lancelot, and nigh a four-and-twenty knights slain. "Ah, Jesu, save me my two brethren!" said Sir Gawain. "For full well wist I," said Sir Gawain, "that Sir Lancelot would rescue her, other else he would die in that field. And to say the truth he were not of worship but if he had[9] rescued the Queen, insomuch as she should have been burned for his sake. And as in that," said Sir Gawain, "he hath done but knightly, and as I would have done myself and I had stood in like case. But where are my brethren?" said Sir Gawain. "I marvel that I hear not of them."

Then said that man, "Truly, Sir Gaheris and Sir Gareth be slain."

"Jesu defend!"[1] said Sir Gawain. "For all this world I would not that they were slain, and in especial my good brother Sir Gareth."

"Sir," said the man, "he is slain, and that is great pity."

"Who slew him?" said Sir Gawain.

"Sir Lancelot," said the man, "slew them both."

"That may I not believe," said Sir Gawain, "that ever he slew my good brother Sir Gareth, for I dare say my brother loved him better than me and all his brethren and the King both. Also I dare say, an[2] Sir Lancelot had desired my brother Sir Gareth with him, he would have been with him against

---

9. Kin.
1. Glory.
2. Earthly men.
3. Turmoil.
4. Knew.
5. Unluckily.

6. He will never give me any peace.
7. The loss of my good knights.
8. By.
9. Of honor if he had not.
1. Forbid.
2. If.

the King and us all. And therefore I may never believe that Sir Lancelot slew my brethren."

"Verily, sir," said the man, "it is noised[3] that he slew him."

"Alas," said Sir Gawain, "now is my joy gone." And then he fell down and swooned, and long he lay there as he had been dead. And when he arose out of his swoon, he cried out sorrowfully and said, "Alas!" And forthwith he ran unto the King, crying and weeping, and said, "Ah, mine uncle King Arthur! My good brother Sir Gareth is slain, and so is my brother Sir Gaheris, which were two noble knights."

Then the King wept and he both, and so they fell on swooning. And when they were revived, then spake Sir Gawain and said, "Sir, I will go and see my brother Sir Gareth."

"Sir, ye may not see him," said the King, "for I caused him to be interred and Sir Gaheris both, for I well understood that ye would make overmuch sorrow, and the sight of Sir Gareth should have caused your double sorrow."

"Alas, my lord," said Sir Gawain, "how slew he my brother Sir Gareth? Mine own good lord, I pray you tell me."

"Truly," said the King, "I shall tell you as it hath been told me—Sir Lancelot slew him and Sir Gaheris both."

"Alas," said Sir Gawain, "they bore none arms against him, neither of them both."

"I woot not how it was," said the King, "but as it is said, Sir Lancelot slew them in the thickest of the press and knew them not. And therefore let us shape a remedy for to revenge their deaths."

"My king, my lord, and mine uncle," said Sir Gawain, "wit you well, now I shall make you a promise which I shall hold by my knighthood, that from this day forward I shall never fail[4] Sir Lancelot until that one of us have slain the other. And therefore I require you, my lord and king, dress[5] you unto the wars, for wit you well, I will be revenged upon Sir Lancelot; and therefore, as ye will have my service and my love, now haste you thereto and assay[6] your friends. For I promise unto God," said Sir Gawain, "for the death of my brother Sir Gareth I shall seek Sir Lancelot throughout seven kings' realms, but I shall slay him, other else he shall slay me."

"Sir, ye shall not need to seek him so far," said the King, "for as I hear say, Sir Lancelot will abide me and us all within the castle of Joyous Garde. And much people draweth unto him, as I hear say."

"That may I right well believe," said Sir Gawain, "but my lord," he said, "assay your friends and I will assay mine."

"It shall be done," said the King, "and as I suppose I shall be big[7] enough to drive him out of the biggest tower of his castle."

So then the King sent letters and writs throughout all England, both the length and the breadth, for to summon all his knights. And so unto King Arthur drew many knights, dukes, and earls, that he had a great host, and when they were assembled the King informed them how Sir Lancelot had bereft him his Queen. Then the King and all his host made them ready to lay siege about Sir Lancelot where he lay within Joyous Garde.

---

3. Reported.
4. Give up the pursuit of.
5. Prepare.

6. Appeal to.
7. Strong.

[THE DEATH OF ARTHUR][8]

So upon Trinity Sunday at night King Arthur dreamed a wonderful dream, and in his dream him seemed that he saw upon a chafflet[9] a chair, and the chair was fast to a wheel, and thereupon sat King Arthur in the richest cloth of gold that might be made. And the King thought there was under him, far from him, an hideous deep black water, and therein was all manner of serpents, and worms, and wild beasts, foul and horrible. And suddenly the King thought that the wheel turned upside down, and he fell among the serpents, and every beast took him by a limb. And then the King cried as he lay in his bed, "Help, help!"

And then knights, squires, and yeomen awaked the King, and then he was so amazed that he wist[1] not where he was. And then so he awaked[2] until it was nigh day, and then he fell on slumbering again, not sleeping nor thoroughly waking. So the King seemed[3] verily that there came Sir Gawain unto him with a number of fair ladies with him. So when King Arthur saw him, he said, "Welcome, my sister's son. I weened ye had been dead. And now I see thee on-live, much am I beholden unto Almighty Jesu. Ah, fair nephew and my sister's son, what been these ladies that hither be come with you?"

"Sir," said Sir Gawain, "all these be ladies for whom I have foughten for when I was man living. And all these are tho[4] that I did battle for in righteous quarrels, and God hath given them that grace, at their great prayer, because I did battle for them for their right, that they should bring me hither unto you. Thus much hath given me leave God, for to warn you of your death. For and ye fight as tomorn[5] with Sir Mordred, as ye both have assigned,[6] doubt ye not ye must be slain, and the most party of your people on both parties. And for the great grace and goodness that Almighty Jesu hath unto you, and for pity of you and many mo other good men there[7] shall be slain, God hath sent me to you of his special grace to give you warning that in no wise ye do battle as tomorn, but that ye take a treatise for a month-day.[8] And proffer you largely,[9] so that tomorn ye put in a delay. For within a month shall come Sir Lancelot with all his noble knights and rescue you worshipfully and slay Sir Mordred and all that ever will hold with him."

Then Sir Gawain and all the ladies vanished. And anon the King called upon his knights, squires, and yeomen, and charged them wightly[1] to fetch his noble lords and wise bishops unto him. And when they were come the King told them of his avision,[2] that Sir Gawain had told him and warned him that, and he fought on the morn, he should be slain. Then the King commanded Sir Lucan the Butler[3] and his brother Sir Bedivere the Bold, with

8. The pope arranges a truce, Guinevere is returned to Arthur, and Lancelot and his kin leave England to become rulers of France. At Gawain's instigation Arthur invades France to resume the war against Lancelot. Word comes to the king that Mordred has seized the kingdom, and Arthur leads his forces back to England. Mordred attacks them upon their landing, and Gawain is mortally wounded and dies, although not before he has repented for having insisted that Arthur fight Lancelot and has written Lancelot to come to the aid of his former lord.
9. Scaffold. "Him seemed": it seemed to him.
1. Knew.
2. Lay awake.

3. It seemed to the king.
4. Those.
5. If you fight tomorrow.
6. Decided.
7. I.e., who there. "Mo": more.
8. For a month from today. "Treatise": treaty, truce.
9. Make generous offers.
1. Quickly.
2. Dream.
3. "Butler" here is probably only a title of high rank, although it was originally used to designate the officer who had charge of wine for the king's table.

two bishops with them, and charged them in any wise to take a treatise for a month-day with Sir Mordred. "And spare not: proffer him lands and goods as much as ye think reasonable."

So then they departed and came to Sir Mordred where he had a grim host of an hundred thousand, and there they entreated[4] Sir Mordred long time. And at the last Sir Mordred was agreed for to have Cornwall and Kent by King Arthur's days,[5] and after that, all England, after the days of King Arthur.

Then were they condescended[6] that King Arthur and Sir Mordred should meet betwixt both their hosts, and everich[7] of them should bring fourteen persons. And so they came with this word unto Arthur. Then said he, "I am glad that this is done," and so he went into the field.

And when King Arthur should depart, he warned all his host that, and they see any sword drawn, "Look ye come on fiercely and slay that traitor Sir Mordred, for I in no wise trust him." In like wise Sir Mordred warned his host that "And ye see any manner of sword drawn, look that ye come on fiercely, and so slay all that ever before you standeth, for in no wise I will not trust for this treatise." And in the same wise said Sir Mordred unto his host, "For I know well my father will be avenged upon me."

And so they met as their pointment[8] was and were agreed and accorded thoroughly. And wine was fetched and they drank together. Right so came an adder out of a little heath-bush, and it stung a knight in the foot. And so when the knight felt him so stung, he looked down and saw the adder. And anon he drew his sword to slay the adder, and thought[9] none other harm. And when the host on both parties saw that sword drawn, then they blew beams,[1] trumpets, and horns, and shouted grimly. And so both hosts dressed them[2] together. And King Arthur took his horse and said, "Alas, this unhappy day!" and so rode to his party, and Sir Mordred in like wise.

And never since was there never seen a more dolefuller battle in no Christian land, for there was but rushing and riding, foining[3] and striking; and many a grim word was there spoken of either to other, and many a deadly stroke. But ever King Arthur rode throughout the battle[4] of Sir Mordred many times and did full nobly, as a noble king should do, and at all times he fainted never. And Sir Mordred did his devoir[5] that day and put himself in great peril.

And thus they fought all the long day, and never stinted[6] till the noble knights were laid to the cold earth. And ever they fought still till it was near night, and by then was there an hundred thousand laid dead upon the down. Then was King Arthur wood-wroth[7] out of measure when he saw his people so slain from him. And so he looked about him and could see no mo[8] of all his host, and good knights left no mo on-live, but two knights: the t'one[9] was Sir Lucan the Butler and [the other] his brother Sir Bedivere. And yet they were full sore wounded.

"Jesu, mercy," said the King, "where are all my noble knights become?[1]

---

4. Dealt with.
5. During King Arthur's lifetime.
6. Agreed.
7. Each.
8. Arrangement.
9. Meant.
1. A kind of trumpet.
2. Prepared to come.

3. Lunging.
4. Battalion.
5. Knightly duty.
6. Stopped.
7. Mad with rage.
8. Others.
9. That one, i.e., the first.
1. What has become of all my noble knights?

Alas that ever I should see this doleful day! For now," said King Arthur, "I am come to mine end. But would to God," said he, "that I wist[2] now where were that traitor Sir Mordred that has caused all this mischief."

Then King Arthur looked about and was ware where stood Sir Mordred leaning upon his sword among a great heap of dead men.

"Now give me my spear," said King Arthur unto Sir Lucan, "for yonder I have espied the traitor that all this woe hath wrought."

"Sir, let him be," said Sir Lucan, "for he is unhappy.[3] And if ye pass this unhappy day ye shall be right well revenged upon him. And, good lord, remember ye of your night's dream, and what the spirit of Sir Gawain told you tonight, and yet God of his great goodness hath preserved you hitherto. And for God's sake, my lord, leave off by this,[4] for, blessed be God, ye have won the field: for yet we been here three on-live, and with Sir Mordred is not one on-live. And therefore if ye leave off now, this wicked day of destiny is past."

"Now, tide[5] me death, tide me life," said the King, "now I see him yonder alone, he shall never escape mine hands. For at a better avail[6] shall I never have him."

"God speed you well!" said Sir Bedivere.

Then the King got his spear in both his hands and ran toward Sir Mordred, crying and saying, "Traitor, now is thy deathday come!"

And when Sir Mordred saw King Arthur he ran until him with his sword drawn in his hand, and there King Arthur smote Sir Mordred under the shield, with a foin[7] of his spear, throughout the body more than a fathom.[8] And when Sir Mordred felt that he had his death's wound, he thrust himself with the might that he had up to the burr[9] of King Arthur's spear, and right so he smote his father King Arthur with his sword holden in both his hands, upon the side of the head, that the sword pierced the helmet and the tay[1] of the brain. And therewith Sir Mordred dashed down stark dead to the earth.

And noble King Arthur fell in a swough[2] to the earth, and there he swooned oftentimes, and Sir Lucan and Sir Bedivere ofttimes heaved him up. And so, weakly betwixt them, they led him to a little chapel not far from the seaside, and when the King was there, him thought him reasonably eased. Then heard they people cry in the field. "Now go thou, Sir Lucan," said the King, "and do me to wit[3] what betokens that noise in the field."

So Sir Lucan departed, for he was grievously wounded in many places. And so as he yede[4] he saw and harkened by the moonlight how that pillers[5] and robbers were come into the field to pill and to rob many a full noble knight of brooches and bees[6] and of many a good ring and many a rich jewel. And who that were not dead all out there they slew them for their harness[7] and their riches. When Sir Lucan understood this work, he came to the King as soon as he might and told him all what he had heard and seen. "Therefore by my read,"[8] said Sir Lucan, "it is best that we bring you to some town."

---

2. Knew.
3. I.e., unlucky for you.
4. I.e., with this much accomplished.
5. Betide.
6. Advantage.
7. Thrust.
8. I.e., six feet.
9. Hand guard.

1. Edge.
2. Swoon.
3. Let me know.
4. Walked.
5. Plunderers.
6. Bracelets.
7. Armor. "All out": entirely.
8. Advice.

"I would it were so," said the King, "but I may not stand, my head works[9] so. Ah, Sir Lancelot," said King Arthur, "this day have I sore missed thee. And alas that ever I was against thee, for now have I my death, whereof Sir Gawain me warned in my dream."

Then Sir Lucan took up the King the t'one party[1] and Sir Bedivere the other party; and in the lifting up the King swooned and in the lifting Sir Lucan fell in a swoon that part of his guts fell out of his body, and therewith the noble knight's heart burst. And when the King awoke he beheld Sir Lucan how he lay foaming at the mouth and part of his guts lay at his feet.

"Alas," said the King, "this is to me a full heavy[2] sight to see this noble duke so die for my sake, for he would have holpen[3] me that had more need of help than I. Alas that he would not complain him for[4] his heart was so set to help me. Now Jesu have mercy upon his soul."

Then Sir Bedivere wept for the death of his brother.

"Now leave this mourning and weeping, gentle knight," said the King, "for all this will not avail me. For wit thou well, and[5] I might live myself, the death of Sir Lucan would grieve me evermore. But my time passeth on fast," said the King. "Therefore," said King Arthur unto Sir Bedivere, "take thou here Excalibur[6] my good sword and go with it to yonder water's side; and when thou comest there I charge thee throw my sword in that water and come again and tell me what thou sawest there."

"My lord," said Sir Bedivere, "your commandment shall be done, and [I shall] lightly[7] bring you word again."

So Sir Bedivere departed. And by the way he beheld that noble sword, that the pommel and the haft[8] was all precious stones. And then he said to himself, "If I throw this rich sword in the water, thereof shall never come good, but harm and loss." And then Sir Bedivere hid Excalibur under a tree. And so, as soon as he might, he came again unto the King and said he had been at the water and had thrown the sword into the water.

"What saw thou there?" said the King.

"Sir," he said, "I saw nothing but waves and winds."

"That is untruly said of thee," said the King. "And therefore go thou lightly again and do my commandment; as thou art to me lief[9] and dear, spare not, but throw it in."

Then Sir Bedivere returned again and took the sword in his hand. And yet him thought[1] sin and shame to throw away that noble sword. And so eft[2] he hid the sword and returned again and told the King that he had been at the water and done his commandment.

"What sawest thou there?" said the King.

"Sir," he said, "I saw nothing but waters wap and waves wan."[3]

"Ah, traitor unto me and untrue," said King Arthur, "now hast thou betrayed me twice. Who would have weened that thou that has been to me so lief and dear, and thou art named a noble knight, and would betray me

---

9. Aches.
1. On one side.
2. Sorrowful.
3. Helped.
4. Because.
5. If.
6. The sword that Arthur had received as a young man from the Lady of the Lake; it is presumably she who catches it when Bedivere finally throws it

into the water.
7. Quickly.
8. Handle. "Pommel": rounded knob on the hilt.
9. Beloved.
1. It seemed to him.
2. Again.
3. The phrase seems to mean "waters wash the shore and waves grow dark."

for the riches of this sword. But now go again lightly, for thy long tarrying putteth me in great jeopardy of my life, for I have taken cold. And but if thou do now as I bid thee, if ever I may see thee I shall slay thee mine[4] own hands, for thou wouldest for my rich sword see me dead."

Then Sir Bedivere departed and went to the sword and lightly took it up, and so he went to the water's side; and there he bound the girdle[5] about the hilts, and threw the sword as far into the water as he might. And there came an arm and an hand above the water and took it and clutched it, and shook it thrice and brandished; and then vanished away the hand with the sword into the water. So Sir Bedivere came again to the King and told him what he saw.

"Alas," said the King, "help me hence, for I dread me I have tarried overlong."

Then Sir Bedivere took the King upon his back and so went with him to that water's side. And when they were at the water's side, even fast[6] by the bank hoved[7] a little barge with many fair ladies in it; and among them all was a queen; and all they had black hoods, and all they wept and shrieked when they saw King Arthur.

"Now put me into that barge," said the King; and so he did softly. And there received him three ladies with great mourning, and so they set them[8] down. And in one of their laps King Arthur laid his head, and then the queen said, "Ah, my dear brother, why have ye tarried so long from me? Alas, this wound on your head hath caught overmuch cold." And anon they rowed fromward the land, and Sir Bedivere beheld all tho ladies go froward him.

Then Sir Bedivere cried and said, "Ah, my lord Arthur, what shall become of me, now ye go from me and leave me here alone among mine enemies?"

"Comfort thyself," said the King, "and do as well as thou mayest, for in me is no trust for to trust in. For I must into the vale of Avilion[9] to heal me of my grievous wound. And if thou hear nevermore of me, pray for my soul."

But ever the queen and ladies wept and shrieked that it was pity to hear. And as soon as Sir Bedivere had lost the sight of the barge he wept and wailed and so took the forest, and went[1] all that night. And in the morning he was ware betwixt two holts hoar[2] of a chapel and an hermitage.[3]

* * *

Thus of Arthur I find no more written in books that been authorized,[4] neither more of the very certainty of his death heard I never read,[5] but thus was he led away in a ship wherein were three queens: that one was King Arthur's sister, Queen Morgan la Fée, the t'other[6] was the Queen of North Wales, and the third was the Queen of the Waste Lands. * * *

Now more of the death of King Arthur could I never find but that these

4. I.e., with mine.
5. Sword belt.
6. Close.
7. Waited.
8. I.e., they sat.
9. A legendary island, sometimes identified with the earthly paradise.
1. Walked. "Took": took to.
2. Ancient copses.
3. In the passage here omitted, Sir Bedivere meets

the former bishop of Canterbury, now a hermit, who describes how on the previous night a company of ladies had brought to the chapel a dead body, asking that it be buried. Sir Bedivere exclaims that the dead man must have been King Arthur and vows to spend the rest of his life there in the chapel as a hermit.
4. That have authority.
5. Tell.
6. The second.

ladies brought him to his burials,[7] and such one was buried there that the hermit bore witness that sometime was Bishop of Canterbury.[8] But yet the hermit knew not in certain that he was verily the body of King Arthur, for this tale Sir Bedivere, a Knight of the Table Round, made it to be written. Yet some men say in many parts of England that King Arthur is not dead, but had by the will of our Lord Jesu into another place. And men say that he shall come again and he shall win the Holy Cross. Yet I will not say that it shall be so, but rather I will say, Here in this world he changed his life. And many men say that there is written upon his tomb this verse: *Hic iacet Arthurus, rex quondam, rexque futurus.*[9]

[THE DEATHS OF LANCELOT AND GUINEVERE][1]

And thus upon a night there came a vision to Sir Lancelot and charged him, in remission[2] of his sins, to haste him unto Amesbury: "And by then[3] thou come there, thou shalt find Queen Guinevere dead. And therefore take thy fellows with thee, and purvey them of an horse-bier,[4] and fetch thou the corse[5] of her, and bury her by her husband, the noble King Arthur. So this avision[6] came to Lancelot thrice in one night. Then Sir Lancelot rose up ere day and told the hermit.

"It were well done," said the hermit, "that ye made you ready and that ye disobey not the avision."

Then Sir Lancelot took his eight fellows with him, and on foot they yede[7] from Glastonbury to Amesbury, the which is little more than thirty mile, and thither they came within two days, for they were weak and feeble to go. And when Sir Lancelot was come to Amesbury within the nunnery, Queen Guinevere died but half an hour afore. And the ladies told Sir Lancelot that Queen Guinevere told them all ere she passed that Sir Lancelot had been priest near a twelve-month:[8] "and hither he cometh as fast as he may to fetch my corse, and beside my lord King Arthur he shall bury me." Wherefore the Queen said in hearing of them all, "I beseech Almighty God that I may never have power to see Sir Lancelot with my worldly eyes."

"And thus," said all the ladies, "was ever her prayer these two days till she was dead."

Then Sir Lancelot saw her visage, but he wept not greatly, but sighed. And so he did all the observance of the service himself, both the *dirige*[9] and on the morn he sang mass. And there was ordained[1] an horse-bier, and so with an hundred torches ever burning about the corse of the Queen, and ever Sir Lancelot with his eight fellows went about[2] the horse-bier, singing and reading many an holy orison,[3] and frankincense upon the corse incensed.[4]

Thus Sir Lancelot and his eight fellows went on foot from Amesbury unto

7. Grave.
8. Of whom the hermit, who was formerly bishop of Canterbury, bore witness.
9. "Here lies Arthur, who was once king and king will be again."
1. Guinevere enters a convent at Amesbury where Lancelot, returned with his companions to England, visits her, but she commands him never to see her again. Emulating her example, Lancelot joins the bishop of Canterbury and Bedivere in their hermitage where he takes holy orders and is joined in turn by seven of his fellow knights.

2. For the remission.
3. By the time.
4. Provide them with a horse-drawn hearse.
5. Body.
6. Dream.
7. Went.
8. Nearly twelve months.
9. Funeral service.
1. Prepared.
2. Around.
3. Reciting many a prayer.
4. Burned frankincense over the body.

Glastonbury, and when they were come to the chapel and the hermitage, there she had a *dirige* with great devotion.[5] And on the morn the hermit that sometime[6] was Bishop of Canterbury sang the mass of requiem with great devotion, and Sir Lancelot was the first that offered, and then als[7] his eight fellows. And then she was wrapped in cered cloth of Rennes, from the top[8] to the toe, in thirtyfold, and after she was put in a web[9] of lead, and then in a coffin of marble.

And when she was put in the earth Sir Lancelot swooned and lay long still, while[1] the hermit came and awaked him, and said, "Ye be to blame, for ye displease God with such manner of sorrow-making."

"Truly," said Sir Lancelot, "I trust I do not displease God, for He knoweth mine intent—for my sorrow was not, nor is not, for any rejoicing of sin, but my sorrow may never have end. For when I remember of her beauté and of her noblesse[2] that was both with her king and with her,[3] so when I saw his corse and her corse so lie together, truly mine heart would not serve to sustain my careful[4] body. Also when I remember me how by my defaute and mine orgule[5] and my pride that they were both laid full low, that were peerless that ever was living of Christian people, wit you well," said Sir Lancelot, "this remembered, of their kindness and mine unkindness, sank so to mine heart that I might not sustain myself." So the French book maketh mention.

Then Sir Lancelot never after ate but little meat,[6] nor drank, till he was dead, for then he sickened more and more and dried and dwined[7] away. For the Bishop nor none of his fellows might not make him to eat, and little he drank, that he was waxen by a kibbet[8] shorter than he was, that the people could not know him. For evermore, day and night, he prayed, but sometime he slumbered a broken sleep. Ever he was lying groveling on the tomb of King Arthur and Queen Guinevere, and there was no comfort that the Bishop nor Sir Bors, nor none of his fellows could make him—it availed not.

So within six weeks after, Sir Lancelot fell sick and lay in his bed. And then he sent for the Bishop that there was hermit, and all his true fellows. Then Sir Lancelot said with dreary steven,[9] "Sir Bishop, I pray you give to me all my rights that longeth[1] to a Christian man."

"It shall not need you,"[2] said the hermit and all his fellows. "It is but heaviness of your blood. Ye shall be well mended by the grace of God tomorn."

"My fair lords," said Sir Lancelot, "wit you well my careful body will into the earth; I have warning more than now I will say. Therefore give me my rights."

So when he was houseled and annealed[3] and had all that a Christian man ought to have, he prayed the Bishop that his fellows might bear his body to Joyous Garde. (Some men say it was Alnwick, and some men say it was

---

5. Solemnity.
6. Once.
7. Also. "Offered": made his donation.
8. Head. "Cloth of Rennes": A shroud made of fine linen smeared with wax, produced at Rennes.
9. Afterward she was put in a sheet.
1. Until.
2. Her beauty and nobility.
3. That she and her king both had.

4. Sorrowful.
5. My fault and my haughtiness.
6. Food.
7. Wasted.
8. Grown by a cubit.
9. Sad voice.
1. Pertains. "Rights": last sacrament.
2. You shall not need it.
3. Given communion and extreme unction.

Bamborough.) "Howbeit," said Sir Lancelot, "me repenteth[4] sore, but I made mine avow sometime that in Joyous Garde I would be buried. And because of breaking[5] of mine avow, I pray you all, lead me thither." Then there was weeping and wringing of hands among his fellows.

So at a season of the night they all went to their beds, for they all lay in one chamber. And so after midnight, against[6] day, the Bishop that was hermit, as he lay in his bed asleep, he fell upon a great laughter. And therewith all the fellowship awoke and came to the Bishop and asked him what he ailed.[7]

"Ah, Jesu mercy," said the Bishop, "why did ye awake me? I was never in all my life so merry and so well at ease."

"Wherefore?" said Sir Bors.

"Truly," said the Bishop, "here was Sir Lancelot with me, with mo[8] angels than ever I saw men in one day. And I saw the angels heave[9] up Sir Lancelot unto heaven, and the gates of heaven opened against him."

"It is but dretching of swevens,"[1] said Sir Bors, "for I doubt not Sir Lancelot aileth nothing but good."[2]

"It may well be," said the Bishop. "Go ye to his bed and then shall ye prove the sooth."

So when Sir Bors and his fellows came to his bed, they found him stark dead. And he lay as he had smiled, and the sweetest savor[3] about him that ever they felt. Then was there weeping and wringing of hands, and the greatest dole they made that ever made men. And on the morn the Bishop did his mass of Requiem, and after the Bishop and all the nine knights put Sir Lancelot in the same horse-bier that Queen Guinevere was laid in tofore that she was buried. And so the Bishop and they all together went with the body of Sir Lancelot daily, till they came to Joyous Garde. And ever they had an hundred torches burning about him.

And so within fifteen days they came to Joyous Garde. And there they laid his corse in the body of the choir,[4] and sang and read many psalters[5] and prayers over him and about him. And ever his visage was laid open and naked, that all folks might behold him; for such was the custom in tho[6] days that all men of worship should so lie with open visage till that they were buried.

And right thus as they were at their service, there came Sir Ector de Maris that had seven year sought all England, Scotland, and Wales, seeking his brother, Sir Lancelot. And when Sir Ector heard such noise and light in the choir of Joyous Garde, he alight and put his horse from him and came into the choir. And there he saw men sing and weep, and all they knew Sir Ector, but he knew not them. Then went Sir Bors unto Sir Ector and told him how there lay his brother, Sir Lancelot, dead. And then Sir Ector threw his shield, sword, and helm from him, and when he beheld Sir Lancelot's visage, he fell down in a swoon. And when he waked, it were hard any tongue to tell the doleful complaints that he made for his brother.

---

4. I am sorry.
5. In order not to break.
6. Toward.
7. Ailed him.
8. More.
9. Lift.
1. Illusion of dreams.

2. Has nothing wrong with him.
3. Odor. A sweet scent is a conventional sign in saints' lives of a sanctified death.
4. The center of the chancel, the place of honor.
5. Psalms.
6. Those.

"Ah, Lancelot!" he said, "thou were head of all Christian knights. And now I dare say," said Sir Ector, "thou Sir Lancelot, there thou liest, that thou were never matched of earthly knight's hand. And thou were the courteoust[7] knight that ever bore shield. And thou were the truest friend to thy lover that ever bestrode horse, and thou were the truest lover, of a sinful man,[8] that ever loved woman, and thou were the kindest man that ever struck with sword. And thou were the goodliest person that ever came among press of knights, and thou was the meekest man and the gentlest that ever ate in hall among ladies, and thou were the sternest knight to thy mortal foe that ever put spear in the rest."[9]

Then there was weeping and dolor out of measure.

Thus they kept Sir Lancelot's corse aloft fifteen days, and then they buried it with great devotion. And then at leisure they went all with the Bishop of Canterbury to his hermitage, and there they were together more than a month.

Then Sir Constantine that was Sir Cador's son of Cornwall was chosen king of England, and he was a full noble knight, and worshipfully he ruled this realm. And then this King Constantine sent for the Bishop of Canterbury, for he heard say where he was. And so he was restored unto his bishopric and left that hermitage, and Sir Bedivere was there ever still hermit to his life's end.

Then Sir Bors de Ganis, Sir Ector de Maris, Sir Gahalantine, Sir Galihud, Sir Galihodin, Sir Blamour, Sir Bleoberis, Sir Villiars le Valiant, Sir Clarrus of Clermount, all these knights drew them to their countries. Howbeit[1] King Constantine would have had them with him, but they would not abide in this realm. And there they all lived in their countries as holy men.

And some English books make mention that they went never out of England after the death of Sir Lancelot—but that was but favor of makers.[2] For the French book maketh mention—and is authorized—that Sir Bors, Sir Ector, Sir Blamour, and Sir Bleoberis went into the Holy Land, thereas Jesu Christ was quick[3] and dead, and anon as they had stablished their lands;[4] for the book saith so Sir Lancelot commanded them for to do ere ever he passed out of this world. There these four knights did many battles upon the miscreaunts,[5] or Turks, and there they died upon a Good Friday for God's sake.

Here is the end of the whole book of King Arthur and of his noble knights of the Round Table, that when they were whole together there was ever an hundred and forty. And here is the end of *The Death of Arthur*.[6]

I pray you all gentlemen and gentlewomen that readeth this book of Arthur and his knights from the beginning to the ending, pray for me while I am alive that God send me good deliverance. And when I am dead, I pray you all pray for my soul.

For this book was ended the ninth year of the reign of King Edward the

---

7. Most courteous.
8. Of any man born in original sin.
9. Support for the butt of the lance.
1. However.
2. The authors' bias.
3. Living. "Thereas": where.

4. As soon as they had put their lands in order.
5. Infidels.
6. By the "whole book" Malory refers to the entire work; the *Death of Arthur*, which Caxton made the title of the entire work, refers to the last part of Malory's book.

Fourth, by Sir Thomas Malory, knight, as Jesu help him for His great might,
as he is the servant of Jesu both day and night.

1469–70   1485

ROBERT HENRYSON
ca. 1425–ca. 1500

Robert Henryson is one of a group of Middle Scots poets sometimes referred to as
"Scottish Chaucerians." That term does less than justice to an older tradition of
Scottish literature that carries on into modern times but does indicate the great influence Chaucer exerted on both his English and his Scottish followers. That influence
is nowhere more apparent than in Henryson's *The Testament of Cresseid*, which is a
sequel to Chaucer's other major poem, *Troilus and Criseyde*, and relates the fate of
its heroine. In the sixteenth century, *The Testament* was printed as one of Chaucer's
works. *The Cock and the Fox*, one of fourteen fables that constitute another important
work by Henryson, is a highly original retelling of Chaucer's *Nun's Priest's Tale*.
Henryson clearly enjoyed and shared Chaucer's humor, and the animals in his fables
speak a wonderfully colloquial idiom. He is also a serious moralist: his earnest purpose
and that of his master Aesop, he explains in a *Prologue*, is to show in an entertaining
way how many men behave like beasts.

   Very little is known for certain about Henryson's life. Because he is spoken of as
"master," he probably held a master's degree, and evidence points to his having been
headmaster of a grammar school founded by monks of the town Dunfermline. As a
schoolmaster, Henryson would have regularly used collections of fables to teach boys
their Latin. Such a Latin collection by Walter the Englishman served as Henryson's
main source for *The Fables*.

   One of the chief attractions of Henryson's poetry is the language, which is no more
difficult than Chaucer's. The text here is based on the Oxford edition by Denton Fox
(1981), but spellings have occasionally been altered for easier comprehension. The
notes call attention to some of the main differences between Chaucer's East Midland
and Henryson's Scots dialect. The seven-line stanza of *The Fables* and *The Testament
of Cresseid*, known as rhyme royal, is the one Chaucer used in his *Troilus and Criseyde*
and most of the religious stories in *The Canterbury Tales*. It has been said to derive
its name from the fact that a royal poet, King James I of Scotland, wrote *The Kingis
Quair* (The King's Book) in that stanza.

The Cock and the Fox

Thogh brutal[1] beestes be irrational,
That is to say, wantand,[2] discretioun,
Yit ilk ane° in their[3] kindes natural   *each one*
Has many divers inclinatioun:°   *natural disposition*

---

1. Brute, adj., in the sense of relating to animals,
as in "brute beasts."
2. Wanting, (i.e., lacking). In the Scottish dialect
the normal ending of the present participle is *-and*

instead of *-ing*.
3. Note that Scottish dialect uses *their* and *them*
where Chaucer's East Midland still has *hire* and
hem.

5   The bair° busteous,° the wolf, the wylde lyoun,   *bear/rough, rude*
      The fox fenyeit,° craftie and cautelous,°   *deceitful/cunning*
      The dog to bark on night and keep the hous.

      Sa[4] different they are in properteis°   *qualities*
      Unknawin° unto man and infinite,   *unknown*
10   In kind havand sa fel° diversiteis,   *having so many*
      My cunning° it excedis[5] for to dyte.°   *skill/write*
      Forthy° as now, I purpose for to wryte   *therefore*
      Ane case I fand whilk fell this other yeer[6]
      Betwix° ane fox and gentil° Chauntecleer.   *between/noble*

15   Ane widow dwelt intill ane drop they dayis[7]
      Whilk wan hir food off[8] spinning on hir rok,°   *distaff*
      And na mair° had, forsooth, as the fabill sayis,   *no more*
      Except of hennes scho° had ane lyttel flok,   *she*
      And them to keep scho had ane jolie cok,
20   Right corageous, that to this widow ay°   *always*
      Divided night[9] and crew before the day.

      Ane lyttel fra° this foresaid widow's hous,   *from*
      Ane thornie schaw° there was of greet defence,   *thicket*
      Wherein ane foxe, craftie and cautelous,°   *cunning*
25   Made his repair and daylie residence,
      Whilk° to this widow did greet violence   *which*
      In pyking off pultrie° baith° day and night,   *poultry/both*
      And na way be revengit on him scho might.

      This wylie tod,° when that the lark couth sing,[1]   *fox*
30   Full sair° and hungrie unto the toun him drest,° *sorely, painfully/proceeded*
      Where Chauntecleer, in to the gray dawing,°   *dawn*
      Werie for° night, was flowen fra his nest.   *weary of*
      Lowrence[2] this saw and in his mind he kest°   *cast, considered*
      The jeperdies, the wayes, and the wyle,[3]
35   By what menis° he might this cok begyle.   *means*

      Dissimuland in to countenance and cheer,[4]
      On knees fell and simuland thus he said,
      "Gude morne, my maister, gentil Chantecleer!"
      With that the cok start bakwart in ane braid.°   *with a start*
40   "Schir,"° by my saul,° ye need not be effraid,   *sir/soul*
      Nor yit for me to start nor flee abak;
      I come bot here service to you to mak.

4. So. Note that in Scottish dialect long *a* is pronounced for long *o*.
5. Note that the third person singular of verbs ends in-*s* or-*is* instead of-*th* as in Chaucer.
6. A case I found which happened a year or two ago. "Ane": a. The same word as *one*, which functions as the indefinite article.
7. In a village [in] those days.
8. Who made her living (literally: won her food) by.

9. I.e., kept the hours at night by crowing. Cf. *The Miller's Tale*, line 567, and *The Nun's Priest's Tale*, lines 33–38.
1. When the lark could sing, i.e., at dawn.
2. Generic name for a fox, perhaps invented here by Henryson.
3. The stratagems, the devices, and the trickery.
4. Dissimulating in facial expression and manner.

"Wald I not serve to you, it wer bot blame,[5]
As I have done to your progenitouris.
45   Your father oft fulfillit has my wame,°   *belly*
  And sent me meit° fra midding° to the muris,°   *food/refuse pile/moors*
  And at his end I did my besie curis°   *busy cares*
  To held his heed and gif him drinkis warme,
  Syne° at the last, the sweit° swelt° in my arme!"   *then/sweet (man)/died*

50   "Knew ye my father?" quad the cok, and leuch.°   *laughed*
  "Yea, my fair son, forsooth I held his heed
  When that he deit° under ane birkin beuch,°   *died/birch bough*
  Syne said the Dirigie[6] when that he was deed.
  Betwix us twa how suld there be ane feid?[7]
55   Wham suld ye traist° bot me, your servitour   *whom should you trust*
  That to your father did so greet honour?

  When I beheld your fedderis° fair and gent,   *feathers*
  Your beck, your breast, your hekill,° and your kame°— *hackle/comb*
  Schir, by my saul, and the blissit sacrament,[8]
60   My heart warmis, me think I am at hame.
  You for to serve, I wald creep on my wame°   *belly*
  In froist and snaw, in wedder wan and weit°   *dark and wet*
  And lay my lyart° lokkes under your feit."   *gray*

  This fenyeit fox, fals and dissimulate,
65   Made to this cok ane cavillatioun:°   *a critical remark*
  "Ye are, me think, changed and degenerate
  Fra your father and his conditioun,
  Of craftie crawing he might beer the croun,[9]
  For he weld on his tais° stand and craw.   *toes*
70   This is no le;° I stude beside and saw."   *lie*

  With that the cok, upon his tais° hie,   *toes*
  Kest up his beek and sang with all his might.
  Quod schir Lowrence, "Well said, sa mot I the.[1]
  Ye are your fatheris son and heir upright,°   *rightful*
75   Bot of his cunning yit ye want ane slight."°   *trick*
  "What?" quad the cok. "He wald, and have na dout,
  Baith wink, and craw, and turne him thryis about."[2]

  The cok, inflate with wind and fals vanegloir,°   *vainglory*
  That mony puttes unto confusioun,
80   Traisting to win ane greet worship therefoir,
  Unwarlie winkand[3] walkit up and doun,
  And syne° to chant and craw he made him boun°—   *then/ready*

---

5. It would be just a shame if I were not to serve you. "Serve" has both the feudal sense of service and a second sense.
6. *Dirigie* (>modern "dirge"): the first word of the anthem beginning the funeral service, which designates the prayer itself or the whole Office for the Dead: *"Dirige Dominus Deus meus"*—Lead me O Lord my God (Psalm 5.9).
7. Between the two of us how should there be a feud? "Suld": should. The future of "shall" is "sall."
8. The Eucharist.
9. He might bear the crown of skilfull crowing.
1. So may I prosper.
2. Both shut his eyes, and crow, and turn himself around thrice.
3. Unwarily shutting his eyes.

And suddandlie, by° he had crawin ane note   *by the time that*
The fox was war, and hent° him be the throte.   *seized*

85 Syne to the wood but tarie° with him hyit,°   *without delay/hurried*
Of countermaund havand but lytil dout.[4]
With that Pertok, Sprutok, and Coppok cryit,
The widow heard, and with ane cry come out.
Seand the case scho sighit and gaif[5] ane schout,
90 "How, murther, reylok!"[6] with ane hiddeous beir,° *noise*
"Allas, now lost is gentil Chauntecleer!"

As scho were wod° with mony yell and cry,   *mad*
Ryvand hir hair, upon hir breist can beit,[7]
Syne pale of hew,° half in ane extasy,°   *hue/frenzy*
95 Fell doun for care in swoning° and in sweit.° *fainting/sweating*
With that the selie° hennes left their meit,°   *poor/food*
And whyle this wyfe was lyand thus in swoon,
Fell of that case in disputacioun.

"Allas," quod Pertok, makand sair murning,[8]
100 With teeris greet attour hir cheekis fell,[9]
"Yon was our drowrie° and our day's darling,   *beloved*
Our nightingal, and als° our orlege° bell,   *also/clock*
Our walkrife watch,° us for to warne and tell *wakeful sentinel*
When that Aurora with hir curcheis° gray   *headcovers, scarves*
105 Put up hir heid° betwix the night and day.   *head*

"Wha sall° our lemman° be? Who sall us leid?° *who shall/lover/lead*
When we are sad wha sall unto us sing?
With his sweet bill he wald breke us the breid;°   *bread*
In all this warld was there ane kynder thing?
110 In paramouris° he wald do us plesing,   *making love*
At his power, as nature list him geif.[1]
Now efter him, allas, how sall we leif?"°   *live*

Quod Sprutok than, "Ceis,° sister of your sorrow, *cease*
Ye be too mad, for him sic murning mais.[2]
115 We sall fare well, I find Sanct John to borrow;[3]
The proverb sayis, 'Als gude lufe cummis as gais.'[4]
I will put on my haly-dayis clais°   *holiday clothes*
And mak me fresch agane this jolie May,
Syne chant this sang, 'Was never widow sa gay!'

120 "He was angry and held us ay in aw,°   *always in fear*
And wounded with the speir° of jelowsy.   *spear*
Of chalmerglew,[5] Pertok, full well ye knaw,
Wasted he was, of nature cauld and dry.[6]

---

4. Having but little fear of prevention.
5. Gave. Note the hard g where the Chaucerian form would be *yaf.* "Seand": seeing.
6. Ho [Stop], murder, robbery.
7. Tearing her hair did beat upon her breast.
8. Making sore mourning.
9. While great tears fell down over her cheeks.
1. To the extent of the potency nature was pleased to give him.

2. You are too silly—you make such mourning for him.
3. I take St. John to be my guarantor; an expression used at parting.
4. As good love comes as goes.
5. Chamber-joy, i.e., performance in the bedroom.
6. A preponderance of black bile, the humor that is cold and dry like earth, enfeebled his potency.

Sen° he is gone, therefore, sister, say I,   *since*
125 Be blythe in baill,⁷ for that is best remeid.°   *remedy*
Let quik° to quik, and deid° ga to the deid."   *living/dead*

Than Pertok spak, that feinyeit° faith before,   *pretended*
In lust but° lufe that set all hir delyte,   *without*
"Sister, ye wait° of sic° as him ane score   *know/such*
130 Wald not suffice to slake our appetyte.
I hecht° you by my hand, sen ye are quyte,°   *promise/free*
Within ane oulk,° for schame and I durst speik,   *week*
To get ane berne suld better claw oure breik."⁸

Than Coppok like ane curate° spak full crous:°   *priest/smugly*
135 "Yon was ane verray vengeance from the hevin.
He was sa lous° and sa lecherous,   *loose, dissolute*
Ceis coud he noght with kittokis ma than sevin,⁹
But righteous God, haldand the balance evin,¹
Smytis right sair,° thoght he be patient,   *sore*
140 Adulteraris° that list them not repent.   *adulterers*

"Prydeful he was, and joyit of his sin,
And comptit° not for Goddis favor nor feid.°   *cared/enmity*
Bot traisted ay to rax and sa to rin,²
Whil at the last his sinnis can° him leid°   *did/lead*
145 To schameful end and to yon suddand deid.°   *sudden death*
Therefore it is the verray hand of God
That causit him be werryit° with the tod."°   *seized by the throat/fox*

When this was said, this widow fra hir swoun
Start up on fute, and on hir kennettis° cryde,   *small hunting dogs*
150 "How,° Birkye, Berrie, Bell, Bawsie, Broun,   *what*
Rype Schaw, Rin Weil, Curtes, Nuttieclyde!
Togidder all but grunching furth ye glyde!³
Reskew my nobil cok ere he be slane,°   *slain*
Or ellis to me see ye come never agane!°   *again*

155 With that, but baid, they braidet over the bent,⁴
As fire off flint they over the feildis flaw,°   *flew*
Full wichtlie° they through wood and wateris went,   *swiftly*
And ceissit not, schir Lowrence while they saw.⁵
But when he saw the raches° come on raw,°   *dogs/in a line*
160 Unto the cok in mind° he said, "God sen°   *thought/grant*
That I and thou were fairlie in my den."

Then spak the cok, with sum gude spirit inspyrit,
"Do my counsall⁶ and I sall warrand° thee.   *guarantee*
Hungrie thou art, and for greet travel° tyrit,°   *labor/tired*

7. Be merry in misery.
8. If I dare speak, shame not withstanding, to get
a man who should better claw our tail.
9. He could not stop [even] with more than seven
wenches. "Kittock" is a Scots diminutive for Katherine (as-*ok* is a diminutive in the names of the
hens), used here as a generic term for "girl."

1. Holding the scales (of judgment) level.
2. And trusted always to have rule and so to reign.
3. Glide forth all together without grumbling.
4. Without delay they rushed over the ground.
5. And did not stop as long as they saw sir Lowrence.
6. Take my advice.

165	Right faint of force° and may not ferther flee:
	Swyth° turn agane and say that I and ye
	Freindes are made and fellowis for ane yeir.°
	Than will they stint,° I stand for it, and not steir."[7]

strength
quickly
year
stop

	This tod, thogh he were fals and frivolous,°
170	And had fraudis, his querrel° to defend,
	Desavit° was by menis° right marvelous,
	For falset° failis ay at the latter end.
	He start about, and cryit as he was kend°—
	With that the cok he braid° unto a bewch.°
175	Now juge ye all whereat schir Lowrence lewch.[8]

untrustworthy
cause
deceived / means
falsehood
instructed
moved quickly / bough

	Begylit° thus, the tod under the tree
	On knees fell, and said, "Gude Chauntecleer,
	Come doun agane, and I but meit or fee[9]
	Sall be your man and servant for ane yeir."
180	"Na, murther, theif, and revar, stand on reir.[1]
	My bludy hekill° and my nek sa bla°
	Has partit love for ever betwene us twa.

deceived
bloody hackle / blue

	"I was unwise that winkit° at thy will,
	Wherethrough almaist I loissit° had my heid."°
185	"I was mair fule,"[2] quod he, "coud noght be still,
	Bot spake to put my pray into pleid."[3]
	"Fare on, fals theef, God keep me fra thy feid."°
	With that the cok over the feildis tuke his flight,
	And in at the widow's lewer[4] couth he light.

shut my eyes
lost / head
enmity, feud

Moralitas°

moral

190	Now worthie folk, suppose this be ane fabill,
	And overheillit with typis figural,[5]
	Yit may ye find ane sentence° right agreabill°
	Under their fenyeit termis textual.[6]
	To our purpose this cok well may we call
195	Nyce° proud men, woid° and vaneglorious
	Of kin and blude, whilk is presumptuous.[7]

meaning / suitable
foolish / mad

	Fy, puffed up pride, thou is full poysonabill!°
	Wha favoris thee, on force man have ane fall,[8]
	Thy strength is noght, thy stule° standis unstabill.
200	Tak witnes of the feyndes infernall,
	Whilk° houndit doun was fra that hevinlie° hall[9]

poisonous
stool
who / heavenly

---

7. I guarantee it and [will] not move.
8. Laughed, i.e., he had no reason whatsoever to laugh.
9. Without board or wages.
1. No, murderer, thief, and robber, back off (literally, "stand in the rear").
2. The greater fool. (Said by the fox.)
3. To make my prey a subject of a plea (i.e., a legal argument).
4. Louver, i.e., a hole in a roof for letting out smoke.

5. And covered over with figural symbols, i.e., a hidden allegory.
6. Beneath the feigned words of the text, i.e., referring to the interpretation of scripture allegorically, not by the "letter" but by the "spirit."
7. Of family and bloodline, which (pride) is arrogant.
8. Whoever favors thee necessarily must have a fall.
9. The fallen angels who were cast from heaven into hell because they rebelled against God.

To hellis hole and to that hiddeous hous,
Because in pride they were presumptous.

This fenyeit foxe may well be figurate°   *serve as a figure for*
To flatteraris with plesand wordis white,
With fals mening and mynd maist toxicate,°   *most poisonous*
To loif and le that settis their hail delyte.[1]
All worthie folk at sic suld haif despite[2]—
For where is there mair perrelous pestilence?—
205 Nor give to learis° haistelie credence.   *liars*

The wickit mind and adullatioun,°   *excessive praise*
Of sucker sweet haifand similitude,[3]
Bitter as gall and full of fell poysoun
To taste it is, wha cleirlie understude,[4]
210 Forthy° as now schortlie to conclude,   *therefore*
Thir° twa sinnis, flatterie and vanegloir.   *these*
Are venomous: gude folk, flee them thairfoir!

1. Who set their whole delight in lauding and lying.
2. Should have contempt for such people.
3. Having resemblance to sweet sugar.
4. Whoever clearly understands it.

EVERYMAN
after 1485

Everyman is a late example of a kind of medieval drama known as the morality play. Morality plays apparently evolved side by side with the mystery plays, although they were composed individually and not in cycles. They too have a primarily religious purpose, but their method of attaining it is different. The mysteries dramatized significant events in biblical and sacred history from the creation of the world to Judgment Day in order to bring out the meaning of God's scheme of salvation. The moralities, on the other hand, employed allegory to show this scheme in the lifespan of a representative figure called "Mankind" or "Everyman." *Everyman* is about the day of judgment that every individual human being must face eventually. The play represents allegorically the forces—both outside the protagonist and within—that can help to save Everyman and those that cannot or that obstruct his salvation.

 Everyman lacks the broad (even slapstick) humor of some morality plays that portray as clowns the vices that try to lure the Everyman figure away from salvation. The play does contain a certain grim humor in showing the haste with which the hero's fair-weather friends abandon him when they discover what his problem is. The play inculcates its austere lesson by the simplicity and directness of its language and of its approach. A sense of urgency builds—one by one Everyman's supposed resources fail him as time is running out. Ultimately Knowledge teaches him the lesson that every Christian must learn in order to be saved.

 The play was written near the end of the fifteenth century. It is probably a translation of a Flemish play, although it is possible that the Flemish play is the translation and the English *Everyman* the original.

Everyman[1]

CAST OF CHARACTERS

MESSENGER	KNOWLEDGE
GOD	CONFESSION
DEATH	BEAUTY
EVERYMAN	STRENGTH
FELLOWSHIP	DISCRETION
KINDRED	FIVE-WITS
COUSIN	ANGEL
GOODS	DOCTOR
GOOD DEEDS	

HERE BEGINNETH A TREATISE HOW THE HIGH FATHER OF HEAVEN SENDETH DEATH TO SUMMON EVERY CREATURE TO COME AND GIVE ACCOUNT OF THEIR LIVES IN THIS WORLD, AND IS IN MANNER OF A MORAL PLAY

[*Enter* MESSENGER.]

MESSENGER   I pray you all give your audience,
And hear this matter with reverence,
By figure° a moral play.   *in form*
The Summoning of Everyman called it is,
5   That of our lives and ending shows
How transitory we be all day.°   *always*
The matter is wonder precious,
But the intent of it is more gracious
And sweet to bear away.
10   The story saith: Man, in the beginning
Look well, and take good heed to the ending,
Be you never so gay.
You think sin in the beginning full sweet,
Which in the end causeth the soul to weep,
15   When the body lieth in clay.
Here shall you see how fellowship and jollity,
Both strength, pleasure, and beauty,
Will fade from thee as flower in May.
For ye shall hear how our Heaven-King
20   Calleth Everyman to a general reckoning.
Give audience and hear what he doth say.

[*Exit* MESSENGER.—*Enter* GOD.]

GOD   I perceive, here in my majesty,
How that all creatures be to me unkind,°   *thoughtless*

---

1. The text is based on the earliest printing of the play (no manuscript is known) by John Skot about 1530, as reproduced by W. W. Greg (1904). The spelling has been modernized except where modernization would spoil the rhyme, and modern punctuation has been added. The stage directions have been amplified.

Living without dread in worldly prosperity.
25 Of ghostly° sight the people be so blind,   *spiritual*
Drowned in sin, they know me not for their God.
In worldly riches is all their mind:
They fear not of my righteousness the sharp rod;
My law that I showed when I for them died
30 They forget clean, and shedding of my blood red.
I hanged between two,[2] it cannot be denied:
To get them life I suffered to be dead.
I healed their feet, with thorns hurt was my head.
I could do no more than I did, truly—
35 And now I see the people do clean forsake me.
They use the seven deadly sins damnable,
As pride, coveitise,° wrath, and lechery[3]   *avarice*
Now in the world be made commendable.
And thus they leave of angels the heavenly company.
40 Every man liveth so after his own pleasure,
And yet of their life they be nothing sure.
I see the more that I them forbear,
The worse they be from year to year:
All that liveth appaireth° fast.   *degenerates*
45 Therefore I will, in all the haste,
Have a reckoning of every man's person.
For, and° I leave the people thus alone   *if*
In their life and wicked tempests,
Verily they will become much worse than beasts;
50 For now one would by envy another up eat.
Charity do they all clean forgeet.
I hoped well that every man
In my glory should make his mansion,
And thereto I had them all elect.°   *chosen*
55 But now I see, like traitors deject,°   *abased*
They thank me not for the pleasure that I to° them meant,   *for*
Nor yet for their being that I them have lent.
I proffered the people great multitude of mercy,
And few there be that asketh it heartily.°   *sincerely*
60 They be so cumbered° with worldly riches   *encumbered*
That needs on them I must do justice—
On every man living without fear.
Where art thou, Death, thou mighty messenger?

     [*Enter* DEATH.]

   DEATH   Almighty God, I am here at your will,
65   Your commandment to fulfill.
     GOD   Go thou to Everyman,
     And show him, in my name,

2. I.e., the two thieves between whom Christ was crucified.

3. The other three deadly sins are envy, gluttony, and sloth.

A pilgrimage he must on him take,
Which he in no wise may escape;
70 And that he bring with him a sure reckoning
Without delay or any tarrying.
DEATH   Lord, I will in the world go run over all,°   *everywhere*
And cruelly out-search both great and small.

[*Exit* GOD.]

Everyman will I beset that liveth beastly
75 Out of God's laws, and dreadeth not folly.
He that loveth riches I will strike with my dart,
His sight to blind, and from heaven to depart°   *separate*
Except that Almsdeeds be his good friend—
In hell for to dwell, world without end.
80 Lo, yonder I see Everyman walking:
Full little he thinketh on my coming;
His mind is on fleshly lusts and his treasure,
And great pain it shall cause him to endure
Before the Lord, Heaven-King.

[*Enter* EVERYMAN.]

85 Everyman, stand still! Whither art thou going
Thus gaily? Hast thou thy Maker forgeet?°   *forgotten*
EVERYMAN   Why askest thou?
Why wouldest thou weet?°   *know*
DEATH   Yea, sir, I will show you:
90 In great haste I am sent to thee
From God out of his majesty.
EVERYMAN   What! sent to me?
DEATH   Yea, certainly.
Though thou have forgot him here,
95 He thinketh on thee in the heavenly sphere,
As, ere we depart, thou shalt know.
EVERYMAN   What desireth God of me?
DEATH   That shall I show thee:
A reckoning he will needs have
100 Without any longer respite.
EVERYMAN   To give a reckoning longer leisure I crave.
This blind° matter troubleth my wit.   *unexpected*
DEATH   On thee thou must take a long journay:
Therefore thy book of count° with thee thou bring,   *accounts*
105 For turn again thou cannot by no way.
And look thou be sure of thy reckoning,
For before God thou shalt answer and shew
Thy many bad deeds and good but a few—
How thou hast spent thy life and in what wise,
110 Before the Chief Lord of Paradise.

Have ado that we were in that way,[4]
For weet thou well thou shalt make none attornay.[5]

EVERYMAN Full unready I am such reckoning to give.
I know thee not. What messenger art thou?

115 DEATH I am Death that no man dreadeth,[6]
For every man I 'rest,° and no man spareth;   *arrest*
For it is God's commandment
That all to me should be obedient.

EVERYMAN O Death, thou comest when I had thee least in mind.

120 In thy power it lieth me to save:
Yet of my good° will I give thee, if thou will be kind,   *goods*
Yea, a thousand pound shalt thou have—
And defer this matter till another day.

DEATH Everyman, it may not be, by no way.

125 I set nought by[7] gold, silver, nor riches,
Nor by pope, emperor, king, duke, nor princes,
For, and° I would receive gifts great,   *if*
All the world I might get.
But my custom is clean contrary:

130 I give thee no respite. Come hence and not tarry!

EVERYMAN Alas, shall I have no longer respite?
I may say Death giveth no warning.
To think on thee it maketh my heart sick,
For all unready is my book of reckoning.

135 But twelve year and I might have a biding,[8]
My counting-book I would make so clear
That my reckoning I should not need to fear.
Wherefore, Death, I pray thee, for God's mercy,
Spare me till I be provided of remedy.

140 DEATH Thee availeth not to cry, weep, and pray;
But haste thee lightly° that thou were gone that journay   *quickly*
And prove° thy friends, if thou can.   *test*
For weet° thou well the tide° abideth no man,   *know / time*
And in the world each living creature

145 For Adam's sin must die of nature.[9]

EVERYMAN Death, if I should this pilgrimage take
And my reckoning surely make,
Show me, for saint° charity,   *holy*
Should I not come again shortly?

150 DEATH No, Everyman. And thou be once there,
Thou mayst never more come here,
Trust me verily.

EVERYMAN O gracious God in the high seat celestial,
Have mercy on me in this most need!

155 Shall I have company from this vale terrestrial
Of mine acquaintance that way me to lead?

---

4. I.e., let's get started at once.   7. I care nothing for.
5. I.e., none to appear in your stead.   8. If I might have a delay for just twelve years.
6. That fears nobody.   9. Naturally.

DEATH   Yea, if any be so hardy
      That would go with thee and bear thee company.
      Hie° thee that thou were gone to God's magnificence,   *hasten*
160   Thy reckoning to give before his presence.
      What, weenest° thou thy life is given thee,   *suppose*
      And thy worldly goods also?
EVERYMAN   I had weened so, verily.
DEATH   Nay, nay, it was but lent thee.
165   For as soon as thou art go,
      Another a while shall have it and then go therefro,
      Even as thou hast done.
      Everyman, thou art mad! Thou hast thy wits° five,   *senses*
      And here on earth will not amend thy live![1]
170   For suddenly I do come.
EVERYMAN   O wretched caitiff! Whither shall I flee
      That I might 'scape this endless sorrow?
      Now, gentle Death, spare me till tomorrow,
      That I may amend me
175   With good advisement.°   *preparation*
DEATH   Nay, thereto I will not consent,
      Nor no man will I respite,
      But to the heart suddenly I shall smite,
      Without any advisement.
180   And now out of thy sight I will me hie:
      See thou make thee ready shortly,
      For thou mayst say this is the day
      That no man living may 'scape away.

          [*Exit* DEATH.]

EVERYMAN   Alas, I may well weep with sighs deep:
185   Now have I no manner of company
      To help me in my journey and me to keep.°   *guard*
      And also my writing° is full unready—   *ledger*
      How shall I do now for to excuse me?
      I would to God I had never be geet!°   *been forgotten*
190   To my soul a full great profit it had be.
      For now I fear pains huge and great.
      The time passeth: Lord, help, that all wrought!
      For though I mourn, it availeth nought.
      The day passeth and is almost ago:°   *gone by*
195   I wot° not well what for to do.   *know*
      To whom were I best my complaint to make?
      What and I to Fellowship thereof spake,
      And showed him of this sudden chance?
      For in him is all mine affiance,°   *trust*
200   We have in the world so many a day
      Be good friends in sport and play.

1. In thy life.

I see him yonder, certainly.
I trust that he will bear me company.
Therefore to him will I speak to ease my sorrow.

[*Enter* FELLOWSHIP.]

205 Well met, good Fellowship, and good morrow!
    FELLOWSHIP Everyman, good morrow, by this day!
      Sir, why lookest thou so piteously?
      If anything be amiss, I pray thee me say,
      That I may help to remedy.
210 EVERYMAN Yea, good Fellowship, yea:
      I am in great jeopardy.
    FELLOWSHIP My true friend, show to me your mind.
      I will not forsake thee to my life's end
      In the way of good company.
215 EVERYMAN That was well spoken, and lovingly!
    FELLOWSHIP Sir, I must needs know your heaviness.°   *sorrow*
      I have pity to see you in any distress.
      If any have you wronged, ye shall revenged be,
      Though I on the ground be slain for thee,
220 Though that I know before that I should die.
    EVERYMAN Verily, Fellowship, gramercy.°   *many thanks*
    FELLOWSHIP Tush! by thy thanks I set not a stree.°   *straw*
      Show me your grief and say no more.
    EVERYMAN If I my heart should to you break,°   *disclose*
225 And then you to turn your mind fro me,
      And would not me comfort when ye hear me speak,
      Then should I ten times sorrier be.
    FELLOWSHIP Sir, I say as I will do, indeed.
    EVERYMAN Then be you a good friend at need.
230 I have found you true herebefore.
    FELLOWSHIP And so ye shall evermore.
      For, in faith, and° thou go to hell,   *if*
      I will not forsake thee by the way.
    EVERYMAN Ye speak like a good friend. I believe you well.
235 I shall deserve° it, and° I may.   *repay / if*
    FELLOWSHIP I speak of no deserving, by this day!
      For he that will say and nothing do
      Is not worthy with good company to go.
      Therefore show me the grief of your mind,
240 As to your friend most loving and kind.
    EVERYMAN I shall show you how it is:
      Commanded I am to go a journey,
      A long way, hard and dangerous,
      And give a strait° count,° without delay,   *strict / accounting*
245 Before the high judge Adonai.°   *God*
      Wherefore I pray you bear me company,
      As ye have promised, in this journay.
    FELLOWSHIP This is matter indeed! Promise is duty—

But, and I should take such a voyage on me,
250 I know it well, it should be to my pain.
Also it maketh me afeard, certain.
But let us take counsel here, as well as we can—
For your words would fear° a strong man.   *frighten*

EVERYMAN   Why, ye said if I had need,
255 Ye would me never forsake, quick ne dead,
Though it were to hell, truly.

FELLOWSHIP   So I said, certainly,
But such pleasures° be set aside, the sooth to say.   *jokes*
And also, if we took such a journay,
260 When should we again come?

EVERYMAN   Nay, never again, till the day of doom.

FELLOWSHIP   In faith, then will not I come there!
Who hath you these tidings brought?

EVERYMAN   Indeed, Death was with me here.

265 FELLOWSHIP   Now by God that all hath bought,°   *redeemed*
If Death were the messenger,
For no man that is living today
I will not go that loath° journay—   *loathsome*
Not for the father that begat me!

270 EVERYMAN   Ye promised otherwise, pardie.°   *by God*

FELLOWSHIP   I wot well I said so, truly.
And yet, if thou wilt eat and drink and make good cheer,
Or haunt to women the lusty company,[2]
I would not forsake you while the day is clear,
275 Trust me verily!

EVERYMAN   Yea, thereto ye would be ready—
To go to mirth, solace,° and play: *pleasure*
Your mind to folly will sooner apply°   *attend*
Than to bear me company in my long journay.

280 FELLOWSHIP   Now in good faith, I will not that way.
But, and thou will murder or any man kill,
In that I will help thee with a good will.

EVERYMAN   O that is simple° advice, indeed!   *foolish*
Gentle fellow, help me in my necessity:
285 We have loved long, and now I need—
And now, gentle Fellowship, remember me!

FELLOWSHIP   Whether ye have loved me or no,
By Saint John, I will not with thee go!

EVERYMAN   Yet I pray thee take the labor and do so much for me,
290 To bring me forward,° for saint charity,   *escort me*
And comfort me till I come without the town.

FELLOWSHIP   Nay, and° thou would give me a new gown,   *if*
I will not a foot with thee go.
But, and thou had tarried, I would not have left thee so.
295 And as now, God speed thee in thy journey!
For from thee I will depart as fast as I may.

2. Or frequent the lusty company of women.

EVERYMAN   Whither away, Fellowship? Will thou forsake me?

FELLOWSHIP   Yea, by my fay!° To God I betake° thee.   *faith / commend*

EVERYMAN   Farewell, good Fellowship! For thee my heart is sore.

300   Adieu forever—I shall see thee no more.

FELLOWSHIP   In faith, Everyman, farewell now at the ending:

For you I will remember that parting is mourning.

[*Exit* FELLOWSHIP.]

EVERYMAN   Alack, shall we thus depart° indeed—   *part*

Ah, Lady, help!—without any more comfort?

305   Lo, Fellowship forsaketh me in my most need!

For help in this world whither shall I resort?

Fellowship herebefore with me would merry make,

And now little sorrow for me doth he take.

It is said, "In prosperity men friends may find

310   Which in adversity be full unkind."

Now whither for succor shall I flee,

Sith° that Fellowship hath forsaken me?   *since*

To my kinsmen I will, truly,

Praying them to help me in my necessity.

315   I believe that they will do so,

For kind will creep where it may not go.[3]

I will go 'say°—for yonder I see them—   *assay*

Where° be ye now my friends and kinsmen.   *whether*

[*Enter* KINDRED *and* COUSIN.]

KINDRED   Here be we now at your commandment:

320   Cousin, I pray you show us your intent

In any wise, and not spare.

COUSIN   Yea, Everyman, and to us declare

If ye be disposed to go anywhither.

For, weet° you well, we will live and die togither.   *know*

325   KINDRED   In wealth and woe we will with you hold,

For over his kin a man may be bold.[4]

EVERYMAN   Gramercy,° my friends and kinsmen kind.   *much thanks*

Now shall I show you the grief of my mind.

I was commanded by a messenger

330   That is a high king's chief officer:

He bade me go a pilgrimage, to my pain—

And I know well I shall never come again.

Also I must give a reckoning strait,°   *strict*

For I have a great enemy that hath me in wait,[5]

335   Which intendeth me to hinder.

KINDRED   What account is that which ye must render?

That would I know.

3. For kinship will creep where it cannot walk (i.e., kinsmen will suffer hardship for one another).
4. I.e., for a man may make demands of his kins-men.
5. I.e., Satan lies in ambush for me.

EVERYMAN   Of all my works I must show
　　　How I have lived and my days spent;
340　Also of ill deeds that I have used
　　　In my time sith life was me lent,
　　　And of all virtues that I have refused.
　　　Therefore I pray you go thither with me
　　　To help me make mine account, for saint charity.
345　COUSIN   What, to go thither? Is that the matter?
　　　Nay, Everyman, I had liefer fast[6] bread and water
　　　All this five year and more!
　　　EVERYMAN   Alas, that ever I was bore!°　　　　　　　*born*
　　　For now shall I never be merry
350　If that you forsake me.
　　　KINDRED   Ah, sir, what? Ye be a merry man:
　　　Take good heart to you and make no moan.
　　　But one thing I warn you, by Saint Anne,
　　　As for me, ye shall go alone.
355　EVERYMAN   My Cousin, will you not with me go?
　　　COUSIN   No, by Our Lady! I have the cramp in my toe:
　　　Trust not to me. For, so God me speed,
　　　I will deceive you in your most need.
　　　KINDRED   It availeth you not us to 'tice.°　　　　　　*entice*
360　Ye shall have my maid with all my heart:
　　　She loveth to go to feasts, there to be nice,°　　　*wanton*
　　　And to dance, and abroad to start.[7]
　　　I will give her leave to help you in that journey,
　　　If that you and she may agree.
365　EVERYMAN   Now show me the very effect° of your mind:　*bent*
　　　Will you go with me or abide behind?
　　　KINDRED   Abide behind? Yea, that will I and I may!
　　　Therefore farewell till another day.

　　　　　　　[*Exit* KINDRED.]

　　　EVERYMAN   How should I be merry or glad?
370　For fair promises men to me make,
　　　But when I have most need they me forsake.
　　　I am deceived. That maketh me sad.
　　　COUSIN   Cousin Everyman, farewell now,
　　　For verily I will not go with you;
375　Also of mine own an unready reckoning
　　　I have to account—therefore I make tarrying.
　　　Now God keep thee, for now I go.

　　　　　　　[*Exit* COUSIN.]

　　　EVERYMAN   Ah, Jesus, is all come hereto?°　　　　　*to this*
　　　Lo, fair words maketh fools fain:°　　　　　　　　*glad*

---

6. I.e., rather fast on.　　　　　　7. To go gadding about.

380 They promise and nothing will do, certain.
My kinsmen promised me faithfully
For to abide with me steadfastly,
And now fast away do they flee.
Even so Fellowship promised me.
385 What friend were best me of to provide?
I lose my time here longer to abide.
Yet in my mind a thing there is:
All my life I have loved riches;
If that my Good° now help me might,   *Goods*
390 He would make my heart full light.
I will speak to him in this distress.
Where art thou, my Goods and riches?
GOODS [*within*] Who calleth me? Everyman? What, hast thou haste?
I lie here in corners, trussed and piled so high,
395 And in chests I am locked so fast—
Also sacked in bags—thou mayst see with thine eye
I cannot stir, in packs low where I lie.
What would ye have? Lightly° me say.   *quickly*
EVERYMAN Come hither, Good, in all the haste thou may,
400 For of counsel I must desire thee.

[*Enter* GOODS.]

GOODS Sir, and° ye in the world have sorrow or adversity,   *if*
That can I help you to remedy shortly.
EVERYMAN It is another disease° that grieveth me: *distress*
In this world it is not, I tell thee so.
405 I am sent for another way to go,
To give a strait count general
Before the highest Jupiter° of all.   *God*
And all my life I have had joy and pleasure in thee:
Therefore I pray thee go with me,
410 For, peradventure, thou mayst before God Almighty
My reckoning help to clean and purify.
For it is said ever among°   *now and then*
That money maketh all right that is wrong.
GOODS Nay, Everyman, I sing another song:
415 I follow no man in such voyages.
For, and° I went with thee,   *if*
Thou shouldest fare much the worse for me;
For because on me thou did set thy mind,
Thy reckoning I have made blotted and blind,°   *illegible*
420 That thine account thou cannot make truly—
And that hast thou for the love of me.
EVERYMAN That would grieve me full sore
When I should come to that fearful answer.
Up, let us go thither together.
425 GOODS Nay, not so, I am too brittle, I may not endure.
I will follow no man one foot, be ye sure.

EVERYMAN   Alas, I have thee loved and had great pleasure
    All my life-days on good and treasure.
GOODS   That is to thy damnation, without leasing,°   *lie*
430   For my love is contrary to the love everlasting.
    But if thou had me loved moderately during,°   *in the meanwhile*
    As to the poor to give part of me,
    Then shouldest thou not in this dolor be,
    Nor in this great sorrow and care.
435 EVERYMAN   Lo, now was I deceived ere I was ware,
    And all I may wite° misspending of time.   *blame on*
GOODS   What, weenest° thou that I am thine?   *suppose*
EVERYMAN   I had weened so.
GOODS   Nay, Everyman, I say no.
440   As for a while I was lent thee;
    A season thou hast had me in prosperity.
    My condition° is man's soul to kill;   *disposition*
    If I save one, a thousand I do spill.°   *ruin*
    Weenest thou that I will follow thee?
445   Nay, from this world, not verily.
EVERYMAN   I had weened otherwise.
GOODS   Therefore to thy soul Good is a thief;
    For when thou art dead, this is my guise°—   *custom*
    Another to deceive in the same wise
450   As I have done thee, and all to his soul's repreef.°   *shame*
EVERYMAN   O false Good, cursed thou be,
    Thou traitor to God, that hast deceived me
    And caught me in thy snare!
GOODS   Marry, thou brought thyself in care,°   *sorrow*
455   Whereof I am glad:
    I must needs laugh, I cannot be sad.
EVERYMAN   Ah, Good, thou hast had long my heartly° love;   *sincere*
    I gave thee that which should be the Lord's above.
    But wilt thou not go with me, indeed?
460   I pray thee truth to say.
GOODS   No, so God me speed!
    Therefore farewell and have good day.

        [*Exit* GOODS.]

EVERYMAN   Oh, to whom shall I make my moan
    For to go with me in that heavy° journay?   *sorrowful*
465   First Fellowship said he would with me gone:°   *go*
    His words were very pleasant and gay,
    But afterward he left me alone.
    Then spake I to my kinsmen, all in despair,
    And also they gave me words fair—
470   They lacked no fair speaking,
    But all forsake me in the ending.
    Then went I to my Goods that I loved best,
    In hope to have comfort; but there had I least,

For my Goods sharply did me tell
475 That he bringeth many into hell.
Then of myself I was ashamed,
And so I am worthy to be blamed:
Thus may I well myself hate.
Of whom shall I now counsel take?
480 I think that I shall never speed
Till that I go to my Good Deed.
But alas, she is so weak
That she can neither go° nor speak.   *walk*
Yet will I venture° on her now.   *gamble*
485 My Good Deeds, where be you?
  GOOD DEEDS [*speaking from the ground*] Here I lie, cold in the
    ground:
  Thy sins hath me sore bound
  That I cannot stear.°   *stir*
  EVERYMAN O Good Deeds, I stand in fear:
490 I must you pray of counsel,
For help now should come right well.
  GOOD DEEDS Everyman, I have understanding
  That ye be summoned, account to make,
  Before Messiah of Jer'salem King.
495 And you do by me,[8] that journey with you will I take.
  EVERYMAN Therefore I come to you my moan to make:
  I pray you that ye will go with me.
  GOOD DEEDS I would full fain, but I cannot stand, verily.
  EVERYMAN Why, is there anything on you fall?°   *fallen*
500 GOOD DEEDS Yea, sir, I may thank you of all:
  If ye had perfectly cheered me,
  Your book of count full ready had be.

    [GOOD DEEDS *shows him the account book.*]

Look, the books of your works and deeds eke,°   *also*
As how they lie under the feet,
505 To your soul's heaviness.°   *distress*
  EVERYMAN Our Lord Jesus help me!
  For one letter here I cannot see.
  GOOD DEEDS There is a blind° reckoning in time of distress! *illegible*
  EVERYMAN Good Deeds, I pray you help me in this need,
510 Or else I am forever damned indeed.
Therefore help me to make reckoning
Before the Redeemer of all thing
That King is and was and ever shall.
  GOOD DEEDS Everyman, I am sorry of° your fall   *for*
515 And fain would help you and° I were able.   *if*
  EVERYMAN Good Deeds, your counsel I pray you give me.
  GOOD DEEDS That shall I do verily,

8. I.e., if you do what I say.

Though that on my feet I may not go;
I have a sister that shall with you also,
520   Called Knowledge, which shall with you abide
To help you to make that dreadful reckoning.

[*Enter* KNOWLEDGE.]

KNOWLEDGE   Everyman, I will go with thee and be thy guide,
In thy most need to go by thy side.
EVERYMAN   In good condition I am now in everything,
525   And am whole content with this good thing,
Thanked be God my Creator.
GOOD DEEDS   And when she hath brought you there
Where thou shalt heal thee of thy smart,°   pain
Then go you with your reckoning and your Good Deeds together
530   For to make you joyful at heart
Before the blessed Trinity.
EVERYMAN   My Good Deeds, gramercy!
I am well content, certainly,
With your words sweet.
535   KNOWLEDGE   Now go we together lovingly
To Confession, that cleansing river.
EVERYMAN   For joy I weep—I would we were there!
But I pray you give me cognition,°   knowledge
Where dwelleth that holy man Confession?
540   KNOWLEDGE   In the House of Salvation:
We shall us comfort, by God's grace.

[KNOWLEDGE *leads* EVERYMAN *to* CONFESSION.]

Lo, this is Confession: kneel down and ask mercy,
For he is in good conceit° with God Almighty.   esteem
545   EVERYMAN   [*kneeling*] O glorious fountain that all
uncleanness doth clarify,°   purify
Wash from me the spots of vice unclean,
That on me no sin may be seen.
I come with Knowledge for my redemption,
Redempt° with heart and full contrition,   redeemed
550   For I am commanded a pilgrimage to take
And great accounts before God to make.
Now I pray you, Shrift,° mother of Salvation,   confession
Help my Good Deeds for my piteous exclamation.
CONFESSION   I know your sorrow well, Everyman:
555   Because with Knowledge ye come to me,
I will you comfort as well as I can,
And a precious jewel I will give thee,
Called Penance, voider° of adversity.   expeller
Therewith shall your body chastised be—
560   With abstinence and perseverance in God's service.
Here shall you receive that scourge of me,

Which is penance strong° that ye must endure,   *harsh*
To remember thy Saviour was scourged for thee
With sharp scourges, and suffered it patiently.
565 So must thou ere thou 'scape that painful pilgrimage.
Knowledge, keep° him in this voyage,   *guard*
And by that time Good Deeds will be with thee.
But in any wise be secure° of mercy—   *certain*
For your time draweth fast—and ye will saved be.
570 Ask God mercy and he will grant, truly.
When with the scourge of penance man doth him° bind,   *himself*
The oil of forgiveness then shall he find.
EVERYMAN   Thanked be God for his gracious work,
For now I will my penance begin.
575 This hath rejoiced and lighted my heart,
Though the knots be painful and hard within.[9]
KNOWLEDGE   Everyman, look your penance that ye fulfill,
What pain that ever it to you be;
And Knowledge shall give you counsel at will
580 How your account ye shall make clearly.
EVERYMAN   O eternal God, O heavenly figure,
O way of righteousness, O goodly vision,
Which descended down in a virgin pure
Because he would every man redeem,
585 Which Adam forfeited by his disobedience;
O blessed Godhead, elect and high Divine,°   *divinity*
Forgive my grievous offense!
Here I cry thee mercy in this presence:
O ghostly Treasure, O Ransomer and Redeemer,
590 Of all the world Hope and Conduiter,°   *guide*
Mirror of joy, Foundator° of mercy,   *Founder*
Which enlumineth° heaven and earth thereby,   *lights up*
Hear my clamorous complaint, though it late be;
Receive my prayers, of thy benignity.
595 Though I be a sinner most abominable,
Yet let my name be written in Moses' table.[1]
O Mary, pray to the Maker of all thing
Me for to help at my ending,
And save me from the power of my enemy,
600 For Death assaileth me strongly.
And Lady, that I may by mean of thy prayer
Of your Son's glory to be partner—
By the means of his passion I it crave.
I beseech you help my soul to save.
605 Knowledge, give me the scourge of penance:
My flesh therewith shall give acquittance.°   *satisfaction for sins*
I will now begin, if God give me grace.

9. I.e., to my senses. "Knots": i.e., the knots on the scourge (whip) of penance.
1. "Moses' table" is here the tablet on which are recorded those who have been baptized and have done penance.

KNOWLEDGE   Everyman, God give you time and space!°   *opportunity*
    Thus I bequeath you in the hands of our Saviour:
610   Now may you make your reckoning sure.
EVERYMAN   In the name of the Holy Trinity
    My body sore punished shall be:
    Take this, body, for the sin of the flesh!
    Also° thou delightest to go gay and fresh,   *as*
615   And in the way of damnation thou did me bring,
    Therefore suffer now strokes of punishing!
    Now of penance I will wade the water clear,
    To save me from purgatory, that sharp fire.
GOOD DEEDS   I thank God, now can I walk and go,
620   And am delivered of my sickness and woe.
    Therefore with Everyman I will go, and not spare:
    His good works I will help him to declare.
KNOWLEDGE   Now, Everyman, be merry and glad:
    Your Good Deeds cometh now, ye may not be sad.
625   Now is your Good Deeds whole and sound,
    Going° upright upon the ground.   *walking*
EVERYMAN   My heart is light, and shall be evermore.
    Now will I smite faster than I did before.
GOOD DEEDS   Everyman, pilgrim, my special friend,
630   Blessed be thou without end!
    For thee is preparate° the eternal glory.   *prepared*
    Ye have me made whole and sound
    Therefore I will bide by thee in every stound.°   *trial*
EVERYMAN   Welcome, my Good Deeds! Now I hear thy voice,
635   I weep for very sweetness of love.
KNOWLEDGE   Be no more sad, but ever rejoice:
    God seeth thy living in his throne above.
    Put on this garment to thy behove,°   *advantage*
    Which is wet with your tears—
640   Or else before God you may it miss
    When ye to your journey's end come shall.
EVERYMAN   Gentle Knowledge, what do ye it call?
KNOWLEDGE   It is a garment of sorrow;
    From pain it will you borrow:°   *redeem*
645   Contrition it is
    That getteth forgiveness;
    It pleaseth God passing° well.   *surpassingly*
GOOD DEEDS   Everyman, will you wear it for your heal?° *welfare*
EVERYMAN   Now blessed be Jesu, Mary's son,
650   For now have I on true contrition.
    And let us go now without tarrying.
    Good Deeds, have we clear our reckoning?
GOOD DEEDS   Yea, indeed, I have it here.
EVERYMAN   Then I trust we need not fear.
655   Now friends, let us not part in twain.
KNOWLEDGE   Nay, Everyman, that will we not, certain.

GOOD DEEDS   Yet must thou lead with thee
 Three persons of great might.
EVERYMAN   Who should they be?
660 GOOD DEEDS   Discretion and Strength they hight,°   *are called*
 And thy Beauty may not abide behind.
KNOWLEDGE   Also ye must call to mind
 Your Five-Wits° as for your counselors.   *senses*
GOOD DEEDS   You must have them ready at all hours.
665 EVERYMAN   How shall I get them hither?
KNOWLEDGE   You must call them all togither,
 And they will be here incontinent.°   *at once*
EVERYMAN   My friends, come hither and be present,
 Discretion, Strength, my Five-Wits, and Beauty!

[*They enter.*]

670 BEAUTY   Here at your will we be all ready.
 What will ye that we should do?
GOOD DEEDS   That ye would with Everyman go
 And help him in his pilgrimage.
 Advise you:° will ye with him or not in that voyage? *take thought*
675 STRENGTH   We will bring him all thither,
 To his help and comfort, ye may believe me.
DISCRETION   So will we go with him all togither.
EVERYMAN   Almighty God, loved° might thou be!   *praised*
 I give thee laud that I have hither brought
680 Strength, Discretion, Beauty, and Five-Wits—lack I nought—
 And my Good Deeds, with Knowledge clear,
 All be in my company at my will here:
 I desire no more to my business.
STRENGTH   And I, Strength, will by you stand in distress,
685 Though thou would in battle fight on the ground.
FIVE-WITS   And though it were through the world round,
 We will not depart for sweet ne sour.
BEAUTY   No more will I, until death's hour,
 Whatsoever thereof befall.
690 DISCRETION   Everyman, advise you first of all:
 Go with a good advisement° and deliberation.   *preparation*
 We all give you virtuous° monition°   *confident / prediction*
 That all shall be well.
EVERYMAN   My friends, hearken what I will tell;
695 I pray God reward you in his heaven-sphere;
 Now hearken all that be here,
 For I will make my testament,
 Here before you all present:
 In alms half my good° I will give with my hands twain, *goods*
700 In the way of charity with good intent;
 And the other half, still° shall remain,   *which still*
 I 'queath° to be returned there it ought to be.   *bequeath*

This I do in despite of the fiend of hell,
To go quit out of his perel,[2]
705   Ever after and this day.
    KNOWLEDGE   Everyman, hearken what I say:
Go to Priesthood, I you advise,
And receive of him, in any wise,°   at all costs
The holy sacrament and ointment° togither;   extreme unction
710   Then shortly see ye turn again hither:
We will all abide you here.
    FIVE-WITS   Yea, Everyman, hie you that ye ready were.
There is no emperor, king, duke, ne baron,
That of God hath commission
715   As hath the least priest in the world being:
For of the blessed sacraments pure and bening°   benign
He beareth the keys, and thereof hath the cure°   care
For man's redemption—it is ever sure—
Which God for our souls' medicine
720   Gave us out of his heart with great pine,°   torment
Here in this transitory life for thee and me.
The blessed sacraments seven there be:
Baptism, confirmation, with priesthood° good,   ordination
And the sacrament of God's precious flesh and blood,
725   Marriage, the holy extreme unction, and penance:
These seven be good to have in remembrance,
Gracious sacraments of high divinity.
    EVERYMAN   Fain° would I receive that holy body,   gladly
And meekly to my ghostly° father I will go.   spiritual
730   FIVE-WITS   Everyman, that is the best that ye can do:
God will you to salvation bring.
For priesthood exceedeth all other thing:
To us Holy Scripture they do teach,
And converteth man from sin, heaven to reach;
735   God hath to them more power given
Than to any angel that is in heaven.
With five words[3] he may consecrate
God's body in flesh and blood to make,
And handleth his Maker between his hands.
740   The priest bindeth and unbindeth all bands,[4]
Both in earth and in heaven.
Thou ministers° all the sacraments seven;   administer
Though we kiss thy feet, thou were worthy;
Thou art surgeon that cureth sin deadly;
745   No remedy we find under God
But all only priesthood.[5]
Everyman, God gave priests that dignity

2. In order to go free of danger from him.
3. The five words ("For this is my body") spoken by the priest when he offers the wafer at communion.
4. A reference to the power of the keys, inherited

by the priesthood from St. Peter, who received it from Christ (Matthew 16.19) with the promise that whatever St. Peter bound or loosed on earth would be bound or loosed in heaven.
5. Except from priesthood alone.

And setteth them in his stead among us to be.
Thus be they above angels in degree.

[*Exit* EVERYMAN.]

750 KNOWLEDGE   If priests be good, it is so, surely.
But when Jesu hanged on the cross with great smart,°   *pain*
There he gave out of his blessed heart
The same sacrament in great torment,
He sold them not to us, that Lord omnipotent:
755 Therefore Saint Peter the Apostle doth say
That Jesu's curse hath all they
Which God their Saviour do buy or sell,[6]
Or they for any money do take or tell.[7]
Sinful priests giveth the sinners example bad:
760 Their children sitteth by other men's fires, I have heard;
And some haunteth women's company
With unclean life, as lusts of lechery.
These be with sin made blind.
FIVE-WITS   I trust to God no such may we find.
765 Therefore let us priesthood honor,
And follow their doctrine for our souls' succor.
We be their sheep and they shepherds be
By whom we all be kept in surety.
Peace, for yonder I see Everyman come,
770 Which hath made true satisfaction.
GOOD DEEDS   Methink it is he indeed.

[*Re-enter* EVERYMAN.]

EVERYMAN   Now Jesu be your alder speed![8]
I have received the sacrament for my redemption,
And then mine extreme unction.
775 Blessed be all they that counseled me to take it!
And now, friends, let us go without longer respite.
I thank God that ye have tarried so long.
Now set each of you on this rood° your hond   *cross*
And shortly follow me:
780 I go before there° I would be. God be our guide!   *where*
STRENGTH   Everyman, we will not from you go
Till ye have done this voyage long.
DISCRETION   I, Discretion, will bide by you also.
KNOWLEDGE   And though this pilgrimage be never so strong,°   *harsh*
785 I will never part you fro.
STRENGTH   Everyman, I will be as sure by thee
As ever I did by Judas Maccabee.[9]

---

6. To give or receive money for the sacraments is simony, named after Simon, who wished to buy the gift of the Holy Ghost and was cursed by St. Peter. 7. Or who, for any sacrament, take or count out money.

8. The prosperer of you all. 9. Judas Maccabaeus was an enormously powerful warrior in the defense of Israel against the Syrians in late Old Testament times.

EVERYMAN   Alas, I am so faint I may not stand—
    My limbs under me doth fold!
790   Friends, let us not turn again to this land,
    Not for all the world's gold.
    For into this cave must I creep
    And turn to earth, and there to sleep.
BEAUTY   What, into this grave, alas?
795   EVERYMAN   Yea, there shall ye consume,° more and lass.[1]   *decay*
BEAUTY   And what, should I smother here?
EVERYMAN   Yea, by my faith, and nevermore appear.
    In this world live no more we shall,
    But in heaven before the highest Lord of all.
800   BEAUTY   I cross out all this! Adieu, by Saint John—
    I take my tape in my lap and am gone.[2]
EVERYMAN   What, Beauty, whither will ye?
BEAUTY   Peace, I am deaf—I look not behind me,
    Not and thou wouldest give me all the gold in thy chest.

        [*Exit* BEAUTY.]

805   EVERYMAN   Alas, whereto may I trust?
    Beauty goeth fast away fro me—
    She promised with me to live and die!
STRENGTH   Everyman, I will thee also forsake and deny.
    Thy game liketh° me not at all.   *pleases*
810   EVERYMAN   Why then, ye will forsake me all?
    Sweet Strength, tarry a little space.
STRENGTH   Nay, sir, by the rood of grace,
    I will hie me from thee fast,
    Though thou weep till thy heart tobrast.°   *break*
815   EVERYMAN   Ye would ever bide by me, ye said.
STRENGTH   Yea, I have you far enough conveyed!°   *escorted*
    Ye be old enough, I understand,
    Your pilgrimage to take on hand:
    I repent me that I hither came.
820   EVERYMAN   Strength, you to displease I am to blame,[3]
    Yet promise is debt, this ye well wot.°   *know*
STRENGTH   In faith, I care not:
    Thou art but a fool to complain;
    You spend your speech and waste your brain.
825   Go, thrust thee into the ground.

        [*Exit* STRENGTH.]

EVERYMAN   I had weened° surer I should you have found.   *supposed*
    He that trusteth in his Strength
    She him deceiveth at the length.

---

1. More and less (i.e., all of you).   3. I'm to blame for displeasing you.
2. I tuck my skirts in my belt and am off.

Both Strength and Beauty forsaketh me—
830   Yet they promised me fair and lovingly.
DISCRETION   Everyman, I will after Strength be gone:
    As for me, I will leave you alone.
EVERYMAN   Why Discretion, will ye forsake me?
DISCRETION   Yea, in faith, I will go from thee.
835   For when Strength goeth before,
    I follow after evermore.
EVERYMAN   Yet I pray thee, for the love of the Trinity,
    Look in my grave once piteously.
DISCRETION   Nay, so nigh will I not come.
840   Farewell everyone!

        [*Exit* DISCRETION.]

EVERYMAN   O all thing faileth save God alone—
    Beauty, Strength, and Discretion.
    For when Death bloweth his blast
    They all run fro me full fast.
845   FIVE-WITS   Everyman, my leave now of thee I take.
    I will follow the other, for here I thee forsake.
EVERYMAN   Alas, then may I wail and weep,
    For I took you for my best friend.
FIVE-WITS   I will no longer thee keep.°   *watch over*
850   Now farewell, and there an end!

        [*Exit* FIVE-WITS.]

EVERYMAN   O Jesu, help, all hath forsaken me!
GOOD DEEDS   Nay, Everyman, I will bide with thee:
    I will not forsake thee indeed;
    Thou shalt find me a good friend at need.
855   EVERYMAN   Gramercy, Good Deeds! Now may I true friends see.
    They have forsaken me every one—
    I loved them better than my Good Deeds alone.
    Knowledge, will ye forsake me also?
KNOWLEDGE   Yea, Everyman, when ye to Death shall go,
860   But not yet, for no manner of danger.
EVERYMAN   Gramercy, Knowledge, with all my heart!
KNOWLEDGE   Nay, yet will I not from hence depart
    Till I see where ye shall become.[4]
EVERYMAN   Methink, alas, that I must be gone
865   To make my reckoning and my debts pay,
    For I see my time is nigh spent away.
    Take example, all ye that this do hear or see,
    How they that I best loved do forsake me,
    Except my Good Deeds that bideth truly.
870   GOOD DEEDS   All earthly things is but vanity.

4. Till I see what shall become of you.

Beauty, Strength, and Discretion do man forsake,
Foolish friends and kinsmen that fair spake—
All fleeth save Good Deeds, and that am I.
EVERYMAN   Have mercy on me, God most mighty,
875   And stand by me, thou mother and maid, holy Mary!
GOOD DEEDS   Fear not: I will speak for thee.
EVERYMAN   Here I cry God mercy!
GOOD DEEDS   Short our end, and 'minish our pain.[5]
Let us go, and never come again.
880   EVERYMAN   Into thy hands, Lord, my soul I commend:
Receive it, Lord, that it be not lost.
As thou me boughtest,° so me defend,   redeemed
And save me from the fiend's boast,
That I may appear with that blessed host
885   That shall be saved at the day of doom.
In manus tuas, of mights most,
Forever *commendo spiritum meum.*[6]

[EVERYMAN *and* GOOD DEEDS *descend into the grave.*]

KNOWLEDGE   Now hath he suffered that we all shall endure,
The Good Deeds shall make all sure.
890   Now hath he made ending,
Methinketh that I hear angels sing
And make great joy and melody
Where Everyman's soul received shall be.
ANGEL   [*within*] Come, excellent elect° spouse to Jesu![7]   chosen
895   Here above thou shalt go
Because of thy singular virtue.
Now the soul is taken the body fro,
Thy reckoning is crystal clear:
Now shalt thou into the heavenly sphere—
900   Unto the which all ye shall come
That liveth well before the day of doom.

[*Enter* DOCTOR.[8]]

DOCTOR   This memorial° men may have in mind: reminder
Ye hearers, take it of worth,° old and young,   prize it
And forsake Pride, for he deceiveth you in the end.
905   And remember Beauty, Five-Wits, Strength, and Discretion,
They all at the last do Everyman forsake,
Save his Good Deeds there doth he take—
But beware, for and they be small,
Before God he hath no help at all—
910   None excuse may be there for Everyman.

---

5. I.e., make our dying quick and diminish our
pain.
6. Into thy hands, O greatest of powers, I commend my spirit forever.

7. The soul is often referred to as the bride of
Jesus.
8. The Doctor is the learned theologian who
explains the meaning of the play.

Alas, how shall he do than?°   *then*
For after death amends may no man make,
For then mercy and pity doth him forsake.
If his reckoning be not clear when he doth come,
915   God will say, *"Ite, maledicti, in ignem eternum!"*[9]
And he that hath his account whole and sound,
High in heaven he shall be crowned,
Unto which place God bring us all thither,
That we may live body and soul togither.
920   Thereto help, the Trinity!
Amen, say ye, for saint charity.

9. Depart, ye cursed, into everlasting fire.

them

Alas, how shall he do than?
For after death amends may no man make,
For then mercy and pity doth him forsake.
If his reckoning be not clear when he doth come,
God will say, "Ite, maledicti, in ignem aeternum."
And he that hath his account whole and sound,
High in heaven he shall be crowned,
Unto which place God bring us all thither,
That we may live body and soul together.
Thereto help, the Trinity!
Amen, say ye, for saint charity.

9. Depart, ye cursed, into everlasting fire.

Poems in Process

In all ages some poets have claimed that their poems were not willed but were inspired, whether by a muse, by divine visitation, or by sudden emergence from the author's unconscious mind. But as the poet Richard Aldington has remarked, "genius is not enough; one must also work." The working manuscripts of the greatest writers show that, however involuntary the origin of a poem, vision was usually followed by laborious revision before the work achieved the seeming inevitability of its final form.

Milton is the first major English author for whom we possess drafts of poems indubitably written in his own hand; the excerpt below from his manuscript of *Lycidas* shows the extent to which he worked over and expanded his initial attempts. It is no surprise to find Pope, one of the most meticulous of craftsmen, working and reworking his drafts, and radically enlarging *The Rape of the Lock* even after the success that attended its first printed version. But the manuscript of Samuel Johnson's greatest poem, *The Vanity of Human Wishes*, discovered in the 1940s, is a surprise, for it shows that this neoclassic writer who, in his critical theory, regarded poetry as primarily an art of achieving preconceived ends by tested means in fact composed with even greater speed and assurance than the Romantic Byron, who liked to represent himself to his readers as dashing off his verses with unreflecting ease. In the manuscript of Gray's *Elegy Written in a Country Churchyard* we find that the poet, by late afterthought, converted a relatively simple elegiac meditation into a longer and much more complex apologia for his chosen way of life. In all these selections we look on as poets, no matter how rapidly they achieve a result they are willing to let stand, carry on their inevitably tentative efforts to meet the multiple requirements of meaning, syntax, meter, sound pattern, and the constraints imposed by a chosen stanza. And because these are all very good poets, the seeming conflict between the necessities of significance and form results not in the distortion but in the perfecting of the poetic statement.

Our transcriptions from the poets' drafts attempt to reproduce, as accurately as the change from script to print will allow, the appearance of the manuscript page. A poet's first attempt at a line or phrase is reproduced in larger type, the revisions in smaller type. The line numbers that are used to identify an excerpt are those of the final form of the complete poem, as reprinted in this anthology. The marginal numbers beside the extract from *The Vanity of Human Wishes* are Johnson's own additions.

SELECTED BIBLIOGRAPHY

Autograph Poetry in the English Language, 2 vols., 1973, compiled by P. J. Croft, reproduces and transcribes one or more pages of manuscript in the poet's own hand, from the 14th century to the present time; volume 1 includes many of the poets represented in this volume of *The Norton Anthology of English Literature*, from John Skelton to George Crabbe. Books that discuss the process of poetic composition and revision, with examples from manuscripts and printed versions, are Charles D. Abbott, ed., *Poets at Work*, 1948; Phyllis Bartlett, *Poems in Process*, 1951; A. F. Scott, *The Poet's Craft*, 1957. In *Word for Word: A Study of Authors' Alterations*, 1965, Wallace Hildick analyzes the composition of prose fiction, as well as poems.

JOHN MILTON

From Lycidas[1]

[*Lines 1–14*][2]

yet once more O ye laurells and once more

ye myrtl's browne wth Ivie never sere

I come to pluck yor berries harsh and crude

~~before the mellowing yeare~~ and wth forc't fingers rude

~~and crop yor young~~ shatter yor leaves before ye mellowing yeare
bitter constraint, and sad occasion deare

compells me to disturbe yor season due
for ~~young~~ Lycidas is dead, dead ere his prime
young Lycidas and hath not left his peere

           not
who would ∧ sing for Lycidas he well knew
himselfe to sing & build the loftie rime
he must not flote upon his watrie beare
unwept, and welter to the parching wind
without the meed of some melodious teare

[*Lines 56–63*]

ay mee I fondly dreame
~~had yee~~ bin there, ~~for~~ what could that have don?
~~what could the golden hayrd Calliope~~
for her inchaunting son ——————
~~when shee beheld~~ (the gods farre sighted bee)
~~his goarie scalpe rowle downe the Thracian lee~~

✳ whome universal nature
  might lament
  ~~and heaven and hel deplore~~
  ~~when his divine head downe~~
  the streame was sent
  downe the Swift Hebrus to the
    Lesbian shore.

[THE THIRD AND FOLLOWING LINES ARE REWRITTEN
ON A SEPARATE PAGE]

✳ what could the muse her selfe that Orpheus bore
  the muse her selfe for her inchanting son
~~for her inchanting son~~

          did
whome universal nature ~~might~~ lament
when by the rout that made the hideous roare
     gorie
✳ goarie his ~~divine~~ visage down the streame was sent
downe the swift Hebrus to ye Lesbian shoare.

1. Transcribed from a manuscript of fifty pages in the library of Trinity College, Cambridge. Among the poems written in Milton's own hand are *Lycidas*, *Comus*, seven sonnets, and several other short poems. The manuscript has been photographically reproduced, with printed transcriptions, by W.

Aldis Wright, *Facsimile of the Manuscript of Milton's Minor Poems* (Cambridge, England, 1899).
2. This draft is written on a separate page of the manuscript, which also contains drafts of the passages, "What could the muse her selfe" and "Bring the rathe primrose," transcribed below.

[*Lines 132–53*]

Returne Alpheus the dred voice is past
    that shrunk thy streams, returne Sicilian Muse
    and call the vales and bid them hither cast
    thire bells, and flowrets of a thousand hues
    yee vallies low where the mild wispers use

                          u
    of shades, and wanton winds, and goshing brooks ✱ ✱
                         ✱   sparely
    on whose fresh lap the swart starre sparely looks —faintly
✱
 —bring hither all yor quaint enamel'd eyes ✱ throw
    that on the greene terfe suck the honied showrs
                    th
    and purple all the ground wth vernal flowrs
                              ———— Bring the rathe &c.[3]
    to strew the laureat herse where Lycid' lies
    for so to interpose a little ease
       ✱ fraile
    let our sad thoughts dally wth false surmise ✱ fraile

[LINES 142–50 ARE DRAFTED ON A SEPARATE PAGE, AS FOLLOWS]

    Bring the rathe primrose that unwedded dies
 —collu colouring the pale cheeke of uninjoyd love
    and that sad floure that stroye
    to write his owne woes on the vermeil graine
                  t
    next adde Narcissus y^t still weeps in vaine
                   e   th
    the woodbine and ye pancie freak't wth jet
    the glowing violet
    the cowslip wan that hangs his pensive head
    and every bud that sorrows liverie weares
                        with
    let Daffadillies fill thire cups teares
    bid Amaranthus all his beautie shed
    to strew the laureat herse &c.

    Bring the rathe primrose that forsaken dies
    the tufted crowtoe and pale Gessamin
                  ye
    the white pinke, and pansie freakt wth jet
    the glowing violet
               the well-attired woodbine
    the muske rose and the garish columbine—
    wth cowslips wan that hang the pensive head
                     ✱ weare ✱   weares
    and every flower that sad escutcheon beares imbroidrie beares
 &
 2 let daffadillies fill thire cups wth teares
 1 bid Amaranthus all his beauties shed
    to strew &c.

3. I.e., Milton plans to insert here the passage that follows, lines 142–50.

ALEXANDER POPE
From The Rape of the Lock[1]
[1712 Version: Canto 1, Lines 1–24]

WHAT dire Offence from Am'rous Causes springs,
    What mighty Quarrels rise from Trivial Things,
        I sing—This Verse to C—l, Muse! is due;
This, ev'n *Belinda* may vouchsafe to view:
Slight is the Subject, but not so the Praise,
If she inspire, and He approve my Lays.
    Say what strange Motive, Goddess! cou'd compel
A well-bred *Lord* t'assault a gentle *Belle?*
Oh say what stranger Cause, yet unexplor'd,
Cou'd make a gentle *Belle* reject a *Lord?*
And dwells such Rage in *softest Bosoms* then?
And lodge such daring Souls in *Little Men?*
    Sol thro' white Curtains did his Beams display,
And op'd those Eyes which brighter shine than they;
Shock just had giv'n himself the rowzing Shake,
And Nymphs prepar'd their *Chocolate* to take;
Thrice the wrought Slipper knock'd against the Ground,
And striking Watches the tenth Hour resound.
Belinda rose, and 'midst attending Dames
Launch'd on the Bosom of the silver *Thames:*
A Train of well-drest Youths around her shone,
And ev'ry Eye was fix'd on her alone;
On her white Breast a sparking *Cross* she wore,
Which *Jews* might kiss, and Infidels adore.

[Revised Version: Canto 1, Lines 1–22]

WHAT dire Offence from am'rous Causes springs,
    What mighty Contests rise from trivial Things,
        I sing—This Verse to *Caryll,* Muse! is due;
This, ev'n *Belinda* may vouchsafe to view:
Slight is the Subject, but not so the Praise,
If She inspire, and He approve my Lays.
    Say what strange Motive, Goddess! cou'd compel
A well-bred *Lord* t'assault a gentle *Belle?*
Oh say what stranger Cause, yet unexplor'd,
Cou'd make a gentle *Belle* reject a *Lord?*

1. The first version of *The Rape of the Lock*, published 1712, consisted of two cantos and a total of 334 lines. Two years later, in 1714, Pope published an enlarged version of five cantos and 794 lines, in which he added the supernatural "machinery" of the Sylphs and Gnomes as well as a number of mock-epic episodes. The excerpts reprinted here show how Pope revised and expanded passages that he retained from the first version of the poem. The revised version includes changes that Pope added in later editions of the enlarged text of 1714.

In Tasks so bold, can Little Men engage,
And in soft Bosoms dwells such mighty Rage?
    Sol thro' white Curtains shot a tim'rous Ray,
And op'd those Eyes that must eclipse the Day;
Now Lapdogs give themselves the rowzing Shake,
And sleepless Lovers, just at Twelve, awake:
Thrice rung the Bell, the Slipper knock'd the Ground,
And the press'd Watch return'd a silver Sound.
Belinda still her downy Pillow prest,
Her Guardian *Sylph* prolong'd the balmy Rest.
'Twas he had summon'd to her silent Bed
The Morning-Dream that hover'd o'er her Head.

[*Revised Version: Canto 2, Lines 1–8*]

Not with more Glories, in th' Etherial Plain,
The Sun first rises o'er the purpled Main,
Than issuing forth, the Rival of his Beams
Launch'd on the Bosom of the Silver *Thames*.
Fair Nymphs, and well-drest Youths around her shone,
But ev'ry Eye was fix'd on her alone.
On her white Breast a sparkling *Cross* she wore,
Which *Jews* might kiss, and Infidels adore.

From An Essay on Man[1]

[*From the First Manuscript*]

                            we ourselves
1. Learn ~~then thyself,~~ not God presume to scan,
        But
    ~~And~~ know, the Study of Mankind is Man.
Plac'd on this Isthmus of a Middle State,
A Being darkly wise, & rudely great.
With too much knowledge for the Sceptic side,
And too much Weakness for a Stoic's Pride,
He hangs between, uncertain where to rest;
Whether to deem himself a God or Beast;
Whether his Mind or Body to prefer,
Born but to die, & reas'ning but to err;
                        his
Alike in Ignorance, (~~that~~ Reason such)
    ~~Who~~   ~~who thinks~~
Whether he thinks too little or too much:
Chaos of Thought & Passion, all confus'd,
Still by himself abus'd & dis-abus'd:

---

1. Two of Pope's holograph manuscripts of *An Essay on Man* have survived. The earlier one is at the Pierpont Morgan Library in New York. The second one, at the Houghton Library, Harvard, was evidently intended as a fair copy for printing; but Pope, who was an inveterate reviser, introduced some last-minute changes. The passage transcribed here from each of these manuscripts is Pope's famed description of man's "middle state" in the great chain of being; in the published version, it opens Epistle 2, lines 1–18.

Created half to rise, & half to fall;
Great <u>Lord</u> of all things, yet a <u>prey</u> to all;
Sole <u>Judge</u> of <u>Truth</u>, in endless <u>Error</u> hurl'd;
The <u>Glory</u>, <u>Jest</u>, and <u>Riddle</u> of the World.

[*From the Second Manuscript*]²

~~Incipit I~~   Know
~~Incipit III~~   ~~Learn~~ we ourselves, not God presume to scan,
The only Science   Convinc'd,
          ~~But know,~~ the Study of Mankind is <u>Man</u>;
     (Plac'd on this Isthmus of a Middle <u>State</u>,
     A Being darkly wise, and rudely great;
     With too much Knowledge for the Sceptic side,
          With
     ~~And~~ too much Weakness for a Stoic's Pride,
                    in doubt to act or
     He hangs between, ~~uncertain where to~~ rest,
                              Part of
     Whether ╱o deem himself a ⌃God or Beast;
          In doubt
     Whether his Mind, or Body to prefer.
     ~~This born~~   ~~that~~
     Born but to die, and reas'ning but to err;
     Alike in Ignorance, his Reason such,
          Whether he thinks   or too much.
     ~~Who thinks~~ too little, ~~or who thinks too much:~~
     Chaos of Thought and Passion, all confus'd,
     Still by himself abus'd and dis-abus'd:
     Created half to rise, and half to fall;
     Great Lord of all things, yet a prey to all;
     Sole Judge of Truth, in endless error hurl'd;
     The Glory, Jest, and Riddle of the World!

2. In this version of the manuscript, Pope inserted some marginal glosses. In the right-hand margin (next to the line beginning "Learn we ourselves . . ."), he wrote, "Of Man, as an Individual," while next to the line beginning "Plac'd on this Isthmus . . . ," he wrote, "His Middle Nature." And in the left-hand margin, a little below the line beginning "With too much knowledge . . . ," he wrote, "His Powers, and Imperfections."

SAMUEL JOHNSON

Johnson told Boswell in 1766 that when composing verses "I have generally had them in my mind, perhaps fifty at a time, walking up and down in my room; and then I have written them down, and often, from laziness, have written only half lines. . . . I remember I wrote a hundred lines of *The Vanity of Human Wishes* in a day." When the first manuscript draft of this poem turned up in the 1940s among Boswell's papers at Malahide Castle, it supported Johnson's account, for it had been written and corrected in haste, with only sparse punctuation; also the second half of each line had been filled out, obviously from memory, at some time after the writing of the first half, in a darker ink. In the transcriptions from this manuscript (which is in the collection of Mary Hyde, Somerville, New Jersey), the half-lines and emendations that Johnson added to his initial draft are printed in boldface type.

The draft was written on the right-hand pages of a small homemade pocket book;

some words in the added half-line, impinging on the right margin of the page, had to be completed above or below the line. The two added lines, "See Nations slowly wise . . . the tardy Bust," were written on the blank left-hand page, at the place where they were to be inserted. The numeration of every tenth line was added by Johnson in the manuscript and incorporates these two additional lines.

Johnson published the poem in 1749 and revised it for a second publication in 1755, when it achieved the final form printed in the selections from Johnson, above. It was in 1755 that Johnson introduced his most famous emendation, when, after his disillusionment with Lord Chesterfield as literary patron, he substituted in line 162 the word "patron" for "garret": "Toil, envy, want, the patron, and the jail."

From The Vanity of Human Wishes

[*Lines 135–64*]

When first the College Rolls receive his nam^e
The young Enthusiast quits his ease for fame

Quick fires his breast
~~Each act betrays~~ the fever of renown
Caught from the strong Contagion of the Gown
On Isis banks he wakes, from noise withdrawn
140 In sober state th' imaginary Lawn
O'er Bodley's Dome his future Labours spread
And Bacon's Mansion trembles o'er his head.
Are these thy views, proceed illustrious Youth
And Virtue guard thee to the throne of Trut^h
Yet should thy ~~fate~~ Soul indulge the gen'rous
                                                        Heat
Till Captive Science yields her last Retreat
Should Reason guide thee with her brightest Ray
And pour on misty Doubt resistless day
Should no false kindness lure to loose delight
150 Nor Praise relax, nor difficulty fright
Should tempting Novelty thy cell refrain
                                                        vain
And Sloth's bland opiates shed their fumes in
sShould Beuty blunt on fops her fatal dart
Nor claim the triumph of a letter'd heart
~~S Nor~~ Should no Disease thy torpid veins invade
Nor Melancholys Spectres haunt thy Shade
                    hope
Yet ~~dream~~ not Life from Grief or Danger free,
Nor think the doom of Man revers'd for thee
Deign   passing   to
~~Turn~~ on the world ~~awhile~~ turn thine eyes
160 And pause awhile from Learning to be wise
There mark what ill the Scholar's life assail
                                                the
See Nations slowly wise, and meanly just,   Toil envy Want ~~a~~ Garret and the Jayl
To buried merit raise the tardy Bust.   Dreams
                                             If ~~Hope~~ yet flatter once again attend
                                             Hear Lydiats life and Galileo's End.

THOMAS GRAY

There are three manuscript versions of the *Elegy* in Gray's handwriting. The one reproduced here in part is the earliest of these, preserved at Eton College, England; Gray entitled it "Stanzas wrote in a Country Church-Yard."

It is evident that Gray originally intended to conclude his poem at the end of the fifth stanza transcribed below. At some later time he bracketed off the last four stanzas, introduced a transitional stanza that incorporated the last two lines of the original conclusion, and then went on to write a new and much enlarged conclusion to the poem, which includes the closing "Epitaph." A comparison with the final version of the *Elegy*, above, will show that the author deleted some of these added stanzas, and also made a number of verbal changes, in his published texts of the poem.

From Elegy Written in a Country Churchyard

[*Lines 69–128*]

The struggleing Pangs of conscious Truth to hide,
To quench the Blushes of ingenuous Shame,
       crown
And at the Shrine of Luxury & Pride
 With   by
~~Burn~~ Incense hallowd in the Muse's Flame.
      kindled at

The thoughtless World to Majesty may bow
Exalt the brave, & idolize Success
But more to Innocence their Safety owe
Than Power & Genius e'er conspired to bless

And thou, who mindful of the unhonour'd Dead
             eir
Dost in these notes thy artless Tale relate
By Night & lonely Contemplation led
To linger in the gloomy Walks of Fate

Hark how the sacred Calm, that broods around
Bids ev'ry fierce tumultuous Passion cease
In still small Accents whisp'ring from the Ground
A grateful Earnest of eternal Peace

No more with Reason & thyself at Strife
Give anxious Cares & endless Wishes room
But thro' the cool sequester'd Vale of Life
Pursue the silent Tenour of thy Doom.

Far from the madding Crowd's ignoble Strife;
Their sober Wishes never knew to stray:
Along the cool sequester'd Vale of Life
        noiseless
They kept the silent Tenour of their Way.

Yet even these Bones from Insult to protect
Some frail Memorial still erected nigh

With
~~In~~ uncouth Rhime, & shapeless Sculpture deckt
Implores the passing Tribute of a Sigh.

Their Name, their Years, spelt by th' unletter'd Muse
The Place of Fame, & Epitaph supply,
And many a holy Text around she strews
That teach the rustic Moralist to die.

For who to dumb Forgetfulness a Prey
This pleasing anxious Being e'er resign'd;
Left the warm Precincts of the chearful Day,
Nor cast one longing lingring Look behind?

On some fond Breast the parting Soul relies,
Some pious Drops the closing Eye requires:
Even from the Tomb the Voice of Nature cries,
And buried Ashes glow with social Fires
      For Thee, who mindful &c: as above.[1]

If chance that e'er some pensive Spirit more,
By sympathetic Musings here delay'd,
With vain, tho' kind, Enquiry shall explore
Thy once-loved Haunt, this long-deserted Shade.

Haply some hoary-headed Swain shall say,[2]
Oft have we seen him at the Peep of Dawn
With hasty Footsteps brush the Dews away
On the high Brow of yonder hanging Lawn
Him have we seen the Green-wood Side along,
While o'er the Heath we hied, our Labours done,
Oft as the Woodlark piped her farewell Song
With whistful Eyes pursue the setting Sun.
                              spreading   nodding
Oft at the Foot of yonder hoary Beech
That wreathes its old fantastic Roots so high
His listless Length at Noontide would he stretch,
And pore upon the Brook that babbles by.
With Gestures quaint now smileing as in Scorn,
                    wayward fancies   ~~loved~~ would he
Mutt'ring his fond Conceits he ~~wont to~~ rove:
          drooping,
Now woeful wan, ~~he droop'd,~~ as one forlorn
Or crazed with Care, or cross'd in hopeless Love.
      One Morn we miss'd him on th' accustom'd Hill,
      Along the   near
By the Heath-~~side,~~ & at his fav'rite Tree.
Another came, nor yet beside the Rill,
                              by
Nor up the Lawn, nor at the Wood was he.

---

1. I.e., Gray indicates that the second bracketed stanza, above, is to be inserted here, except that the opening "And thou" is to be altered to "For Thee."
2. At this point in the manuscript Gray ceases to leave a space between the stanzas. The first edition of 1751, at Gray's request, was printed without such spaces. They were, however, inserted in later editions printed during Gray's lifetime.

~~There scatter'd oft, the earliest~~
The next with Dirges meet in sad Array
    by
Slow thro the Church-way Path we saw him born
Approach & read, for thou can'st read the Lay
  Graved carved   yon
Wrote on the Stone beneath that ancient Thorn
                                 Year
There scatter'd oft the earliest of y^e ~~Spring~~
                        showers of
By Hands unseen are frequent Vi'lets found
  Redbreast
The Robin loves to build & warble there,
And little Footsteps lightly print the Ground.

Here rests his Head upon the Lap of Earth[3]
A Youth to Fortune & to Fame unknown
Fair Science frown'd not on his humble Birth
And Melancholy mark'd him for her own

Large was his Bounty & his Heart sincere;
Heaven did a Recompence as largely send.
He gave to Mis'ry all he had, a Tear.
He gain'd from Heav'n, 'twas all he wish'd, a Friend

No farther seek his Merits to disclose,
  think
Nor seek to draw them from their dread Abode
(His Frailties there in trembling Hope repose)
The Bosom of his Father & his God.

---

3. These last three stanzas (which Gray in the first edition of 1751 labeled "The Epitaph") are written in the right-hand margin, with the page turned crosswise.

Selected Bibliographies

The Selected Bibliographies consist of a list of Suggested General Readings on English literature, followed by bibliographies for each of the literary periods in this volume. For ease of reference, the authors within each period are arranged in alphabetical order. Entries for certain classes of writings (e.g., "Literature of the Sacred") are included, in alphabetical order, within the listings for individual authors.

SUGGESTED GENERAL READINGS

Histories of England and of English Literature

New research and new perspectives have made even the most distinguished of the comprehensive, general histories written in past generations seem outmoded. Innovative research in social, cultural, and political history has made it difficult to write a single, coherent account of England from the Middle Ages to the present, let alone to accommodate in a unified narrative the complex histories of Scotland, Ireland, and Wales. Readers who wish to explore the historical matrix out of which the works of literature collected in this anthology emerged are advised to consult the studies of particular periods listed in the appropriate sections of this bibliography. The multivolume *Oxford History of England* is useful, as are the three-volume *Peoples of the British Isles: A New History*, ed. Stanford Lehmberg, 1992, and the nine-volume *Cambridge Cultural History of Britain*, ed. Boris Ford, 1992. Albert Baugh et al., *A Literary History of England*, rev. 1967, remains a convenient source of factual materials about authors, works, and chronology. Given the cultural centrality of London, readers may find Roy Porter's *London: A Social History*, 1994, valuable. Similar observations may be made about literary history. In the light of such initiatives as women's studies, new historicism, and postcolonialism, the range of authors deemed most significant has expanded in recent years, along with the geographical and conceptual boundaries of literature in English. Attempts to capture in a unified account the great sweep of literature from *Beowulf* to late last night have largely given way to studies of individual genres, carefully delimited time periods, and specific authors. For these more focused accounts, see the listings by period.

Among the large-scale literary surveys, *The Cambridge Guide to Literature in English*, 1993, is useful, as is *The Penguin History of Literature*. *The Feminist Companion to Literature in English*, ed. Virginia Blain, Isobel Grundy, and Patricia Clements, 1990, is an important resource, and the editorial materials in *The Norton Anthology of Literature by Women*, 2nd ed., 1996, ed. Sandra M. Gilbert and Susan Gubar, constitute a concise history and set of biographies of women authors since the Middle Ages. *Annals of English Literature, 1475–1950*, rev. 1961, lists important publications year by year, together with the significant literary events for each year. David Daiches, *A Critical History of English Literature*, 2 vols., rev. 1970, provides a running literary appreciation.

Helpful treatments and surveys of English meter, rhyme, and stanza forms are Paul Fussell Jr., *Poetic Meter and Poetic Form*, rev. 1979; Donald Wesling, *The Chances of Rhyme: Device and Modernity*, 1980; Derek Attridge, *The Rhythms of English Poetry*, 1982; Charles O. Hartman, *Free Verse: An Essay in Prosody*, 1983; John Hollander, *Vision and Resonance: Two Senses of Poetic Form*, rev. 1985; and Robert Pinsky, *The Sounds of Poetry: A Brief Guide*, 1998.

On the development of the novel as a form, see Ian Watt, *The Rise of the Novel*, 1957; *The Columbia History of the British Novel*, ed. John Richetti, 1994; and Margaret Doody, *The True Story of the Novel*, 1996. On women novelists and readers, see Nancy Armstrong, *Desire and Domestic Fiction: A Political History of the Novel*, 1987; and Catherine Gallagher, *Nobody's Story: The Vanishing Acts of Women Writers in the Marketplace, 1670–1820*, 1994.

On the history of playhouse design, see Richard Leacroft, *The Development of the English Playhouse: An Illustrated Survey of Theatre Building in England from Medieval to Modern Times*, 1988. For a survey of the plays that have appeared on these and other stages, see Allardyce Nicoll, *British Drama*, rev. 1962, and the eight-volume *Revels History of Drama in English*, gen. eds. Clifford Leech and T. W. Craik, 1975–83.

On some of the key intellectual currents that are at once reflected in and shaped by English literature, Arthur O. Lovejoy's classic studies *The Great*

Chain of Being, 1936, and *Essays in the History of Ideas,* 1948, remain valuable, along with such works as Lovejoy and George Boas, *Primitivism and Related Ideas in Antiquity,* 1935; Ernst Kantorowicz, *The King's Two Bodies: A Study in Medieval Political Theology,* 1957, new ed. 1997; Richard Popkin, *The History of Skepticism from Erasmus to Descartes,* 1960; M. H. Abrams, *Natural Supernaturalism: Tradition and Revolution in Romantic Literature,* 1971; and Michel Foucault, *Madness and Civilization: A History of Insanity in the Age of Reason,* Eng. trans. 1965, and *The Order of Things: An Archaeology of the Human Sciences,* Eng. trans. 1970.

Reference Works

The single most important tool for the study of literature in English is the *Oxford English Dictionary,* 2nd ed., 1989, also available on CD-ROM. The *OED* is written on historical principles: that is, it attempts not only to describe current word use but also to record the history and development of the language from its origins before the Norman conquest to the present. It thus provides, for familiar as well as archaic and obscure words, the widest possible range of meanings and uses, organized chronologically and illustrated with quotations. Beyond the *OED* there are many other valuable dictionaries, such as *The American Heritage Dictionary, The Oxford Dictionary of Etymology,* and an array of reference works from *The Cambridge Encyclopedia of the English Language,* ed. David Crystal, 1995, to guides to specialized vocabularies, slang, regional dialects, and the like.

There is a steady flow of new editions of most major and many minor writers in English, along with a ceaseless outpouring of critical appraisals and scholarship. The *MLA International Bibliography* (also on line) is the best way to keep abreast of the most recent work and to conduct bibliographic searches. *The New Cambridge Bibliography of English Literature* ed. George Watson, 1969–77, updated shorter ed. 1981, is a valuable guide to the huge body of earlier literary criticism and scholarship. *A Guide to English and American Literature,* ed. F. W. Bateson and Harrison Meserole, rev. 1976, is a selected list of editions, as well as scholarly and critical treatments. Further bibliographical aids are described in Arthur G. Kennedy, *A Concise Bibliography for Students of English,* rev. 1972; Richard D. Altick and Andrew Wright, *Selective Bibliography for the Study of English and American Literature* rev. 1979, and James L. Harner, *Literary Research Guide,* rev. 1998.

For compact biographies of English authors, see the multivolume *Dictionary of National Biography,* ed. Leslie Stephen and Sidney Lee, 1885–1900, with supplements that carry the work to 1980; condensed biographies will be found in the *Concise Dictionary of National Biography,* 2 parts (1920, 1988). Handy reference books of authors, works, and various literary terms and allusions are *The Oxford Companion to the Theatre,* Phyllis Hartnoll,

rev. 1990; *Princeton Encyclopedia of Poetry and Poetics,* ed. Alex Preminger and others, rev. 1993; and *The Oxford Companion to English Literature,* ed. Margaret Drabble, rev. 1998. Low-priced handbooks that define and illustrate literary concepts and terms are *The Penguin Dictionary of Literary Terms and Literary Theory,* ed. J. A. Cuddon, 1991; W. F. Thrall and Addison Hibbard, *A Handbook to Literature,* ed. C. Hugh Holman, rev. 1992; *Critical Terms for Literary Study,* ed. Frank Lentricchia and Thomas McLaughlin, rev. 1995; and M. H. Abrams, *A Glossary of Literary Terms,* rev. 1992. On Greek and Roman background, see G. M. Kirkwood, *A Short Guide to Classical Mythology,* 1959; *The Oxford Classical Dictionary,* rev. 1996; and *The Oxford Companion to Classical Literature,* ed. M. C. Howatson and Ian Chilvers, rev. 1993.

Literary Criticism and Theory

Three volumes of the *Cambridge History of Literary Criticism* have been published, 1989–: *Classical Criticism,* ed. George A. Kennedy; *The Eighteenth Century,* ed. H. B. Nisbet and Claude Rawson; and *From Formalism to Poststructuralism,* ed. Raman Selden. See also M. H. Abrams, *The Mirror and the Lamp: Romantic Theory and the Critical Tradition,* 1953; William K. Wimsatt and Cleanth Brooks, *Literary Criticism: A Short History,* 1957; George Watson, *The Literary Critics,* 1962; René Wellek, *A History of Modern Criticism: 1750–1950,* 9 vols., 1955–1993; Frank Lentricchia, *After the New Criticism,* 1980; and *Redrawing the Boundaries: The Transformation of English and American Literary Studies,* ed. Stephen Greenblatt and Giles Gunn, 1992. Raman Selden, Peter Widdowson, and Peter Brooker have written *A Reader's Guide to Contemporary Literary Theory,* 1997.

The following is a selection of books in literary criticism that have been notably influential in shaping modern approaches to English literature and literary forms: Lionel Trilling, *The Liberal Imagination,* 1950; T. S. Eliot, *Selected Essays,* 3rd ed. 1951, and *On Poetry and Poets,* 1957; Erich Auerbach, *Mimesis: The Representation of Reality in Western Literature,* 1953; William Empson, *Seven Types of Ambiguity,* 3rd ed. 1953; William K. Wimsalt, *The Verbal Icon,* 1954; Northrop Frye, *Anatomy of Criticism,* 1957; Wayne C. Booth, *The Rhetoric of Fiction,* 1961, rev. ed. 1983; W. J. Bate, *The Burden of the Past and the English Poet,* 1970; Harold Bloom, *The Anxiety of Influence,* 1973; and Paul de Man, *Allegories of Reading,* 1979.

René Wellek and Austin Warren, *Theory of Literature,* rev. 1970, is a useful introduction to the variety of scholarly and critical approaches to literature up to the time of its publication. Jonathan Culler's *Literary Theory: A Very Short Introduction,* 1997, discusses recurrent issues and debates. Modern feminist literary criticism was fashioned by such works as Patricia Meyers Spacks, *The Female Imagination,* 1975; Ellen Moers, *Literary Women,* 1976; Elaine Showalter, *A Literature of Their Own,* 1977; and Sandra Gilbert and Susan Gubar, *The Mad-*

woman in the Attic, 1979. More recent studies include Jane Gallop, *The Daughter's Seduction: Feminism and Psychoanalysis*, 1982; Gayatri Chakravorty Spivak, *In Other Worlds: Essays in Cultural Politics*, 1987; Sandra Gilbert and Susan Gubar, *No Man's Land: The Place of the Woman Writer in the Twentieth Century*, 2 vols., 1988–89; Barbara Johnson, *A World of Difference*, 1989; Judith Butler, *Gender Trouble*, 1990; and the critical views sampled in Elaine Showalter, *The New Feminist Criticism*, 1985; *Feminist Literary Theory: A Reader*, ed. Mary Eagleton, 2nd ed., 1995; and *Feminisms: An Anthology of Literary Theory and Criticism*, ed. Robyn R. Warhol and Diane Price Herndl, 2nd ed. 1997. Gay and lesbian studies and criticism are represented in *The Lesbian and Gay Studies Reader*, ed. Henry Abelove, Michele Barale, and David Halperin, 1993, and by such books as Eve Sedgwick, *Between Men: English Literature and Male Homosocial Desire*, 1985, and *Epistemology of the Closet*, 1990; Diana Fuss, *Essentially Speaking: Feminism, Nature, and Difference*, 1989; and Gregory Woods, *A History of Gay Literature: The Male Tradition*, 1998. Convenient introductions to structuralist literary criticism include Robert Scholes, *Structuralism in Literature: An Introduction*, 1974, and Jonathan Culler, *Structuralist Poetics*, 1975. The poststructuralist challenges to this approach are discussed in Jonathan Culler, *On Deconstruction*, 1982; Fredric Jameson, *Poststructuralism; or the Cultural Logic of Late Capitalism*, 1991; John

McGowan, *Postmodernism and Its Critics*, 1991; and *Beyond Structuralism*, ed. Wendell Harris, 1996. New historicism is represented in Stephen Greenblatt, *Learning to Curse*, 1990, and in the essays collected in *The New Historicism*, ed. Harold Veeser, 1989, and *New Historical Literary Study: Essays on Reproducing Texts, Representing History*, ed. Jeffrey N. Cox and Larry J. Reynolds, 1993. The related social and historical dimension of texts is discussed in Jerome McGann, *Critique of Modern Textual Criticism*, 1983, and D. F. McKenzie, *Bibliography and Sociology of Texts*, 1986. Characteristic of new historicism is an expansion of the field of literary interpretation extended still further in cultural studies; for a broad sampling of the range of interests, see *The Cultural Studies Reader*, ed. Simon During, 1993, and *A Cultural Studies Reader: History, Theory, Practice*, ed. Jessica Munns and Gita Rajan, 1997. This expansion of the field is similarly reflected in postcolonial studies: see *The Post-Colonial Studies Reader*, ed. Bill Ashcroft, Gareth Griffiths, and Helen Tiffin, 1995, and such influential books as Ranajit Guha and Gayatri Chakravorti Spivak, *Selected Subaltern Studies*, 1988; Edward Said, *Culture and Imperialism*, 1993; and Homi Bhabha, *The Location of Culture*, 1994.

Anthologies representing a range of recent approaches include *Modern Criticism and Theory*, ed. David Lodge, 1988, and *Contemporary Literary Criticism*, ed. Robert Con Davis and Ronald Schlieffer, rev. 1998.

THE MIDDLE AGES

Scholarship during this era has been divided into the same three periods as in the General Introduction: Anglo-Saxon England, Anglo-Norman England, and Middle English Literature of the Fourteenth and Fifteenth Centuries. A reference book for the whole era is Joseph Strayer et al., *Dictionary of the Middle Ages*, 1982–.

Anglo-Saxon England

D. Whitelock, *The Beginnings of English Society*, 1952, provides concise historical background for the literature of the period. The most detailed history is F. M. Stenton's authoritative *Anglo-Saxon England*, 3rd ed., 1971. Also highly informative are P. Hunter Blair, *An Introduction to Anglo-Saxon England*, 1956, and *Roman Britain and Early England, 55 B.C.–A.D. 871*, 1963. The classic study of the culture of the primitive Germanic peoples is H. M. Chadwick, *The Heroic Age*, 1912. For those who wish to sample basic historical documents of the period, there is available the translation by G. N. Garmonsway of *The Anglo-Saxon Chronicle*, 1953. *The Age of Bede*, ed. D. H. Farmer, rev. 1983, and *Alfred the Great*, ed. S. Keynes and M. Lapidge, 1983, contain texts documenting two crucial periods of Anglo-Saxon history. Bede's *Ecclesiastical History of the English People* is

translated and edited by B. Colgrave and R. A. B. Mynors, 1969. For studies of Bede, see G. H. Brown, *Bede, the Venerable*, 1987, and J. M. Wallace-Hadrill, *Bede's Ecclesiastical History of the English People: A Historical Commentary*, 1993. A lavishly and finely illustrated introduction to Anglo-Saxon England is *The Anglo-Saxons*, ed. J. Campbell, 1982. C. Fell, *Women in Anglo-Saxon England*, 1984, is pertinent to women's studies. The journal *Anglo-Saxon England* is devoted to all aspects of the history and culture of the period.

All the surviving poetry in Old English is contained in the six volumes edited by G. P. Krapp and E. V. K. Dobbie, *The Anglo-Saxon Poetic Records*, 1931–53, but the absence of glossaries makes this edition difficult for nonspecialists. Excellent texts of the shorter poems translated in this anthology are contained in J. C. Pope, *Seven Old English Poems*, 1966, rev. 1981. The standard text of *Beowulf and the Fight of Finnsburg* is F. Klaeber's 3rd ed., 1950; C. L. Wrenn's edition, *Beowulf, with the Finnsburg Fragment*, rev. W. F. Bolton, 1973, rev. 1988, is very useful; H. D. Chickering Jr. has made a dual-language edition with extensive commentary, and G. B. Jack has prepared *Beowulf: A Student Edition*, 1994. There are individual editions of *The Dream of the Rood* by M. Swanton, 1970; of *The Wanderer* by T. P. Dunning and A. J. Bliss, 1969. *The Wanderer* and *The Wife's Lament* are included in *The Old English Elegies: A Critical Edition and Genre Study*, ed. A. L. Klinck, 1992. Modern English translations of many of the Old English poems have been published under various titles by R. K. Gordon, C. W. Kennedy, M. Alexander, S. A. J. Bradley, and K. Crossley-Holland. Many translations of *Beowulf* are available. E. T. Donaldson's translation is used in *Beowulf*, A Norton Critical Edition, ed. J. F. Tuso, 1975.

General discussions of Old English literature will be found in Vol. 1 of the *Cambridge History of English Literature*; S. B. Greenfield and D. G. Calder, *New Critical History of Old English Literature*, 1986; C. L. Wrenn, *A Study of Old English Literature*; M. Alexander, *Old English Literature*, 1983; and *The Cambridge Companion to Old English Literature*, ed. M. Godden and M. Lapidge, 1991.

Some useful studies and collections devoted exclusively to Old English poetry are S. B. Greenfield, *The Interpretation of Old English Poems*, 1972; T. A. Shippey, *Old English Verse*, 1972; J. B. Bessinger Jr. and S. J. Kahrl, *Essential Articles for the Study of Old English Poetry*, 1977; D. A. Pearsall, *Old and Middle English Poetry*, 1977; B. C. Raw, *The Art and Background of Old English Poetry*, 1978; *Old English Poetry: Essays on Style*, ed. D. G. Calder, 1979; *The Old English Elegies*, ed. M. Green, 1983; S. B. Greenfield, *Hero and Exile: The Art of Old English Poetry*, 1989; *De Gustibus*, ed. J. M. Foley et al., 1992; *Heroic Poetry in the Anglo-Saxon Period*, ed. H. Damico and J. Leyerle, 1993; *Companion to Old English Poetry*, ed. H. Aertsen and R. H. Bremmer Jr., 1994; and *Old English Shorter Poems: Basic Readings*, ed. K. O'Brien O'Keeffe, 1994.

General collections of essays on Old English literature include *Old English Literature in Context*, ed. J. D. Niles, 1980; *Literature and Learning in Anglo-Saxon England*, ed. M. Lapidge and H. Gneuss, 1985; *Modes of Interpretation in Old English Literature*, ed. P. R. Brown et al., 1986; F. C. Robinson, *The Tomb of Beowulf and Other Essays on Old English*, 1993; and *Studies in English Language and Literature*, ed. M. J. Toswell and E. M. Tyler, 1996.

Some studies of special topics in Old English literature are J. Chance, *Woman as Hero in Old English Literature*, 1986; *New Readings on Women in Old English Literature*, ed. Helen Damico and A. H. Olsen, 1990; A. J. Frantzen, *Desire for Origins: New Language, Old English, and Teaching the Tradition*, 1990; *The Battle of Maldon AD 991*, ed. D. Scragg, 1991; *Class and Gender in Early English Literature*, ed. B. J. Harwood and G. R. Overing, 1994; and *Holy Men, Holy Women: Old English Prose Saints' Lives and Their Contexts*, ed. P. Szarmach, 1996.

Beowulf

Essential backgrounds to the study of the poem are provided by R. W. Chambers, *Beowulf: An Introduction to the Study of the Poem*, 3rd ed., with a supplement by C. L. Wrenn, 1959; and a wide-ranging overview of *Beowulf* scholarship is furnished by *A Beowulf Handbook*, ed. R. E. Bjork and J. D. Niles, 1997. Important critical studies of the poem are found in D. Whitelock, *The Audience of Beowulf*, 1951; A. G. Brodeur, *The Art of Beowulf*, 1959; E. B. Irving Jr., *A Reading of Beowulf*, 1968, *Introduction to Beowulf*, 1969, and *Rereading Beowulf*, 1990; T. A. Shippey, *Beowulf*, 1978; J. D. Niles, *Beowulf: The Poem and Its Tradition*, 1983; G. Clark, *Beowulf*, 1990; J. W. Earl, *Thinking about Beowulf*, 1994; J. M. Hill, *The Cultural World in Beowulf*, 1995; and C. R. Davis, *Beowulf and the Demise of Germanic Legend in England*, 1996.

For anthologies of criticism, see *The Beowulf Poet*, ed. D. K. Fry, 1968; *Beowulf*, A Norton Critical Edition, ed. J. Tuso, 1975; *Interpretations of Beowulf*, ed. R. D. Fulk, 1991; and *Beowulf: Basic Readings*, ed. P. S. Baker, 1995. Special mention should be made of J. R. R. Tolkien's famous lecture, *Beowulf, the Monsters and the Critics*, 1937, reprinted in the anthologies of Fry and Fulk.

Anglo-Norman England

For accounts of the Norman conquest and its historical consequences, see C. Brooke, *From Alfred to Henry III, 871–1272*, 2 vols., 1961; R. A. Brown, *The Normans*, 1984; A. L. Poole, *From Domesday Book to Magna Carta*, 1955; P. Stafford, *A Political and Social History of England in the Tenth and Eleventh Centuries*, 1989; and F. M. Powicke, *The Thirteenth Century, 1216–1307*, 1953. The *Peterborough Chronicle*, a continuation of the *Anglo-Saxon Chronicle* to the year 1154, relates events from the point of view of English monks and can be read in translation in *The Anglo-Saxon Chronicle: a Revised Translation*, ed. by D. Whitelock with D. C. Douglas and S. I. Tucker, 1961, rev. 1965.

Studies of historical writing within the period itself, including the legendary histories of the kings of Britain, are J. S. P. Tatlock, *The Legendary History of Britain*, 1950; R. W. Hanning, *The Vision of History in Early Britain: From Gildas to Geoffrey of Monmouth*, 1966; and M. Otter, *Inventiones: Fiction and Referentiality in Twelfth-Century Historical Writing*.

On **Geoffrey of Monmouth**, in addition to the texts mentioned above, see the translation of his *History of the Kings of Britain* by Lewis Thorpe, 1966; R. W. Leckie Jr., *The Passage of Dominion: Geoffrey of Monmouth and the Periodization of Insular History in the Twelfth Century*, 1981; and M. J. Curley, *Geoffrey of Monmouth*, 1994. The *Brut* of **Layamon** is available in translations by D. G. Bzdyl, 1989; Rosamund Allen, 1992; and in an edition of the Middle English text with facing translation, notes, and commentary by W. R. J. Barron and S. C. Weinberg, 1989. The Arthurian sections of Wace's *Roman de Brut*, translated by Judith Weiss, and of Layamon in Allen's translation are printed together as *The Life of King Arthur*, 1997.

M. D. Legge, *Anglo-Norman Literature and Its Background*, 1963, is the standard history. The lais of **Marie de France** have been translated by R. H. Hanning and J. Ferrante, 1978, and by G. S. Burgess and K. Busby, 1986. For background and critical interpretations of Marie de France's works, see E. J. Mickel, *Marie de France*, 1974; P. M. Clifford, *Marie de France, Lais*, 1982; and G. S. Burgess, *The Lais of Marie de France*, 1987.

R. M. Wilson's *Early Middle English Literature* focuses primarily on this period. Vol. 1 of the *Oxford History of English Literature*, by J. A. W. Bennett and D. Gray, *Middle English Literature*, 1986, which goes up to 1400 (exclusive of Chaucer), contains excellent discussions of early Middle English texts. Selections of texts from this era with a valuable introduction to the language and annotations are contained in the anthology edited by J. A. W. Bennett and G. V. Smithers, *Early Middle English Verse and Prose*, 2nd ed, 1968. The **Ancrene Riwle** (Anchoresses' rule) is available in a modern translation by Mary Salu, 1963. For a study of the work, called by its variant title *Ancrene Wisse* (Anchoresses' guide), and related early Middle English texts, see B. Millett with G. B. Jack and Y. Wada, *Ancrene Wisse, the Katherine Group, and the Wooing Group*, 1996. For a fine essay on the language and culture of the work, see J. R. R. Tolkien, "*Ancrene Wisse* and *Hali Meidenhad*" in *Essays and Studies*, 14.104–26, 1929. See also the commentary in *Medieval English Prose for Women*, ed. B. Millett and J. Wogan-Browne, 1990, from which the translation printed in this anthology is taken.

Translations of Old Irish literature are available by T. Kinsella in *The Táin from the Irish Epic Táin Bó Cuailnge*, 1969, from which **Exile of the Sons of Uisliu** is taken, and by Jeffrey Gantz, *Early Irish Myths and Sagas*, 1981. For background, see K. H. Jackson, *The Oldest Irish Tradition: A Window on the Iron Age*, 1964; K. McCone, *Pagan Past and Christian Present in Early Irish Literature*, 1990; and J. E. Caerwyn Williams and P. K. Ford, *The Irish Literary Tradition*, 1992.

Llud and Lleuelys is taken from P. K. Ford's translation, *The Mabinogi and Other Medieval Welsh Tales*, 1977. Jeffrey Gantz has also translated the *Mabinogion*, 1976, with a useful introduction, bibliography, and commentary on individual selections. On Welsh literature in general, see K. Jackson, *Language and History in Early Britain*, 1953, and *A Guide to Welsh Literature*, vol. 1, ed. A. O. H. Jarman and G. R. Hughes, 1976. Specific commentary on the *Mabinogion* may be found in S. Davies, *The Four Branches of The Mabinogi*, 1993; C. Matthews, *Mabon and the Mysteries of Britain: An Exploration of The Mabinogion*, 1987; P. MacCana, *The Mabinogi*, 1992; and W. J. Gruffyd, *Folklore and Myth in The Mabinogion*, 1994.

For discussions of the Arthurian materials in Geoffrey of Monmouth, Wace, Marie de France, Layamon, and the *Mabinogi*, see chaps. 4 and 8 to 11 in *Arthurian Literature in the Middle Ages*, ed. R. S. Loomis, 1959.

Middle English Literature of the Fourteenth and Fifteenth Centuries

Histories of the period include G. Holmes, *The Later Middle Ages, 1272–1485*, 1962; M. McKisack, *The Fourteenth Century, 1307–99*, 1959; and E. F. Jacob, *The Fifteenth Century*, 1961. Accounts of life and society during this period are provided by G. G. Coulton in *Chaucer and His England*, 1908, *The Medieval Scene*, 1930, and *Medieval Panorama*, 1938; E. Rickert, *Chaucer's World*, 1948; G. M. Trevelyan, *Chaucer's England and the Early Tudors*, vol. 1 of *The Illustrated English Social History*, 1949; and M. Keen, *English Society in the Later Middle Ages*, 1990. See also the picture books listed under Chaucer. J. Huizinga has written a famous account of the culture and spirit of the late fourteenth to fifteenth centuries, formerly translated as *The Waning of the Middle Ages*, 1924, now available in a fuller text under the more accurate title, *The Autumn of the Middle Ages*, trans. R. J. Payton and U. Mammitzsch, 1996. F. R. H. Du Boulay complements and qualifies Huizinga in *An Age of Ambition*, 1970. Chaps. 6 to 10 in E. Auerbach's *Mimesis: The Representation of Reality in Western Literature*, trans. by W. R. Trask, 1953, although it does not deal with works in this anthology, gives penetrating insights into the reading of medieval texts. C. S. Lewis, *The Discarded Image: An Introduction to Medieval and Renaissance Literature*, 1964, seeks to restore for modern readers the perspective and sensibilities of the earlier age.

For general discussion of late Middle English literature, see the *The Oxford History of English Literature*: J. A. W. Bennett and D. Gray, *Middle English Literature*, 1986, vol. 1, part 2 (up to 1400, exclusive of Chaucer); H. S. Bennett, *Chaucer and the Fifteenth Century*, vol. 2, part 1, 1947, and E. K. Chambers, *English Literature at the Close of the Middle Ages*, vol. 2, part 2, 1954; also D. A. Pearsall, *Old and Middle English Poetry*, 1977; J. A. Burrow, *Middle English Literature and Its Background*, 1982; and D. S. Brewer, *English Gothic Literature*, 1983.

Critical works devoted to more than one author or genre in the period are G. Kane, *Middle English Literature*, 1951 (chapters on the romances, the religious lyrics, and *Piers Plowman*); J. A. Burrow, *Ricardian Poetry: Chaucer, Gower, Langland, and the Gawain Poet*, 1971; C. Muscatine, *Poetry and Crisis in the Age of Chaucer*, 1972; A. C. Spearing, *Medieval Dream Poetry*, 1976, and *Readings in Medieval Poetry*, 1987; T. Turville-Petre, *The Alliterative Revival*, 1977; *Medieval Literature: Chaucer and the Alliterative Tradition*, vol. 1 of *The New Pelican Guide to English Literature*, ed. Boris Ford, 1982; D. Despres, *Ghostly Sights: Visual Meditation in Late-Medieval Literature*, 1989; S. Justice, *Writing and Rebellion: England in 1381*, 1994; and G. Margherita, *The Romance of Origins: Language and Sexual Difference in Middle English Literature*, 1994. *Middle English Survey: Critical Essays*, ed. E. Vasta, 1965, contains commentary on Langland, *Gawain*, and drama.

For the Middle English language, see Helge Kökeritz, *A Guide to Chaucer's Pronunciation*, 1954; David Burnley, *A Guide to Chaucer's Language*, 1983; and J. A. Burrow and T. Turville-Petre, *A Book of Middle English*, 1996.

The standard bibliography is *A Manual of the Writings in Middle English, 1050–1500*, 6 vols., ed. J. B. Severs, A. E. Hartung, et al., 1967–80, which is based on and supersedes the *Manual* of J. E. Wells, 1916, with nine supplements through 1945.

Geoffrey Chaucer

The standard edition of Chaucer's writing is *The Riverside Chaucer*, 3rd ed., ed. L. D. Benson et al., 1987, based on F. N. Robinson's edition. E. Talbot Donaldson, *Chaucer's Poetry*, 2nd ed., 1975, from which are taken the selections printed here, is helpful to the nonspecialist, as are John H. Fisher, *The Complete Poetry and Prose of Geoffrey Chaucer*, 2nd ed., 1989, and V. A. Kolve and Glending Olson, *The Canterbury Tales: Nine Tales and The "General Prologue,"* Norton Critical Edition, 1989. Vivid presentations of Chaucer in the background of fourteenth-century England are found in D. S. Brewer, *Chaucer and His World*, 1978, which is beautifully illustrated, and *A New Introduction to Chaucer*, 2nd ed., 1998. Pictorial companions to Chaucer's works, especially the *Canterbury Tales*, include R. S. Loomis, *A Mirror of Chaucer's World*, 1965, Maurice Hussey, *Chaucer's World*, 1967, Ian Serraillier, *Chaucer and His World*, 1968, and Roger Hart, *English Life in Chaucer's Day*, 1973.

The raw material for Chaucer's biography is contained in *Chaucer Life-Records*, ed. M. M. Crow and C. C. Olson, 1966. D. R. Howard, *Chaucer: His Life, His Works, His World*, 1987, and D. A. Pearsall, *The Life of Geoffrey Chaucer*, 1992, contain extensive background and interpretation. For succinct accounts of the sources and literary background of Chaucer's works, see R. D. French, *A Chaucer Handbook*, 2nd ed., 1947; reproductions of many of the known sources of the *Canterbury Tales* are contained in *Sources and Analogues of Chaucer's Canterbury Tales*, ed. W. F. Bryan and Germaine Dempster, 1941, 1958. Useful literary materials are collected in R. P. Miller, *Chaucer: Sources and Backgrounds*, 1977. Muriel Bowden, *A Commentary on the General Prologue to the Canterbury Tales*, 1948, provides a wealth of background information on the individual Canterbury pilgrims; see also Jill Mann, *Chaucer and Medieval Estates Satire*, 1973. Various aspects of Chaucer's work are treated by a number of scholars in *Chaucer and Chaucerians*, ed. D. S. Brewer, 1966; *Geoffrey Chaucer (Writers and Their Background)*, ed. D. S. Brewer, 1974; *Companion to Chaucer Studies*, ed. Beryl Rowland, rev. 1979; and *The Cambridge Chaucer Companion*, ed. Piero Boitani and Jill Mann, 1986.

For literary criticism on both *The Canterbury Tales* and other works by Chaucer, the following contain stimulating discussions: G. L. Kittredge, *Chaucer and His Poetry*, 1915; J. L. Lowes, *Geoffrey Chaucer and the Development of His Genius*, 1934; C. Muscatine, *Chaucer and the French Tradition*, 1957; W. C. Curry, *Chaucer and the Medieval Sciences*, rev. 1960; R. O. Payne, *The Key of Remembrance*, 1963; M. Hussey, A. C. Spearing, and J. Winny, *An Introduction to Chaucer*, 1965; E. T. Donaldson, *Speaking of Chaucer*, 1970; T. Ross, *Chaucer's Bawdy*, 1972; D. S. Brewer, *Chaucer*, 3rd ed., 1973; P. Elbow, *Oppositions in Chaucer*, 1975; A. David, *The Strumpet Muse: Art and Morals in Chaucer's Poetry*, 1976; R. Burlin, *Chaucerian Fiction*, 1977; G. Kane, *Chaucer*, 1984; S. Knight, *Geoffrey Chaucer*, 1986; D. Wallace, *Chaucerian Polity: Absolutist Lineages and Associational Forms in England and Italy*, 1997; and R. P. McGerr, *Chaucer's Open Book: Resistance to Closure in Medieval Discourse*, 1998.

Criticism that deals mainly with *The Canterbury Tales* and with earlier commentary on it includes P. Ruggiers, *The Art of The Canterbury Tales*, 1964; D. R. Howard, *The Idea of The Canterbury Tales*, 1976; T. Lawler, *The One and the Many in The Canterbury Tales*, 1980; D. Pearsall, *The Canterbury Tales*, 1985; C. D. Benson, *Chaucer's Drama of Style: Poetic Variety in The Canterbury Tales*, 1986; W. Wetherbee, *Geoffrey Chaucer: The Canterbury Tales*, 1989; H. M. Leicester Jr., *The Disenchanted Self: Representing the Subject in The Canterbury Tales*, 1990; S. Crane, *Gender and Romance in Chaucer's Canterbury Tales*, 1994; and H. Cooper, *The Canterbury Tales*, Oxford Guides to Chaucer, 2nd ed., 1996.

D. W. Robertson's *A Preface to Chaucer*, 1962, is a learned and stimulating introduction to the reading of Chaucer in the light of medieval aesthetic doctrines. V. A. Kolve, *Chaucer and the Imagery of Narrative*, 1984, relates the first five of the *Canterbury Tales* to medieval art. Several recent books stress the importance of oral delivery, performance, and storytelling in the *Canterbury Tales*: Betsy Bowden, *Chaucer Aloud*, 1987; Carl Lindahl, *Earnest Games: Folkloric Patterns in The Canterbury Tales*, 1987; L. M. Koff, *Chaucer and the Art of Storytelling*, 1988; and J. M. Ganim, *Chaucerian Theatricality*, 1990. The following studies relate Chaucer's works to their social and historical background: Paul Strohm, *Social Chaucer*, 1989; Peggy Knapp, *Chaucer and the Social Contest*, 1990; Peter Brown and Andrew Butcher, *The Age of Saturn: Literature and History in The Canterbury Tales*, 1991; and Lee Patterson, *Chaucer and the Subject of History*, 1991. A pioneer feminist study of Chaucer is Carolyn Dinshaw, *Chaucer's Sexual Poetics*, 1989; see also E. T. Hansen, *Chaucer and the Fictions of Gender*, 1992.

The following are collections of critical essays: *Chaucer: Modern Essays in Criticism*, ed. E. C. Wagenknecht, 1959; *Chaucer Criticism: The Canterbury Tales*, ed. R. J. Schoeck and J. Taylor, 1960; *Discussions of The Canterbury Tales*, ed. C. J. Owen, 1961; *Geoffrey Chaucer: A Critical Anthology*, ed. J. A. Burrow, 1969; and *Geoffrey Chaucer Contemporary Studies in Literature*, ed. G. D. Economou,

1975. See also the prefatory remarks on individual works and tales in *The Riverside Chaucer* and the commentary in E. Talbot Donaldson's anthology, cited above.

Perhaps the most reliable glossary is that edited by Norman Davis et al., 1979. The standard bibliographies are E. P. Hammond, *Chaucer: A Bibliographical Manual*, 1908; D. D. Griffith, *Bibliography of Chaucer*, 1955; W. R. Crawford, *1954–63*, 1967; L. Y. Baird, *1964–73*, 1977; and L. Y. Baird-Lange and H. Schnutgen, *1974–85*, 1988. Two very useful annotated bibliographies are by Mark Allen and J. H. Fisher, *The Essential Chaucer*, 1987, and John Leyerle and Anne Quick, *Chaucer: A Bibliographical Introduction*, 1986. *Studies in the Age of Chaucer*, the journal of The New Chaucer Society publishes a current bibliography as well as articles on Chaucer and other medieval literature. See also Caroline Spurgeon, *Five Hundred Years of Chaucer Criticism and Allusion, 1357–1900*, 1925.

Everyman
See entries under **Mystery Plays; Everyman.**

Robert Henryson
The Poems of Robert Henryson, ed. D. Fox, 1980 and 1987, is the standard edition. *The Moral Fables of Aesop*, ed. G. D. Copen, 1987, has a facing page prose translation. For background and criticism, see J. MacQueen, *Robert Henryson: A Study of the Major Poems*, 1967, and D. Gray, *Robert Henryson*, 1979.

Julian of Norwich
The standard Middle English text with a wealth of commentary is *A Book of Showings to the Anchoress Julian of Norwich*, 2 vols., ed. Edmund Colledge and James Walsh, 1978. The editors' translation is published as *Julian of Norwich: Showings*, 1978; another translation of the long text by Clifton Walters is published under the title *Revelations of Divine Love*, 1966. Another edition of the long text, ed. G. R. Crampton, 1994, published for TEAMS (Consortium for the Teaching of the Middle Ages) is designed for students.

General studies of mystical writing in England and on the Continent are W. Riehle, *The Middle English Mystics*, trans. B. Standring, 1981; *An Introduction to the Medieval Mystics of Europe*, ed. P. Szarmach, 1984; A. K. Warren, *Anchorites and their Patrons in Medieval England*, 1985; F. Beer, *Women and Mystical Experience in the Middle Ages*, 1992; S. Beckwith, *Christ's Body: Identity, Culture, and Society in Late Medieval Writings*, 1993; and D. Aers and L. Staley, *The Powers of the Holy: Religion, Politics, and Gender in Late Medieval English Culture*, 1996. Studies helpful to understanding the mystical thought of Julian of Norwich are B. Pelphrey, *Christ Our Mother*, 1989, and D. N. Baker, *Julian of Norwich's Showing: From Vision to Book*, 1994.

Margery Kempe
The standard Middle English text of *The Book of Margery Kempe* is that of S. B. Meech and H. E.

Allen, 1940. Another edition, ed. L. Staley, 1996, for TEAMS (Consortium for the Teaching of Middle English) is designed for students. Barry Windeatt has made a translation, 1985, with notes and a helpful introduction. For general studies of mystical writings, see under Julian of Norwich. Studies of Kempe are C. W. Atkinson, *Mystic and Pilgrim: The Book and the World of Margery Kempe*, 1983; K. Lochrie, *Margery Kempe and Translations of the Flesh*, 1991; *Margery Kempe: A Book of Essays*, S. McEntire, ed., 1992; and L. S. Johnson, *Margery Kempe's Dissenting Fictions*, 1994. Gibson, cited under **Mystery Plays**, provides background on Kempe's region and includes a chapter on Kempe.

William Langland
The most handy edition is A. V. C. Schmidt, *The Vision of Piers Plowman: A Complete Edition of the B-Text*, 1978. W. W. Skeat, *The Vision of William Concerning Piers the Plowman . . .* , 2 vols., 1886, gives all three versions side by side; the commentary and notes in volume 2 remain invaluable. The Athlone edition, based on all extant manuscripts, has the A text, ed. G. Kane, 1960, the B text, ed. Kane and E. T. Donaldson, 1975, and the C text, ed. Kane and G. H. Russell, 1997. J. A. W. Bennett's edition of the first eight passus of the B text, 1972, is very useful, as is D. A. Pearsall's edition of the C text, 1978. The selections here are taken from E. T. Donaldson's *Piers Plowman: An Alliterative Verse Translation*, 1990. A literal prose translation is J. F. Goodridge, *Langland: Piers the Ploughman*, rev. 1966. The best general account of the poem is in chap. 4 and 5 of R. W. Chambers, *Man's Unconquerable Mind*, 1939; see also Kane's chapter in *Middle English Literature. A Companion to Piers Plowman*, ed. J. A. Alford, 1988, has essays and extensive bibliographies on many aspects of the poem. Book-length studies helpful to the student as well as the specialist include R. W. Frank, *Piers Plowman and the Scheme of Salvation*, 1957; Elizabeth Salter, *Piers Plowman: An Introduction*, 1962; E. D. Kirk, *The Dream Thought of Piers Plowman*, 1972; David Aers, *Piers Plowman and Christian Allegory*, 1975; James Simpson, *Piers Plowman: An Introduction to the B-Text*, 1990; J. A. Burrow, *Langland's Fictions*, 1993; J. Wittig, *William Langland Revisited*, 1997; and S. Justice and K. Kerby-Fulton, *Written Work: Langland, Labor, and Authorship*, 1997. Collections of critical essays have been made by Edward Vasta, *Interpretations of Piers Plowman*, 1968; R. J. Blanch, *Style and Symbolism in Piers Plowman*, 1969; and S. S. Hussey, *Piers Plowman: Critical Approaches*, 1969. Useful background material has been collected by Jeanne Krochalis and Edward Peters in *The World of Piers Plowman*, 1975. F. R. H. DuBoulay, *The England of Piers Plowman*, 1991, places the poem in its historical and cultural setting.

Sir Thomas Malory
The Winchester manuscript of Malory's *Morte Darthur*, with full commentary and valuable discussion,

is given in Eugène Vinaver's *The Works of Sir Thomas Malory*, 3 vols., 2nd ed., 1967; the one-volume edition, 2nd ed., Oxford, 1970, contains the text only. The Caxton version is most readily available in *Caxton's Malory*, ed. J. W. Spisak, 1983. Vinaver, *Malory*, 1929, surveys Malory's life and career; see also, P. J. C. Field, *The Life and Times of Sir Thomas Malory*, 1993. Guides to Malory are B. Dillon, *A Malory Handbook*, 1978; Terence McCarthy, *An Introduction to Malory*, rev. ed., 1991; and E. Archibald and A. S. G. Edwards, *A Companion to Malory*, 1996. A number of critical problems in Malory's work, especially its unity, are discussed in three collections of essays by various scholars: *Essays on Malory*, ed. J. A. W. Bennett, 1963, *Malory's Originality*, ed. by R. M. Lumiansky, 1964, and *Studies in Malory*, ed. J. W. Spisak, 1985. Other studies of Malory and the *Morte Darthur* include Mark Lambert, *Malory: Style and Vision in Le Morte Darthur*, 1975; L. D. Benson, *Malory's Morte Darthur*, 1976; and Felicity Riddy, *Sir Thomas Malory*, 1987.

For reference books and discussions of the development and of the political and social significance of the Arthurian tradition in England, see R. S. Loomis, *The Development of Arthurian Romance*, 1963; S. Knight, *Arthurian Literature and Society*, 1983; *The Arthurian Handbook*, ed. N. J. Lacy and G. Ashe, 2nd ed., 1998; *The New Arthurian Encyclopedia*, ed. N. J. Lacy, 1991; *Approaches to Teaching the Arthurian Tradition*, ed. M. Fries and J. Watson, 1992; *Culture and the King: the Social Implications of the Arthurian Legend*, ed. M. Schichtman and J. Carley, 1994; *Arthurian Women: A Casebook*, ed. T. Fenster, 1996; and *King Arthur: A Casebook*, ed. E. D. Kennedy, 1996.

Middle English Lyrics

The best selections of Middle English lyrics are *Medieval English Lyrics: A Critical Anthology*, ed. R. T. Davies, 1963; *Middle English Lyrics*, A Norton Critical Edition, ed. M. S. Luria and R. L. Hoffman, 1974; *The Oxford Book of Medieval English Verse*, ed. Celia and Kenneth Sisam, 1970; *English Lyrics before 1500*, ed. Theodore Silverstein, 1971. For criticism see A. K. Moore, *The Secular Lyric in Middle English*, 1951; Kane's chapter in *Middle English Literature*; Stephen Manning, *Wisdom and Number*, 1962; Rosemary Woolf, *The English Religious Lyric in the Middle Ages*, 1968; and D. Gray, *Themes and Images in the Medieval English Religious Lyric*, 1972.

For general studies of English and Continental lyric poetry, see P. Dronke, *The Medieval Lyric*, 3rd ed., 1996, and *Vox Feminae: Studies in Medieval Woman's Song*, ed. J. F. Plummer, 1981.

Mystery Plays; Everyman

E. K. Chambers's classic *The Medieval Stage*, 1905, remains a mine of information, although its views about the evolution of medieval drama are no longer accepted. A new understanding and appreciation of medieval drama begins with O. B. Hardison, *Christian Rite and Christian Drama in the Middle Ages*, 1965; and for the mysteries, with V. A. Kolve, *The Play Called Corpus Christie*, 1966. Rosemary Woolf, *The English Mystery Plays*, 1972, makes detailed comparisons among the extant plays. Individual cycles are studied by Peter Travis in *Dramatic Design in the Chester Cycle*, 1982, and by Martin Stevens in *Four Middle English Mystery Cycles: Textual, Contextual, and Critical Interpretations*, 1987. G. M. Gibson fills in the social and religious background in *The Theater of Devotion: East Anglian Drama and Society in the Late Middle Ages*, 1989. Good selections of Middle English plays are presented by A. C. Cawley, *Everyman and Medieval Miracle Plays*, 1960; and by D. M. Bevington, *Medieval Drama*, 1975; and by Peter Happé, *The English Mystery Plays*, 1975. Cawley, *The Wakefield Pageants in the Towneley Cycle*, 1958, has a discussion of the work of the "Wakefield Master" whose hand is seen in the *Second Shepherds' Play*. A collection of critical essays has been made by Jerome Taylor and A. H. Nelson in *Medieval English Drama*, 1972. *Approaches to Teaching Medieval Drama*, ed. Richard Emmerson, 1990, contains essays by many hands and makes up a nontechnical survey of current opinion. For commentary on *Everyman*, see the introduction to A. C. Cawley's 1961 edition and Robert Potter's comprehensive *The English Morality Play: Origins, History, and Influence of a Dramatic Tradition*, 1975.

Sir Gawain and the Green Knight

The standard Middle English edition of the poem is by J. R. R. Tolkien and E. V. Gordon, rev. Norman Davis, 1967. Easier to use are the editions by R. A. Waldron, 1970, rev. for *The Poems of the Pearl Manuscript*, 1978; and by J. A. Burrow, 1972. For a guide to the poems in the manuscript, see A. Putter, *An Introduction to the Gawain-Poet*, 1996, and *A Companion to the Gawain Poet*, ed. D. S. Brewer and J. Gibson, 1997. Discussions of various aspects of the poem appear in Marie Borroff, *Sir Gawain and the Green Knight: A Stylistic and Metrical Study*, 1962; L. D. Benson, *Art and Tradition in Sir Gawain and the Green Knight*, 1965; J. A. Burrow, *A Reading of Sir Gawain and the Green Knight*, 1965; A. C. Spearing, *The Gawain Poet: A Critical Study*, 1971; And W. Clein, *Concepts of Chivalry in Sir Gawain and the Green Knight*, 1984.

Collections of essays have been compiled by R. J. Blanch, *Sir Gawain and Pearl*, 1966, and *Text and Matter: New Critical Perspectives of the Pearl-Poet*, 1991 D. Fox, *Twentieth-Century Interpretations of Sir Gawain and the Green Knight*, 1968; and D. R. Howard and C. K. Zacher, *Critical Studies of Sir Gawain and the Green Knight*, 1968.

The Persistence of English

If you measure the success of a language in purely quantitative terms, English is entering the twenty-first century at the moment of its greatest triumph. It has between 400 and 450 million native speakers, perhaps 300 million more who speak it as a second language—well enough, that is, to use it in their daily lives—and somewhere between 500 and 750 million who speak it as a foreign language with various degrees of fluency. The resulting total of between 1.2 billion and 1.5 billion speakers, or roughly a quarter of the world's population, gives English more speakers than any other language (though Chinese has more native speakers). Then, too, English is spoken over a much wider geographical area than any other language and is the predominant lingua franca of most fields of international activity, such as diplomacy, business, travel, science, and technology.

But figures like these can obscure a basic question: what exactly do we mean when we talk about the "English language" in the first place? There is, after all, an enormous range of variation in the forms of speech that go by the name of English in the various parts of the world—or often, even within the speech of a single nation—and it is not obvious why we should think of all of these as belonging to a single language. Indeed, there are some linguists who prefer to talk about "world Englishes," in the plural, with the implication that these varieties may not have much more to unite them than a single name and a common historical origin.

To the general public, these reservations may be hard to understand; people usually assume that languages are natural kinds like botanical species, whose boundaries are matters of scientific fact. But as linguists observe, there is nothing in the forms of English themselves that tells us that it is a single language. It may be that the varieties called "English" have a great deal of vocabulary and structure in common and that English-speakers can usually manage to make themselves understood to one another, more or less (though films produced in one part of the English-speaking world often have to be dubbed or subtitled to make them intelligible to audiences in another). But there are many cases where we find linguistic varieties that are mutually intelligible and grammatically similar, but where speakers nonetheless identify separate languages—for example, Danish and Norwegian, Czech and Slovak, or Dutch and Afrikaans. And on the other hand, there are cases where speakers identify varieties as belonging to a single language even though they are linguistically quite distant from one another: the various "dialects" of Chinese are more different from one another than the Latin offshoots that we identify now as French, Italian, Spanish, and so forth.

Philosophers sometimes compare languages to games, and the analogy is apt here, as well. Trying to determine whether American English and British English or Dutch and Afrikaans are "the same language" is like trying to determine whether baseball and softball are "the same game"—it is not something you can find out just by looking at their rules. It is not surprising, then, that linguists should throw up their hands when someone asks them to determine on linguistic grounds alone whether two varieties belong to a single language. That, they answer, is a political or social determination, not a linguistic one, and they usually go on to cite a well-known quip: "a language is just a dialect with an army and a navy."

There is something to this remark. Since the eighteenth century, it has been widely believed that every nation deserved to have its own language, and declarations of political independence have often been followed by declarations of linguistic independence. Until recently, for example, the collection of similar language varieties that were spoken in most of central Yugoslavia was regarded as a single language, Serbo-Croatian, but once the various regions became independent, their inhabitants began to speak of Croatian, Serbian, and Bosnian as separate languages, even though they are mutually comprehensible and grammatically almost identical.

The English language has avoided this fate (though on occasion it has come closer to breaking up than most people realize). But the unity of a language is never a foregone conclusion. In any speech-community, there are forces always at work to create new differences and varieties: the geographic and social separation of speech-communities, their distinct cultural and practical interests, their contact with other cultures and other languages, and, no less important, a universal fondness for novelty for its own sake, and a desire to speak differently from one's parents or the people in the next town. Left to function on their own, these centrifugal pressures can rapidly lead to the linguistic fragmentation of the speech-community. That is what happened, for example, to the vulgar (that is, "popular") Latin of the late Roman Empire, which devolved into hundreds or thousands of separate dialects (the emergence of the eight or ten standard varieties that we now think of as the Romance languages was a much later development).

Maintaining the unity of a language over an extended time and space, then, requires a more or less conscious determination by its speakers that they have certain communicative interests in common that make it worthwhile to try to curb or modulate the natural tendency to fragmentation and isolation. This determination can be realized in a number of ways. The speakers of a language may decide to use a common spelling system even when dialects become phonetically distinct, to defer to the same set of literary models, to adopt a common format for their dictionaries and grammars, or to make instruction in the standard language a part of the general school curriculum, all of which the English-speaking world has done to some degree. Or in some other places, the nations of the linguistic community may establish academies or other state institutions charged with regulating the use of the language, and even go so far as to publish lists of words that are unacceptable for use in the press or in official publications, as the French government has done in recent years. Most important, the continuity of the language rests on speakers' willingness to absorb the linguistic and cultural influences of other parts of the linguistic community.

THE EMERGENCE OF THE ENGLISH LANGUAGE

To recount the history of a language, then, is not simply to trace the development of its various sounds, words, and constructions. Seen from that exclusively linguistic point of view, there would be nothing to distinguish the evolution of Anglo-Saxon into the varieties of modern English from the evolution of Latin into modern French, Italian, and so forth—we would not be able to tell, that is, why English continued to be considered a single language while the Romance languages did not. We also have to follow the play of centrifugal and centripetal forces that kept the language always more or less a unity—the continual process of creation of new dialects and varieties, the countervailing rise of new standards and of mechanisms aimed at maintaining the linguistic center of gravity.

Histories of the English language usually put its origin in the middle of the fifth century, when several Germanic peoples first landed in the place we now call England and began to displace the local inhabitants, the Celts. There is no inherent linguistic reason why we should locate the beginning of the language at this time, rather than with the Norman Conquest of 1066 or in the fourteenth century, say, and in fact the determination that English began with the Anglo-Saxon period was not generally accepted until the nineteenth century. But this point of view has been to a certain extent self-justifying, if only because it has led to the addition of Anglo-Saxon works to the canon of English literature, where they remain. Languages are constructions over time as well as over space.

Wherever we place the beginnings of English, though, there was never a time when the language was not diverse. The Germanic peoples who began to arrive in England in the fifth century belonged to a number of distinct tribes, each with its own dialect, and tended to settle in different parts of the country—the Saxons in the southwest, the Angles in the east and north, the Jutes (and perhaps some Franks) in Kent. These differences were the first source of the distinct dialects of the language we now refer to as Anglo-Saxon or Old English. As time went by, the linguistic divisions were reinforced by geography and by the political fragmentation of the country, and later, through contact with the Vikings who had settled the eastern and northern parts of England in the eighth through eleventh centuries.

Throughout this period, though, there were also forces operating to consolidate the language of England. Over the centuries, cultural and political dominance passed from Northumbria in the north to Mercia in the center and then to Wessex in the southwest, where a literary standard emerged in the ninth century, owing in part to the unification of the kingdom and in part to the singular efforts of Alfred the Great (849–899), who encouraged literary production in English and himself translated Latin works into the language. The influence of these standards and the frequent communication between the regions worked to level many of the dialect differences. There is a striking example of the process in the hundreds of everyday words derived from the language of the Scandinavian settlers, which include *dirt, lift, sky, skin, die, birth, weak, seat,* and *want*. All of these spread to general usage from the northern and eastern dialects in which they were first introduced, an indication of how frequent and ordinary were the contacts among the

Anglo-Saxons of various parts of the country—and initially, between the Anglo-Saxons and the Scandinavians themselves. (By contrast, the Celtic peoples that the Anglo-Saxons had displaced made relatively few contributions to the language, apart from place-names like *Thames, Avon,* and *Dover.*)

The Anglo-Saxon period came to an abrupt end with the Norman Conquest of 1066. With the introduction of a French-speaking ruling class, the written use of English was greatly reduced for 150 years. English did not reappear extensively in written records until the beginning of the thirteenth century, and even then it was only one of the languages of a multilingual community: French was widely used for another two hundred years or so (Parliament was conducted in French until 1362), and Latin was the predominant language of scholarship until the Renaissance. The English language that re-emerged in this period was considerably changed from the language of Alfred's period. Its grammar was simplified, continuing a process already under way before the Conquest, and its vocabulary was enriched by thousands of French loan words. Not surprisingly, given the preeminent role of French among the elite, these included the language of government (*majesty, state, rebel*); of religion (*pastor, ordain, temptation*); of fashion and social life (*button, adorn, dinner*); and of art, literature, and medicine (*painting, chapter, paper, physician*). But the breadth of French influence was not limited to those domains; it also provided simple words like *move, aim, join, solid, chief, clear, air,* and *very.* All of this left the language sufficiently different from Old English to warrant describing it with the name of Middle English, though we should bear in mind that language change is always gradual and that the division of English into neat periods is chiefly a matter of scholarly convenience.

Middle English was as varied a language as Old English was: Chaucer wrote in *Troilus and Criseyde* that "ther is so gret diversite in Englissh" that he was fearful that the text would be misread in other parts of the country. It was only in the fifteenth century or so that anything like a standard language began to emerge, based in the speech of the East Midlands and in particular of London, which reflected the increased centralization of political and economic power in that region. Even then, though, dialect differences remained strong; the scholar John Palsgrave complained in 1540 that the speech of university students was tainted by "the rude language used in their native countries [i.e., counties]," which left them unable to express themselves in their "vulgar tongue."

The language itself continued to change as it moved into what scholars describe as the Early Modern English period, which for convenience's sake we can date from the year 1500. Around this time, it began to undergo the Great Vowel Shift, as the long vowels engaged in an intricate dance that left them with new phonetic values. (In Chaucer's time, the word *bite* had been pronounced roughly as "beet," *beet* as "bate," *name* as "nahm," and so forth.) The grammar was changing as well; for example, the pronoun *thee* began to disappear, as did the verbal suffix-*eth,* and the modern form of questions began to emerge: in place of "See you that house?" people began to say "Do you see that house?" Most significantly, at least so far as contemporary observers were concerned, the Elizabethans and their successors coined thousands of new words based on Latin and Greek in an effort to make English an adequate replacement for Latin in the writing of philosophy, science, and literature. Many of these words now seem quite ordinary to us—for example, *accommodation, frugal, obscene, premeditated*, and *submerge*, all of which are recorded for the first time in Shakespeare's works. A large proportion of these linguistic experiments, though, never gained a foothold in the language—for example, *illecebrous* for "delicate," *deruncinate* for "to weed," *obtestate* for "call on," or Shakespeare's *disquantity* to mean "diminish." Indeed, some contemporaries ridiculed the pretension and obscurity of these "inkhorn words" in terms that sound very like modern criticisms of bureaucratic and corporate jargon—the rhetorician Thomas Wilson wrote in 1540 of the writers who affected "outlandish English" such that "if some of their mothers were alive, they were not able to tell what they say." But this effect was inevitable: The additions to the standard language that made it a suitable vehicle for art and scholarship could only increase the linguistic distance between the written language used by the educated classes and the spoken language used by other groups.

DICTIONARIES AND RULES

These were essentially growing pains for the standard language, which continued to gain ground in the sixteenth and seventeenth centuries, abetted by a number of developments: the ever-increasing dominance of London and the Southeast, the growth in social and geographic mobility, and in particular the introduction and spread of print, which led both to higher levels of literacy and schooling and to the gradual standardization of English spelling. But even as this process was going on, other developments were both creating new distinctions and investing existing ones with a new importance. For one thing, people were starting to pay more attention to accents based on social class, rather than region, an understandable preoccupation as social mobility increased and speech became a more important indicator of social background. Not surprisingly, the often imperfect efforts of the emerging middle class to speak and dress like their social superiors occasioned some ridicule; Thomas Gainsford wrote in 1616 of the "foppish mockery" of commoners who tried to imitate gentlemen by altering "habit, manner of life, conversation, and even their phrase of speech." Yet even the upper classes were paying more attention to speech as a social indicator than they had in previous ages; as one writer put it, "it is a pitty when a Noble man is better distinguished from a Clowne by his golden laces, than by his good language." (Shakespeare plays on this theme in *1 Henry IV* [3.1.250, 257–58] when he has Hotspur tease his wife for swearing too daintily, which makes her sound like "a comfit-maker's wife," rather than "like a lady as thou art," who swears with "a good mouth-filling oath.")

Over the course of the seventeenth and eighteenth centuries, print began to exercise a paradoxical effect on the perception of the language: even as it was serving to codify the standard, it was also making people more aware of variation and more anxious about its consequences. This was largely the result of the growing importance of print, as periodicals, novels, and other new forms became increasingly influential in shaping public opinion, together with the perception that the contributors to the print discourse were drawn from a wider range of backgrounds than in previous periods. As Samuel Johnson wrote: "The present age . . . may be styled, with great propriety, the Age of Authors; for, perhaps, there was never a time when men of all degrees of ability, of every kind of education, of every profession and employment were posting with ardor so general to the press. . . . "

This anxiety about the language was behind the frequent eighteenth-century lamentations that English was "unruled," "barbarous," or, as Johnson put it, "copious without order, and energetick without rule." Some writers looked for a remedy in public institutions modeled on the French Academy. This idea was advocated by John Dryden, Daniel Defoe, Joseph Addison, and most notably by Jonathan Swift, in a 1712 pamphlet called *A Proposal for Correcting, Improving, and Ascertaining* [i.e., "fixing"] *the English Tongue*, which did receive some official attention from the Tory government. But the idea was dropped as a Tory scheme when the Whigs came to power two years later, and by the middle of the eighteenth century, there was wide agreement among all parties that an academy would be an unwarranted intervention in the free conduct of public discourse. Samuel Johnson wrote in the Preface to his *Dictionary* of 1775 that he hoped that "the spirit of English liberty will hinder or destroy" any attempt to set up an academy; and the scientist and radical Joseph Priestly called such an institution "unsuitable to the genius of a *free nation.*"

The rejection of the idea of an academy was to be important in the subsequent development of the language. From that time forward, it was clear that the state was not to play a major role in regulating and reforming the language, whether in England or in the other nations of the language community—a characteristic that makes English different from many other languages. (In languages like French and German, for example, spelling reforms can be introduced by official commissions charged with drawing up rules which are then adopted in all textbooks and official publications, a procedure that would be unthinkable in any of the nations of the English-speaking world.) Instead, the task of determining standards was left to private citizens, whose authority rested on their ability to gain general public acceptance.

The eighteenth century saw an enormous growth in the number of grammars and handbooks, which formulated most of the principles of correct English that, for better or worse, are still with us today—the rules for using *who* and *whom*, for example, the injunction against constructions like "very unique," and the curious prejudice against the split infinitive. Even more important was the development of the modern English dictionary. Before 1700, English speakers had to make do with alphabetical lists of "hard-words," a bit like the vocabulary improvement books that are still frequent today; it was only in the early 1700s that scholars began to produce anything like a comprehensive dictionary in the modern sense, a process that culminated in the publication of Samuel Johnson's magisterial *Dictionary* of 1755. It would be hard to argue that these dictionaries did much in fact to reduce variation or to arrest the process of linguistic change (among the words that Johnson objected to, for example, were *belabor, budge, cajole, coax, doff, gambler,* and *job,* all of which have since become part of the standard language). But they did serve to ease the sense of linguistic crisis, by providing a structure for describing the language and points of reference for resolving disputes about grammar and meaning. And while both the understanding of language and the craft of lexicography have made a great deal of progress since Johnson's time, the form of the English-language dictionary is still pretty much as he laid it down. (In this regard, Johnson's *Dictionary* is likely to present a much more familiar appearance to a modern reader than his poetry or periodical essays.)

THE DIFFUSION OF ENGLISH

The Modern English period saw the rise of another sort of variation, as well, as English began to spread over an increasingly larger area. By Shakespeare's time, English was displacing the Celtic languages in Wales, Cornwall, and Scotland, and then in Ireland, where the use of Irish was brutally repressed on the assumption—in retrospect a remarkably obtuse one—that people who were forced to become English in tongue would soon become English in loyalty as well. People in these new parts of the English-speaking world—a term we can begin to use in this period, for English was no longer the language of a single country—naturally used the language in accordance with their own idiom and habits of thought and mixed it with words drawn from the Celtic languages, a number of which eventually entered the speech of the larger linguistic community, for example, *baffle, bun, clan, crag, drab, galore, hubbub, pet, slob, slogan,* and *trousers.*

The development of the language in the New World followed the same process of differentiation. English settlers in North America rapidly developed their own characteristic forms of speech. They retained a number of words that had fallen into disuse in England (*din, clod, trash,* and *fall* for *autumn*) and gave old words new senses (like *corn,* which in England meant simply "grain," or *creek,* originally "an arm of the sea"). They borrowed freely from the other languages they came in contact with. By the time of the American Revolution, the colonists had already taken *chowder, cache, prairie,* and *bureau* from French; *noodle* and *pretzel* from German; *cookie, boss,* and *scow* and *yankee* from the Dutch; and *moose, skunk, chipmunk, succotash, toboggan,* and *tomahawk* from various Indian languages. And they coined new words with abandon. Some of these answered to their specific needs and interests—for example, *squatter, clearing, foothill, watershed, congressional, sidewalk*—but there were thousands of others that had no close connection to the American experience as such, many of which were ultimately adopted by the other varieties of English. *Belittle, influential, reliable, comeback, lengthy, turn down, make good*—all of these were originally American creations; they and other words like them indicate how independently the language was developing in the New World.

This process was repeated wherever English took root—in India, Africa, the Far East, the Caribbean, and Australia and New Zealand; by the late nineteenth century, English bore thousands of souvenirs of its extensive travels. From Africa (sometimes via Dutch) came words like *banana, boorish, palaver, gorilla,* and *guinea;* from the aboriginal languages of Australia came *wombat* and *kangaroo;* from the Caribbean languages came *cannibal, hammock, potato,* and *canoe;* and from the languages of India came *bangle, bungalow, chintz, cot, dinghy, jungle, loot, pariah, pundit,* and *thug.* And even lists like these are misleading, since they include only words that worked their way into the general English vocabulary and don't give a sense of the thousands of borrowings and coinages that were used only locally. Nor do they touch on the variation in grammar from one variety to the next. This kind of variation occurs everywhere, but it is particularly marked in regions like the Caribbean and Africa, where the local varieties of English are heavily influenced by English-based creoles—that is, language varieties that use English-based vocabulary with grammars largely derived from spoken—in this case, African—languages. This is the source, for example, of a number of the distinctive syntactic features of the variety used by many inner-city African Americans, like the "invariant *be*" of sentences like *We be living in Chicago*, which signals a state of affairs that holds for an extended period. (Some linguists have suggested that Middle English, in fact, could be thought of as a kind of creolized French.)

The growing importance of these new forms of English, particularly in America, presented a new challenge to the unity of the language. Until the eighteenth century, English was still thought of as essentially a national language. It might be spoken in various other nations and colonies under English control, but it was nonetheless rooted in the speech of England and subject to a single standard. Not surprisingly, Americans came to find this picture uncongenial, and when the United States first declared its independence from Britain, there was a strong sentiment for declaring that "American," too, should be recognized as a separate language. This was the view held by John Adams, Thomas Jefferson, and above all by America's first and greatest lexicographer, Noah Webster, who argued that American culture would naturally come to take a distinct form in the soil of the New World, free from what he described as "the old feudal and hierarchical establishments of England." And if a language was naturally the product and reflection of a national culture, then Americans could scarcely continue to speak "English." As Webster wrote in 1789: "Culture, habits, and language, as well as government should be national. America should have her own distinct from the rest of the world. . . ." It was in the interest of symbolically distinguishing American from English that Webster introduced a variety of spelling changes, such as *honor* and *favor* for *honour* and *favour*, *theater* for *theatre*, *traveled* for *travelled*, and so forth—a procedure that new nations often adopt when they want to make their variety of a language look different from its parent tongue.

In fact Webster's was by no means an outlandish suggestion. Even at the time of American independence, the linguistic differences between America and Britain were as great as those that separate many languages today, and the differences would have become much more salient if Americans had systematically adopted all of the spelling reforms that Webster at one time proposed, such as *wurd, reezon, tung, iz*, and so forth, which would ultimately have left English and American looking superficially no more similar than German and Dutch. Left to develop on their own, English and American might soon have gone their separate ways, perhaps paving the way for the separation of the varieties of English used in other parts of the world.

In the end, of course, the Americans and British decided that neither their linguistic nor their cultural and political differences warranted recognizing distinct languages. Webster himself conceded the point in 1828, when he entitled his magnum opus *An American Dictionary of the English Language*. And by 1862 the English novelist Anthony Trollope could write:

An American will perhaps consider himself to be as little like an Englishman as he is like a Frenchman. But he reads Shakespeare through the medium of his own vernacular, and has to undergo the penance of a foreign tongue before he can understand Molière. He separates himself from England in politics and perhaps in affection; but he cannot separate himself from England in mental culture.

ENGLISH AND ENGLISHNESS

This was a crucial point of transition, which set the English language on a very different course from most of the European languages, where the association of language and national culture was being made more strongly than ever before. But the detachment of English from Englishness did not take place overnight. For Trollope and his Victorian contemporaries, the "mental culture" of the English-speaking world was still a creation of England, the embodiment of English social and political values. "The English language," said G. C. Swayne in 1862, "is like the English constitution . . . and perhaps also the English Church, full of inconsistencies and anomalies, yet flourishing in defiance of theory." The monumental *Oxford English Dictionary* that the Victorians undertook was conceived in this patriotic spirit. In the words of Archbishop Richard Chevenix Trench, one of the guiding spirits of the OED project:

> We could scarcely have a lesson on the growth of our English tongue, we could scarcely follow upon one of its significant words, without having unawares a lesson in English history as well, without not merely falling upon some curious fact illustrative of our national life, but learning also how the great heart which is beating at the centre of that life, was being gradually shaped and moulded.

It was this conception of the significance of the language that led, too, to the insistence that the origin of the English language should properly be located in Anglo-Saxon, rather than in the thirteenth or fourteenth century, as scholars argued that contemporary English laws and institutions could be traced to a primordial "Anglo-Saxon spirit" in an almost racial line of descent, and that the Anglo-Saxon language was "immediately connected with the original introduction and establishment of their present language and their laws, their liberty, and their religion."

This view of English as the repository of "Anglo-Saxon" political ideals had its appeal in America, as well, particularly in the first decades of the twentieth century, when the crusade to "Americanize" recent immigrants led a number of states to impose severe restrictions on the use of other languages in schools, newspapers, and public meetings, a course that was often justified on the grounds that only speakers of English were in a position to fully appreciate the nuances of democratic thought. As a delegate to a New York State constitutional convention in 1916 put the point: "You have got to learn our language because that is the vehicle of the thought that has been handed down from the men in whose breasts first burned the fire of freedom at the signing of the Magna Carta."

But this view of the language is untenable on both linguistic and historical grounds. It is true that the nations of the English-speaking world have a common political heritage that makes itself known in similar legal systems and an (occasionally shaky) predilection for democratic forms of government. But while there is no doubt that the possession of a common language has helped to reinforce some of these connections, it is not responsible for them. Languages do work to create a common worldview, but not at such a specific level. Words like *democracy* move easily from one language to the next, along with the concepts they name—a good thing for the English-speaking world, since a great many of those ideals of "English democracy," as the writer calls it, owe no small debt to thinkers in Greece, Italy, France, Germany, and a number of other places, and those ideals have been established in many nations that speak languages other than English. (Thirteenth-century England was one of them. We should bear in mind that the Magna Carta that people sometimes like to mention in this context was a Latin document issued by a French-speaking king to French-speaking barons.) For that matter, there are English-speaking nations where democratic institutions have not taken root—nor should we take their continuing health for granted even in the core nations of the English-speaking world.

In the end, the view of English as the repository of Englishness has the effect of marginalizing or disenfranchising large parts of the English-speaking world, particularly those who do not count the political and cultural imposition of Englishness as an unmixed blessing. In most of the places where English has been planted, after all, it has had the British flag flying above it. And for many nations, it has been hard to slough off the sense of English as a colonial language. There is a famous passage in James Joyce's *Portrait of the Artist as a Young Man*, for example, where Stephen Daedelus says of the speech of an English-born dean, "The language in which we are speaking is his not mine," and there are still many people in Ireland and other parts of the English-speaking world who have mixed feelings about the English language: they may use and even love English, but they resent it, too.

Today the view of English as an essentially English creation is impossible to sustain even on purely linguistic grounds; the influences of the rest of the English-speaking world have simply been too great. Already in Trollope's time there were vociferous complaints in England about the growing use of Americanisms, a sign that the linguistic balance of payments between the two communities was tipping westward, and a present-day English writer would have a hard time producing a single paragraph that contained no words that originated in other parts of the linguistic community. Nor, what is more important, could you find a modern British or North American writer whose work was not heavily influenced, directly or indirectly, by the literature of the rest of the linguistic community, particularly after the extraordinary twentieth-century efflorescence of the English-language literatures of other parts of the world. Trying to imagine modern English literature without the contributions of writers like Yeats, Shaw, Joyce, Beckett, Heaney, Walcott, Lessing, Gordimer, Rushdie, Achebe, and Naipaul (to take only some of the writers who are included in this collection) is like trying to imagine an "English" cuisine that made no use of potatoes, tomatoes, corn, noodles, eggplant, olive oil, almonds, bay leaf, curry, or pepper.

THE FEATURES OF "STANDARD ENGLISH"

Where should we look, then, for the common "mental culture" that English-speakers share? This is always a difficult question to answer, partly because the understanding of the language changes from one place and time to the next, and partly because it is hard to say just what sorts of things languages are in the abstract. For all that we may want to think of the English-speaking world as a single community united by a common worldview, it is not a social group comparable to a tribe or people or nation—the sorts of groups that can easily evoke the first-person plural pronoun we. (Americans and Australians do not travel around saying "We gave the world Shakespeare," even though one might think that as paid-up members of the English-speaking community they would be entirely within their rights to do so.)

But we can get some sense of the ties that connect the members of the English-speaking community by starting with the language itself—not just in its forms and rules, but in the centripetal forces spoken of earlier. Forces like these are operating in every language community, it's true, but what gives each language its unique character is the way they are realized, the particular institutions and cultural commonalties which work to smooth differences and create a basis for continued communication—which ensure, in short, that English will continue as a single language, rather than break up into a collection of dialects that are free to wander wherever they will.

People often refer to this basis for communication as "Standard English," but that term is misleading. There are many linguistic communities that do have a genuine standard variety, a fixed and invariant form of the language that is used for certain kinds of communication. But that notion of the standard would be unsuitable to a language like English, which recognizes no single cultural center and has to allow for a great deal of variation even in the language of published texts. (It is rare to find a single page of an English-language novel or newspaper that does not reveal what nation it was written in.) What English does have, rather, is a collection of standard features—of spelling, of grammar, and of word use—which taken together ensure that certain kinds of communication will be more or less comprehensible in any part of the language community.

The standard features of English are as notable for what they don't contain as for what they do. One characteristic of English, for example, is that it has no standard pronunciation. People pronounce the language according to whatever their regional practice happens to be, and while certain pronunciations may be counted as "good" or "bad" according to local standards, there are no general rules about this, the way there are in French or Italian. (Some New Yorkers may be stigmatized for pronouncing words like car and bard as 'kah' and 'bahd', but roughly the same r-less pronunciation is standard in parts of the American South and in England, South Africa, Australia, and New Zealand.) In this sense, "standard English" exists only as a written language. Of course there is some variation in the rules of written English, as well, such as the American spellings that Webster introduced, but these are relatively minor and tend to date from earlier periods. A particular speech-community can pronounce the words half or car however it likes, but it can't unilaterally change the way the words are spelled. Indeed, this is one of the unappreciated advantages of the notoriously irregular English spelling system—it is so plainly *un*phonetic that there's no temptation to take it as codifying any particular spoken variety. When you want to define a written standard in a linguistic community that embraces no one standard accent, it's useful to have a spelling system that doesn't tip its hand.

The primacy of the written language is evident in the standard English vocabulary, too, if only indirectly. The fact is that English as such does not give us a complete vocabulary for talking about the world, but only for certain kinds of topics. If you want to talk about vegetables in English, for example, you have to choose among the usages common in one or another region: Depending on where you do your shopping, you will talk about *rutabagas*, *scallions*, and *string beans* or *Swedes*, *spring onions*, and *French beans*. That is, you can only talk about vegetables in your capacity as an American, an Englishman, or whatever, not in your capacity as an English-speaker in general. And similarly for fashion (*sweater* vs. *jumper*, *bobby pin* vs. *hair grip*, *vest* vs. *waistcoat*), for car parts (*hood* vs. *bonnet*, *trunk* vs. *boot*), and for food, sport, transport, and furniture, among many other things.

The English-language vocabulary is much more standardized, though, in other areas of the lexicon. We have a large common vocabulary for talking about aspects of our social and moral life—*blatant*, *vanity*, *smug*, *indifferent*, and the like. We have a common repertory of grammatical constructions and "signpost" expressions—for example, adverbs like *arguably*, *literally*, and *of course*—which we use to organize our discourse and tell readers how to interpret it. And there is a large number of common words for talking about the language itself—for example, *slang*, *usage*, *jargon*, *succinct*, and *literate*. (It is striking how many of these words are particular to English. No other language has an exact synonym for *slang*, for example, or a single word that covers the territory that *literate* covers in English, from "able to read and write" to "knowledgeable or educated.")

The common "core vocabulary" of English is not limited to these notions, of course—for example, it includes as well the thousands of technical and scientific terms that are in use throughout the English-speaking world, like *global warming* and *penicillin*, which for obvious reasons are not particularly susceptible to cultural variation. Nor would it be accurate to say that the core vocabulary includes all the words we use to refer to our language or to our social and moral life, many of which have a purely local character. But the existence of a core vocabulary of common English words, as fuzzy as it may prove to be, is an indication of the source of our cultural commonalities. What is notable about words like *blatant*, *arguably*, and *succinct* is that their meanings are defined by reference to our common literature, and in particular to the usage of what the eighteenth-century philosopher George Campbell described as "authors of reputation"—writers whose authority is determined by "the esteem of the public." We would not take the usage of Ezra Pound or Bernard Shaw as authoritative in deciding what words like *sweater* or *rutabaga* mean—they could easily have been wrong about either— but their precedents carry a lot of weight when we come to talking about the meaning of *blatant* and *succinct*. In fact the body of English-language "authors of reputation" *couldn't* be wrong about the meanings of words like these, since it is their usage by these authors that collectively determines what these words mean. And for purposes of defining these words it does not matter where a writer is from. The *American Heritage Dictionary*, for example, uses citations from the Irish writer Samuel Beckett to illustrate the meanings of *exasperate* and *impulsion*, from the Persian-born Doris Lessing, raised in southern Africa, to illustrate the meaning of *efface*, and from the Englishman E. M. Forster to illustrate the meaning of *solitude*; and dictionaries from other communities feel equally free to draw on the whole of English literature to illustrate the meanings of the words of the common vocabulary.

It is this strong connection between our common language and our common literature that gives both the language and the linguistic community their essential unity. Late in the eighteenth century, Samuel Johnson said that Britain had become "a nation of readers," by which he meant not just that people were reading more than ever before, but that participation in the written discourse of English had become in some sense constitutive of the national identity. And while the English-speaking world and its ongoing conversation can no longer be identified with a single nation, that world is still very much a community of readers in this sense. Historically, at least, we use the language in the same way because we read and talk about the same books—not *all* the same books, of course, but a loose and shifting group of works that figure as points of reference for our use of language.

This sense of the core vocabulary based on a common literature is intimately connected to the linguistic culture that English-speakers share—the standards, beliefs, and institutions that keep the various written dialects of the language from flying apart. The English dictionary is a good example. It is true that each part of the linguistic community requires its own dictionaries, given the variation in vocabulary and occasionally in spelling and the rest, but they are all formed on more or less the same model, which is very different from that of the French or the Germans. They all organize their entries in the same way, use the same form of definitions, include the same kind of information, and so on, to the point where we often speak of "*the* dictionary," as if the book were a single, invariant text like "the periodic table." By the same token, the schools in every English-speaking nation generally teach the same principles of good usage, a large number of which date from the grammarians of the eighteenth century. There are a few notable exceptions to this generality (Americans and most other communities outside England abandoned some time ago the effort to keep *shall* and *will* straight and seem to be none the worse off for it), but even in these cases grammarians justify their prescriptions using the same terminology and forms of argument.

THE CONTINUITY OF ENGLISH

To be sure, our collective agreement on standards of language and literature is never more than approximate and is always undergoing redefinition and change. Things could hardly be otherwise, given the varied constitution of the English-speaking community, the changing social background, and the insistence of English-speakers that they must be left to decide these matters on their own, without the intervention of official commissions or academies. It is not surprising that the reference points that we depend on to maintain the continuity of the language should often be controversial, even within a single community, and even less so that different national communities should have different ideas as to who counts as authority or what kinds of texts should be relevant to defining the common core of English words. The most we can ask of our common linguistic heritage is that it give us a general format for adapting the language to new needs and for reinterpreting its significance from one time and place to another.

This is the challenge posed by the triumph of English. Granted, there is no threat to the hegemony of English as a worldwide medium for practical communication. It is a certainty that the nations of the English-speaking community will continue to use the various forms of English to communicate with each other, as well as with the hundreds of millions of people who speak English as a second language (and who in fact outnumber the native speakers of the language by a factor of two or three to one). And with the growth of travel and trade and of media like the Internet, the number of English-speakers is sure to continue to increase.

But none of this guarantees the continuing unity of English as a means of cultural expression. What is striking about the accelerating spread of English over the past two centuries is not so much the number of speakers that the language has acquired, but the remarkable variety of the cultures and communities who use it. The heterogeneity of the linguistic community is evident not just in the emergence of the rich new literatures of Africa, Asia, and the Caribbean, but also in the literatures of what linguists sometimes call the "inner circle" of the English-speaking world—nations like Britain, the United States, Australia, and Canada—where the language is being asked to describe a much wider range of experience than ever before, particularly on behalf of groups who until recently have been largely excluded or marginalized from the collective conversation of the English-speaking world.

Not surprisingly, the speakers of the "new Englishes" use the language with different voices and different rhythms and bring to it different linguistic and cultural backgrounds. The language of a writer like Chinua Achebe reflects the influence not just of Shakespeare and Wordsworth but of proverbs and other forms of discourse drawn from West African oral traditions. Indian writers like R. K. Narayan and Salman Rushdie ground their works not just in the traditional English-language canon but in Sanskrit classics like the epic *Rāmāyana*. The continuing sense that all English-speakers are engaged in a common discourse depends on the linguistic community's being able to accommodate and absorb these new linguistic and literary influences, as it has been able to do in the past.

In all parts of the linguistic community, moreover, there are questions posed by the new media of discourse. Over the past hundred years, the primacy of print has been challenged first by the growth of film, recordings, and the broadcast media, and more recently by the remarkable growth of the Internet, each of which has had its effects on the language. With film and the rest, we have begun to see the emergence of spoken standards that coexist with the written standard of print, not in the form of a standardized English pronunciation—if anything, pronunciation differences among the communities of the English-speaking world have become more marked over the course of the century—but rather in the use of words, expressions, and rhythms that are particular to speech (there is no better example of this than the universal adoption of the particle *okay*). And the Internet has had the effect of projecting what were previously private forms of written communication, like the personal letter, into something more like models of public discourse, but with a language that is much more informal than the traditional discourse of the novel or newspaper.

It is a mistake to think that any of these new forms of discourse will wholly replace the discourse of print (the Internet, in particular, has shown itself to be an important vehicle for marketing and diffusing print works with much greater efficiency than has ever been possible before). It seems reasonable to assume that a hundred years from now the English-speaking world will still be at heart a community of readers—and of readers of books, among other things. And it is likely, too, that the English language will still be at heart a means of written expression, not just for setting down air schedules and trade statistics, but for doing the kind of cultural work that we have looked for literature to do for us in the past; a medium, that is, for poetry, criticism, history, and fiction. But only time will tell if English will remain a single language—if in the midst of all the diversity, cultural and communicative, people will still be able to discern a single "English literature" and a characteristic English-language frame of mind.

GEOFFREY NUNBERG
Stanford University and Xerox Palo Alto Research Center

Geographic Nomenclature: England, Great Britain, The United Kingdom

The British Isles refers to the prominent group of islands off the northwest coast of Europe, especially to the two largest, **Great Britain** and **Ireland**. At present these comprise two sovereign states: **The Republic of Ireland**, or **Eire**, and **The United Kingdom of Great Britain and Northern Ireland**—known for short as **The United Kingdom** or **The U.K.** Most of the smaller islands are part of **The U.K.** but a few, like the **Isle of Man** and the tiny **Channel Islands**, are very largely independent. **The U.K.** is often loosely referred to as **"Britain"** or **"Great Britain"** and is sometimes simply called **"England."** The latter usage, though technically inaccurate and occasionally confusing, is common among Englishmen as well as foreigners, though, for obvious reasons, it is rarely heard among the inhabitants of the other countries of **The U.K.**—**Scotland**, **Wales**, and **Northern Ireland** (sometimes called **Ulster**). England is by far the most populous part of the kingdom, as well as the seat of its capital, London.

From the first to the fifth century C.E. most of what is now **England** and **Wales** was a province of the Roman Empire called **Britain** (in Latin, **Britannia**). After the fall of Rome, much of the island was invaded and settled by peoples from northern Germany and Denmark speaking what we now call Old English. They are collectively known as the Anglo-Saxons, and the word **England** is related to the first element of their name. By the time of the Norman Conquest (1066) most of the kingdoms founded by the Anglo-Saxons and subsequent Viking invaders had coalesced into the kingdom of **England**, which, in the latter Middle Ages, conquered and largely absorbed the neighboring Celtic kingdom of **Wales**. In 1603 James VI of **Scotland** inherited the island's other throne as James I of **England**, and for the next hundred years—except for the brief period of Puritan rule—**Scotland** and **England** (with **Wales**) were two kingdoms under a single king. In 1707 the Act of Union welded them together as **The United Kingdom of Great Britain**, which, upon the incorporation of **Ireland** in 1801, became **The United Kingdom of Great Britain and Ireland**. With the division of Ireland and the establishment of **The Irish Free State** after World War I, this name was modified to its present form. In 1949 **The Irish Free State** became **The Republic of Ireland**; and in 1997 **Scotland** voted to restore the separate parliament it had relinquished in 1707, without, however, ceasing to be part of **The United Kingdom**.

The **British Isles** are further divided into counties, which in **Great Britain** are also known as shires. This word, with its vowel shortened in pronunciation, forms the suffix in the names of many counties, such as **Yorkshire, Wiltshire, Somersetshire**.

The Latin names **Britannia (Britain), Caledonia (Scotland)**, and **Hibernia (Ireland)** are sometimes used in poetic diction; so too is **Britain**'s ancient Celtic name, **Albion**. Because of its accidental resemblance to *albus* (Latin for "white"), **Albion** is especially associated with the chalk cliffs which seem to gird much of the English coast like defensive walls.

The **British Empire** took its name from **The British Isles** because it was created not only by the **English** but by the **Irish, Scots,** and **Welsh**, as well as by civilians and servicemen from other constituent countries of the Empire.

British Money

Since 1971, British money has been calculated on the decimal system, with 100 pence to the pound; the pound has fluctuated from a bit more than 2 American dollars to virtual parity—whatever dollars may be worth. Before 1971, the pound consisted of 20 shillings, each containing 12 pence, making 240 pence to the pound. In paper money the change has not been great; 5- and 10-pound notes constitute the mass of bills under both the old and the new systems; nowadays, in addition, 20- and 50-pound notes have been added. But in the smaller coinage the change has been considerable and the simplification remarkable. Most notable is the abolition of the shilling, which goes into retirement now with the mark (worth in its day two-thirds of a pound or 13 shillings 4 pence) and the angel (once 10 shillings but replaced by the 10-shilling note, now in its turn abolished). The guinea, an oddity of the old currency, amounted to a pound and a shilling; though it has not been minted since 1813, a very few quality items or prestige awards (like horse races) may still be quoted in guineas. Colloquially, a pound was (and is) called a quid; a shilling a bob; sixpence a tanner; a penny, half-penny, or farthing, a copper. The common signs were £ for pound, s. for shilling, d. for a penny (from Latin *denarius*). A sum would normally be written £2.19.3, i.e., 2 pounds, 19 shillings, 3 pence. In Joyce's *Ulysses*, that is Leopold Bloom's budget for June 16, 1904. In new currency, it would be about £2.96.

Old	*New*
1 pound note	1 pound coin (or note in Scotland)
10 shilling (half-pound note)	50 pence
5 shilling (crown)	
	20 pence
2½ shilling (half crown)	
2 shilling (florin)	10 pence
1 shilling	5 pence
6 pence	
2½ pence	1 penny
2 pence	
1 penny	
½ penny	
¼ penny (farthing)	

What the pound was worth at any point in history is ever easy to state. In the first part of the twentieth century, 1 pound equaled about 5 American dollars; but those dollars bought three or four times what they would today. Historians sometimes attempt to calculate the value of the pound in terms of the goods and services it would purchase, but these too vary radically with special circumstances such as wars and poor harvests. Nevertheless, it is clear that money used to be worth much more than it is now. In the early sixteenth century, according to Hugh Latimer, people would say, "Oh, he's a rich man, he's worth £500." Four centuries later, Virginia Woolf argued that £500 a year (along with a room of one's own) was the bare minimum necessary for a woman to be able to write. Whatever Latimer meant by "rich," or Woolf by "necessary," it is clear that the value of the pound had declined drastically over this period, as it has continued to do in the course of the twentieth century. In Britain today, a worker on minimum wage earns more than £500 a month, an income associated with severe poverty.

In the Anglo-Saxon period, the silver penny was the biggest coin in general circulation; 4 of them would buy a sheep. Peasants and craftsmen before the Black Death of the fourteenth century made at most 2 or 3 pence a day—an annual income of £3 or £4; after the onset of the plague, wages nearly doubled, due to the shortage of laborers. Throughout the medieval period, kings and commoners worried less about inflation than about the debasement of the silver currency. In 1124, dozens of mint-masters had their right hands chopped off on Christmas Day for issuing inferior coinage. In the early sixteenth century, under Henry VIII and his son Edward VI, the silver content of coins fell as low as 25 percent. Elizabeth I considered the revaluation of the silver coinage to be one of her greatest achievements as queen. Nevertheless, her reign was marked by sustained inflation of prices, caused in part by the influx of gold and silver from the New World, and in part by the rising population.

In the Elizabethan era, admission to the public theaters cost a penny for those who stood throughout the performance. Playwrights were paid about £6 for each play, so to make a living a writer had to be prolific (or, like Shakespeare, own shares in the theater company). In the same period, 40 pounds a year in independent income (generally rent from lands) was the minimum requirement for a justice of the peace; it marked the threshold of gentry status and was also the sum fixed by King James I at which a man could be forced to accept knighthood (paying a fee to the crown). In 1661, following further inflation, Samuel Pepys calculated his worth at a modest £650 just after he had begun working for the navy; five years later, that good bourgeois was worth more than £6000, and his annual income was about £3000. Of course, he was working for most of this income. Pepys was a rising official and would become a very important one; but he never achieved a title or even knighthood because the smell of commerce had never been washed from his money by possession of land.

Various writers provide examples of the incomes of rich and poor in the eighteenth and nineteenth centuries. Joseph Andrews (in Fielding's novel, published 1742) worked as a footman in the house of Lady Booby for £8 a year; in addition, he got his room, board, and livery, plus the occasional tip. Among the comfortable classes, Mr. Bennet of Jane Austen's *Price and Prejudice* (1813) enjoyed an income of £2000 a year (with a family of five nonearning females to support), while Mr. Darcy had close to £10,000, nearing the level of the aristocracy. In his deepest degradation David Copperfield (of Dickens's 1850 novel) worked in the warehouse of Murdstone & Grinby for 6 or 7 shillings a week (£15 to £18 a year). Mr. Murdstone paid extra for his lodging and laundry, but even so the boy was bitterly impoverished, though he had only himself to feed. When his father died, his mother was thought to be pretty well taken care of with £105 a year, less than £9 per month. Even in 1888, Annie Besant reports workers in Bryant and May's match factory made 4 to 9 shillings a week and paid for their own lodging—this, in the words of Ada Nield Chew, was not a living wage, but "a lingering, dying wage." Far removed from this world is Jack Worthing in Wilde's comedy *The Importance of Being Earnest* (1895), who receives £7000 or £8000 a year from investments and has a country house with about fifteen hundred acres attached to it, though it yields no income worth talking about.

While incomes have risen enormously over the centuries, and the value of the pound declined accordingly, the gap between rich and poor has remained. So too has the gap between the country and the city: London has always been very expensive, and elsewhere a small income goes further. To a large extent, one's position in terms of class and geography determines not only what money can buy but what it means.

We have only to contrast Jack Worthing's vague estimate of his income with the factory workers' exact sense of the value of a shilling. As Woolf acknowledged, having a purse with the power "to breed ten-shilling notes automatically," changes one's view of money and of the world. Perhaps it is because British currency has been so important in shaping people's views of themselves and their society that many Britons are reluctant to let it go. The question of whether the United Kingdom should relinquish the pound and the penny to join the single European currency (the Euro) is a matter of fierce and prolonged debate. For some, the pound, far more than the flag, is an enduring symbol of the nation. Whether or not one holds this view, it can at least be said that over the centuries the pound has undergone as many crises and transformations as the nation itself.

The British Baronage

The English monarchy is in principle hereditary, though at times during the Middle Ages the rules were subject to dispute. In general, authority passes from father to eldest surviving son, from daughters in order of seniority if there is no son, to a brother if there are no children, and in default of direct descendants to collateral lines (cousins, nephews, nieces) in order of closeness. There have been breaks in the order of succession (1066, 1399, 1688), but so far as possible the usurpers have always sought to paper over the break with a legitimate, i.e., a hereditary claim. When a queen succeeds to the throne and takes a husband, he does not become king unless he is in the line of blood succession; rather, he is named prince consort, as Albert was to Victoria. He may father kings, but is not one himself.

The original Saxon nobles were the king's thanes, ealdormen, or earls, who provided the king with military service and counsel in return for booty, gifts, or landed estates. William the Conqueror, arriving from France, where feudalism was fully developed, considerably expanded this group. In addition, as the king distributed the lands of his new kingdom, he also distributed dignities to men who became known collectively as "the baronage." "Baron" in its root meaning signifies simply "man," and barons were the king's men. As the title was common, a distinction was early made between greater and lesser barons, the former gradually assuming loftier and more impressive titles. The first English "duke" was created in 1337; the title of "marquess," or "marquis" (pronounced "markwis"), followed in 1385, and "viscount" ("vyekount") in 1440. Though "earl" is the oldest title of all, it now comes between a marquess and a viscount in order of dignity and precedence, and the old term "baron" now designates a rank just below viscount. "Baronets" were created in 1611 as a means of raising revenue for the crown (the title could be purchased for about £1000); they are marginal nobility and do not sit in the House of Lords.

Kings and queens are addressed as "Your Majesty," princes and princesses as "Your Highness," the other hereditary nobility as "My Lord" or "Your Lordship." Peers receive their titles either by inheritance (like Lord Byron, the sixth baron of that line) or from the monarch (like Alfred Lord Tennyson, created first Baron Tennyson by Victoria). The children, even of a duke, are commoners unless they are specifically granted some other title or inherit their father's title from him. A peerage can be forfeited by act of attainder, as for example when a lord is convicted of treason; and, when forfeited, or lapsed for lack of a successor, can be bestowed on another family. Thus Robert Cecil was made in 1605 first earl of Salisbury in the third creation, the first creation dating from 1149, the second from 1337, the title having been in abeyance since 1539. Titles descend by right of succession and do not depend on tenure of land; thus, a title does not always indicate where a lord dwells or holds power. Indeed, noble titles do not always refer to a real place at all. At Prince Edward's marriage in 1999, the queen created him earl of Wessex, although the old kingdom of Wessex has had no political existence since the Anglo-Saxon period, and the name was all but forgotten until it was resurrected by Thomas Hardy as the setting of his novels. (This is perhaps but one of many ways in which the world of the aristocracy increasingly resembles the realm of literature.)

The king and queen	(These are all of the royal line.)
Prince and princess	

Duke and duchess	(These may or may not be of the royal line, but are
Marquess and marchioness	ordinarily remote from the succession.)
Earl and countess	
Viscount and viscountess	
Baron and baroness	
Baronet and lady	

Scottish peers sat in the parliament of Scotland, as English peers did in the parliament of England, till at the Act of Union (1707) Scots peers were granted sixteen seats in the English House of Lords, to be filled by election. Similarly, Irish peers, when the Irish parliament was abolished in 1801, were granted the right to elect twenty-eight of their number to the House of Lords in Westminster. (Now that the Republic of Ireland is a separate nation, of course, this no longer applies.) The House of Lords still retains some power to influence or delay legislation. But this upper house is now being reformed. All or most of the hereditary peers are to be expelled, while recipients of nonhereditary Life Peerages will remain and vote as before.

Below the peerage the chief title of honor is "knight." Knighthood, which is not hereditary, is generally a reward for services rendered. A knight (Sir John Black) is addressed, using his first name, as "Sir John"; his wife, using the last name, is "Lady Black"—unless she is the daughter of an earl or nobleman of higher rank, in which case she will be "Lady Arabella." The female equivalent of a knight bears the title of "Dame."

Though the word itself comes from the Anglo-Saxon *cniht*, there seems to be some doubt as to whether knighthood amounted to much before the arrival of the Normans. The feudal system required military service as a condition of land tenure, and a man who came to serve his king at the head of an army of tenants required a title of authority and badges of identity—hence the title of knighthood and the coat of arms. During the Crusades, when men were far removed from their land (or had even sold it in order to go on crusade), more elaborate forms of fealty sprang up that soon expanded into orders of knighthood. The Templars, Hospitallers, Knights of the Teutonic Order, Knights of Malta, and Knights of the Golden Fleece were but a few of these companionships; not all of them were available at all times in England.

Gradually, with the rise of centralized government and the decline of feudal tenures, military knighthood became obsolete, and the rank largely honorific; sometimes, as under James I, it degenerated into a scheme of the royal government for making money. For hundreds of years after its establishment in the fourteenth century, the Order of the Garter was the only English order of knighthood, an exclusive courtly companionship. Then, during the late seventeenth, the eighteenth, and the nineteenth centuries, a number of additional orders were created, with names such as the Thistle, Saint Patrick, the Bath, Saint Michael and Saint George, plus a number of special Victorian and Indian orders. They retain the terminology, ceremony, and dignity of knighthood, but the military implications are vestigial.

Although the British Empire now belongs to history, appointments to the Order of the British Empire continue to be conferred for services to that empire at home or abroad. Such honors (commonly referred to as "gongs") are granted by the monarch in her New Year's and Birthday lists, but the decisions are now made by the government in power. In recent years there have been efforts to popularize and democratize the dispensation of honors, with recipients including rock stars and actors. But this does not prevent large sectors of British society from regarding both knighthood and the peerage as largely irrelevant to modern life.

The Royal Lines of England and Great Britain

England

SAXONS AND DANES

Egbert, king of Wessex	802–839
Ethelwulf, son of Egbert	839–858
Ethelbald, son of Ethelwulf	858–860
Ethelbert, second son of Ethelwulf	860–866
Ethelred I, third son of Ethelwulf	866–871
Alfred the Great, fourth son of Ethelwulf	871–899
Edward the Elder, son of Alfred	899–924
Athelstan the Glorious, son of Edward	924–940
Edmund I, third son of Edward	940–946
Edred, fourth son of Edward	946–955
Edwy the Fair, son of Edmund	955–959
Edgar the Peaceful, second son of Edmund	959–975
Edward the Martyr, son of Edgar	975–978 (murdered)
Ethelred II, the Unready, second son of Edgar	978–1016
Edmund II, Ironside, son of Ethelred II	1016–1016
Canute the Dane	1016–1035
Harold I, Harefoot, natural son of Canute	1035–1040
Hardecanute, son of Canute	1040–1042
Edward the Confessor, son of Ethelred II	1042–1066
Harold II, brother-in-law of Edward	1066–1066 (died in battle)

HOUSE OF NORMANDY

William I the Conqueror	1066–1087
William II, Rufus, third son of William I	1087–1100 (shot from ambush)
Henry I, Beauclerc, youngest son of William I	1100–1135

HOUSE OF BLOIS

Stephen, son of Adela, daughter of William I	1135–1154

HOUSE OF PLANTAGENET

Henry II, son of Geoffrey Plantagenet by Matilda, daughter of Henry I	1154–1189
Richard I, Coeur de Lion, son of Henry II	1189–1199
John Lackland, son of Henry II	1199–1216
Henry III, son of John	1216–1272
Edward I, Longshanks, son of Henry III	1272–1307
Edward II, son of Edward I	1307–1327
Edward III of Windsor, son of Edward II	1327–1377
Richard II, grandson of Edward III	1377–1400

HOUSE OF LANCASTER

Henry IV, son of John of Gaunt, son of Edward III	1399–1413
Henry V, Prince Hal, son of Henry IV	1413–1422
Henry VI, son of Henry V	1422–1471 (deposed)

HOUSE OF YORK

Edward IV, great-great-grandson of Edward III	1461–1483
Edward V, son of Edward IV	1483–1483 (murdered)
Richard III, Crookback	1483–1485 (died in battle)

HOUSE OF TUDOR

Henry VII, married daughter of Edward IV	1485–1509
Henry VIII, son of Henry VII	1509–1547
Edward VI, son of Henry VIII	1547–1553
Mary I, "Bloody," daughter of Henry VIII	1553–1558
Elizabeth I, daughter of Henry VIII	1558–1603

HOUSE OF STUART

James I (James VI of Scotland)	1603–1625
Charles I, son of James I	1625–1649 (executed)

COMMONWEALTH & PROTECTORATE

Council of State	1649–1653
Oliver Cromwell, Lord Protector	1653–1658
Richard Cromwell, son of Oliver	1658–1660 (resigned)

HOUSE OF STUART (RESTORED)

Charles II, son of Charles I	1660–1685
James II, second son of Charles I	1685–1688

(INTERREGNUM, 11 DECEMBER 1688 TO 13 FEBRUARY 1689)

William III of Orange, by Mary, daughter of Charles I	1685–1701
and Mary II, daughter of James II	–1694
Anne, second daughter of James II	1702–1714

Great Britain

HOUSE OF HANOVER

George I, son of Elector of Hanover and Sophia, granddaughter of James I	1714–1727
George II, son of George I	1727–1760
George III, grandson of George II	1760–1820
George IV, son of George III	1820–1830
William IV, third son of George III	1830–1837
Victoria, daughter of Edward, fourth son of George III	1837–1901

HOUSE OF SAXE-COBURG AND GOTHA

Edward VII, son of Victoria   1901–1910

HOUSE OF WINDSOR (NAME ADOPTED 17 JULY 1917)

George V, second son of Edward VII   1910–1936
Edward VIII, eldest son of George V   1936–1936 (abdicated)
George VI, second son of George V   1936–1952
Elizabeth II, daughter of George VI   1952–

Religions in England

Religious distinctions and denominations are important in British social history, hence deeply woven into the nation's literature. The numerous (over three hundred) British churches and sects divide along a scale from high to low, depending on the amount of authority they give to the church or the amount of liberty they concede to the individual conscience. At one end of the scale is the Roman Catholic Church, asserting papal infallibility, universal jurisdiction, and the supreme importance of hierarchy as guide and intercessor. For political and social reasons, Catholicism struck deep roots in Ireland but in England was the object of prolonged, bitter hatred on the part of Protestants from the Reformation through the nineteenth century. The Established English (Anglican) Episcopal church has been the official national church since the sixteenth century; it enjoys the support (once direct and exclusive, now indirect and peripheral) of the national government. Its creed is defined by Thirty-Nine Articles, but these are intentionally vague, so there are numerous ways of adhering to the Church of England. Roughly and intermittently, the chief classes of Anglicans have been known as High Church (with its highest portion calling itself Anglo-Catholic); Broad Church, or Latitudinarian (when they get so broad that they admit anyone believing in God, they may be known as Deists, or some may leave the church altogether and be known as Unitarians); and Low Church, whose adherents may stay in the English church and yet come close to shaking hands with Presbyterians or Methodists. These various groups may be arranged, from the High down to the Low Church, in direct relation to the amount of ritual each prefers and in the degree of authority conceded to the upper clergy—and in inverse relation to the importance ascribed to a saving faith directly infused by God into an individual conscience.

All English Protestants who decline to subscribe to the English established church are classed as Dissenters or Nonconformists; for a time in the sixteenth and seventeenth centuries, they were also known as Puritans. (Nowadays, though Puritanism has less distinct theological meaning, it marks a distinct character type; because of his passionate emphasis on individual conscience and moral economy, Bernard Shaw was a prototypical Puritan.) The Presbyterians model their church government on that established by John Calvin in the Swiss city of Geneva. It has no bishops, and therefore is more democratic for the clergy; but it gains energy by associating lay elders with clergymen in matters of social discipline and tends to be strict with the ungodly. From its first reformation the Scottish Kirk was fixed on the Presbyterian model. During the civil wars of the seventeenth century, a great many sects sprang up on the left wing of the Presbyterians, most of them touched by Calvinism but some rebelling against it; a few of these still survive. The Independents became our modern Congregationalists; the Quakers are still Quakers, as Baptists are still Baptists, though multiply divided. But many of the sects flourished and perished within the space of a few years. Among these now vanished groups were the Shakers (though a few groups still exist in America), the Seekers, the Ranters, the Anabaptists, the Muggletonians, the Fifth Monarchy Men, the Family of Love, the Sweet Singers of Israel, and many others, forgotten by all except scholars. During the eighteenth and nineteenth centuries, new sects arose, supplanting old ones; the Methodists, under John and Charles Wesley, became numerous and important, taking root particularly in Wales. (The three "subject" nationalities, Ireland, Scotland, and Wales, thus turned three different ways to avoid the Anglican church.) With the passage of time a small number of Swedenborgians sprang up, followers of the Swedish mystic Emanuel Swedenborg—to be followed by the Plymouth Brethren, Christian Scientists, Jehovah's Witnesses, and countless other nineteenth-century groups. All these sects constantly grow, shrink, split, and occasionally disappear as they succeed or fail in attracting new converts.

Within the various churches and sects, independent of them all but amazingly persistent, there has always survived a stream of esoteric or hermetic thought—a belief in occult powers, and sometimes in magic also, exemplified by the pseudo-sciences of astrology and alchemy but taking many other forms as well. From the mythical Egyptian seer Hermes Trismegistus through Paracelsus, Cornelius Agrippa, Giordano Bruno, Jakob Boehme, the society of Rosicrucians, and a hundred other shadowy figures, the line can be traced to William Blake and William Butler Yeats, who both in their different ways brought hermetic Protestantism close to its ultimate goal, a mystic church of a single consciousness, poised within its mind-elaborated cosmos.

Christianity is not, of course, the only religion present on the British Isles. The few Jews in medieval England were regarded as resident aliens, as were those in other European countries. In 1290 all English Jews who refused baptism were expelled from the kingdom, and officially, there were no Jews living in England between that time and the mid-1650s, when Cromwell encouraged Jewish merchants to settle in London. A considerable number of east European Jews emigrated to England in the first half of the twentieth century (many as refugees), but the country's Jewish population as a whole remains quite small (less than half a million). Hardly any Muslims or Hindus lived in the U.K. before the dissolution of the Empire shortly after World War II. Today both religions have a large and growing representation among ex-colonial immigrants and their children.

Poetic Forms and
Literary Terminology

Systematic literary theory and criticism in English began in the sixteenth century, at a time when the standard education for upper-class students emphasized the study of the classical languages and literatures. As a consequence, the English words that were introduced to describe meter, figures of speech, and literary genres often derive from Latin and Greek roots.

RHYTHM AND METER

Verse is generally distinguished from prose as a more compressed and more regularly rhythmic form of statement. This approximate truth underlines the importance of **meter** in poetry, as the means by which rhythm is measured and described.

In Latin and Greek, meter was established on a **quantitative** basis, by the regular alternation of long and short syllables (that is, syllables classified according to the time taken to pronounce them). Outside of a few experiments (and the songs of Thomas Campion), this system has never proved congenial to Germanic languages such as English, which distinguish, instead, between **stressed** and **unstressed**, or accented and unaccented syllables. Two varieties of accented stress may be distinguished. On the one hand, there is the natural stress pattern of words themselves; *sýllable* is accented on the first syllable, *deplórable* on the second, and so on. Then there is the sort of stress that indicates rhetorical emphasis. If the sentence "You went to Greece?" is given a pronounced accent on the last word, it implies "Greece (of all places)?" If the accent falls on the first word, it implies "you (of all people)?" The meter of poetry—that is, its rhythm—is ordinarily built up out of a regular recurrence of accents, whether established as **word accents** or **rhetorical accents;** once started, it has (like all rhythm) a tendency to persist in the reader's mind.

The unit that is repeated to give steady rhythm to a poem is called a **foot;** in English it usually consists of accented and unaccented syllables in one of five fairly simple patterns:

The **iambic foot** (or **iamb**) consists of an unstressed followed by a stressed syllable, as in *uníte, repeát,* or *insíst.* Most English verse falls naturally into the iambic pattern.

The **trochaic foot** (**trochee**) inverts this order; it is a stressed followed by an unstressed syllable—for example, *únit, réaper,* or *ínstant.*

The **anapestic foot** (**anapest**) consists of two unstressed syllables followed by a stressed syllable, as in *intercéde, disarránged,* or *Cameróon.*

The **dactylic foot** (**dactyl**) consists of a stressed syllable followed by two unstressed syllables, as in *Wáshington, Écuador,* or *ápplejack.*

The **spondaic foot** (**spondee**) consists of two successive stressed syllables, as in *heartbreak, headline,* or *Kashmir.*

In all the examples above, word accent and the quality of the metrical foot coincide exactly. But the metrical foot may well consist of several words, or, on the other hand, one word may well consist of several metrical feet. *Phótolithógraphy* consists of two dactyls in a single word; *dárk and with spóts on it,* though it consists of six words rather than one, is also two dactyls. When we read a piece of poetry with the intention of discovering its underlying metrical pattern, we are said to **scan** it—that is, we go through it line by line, indicating by conventional signs which are the accented and which the unaccented syllables within the feet. We also count the number of feet in each line; a line is, formally, also called a **verse** (from Latin *versus,* which means one "row" of metrical feet). Verse lengths are conventionally described in terms derived from the Greek:

Monometer: one foot (of rare occurrence)
Dimeter: two feet (also rare)
Trimeter: three feet
Tetrameter: four feet
Pentameter: five feet
Hexameter: six feet (six iambic feet make what is called an **Alexandrine**)
Heptameter: seven feet (also rare)

Samuel Johnson wrote a little parody of simpleminded poets which can be scanned this way:

> Ĭ pút m̆y hát ŭpón m̆y héad
> Ănd wálked ĭntó thĕ Stránd
> Ănd thére Ĭ mét ănóthĕr mán
> Whŏse hát wăs ín hĭs hánd.

The poem is iambic in rhythm, alternating tetrameter and trimeter in the length of the verse-lines. The fact that it scans so nicely is, however, no proof that it is good poetry. Quite the contrary. Many of poetry's most subtle effects are achieved by establishing an underlying rhythm and then varying it by means of a whole series of devices, some dramatic and expressive, others designed simply to lend variety and interest to the verse. A well-known sonnet of Shakespeare's (*116*) begins,

> Let me not to the marriage of true minds
> Admit impediments. Love is not love
> Which alters when it alteration finds,
> Or bends with the remover to remove.

It is possible to read the first line of this poem as mechanical iambic pentameter:

Lĕt mé nŏt tó thĕ márriăge óf trŭe mińds

But of course nobody ever reads it that way, except to make a point; read with normal English accent and some sense of what it is saying, the line would form a pattern something like this:

Lét mĕ nŏt tŏ thĕ márriăge ŏf trúe mińds

which is neither pentameter nor in any way iambic. The second line is a little more iambic, but, read expressively also falls short of pentameter:

Ădmít ĭmpédĭmeńts. Lóve ĭs nŏt lóve

Only in the third and fourth lines of the sonnet do we get verses that read as five iambic feet.

The fact is that perfectly regular metrical verse is easy to write and dull to read. Among the devices in common use for varying too regular a pattern are the insertion of a trochaic foot among iambics, especially at the opening of a line, where the soft first syllable of the iambic foot often needs stiffening (see line 1 of the sonnet above); the more or less free addition of extra unaccented syllables; and the use of **caesura,** or strong grammatical pause within a line (conventionally indicated, in scanning, by the sign ‖). The second line of the sonnet above is a good example of caesura:

Admit impediments. ‖ Love is not love

The strength of the caesura, and its placing in the line, may be varied to produce striking variations of effect. More broadly, the whole relation between the poem's sound- and rhythm-patterns and its pattern as a sequence of assertions (phrases, clauses, sentences) may be manipulated by the poet. Sometimes the statements fit neatly within the lines, so that each line ends with a strong mark of punctuation; they are then known as **end-stopped lines.** Sometimes the sense flows over the ends of the lines, creating **run-on lines;** this process is also known, from the French, as **enjambment** (literally, "straddling").

End-stopped lines (Marlowe, *Hero and Leander*, lines 45–48):

> So lovely fair was Hero, Venus' nun,
> As Nature wept, thinking she was undone,
> Because she took more from her than she left
> And of such wondrous beauty her bereft.

Run-on lines (Keats, *Endymion* 1.89–93):

> Full in the middle of this pleasantness
> There stood a marble altar, with a tress
> Of flowers budded newly; and the dew
> Had taken fairy fantasies to strew
> Daisies upon the sacred sward, . . .

Following the example of such poets as Blake, Rimbaud, and Whitman, many twentieth-century poets have undertaken to write what is called **free** verse—that is, verse which has neither a fixed metrical foot nor (consequently) a fixed number of feet in its lines, but which depends for its rhythm on a pattern of cadences, or the rise and fall of the voice in utterance, or the pattern indicated to the reader's eye by the breaks between the verse lines. As in traditional versification, free verse is printed in short lines instead of with the continuity of prose; it differs from such versification, however, by the fact that its stressed syllables are not organized into a regular metric sequence.

SENSE AND SOUND

The words of which poetic lines—whether free or traditional—are composed cause them to have different sounds and produce different effects. Polysyllables, being pronounced fast, often cause a line to move swiftly; monosyllables, especially when heavy and requiring distinct accents, may cause it to move heavily, as in Milton's famous line (*Paradise Lost* 2.621):

> Rocks, caves, lakes, fens, bogs, dens, and shades of death

Poetic assertions are often dramatized and reinforced by means of **alliteration**—that is, the use of several nearby words or stressed syllables beginning with the same consonant. When Shakespeare writes (*Sonnet 64*),

> Ruin hath taught me thus to ruminate
> That Time will come and take my love away,

the alliterative *r*'s and rich internal echoes of the first line contrast with the sharp anxiety and directness of the alliterative *t*'s in the second. When Dryden starts *Absalom and Achitophel* with the couplet,

> In pious times, ere priestcraft did begin,
> Before polygamy was made a sin,

the satiric undercutting is strongly reinforced by the triple alliteration that links "*p*ious" with "*p*riestcraft" and "*p*olygamy."

Assonance, or repetition of the same or similar vowel sounds within a passage (usually in accented syllables), also serves to enrich it, as in two lines from Keats's *Ode on Melancholy*:

> For shade to shade will come too drowsily,
> And drown the wakeful anguish of the soul.

It is clear that the round, hollow tones of "drowsily," repeated in "drown" and darkening to the full *o*-sound of "soul," have much to do with the effect of the passage. A related device is **consonance**, or the repetition of a pattern of consonants with changes in the intervening vowels—for example: *linger, longer, languor; rider, reader, raider, ruder.*

The use of words that seem to reproduce the sounds they designate (known as **onomatopoeia**) has been much attempted, from Virgil's galloping horse—

Quadrupedante putrem sonitu quatit ungula campum—

through Tennyson's account, in *The Princess*, of

> The moan of doves in immemorial elms,
> And murmuring of innumerable bees—

to many poems in the present day.

RHYME AND STANZA

Rhyme consists of a repetition of accented sounds in words, usually those falling at the end of verse lines. If the rhyme sound is the very last syllable of the line (*rebound, sound*), the rhyme is called **masculine**; if the accented syllable is followed by an unaccented syllable (*hounding, bounding*), the rhyme is called **feminine**. Rhymes amounting to three or more syllables, like forced rhymes, generally have a comic effect in English, and have been freely used for this purpose, e.g., by Byron (*intellectual, henpecked-you-all*). Rhymes occurring within a single line are called **internal**; for instance, the Mother Goose rhyme "Mary, Mary, quite contrary," or from Coleridge's *Ancient Mariner* ("We were the first that ever burst / Into that silent sea"). **Eye rhymes** are words used as rhymes that look alike but actually sound different (for example, *alone, done; remove, love*); **off rhymes** (sometimes called **partial, imperfect,** or **slant rhymes**) are occasionally the result of pressing exigencies or lack of skill, but are also, at times, used deliberately by modern poets for special effects. For instance, a poem by Wilfred Owen (*Strange Meeting*) contains such paired words (which Owen called "para-rhymes") as *years / yours* or *tigress / progress*.

Blank verse is unrhymed iambic pentameter; until the recent advent of free verse, it was the only unrhymed measure to achieve general popularity in English. Though first used by the earl of Surrey in translating Virgil's *Aeneid*, blank verse was during the sixteenth century employed primarily in plays; *Paradise Lost* was one of the first nondramatic poems in English to use it. But Milton's authority and his success were so great that during the eighteenth and nineteenth centuries blank verse came to be used for a great variety of discursive, descriptive, and philosophical poems—besides remaining the standard metrical form for epics. Thomson's *Seasons*, Cowper's *Task*, Wordsworth's *Prelude*, and Tennyson's *Idylls of the King* were all written in blank verse.

A **stanza** is a recurring unit of a poem, consisting of a number of verses. Certain poems (for example, Dryden's *Alexander's Feast*) have stanzas comprising a variable number of verses, of varying lengths. Others are more regular, and are identified by particular names.

The simplest form of stanza is the **couplet**; it is two lines rhyming together. A single couplet considered in isolation is sometimes called a **distich;** when it expresses a complete thought, ending with a terminal mark of punctuation such as a semicolon or period, it is called a **closed couplet.** The development of very regular end-stopped couplets, their use in so-called heroic tragedies, and their consequent acquisition of the name **heroic couplets** took place for the most part during the mid-seventeenth century. The heroic couplet was the principal form in English neoclassical poems.

Another traditional and challenging form of couplet is the **tetrameter, or four-beat couplet.** All rhymed couplets are hard to manage without monotony; and since, in addition, a four-beat line is hard to divide by caesura without splitting it into two tick-tock dimeters, tetrameter couplets have posed a perpetual challenge to poets, and still provide an admirable finger-exercise for aspiring versifiers. An instance of tetrameter couplets managed with marvelous variety, complexity, and expressiveness is Marvell's *To His Coy Mistress*:

> Thou by the Indian Ganges' side
> Shouldst rubies find; I by the tide
> Of Humber would complain. I would
> Love you ten years before the Flood,
> And you should, if you please, refuse
> Till the conversion of the Jews.

English has not done much with rhymes grouped in threes, but has borrowed from Italian the form known as **terza rima,** in which Dante composed his *Divine Comedy*. This form consists of linked groups of three rhymes according to the following pattern: *aba bcb cdc ded*, etc. Shelley's *Ode to the West Wind* is composed in stanzas of *terza rima*, the poem as a whole ending with a couplet.

Quatrains are stanzas of four lines; the lines usually rhyme alternately, *abab*, or in the second and fourth lines, *abcb*. When they alternate tetrameter and trimeter lines, as in Johnson's little poem about men in hats (above), or as in *Sir Patrick Spens*, they are called **ballad stanza.** Dryden's *Annus Mirabilis* and Gray's *Elegy Written in a Country Churchyard* are in **heroic quatrains;** these rhyme alternately *abab*, and employ five-stress iambic verse throughout. Tennyson used for *In Memoriam* a tetrameter quatrain rhymed *abba*, and FitzGerald translated *The Rubáiyát of Omar Khayyám* into a pentameter quatrain rhymed *aaba*; but these forms have not been widely adopted.

Chaucer's *Troilus and Criseide* is the premier example in English of **rhyme royal,** a seven-line iambic pentameter stanza consisting essentially of a quatrain dovetailed onto two couplets, according to the rhyme scheme *ababbcc* (the fourth line serves both as the final line of the quatrain and as the first line of the first couplet). Closely akin to rhyme royal, but differentiated by an extra *a*-rhyme between the two *b*-rhymes, is **ottava rima,** that is, an eight-line stanza rhyming *abababcc*. As its name suggests, ottava rima is of Italian origin; it was first used in English by Wyatt. Its final couplet, being less prepared for than in rhyme royal, and usually set off as a separate verbal unit, is capable of manifesting a witty snap, for which Byron found good use in *Don Juan*.

The longest and most intricate stanza generally used for narrative purposes in English is that devised by Edmund Spenser for *The Faerie Queene*. The **Spenserian stanza** has nine lines rhyming *ababbcbcc*; the first eight lines are pentameter, the last line an Alexandrine. Slow-moving, intricate of pattern, and very demanding in its rhyme scheme (the *b*-sound recurs four times, the *c*-sound three), the Spenserian stanza has nonetheless appealed widely to poets who seek a rich and complicated metrical form. Keats's *Eve of St. Agnes* and Shelley's *Adonais* are brilliantly successful nineteenth-century examples of its use.

The **sonnet,** originally a stanza of Italian origin that has developed into an independent lyric form, is usually defined nowadays as fourteen lines of iambic pentameter. None of the elements in this definition is absolute and in earlier centuries there were sonnets in hexameters (the first of Sidney's *Astrophil and Stella*), and sonnets of as many as twenty lines (Milton's *On the New Forcers of Conscience*). Most, however, approximate the definition. Most Elizabethan sonnets dealt with love; and some poets, like Sidney, Spenser, and Shakespeare, imitated Petrarch in grouping together their sonnets dealing with a particular lady or situation. The term for these gatherings is **sonnet sequences;** the extent to which they tell a sequential story, and the extent to which such stories are autobiographical, vary greatly. Since Elizabethan times, the sonnet has been applied to a wide range of subject matters—religious, political, satiric, moral, and philosophic.

In blank verse or irregularly rhymed verse, where stanzaic divisions do not exist or are indistinct, the poetry sometimes falls into **verse paragraphs,** which are in effect divisions of sense like prose paragraphs. This division can be clearly seen in Milton's *Lycidas* and *Paradise Lost.* An intermediate form, clearly stanzaic but with stanzas of varying patterns of line-length and rhyme, is illustrated by Spenser's *Epithalamion*; in this instance, the division into stanzas is reinforced by a **refrain,** which is simply a line repeated at the end of each stanza. Ballads also customarily have refrains; for example, the refrain of *Lord Randall* is

> mother, make my bed soon,
> For I'm weary wi' hunting, and fain wald lie down.

FIGURATIVE LANGUAGE

The act of bringing words together into rich and vigorous poetic lines is complex and demanding, chiefly because so many variables require control. There is the "thought" of the lines, their verbal texture, their emotional resonance, the developing perspective of the reader—all these to be managed at once. One of the poet's chief resources toward this end is figurative language. Here, as in matters of meter, one may distinguish a great variety of devices, some of which we use in everyday speech without special awareness of their names and natures. When we say someone eats "like a horse" or "like a bird," we are using a **simile,** that is, a comparison marked out by a specific word of likening—"like" or "as." When we omit the word of comparison but imply a likeness—as in the sentence "That hog has guzzled all the champagne"—we are making use of **metaphor.** The **epic simile,** frequent in epic poetry, is an extended simile in which the thing compared is described as an object in its own right, beyond its point of likeness with the main subject. Milton starts to compare Satan to Leviathan, but concludes his simile with the story of a sailor who moored his ship by mistake, one night, to a whale (*Paradise Lost* 1.200–208). Metaphors and similes have been distinguished according to their special effects; they may be, for instance, violent, comic, degrading, decorative, or ennobling.

When we speak of "forty head of cattle" or ask someone to "lend a hand" with a job, we are using **synecdoche,** a figure that substitutes the part for the whole. When we speak of a statement coming "from the White House," or a man much interested in "the turf," (that is, the race-course), we are using **metonymy,** or the substitution of one term for another with which it is closely associated. **Antithesis** is a device for placing opposing ideas in grammatical parallel, as, for example, in the following passage from Alexander Pope's *Rape of the Lock* (5.25–30), where there are more examples of antithesis than there are lines:

> But since, alas! frail beauty must decay,
> Curled or uncurled, since locks will turn to gray;
> Since painted, or not painted, all shall fade,
> And she who scorns a man must die a maid;
> What then remains but well our power to use,
> And keep good humor still whate'er we lose?

Irony is a verbal device that implies an attitude quite different from (and often opposite to) that which is literally expressed. In Pope's *The Rape of the Lock* (4.131–32), after poor Sir Plume has stammered an incoherent request to return the stolen lock of hair, the Baron answers ironically:

> "It grieves me much," replied the Peer again,
> "Who speaks so well should ever speak in vain."

And when Donne "proves," in *The Canonization*, that he and his mistress are going to found a new religion of love, he seems to be inviting us to take a subtly ironic attitude toward religion as well as love.

Because it is easy to see through, **hyperbole,** or willful exaggeration, is a favorite device of irony—which is not to say that it may not be "serious" as well. When she hears that a young man is "dying for love" of her, a sensible young woman does not accept this statement literally, but it may convey a serious meaning to her nonetheless. The **pun,** or play on words (known to the learned, sometimes, as **paronomasia**), may also be serious or comic in intent; witness, for example, the famous series of puns on Donne's name in his *Hymn to God the Father.* **Oxymoron** is a conjunction of two terms that in ordinary use are contraries or incompatible—for instance, Milton's famous description of hell as containing "darkness visible" (*Paradise Lost* 1.63). A **paradox** is a statement that seems absurd but turns out to have rational meaning after all, usually in some unexpected sense; Donne speaks of fear being great courage and high valor (*Satire* 3, line 16), and turns out to mean that fear of God is greater courage than any earthly bravery. A **conceit** is a far-fetched and unusually elaborate comparison. Writing in the fourteenth century, the Italian poet Petrarch popularized a great number of conceits handy for use in love poetry, and readily adapted by his English imitators. Wyatt, for example, is using **Petrarchan conceits** when he compares love to a warrior, or the lover's state to that of a storm-tossed ship; and a hundred other sonneteers developed the themes of the lady's stony heart, incendiary glances, and so forth. On the other hand, the **metaphysical conceit** was a more intellectualized, many-leveled comparison, giving a strong sense of the poet's ingenuity in overcoming obstacles—for instance, Donne's comparison of separated lovers to the legs of a compass (A *Valediction: Forbidding Mourning*) or Herbert's comparison of devotion to a pulley, in the poem of that name.

Personification (or in the term derived from Latin **prosopopoeia**) is the attribution of human qualities to an inanimate object (for example, the Sea) or an abstract concept (Freedom); a special variety of it is called (in a term of John Ruskin's invention) the **pathetic fallacy.** When we speak of leaves "dancing" or a lake "smiling," we attribute human traits to nonhuman objects. Ruskin thought this was false and therefore "morbid"; modern criticism tends to view the practice as artistically and morally neutral. A more formal and abstract variety of personification is **allegory,** in which a narrative (such as *Pilgrim's Progress*) is constructed by representing general concepts (Faithfulness, Sin, Despair) as persons who act out the plot. A **fable** (like Chaucer's *The Nun's Priest's Tale*) represents beasts behaving like humans; a **parable** is a brief story, or simply an observation, with strong moral application; and an **exemplum** is a story told to illustrate a point in a sermon.

A special series of devices, nearly obsolete today, used to be available to poets who could count on readers trained in the classics. These were the devices of **classical allusion**—that is, reference to the mythology (stories about the actions of gods and other supernatural beings) of the Greeks and Romans. In their simplest form, the classic **myths** used to provide a repertoire of agreeable stage properties, and a convenient shorthand for expressing emotional attitudes. Picturesque creatures like centaurs, satyrs, and sphinxes, heroes and heroines like Hector and Helen, and the whole pantheon of Olympic deities could be used to make ready reference to a great many aspects of human nature. One does not have to explain the problems of a man who is "cleaning the Augean stables"; if he is afflicted with an "Achilles' heel," or is assailing "Hydra-headed difficulties," his state is clear. These descriptive phrases, making **allusion** to mythological stories, suggest in a phrase situations that would normally require cumbersome explanations. But because it used to be taken for granted that the classical mythology was the common possession of all educated readers, the classic myths entered into English literature as early as Chaucer. In poets like Spenser and Milton, classical allusion becomes a kind of enormously learned game, in which the poet seeks to make his points as indirectly as possible. For instance, Spenser writes in the *Epithalamion*, lines 328–29:

> Lyke as when Jove with fayre Alcmena lay,
> When he begot the great Tirynthian groome.

The mere mention of Alcmena in the first line suggests, to the informed reader, Hercules, the son of Jupiter (Jove) by Alcmena. Spenser's problem in the second line is to find a way of referring to him that is neither redundant nor heavy-handed. "Tirynthian" reminds the reader of Hercules' long connection with the city of Tiryns, stretching our minds (as it were) across his whole career; and "groome" compresses references to a man-child, a servant, and a bridegroom, all of which apply to different aspects of Hercules' history. Thus, far from simply avoiding redundancy, Spenser has enriched, for the reader who possesses the classical information, the whole texture of his verse, thought, and feeling.

SCHOOLS

Literary scholars and critics often group together in **schools** writers who share stylistic traits or thematic concerns. Whether they considered themselves a group doesn't much matter; although in some cases—for example, the Imagists or the Beat poets—the writers themselves have identified themselves as belonging to a group. None of the **Romantic poets** knew they were being romantic, although Hazlitt, Shelley, and other writers of the time recognized shared features that they called "the spirit of the age." The followers of Spenser are known as **Spenserians**; they knew they admired and to some extent wrote like Spenser, but didn't realize that made them a group. **Cavalier** poets are set decisively apart from **Metaphysical** poets, though pretty surely none of the two-dozen-odd men involved knew that was what they were. And so with the **Gothic novelists,** and the so-called **Graveyard School** of the eighteenth century; these schools are generally grouped, defined, and named by scholars and critics after the event.

Intellectual affinities have led some writers to be classified under the names of the philosophical schools of Greece and Rome. These are chiefly the **Epicureans,** who specify that the aim of life and the source of value is pleasure; the **Stoics,** who emphasize stern virtue and the dignified endurance of what cannot be avoided; and the **Skeptics,** who doubt that anything can be known for certain. These categories are useful as capsule descriptions, but they aren't very tidy, as they are omissive, overlap one another, and cut across other categories. Dryden is an author strongly tinged with skepticism, but many of his poems suggest an unabashed epicureanism. *The Vanity of Human Wishes*, by Samuel Johnson, is the classic poem in English of stoic philosophy, but it also expresses a particularly strong coloring of Christian humanism.

TERMS OF LITERARY ART

The following section defines frequently used literary terms, especially frequently used terms that are closely related or tend to be mistaken for each other.

Allegory, Symbol, Emblem, Type. Allegory is a narrative in which the agents, and sometimes also the setting, are personified concepts or character-types, and the plot represents a doctrine or thesis. John Bunyan's *Pilgrim's Progress*, for example, allegorizes the Christian doctrine of salvation by narrating how the character named Christian, warned by Evangelist, flees the City of Destruction and makes his laborious way to the Celestial City; en route he meets such characters as Faithful and the Giant Despair, and passes through places like the Slough of Despond and Vanity Fair. A literary **symbol** is the representation of an object or event which has a further range of reference beyond itself. Examples of sustainedly symbolic poems are William Blake's *The Sick Rose* and William Butler Yeats's *Sailing to Byzantium*. In the sixteenth and seventeenth centuries, an **emblem** was an enigmatic picture of a physical object, to which was attached a motto and a verse explaining its significance. In present-day usage, an emblem is any object which is widely understood to signify an abstract concept; thus a dove is an emblem of peace, and a cross, of Christianity. In what was once a widespread Christian mode of biblical interpretation, a **type** was a person or event in the Old Testament which was regarded as historically real, but also as "prefiguring" a person or event in the New Testament. Thus Adam was often said to be a type of Christ, and the act of Moses in liberating the children of Israel was said to prefigure Christ in freeing men from Satan.

Baroque and **Mannerist** are terms imported into literary study from the history of art, and applied by analogy. Michelangelo is a **baroque** artist; he holds great masses in powerful dynamic tension, his style is heavily ornamented and restless. In these respects he is sometimes compared to Milton. El Greco is a **mannerist,** whose gaunt and distorted figures often seem to be laboring under great spiritual stress, whose light seems to be focused in spots against a dark background. He has been compared to Donne. Analogies of this sort are occasionally suggestive, but can readily deteriorate into parallels that are forced and nominal rather than substantial.

Bathos. See **Pathos,** the **Sublime,** and **Bathos.**

Burlesque and **Mock Heroic** differ in that the former makes its subject ludicrous by directly cutting it down, the latter by inflating it. In Pope's mock-heroic *Dunciad*, the figure of Dulness (Colley Cibber) is given inappropriately heroic dimensions; in Butler's burlesque *Hudibras*, the knightly hero is characterized by low and vulgar attributes, and persistently engages in inappropriately low behavior. Burlesque contributed to the development of the English novel; and during the nineteenth century, when formal drama tended to be stagy and melodramatic, a vigorous burlesque stage flourished in England, making fun of the classics. See **Imitation** and **Parody.**

Catastrophe and **Catharsis.** The **catastrophe** is the conclusion of a play; the word means "down-turning," and is usually applied only to tragedies, in which a frequent kind of catastrophe is the death of the protagonist. (A term for the precipitating final scene that applies both to tragedy and to comedy is **denouement,** which in French means "unknotting.") **Catharsis** in Greek signifies "purgation" or "purification." In Aristotle's *Poetics*, the special effect of tragedy is the "catharsis" of the "emotions of pity and fear" that have been aroused in the audience by the events of the drama.

Chiasmus and **Zeugma. Chiasmus** is an inversion of the word order in two parallel phrases, as in John Denham's *Cooper's Hill*: "Strong without rage, without o'erflowing full." **Zeugma** is the use of a single verb or adjective to control two nouns, as in Pope's *The Rape of the Lock*: "Or stain her honor, or her new brocade."

Classic and **Neoclassic.** See **Gothic, Classic, Neoclassic.**

Convention and **Tradition. Conventions** are agreed-upon artistic procedures peculiar to an art form. None of Shakespeare's contemporaries spoke blank verse in everyday life, but characters in his plays do, and the audience accepts it—as the audience at an opera accepts that characters will sing arias to express their feelings. A **tradition** consists of beliefs, attitudes, and ways of representing things that is widely shared by writers over a span of time; it generally includes a number of conventions.

Didactic poetry is designed to teach a branch of knowledge, or to embody in fictional form a moral, religious, or philosophical doctrine. The term is not derogatory. John Milton's *Paradise Lost*, for example, can be called didactic, insofar as it is organized, as Milton claimed in his invocation, to "assert Eternal Providence / And justify the ways of God to men." In the eighteenth century, a number of poets wrote didactic poems called **georgics** (modeled on the Roman Virgil's *Georgics* on rural life and farming), which described such applied arts as making cider or running a sugar plantation.

Dramatic irony and **Dramatic monologue** are quite different literary modes. In **dramatic irony** a stage character says something that has one meaning for him, but quite another for the audience who possesses relevant knowledge that the speaker lacks. The **dramatic monologue** is a form that was perfected by Robert Browning in such poems as *My Last Duchess* and *The Bishop Orders His Tomb*. In it, the poetic speaker unintentionally reveals to the reader his character and temperament by what he says, usually to another person whose presence we infer from the utterance of the speaker.

Eclogue. See **Pastorals.**

Emblem. See **Allegory, Symbol, Emblem, Type.**

Epigram, Epigraph, Epitaph. An **epigram** is a short, witty statement in verse or prose. One of Oscar Wilde's characters remarks, "I can resist everything, except temptation." An **epigraph** is an apposite quotation placed at the beginning of a book or a section of it. An **epitaph** is a brief statement about someone who has died; usually, it is intended to be inscribed on a tombstone.

Eulogy and **Elegy.** The **eulogy** is a work of praise, in prose or poetry, for a person either very distinguished or recently dead. In its usual modern sense, an **elegy** is a formal, and usually long, poetic lament for someone who has died. In an extended sense, the term is also used to designate poems on the transience of earthly things (such as the Old English *The Seafarer*) or poetic meditations on mortality (such as Thomas Gray's *Elegy Written in a Country Churchyard*).

Euphemism and **Euphuism. Euphemism,** or "fine speech," is a verbal device for avoiding an unpleasant concept or expression, as when, instead of saying a person "died," we say he "passed away." Euphues was the hero of a prose romance (published 1579–80) by John Lyly; his adventures are recounted in a mannered style full of puns, alliteration, and antithetical "points." Under the name of **Euphuism** this courtly style enjoyed a brief vogue in the Elizabethan era.

Fancy and **Imagination.** The distinction between these two mental powers was central to the literary theory of S. T. Coleridge. **Fancy** (a word directly derived by contraction from "fantasy") was defined by Coleridge as the power of combining several known properties into new combinations; **imagination,** on the other hand, was the faculty of using such properties to create an integral whole that is entirely new.

Folios, Quartos, etc., are terms used to specify the size of book pages. To make a **folio,** a sheet of paper (14" × 20" or larger) is folded just once (producing thereby four pages); **quartos** are folded twice (producing eight pages). Shakespeare's plays were first printed in quartos (often in several different editions), but when they were collected together, in 1623, they appeared as the First Folio edition.

Genre, Decorum. A genre is an established literary form or type, such as stage comedy, the picaresque novel, the epic, the sonnet. Works belonging to a certain genre tend to represent certain characters and events, and to seek a similar effect. **Decorum,** in literary criticism—where it was a central concept from the Renaissance through the eighteenth century—designates the requirement that there should be a propriety, or fitness, in the way that the character, actions, and style are matched to each other in a particular genre. Low characters, actions, and style, for example, were thought appropriate for satire, while epic demanded characters of high estate, engaged in great actions, and speaking in an appropriately high style.

Gothic, Classic, Neoclassic. These terms are used to distinguish prominent tendencies in literature and the other arts. The term **Gothic** originally referred to the Goths, an early Germanic tribe, then came to signify "medieval." In the eighteenth century "Gothic" connoted primitive and irregular work, possessing the qualities of the relatively barbaric North. **Gothic novels** were a very popular type of prose fiction, inaugurated by Horace Walpole's *Castle of Otranto* (1764), usually set in a medieval castle, which aimed to evoke chilling terror from their readers. **Classic** implies lucid, rational, and orderly works, such as are usually attributed to the writers and thinkers in the classic era of the Greeks and Romans. **Neoclassic**— a term often applied to the period in England from 1660 through most of the eighteenth century—implies an ideal of life, art, and thought deliberately modeled on Greek and Roman examples.

Heroic poems, Heroic drama, Heroic couplets. Because they concentrate on the figure of a typical hero (Achilles, Aeneas), epic poems were frequently called "**heroic.**" Trying to transfer epic grandeur to the stage, playwrights of the Restoration period wrote what was called **heroic drama,** but usually achieved only grandiosity. The stately iambic pentameter couplets in which they made their characters speak became known as **heroic couplets.**

Humor. See **Wit** and **Humor.**

Humors and **Temperaments** are psychological terms used by Renaissance writers. It was believed that every person's constitution contained four basic humors: the **choleric** (bile), the **sanguine** (blood), the **phlegmatic** (phlegm), and the **melancholy** (black bile). The **temperament,** or mixture, of these four humors was held to determine both a person's physical condition and a person's type of character. When a particular humor predominated, it pushed the character in that direction: choler = anger; sanguine = geniality; phlegm = cold torpor; and melancholy = gloomy self-absorption.

Imagination. See **Fancy** and **Imagination.**

Imitation and **Parody** are forms in which a literary work refers back to a predecessor. In the eighteenth century, an "imitation" was a poem that deliberately echoed an older work, but adapted it to subject matter in the writer's own era, usually with a satirical aim directed against that subject matter; Alexander Pope, for example, wrote a number of satires on contemporary life that he entitled *Imitations of Horace*. A **parody** imitates the characteristic style and other features of a particular literary work—or else of a particular literary type—but in such a way as to satirize that work, by making it either amusing or ridiculous. *Northanger Abbey* (1818) by Jane Austen was a good-humored parody of the popular horror-narratives known as gothic novels. (See **Burlesque** and **Gothic**.)

Irony, Sarcasm. Irony and **sarcasm** are both ways of saying one thing but implying something sharply different, often opposite; they differ, however, in the way they go about doing so. **Sarcasm** is a broad and taunting form of using apparent praise in order in fact to denigrate. The patriarch Job is bitterly sarcastic when he replies to his would-be comforters (12.2), "No doubt but ye are the people, and wisdom shall die with you." On the other hand, Jane Austen, in the first sentence of *Pride and Prejudice*, overstates the case just enough to make it drily **ironic** when she writes, "It is a truth universally acknowledged, that a single man in possession of a good fortune, must be in want of a wife." (See **Irony**, in the section "Figurative Language," above.)

Legend. See **Myth** and **Legend**.

Logic. See **Rhetoric** and **Logic**.

Masque. The **Masque**, which flourished during the reigns of Elizabeth I, James I, and Charles I, was an elaborate court entertainment that combined poetic drama, music, song, dance, and splendid costumes and settings. For a discussion of the English masque, see the introduction to Jonson's *Pleasure Reconciled to Virtue*.

Myth and Legend. **Myths** are hereditary narratives that purport to account, in supernatural terms, for why the world is as it is, and why people act as they do; they also often provide the rules by which people conduct their lives. Myths often spring up to explain rituals, the original meanings of which have been forgotten. A system of related myths is called a **mythology**—a body of supernatural narratives believed to be true by a particular cultural group. The term "myth" is frequently extended to a set of supernatural narratives that are developed by individual poets such as William Blake and W. B. Yeats. Three great mythologies that have been exploited by poets long after they ceased to be believed are the classical (Greek and Roman), the Celtic, and the Germanic. A **legend** is an old and popularly repeated story, of which the protagonist is not supernatural, but a human being. If a hereditary story concerns supernatural beings who are not gods, and the story is not part of a systematic mythology, it is usually classified as a **folktale**.

Naturalism. See **Realism** and **Naturalism**.

Neo-Classic. See **Gothic, Classic, Neoclassic**.

Novel. See **Romance, Novel**.

Ode. A long lyric poem serious in subject and treatment, written in an elevated style and, usually, in an elaborate stanza. See the discussion of English odes in the headnote to Jonson's *Ode on Cary and Morison*.

Pastoral, Eclogue, and Pastoral Elegy. **Pastorals** (from the Latin word for "shepherd") are deliberately conventional poems that project a cultivated poet's nostalgic image of the peace and simplicity of the life of shepherds and other rural folk in an idealized natural setting. The form was established by the Greek poet Theocritus in the third century B.C.E.; it is sometimes also called an **eclogue,** which was the title that the Roman poet Virgil gave to his collection of pastorals. The pastorals by Theocritus and later classical poets often included a poem in which a shepherd mourns the death of a fellow shepherd; from these poems developed the highly conventional **pastoral elegy,** a type that includes such great laments as Milton's *Lycidas* and Shelley's *Adonais. Lycidas* is also an example of the extension of the classical pastoral to a Christian range of reference, by way of the use of the term "pastor" (shepherd) for a parish priest or minister and the frequent representation of Christ as "the Good Shepherd."

Pathos, the **Sublime,** and **Bathos.** In Greek, **pathos** signified deep feeling, especially suffering; in modern criticism, it is used in a more limited way to signify a scene or passage designed to evoke the feelings of pity or sympathetic sorrow from an audience. An example is the passage in which King Lear is briefly reunited with his daughter Cordelia, beginning

> Pray, do not mock me.
> I am a very foolish fond old man . . .

In the first century the Greek rhetorician Longinus wrote a treatise *On the Sublime,* in which he proposed that sublimity ("loftiness") is the greatest of stylistic qualities in literature; the effect of the sublime on the reader is *elestasis* ("transport"). In 1757 Edmund Burke published a highly influential treatise on *The Sublime and Beautiful,* in which he distinguished the sublime from the beautiful, not as a stylistic quality, but as the representation of objects that are vast, obscure, and powerful, which evoke from the reader a "delightful horror" that combines pleasure and terror. **Bathos** (Greek for "depth") was used by Pope, in a parodic parallel to Longinus' "sublime," to signify an unintentional descent in literature, when an author, straining to be passionate or elevated, overshoots the mark and falls into the trivial or the ridiculous.

Poetic diction, Poetic license, Poetic justice. Poetic diction denotes a distinctive language used by a poet which is not current in the discourse of the age; an example is the deliberately archaic language of Spenser's *The Faerie Queene.* In modern critical discussion, the term is applied especially to the style of eighteenth-century poets who, according to the reigning principle of decorum (see **Decorum**), believed that a poet must adapt the level of his diction to the dignity of the high genres of epic, tragedy, and ode. The results were such phrases as "the finny tribe" for "fish" and "the bleating kind" for "sheep." **Poetic license** designates the freedom of a poet or other literary writer to depart, for special effects, from the norms of common discourse and of literal or historical truth. Examples: the use of archaic words, meter, and rhyme, and the use of other literary conventions. (See **Convention.**) **Poetic justice** was coined by Thomas Rymer, in the later seventeenth century, to denote his claim that a narrative or drama should, at the end, distribute rewards and punishments in proportion to the virtues and vices of each character. No important critic since Rymer has adopted this doctrine, except in a highly qualified way.

Quarto. See **Folios, Quartos.**

Realism and **Naturalism** are both terms applied to prose fictions that aim at a faithful representation of actual existence; they differ, however, in the aspects of that existence that they represent and in the manner in which they represent them. The realistic novel attempts to give the effect of representing ordinary life as it commonly occurs. Realistic novelists such as George Eliot in England and William Dean Howells in America present everyday characters experiencing ordinary events, rendered in great detail. **Naturalism,** which the French novelist Émile Zola developed in the 1870s and later, is based on the philosophy that a human being is merely a higher-order animal, whose character and behavior are determined by heredity and environment. Zola, followed by such later naturalistic novelists as the Americans Frank Norris and Theodore Dreiser, typically represents characters who inherit such compulsive instincts as greed and the sexual drive and are shaped by the social and economic forces of family, class, and the milieu into which they are born. Naturalistic novelists also often display an almost medical candor in describing human activities and bodily functions largely unmentioned in earlier fiction.

Rhetoric and **Logic. Rhetoric** was developed by Greek and Roman theorists as the art of using all available means of persuading an audience, either by speech or in writing; it had a great influence on literary criticism in the Renaissance and through the eighteenth century. Rhetorical theorists developed a detailed analysis of figures of speech, largely as effective means to the overall aim of persuasion. In the present century, however, the analysis of such figures has been excerpted from this rhetorical context and made an independent and central concern of language theorists and literary critics. See **Figurative language. Logic** is the study of the principles of reasoning. Logic may be used to persuade an audience, but it does not, like rhetoric, avail itself of all means of persuasion, emotional as well as rational; instead, logic limits itself to a concern with the formal procedures of reasoning from sound premises to valid conclusions.

Romance and **Novel.** Medieval **romances** were verse narratives of adventure, usually about a knightly hero on a quest to gain a lady's favor, who encounters both natural tribulations and supernatural marvels. The term "romance" has since come to be opposed to realism (see **Realism** and **Naturalism**) and is applied to prose fictions that represent characters and events which are more picturesque, fantastic, adventurous, or heroic than one encounters in ordinary life. The **novel,** as distinguished from the prose romance, undertakes to be a more realistic representation of common life and social relationships and tends to avoid the fantastic, the fabulous, and the realm of high derring-do. (See **Realism.**)

Sarcasm. See **Irony, Sarcasm.**

Satire designates literary forms which diminish or derogate a subject by making it ridiculous and by evoking toward it amusement, or scorn, or indignation. In **formal satire,** such as Alexander Pope's *Moral Essays,* the satire is accomplished in a direct, first-person address, either to the audience or to a listener within the work. **Indirect satire** is not a direct address, but is cast in the form of a fictional narrative, as in Swift's *Gulliver's Travels* or Byron's *Don Juan.* For a discussion of the backgrounds of English satire, see the introduction to Donne's *Satire 3.*

Sublime. See **Pathos, the Sublime,** and **Bathos.**

Symbol. See **Allegory, Symbol, Emblem, Type.**

Tradition. See **Convention** and **Tradition.**

Type. See **Allegory, Symbol, Emblem, Type.**

Wit and **Humor,** in their present use, designate elements in a literary work which are designed to amuse or to excite mirth in the reader or audience. **Wit,** through the seventeenth century, had a broad range of meanings, including general intelligence, mental acuity, and ingenuity in literary invention, especially in a brilliant and paradoxical style. From this last application there derived the most common present use of "wit" to denote a kind of verbal expression that is brief, deft, and contrived to produce a shock of comic surprise; a characteristic form of wit, in this sense, is the epigram. (See **Epigram.**) **Humor** goes back to the ancient theory of the four humors and the application of the term "humorous" to a comically eccentric character who has an imbalance of the humors in his or her temperament. (See **Humors** and **Temperament.**) As we now use the word, **humor** is ascribed both to a comic utterance and to the comic appearance or behavior of a literary character. A humorous utterance, unlike a witty utterance, need not be intended to be comic by the speaker, and is not cast in the neat epigrammatic form of a witty saying. In Shakespeare's *Twelfth Night,* for example, Malvolio's utterances, as well as his appearance and behavior, are all found humorous by the audience, but his utterances are never witty and are humorous despite his own very solemn intentions.

Zeugma. See **Chiasmus** and **Zeugma.**

THE UNIVERSE ACCORDING TO PTOLEMY

Ptolemy was a Roman astronomer of Greek descent, born in Egypt during the second century C.E.; after his death, for nearly fifteen hundred years his account of the design of the universe was accepted as standard. During that long period, the basic pattern underwent many detailed modifications and was fitted out with many astrological and pseudoscientific trappings. But in essence Ptolemy's followers agreed in portraying the earth as the center of the universe, with the sun, planets, and fixed stars set in transparent spheres orbiting around it. In this scheme of things, as modified for Christian usage, Hell was usually placed under the earth's surface at the center of the cosmic globe, while Heaven, the abode of the blessed spirits, was in the outermost, uppermost circle, the empyrean. But in 1543 the Polish astronomer Copernicus proposed an alternative hypothesis—that the earth rotates around the sun, not vice versa; and despite theological opposition, observations with the new telescope and careful mathematical calculations insured ultimate acceptance of the new view.

The map of the Ptolemaic universe represented here is a simplified version of a diagram in Peter Apian's *Cosmography* (1584). In such a diagram, the Firmament is the sphere which contained the fixed stars; the Crystalline Sphere, which contained no heavenly bodies, is a late innovation, included to explain certain anomalies in the observed movement of the heavenly bodies; and the Prime Mover is the sphere which, itself put into motion by God, imparts rotation around the earth to all the other spheres.

Milton, writing in mid-seventeenth century, made use of two universes. The Copernican universe, though he alludes to it, was too large, formless, and unfamiliar to serve as the setting for the war between Heaven and Hell in *Paradise Lost.* He therefore adopted as his setting the Ptolemaic cosmos, but placed Heaven well outside this smaller earth-centered universe, Hell far beneath it, and assigned the vast middle space to Chaos.

therefore adopted as His sphere, the Ptolemaic cosmos but placed Heaven well outside this smaller earth-centred universe. Hell far beneath it and assigned the outermost sphere to Chaos.

The Empyrean
The Prime Mover
The Crystalline Sphere
The Firmament
The Sphere of Saturn
The Sphere of Jupiter
The Sphere of Mars
The Sphere of the Sun
The Sphere of Venus
The Sphere of Mercury
The Sphere of the Moon

Index

Adam Lay Bound, 354
Adam lay ybounden, bounden in a bond, 354
Alison, 351
Ancrene Riwle (Rule for Anchoresses), 153
Anglo-Saxon Chronicle, The, 110
Another lay to you I'll tell, 127

Battle of Maldon, The, 103
Bede, 23
Beowulf, 29
Bitweene Merch and Averil, 351
Book of Margery Kempe, The, 367
Book of Showings to the Anchoress Julian of Norwich, A, 356
Brut, 122, 125

Caedmon's Hymn, 23
Canterbury Tales, The, 213
Chaucer, Geoffrey, 210
Chaucer's Retraction, 313
Cock and the Fox, The, 439
Complaint to His Purse, 316
Corpus Christi Carol, The, 354
Cuckoo Song, The, 350

Dream of the Rood, The, 26

Everyman, 445
Exile of the Sons of Uisliu, 142

Flee fro the press and dwelle with soothfast-nesse, 315

General Prologue, The, 214
Geoffrey of Monmouth, 115, 125

Henryson, Robert, 439
History of the Kings of Britain, The, 116, 125

I Am of Ireland, 352
Ich am of Irlonde, 352
If no love is, O God, what feele I so?, 314
I Sing of a Maiden, 353

Julian of Norwich, 355

Kempe, Margery, 366

Langland, William, 317
Lanval, 127
Layamon, 122, 125
Legendary Histories of Britain, 115
Lludd and Lleuelys, 150
Lully, lullay, lully, lullay, 354

Malory, Sir Thomas, 419
Man of Law's Epilogue, The, 252
Marie de France, 126
Miller's Prologue and Tale, 235
Morte Darthur, 421
My Lief Is Faren in Londe, 352
Myth of Arthur's Return, The, 124

Noah's Flood, 38
Now gooth sunne under wode, 353
Nun's Priest's Tale, The, 296

Once long ago a wolf strolled down, 141

Pardoner's Prologue and Tale, The, 281
Parson's Tale, The, 311
Piers Plowman, The Vision of, 319

Roman de Brut, Le, 118, 125

Second Shepherds' Play, 391
Sir Gawain and the Green Knight, 156
So. The Spear-Danes in days gone by, 32
Sumer is ycomin in, 350
Sunset on Calvary, 353

This tells of wolf and lamb who drank, 140
Thogh brutal beestes be irrational, 439
To you, my purs, and to noon other wight, 316
Troilus's Song, 314
Truth, 315

Wace, 118, 125
Wanderer, The, 99
Western Wind, 352
Westron wind, when will thou blow?, 352
What is he, this lordling, that cometh from the fight, 352
Wife of Bath's Prologue and Tale, 253
Wife's Lament, The, 102
Wolf and the Lamb, The, 140
Wolf and the Sow, The, 141

Ye That Pasen by the Weye, 353